GARETH STEVENS
ATLAS
— OF THE —
WORLD

Maps created by
MapQuest.com, Inc.

Gareth Stevens Publishing
A WORLD ALMANAC EDUCATION GROUP COMPANY

World Almanac Education Group Staff

Editorial Director
William A. McGeveran, Jr.

Director–Purchasing and Production
Edward A. Thomas

Managing Editor
Lori Wiesenfeld

Associate Editors
Erik Gopel, Kevin Seabrooke

Desktop Production Manager
Lisa Lazzara

Publisher
Ken Park

Cover Design
Eileen Svajger

MapQuest.com/Digital Mapping Services Staff

Project Managers
Keith Winters, Robert Woolley

Project Coordinators
Matt DiBerardino, Andrew Green, Matt Tharp

Research & Compilation
Marley Amstutz, Laura Hartwig, Bill Truninger

Research Librarian
Craig Haggit

GIS
Mark Leitzell

Cartographers
Brian Goudreau, Kendall Marten, Jeff Martz, Hylon Plumb

Editors
Robert Harding, Dana Wolf

Production Support
Shawna Roberts

Gareth Stevens Staff

Cover Design
Scott M. Krall

Editorial
Jacqueline Laks Gorman
JoAnn Early Macken
Mark J. Sachner

Copyright © 2004
MapQuest.com, Inc.

Please visit our web site at:
www.garethstevens.com
For a free color catalog describing Gareth Stevens' list of high-quality books and multimedia programs, call 1-800-542-2595 (USA) or 1-800-387-3178 (Canada). Gareth Stevens Publishing's fax: (414) 332-3567.

Library of Congress Cataloging-in-Publication Data available on request from publisher. Fax (414) 336-0157 for the attention of the Publishing Records Department.

ISBN 0-8368-4091-7

This edition first published in 2004 by
Gareth Stevens Publishing
A World Almanac Education Group Company
330 West Olive Street, Suite 100
Milwaukee, WI 53212 USA

Printed in the United States of America

1 2 3 4 5 6 7 8 9 08 07 06 05 04

TABLE OF CONTENTS

PORTRAIT OF THE U.S.
THE WORLD IN THE 21ST CENTURY

4 WORLD

6 ASIA and OCEANIA

8 Japan
9 North Korea, South Korea, Taiwan
10 China
11 Vietnam, Laos, Cambodia, Mongolia
12 Thailand, Myanmar (Burma), Philippines
13 Indonesia, Brunei, Singapore, Malaysia
14 Australia
15 Papua New Guinea, New Zealand, East Timor, Micronesia
16 Marshall Is., Nauru, Solomon Is., Tuvalu
17 Kiribati, Fiji, Palau, Tonga
18 Vanuatu, New Caledonia & Dependencies, Samoa, American Samoa
19 Nepal, Maldives, Bhutan, Sri Lanka
20 India
21 Bangladesh, Pakistan
22 Afghanistan, Iran, Turkmenistan
23 Kazakhstan, Uzbekistan, Kyrgyzstan, Tajikistan
24 Iraq, Kuwait, Saudi Arabia
25 Bahrain, Qatar, United Arab Emirates, Yemen, Oman
26 Lebanon, Israel, Jordan
27 Turkey, Cyprus, Syria

28 EUROPE

30 Great Britain & Northern Ireland
31 Republic of Ireland
32 Denmark, Netherlands
33 Belgium, Liechtenstein, Luxembourg
34 France
35 Monaco, Switzerland
36 Portugal, Malta, Gibraltar, Andorra
37 Spain
38 Italy
39 Austria, Vatican City, San Marino
40 Germany
41 Poland
42 Czech Republic, Slovakia
43 Hungary, Romania
44 Russia
45 Armenia, Georgia, Azerbaijan
46 Estonia, Latvia, Lithuania
47 Belarus, Ukraine
48 Slovenia, Croatia, Bosnia & Herzegovina, F.Y.R. Macedonia
49 Albania, Serbia and Montenegro
50 Moldova, Bulgaria
51 Greece
52 Iceland, Norway
53 Sweden, Finland

54 AFRICA

56 Egypt, Libya
57 Algeria, Tunisia, Morocco
58 Western Sahara, Cape Verde, Mali, Mauritania
59 Chad, Niger, Sudan
60 Eritrea, Djibouti, Ethiopia, Somalia
61 Kenya, Uganda, Rwanda, Burundi
62 Senegal, The Gambia, Guinea, Guinea-Bissau
63 Sierra Leone, Côte d'Ivoire, São Tomé & Príncipe, Liberia
64 Ghana, Burkina Faso, Benin, Togo
65 Nigeria, Cameroon
66 Equatorial Guinea, Republic of the Congo, Gabon, Central African Republic
67 Comoros, Democratic Republic of the Congo, Zambia
68 Tanzania, Malawi, Mozambique
69 Mauritius, Zimbabwe, Botswana, Madagascar
70 Angola, Namibia, Seychelles
71 South Africa, Swaziland, Lesotho

72 SOUTH AMERICA

74 Argentina
75 Paraguay, Uruguay
76 Chile
77 Peru, Bolivia
78 Colombia
79 Ecuador, Venezuela
80 Guyana, Suriname, French Guiana
81 Brazil

82 NORTH AMERICA

84 Mexico
85 Belize, Guatemala
86 Honduras, El Salvador, Costa Rica
87 Nicaragua, Panama
88 Cuba, Jamaica
89 Dominican Republic, Haiti, Bahamas, Turks & Caicos Is.
90 Puerto Rico, Antigua & Barbuda, St. Kitts & Nevis, Dominica
91 St. Lucia, Barbados, St. Vincent & the Grenadines, Grenada, Trinidad & Tobago
92 Canada
93 Canadian Provincial & Territorial Flags
94 Alberta
95 British Columbia
96 Manitoba
97 New Brunswick
98 Newfoundland and Labrador
99 Northwest Territories, Nunavut
100 Nova Scotia, Prince Edward Island
101 Ontario, Québec
102 Southern Ontario
103 Southern Québec
104 Saskatchewan
105 Yukon Territory

POLAR REGIONS

106 Arctic Regions, Greenland
107 Antarctica

108 WORLD INDEX

UNITED STATES

126 U.S. Political
127 U.S. Physical
128 Alabama
129 Alaska
130 Arizona
131 Arkansas
132 California
133 Colorado
134 Connecticut
135 Delaware
136 Florida
137 Georgia
138 Hawaii
139 Idaho
140 Illinois
141 Indiana
142 Iowa
143 Kansas
144 Kentucky
145 Louisiana
146 Maine
147 Maryland
148 Massachusetts
149 Michigan
150 Minnesota
151 Mississippi
152 Missouri
153 Montana
154 Nebraska
155 Nevada
156 New Hampshire
157 New Jersey
158 New Mexico
159 New York
160 North Carolina
161 North Dakota
162 Ohio
163 Oklahoma
164 Oregon
165 Pennsylvania
166 Rhode Island
167 South Carolina
168 South Dakota
169 Tennessee
170 Texas
171 Utah
172 Vermont
173 Virginia
174 Washington
175 West Virginia
176 Wisconsin
177 Wyoming

178 STATE INDEXES

General

⊛ National Capital
★ Territorial Capital
• Other City

International Boundary (subject area)
International Boundary (non-subject)
Internal Boundary (state, province, etc.)
‐ ‐ ‐ ‐ Disputed Boundary

Perennial River
Intermittent River
Canal
Dam

U.S. States, Canadian Provinces & Territories
(additions and changes to general legend)

★ State Capital
• County Seat
Built Up Area
State Boundary
County Boundary
National Park
Other Park, Forest, Grassland
Indian, Other Reservation

■ Point of Interest
▲ Mountain Peak
·········· Continental Divide
······· Time Zone Boundary

Limited Access Highway
Other Major Road
(90) Highway Shield

PROJECTION

The only true representation of the Earth, free of distortion, is a globe. Maps are flat, and the process by which the geographic locations (latitude and longitude) are transformed from a three-dimensional sphere to a two-dimensional flat map is called a Projection.

For a detailed explanation of Projections, see *MapScope* in Volume 2 of *Funk & Wagnalls New Encyclopedia*.

TYPES OF SCALE

VISUAL SCALE

Every map has a bar scale, or a Visual Scale, that can be used for measuring. It shows graphically the relationship between map distance and ground distance.

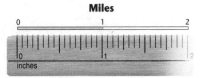

Miles

One inch represents 1 mile

Kilometers

One centimeter represents 10 kilometers

REPRESENTATIVE FRACTION

The scale of a map, expressed as a numerical ratio of map distance to ground distance, is called a Representative Fraction (or RF). It is usually written as 1/50,000 or 1:50,000, meaning that one unit of measurement on the map represents 50,000 of the same units on the ground.

This example is used on pages 20, 21 for India, Bangladesh, and Pakistan.

— The Globe is centered on the continent of Asia, as shown on pages 6, 7.

— The subject countries are shown in a stronger red/brown color.

LOCATOR

United States Population, 2000-2002

The following four pages look at recent population trends in the United States. Here's some news from the U.S. Census Bureau, the government agency that measures the nation's population and studies its many characteristics.

- Between April 1, 2000, and July 1, 2002, the U.S. population increased 2.4%, from 281,422,509 to 288,368,698.
- The Hispanic community became the nation's largest minority community in 2002. The Census Bureau estimated that 38.8 million people were of Hispanic or Latino origin–13.5% of the total U.S. population.
- In 2002, Nevada was the fastest growing state in the nation–for the sixteenth year in a row.
- The foreign-born population—those who were born in another country, but live in the U.S.—reached a record 32.5 million people in 2002. The foreign born made up 11.5% of the total population, the highest percentage since 1930. Among this group, about 36.4% came from Central America, 25.5% from Asia, 14% from Europe, 9.6% from the Caribbean, and 6.2% from South America.

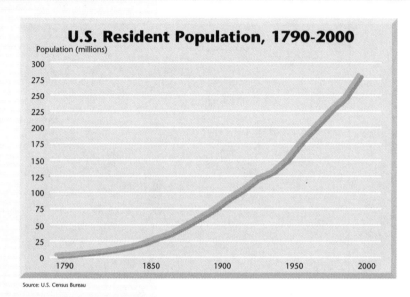

U.S. Resident Population, 1790-2000

Source: U.S. Census Bureau

United States Resident Population per Census

Year	Population
2000	281,421,906
1990	248,709,873
1980	226,542,199
1970	203,302,031
1960	179,323,175
1950	151,325,798
1940	132,164,569
1930	123,202,624
1920	106,021,537
1910	92,228,496
1900	76,212,168
1890	62,979,766
1880	50,189,209
1870	38,558,371
1860	31,443,321
1850	23,191,876
1840	17,063,353
1830	12,860,702
1820	9,638,453
1810	7,239,881
1800	5,308,483
1790	3,929,214

Source: U.S. Census Bureau

Population Density, 2000
(persons per sq. mi., land area only)

© MapQuest.com, Inc.

Population Density, 2000
- ≥500 Persons
- 250–499 Persons
- 100–249 Persons
- 50–99 Persons
- 25–49 Persons
- 0–24 Persons

Most People per Sq. Mi.
Washington, D.C.	9,378.0
New Jersey	1,134.5
Rhode Island	1,003.2
Massachusetts	809.8
Connecticut	702.9

Fewest People per Sq. Mi.
Alaska	1.1
Wyoming	5.1
Montana	6.2
North Dakota	9.3
South Dakota	9.9

New Apportionment in U.S. House of Representatives

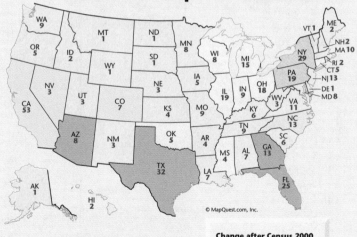

© MapQuest.com, Inc.

Apportionment is the process of dividing the 435 seats in the U.S. House of Representatives among the states. The apportionment calculation is based upon the total resident population of each state as determined by the latest U.S. Census.

Change after Census 2000
- Gain two seats
- Gain one seat
- No change
- Lose one seat
- Lose two seats

red fig. Number of seats in 108th Congress (January 2003)

Percent Change in State Population, 1990-2000

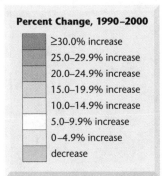

Percent Change, 1990–2000

- ≥30.0% increase
- 25.0–29.9% increase
- 20.0–24.9% increase
- 15.0–19.9% increase
- 10.0–14.9% increase
- 5.0–9.9% increase
- 0–4.9% increase
- decrease

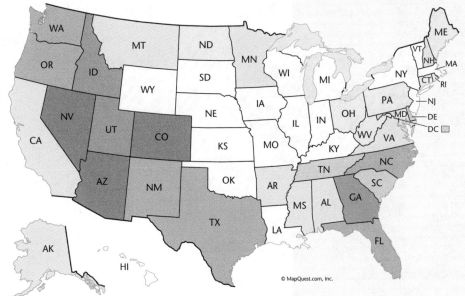

© MapQuest.com, Inc.

Population by State, 2000-2002

Source: U.S. Census Bureau

State	2002 Pop.	2000 Pop.	Percent Change
Alabama	4,486,508	4,447,100	0.9
Alaska	643,786	626,931	2.7
Arizona	5,456,453	5,130,632	6.4
Arkansas	2,710,079	2,673,398	1.4
California	35,116,033	33,871,648	3.7
Colorado	4,506,542	4,301,331	4.8
Connecticut	3,460,503	3,405,565	1.6
Delaware	807,385	783,600	3.0
District of Columbia	570,898	572,059	-0.2
Florida	16,713,149	15,982,400	4.6
Georgia	8,560,310	8,186,486	4.6
Hawaii	1,244,898	1,211,537	2.8
Idaho	1,341,131	1,293,953	3.6
Illinois	12,600,620	12,419,296	1.5
Indiana	6,159,068	6,080,485	1.3
Iowa	2,936,760	2,926,327	0.4
Kansas	2,715,884	2,688,418	1.0
Kentucky	4,092,891	4,042,209	1.3
Louisiana	4,482,646	4,468,979	0.3
Maine	1,294,464	1,274,923	1.5
Maryland	5,458,137	5,296,483	3.1
Massachusetts	6,427,801	6,349,097	1.2
Michigan	10,050,446	9,938,444	1.1
Minnesota	5,019,720	4,919,479	2.0
Mississippi	2,871,782	2,844,658	1.0
Missouri	5,672,579	5,595,211	1.4
Montana	909,453	902,195	0.8
Nebraska	1,729,180	1,711,263	1.0
Nevada	2,173,491	1,998,257	8.8
New Hampshire	1,275,056	1,235,786	3.2
New Jersey	8,590,300	8,414,350	2.1
New Mexico	1,855,059	1,819,046	2.0
New York	19,157,532	18,976,457	1.0
North Carolina	8,320,146	8,049,474	3.4
North Dakota	634,110	642,200	-1.3
Ohio	11,421,267	11,353,008	0.6
Oklahoma	3,493,714	3,450,656	1.2
Oregon	3,521,515	3,421,405	2.9
Pennsylvania	12,335,091	12,281,054	0.4
Rhode Island	1,069,725	1,048,319	2.0
South Carolina	4,107,183	4,012,010	2.4
South Dakota	761,063	754,844	0.8
Tennessee	5,797,289	5,689,277	1.9
Texas	21,779,893	20,851,812	4.5
Utah	2,316,256	2,233,169	3.7
Vermont	616,592	608,827	1.3
Virginia	7,293,542	7,078,499	3.0
Washington	6,068,996	5,894,119	3.0
West Virginia	1,801,873	1,808,350	-0.4
Wisconsin	5,441,196	5,363,701	1.4
Wyoming	498,703	493,782	1.0

Distribution of Population by Region, 1900, 1950, 2000

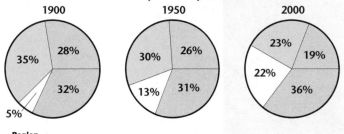

1900 — 35%, 28%, 32%, 5%

1950 — 30%, 26%, 13%, 31%

2000 — 23%, 19%, 22%, 36%

Region

- Northeast - CT, ME, MA, NH, NJ, NY, PA, RI, VT
- South - AL, AR, DE, DC, FL, GA, KY, LA, MD, MS, NC, OK, SC, TN, TE, VA, WV
- Midwest - IL, IN, IA, KS, MI, MN, MO, NE, ND, OH, SD, WI
- West - AK, AZ, CA, CO, HI, ID, MT, NV, NM, OR, UT, WA, WY

Source: U.S. Census Bureau

U.S. Center of Population

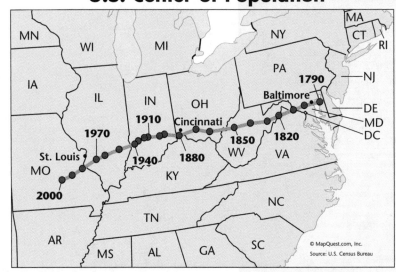

© MapQuest.com, Inc.
Source: U.S. Census Bureau

U.S. Center of Population = center of population gravity, or the point on which the U.S. would balance if it were a rigid plane, assuming all individuals weigh the same and exert influence proportional to their distance from a central point

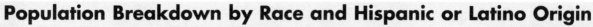

Population Breakdown by Race and Hispanic or Latino Origin

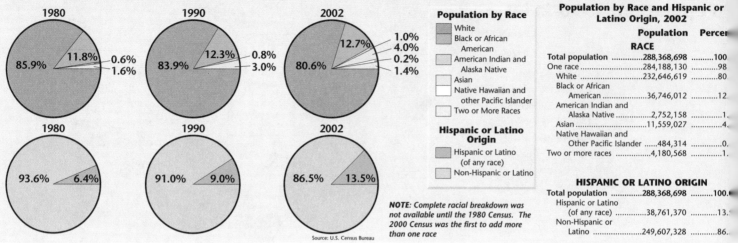

1980
85.9% 11.8% 0.6% 1.6%

1990
83.9% 12.3% 0.8% 3.0%

2002
12.7% 1.0% 4.0% 0.2% 1.4% 80.6%

Population by Race
- White
- Black or African American
- American Indian and Alaska Native
- Asian
- Native Hawaiian and other Pacific Islander
- Two or More Races

1980
93.6% 6.4%

1990
91.0% 9.0%

2002
86.5% 13.5%

Hispanic or Latino Origin
- Hispanic or Latino (of any race)
- Non-Hispanic or Latino

NOTE: Complete racial breakdown was not available until the 1980 Census. The 2000 Census was the first to add more than one race

Source: U.S. Census Bureau

Population by Race and Hispanic or Latino Origin, 2002

	Population	Percen
RACE		
Total population	288,368,698	100
One race	284,188,130	98
White	232,646,619	80
Black or African American	36,746,012	12
American Indian and Alaska Native	2,752,158	1.
Asian	11,559,027	4.
Native Hawaiian and Other Pacific Islander	484,314	0.
Two or more races	4,180,568	1.
HISPANIC OR LATINO ORIGIN		
Total population	288,368,698	100.
Hispanic or Latino (of any race)	38,761,370	13.
Non-Hispanic or Latino	249,607,328	86.

20 Largest Metropolitan Areas, 2000 Census

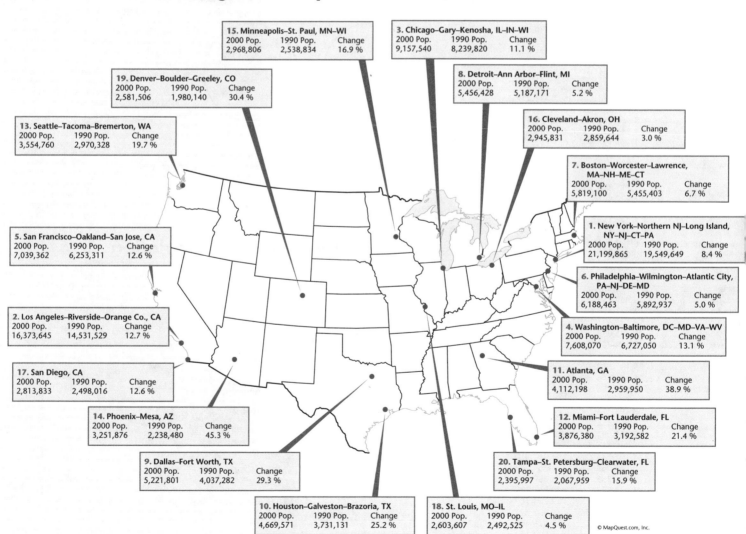

15. Minneapolis–St. Paul, MN–WI
2000 Pop.	1990 Pop.	Change
2,968,806	2,538,834	16.9 %

3. Chicago–Gary–Kenosha, IL–IN–WI
2000 Pop.	1990 Pop.	Change
9,157,540	8,239,820	11.1 %

19. Denver–Boulder–Greeley, CO
2000 Pop.	1990 Pop.	Change
2,581,506	1,980,140	30.4 %

8. Detroit–Ann Arbor–Flint, MI
2000 Pop.	1990 Pop.	Change
5,456,428	5,187,171	5.2 %

13. Seattle–Tacoma–Bremerton, WA
2000 Pop.	1990 Pop.	Change
3,554,760	2,970,328	19.7 %

16. Cleveland–Akron, OH
2000 Pop.	1990 Pop.	Change
2,945,831	2,859,644	3.0 %

7. Boston–Worcester–Lawrence, MA–NH–ME–CT
2000 Pop.	1990 Pop.	Change
5,819,100	5,455,403	6.7 %

5. San Francisco–Oakland–San Jose, CA
2000 Pop.	1990 Pop.	Change
7,039,362	6,253,311	12.6 %

1. New York–Northern NJ–Long Island, NY–NJ–CT–PA
2000 Pop.	1990 Pop.	Change
21,199,865	19,549,649	8.4 %

6. Philadelphia–Wilmington–Atlantic City, PA–NJ–DE–MD
2000 Pop.	1990 Pop.	Change
6,188,463	5,892,937	5.0 %

2. Los Angeles–Riverside–Orange Co., CA
2000 Pop.	1990 Pop.	Change
16,373,645	14,531,529	12.7 %

4. Washington–Baltimore, DC–MD–VA–WV
2000 Pop.	1990 Pop.	Change
7,608,070	6,727,050	13.1 %

17. San Diego, CA
2000 Pop.	1990 Pop.	Change
2,813,833	2,498,016	12.6 %

11. Atlanta, GA
2000 Pop.	1990 Pop.	Change
4,112,198	2,959,950	38.9 %

14. Phoenix–Mesa, AZ
2000 Pop.	1990 Pop.	Change
3,251,876	2,238,480	45.3 %

12. Miami–Fort Lauderdale, FL
2000 Pop.	1990 Pop.	Change
3,876,380	3,192,582	21.4 %

9. Dallas–Fort Worth, TX
2000 Pop.	1990 Pop.	Change
5,221,801	4,037,282	29.3 %

20. Tampa–St. Petersburg–Clearwater, FL
2000 Pop.	1990 Pop.	Change
2,395,997	2,067,959	15.9 %

10. Houston–Galveston–Brazoria, TX
2000 Pop.	1990 Pop.	Change
4,669,571	3,731,131	25.2 %

18. St. Louis, MO–IL
2000 Pop.	1990 Pop.	Change
2,603,607	2,492,525	4.5 %

© MapQuest.com, Inc.

20 Largest Cities, 2002

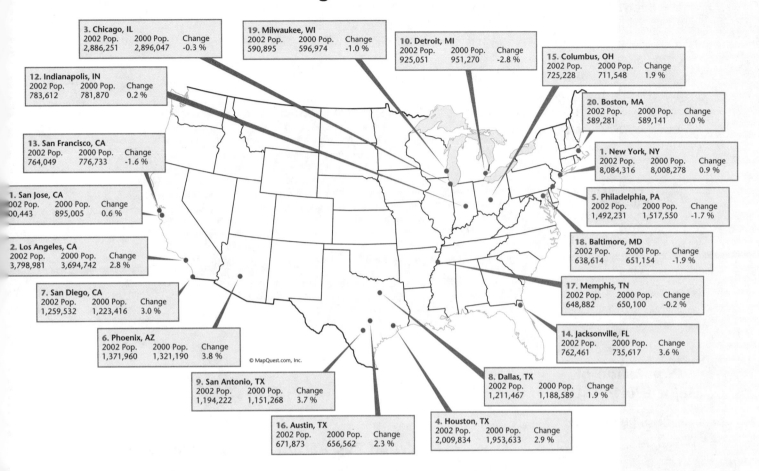

3. Chicago, IL
2002 Pop.	2000 Pop.	Change
2,886,251	2,896,047	-0.3 %

19. Milwaukee, WI
2002 Pop.	2000 Pop.	Change
590,895	596,974	-1.0 %

10. Detroit, MI
2002 Pop.	2000 Pop.	Change
925,051	951,270	-2.8 %

15. Columbus, OH
2002 Pop.	2000 Pop.	Change
725,228	711,548	1.9 %

12. Indianapolis, IN
2002 Pop.	2000 Pop.	Change
783,612	781,870	0.2 %

20. Boston, MA
2002 Pop.	2000 Pop.	Change
589,281	589,141	0.0 %

13. San Francisco, CA
2002 Pop.	2000 Pop.	Change
764,049	776,733	-1.6 %

1. New York, NY
2002 Pop.	2000 Pop.	Change
8,084,316	8,008,278	0.9 %

11. San Jose, CA
2002 Pop.	2000 Pop.	Change
00,443	895,005	0.6 %

5. Philadelphia, PA
2002 Pop.	2000 Pop.	Change
1,492,231	1,517,550	-1.7 %

2. Los Angeles, CA
2002 Pop.	2000 Pop.	Change
3,798,981	3,694,742	2.8 %

18. Baltimore, MD
2002 Pop.	2000 Pop.	Change
638,614	651,154	-1.9 %

7. San Diego, CA
2002 Pop.	2000 Pop.	Change
1,259,532	1,223,416	3.0 %

17. Memphis, TN
2002 Pop.	2000 Pop.	Change
648,882	650,100	-0.2 %

6. Phoenix, AZ
2002 Pop.	2000 Pop.	Change
1,371,960	1,321,190	3.8 %

© MapQuest.com, Inc.

14. Jacksonville, FL
2002 Pop.	2000 Pop.	Change
762,461	735,617	3.6 %

9. San Antonio, TX
2002 Pop.	2000 Pop.	Change
1,194,222	1,151,268	3.7 %

8. Dallas, TX
2002 Pop.	2000 Pop.	Change
1,211,467	1,188,589	1.9 %

16. Austin, TX
2002 Pop.	2000 Pop.	Change
671,873	656,562	2.3 %

4. Houston, TX
2002 Pop.	2000 Pop.	Change
2,009,834	1,953,633	2.9 %

Percent of Population by Race and Hispanic or Latino Origin for the 20 Largest Cities, 2000

	City	2000 Population	White	Black or African American	American Indian, Alaska Native	Asian	Hawaiian & Other Pacific Islander	Some Other Race	Two or More Races	Hispanic or Latino (of any race)
1	New York ....NY	8,008,278	44.7	26.6	0.5	9.8	0.1	13.4	4.9	27.0
2	Los Angeles ....CA	3,694,820	46.9	11.2	0.8	10.0	0.2	25.7	5.2	46.5
3	Chicago IL	2,896,016	42.0	36.8	0.4	4.3	0.1	13.6	2.9	26.0
4	Houston ....TX	1,953,631	49.3	25.3	0.4	5.3	0.1	16.5	3.1	37.4
5	Philadelphia..........PA	1,517,550	45.0	43.2	0.3	4.5	0.0	4.8	2.2	8.5
6	Phoenix ......AZ	1,321,045	71.1	5.1	2.0	2.0	0.1	16.4	3.3	34.1
7	San Diego ....CA	1,223,400	60.2	7.9	0.6	13.6	0.5	12.4	4.8	25.4
8	Dallas ....TX	1,188,580	50.8	25.9	0.5	2.7	0.1	17.2	2.7	35.6
9	San Antonio ....TX	1,144,646	67.7	6.8	0.8	1.6	0.1	19.3	3.7	58.7
10	Detroit ....MI	951,270	12.3	81.6	0.3	1.0	0.0	2.5	2.3	5.0
11	San Jose ....CA	894,943	47.5	3.5	0.8	26.9	0.4	15.9	5.0	30.2
12	Indianapolis..........IN	791,926	69.3	25.3	1.4	0.0	2.0	1.6	3.9	
13	San Francisco ....CA	776,733	49.7	7.8	0.4	30.8	0.5	6.5	4.3	14.1
14	Jacksonville ....FL	735,617	64.5	29.0	0.3	2.8	0.1	1.3	2.0	4.2
15	Columbus ....OH	711,470	67.9	24.5	0.3	3.4	0.1	1.2	2.6	2.5
16	Austin ....TX	656,562	65.4	10.0	0.6	4.7	0.1	16.2	3.0	30.5
17	Baltimore..........MD	651,154	31.6	64.3	0.3	1.5	0.0	0.7	1.5	1.7
18	Memphis ....TN	650,100	34.4	61.4	0.2	1.5	0.0	1.5	1.0	3.0
19	Milwaukee ....WI	596,974	50.0	37.3	0.9	2.9	0.1	6.1	2.7	12.0
20	Boston ....MA	589,141	54.5	25.3	0.4	7.5	0.1	7.8	4.4	14.4

Source: U.S. Census Bureau

THE WORLD IN THE 21ST CENTURY

The following four pages look at the growing world population and the latest trends in health and mortality. Some highlights:

- The world population has passed 6.1 billion, with 1.3 billion people in China alone.

- By 2050 the world population may pass 11 billion, with most of the growth in urban areas and developing countries.

- The highest life expectancies and lowest infant mortality rates are in North America, Western Europe, and Australia.

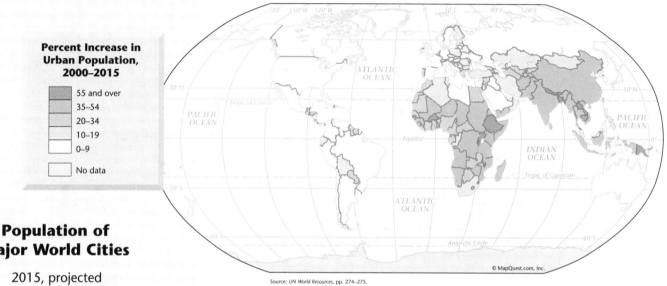

Percent Increase in Urban Population, 2000–2015
- 55 and over
- 35–54
- 20–34
- 10–19
- 0–9
- No data

Source: *UN World Resources*, pp. 274–275.

© MapQuest.com, Inc.

Population of Major World Cities

2015, projected

1	Tokyo	27,190,000
2	Dhaka	22,766,000
3	Mumbai	22,577,000
4	São Paulo	21,229,000
5	Delhi	20,884,000
6	Mexico City	20,434,000
7	New York	17,944,000
8	Jakarta	17,268,000
9	Kolkata	16,747,000
10	Karachi	16,197,000
11	Lagos	15,966,000
12	Los Angeles	14,494,000
13	Shanghai	13,598,000
14	Buenos Aires	13,185,000
15	Manila	12,579,000

These figures are for "urban agglomerations," which are densely populated urban areas, larger than the cities by themselves.

Source: UN, Dept. for Economic and Social Information and Policy Analysis

© MapQuest.com, Inc.

Urban Population Growth, 2000–2015

The world population will become increasingly urbanized in the early 21st century. It is predicted that the largest increases in urban population will occur in Africa and southern and eastern Asia.

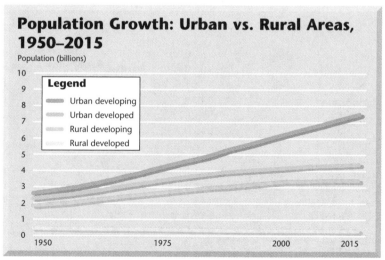

Population Growth: Urban vs. Rural Areas, 1950–2015

Population (billions)

Legend
- Urban developing
- Urban developed
- Rural developing
- Rural developed

Source: *UN World Resources*, p. 146.

Population growth in rural areas will taper off where it has not already. But urban growth will increase, especially in the developing nations.

Developed regions include United States, Canada, Japan, Europe, and Australia and New Zealand.

Developing regions include Africa, Asia (excluding Japan), South America and Central America, Mexico, and Oceania (excluding Australia and New Zealand). The European successor states of the former Soviet Union are classified as developed regions, while the Asian successor states are classified as developing regions.

Population Density, 2000

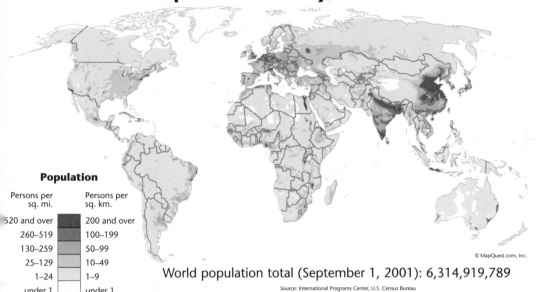

Population

Persons per sq. mi.	Persons per sq. km.
520 and over	200 and over
260–519	100–199
130–259	50–99
25–129	10–49
1–24	1–9
under 1	under 1

© MapQuest.com, Inc.

World population total (September 1, 2001): 6,314,919,789

Source: International Programs Center, U.S. Census Bureau

Population Density, Largest Countries

2000
People per square mile

China	330
India	800
United States	70
Indonesia	290
Brazil	50
Russia	20

2050
People per square mile

China	360
India	1,400
United States	100
Indonesia	450
Brazil	70
Russia	20

The world is becoming more crowded in the 21st century. In mid-2002, China had the highest population in the world, with an estimated 1.3 billion people, more than one-fifth of the total population. India had passed 1 billion, while the United States had the world's third-largest population, with about 288 million, followed by Indonesia, Brazil, and Pakistan.

Source: U.S. Census Bureau

Anticipated World Population Growth

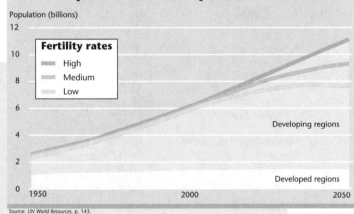

Population (billions)

Fertility rates
- High
- Medium
- Low

Developing regions

Developed regions

1950 2000 2050

Source: *UN World Resources*, p. 143.

The world population has grown from about 2 billion in 1950 to more than 6 billion today, and could almost double by 2050. Most of the growth will continue to occur in developing regions, where fertility rates (number of children born per woman of childbearing age) are relatively high.

Where the fertility rate is around 2 children per woman of childbearing age, the population will tend to stabilize. This figure indicates roughly that couples, over a lifetime, are replacing themselves without adding to the population.

Population experts at the United Nations actually give three different projections for future population growth. Under a **high** fertility-rate projection, which assumes rates would stabilize at an average of 2.6 in high-fertility regions and 2.1 in low-fertility regions, the global population would reach 11.2 billion by 2050. Under a **medium** projection, which assumes rates would ultimately stabilize at around replacement levels, the population would rise to 9.4 billion by 2050. Under a **low** fertility-rate projection, which assumes rates would eventually stabilize at lower-than-replacement levels, the world population would still reach about 7.7 billion by 2050.

Population Projections by Continent

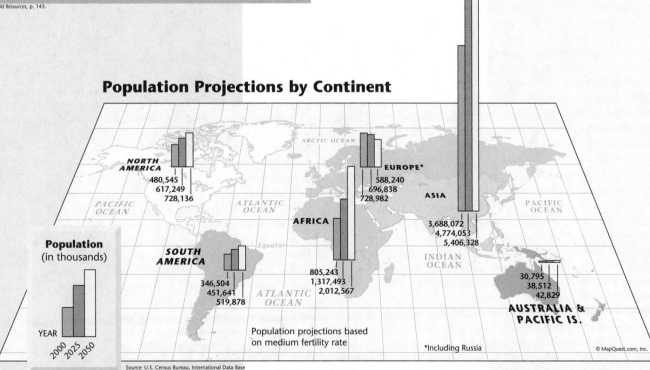

Population (in thousands)

YEAR 2000 2025 2050

NORTH AMERICA
480,545
617,249
728,136

EUROPE*
588,240
696,838
728,982

AFRICA
805,243
1,317,493
2,012,567

ASIA
3,688,072
4,774,053
5,406,328

SOUTH AMERICA
346,504
451,641
519,878

AUSTRALIA & PACIFIC IS.
30,795
38,512
42,829

Population projections based on medium fertility rate

*Including Russia

© MapQuest.com, Inc.

Source: U.S. Census Bureau, International Data Base

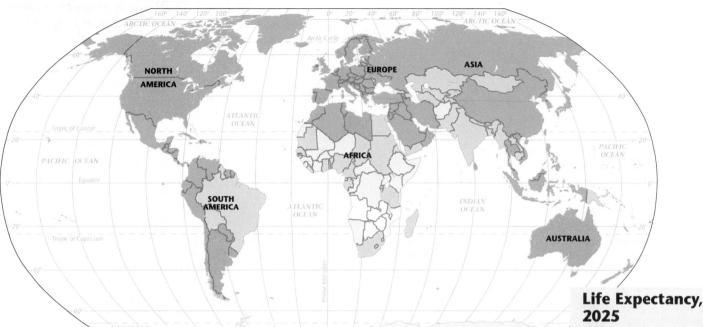

World Life Expectancy, 2000

Life Expectancy
(in years)

- 75–84
- 65–74
- 50–64
- 40–49
- Less than 40
- No data

Life expectancy at birth is a common measure of the number of years a person may expect to live. There are many factors, such as nutrition, sanitation, health and medical services, that contribute to helping people live longer.

As some of the above factors improve in the developing countries, life expectancy there should increase. But most of Sub-Saharan Africa will have less than average life expectancies.

Although it is not indicated here, females almost always have a longer life expectancy than males.

World Life Expectancy, 2025

Life Expectancy, 2025

World Average	70
United States	79

Highest

Andorra	84
Austria	84
Australia	83
Canada	82
Cyprus	82
Dominica	82
Israel	82
Japan	82
Kuwait	82
Monaco	82
San Marino	82
Singapore	82
Taiwan	82

Lowest

Malawi	45
Ethiopia	47
Zambia	47
Rwanda	48
Swaziland	48
Botswana	49
Namibia	50
Zimbabwe	50
Kenya	53
Lesotho	53

Source: U.S. Bureau of the Census, World Population Profile: 1998

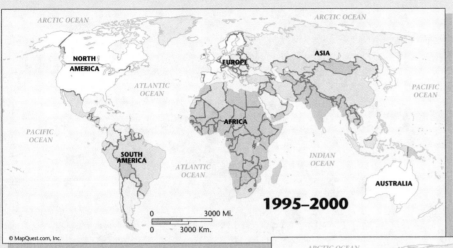

1995–2000

© MapQuest.com, Inc.

Infant Mortality Averages, 2015–2020

by continent with highest and lowest country

World Average 35

Africa	55	Europe	8
Sierra Leone	114	Albania	20
Mauritius	8	Austria & 14 others	5
Asia	32		
Afghanistan	118	North America	22
Japan	4	Haiti	82
		Canada	5
		U.S.	5
Australia & Oceania	15		
Papua		South America	23
New Guinea	37	Guyana	37
Australia	5	Chile	9

Infant Mortality

Infant mortality means the number of deaths before the age of one per 1,000 live births. It is a fairly common way of judging how healthy a country is. Presently there are about 14 countries with infant mortality rates lower than that of the United States.

With improvements in sanitation and health care, it is expected that infant mortality will decline substantially in the 21st century. However, it will continue to be a serious problem especially in Sub-Saharan Africa and other developing regions.

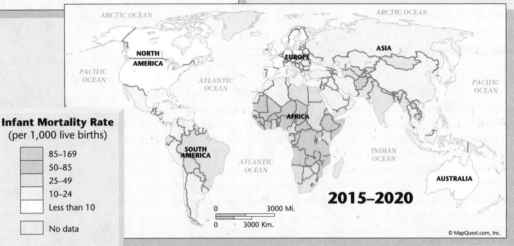

Infant Mortality Rate
(per 1,000 live births)

- 85–169
- 50–85
- 25–49
- 10–24
- Less than 10
- No data

2015–2020

© MapQuest.com, Inc.

Source: UN Population Division and UN Children's Fund

Food & Nutrition

There has been a general trend towards better nutrition, but Sub-Saharan Africa remains a problem area: increasing numbers of people will be suffering from undernutrition.

On a worldwide basis, the food supply seems adequate. Unfortunately the availability of food and the distribution of people don't always match up.

Undernutrition in Developing Countries, 1969-2010

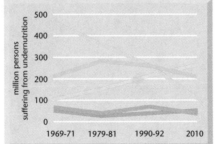

million persons suffering from undernutrition

500, 400, 300, 200, 100

1969-71   1979-81   1990-92   2010

Legend
- Latin America and the Caribbean
- Near East and North Africa
- Sub-Saharan Africa
- East and Southeast Asia
- South Asia

Fertility

This rate is the number of births related to the number of women of childbearing age. Currently the rate for developed nations is about 1.6, but it is about 2.9 in developing nations.

Africa shows the slowest reduction in the fertility rate. With improvements in infant mortality and the implementation of family planning programs, the rate should stabilize.

Average Daily per Capita Calorie Supply, 1999

by continent with highest and lowest country

PORTUGAL 3,768
CROATIA 2,617
ISRAEL 3,542
AFGHANISTAN 1,755
UNITED STATES 3,754
HAITI 1,977
VENEZUELA 2,229
PAPUA NEW GUINEA 2,186
TUNISIA 3,388
SOMALIA 1,555
ARGENTINA 3,176
NEW ZEALAND 3,152

Source: UN Food and Agriculture Organization, UN Population Division, U.S. Department of Agriculture

© MapQuest.com, Inc.

Trends in Fertility Rates

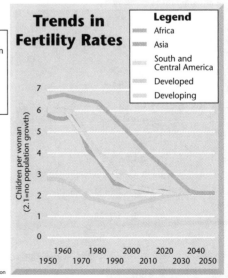

Legend
- Africa
- Asia
- South and Central America
- Developed
- Developing

Children per woman (2.1=no population growth)

7, 6, 5, 4, 3, 2, 1, 0

1950 1960 1970 1980 1990 2000 2010 2020 2030 2040 2050

Source: UN Population Division

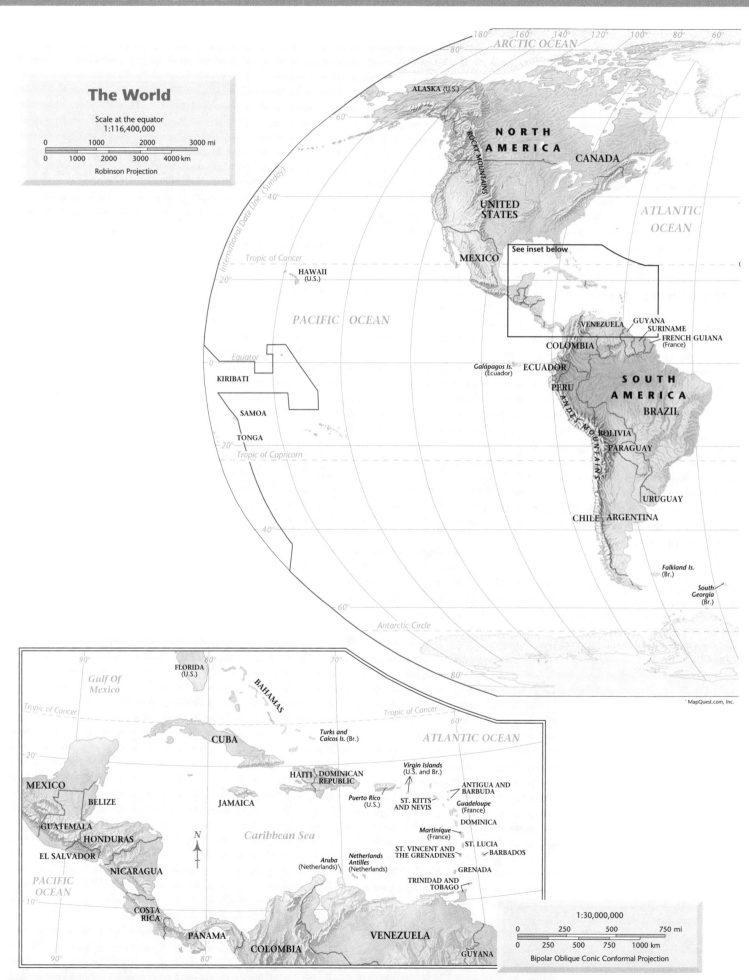

The World

Scale at the equator
1:116,400,000

0   1000   2000   3000 mi
0   1000   2000   3000   4000 km

Robinson Projection

ARCTIC OCEAN

180°   160°   140°   120°   100°   80°   60°

80°

ALASKA (U.S.)

60°

NORTH AMERICA

ROCKY MOUNTAINS

CANADA

40°

UNITED STATES

ATLANTIC OCEAN

MEXICO

See inset below

Tropic of Cancer

20°

HAWAII (U.S.)

PACIFIC OCEAN

VENEZUELA   GUYANA
SURINAME
FRENCH GUIANA
(France)

COLOMBIA

Galápagos Is.
(Ecuador)   ECUADOR

Equator

0°

KIRIBATI

PERU

SOUTH AMERICA

BRAZIL

ANDES MOUNTAINS

SAMOA

BOLIVIA

TONGA   PARAGUAY

Tropic of Capricorn

20°

URUGUAY

CHILE   ARGENTINA

40°

Falkland Is.
(Br.)

South
Georgia
(Br.)

60°

Antarctic Circle

80°

' MapQuest.com, Inc.

International Date Line (Sunday)

90°   80°   FLORIDA
(U.S.)   70°

Gulf Of
Mexico   BAHAMAS

Tropic of Cancer   Tropic of Cancer

60°

ATLANTIC OCEAN

20°   CUBA   Turks and
Caicos Is. (Br.)

Virgin Islands
(U.S. and Br.)

MEXICO   HAITI   DOMINICAN
REPUBLIC

ANTIGUA AND
BARBUDA

BELIZE   JAMAICA   Puerto Rico
(U.S.)   ST. KITTS
AND NEVIS   Guadeloupe
(France)

GUATEMALA   N   DOMINICA

HONDURAS   Caribbean Sea   Martinique
(France)   ST. LUCIA

EL SALVADOR   ST. VINCENT AND
THE GRENADINES   BARBADOS

NICARAGUA   Aruba
(Netherlands)   Netherlands
Antilles
(Netherlands)   GRENADA

PACIFIC
OCEAN

10°   TRINIDAD AND
TOBAGO

COSTA
RICA

PANAMA

COLOMBIA   VENEZUELA

GUYANA

90°   80°

1:30,000,000

0   250   500   750 mi
0   250   500   750   1000 km

Bipolar Oblique Conic Conformal Projection

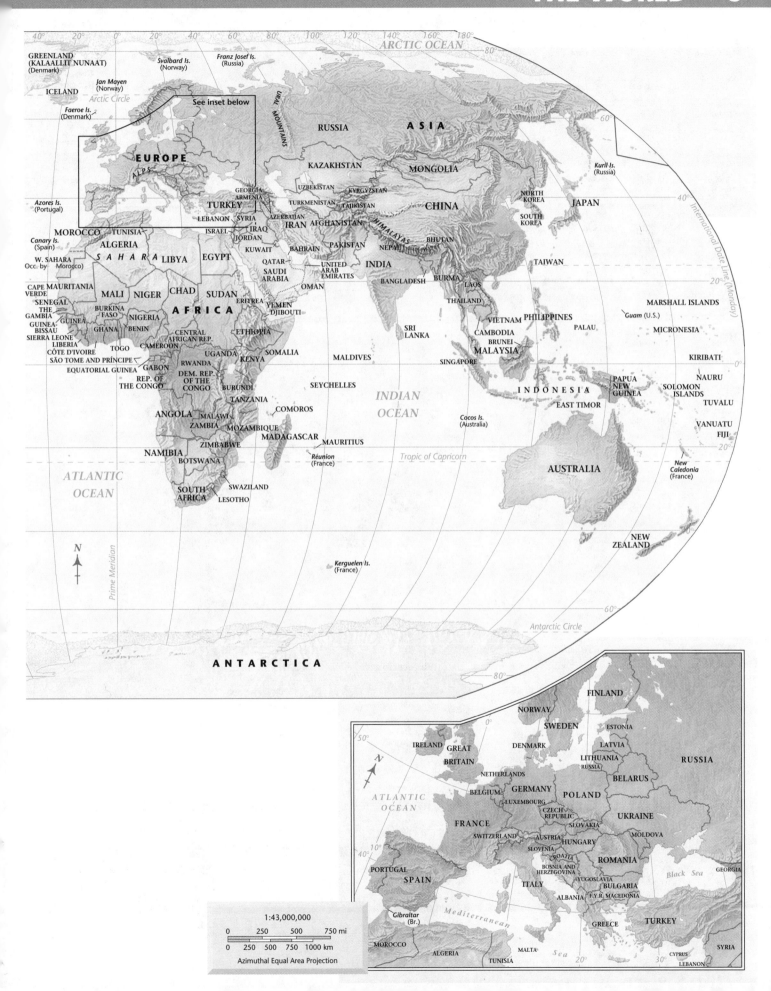

ARCTIC OCEAN

GREENLAND
(KALAALLIT NUNAAT)
(Denmark)

Svalbard Is.
(Norway)

Franz Josef Is.
(Russia)

Jan Mayen
(Norway)

ICELAND

Arctic Circle

Faeroe Is.
(Denmark)

See inset below

URAL MOUNTAINS

RUSSIA

A S I A

EUROPE

ALPS

KAZAKHSTAN

MONGOLIA

Kuril Is.
(Russia)

Azores Is.
(Portugal)

GEORGIA
ARMENIA
TURKEY

UZBEKISTAN
KYRGYZSTAN
TURKMENISTAN
TAJIKISTAN

CHINA

NORTH
KOREA

JAPAN

SOUTH
KOREA

LEBANON SYRIA
AZERBAIJAN

Canary Is.
(Spain)

MOROCCO TUNISIA

ISRAEL
JORDAN

IRAQ

IRAN AFGHANISTAN

HIMALAYAS

TAIWAN

ALGERIA

S A H A R A LIBYA

EGYPT

KUWAIT

PAKISTAN

NEPAL

BHUTAN

W. SAHARA
Occ. by Morocco

QATAR
SAUDI
ARABIA

BAHRAIN

UNITED
ARAB
EMIRATES

INDIA

BANGLADESH

BURMA

LAOS

MARSHALL ISLANDS

CAPE
VERDE

MAURITANIA

MALI
NIGER

CHAD
SUDAN

OMAN

ERITREA

YEMEN
DJIBOUTI

THAILAND

Guam (U.S.)

SENEGAL
THE
GAMBIA
GUINEA-
BISSAU

BURKINA
FASO
GUINEA

NIGERIA
BENIN

A F R I C A

ETHIOPIA

SRI
LANKA

VIETNAM
PHILIPPINES

MICRONESIA

PALAU

SIERRA LEONE
LIBERIA
CÔTE D'IVOIRE
SÃO TOME AND PRÍNCIPE

GHANA

TOGO

CAMEROON

CENTRAL
AFRICAN REP.

UGANDA
KENYA

SOMALIA

MALDIVES

CAMBODIA
BRUNEI

MALAYSIA

KIRIBATI

EQUATORIAL GUINEA
REP. OF
THE CONGO

GABON

RWANDA
DEM. REP.
OF THE
CONGO

BURUNDI

SINGAPORE

I N D O N E S I A

PAPUA
NEW
GUINEA

NAURU

SOLOMON
ISLANDS

TUVALU

TANZANIA

SEYCHELLES

EAST TIMOR

ANGOLA

MALAWI

ZAMBIA

MOZAMBIQUE

COMOROS

MADAGASCAR

INDIAN
OCEAN

Cocos Is.
(Australia)

VANUATU
FIJI

ZIMBABWE

MAURITIUS

NAMIBIA

BOTSWANA

Réunion
(France)

Tropic of Capricorn

AUSTRALIA

New
Caledonia
(France)

ATLANTIC
OCEAN

SOUTH
AFRICA

SWAZILAND

LESOTHO

N

Prime Meridian

Kerguelen Is.
(France)

NEW
ZEALAND

Antarctic Circle

A N T A R C T I C A

1:43,000,000

| 0 | 250 | 500 | 750 mi |
| 0 | 250 | 500 | 750 | 1000 km |

Azimuthal Equal Area Projection

FINLAND

NORWAY

SWEDEN

ESTONIA

IRELAND
GREAT
BRITAIN

DENMARK

LATVIA

RUSSIA

LITHUANIA
RUSSIA

NETHERLANDS

BELARUS

N

ATLANTIC
OCEAN

BELGIUM
LUXEMBOURG

GERMANY

POLAND

UKRAINE

CZECH
REPUBLIC

FRANCE

SWITZERLAND

AUSTRIA

SLOVAKIA

MOLDOVA

SLOVENIA
CROATIA

HUNGARY

ROMANIA

PORTUGAL

SPAIN

ITALY

BOSNIA AND
HERZEGOVINA

YUGOSLAVIA

BULGARIA

Black Sea

GEORGIA

ALBANIA

F.Y.R. MACEDONIA

Gibraltar
(Br.)

Mediterranean

GREECE

TURKEY

MOROCCO

ALGERIA

TUNISIA

MALTA

Sea

CYPRUS
LEBANON

SYRIA

MAJOR CITIES

Afghanistan (metro)
Kabul 2,602,000

Bahrain
Manama 150,000

Bangladesh (metro)
Dhaka 13,181,000

Bhutan
Thimphu 32,000

Brunei
Band. Seri Begawan 46,000

Cambodia (metro)
Phnom Penh 1,109,000

China (metro)
Shanghai 12,887,000
Beijing 10,836,000
Tianjin 9,156,000
Hong Kong 6,860,000
Wuhan 5,169,000
Chongqing 4,900,000
Shenyang 4,828,000
Guangzhou 3,893,000
Chengdu 3,294,000
Xi'an 3,123,000
Harbin 2,928,000
Nanjing 2,740,000
Zibo 2,675,000

Cyprus
Nicosia 199,000

East Timor
Dili 140,000

India (metro)
Mumbai
(Bombay) 16,086,000
Kolkata
(Calcutta) 13,058,000
Delhi 12,441,000
Madras 6,353,000
Bangalore 5,567,000
Hyderabad 5,445,000

Indonesia (metro)
Jakarta 11,018,000
Bandung 3,409,000
Surabaya 2,461,000
Medan 1,879,000

Iran (metro)
Tehran 6,979,000
Mashhad 1,990,000
Esfahan 1,381,000

Iraq (metro)
Baghdad 4,865,000
Irbil 2,369,000
Basra 1,337,000
Mosul 1,131,000

Israel (metro)
Tel Aviv-Jaffa 2,001,000
Jerusalem 661,000

Japan (metro)
Tokyo 26,546,000
Osaka 11,013,000
Nagoya 3,157,000
Kitakyushu 2,750,000
Kyoto 1,849,000
Sapporo 1,813,000
Sendai 953,000
Hiroshima 866,000

Jordan (metro)
Amman 1,181,000

Kazakhstan (metro)
Almaty
(Alma-Ata) 1,130,000
Astana 328,000

North Korea (metro)
P'yŏngyang 3,124,000
Nampo 1,022,000

South Korea (metro)
Seoul 9,888,000
Pusan 3,830,000
Inch'on 2,884,000
Taegu 2,675,000

Kuwait (metro)
Kuwait 879,000

Kyrgyzstan
Bishkek 736,000

Laos
Vientiane 633,000

Lebanon (metro)
Beirut 2,070,000

Malaysia (metro)
Kuala Lumpur 1,379,000

Maldives
Male 84,000

Mongolia (metro)
Ulaanbaatar 781,000

Myanmar (Burma) (metro)
Yangon
(Rangoon) 4,504,000
Mandalay 770,000

Nepal
Kathmandu 755,000

Oman
Muscat 540,000

Pakistan (metro)
Karachi 10,032,000
Lahore 5,452,000
Faisalabad 2,142,000
Islamabad 636,000

Philippines (metro)
Manila 9,950,000
Quezon City 2,160,000
Davao 1,146,000

Qatar
Doha 285,000

Russia (Asian) (metro)
Novosibirsk 1,321,000
Yekaterinburg 1,218,000
Omsk 1,174,000
Chelyabinsk 1,045,000

Saudi Arabia (metro)
Riyadh 4,549,000
Jeddah 3,192,000
Mecca 1,335,000
Medina 891,000

Singapore (metro)
Singapore 4,018,000

Sri Lanka
Colombo 615,000

Syria (metro)
Halab (Aleppo) 2,229,000
Damascus 2,144,000
Homs 811,000

Taiwan (metro)
Taipei 2,596,000
Kaohsiung 1,435,000
T'aichung 881,870

Tajikistan
Dushanbe 522,000

Thailand (metro)
Bangkok 7,372,000

Turkey (Asian) (metro)
Ankara 3,155,000
Izmir 2,214,000

Turkmenistan
Ashgabat 558,000

United Arab Emirates
Dubai (metro) 886,000
Abu Dhabi 471,000

Uzbekistan (metro)
Tashkent 2,148,000

Vietnam (metro)
Ho Chi Minh City 4,619,000
Hanoi 3,751,000
Haiphong 1,676,000

Yemen (metro)
Sanaa 1,410,000

International comparability of city population data is limited by various data inconsistencies.

© MapQuest.com, Inc.

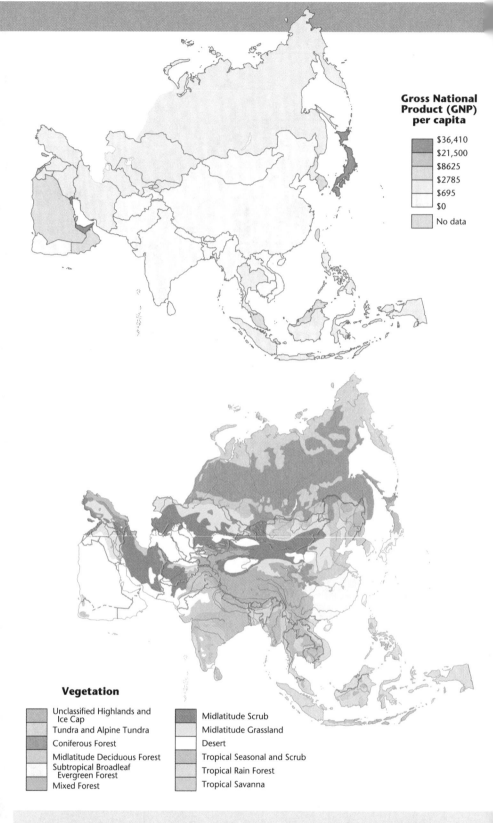

Gross National Product (GNP) per capita

- $36,410
- $21,500
- $8625
- $2785
- $695
- $0
- No data

Vegetation

- Unclassified Highlands and Ice Cap
- Tundra and Alpine Tundra
- Coniferous Forest
- Midlatitude Deciduous Forest
- Subtropical Broadleaf Evergreen Forest
- Mixed Forest
- Midlatitude Scrub
- Midlatitude Grassland
- Desert
- Tropical Seasonal and Scrub
- Tropical Rain Forest
- Tropical Savanna

Asia: Population, by nation (in millions)*

CHINA	INDIA	INDON.	PAKIS.	BANGL.	JAPAN	PHILIP.	All other Asian countries
1304.2	1065.5	219.9	153.6	146.7	127.7	80.0	719.0*

*Excluding Russia

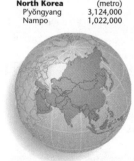

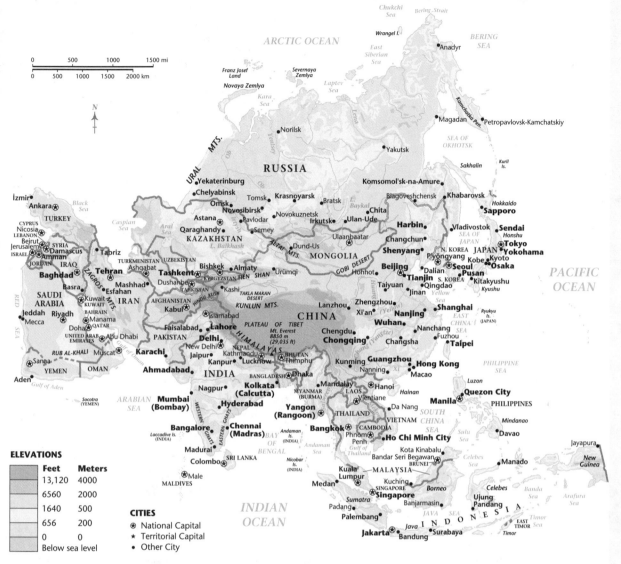

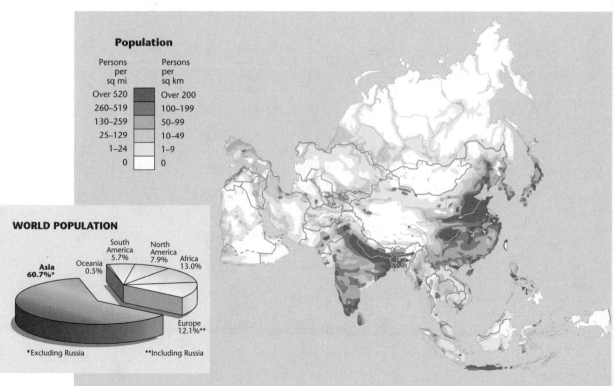

CLIMATE

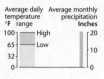

Average daily temperature °F range — High / Low
Average monthly precipitation Inches

ALMATY, Kazakhstan
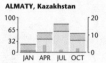

BEIRUT, Lebanon
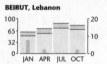

COLOMBO, Sri Lanka
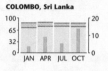

DHAKA, Bangladesh
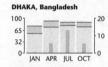

HONG KONG, China
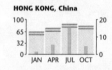

JAKARTA, Indonesia

NEW DELHI, India
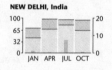

RIYADH, Saudi Arabia
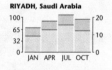

TEHRAN, Iran
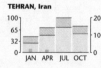

TIANJIN, China
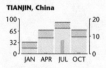

TOKYO, Japan
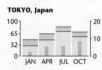

YAKUTSK, Russia

ELEVATIONS

Feet	Meters
13,120	4000
6560	2000
1640	500
656	200
0	0
Below sea level	

CITIES

⊛ National Capital
★ Territorial Capital
• Other City

Population

Persons per sq mi	Persons per sq km
Over 520	Over 200
260–519	100–199
130–259	50–99
25–129	10–49
1–24	1–9
0	0

WORLD POPULATION

Asia 60.7%*
Oceania 0.5%
South America 5.7%
North America 7.9%
Africa 13.0%
Europe 12.1%**

*Excluding Russia   **Including Russia

Japan

★ National Capital
• Other City

1:7,500,000

0   50   100   150 mi
0 50 100 150 km

Lambert Conformal Conic Projection

Inset I — Hokkaido

HOKKAIDO (see inset)

Sea of Okhotsk

La Pérouse Strait
Point Soya
Rebun
Rishiri
Wakkanai
Kitami Mts.
Mombetsu
Haboro
Teshio
Ishikari
Kitami
Cape Shiretoko
Kunashir (Russia)
Asahikawa
Asahi Dake 2290 m (7513 ft)
Cape Kamui
Otaru
Yubari
Sapporo
Obihiro
Kushiro
Tomakomai
Chitose
HIDAKA MTS.
Tokachi
Nemuro
Nemuro Strait
Cape Erimo
Okushiri
Uchiura Bay
Muroran
Oshima Pen.
Hakodate
Matsumae
Tsugaru Strait

same scale as main map

Main map — Honshu / Kyushu / Shikoku

SOUTH KOREA

Sea of Japan

P'ohang
Pusan
Korea Strait
Tsu
Izuhara
Iki

East China Sea

Oki Is.
Dogo
Dozen

HOKKAIDO (see inset)
Okushiri
Oshima Pen.
Hakodate
Matsumae
Cape Henashi
Tsugaru Strait
Mutsu
Aomori
Hirosake
AOMORI
Towada L.
Hachinohe
Akita
Miyako
Morioka
AKITA
IWATE
Ou Mts.
Kitakami
Tsuruoka
MIYAGI
Ishinomaki
YAMAGATA
Sendai
Ishinomaki Bay
Yamagata
Zao 1841 m (6040 ft)
Mogami
Sado
Ryotsu
Niigata
Fukushima
NIIGATA
Aizuwakamatsu
Nagaoka
Koriyama
FUKUSHIMA
Iwaki
HONSHU
Noto Peninsula
Joetsu
TOCHIGI
Nikko
IBARAKI
Hitachi
Toyama Bay
ISHIKAWA
Toyama
Nagano
GUMMA
Maebashi
Utsunomiya
Mito
Kanazawa
TOYAMA
Komatsu
Asama 2542 m (8340 ft)
Koshigaya
Kawaguchi
SAITAMA
Urawa
Matsudo
Fukui
Matsumoto
NAGANO
Kawagoe
Omiya
Kashiwa
FUKUI
Tsuruga
Yariga 3180 m (10,433 ft)
Japanese Alps
Kofu
Tokorozawa
Ichikawa
Hachioji
TOKYO
Chiba
Shirane 3192 m (10,472 ft)
YAMANASHI
Machida
Ichihara
Wakasa Bay
Maizuru
SHIGA
GIFU
Gifu
Sagamihara
Fuji 3776 m (12,388 ft)
KANAGAWA
Yokohama
Kawasaki
Matsue
Tottori
HYOGO
KYOTO
Ichinomiya
AICHI
Numazu
SHIZUOKA
CHIBA
Boso Pen.
Yokosuka
Fujisawa
Cape Hino
Yonago
TOTTORI
Biwa Lake
Otsu
Kyoto
Nagoya
Kuwana
Toyota
Shimizu
Izu Pen.
Sagami Bay
SHIMANE
Ibaraki
Toyonaka
Nishinomiya
Nara
Okazaki
Yokkaichi
Hamamatsu
Cape Nojima
Gotsu
CHUGOKU
Okayama
HIROSHIMA
Kurashiki
Himeji
Akashi
Kobe
Suita
Sakai
Yao
Higashiosaka
MIE
Toyohashi
Ise Bay
Kozu
Nii
Miyake
Masuda
OKAYAMA
Amagasaki
Takatsuki
Hirakata
Neyagawa
Osaka
NARA
Izu Islands
Mikura
Yamaguchi
Hiroshima
YAMAGUCHI
Fukuyama
Kure
Takamatsu
KAGAWA
Awaji
Wakayama
WAKAYAMA
Kii Peninsula
Kinokawa
Kii Channel
PACIFIC OCEAN
Shimonoseki
Tokuyama
Iwakuni
Inland Sea
Niihama
TOKUSHIMA
Tokushima
Kozu
Hachijo
Kitakyushu
Ube
Matsuyama
Ishizuchi 1981 m (6499 ft)
KOCHI
Yoshinogawa
Fukuoka
Kurume
EHIME
Kochi
Tosa Bay
Cape Muroto
Bonin Is. (see inset)
Sasebo
SAGA
Saga
OITA
Oita
Uwajima
SHIKOKU
Cape Ashizuri
Cape Shiono
Nakadori
Omuta
NAGASAKI
Nagasaki
Kumamoto
KYUSHU
Aso 1592 m (5223 ft)
Nobeoka
Cape Sata
Fukue
Fukue
Yatsushiro
Amakusa Is.
KUMAMOTO
MIYAZAKI
Koshiki Is.
KAGOSHIMA
Miyazaki
Miyakonojo
Kagoshima
Osumi Pen.
Satsuma Peninsula
Cape Sata
Osumi Strait
Osumi Is.
Tanega
Yaku
Kuchino
Nakano
Suwanose
Akuseki
Tokara Islands
Takara
RYUKYU ISLANDS (see inset)

Inset II — Ryukyu Islands

RYUKYU ISLANDS
AMAMI ISLANDS
Amami
Naze
Kakeroma
Tokuno
Okino Erabu
Yoron
Okinawa Islands
Kume
Okinawa
Gushikawa
Naha
OKINAWA
Senkaku Islands
Miyako
Hirara
Yonaguni
Ishigaki
Iriomote
Sakishima Islands

0   50   100 mi
0 50 100 km

Inset III — Bonin / Volcano Islands

Nishino
Muko
Nishino
Chichi
Haha
Bonin Islands
Kita
Iwo Jima
Volcano Islands
Minami

0   50   100 mi
0 50 100 km

N

Japan

Capital: Tokyo
Area: 145,850 sq. mi.
          377,850 sq. km.
Population: 127,654,000
Largest City: Tokyo
Language: Japanese
Monetary Unit: Yen

Cities and Towns

Aizuwakamatsu	C2
Akashi	B3
Akita	D2
Amagasaki	B3
Aomori	D1
Asahikawa	Inset I
Ashikaga	B3
Awaji	B3
Chiba	D3
Chitose	Inset I
Fujisawa	C3
Fukue	A3
Fukui	C2
Fukuoka	A3
Fukushima	D2
Fukuyama	B3
Funabashi	D3
Gifu	C3
Gotsu	B3
Gushikawa	Inset II
Haboro	Inset I
Hachinohe	D1
Hachioji	C3
Hakodate	D1, Inset I
Hamamatsu	C3
Higashiosaka	B3
Himeji	B3
Hirakata	B3
Hirara	Inset II
Hirosake	D1
Hiroshima	B3
Hitachi	D2
Ibaraki	B3
Ichihara	D3
Ichikawa	D3
Ichinomiya	C3
Ise	C3
Ishinomaki	D2
Iwaki	D2
Iwakuni	B3
Izuhara	A3
Joetsu	C2
Kagoshima	A4
Kanazawa	C2
Kashiwa	D3
Kasugai	C3
Kawagoe	C3
Kawaguchi	C3
Kawasaki	C3
Kitakyushu	A3
Kitami	Inset I
Kobe	B3
Kochi	B3
Kofu	C3
Komatsu	C2
Koriyama	D2
Koshigaya	C3
Kumamoto	A3
Kurashiki	B3
Kure	B3
Kurume	A3
Kushiro	Inset I
Kyoto	B3
Machida	C3
Maebashi	C2
Maizuru	B3
Masuda	A3
Matsudo	C3
Matsue	B3
Matsumae	D1, Inset I
Matsumoto	C2
Matsuyama	B3
Mito	D2
Miyako	D2
Miyakonojo	A4
Miyazaki	A4
Mombetsu	Inset I
Morioka	D2
Muroran	D1, Inset I
Mutsu	D1
Nagano	C2
Nagaoka	C2
Nagasaki	A3
Nagoya	C3
Naha	Inset II
Nara	B3
Naze	Inset II
Nemuro	Inset I
Neyagawa	B3
Niigata	C2
Niihama	B3
Nikko	C2
Nishinomiya	B3
Nobeoka	A3
Numazu	C3
Obihiro	Inset I
Oita	A3
Okayama	B3
Okazaki	C3
Omiya	C3
Omuta	A3
Osaka	B3
Otaru	Inset I
Otsu	B3
Ryotsu	C2
Saga	A3
Sagamihara	C3
Sakai	B3
Sapporo	Inset I
Sasebo	A3
Sendai	D2
Shimizu	C3
Shimonoseki	A3
Shizuoka	C3
Suita	B3
Takamatsu	B3
Takatsuki	B3
Tanabe	B3
Tokorozawa	C3
Tokushima	B3
Tokuyama	A3
Tokyo, capital	C3
Tomakomai	Inset I
Tottori	B3
Toyama	C2
Toyohashi	C3
Toyonaka	B3
Toyota	C3
Tsuruga	C2
Tsuruoka	C2
Ube	A3
Urawa	C3
Utsunomiya	C2
Uwajima	B3
Wakayama	B3
Wakkanai	Inset I
Yamagata	D2
Yamaguchi	A3
Yao	B3
Yatsushiro	A3

Japan: Map Index

Prefectures

Aichi	C3	Gumma	C2	Mie	C3	Shiga	C3
Akita	D2	Hiroshima	B3	Miyagi	D2	Shimane	B3
Aomori	D1	Hokkaido	D1, Inset I	Miyazaki	A3	Shizuoka	C3
Chiba	D3	Hyogo	B3	Nagano	C2	Tochigi	C2
Ehime	B3	Ibaraki	D2	Nagasaki	A3	Tokushima	B3
Fukui	C3	Ishikawa	C2	Nara	B3	Tokyo	C3
Fukuoka	A3	Iwate	D2	Niigata	C2	Tottori	B3
Fukushima	C2	Kagawa	B3	Oita	A3	Toyama	C2
Gifu	C3	Kagoshima	A4	Okayama	B3	Wakayama	B3
		Kanagawa	C3	Okinawa	Inset II	Yamagata	D2
		Kochi	B3	Osaka	B3	Yamaguchi	A3
		Kumamoto	A3	Saga	A3	Yamanashi	C3
		Kyoto	B3	Saitama	C3		

© MapQuest.com, Inc.

NORTH KOREA, SOUTH KOREA, TAIWAN

Japan: Map Index

Yokkaichi C3
Yokohama..........C3
Yokosuka C3
Yonago B3
Yubari ....Inset I

Other Features

Akuseki, *island*..........A4
Amakusa, *islands*..........A3
Amami, *island*..........Inset II
Amami, *islands* ....Inset II
Asahi Dake, *mt.* ....Inset I
Asama, *mt.* C2
Ashizuri, *cape* B3
Aso, *mt.* A3
Awaji, *island* B3
Biwa, *lake* B3
Bonin, *islands*..........Inset III
Boso, *peninsula*..........D3
Bungo, *channel*..........B3
Chichi, *island* ....Inset III
Chugoku, *mts.* B3
Dogo, *island* B2
Dozen, *island* B2
East China, *sea* A4
Erimo, *cape* ....Inset I
Fuji, *mt.* C3
Fukue, *island*..........A3
Hachijo, *island* C3
Haha, *island*..........Inset III
Henashi, *cape* C1
Hidaka, *mts.*..........Inset I
Hino, *cape*..........B3
Hokkaido, *island* ....D1, Inset I
Honshu, *island* C2
Iki, *island*..........A3
Inland, *sea* B3
Iriomote, *island*..........Inset II
Ise, *bay*..........C3
Ishigaki, *island*..........Inset II
Ishikari, *river*..........Inset I
Ishinomaki, *bay* D2
Ishizuchi, *mt.*..........B3
Iwo Jima, *island* ....Inset III
Izu, *islands* C3
Izu, *peninsula* C3
Japan, *sea* B2
Japanese Alps, *mts.* C3
Kakeroma, *island*..........Inset II
Kamui, *cape*..........Inset I
Kii, *channel* B3
Kii, *peninsula*..........B3
Kita, *island*..........Inset III
Kitakami, *river*..........D2
Kitami, *mts.* ....Inset I
Korea, *strait* A3
Koshiki, *islands* A4
Kozu, *island* C3
Kuchino, *island* A4
Kume, *island*..........Inset II
Kyushu, *island*..........A3
La Pérouse, *strait* ....Inset I
Mikura, *island*..........C3
Minami, *island*..........Inset III
Miyake, *island*..........C3
Miyako, *island*..........Inset II
Mogami, *river*..........D2
Muko, *island* ....Inset III
Muroto, *cape* B3
Nakadori, *island* A3
Nakano, *island* A4
Nemuro, *strait*..........Inset I
Nii, *island* C3
Nishino, *island*..........Inset III
Nojima, *cape* D3
Noto, *peninsula* C2
Okhotsk, *sea* ....Inset I
Oki, *islands* B2
Okinawa, *island* ....Inset II
Okinawa, *islands*..........Inset II
Okino Erabu, *island*......Inset II
Okushiri, *island* ......C1, Inset I
Oshima, *peninsula*..D1, Inset I
Osumi, *islands*..........A4
Osumi, *peninsula*..........A4
Osumi, *strait*..........A4
Ou, *mts.* D2
Rebun, *island*..........Inset I
Rishiri, *island* ....Inset I
Ryukyu, *islands* ......A4, Inset II
Sado, *island* C2
Sagami, *bay* C3
Sakishima, *islands* ....Inset II
Sata, *cape*..........A4
Satsuma, *peninsula* A4
Senkaku, *islands* ....Inset II
Shikoku, *island* B3
Shimonoseki, *strait* A3
Shinano, *river* C2
Shiono, *cape*..........B3
Shirane, *mt.* C3
Shiretoko, *cape* ....Inset I
Soya, *point*..........Inset I
Suwanose, *island*..........A4
Takara, *island* A4
Tanega, *island*..........A4
Tenryu, *river* C3
Teshio, *river* ....Inset I
Tokachi, *river* ....Inset I
Tokara, *islands*..........A4
Tokuno, *island*..........Inset II
Tone, *river*..........C2
Tosa, *bay*..........B3
Towada, *lake* D1
Toyama, *bay*..........C2
Tsu, *island*..........A3
Tsugaru, *strait* ....D1, Inset I
Uchiura, *bay* ....Inset I
Volcano, *islands* ....Inset III
Wakasa, *bay* B3
Yaku, *island*..........A4
Yariga, *mt.* C2
Yonaguni, *island* ....Inset II
Yoron, *island*..........Inset II
Yoshino, *river*..........B3
Zao, *mt.* D2

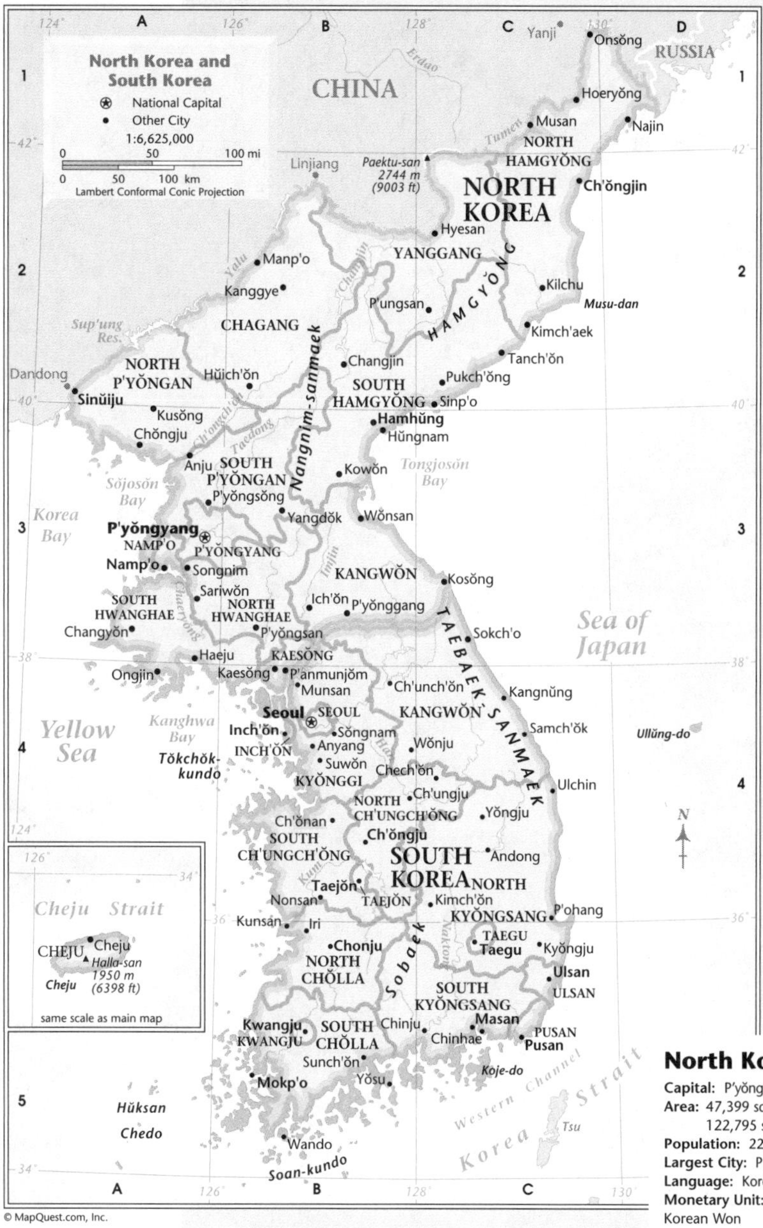

North Korea and South Korea
National Capital
Other City
1:6,625,000
0 50 100 mi
0 50 100 km
Lambert Conformal Conic Projection
CHINA
RUSSIA
NORTH KOREA
SOUTH KOREA
Yellow Sea
Sea of Japan
Korea Bay
Paektu-san 2744 m (9003 ft)
P'yŏngyang
Seoul
Cheju Strait
same scale as main map
Korea Strait
Western Channel
© MapQuest.com, Inc.

North Korea

Capital: P'yŏngyang
Area: 47,399 sq. mi.
122,795 sq. km.
Population: 22,664,000
Largest City: P'yŏngyang
Language: Korean
Monetary Unit: North Korean Won

South Korea

Capital: Seoul
Area: 38,330 sq. mi.
99,301 sq. km.
Population: 47,700,000
Largest City: Seoul
Language: Korean
Monetary Unit: South Korean Won

North Korea: Map Index

Provinces

Chagang B2
Kaesŏng B3
Kangwŏn..........B3
Namp'o..........A3
North Hamgyŏng C1
North Hwanghae..........B3
North P'yŏngan A2
P'yŏngyang..........A3
South Hamgyŏng B2
South Hwanghae..........A3
South P'yŏngan..........B3
Yanggang B2

Cities and Towns

Anju A3
Changjin B2
Changyŏn A3
Ch'ŏngjin C2
Chŏngju A3
Haeju A3
Hamhŭng B3
Hoeryŏng C1
Hŭich'ŏn B2
Hŭngnam B3
Hyesan C2
Ich'ŏn B3
Kaesŏng B4
Kanggye B2
Kilchu C2
Kimch'aek C2
Kosŏng C3
Kowŏn B3
Kusŏng A3
Manp'o B2
Musan C1
Najin..........D1
Namp'o A3
Ongjin..........A4
Onsŏng..........C1
P'anmunjŏm B4
Pukch'ŏng C2
P'ungsan..........C2
P'yŏnggang..........B3
P'yŏngsan B3
P'yŏngsŏng..........A3
P'yŏngyang, *capital*..........A3
Sariwŏn..........A3
Sinp'o C2
Sinŭiju A2
Songnim A3
Tanch'ŏn C2
Wŏnsan..........B3
Yangdŏk B3

Other Features

Chaeryŏng, *river* A3
Changjin, *river* B2
Ch'ongch'ŏn, *river*..........A3
Hamgyŏng, *mts.* C2
Imjin, *river*..........B3
Kanghwa, *bay* A4
Korea, *bay*..........A3
Musu-dan, *point* C2
Nangnim-sanmaek, *mts.*..........B3
Paektu-san, *mt.* C2
Sŏjosŏn, *bay* A3
Sup'ung, *reservoir* A2
Taedong, *river* B3
Tongjosŏn, *bay* B3
Tumen, *river* C1
Yalu, *river*..........B2

South Korea: Map Index

Provinces

Cheju ....Inset
Inch'ŏn B4
Kangwŏn..........B4
Kwangju B5
Kyŏnggi B4
North Chŏlla B5
North Ch'ungch'ŏng B4
North Kyŏngsang C4
Pusan C5
Seoul..........B4
South Chŏlla B5
South Ch'ungch'ŏng B4
South Kyŏngsang C5
Taegu C5
Taejŏn B4
Ulsan C5

Cities and Towns

Andong..........C4
Anyang B4
Chech'ŏn C4
Cheju ....Inset
Chinhae..........C5
Chinju C5
Chonju B5
Ch'ŏnan B4
Ch'ŏngju B4
Ch'unch'ŏn B4
Ch'ungju B4
Inch'ŏn B4
Iri B5
Kangnŭng C4
Kimch'ŏn C4
Kunsan B5
Kwangju B5
Kyŏngju..........C5
Masan..........C5
Mokp'o B5
Munsan B4
Nonsan B4
P'ohang C4
Pusan C5
Samch'ŏk C4
Seoul, *capital*..........B4
Sokch'o C3
Sŏngnam..........B4
Sunch'ŏn..........B5
Suwŏn..........B4
Taegu C5
Taejŏn B4
Ulchin C4
Ulsan C5
Wŏnju B4
Wando B5
Yŏngju C4
Yŏsu B5

Other Features

Cheju, *island*..........Inset
Cheju, *strait* ....Inset
Halla-san, *mt.* ....Inset
Han, *river* B4
Hŭksan Chedo, *islands*..........A5
Kanghwa, *bay*..........A4
Koje-do, *island* C5
Korea, *strait*..........C5
Kum, *river* B4
Naktong, *river*..........C5
Soan-kundo, *islands*..........B5
Sobaek, *mts.* B5
Taebaek-Sanmaek, *mts.* C3
Tŏkchŏk-kundo, *islands* A4
Ullŭng-do, *island*..........D4
Western, *channel* C5

Taiwan
National Capital
Other City
1:10,292,000
0 30 60 mi
0 30 60 km
Lambert Conformal Conic Projection
CHINA
East China Sea
Taiwan Strait
P'enghu Is. (Pescadores)
Taipei
Kaohsiung
Yü Shan 3997 m (13,113 ft)
CHUNG-YANG RANGE
South China Sea
Philippine Sea
Luzon Strait
© MapQuest.com, Inc.

Taiwan

Capital: Taipei
Area: 13,969 sq. mi.
36,189 sq. km.
Population: 22,603,000
Largest City: Taipei
Language: Mandarin Chinese
Monetary Unit: New Taiwan dollar

Taiwan: Map Index

Cities and Towns

Changhua..........B1
Chiai..........B2
Chilung B1
Chunan B1
Chungho B1
Chungli B1
Fangliao..........B2
Fengshan B2
Fengyüan..........B1
Hengch'un..........B2
Hsinchu B1
Hsinchuang B1
Hsintien B1
Hsinying B2
Hualien B2
Ilan B1
Kangshan..........B2
Kaohsiung..........B2
Makung..........A2
Miaoli B1
Nant'ou B2
Panch'iao..........B1
P'ingtung..........B2
Shanchung B1
T'aichung B1
T'ainan B2
Taipei, *capital*..........B1
T'aitung..........B2
Tanshui B1
T'aoyüan..........B1
Touliu B2
Yungho..........B1

Other Features

Choshui, *river*..........B2
Chungyang, *range*..........B2
East China, *sea*..........B1
Kaop'ing, *river* B2
Lan, *island* B2
Lü, *island* B2
Luzon, *strait*..........B3
P'enghu (Pescadores), *islands*..........A2
Pescadores, *channel*..........A2
Philippine, *sea*..........B2
South China, *sea* A2
Taiwan, *strait* A1
Tanshui, *river*..........B1
Tsengwen, *river*..........B2
Yü Shan, *mt.* B2

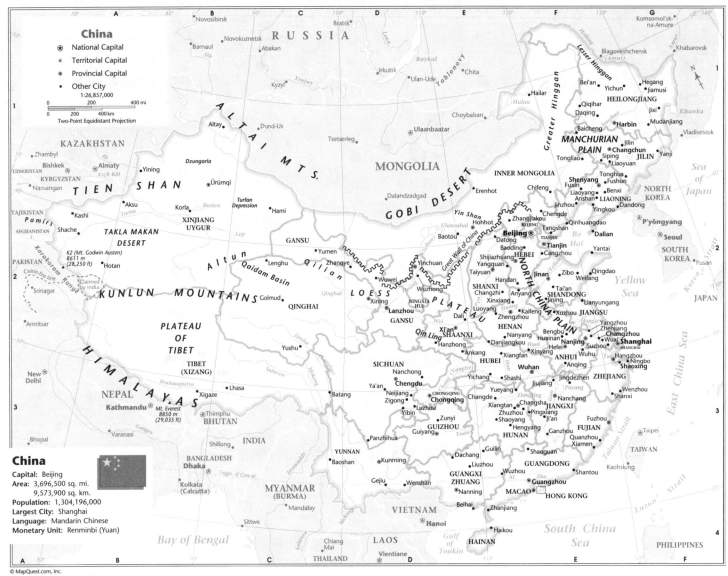

China

- ⊛ National Capital
- ★ Territorial Capital
- ⊚ Provincial Capital
- • Other City

1:26,857,000

0   200   400 mi
0   200   400 km
Two-Point Equidistant Projection

China

Capital: Beijing
Area: 3,696,500 sq. mi.
    9,573,900 sq. km.
Population: 1,304,196,000
Largest City: Shanghai
Language: Mandarin Chinese
Monetary Unit: Renminbi (Yuan)

© MapQuest.com, Inc.

Hong Kong S.A.R.

- • City

1:1,800,000

0   10   20 mi
0   10   20 km
Transverse Mercator Projection

© MapQuest.com, Inc.

China:
Map Index

Internal Divisions
Provinces
Anhui E2
Fujian E3
Gansu C1, D2
Guangdong E3
Guizhou D3
Hainan D4
Hebei E2
Heilongjiang F1
Henan E2
Hubei E2
Hunan E2
Jiangsu E2
Jiangxi E3
Jilin F1
Liaoning F1
Qinghai C2
Shaanxi E2
Shandong E2
Shanxi E2
Sichuan D2
Yunnan C3
Zhejiang E3

Autonomous Regions
Guangxi Zhuang D3
Inner Mongolia E1
Ningxia Hui D2
Tibet (Xizang) B2
Xinjiang Uygur B1

Independent Municipalities
Beijing E1
Chongqing D3
Shanghai F2
Tianjin E2

Special Administrative
Regions (S.A.R.)
Hong Kong ....E3, Inset
Macao E3

Cities and Towns
Aberdeen ....Inset
Aksu B1
Altay B1
Ankang D2
Anqing E2
Anshan F1

Anyang E2
Baicheng F1
Baoding E2
Baoshan C3
Baotou E1
Batang C3
Bei'an F1
Beihai D3
Beijing, capital E2
Bengbu E2
Benxi F1
Cangzhou E2
Changchun F1
Changde E3
Changsha E3
Changzhi E2
Changzhou F2
Chek Keng ....Inset
Chengde E1
Chengdu D2
Chifeng E1
Chongqing D3
Chung Hau ....Inset
Dachang D3
Dali D2
Dalian F2
Dandong F1
Dangjiangkou E2
Daqing F1
Datong E1
Erenhot E1
Fushun F1
Fuxin F1
Fuzhou E3
Ganzhou E3
Gejiu D3
Golmud C2
Guangzhou E3
Guilin D3
Guiyang D3
Haikou E4
Hailar E1
Handan E2
Hangzhou F2
Hanzhong D2
Harbin F1
Hefei E2
Hegang G1
Hengyang E3
Hohhot E1
Hotan A2

Huainan E2
Jiamusi G1
Ji'an E3
Jilin F1
Jinan E2
Jingdezhen E3
Jining E2
Jinzhou F1
Jiujiang E3
Jixi G1
Kaifeng E2
Kashi A2
Korla B1
Kowloon ....Inset
Kunming D3
Lanzhou D2
Lenghu C2
Lhasa C3
Lianyungang E2
Liaoyang F1
Liaoyuan F1
Lo Wu ....Inset
Luoyang E2
Luzhou D3
Mudanjiang F1
Nanchang E3
Nanchong D2
Nanjing E2
Nanning D3
Nanyang E2
Neijiang D2
New Kowloon ....Inset
Ningbo F3
Panzhihua D3
Pingxiang E3
Qingdao E2
Qinhuangdao E2
Qiqihar F1
Quanzhou E3
Sai Kung ....Inset
Shache A2
Shanghai F2
Shantou E3
Shanxi E2
Shaoguan E3
Shaoxing E3
Shaoyang E3
Shashi E2
Sha Tin ....Inset
Shek Pik ....Inset
Shenyang F1

Shijiazhuang E2
Siping F1
Suzhou F2
Tai'an E2
Taiyuan E2
Tangshan E2
Tianjin E2
Tonghua F1
Tongliao F1
Tsuen Wan ....Inset
Tuen Mun ....Inset
Ürümqi B1
Weifang E2
Wenshan D3
Wenzhou F3
Wuhan E2
Wuhu E2
Wuwei D2
Wuxi F2
Wuzhong D2
Wuzhou E3
Xiamen E3
Xi'an D2
Xiangfan E2
Xiangtan E3
Xigaze B3
Xining D2
Xinxiang E2
Xinyang E2
Xuzhou E2
Ya'an D2
Yangguan D2
Yangzhou E2
Yanji F1
Yantai E2
Yibin D3
Yichang E2
Yichun F1
Yinchuan D2
Yingkou F1
Yining A1
Yuen Long ....Inset
Yueyang E3
Yumen C2
Yushu C2
Zhangjiakou E1
Zhangye D2
Zhanjiang D3
Zhengzhou E2
Zhenjiang F2
Zhuzhou E3
Zibo E2

Zigong D3
Zunyi D3

Other Features
Altai, mts. B1
Altun, range B2
Bayan Har, range C2
Bo Hai, gulf E2
Bosten, lake B1
Brahmaputra, river B3
Chang (Yangtze), river .D2, E2
Deep, bay ....Inset
Dongting, lake E3
Dzungaria, desert basin .B1
East China, sea F3
Fen, river E2
Gan, river E3
Gobi, desert D1
Greater Hinggan, range .F1
Great Wall of China D2
Han, river E2
Heilong (Amur), river F1
Himalayas, mts. B3
Hong Kong, island ......Inset
Hongze, lake E2
Huai, river E2
Huang (Yellow), river .D2, E2
Hulun, lake E1
Indus, river A2
Jinsha (Yangtze), river ..C3
Khanka, lake G1
Kunlun, mts. B2
K2 (Godwin Austen), mt. .A2
Lantau, island ....Inset
Lesser Hinggan, range ...F1
Liao, river F1
Loess, plateau D2
Lop, lake C1
Manchurian, plain F1
Mekong, river C2
Nan Ling, mts. D3
New Territories, island .Inset
North China, plain E2
Pamirs, region A2
Poyang, lake E3
Qaidam, basin C2
Qilian, range C2
Qinghai, lake C2
Qin Ling, mts. D2
Salween, river C2
Songhua, river F1
South China, sea .....E4, Inset

Zigong D3
Zunyi D3

Tai, lake F2
Taiwan, strait E3
Takla Makan, desert B2
Tanggula, range C2
Tarim, river B1
Tibet, plateau B2
Tien Shan, range A1
Tonkin, gulf D4
Turfan, depression C1
Ulansuhai, lake D1
Wei, river D2
Xi, river E3
Yalu, river F1
Yangtze, river C2, D2
Yellow, sea F2
Yin Shan, mts. E1
Yuan, river E3
Zhu, river E3

Stonecutters (S.I.), island ..Inset

Vietnam: Map Index

Cities and Towns
Bac Lieu	A5
Bien Hoa	B4
Buon Me Thuot	B4
Ca Mau	A5
Cam Ranh	B4
Can Tho	A4
Cao Bang	B1
Chau Doc	A4
Da Lat	B4
Da Nang	B3
Dien Bien Phu	A2
Dong Hoi	B3
Ha Giang	A1
Haiphong	B2
Hanoi, capital	A2
Hoa Binh	A2
Ho Chi Minh City	B4
Hon Gai	B2
Hue	B3
Khe Sanh	B3
Kontum	B3
Lang Son	B2
Lao Cai	A1
Long Xuyen	A4
My Tho	B4
Nam Dinh	B2
Nha Trang	B4
Phan Rang	B4
Phan Thiet	B4
Pleiku	B4
Quang Ngai	B3
Quang Tri	B3
Qui Nhon	B4
Rach Gia	A4
Soc Trang	A5
Son La	A2
Tay Ninh	B4
Thai Nguyen	A2
Thanh Hoa	A2
Tuy Hoa	B4
Viet Tri	A2
Vinh	A2
Vung Tau- Con Dao	B4
Yen Bai	A2

Other Features
Annam, mts.	A2
Ba, river	B3
Black (Da), river	A2
Ca, river	A2
Central, highlands	B4
Con Son, islands	B5
Cu Lao Thu, island	B4
Dao Phu Quoc, island	A4
Dong Nai, river	B4
Fan Si Pan, mt.	A1
Gam, river	A1
Lo, river	A1
Ma, river	A2
Mekong, delta	B5
Mekong, river	A4
Mui Bai Bung, point	A5
Ngoc Linh, mt.	B3
Red (Hong), river	A2
Tonkin, gulf	B2

Vietnam

Capital: Hanoi
Area: 127,246 sq. mi.
329,653 sq. km.
Population: 81,377,000
Largest City: Ho Chi Minh City
Language: Vietnamese
Monetary Unit: Dong

Laos: Map Index

Cities and Towns
Attapu	D4
Ban Houayxay	A1
Champasak	C4
Louang Namtha	A1
Luang Prabang	B2
Muang Khammouan	C3
Muang Khong	C4
Muang Khôngxédôn	C4
Muang Paklay	A2
Muang Pakxan	B2
Muang Vangviang	B2
Muang Xaignabouri	A2
Muang Xay	A1
Muang Xépôn	D3
Muang Xon	B1
Pakse	C4
Phôngsali	B1
Saravan	D4
Savannakhet	C3
Vientiane, capital	B3
Xam Nua	C1
Xiangkhoang	B2

Other Features
Annam, range	C3
Banghiang, river	C3
Bolovens, plateau	D4
Kong, river	D4
Luang Prabang, range	A3
Mekong, river	A1, C3
Nam Ngum, reservoir	B2
Ou, river	B1
Phou Bia, mt.	B2
Xiangkhoang, plateau	B2

Laos

Capital: Vientiane
Area: 91,429 sq. mi.
236,085 sq. km.
Population: 5,657,000
Largest City: Vientiane
Language: Lao
Monetary Unit: Kip

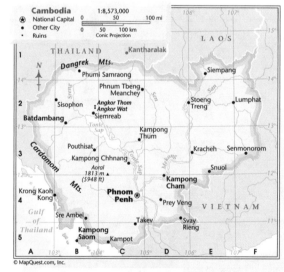

Mongolia

Capital: Ulaanbaatar
Area: 604,800 sq. mi.
1,566,839 sq. km.
Population: 2,594,000
Largest City: Ulaanbaatar
Language: Mongolian
Monetary Unit: Tughrik

Mongolia: Map Index

Cities and Towns
Altay	B2
Arvayheer	C2
Baruun-Urt	D2
Bayanhongor	C2
Bulgan	C2
Buyant-Uhaa	D3
Choybalsan	D2
Dalandzadgad	C3
Darhan	C2
Dund-Us	B2
Erdenet	C2
Mandalgovĭ	C2
Mörön	C2
Ölgiy	A2
Öndörhaan	D2
Sühbaatar	C2
Tamsagbulag	D2
Tsetserleg	C2
Ulaangom	B2
Ulaan-Uul	C2
Ulaanbaatar, capital	C2
Uliastay	B2

Other Features
Altai, mts.	B2
Bööntsagaan, lake	B2
Dörgön, lake	B2
Dzavhan, river	B2
Gobi, desert	C3
Hangayn, mts.	B2
Har Us, lake	B2
Hovd, river	B2
Hövsgöl, lake	C1
Hyargas, lake	B2
Ih Bogd Uul, mt.	C3
Kerulen, river	D2
Mongolian, plateau	C2
Onon, river	D2
Orhon, river	C2
Selenge Mörön, river	C2
Tavan Bogd Uul, mt.	A2
Tesiyn, river	B2
Tuul, river	C2
Uvs, lake	B1

Cambodia

Capital: Phnom Penh
Area: 70,238 sq. mi.
181,964 sq. km.
Population: 14,144,000
Largest City: Phnom Penh
Language: Khmer
Monetary Unit: Riel

Cambodia: Map Index

Cities and Towns
Batdambang	B2
Kampong Cham	D4
Kampong Chhnang	C3
Kampong Saom	B5
Kampong Thum	C3
Kampot	C5
Kracheh	E3
Krong Kaoh Kong	A4
Lumphat	F2
Phnom Penh, capital	C4
Phnum Tbeng Meanchey	C2
Phumi Samraong	B1
Pouthisat	B3
Prey Veng	D4
Senmonorom	F3
Siempang	E1
Siemreab	B2
Sisophon	B2
Snuol	E3
Sre Ambel	B4
Stoeng Treng	D2
Svay Rieng	D4
Takev	C5

Other Features
Angkor Thom, ruins	B2
Angkor Wat, ruins	B2
Aoral, mt.	C3
Cardamom, mts.	A3
Dangrek, mts.	B1
Mekong, river	D3
San, river	E2
Sen, river	C2
Sreng, river	B2
Thailand, gulf	A4
Tonle Sap, lake	B2, C3
Tonle Sap, river	B2

© MapQuest.com, Inc.

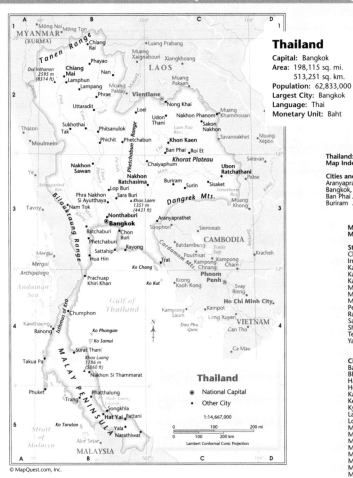

© MapQuest.com, Inc.

Thailand

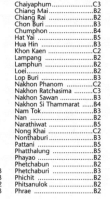

Capital: Bangkok
Area: 198,115 sq. mi.
513,251 sq. km.
Population: 62,833,000
Largest City: Bangkok
Language: Thai
Monetary Unit: Baht

Thailand:
Map Index

Cities and Towns

Aranyaprathet	C3
Bangkok, *capital*	B3
Ban Phai	C2
Buriram	C3
Chaiyaphum	C3
Chiang Mai	B2
Chiang Rai	B2
Chon Buri	B3
Chumphon	B4
Hat Yai	B5
Hua Hin	B3
Khon Kaen	C2
Lampang	B2
Lamphun	B2
Loei	B2
Lop Buri	B3
Nakhon Phanom	C2
Nakhon Ratchasima	C3
Nakhon Sawan	B3
Nakhon Si Thammarat	B4
Nam Tok	B3
Nan	B2
Narathiwat	B5
Nong Khai	C2
Nonthaburi	B3
Pattani	B5
Phatthalung	B5
Phayao	B2
Phetchabun	B2
Phetchaburi	B3
Phichit	B2
Phitsanulok	B2
Phrae	B2
Phra Nakhon Si Ayutthaya	B3
Phuket	B5
Prachuap Khiri Khan	B4
Ranong	B4
Ratchaburi	B3
Rayong	B3
Roi Et	C2
Sakon Nakhon	C2
Sara Buri	B3
Sattahip	B3
Sisaket	C3
Songkhla	B5
Sukhothai	B2
Surat Thani	B4
Surin	C3
Tak	B2
Takua Pa	B4
Trang	B5
Trat	C3
Ubon Ratchathani	C3
Udon Thani	C2
Uttaradit	B2
Yala	B5

Other Features

Bilauktaung, *range*	B3
Chao Phraya, *river*	B3
Chi, *river*	C2
Dangrek, *mts.*	C3
Dawna, *range*	B2
Inthanon, *mt.*	B2
Khorat, *plateau*	C3
Ko Chang, *island*	C3
Ko Kut, *island*	C4
Ko Phangan, *island*	B4
Ko Samui, *island*	B4
Ko Tarutao, *island*	B5
Kra, *isthmus*	B4
Laem, *mt.*	B3
Lam Pao, *reservoir*	C2
Luang, *mt.*	B4
Mae Klong, *river*	B3
Malacca, *strait*	B5
Malay, *peninsula*	B4
Mekong, *river*	C2
Mun, *river*	C3
Nan, *river*	B2
Pa Sak, *river*	B3
Phetchabun, *range*	B2
Ping, *river*	B2
Salween, *river*	A2
Sirinthorn, *reservoir*	C3
Srinagarind, *reservoir*	B3
Tanen, *range*	B2
Thailand, *gulf*	B4
Thale Luang, *lagoon*	B5
Yom, *river*	B2

Thailand

⊛ National Capital

• Other City

1:14,667,000

0   100   200 mi
0   100   200 km
Lambert Conformal Conic Projection

Myanmar (Burma):
Map Index

States and Divisions

Chin, *state*	B2
Irrawaddy, *division*	B3
Kachin, *state*	C1
Karen, *state*	C2
Kayah, *state*	C2
Magwe, *division*	B2
Mandalay, *division*	B2
Mon, *state*	C3
Pegu, *division*	B3
Rakhine, *state*	B2
Sagaing, *division*	B2
Shan, *state*	C2
Tenasserim, *division*	C3
Yangon (Rangoon), *division*	C3

Cities and Towns

Bassein	B3
Bhamo	C1
Haka	B2
Henzada	B3
Kawthaung	C4
Keng Tung	C2
Kyaukpyu	B2
Lashio	C2
Loi-kaw	C2
Mandalay	C2
Maymyo	C2
Meiktila	B2
Mergui	C3
Monywa	B2
Moulmein	C3
Myingyan	B2
Myitkyina	C1
Pa-an	C3
Pegu	C3
Prome	B2
Putao	C1
Sagaing	B2
Shwebo	B2
Sittwe	B2
Tamu	B1
Taunggyi	C2
Tavoy	C3
Toungoo	C3
Yangon (Rangoon), *capital*	C3
Ye	C3

Other Features

Andaman, *sea*	B3
Arakan Yoma, *mts.*	B2
Bengal, *bay*	B3
Bilauktaung, *range*	C3
Cheduba, *island*	B2
Chin, *hills*	B2
Chindwin, *river*	B1
Coco, *islands*	B3
Hkakabo Razi, *mt.*	C1
Irrawaddy, *river*	B2
Martaban, *gulf*	C3
Mekong, *river*	C2
Mergui, *archipelago*	C4
Mouths of the Irrawaddy, *delta*	B3
Preparis, *island*	B3
Ramree, *island*	B2
Salween, *river*	C2
Shan, *plateau*	C2
Sittang, *river*	C2
Tavoy, *point*	C3
Thailand, *gulf*	C4

Myanmar (Burma)

Capital: Yangon (Rangoon)
Area: 261,228 sq. mi.
676,756 sq. km.
Population: 49,485,000
Largest City: Yangon (Rangoon)
Language: Burmese
Monetary Unit: Kyat

Myanmar (Burma)

⊛ National Capital

• Other City

1:24,054,000

0   100   200 mi
0   100   200 km
Lambert Conformal Conic Projection

© MapQuest.com, Inc.

© MapQuest.com, Inc.

Philippines

⊛ National Capital

• Other City

1:16,000,000

0   100   200 mi
0   100   200 km
Lambert Conformal Conic Projection

Philippines

Capital: Manila
Area: 115,860 sq. mi.
300,155 sq. km.
Population: 79,999,000
Largest City: Manila
Languages: Pilipino, English
Monetary Unit: Philippine peso

Philippines:
Map Index

Regions

Bicol	B3
Cagayan Valley	B2
Central Luzon	A3
Central Mindanao	C5
Central Visayas	B4
*Cordillera Autonomous Region	B2
Eastern Visayas	C4
Ilocos	B2
*Moslem Mindanao Autonomous Region	B5
National Capital Region	A3
Northern Mindanao	C5
Southern Mindanao	C5
Southern Tagalog	B3
Western Mindanao	B5
Western Visayas	B4

Cities and Towns

Angeles	B3
Bacolod	B4
Baguio	B2
Basilan	B5
Batangas	B3
Bislig	C4
Butuan	C4
Cabanatuan	B3
Cadiz	B4
Cagayan de Oro	C4
Calapan	B3
Calbayog	C3
Cebu	B4
Cotabato	C5
Dagupan	B2
Davao	C5
Dipolog	B4
Dumaguete	B4
General Santos	C5
Iligan	C4
Iloilo	B4
Jolo	B5
Laoag	B2
Laoang	C3
Legazpi	B3
Lipa	B3
Lucena	B3
Mamburao	B3
Mandaue	B4
Manila, *capital*	B3
Masbate	B3
Naga	B3
Olongapo	B3
Ormoc	C4
Pagadian	B5
Puerto Princesa	A4
Quezon City	B3
Roxas	B4
San Carlos	B4
San Fernando	B2
San Pablo	B3
Silay	B4
Surigao	C4
Tacloban	C4
Tuguegarao	B2
Vigan	B2
Zamboanga	B5

Other Features

Agusan, *river*	C4
Apo, *volcano*	C5
Babuyan, *channel*	B2
Babuyan, *islands*	B2
Balabac, *island*	A5
Balabac, *strait*	A5
Bashi, *channel*	B1
Basilan, *island*	B5
Bataan, *peninsula*	B3
Batan, *islands*	B1
Bohol, *island*	C4
Bohol, *sea*	C4
Cagayan, *islands*	B4
Cagayan, *river*	B2
Cagayan Sulu, *island*	A5
Calamian, *islands*	A3
Caramoan, *peninsula*	C3
Catanduanes, *island*	C3
Cebu, *island*	B4
Celebes, *sea*	B5
Corregidor, *island*	B3
Cordillera Central, *mts.*	B2
Cuyo, *islands*	B4
Davao, *gulf*	C5
Dinagat, *island*	C4
Duata, *mts.*	C4
Jolo, *island*	B5
Laguna de Bay, *lake*	B3
Lamon, *bay*	B3
Leyte, *island*	C4
Lingayen, *gulf*	B2
Luzon, *island*	B3
Luzon, *strait*	B1
Manila, *bay*	B3
Marinduque, *island*	B3
Masbate, *island*	B3
Mayon, *volcano*	B3
Mindanao, *island*	C5
Mindoro, *island*	B3
Mindoro, *strait*	B3
Moro, *gulf*	B5
Negros, *island*	B4
Palawan, *island*	A4
Panay, *gulf*	B4
Panay, *island*	B4
Philippine, *sea*	C3
Pulangi, *river*	C5
Samar, *island*	C3
Samar, *sea*	C3
Siargao, *island*	C4
Sibuyan, *island*	B3
Sibuyan, *sea*	B3
Sierra Madre, *mts.*	B2
South China, *sea*	A3
Sulu, *archipelago*	A5
Sulu, *sea*	A4
Tablas, *island*	B3
Tawi Tawi, *island*	A5
Visayan, *islands*	B4
Visayan, *sea*	B4
Zambales, *mts.*	B3
Zamboanga, *peninsula*	B5
*Not on map	

© MapQuest.com, Inc.

Indonesia: Map Index

Cities and Towns

Amahai D2
Ambon D2
Balikpapan C2
Banda Aceh A1
Bandar Lampung B2
Bandung B2
Banjarmasin C2
Baubau D2
Bengkulu B2
Bogor B2
Cilacap B2
Cirebon B2
Denpasar C2
Ende D2
Fakfak E2
Gorontalo D1
Jakarta, capital B2
Jambi B2
Jayapura F2
Kediri C2
Kendari D2
Kupang D3
Madiun C2
Magelang C2
Malang C2
Manado D1
Manokwari E2
Mataram C2
Medan A1
Merauke F2
Padang B2
Palangkaraya C2
Palembang B2
Palu C2
Pangkalpinang B2
Parepare C2
Pekalongan B2
Pekanbaru B1
Pematangsiantar A1

Pontianak B2
Raba C2
Samarinda C2
Semarang C2
Sorong E2
Sukabumi B2
Surabaya C2
Surakarta C2
Tanjungpinang B1
Tarakan C1
Tasikmalaya B2
Tegal C2
Ternate D1
Ujung Pandang C2
Waingapu D2
Yogyakarta C2

Other Features

Agung, mt. C2
Alor, island D2

Arafura, sea E2
Aru, islands E2
Babar, island D2
Bali, island C2
Banda, sea D2
Bangka, island B2
Belitung, island B2
Biak, island E2
Borneo, island C1
Buru, island D2
Celebes (Sulawesi), island .. D2
Celebes, sea D1
Ceram, island D2
Ceram, sea D2
Digul, river E2
Enggano, island B2
Flores, island D2
Flores, sea C2
Greater Sunda, islands .. B2
Halmahera, island D1

Irian Jaya, region E2
Java, island C2
Java, sea C2
Jaya, mt. E2
Kahayan, river C2
Kai, islands E2
Kalimantan, region C2
Kerinci, mt. B2
Krakatau, island B2
Lesser Sunda, islands .. C2
Lingga, island B2
Lombok, island C2
Madura, island C2
Makassar, strait C2
Malacca, strait A1
Mentawai, islands A2
Misool, island E2
Moa, island D2
Molucca, sea D2
Moluccas, islands D2

Morotai, island D1
Muna, island D2
Natuna Besar, island .. B1
New Guinea, island ... F2
Nias, island A1
Obi, island D2
Peleng, island D2
Savu, sea C2
Semeru, mt. C2
Siberut, island A1
Simeulue, island A1
South China, sea C1
Sudirman, range E2
Sula, islands D2
Sulu, sea D1
Sumatra, island B2
Sumba, island C2
Sumbawa, island C2
Talaud, islands D1
Tanimbar, islands E2

Timor, island D2
Timor, sea D3
Waigeo, island E2
Wetar, island D2
Yapen, island E2

Indonesia

Capital: Jakarta
Area: 741,052 sq. mi.
1,919,824 sq. km.
Population: 219,883,000
Largest City: Jakarta
Language: Bahasa Indonesian
Monetary Unit: Indonesian rupiah

Brunei

Capital: Bandar Seri
Begawan
Area: 2,226 sq. mi.
5,767 sq. km.
Population: 358,000
Largest City: Bandar Seri Begawan
Language: Malay
Monetary Unit: Brunei dollar

Brunei: Map Index

Cities and Towns

Badas A2
Bandar Seri Begawan,
capital B2
Bangar C2
Batang Duri C2
Jerudong B2
Kerangan Nyatan B3
Kuala Abang B2
Kuala Belait A2
Labi A3
Labu B2
Lumut A2
Medit B2
Muara C1
Seria A2
Sukang B3
Tutong B2

Other Features

Belait, river B3
Brunei, bay C1
Brunei, river B2
Bukit Pagon, mt. C3
Pandaruan, river C2
South China, sea A2
Temburong, river B2
Tutong, river B2

Singapore: Map Index

Cities and Towns

Bedok B1
Bukit Panjang B1
Bukit Timah B1
Changi B1
Choa Chu Kang A1
Jurong A1
Kranji B1
Nee Soon B1
Punggol B1
Queenstown B1
Sembawang B1
Serangoon B1
Singapore, capital B1
Tampines B1
Thong Hoe A1
Toa Payoh B1
Tuas A1
Woodlands B1

Other Features

Ayer Chawan, island ... A1
Bukum, island B2
Johor, strait B1
Keppel, harbor B2
Pandan, strait A2
Semakau, island B2
Senang, island A2
Sentosa, island B2
Singapore, island B1
Singapore, strait B2
Tekong, island C1
Timah, hill B1
Ubin, island B1

Singapore

Capital: Singapore
Area: 247 sq. mi.
640 sq. km.
Population: 4,253,000
Largest City: Singapore
Languages: Mandarin Chinese, English,
Malay, Tamil
Monetary Unit: Singapore dollar

Brunei

Capital: Bandar Seri
Begawan
Area: 2,226 sq. mi.
5,767 sq. km.
Population: 358,000
Largest City: Bandar Seri Begawan
Language: Malay
Monetary Unit: Brunei dollar

Malaysia: Map Index

Cities and Towns

Alor Setar A1
Batu Pahat B2
George Town A2
Ipoh A2
Johor Baharu B2
Kelang A2
Keluang B2
Kota Baharu B1
Kota Kinabalu D2
Kuala Lumpur, capital .. A2
Kuala Terengganu B2

Kuantan B2
Kuching C2
Melaka B2
Miri D2
Muar B2
Sandakan D2
Seremban A2
Sibu C2
Tawau D2
Telok Anson A2

Other Features

Banggi, island D1
Baram, river D2
Crocker, range D2
Kinabalu, mt. D1
Kinabatangan, river ... D2
Labuan, island D2
Langkawi, island A1
Malacca, strait A2
Malay, peninsula A1
Pahang, river B2
Peninsular Malaysia, region .. B2
Perak, river A2
Pinang, island A2
Rajang, river C2
Sabah, state D2
Sarawak, state C2
Tahan, mt. B2

Malaysia

Capital: Kuala Lumpur
Area: 127,584 sq. mi.
330,529 sq. km.
Population: 24,425,000
Largest City: Kuala Lumpur
Language: Malay
Monetary Unit: Ringgit

© MapQuest.com, Inc.

Australia:
Map Index

States and Territories
Australian Capital Territory......D3
New South Wales.................D3
Northern Territory...............C2
Queensland......................D2
South Australia..................C2
Tasmania........................D4
Victoria.........................D3
Western Australia................B2

Aboriginal Lands
Alawa-Ngandji...................C1
Balwina.........................B2
Central Australia................B2
Central Desert...................C2
Daly River......................B1
Haasts Bluff....................C2
Lake Mackay.....................B2
Nganyatjara.....................B2
Petermann.......................B2
Pitjantjatjara...................C2
Waani/Garawa....................C1
Yandeyarra......................A2
Unnamed.........................B2
Unnamed.........................C2
Unnamed.........................D1

Cities and Towns
Adelaide, S.A., capital ..C3, Inset II
Albany, W.A.....................A3
Albury, N.S.W...................D3
Alice Springs, N.T...............C2
Altona, Vic.................Inset V
Armadale, W.A.............Inset I
Armidale, N.S.W.................E3
Asquith, N.S.W............Inset IV
Auburn, N.S.W.............Inset IV
Balcatta, W.A.............Inset I
Bald Hills, Qld............Inset III
Ballarat, Vic...................D3
Bankstown, N.S.W.........Inset IV
Bayswater, W.A............Inset I
Beenleigh, Qld............Inset III
Belmont, W.A.............Inset I
Bendigo, Vic...................D3
Berwick, Vic..............Inset V
Blacktown, N.S.W.........Inset IV
Botany, N.S.W............Inset IV

Bourke, N.S.W...................D3
Bowen, Qld.....................D2
Box Hill, Vic.............Inset V
Brighton, S.A.............Inset II
Brighton, Qld.............Inset III
Brighton, Vic.............Inset V
Brisbane, Qld.,
capital.................E2, Inset III
Broadmeadows, Vic........Inset V
Broken Hill, N.S.W..............D3
Broome, W.A....................B1
Brown Plains, Qld.........Inset III
Bunbury, W.A...................A3
Bundaberg, Qld..................E2
Burnside, S.A.............Inset II
Byford, W.A..............Inset I
Cairns, Qld.....................D1
Campbelltown, S.A.........Inset II
Campbelltown, N.S.W......Inset IV
Canberra, A.C.T.,
national capital................D3
Cannington, W.A..........Inset I
Canterbury, N.S.W........Inset IV
Carnarvon, W.A.................A2
Castle Hill, N.S.W........Inset IV
Caulfield, Vic...........Inset V
Ceduna, S.A....................C3
Charleville, Qld................D2
Charters Towers, Qld............D2
Chelsea, Vic.............Inset V
Chermside, Qld...........Inset III
City Beach, W.A..........Inset I
Cleveland, Qld...........Inset III
Cloncurry, Qld.................D1
Coburg, Vic..............Inset V
Coober Pedy, S.A................C2
Coopers Plains, Qld......Inset III
Cranbourne, Vic..........Inset V
Cronulla, N.S.W..........Inset IV
Dampier, W.A...................A2
Dandenong, Vic...........Inset V
Darwin, N.T., capital...........C1
Dee Why, N.S.W...........Inset IV
Devonport, Tas.................D4
Doncaster, Vic...........Inset V
Dubbo, N.S.W...................D3
Elizabeth, S.A...........Inset II
Eltham, Vic..............Inset V
Emerald, Qld...................D2
Enfield, S.A.............Inset II
Epping, N.S.W............Inset IV
Esperance, W.A.................B3
Essendon, Vic............Inset V
Fairfield, N.S.W.........Inset IV
Ferntree Gully, Vic......Inset V
Ferny Grove, Qld.........Inset III

Frankston, Vic...........Inset V
Fremantle, W.A..........A3, Inset I
Geelong, Vic...................D3
Geraldton, W.A.................A2
Gladstone, Qld.................D2
Glenelg, S.A.............Inset II
Glen Forrest, W.A........Inset I
Gold Coast, Qld................E2
Goodna, Qld..............Inset III
Gosford, N.S.W...........Inset III
Gosnells, W.A............Inset I
Grafton, N.S.W.................E2
Grange, S.A..............Inset II
Greenslopes, Qld.........Inset III
Griffith, N.S.W................D3
Gympie, Qld....................E2
Heidelberg, Vic..........Inset V
Hobart, Tas., capital...........D4
Holland Park, Qld........Inset III
Holroyd, N.S.W...........Inset IV
Hornsby, N.S.W...........Inset IV
Hurstville, N.S.W........Inset IV
Inala, Qld...............Inset III
Ipswich, Qld.............Inset III
Kalamunda, W.A...........Inset I
Kalgoorlie-Boulder, W.A.........B3
Katherine, N.T.................C1
Keilor, Vic..............Inset V
Kelmscott, W.A...........Inset I
Kersbrook, S.A...........Inset II
Kwinana, W.A.............Inset I
Kwinana Beach, W.A.......Inset I
La Perouse, N.S.W........Inset IV
Launceston, Tas................D4
Leichhardt, N.S.W........Inset IV
Lilydale, Vic............Inset V
Lismore, N.S.W.................E2
Liverpool, N.S.W.........Inset IV
Lobethal, S.A............Inset II
Logan, Qld...............Inset III
Longreach, Qld.................D2
Mackay, Qld....................D2
Mandurah, W.A..................A3
Manly, Qld...............Inset III
Manly, N.S.W.............Inset IV
Marion, S.A..............Inset II
Maryborough, Qld...............E2
Melbourne, Vic.,
capital..............D3, Inset V
Melville, W.A............Inset I
Merredin, W.A..................A3
Midland, W.A.............Inset I
Mildura, Vic...................D3
Mitcham, S.A.............Inset II
Mona Vale, N.S.W.........Inset V
Moorabbin, Vic...........Inset V

Mordialloc, Vic..........Inset V
Moree, N.S.W.............Inset V
Morningside, Qld.........Inset III
Mosman Park, W.A.........Inset I
Mount Barker, S.A........Inset II
Mount Gambier, S.A.............D3
Mount Gravatt, Qld.......Inset III
Mount Isa, Qld.................C2
Mount Nebo, Qld..........Inset III
Mullaloo, W.A............Inset I
Narrogin, W.A..................A3
Nedlands, W.A............Inset I
Newcastle, N.S.W...............E3
Newman, W.A....................A2
Newmarket, Qld...........Inset III
Noarlunga, S.A...........Inset II
North Adelaide, S.A......Inset II
Northcote, Vic...........Inset V
North Sydney, N.S.W......Inset IV
Nunawading, Vic..........Inset V
Oakleigh, Vic............Inset V
Orange, N.S.W..................D3
Parramatta, N.S.W........Inset IV
Perth, W.A., capital....A3, Inset I
Petrie, Qld..............Inset III
Pickering Brook, W.A.....Inset I
Port Adelaide, S.A.......Inset II
Port Augusta, S.A..............C3
Port Hedland, W.A..............A2
Port Lincoln, S.A..............C3
Port Macquarie, N.S.W..........E3
Port Pirie, S.A................C3
Prahran, Vic.............Inset V
Preston, Vic.............Inset V
Queenstown, Tas................D4
Randwick, N.S.W..........Inset IV
Redcliffe, Qld...........Inset III
Redland Bay, Qld.........Inset III
Reynella, S.A............Inset II
Ringwood, Vic............Inset V
Rockdale, N.S.W..........Inset IV
Rockhampton, Qld...............D2
Roma, Qld......................D2
Ryde, N.S.W..............Inset IV
St. Ives, N.S.W..........Inset IV
St. Kilda, S.A...........Inset II
St. Kilda, Vic...........Inset V
Salisbury, S.A...........Inset II
Samford, Qld.............Inset III
Sandgate, Qld............Inset III
Scarborough, W.A.........Inset I
Spearwood, W.A...........Inset I
Springvale, Vic..........Inset V
Stirling, W.A............Inset I
Stirling, S.A............Inset II
Sunshine, Vic............Inset V

Sutherland, N.S.W........Inset IV
Sydney, N.S.W.,
capital...............E3, Inset IV
Tamworth, N.S.W................E3
Taree, N.S.W...................E3
Tea Tree Gully, S.A......Inset II
Tennant Creek, N.T.............C1
Tom Price, W.A.................A2
Toowoomba, Qld.................E2
Townsville, Qld................D1
Unley, S.A...............Inset II
Victoria Park, W.A.......Inset I
Victoria Point, Qld......Inset III
Wagga Wagga, N.S.W.............D3
Wanneroo, W.A............Inset I
Warrnambool, Vic...............D3
Waverley, Vic............Inset V
Weipa, Qld.....................D1
Whyalla, S.A...................C3
Willoughby, N.S.W........Inset IV
Wollongong, N.S.W..............E3
Woodside, S.A............Inset II
Woodville, S.A...........Inset II
Woomera, S.A...................C3
Wyndham, W.A...................B1
Wynnum, Qld..............Inset III

Other Features
Arafura, sea...................C1
Arnhem, cape...................C1
Arnhem Land, region............C1
Ashburton, river...............A2
Ashmore and Cartier, islands...B1
Australian Alps, mts...........D3
Barkly, tableland..............C1
Bass, strait...................D3
Bate, bay................Inset IV
Blue, mts................Inset IV
Botany, bay..............Inset IV
Brisbane, river..........Inset III
Burdekin, river................D1
Canning, river...........Inset I
Cape York, peninsula...........C1
Carpentaria, gulf..............C1
Coral, sea.....................E1
Daly, river....................C1
Darling, range............A3
Darling, river................D3
Drysdale River Natl. Park......B1
Eyre, lake.....................C2
Eyre, peninsula................C3
Fitzroy, river.................B1
Flinders, range................D1
Flinders, river................D1
Frome, lake....................D2
Gairdner, lake.................C3

Garden, island...........Inset I
Gascoyne, river................A2
Gibson, desert.................B2
Gilbert, river.................D1
Great Artesian, basin..........D2
Great Australian, bight........B3
Great Barrier, reef............D1
Great Dividing, range....D1, D3
Great Sandy, desert............B2
Great Victoria, desert.........B2
Gregory Natl. Park.............C1
Grey, range....................D2
Groote Eylandt, island.........C1
Hamersley, range...............A2
Hobsons, bay.............Inset V
Jackson, port............Inset IV
Kakadu Natl. Park..............C1
Kangaroo, island...............C3
Kimberley, plateau.............B1
King Leopold, range............B1
Kosciusko, mt..................D3
Lakefield Natl. Park...........D1
Leeuwin, cape..................A3
Leichhardt, river..............C1
Leveque, cape..................B1
Loddon, river............Inset III
Macdonnell, ranges.............C1
Melville, island...............C1
Mitchell, river................D1
Moreton, bay.............Inset III
Murchison, river...............A2
Murray, river..................D3
Murrumbidgee, river............D3
Musgrave, ranges...............C2
New England, range.............E3
North West, cape...............A2
Nullarbor, plain...............B3
Port Phillip, bay........Inset V
Roper, river...................C1
Rudall River Natl. Park........B2
St. Vincent, gulf........Inset II
Samsonvale, lake.........Inset III
Simpson, desert................C2
Simpson Desert Natl. Park......C2
Spencer, gulf..................C3
Swan, river..............Inset I
Tasman, sea....................E3
Timor, sea.....................B1
Torrens, lake..................C2
Torrens, river...........Inset II
Torres, strait.................D1
Uluru (Ayers Rock).............C2
Victoria, river................C1
Witjira Natl. Park.............C2
Yampi, sound...................B1
York, cape.....................D1

Australia

Capital: Canberra
Area: 2,966,200 sq. mi.
7,684,456 sq. km.
Population: 19,731,000
Largest City: Sydney
Language: English
Monetary Unit: Australian dollar

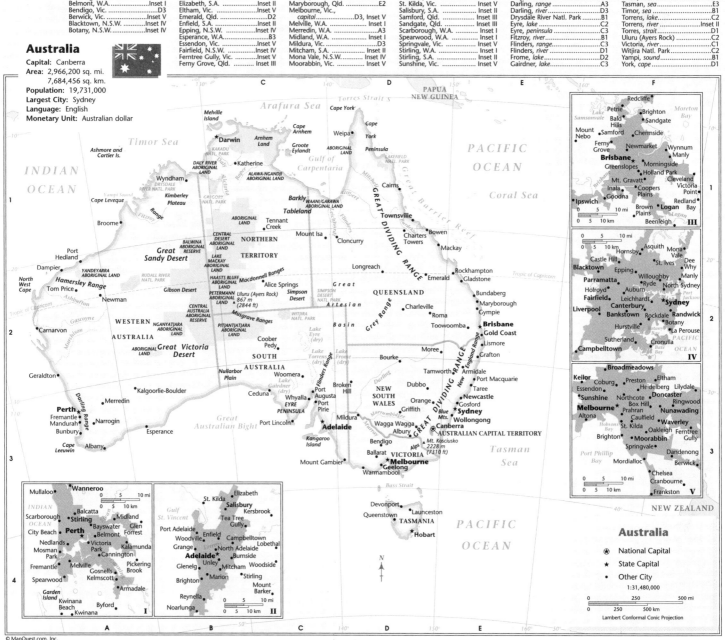

Australia

⊛ National Capital
★ State Capital
• Other City

1:31,480,000

Lambert Conformal Conic Projection

Papua New Guinea: Map Index

Cities and Towns

Alotau	B3
Arawa	B2
Daru	A2
Goroka	A2
Kavieng	B2
Kerema	A2
Kimbe	B2
Lae	A2
Lorengau	A2
Madang	A2
Morehead	A2
Mount Hagen	A2
Popondetta	A2
Port Moresby, *capital*	A2
Rabaul	B2
Vanimo	A2
Wabag	A2
Wau	A2
Wewak	A1

Other Features

Admiralty, *islands*	A2
Bismarck, *archipelago*	A2
Bismarck, *range*	A2
Bismarck, *sea*	A2
Bougainville, *island*	B2
Buka, *island*	B2
Central, *range*	A2
Coral, *sea*	A3
D'Entrecasteaux, *islands*	B2
Feni, *islands*	B2
Fly, *river*	A2
Gazelle, *peninsula*	B2
Green, *islands*	B2
Huon, *peninsula*	A2
Karkar, *island*	A2
Lihir, *group*	B2
Louisiade, *archipelago*	B3
Manus, *island*	A2
Markham, *river*	A2
Milne, *bay*	B3
Murray, *lake*	A2
Mussau, *island*	A2
New Britain, *island*	B2
New Guinea, *island*	A2
New Hanover, *island*	B2
New Ireland, *island*	B2
Ninigo, *group*	A2
Nuguria, *islands*	B2
Owen Stanley, *range*	A2
Papua, *gulf*	A2
Purari, *river*	A2
Ramu, *river*	A2
Rossel, *island*	B3
St. George's, *channel*	B2
Sepik, *river*	A2
Solomon, *sea*	B2
Tabar, *island*	B2
Tagula, *island*	B3
Tanga, *islands*	B2
Tauu, *islands*	B3
Torres, *strait*	A2
Trobriand, *islands*	B2
Umboi, *island*	A2
Whiteman, *range*	A2
Wilhelm, *mt.*	A2
Witu, *island*	A2
Woodlark (Muyua), *island*	B2

Papua New Guinea

Capital: Port Moresby
Area: 178,704 sq. mi.
462,964 sq. km.
Population: 5,711,000
Largest City: Port Moresby
Language: English
Monetary Unit: Kina

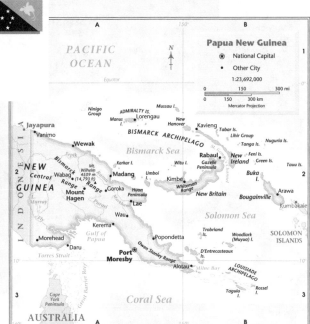

New Zealand

Capital: Wellington
Area: 104,454 sq. mi.
270,606 sq. km.
Population: 3,875,000
Largest City: Auckland
Language: English
Monetary Unit: New Zealand dollar

New Zealand: Map Index

Cities and Towns

Alexandra	A4
Ashburton	B3
Auckland	B2
Blenheim	B3
Christchurch	B3
Collingwood	B3
Dunedin	B4
East Coast Bays	B2
Gisborne	C2
Greymouth	B3
Hamilton	C2
Hastings	C2
Hicks Bay	C2
Invercargill	A4
Kaeo	B2
Kaikoura	B3
Kaitaia	B2
Kawhia	B2
Lower Hutt	B3
Manukau	B2
Milford Sound	A3
Napier	C2
Nelson	B3
New Plymouth	B2
Oamaru	B4
Palmerston North	C3
Queenstown	A3
Rotorua	C2
Taumaruni	C2
Taupo	C2
Tauranga	C2
Timaru	B3
Waimamaku	B2
Wanganui	C2
Wellington, *capital*	B3
Westport	B3
Whakatane	C2
Whangarei	B2

Other Features

Aspiring, *mt.*	A3
Banks, *peninsula*	B3
Canterbury, *bight*	B3
Canterbury, *plains*	B3
Clutha, *river*	A4
Cook, *mt.*	B3
Cook, *strait*	B3
Coromandel, *peninsula*	C2
East, *cape*	C2
Egmont, *cape*	B2
Egmont, *mt.*	B2
Farewell, *cape*	B3
Foveaux, *strait*	A4
Great Barrier, *island*	C2
Hawea, *lake*	A3
Hawke, *bay*	C2
Ngauruhoe, *mt.*	C2
North, *cape*	B1
North, *island*	B2
North Taranaki, *bight*	B2
Palliser, *cape*	C3
Pegasus, *bay*	B3
Plenty, *bay*	C2
Puysegur, *point*	A4
Rangitikei, *river*	C2
Raukumara, *range*	C2
Ruahine, *range*	C2
Ruapehu, *mt.*	C2
South, *island*	A3
Southern Alps, *mts.*	A3
Southland, *plains*	A4
South Taranaki, *bight*	B2
South West, *cape*	A4
Stewart, *island*	A4
Tararua, *range*	C3
Tasman, *bay*	B3
Tasman, *sea*	A2
Taupo, *lake*	C2
Te Anau, *lake*	A4
Tekapo, *lake*	B3
Three Kings, *islands*	B1
Tongariro, *mt.*	C2
Waikato, *river*	B2
Wairau, *river*	B3
Waitaki, *river*	B3
Wanaka, *lake*	A3

MAJOR CITIES

Australia

Sydney	3,907,000
Melbourne	3,232,000
Brisbane	1,622,000
Perth	1,329,000
Adelaide	1,064,000

Papua New Guinea

Port Moresby	173,500

New Zealand

Auckland	1,075,000
Wellington	340,000
Christchurch	334,000
Hamilton	166,000
Napier-Hastings	114,000
Dunedin	107,000

© MapQuest.com, Inc.

East Timor

Capital: Dili
Area: 5,794 sq. mi.
15,007 sq. km.
Population: 778,000
Largest City: Dili
Language: Tetum, Portuguese
Monetary Unit: Indonesian rupiah

East Timor: Map Index

Cities and Towns:

Aileu	B1
Ainaro	B2
Baukau	C1
Dili, *capital*	B1
Ermera	B1
Liquica	B1
Los Palos	C1
Maliana	B1
Manatuto	C1
Pante Makasar	A2
Same	B2
Suai	B2
Vikeke	C1

© MapQuest.com, Inc.

Micronesia

Capital: Palikir
Area: 271 sq. mi.
702 sq. km.
Population: 109,000
Largest City: Palikir
Language: English
Monetary Unit: U.S. dollar

Micronesia: Map Index

Cities and Towns

Colonia	A2
Kosrae	D2
Palikir, *capital*	C2
Weno	C2

Other Features

Caroline, *islands*	B2
Chuuk, *islands*	C2
Eauripik, *atoll*	B2
Faraulep, *atoll*	B2
Kapingamarangi, *atoll*	C2
Kosrae, *island*	D2
Mortlock, *islands*	C2
Murilo, *atoll*	C2
Namoluk, *atoll*	C2
Namonuito, *atoll*	C2
Ngulu, *atoll*	A2
Nukuoro, *atoll*	C2
Oroluk, *atoll*	C2
Pohnpei, *island*	D2
Pulusuk, *island*	B2
Ulithi, *atoll*	B2
Weno, *island*	C2
Yap, *islands*	A2

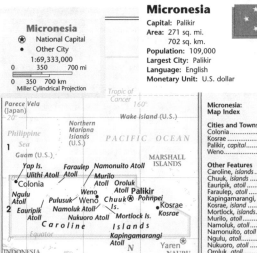

© MapQuest.com, Inc.

Marshall Islands

⊛ National Capital
● Other City

1:25,750,000

0 150 300 mi
0 150 300 km
Mercator Projection

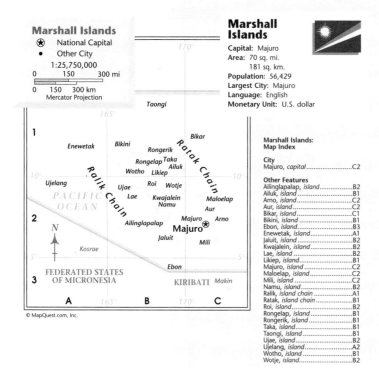

Marshall Islands

Capital: Majuro
Area: 70 sq. mi.
181 sq. km.
Population: 56,429
Largest City: Majuro
Language: English
Monetary Unit: U.S. dollar

Marshall Islands:
Map Index

City
Majuro, capital C2

Other Features
Ailinglapalap, island B2
Ailuk, island B1
Arno, island C2
Aur, island C2
Bikar, island C1
Bikini, island B1
Ebon, island B3
Enewetak, island A1
Jaluit, island B2
Kwajalein, island B2
Lae, island B2
Likiep, island B1
Majuro, island C2
Maloelap, island C2
Mili, island C2
Namu, island B2
Ralik, island chain A1
Ratak, island chain B1
Roi, island B2
Rongelap, island B1
Rongerik, island B1
Taka, island B1
Taongi, island B1
Ujae, island B2
Ujelang, island A2
Wotho, island B1
Wotje, island B2

Nauru

⊛ National Capital
● Other City

1:135,000

0 1 2 mi
0 1 2 km
Lambert Conformal Conic Projection

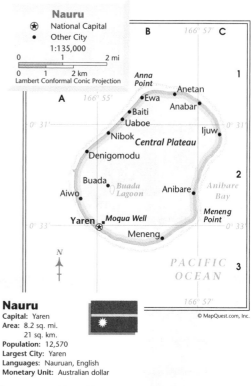

Nauru

Capital: Yaren
Area: 8.2 sq. mi.
21 sq. km.
Population: 12,570
Largest City: Yaren
Languages: Nauruan, English
Monetary Unit: Australian dollar

Nauru:
Map Index

Cities and Towns
Aiwo A2
Anabar C1
Anetan B1
Anibare B2
Baiti B1
Buada B2
Denigomodu A2
Ewa B1
Ijuw C2

Meneng B3
Nibok B2
Uaboe B1
Yaren, capital B3

Other Features
Anibare, bay C2
Anna, point B1
Buada, lagoon B2
Central, plateau B2
Meneng, point C2
Moqua, well B2

Solomon Islands

⊛ National Capital
● Other City

1:24,100,000

0 150 300 mi
0 150 300 km
Mercator Projection

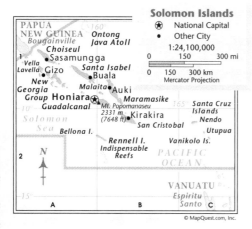

Solomon Islands:
Map Index

Cities and Towns
Auki B1
Buala A1
Gizo A1
Honiara, capital A1
Kirakira B2
Sasamungga A1

Other Features
Bellona, island A2
Choiseul, island A1
Guadalcanal, island A1
Indispensable, reefs B2
Malaita, island B1
Maramasike, island B1
Nendo, island C2
New Georgia Group,
islands A1
Ontong Java, island A1
Popomanaseu, mt. B1
Rennell, island B2
San Cristobal, island B2
Santa Cruz, islands C2
Santa Isabel, island A1
Solomon, sea A2
Utupua, island C2
Vanikolo, islands C2
Vella Lavella, island A1

Solomon Islands

Capital: Honiara
Area: 10,954 sq. mi.
28,378 sq. km.
Population: 477,000
Largest City: Honiara
Language: English
Monetary Unit: Solomon Islands dollar

Tuvalu

Capital: Funafuti
Area: 9.4 sq. mi.
24.4 sq. km.
Population: 11,305
Largest City: Funafuti
Languages: Tuvaluan, English
Monetary Unit: Tuvaluan dollar,
Australian dollar

Tuvalu:
Map Index

City
Funafuti, capital C3

Other Features
Funafuti, island C3
Nanumanga, island B2
Nanumea, island B1
Niulakita, island C4
Niutao, island B2
Nui, island B2
Nukufetau, island C2
Nukulaelae, island C3
Vaitupu, island C2

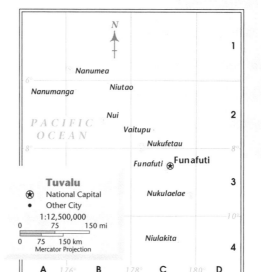

Tuvalu

⊛ National Capital
● Other City

1:12,500,000

0 75 150 mi
0 75 150 km
Mercator Projection

© MapQuest.com, Inc.

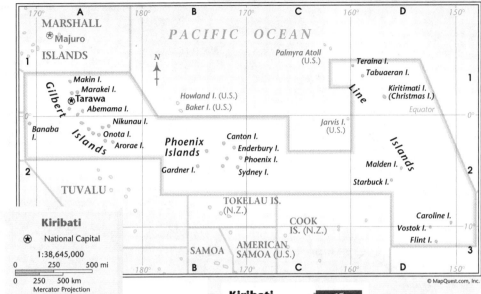

PACIFIC OCEAN

MARSHALL ISLANDS — Majuro

Gilbert Islands — Makin I., Marakei I., Tarawa, Abemama I., Banaba I., Nikunau I., Onota I., Arorae I.

Palmyra Atoll (U.S.)

Teraina I., Tabuaeran I., Kiritimati I. (Christmas I.)

Howland I. (U.S.), Baker I. (U.S.), Jarvis I. (U.S.)

Equator

Phoenix Islands — Canton I., Enderbury I., Phoenix I., Gardner I., Sydney I.

Line Islands — Malden I., Starbuck I.

TUVALU

TOKELAU IS. (N.Z.)

COOK IS. (N.Z.)

Caroline I., Vostok I., Flint I.

SAMOA, AMERICAN SAMOA (U.S.)

© MapQuest.com, Inc.

Kiribati
⊛ National Capital
1:38,645,000
0   250   500 mi
0   250   500 km
Mercator Projection

Kiribati
Capital: Tarawa
Area: 313 sq. mi.
811 sq. km.
Population: 98,549
Largest City: Tarawa
Languages: I-Kiribati (Gilbertese), English
Monetary Unit: Australian dollar

Kiribati: Map Index

City
Tarawa, capital A1

Other Features
Abemama, island A1
Arorae, island A2
Banaba, island A2
Canton, island B2
Caroline, island D2
Enderbury, island B2
Flint, island D3
Gardner, island B2
Gilbert, islands A1
Kiritimati (Christmas), island ...D1
Line, islands D1
Makin, island A1
Malden, island D2
Marakei, island A1
Nikunau, island A2
Onota, island A2
Phoenix, island B2
Phoenix, islands B2
Starbuck, island B2
Sydney, island B2
Tabuaeran, island D1
Teraina, island D1
Vostok, island D3

Fiji: Map Index

Cities and Towns
Galoa B3
Labasa B2
Lami B3
Lautoka A2
Lomawai A3
Nabouwalu B2
Nadi A2
Naduri B2
Nakodu B2
Navua B3
Suva, capital B3
Vunisea B3

Other Features
Beqa, island B3
Bligh Water, sound A2
Cicia, island C2
Cikobia, island C1
Gau, island B3
Great Sea, reef B1
Kadavu, island B3
Kadavu, passage A3
Kioa, island C2
Koro, island B2
Koro, sea B2
Lakeba, island C3
Lakeba, passage C3
Lau, island group C2
Laucala, island C2
Moala, island group B3
Nadi, bay A2
Navua, river A3
Ono, island B3
Ovalau, island B2
Qamea, island C2
Qelelevu, island C2
Rabi, island C2
Soso, bay B3
Taveuni, island C2
Tomanivi, mt. B2
Udu, point C2
Vanua Balavu, island C2
Vanua Levu, island B2
Vatu Lele, island A3
Vetauua, island C1
Viti Levu, island A3
Vunaniu, bay A3
Washington, cape A3
Yasawa, island group A2

Fiji
⊛ National Capital
• Other City
1:8,900,000
0   50   100 mi
0   50   100 km
Azimuthal Equal Area Projection

Fiji
Capital: Suva
Area: 7,056 sq. mi.
18,280 sq. km.
Population: 839,000
Largest City: Suva
Languages: Fijian, Hindi, English
Monetary Unit: Fijian dollar

Cikobia, Vetauua, Udu Point, Great Sea Reef, Vanua Levu, Labasa, Rabi, Kioa, Naduri, Laucala, Qamea, Taveuni, Qelelevu, Yasawa Group, Bligh Water, Viti Levu, Tomanivi 1323 m (4340 ft), Nabouwalu, Koro, Nakodu, Vanua Balavu, Lau Group, Lautoka, Nadi Bay, Nadi, Lami, Ovalau, Koro Sea, Lakeba Passage, Lomawai, Navua, Suva, Gau, Cicia, Galoa, Beqa, Lakeba, Vatu Lele, Kadavu, Ono, Moala Group, Vunisea, Cape Washington, Soso Bay, Kadavu Passage

© MapQuest.com, Inc.

Tonga
⊛ National Capital
• Other City
1:11,000,000
0   75   150 mi
0   75   150 km
Mercator Projection

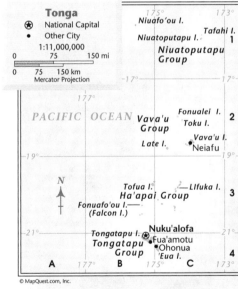

Niuafo'ou I., Tafahi I., Niuatoputapu I., Niuatoputapu Group

PACIFIC OCEAN

Vava'u Group, Fonualei I., Toku I., Late I., Vava'u, Neiafu

Tofua I., Lifuka I., Ha'apai Group, Fonuafo'ou I. (Falcon I.)

Tongatapu I., Nuku'alofa, Tongatapu Group, Fua'amotu, Ohonua, 'Eua I.

© MapQuest.com, Inc.

Tonga
Capital: Nuku'alofa
Area: 301 sq. mi.
780 sq. km.
Population: 104,000
Largest City: Nuku'alofa
Languages: Tongan, English
Monetary Unit: Pa'anga

Tonga: Map Index

Cities and Towns
Fua'amotu B4
Neiafu C2
Nuku'alofa, capital B4
Ohonua C4

Other Features
'Eua, island C4
Fonuafo'ou (Falcon), island B3
Fonualei, island C2
Ha'apai, island group B3
Late, island C2
Lifuka, island C3
Niuafo'ou, island B1
Niuatoputapu, island C1
Niuatoputapu, island group C1
Tafahi, island C1
Tofua, island B3
Toku, island C2
Tongatapu, island B4
Tongatapu, island group B4
Vava'u, island C2
Vava'u, island group C2

Palau: Map Index

Cities and Towns
Kloulklubed B3
Koror, capital B3
Melekeok C3
Meyungs B4
Ngaramasch B4
Ngerkeel B3
Ngermechau C2
Ngetbong C2
Ollei C2

Other Features
Angaur, island B4
Arakabesan, island B3
Arekalong, peninsula C2
Babelthuap, island C3
Cormoran, reef B2
Eli Malk, island B3
Helen, reef ....Inset
Kayangel, islands C1
Koror, island C3
Kossol, passage C2
Kossol, reef C2
Merir, island ....Inset
Ngemelis, islands B3
Peleliu, island B4
Philippine, sea B2
Pulo Anna, island ....Inset
Sar, passage B3
Sonsorol, island ....Inset
Tobi, island ....Inset
Urukthapel, island B3

Palau
⊛ National Capital
• Other City
1:1,900,000
0   5   10 mi
0   5   10 km
Lambert Conformal Conic Projection

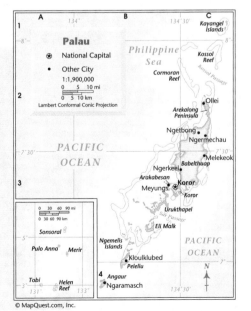

Kayangel Islands, Philippine Sea, Kossol Reef, Cormoran Reef, Aovaop Passage, Ollei, Arekalong Peninsula, Ngetbong, Ngermechau, Ngerkeel, Babelthuap, Melekeok, Arakabesan, Meyungs, Koror, Urukthapel, Sai Passage, Eli Malk, Ngemelis Islands, Kloulklubed, Peleliu, Angaur, Ngaramasch

Sonsoral, Pulo Anna, Merir, Tobi, Helen Reef

PACIFIC OCEAN

© MapQuest.com, Inc.

Palau
Capital: Koror
Area: 177 sq. mi.
458 sq. km.
Population: 19,717
Largest City: Koror
Languages: English, Sonsorolese, Angaur, Japanese, Tobi, Palauan
Monetary Unit: U.S. dollar

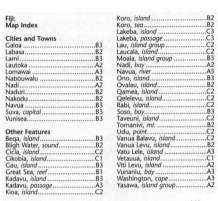

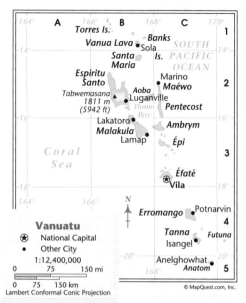

Vanuatu

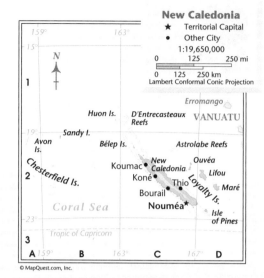

Capital: Vila
Area: 4,707 sq. mi.
  12,194 sq. km.
Population: 212,000
Largest City: Vila
Languages: French, English, Bislama
Monetary Unit: Vatu

Vanuatu: Map Index

Cities and Towns
Anelghowhat............C5
Isangel...............C4
Lakatoro..............B3
Lamap.................B3
Luganville............B2
Marino................C2
Potnarvin.............C4
Sola..................B1
Vila, capital.........C3

Other Features
Ambrym, island........C3
Anatom, island........C5
Aoba, island..........B2
Banks, islands........B1
Coral, sea............C3
Éfaté, island.........C3
Épi, island...........C3
Erromango, island.....C4
Espiritu Santo, island..B2
Futuna, island........C4
Homo, bay.............B2
Maéwo, island.........C2
Malakula, island......B3
Pentecost, island.....C2
Santa Maria, island...B2
Tabwemasana, mt.......B2
Tanna, island.........C4
Torres, islands.......B1
Vanua Lava, island....B1

Vanuatu
⊛ National Capital
• Other City
1:12,400,000
0   75   150 mi
0   75   150 km
Lambert Conformal Conic Projection

© MapQuest.com, Inc.

New Caledonia

★ Territorial Capital
• Other City
1:19,650,000
0   125   250 mi
0   125   250 km
Lambert Conformal Conic Projection

© MapQuest.com, Inc.

New Caledonia: Map Index

Cities and Towns
Bourail...............C2
Koné..................C2
Koumac................C2
Nouméa, capital.......C2
Thio..................C2

Other Features
Astrolabe, reefs......C2

Avon, islands.........A2
Bélep, islands........C2
Chesterfield, islands...A2
Coral, sea............B2
D'Entrecasteaux, reefs..C1
Huon, islands.........B1
Lifou, island.........D2
Loyalty, islands......D2
Maré, island..........D2
New Caledonia, island...C2
Ouvéa, island.........C2
Pines, island.........D2
Sandy, island.........B2

New Caledonia

Capital: Nouméa
Area: 8,548 sq. mi.
  21,912 sq. km.
Population: 228,000
Largest City: Nouméa
Language: French
Monetary Unit: CFP franc

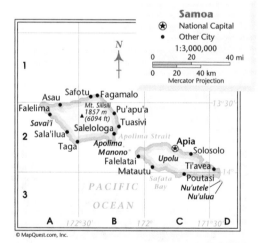

Samoa
⊛ National Capital
• Other City
1:3,000,000
0   20   40 mi
0   20   40 km
Mercator Projection

© MapQuest.com, Inc.

Samoa

Capital: Apia
Area: 1,093 sq. mi.
  2,832 sq. km.
Population: 178,000
Largest City: Apia
Languages: Samoan, English
Monetary Unit: Tala

Samoa: Map Index

Cities and Towns
Apia, capital.........C2
Asau..................A2
Fagamalo..............B1
Falelatai.............B2
Falelima..............A2
Matautu...............C2
Poutasi...............C3
Pu'apu'a..............B2
Safotu................B1
Sala'ilua.............A2
Salelologa............B2
Solosolo..............C2
Taga..................A2
Ti'avea...............D2
Tuasivi...............B2

Other Features
Apolima, island.......B2
Apolima, strait.......B2
Manono, island........B2
Nu'ulua, island.......D3
Nu'utele, island......D3
Safata, bay...........C3
Savai'i, island.......A2
Silisili, mt..........B2
Upolu, island.........C2

American Samoa: Map Index

Cities and Towns
Aoa...................C1
Aua...................C1
Fagasa................B1
Fagatogo..............B1
Faleniu...............B1
Leone.................B2
Nuuuli................B1
Pago Pago, capital....B1
Pavaiai...............B2

Other Features
Aunuu, island.........C1
Ofu, island...........A1
Olosega, island.......A1
Pola, island..........C1
Rose, island..........A1
Swains, island........A1
Tau, island...........A1
Tutuila, island.......A1, C2

American Samoa

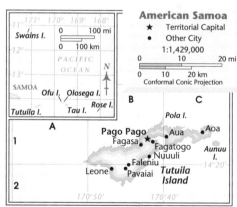

★ Territorial Capital
• Other City
1:1,429,000
0   10   20 mi
0   10   20 km
Conformal Conic Projection

© MapQuest.com, Inc.

American Samoa

Capital: Pago Pago
Area: 77 sq. mi.
  199 sq. km.
Population: 57,844
Largest City: Pago Pago
Language: Samoan, English
Monetary Unit: U.S. dollar

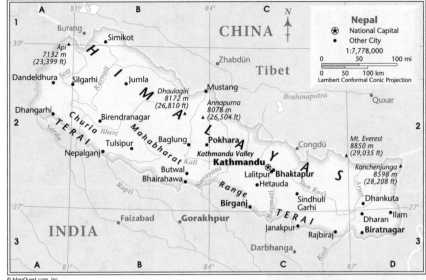

CHINA

Tibet

Brahmaputra

INDIA

Nepal

- ⊛ National Capital
- • Other City

1:7,778,000

0   50   100 mi

0   50   100 km

Lambert Conformal Conic Projection

Nepal: Map Index

Cities and Towns

Baglung	B2
Bhairahawa	B2
Bhaktapur	C2
Biratnagar	D3
Birendranagar	B2
Birganj	C2
Butwal	B2
Dandeldhura	A2
Dhangarhi	A2
Dhankuta	D2
Dharan	D3
Hetauda	C2
Ilam	D3
Janakpur	C3
Jumla	B2
Kathmandu, *capital*	C2
Lalitpur	C2
Mustang	B2
Nepalganj	B2
Pokhara	B2
Rajbiraj	C3
Silgarhi	B2
Simikot	B1
Sindhuli Garhi	C2
Tulsipur	B2

Other Features

Annapurna, *mt.*	B2
Api, *mt.*	A2
Arun, *river*	D2
Bagmati, *river*	C2
Bheri, *river*	B2
Churia, *mts.*	B2
Dhaulagiri, *mt.*	B2
Everest, *mt.*	C2
Himalayas, *mts.*	B2
Kali, *river*	B2
Kanchenjunga, *mt.*	D2
Karnali, *river*	B2
Kathmandu, *valley*	C2
Mahabharat, *range*	B2
Narayani, *river*	B2
Rapti, *river*	B2
Sarda, *river*	A2
Seti, *river*	A2
Sun Kosi, *river*	C2
Terai, *region*	A2, C3

Maldives

Capital: Male
Area: 115 sq. mi.
  298 sq. km.
Population: 318,000
Largest City: Male
Language: Divehi
Monetary Unit: Rufiyaa

INDIAN OCEAN

Maldives

- ⊛ National Capital

1:11,579,000

0   75   150 mi

0   75   150 km

Lambert Conformal Conic Projection

Maldives: Map Index

City

Male, *capital*	A2

Other Features

Addu, *atoll*	A5
Ari, *atoll*	A3
Equatorial, *channel*	A5
Fadiffolu, *atoll*	A2
Felidu, *atoll*	A3
Haddummati, *atoll*	A4
Horsburgh, *atoll*	A2
Ihavandiffulu, *atoll*	A1
Kardiva, *channel*	A2
Kolumadulu, *atoll*	A3
Malcolm, *atoll*	A1
Male, *atoll*	A2
Miladummadulu, *atoll*	A1
Mulaku, *atoll*	A3
Nilandu, *atoll*	A3
North Malosmadulu, *atoll*	A2
One and Half Degree, *channel*	A4
South Male, *atoll*	A3
South Malosmadulu, *atoll*	A2
Suvadiva, *atoll*	A4
Tiladummati, *atoll*	A1
Veimandu, *channel*	A3

Nepal

Capital: Kathmandu
Area: 56,827 sq. mi.
  147,220 sq. km.
Population: 25,164,000
Largest City: Kathmandu
Language: Nepali
Monetary Unit: Nepalese rupee

Sri Lanka: Map Index

Provinces

Central	B4
Eastern	C4
North Central	B3
Northern	B2
North Western	B4
Sabaragamuwa	B5
Southern	B5
Uva	C5
Western	A4

Cities and Towns

Amparai	C4
Anuradhapura	B3
Batticaloa	C4
Colombo, *capital*	A5
Dehiwala-Mt. Lavinia	A5
Galle	B5

Hambantota	C5
Jaffna	B2
Kalutara	A5
Kandy	B4
Kilinochchi	B2
Kurunegala	B4
Mankulam	B2
Mannar	A3
Matale	B4
Matara	B6
Moratuwa	A5
Mullaittivu	B2
Negombo	A4
Nuwara Eliya	B5
Point Pedro	B2
Polonnaruwa	C4
Pottuvil	C5
Puttalam	A3
Ratnapura	B5
Sri Jayawardenepura, *capital*	A5

Trincomalee	C3
Vavuniya	B3

Other Features

Adam's, *peak*	B4
Adam's Bridge, *shoal*	A3
Aruvi, *river*	B3
Bengal, *bay*	C3
Delft, *island*	A2
Dondra Head, *cape*	B6
Jaffna, *lagoon*	B2
Kalu, *river*	B5
Kelani, *river*	B4
Mahaweli Ganga, *river*	C4
Mannar, *gulf*	A3
Mannar, *island*	A2
Palk, *strait*	A2
Pidurutalagala, *mt.*	B4
Trincomalee, *harbor*	C3
Yan, *river*	B3

Sri Lanka

Capital: Colombo,
  Sri Jayawardenepura
Area: 25,332 sq. mi.
  65,627 sq. km.
Population: 19,065,000
Largest City: Colombo
Language: Sinhalese
Monetary Unit: Sri Lankan rupee

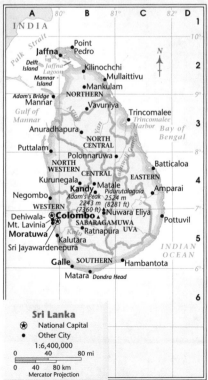

INDIA

NORTHERN

NORTH CENTRAL

NORTH WESTERN

CENTRAL

WESTERN

EASTERN

SABARAGAMUWA

UVA

SOUTHERN

INDIAN OCEAN

Bay of Bengal

Sri Lanka

- ⊛ National Capital
- • Other City

1:6,400,000

0   40   80 mi

0   40   80 km

Mercator Projection

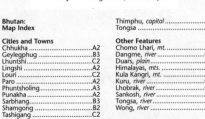

CHINA

HIMALAYAS

Tibet

INDIA

Duars

Brahmaputra

Bhutan

Capital: Thimphu
Area: 18,147 sq. mi.
  47,013 sq. km.
Population: 2,257,000
Largest City: Thimphu
Language: Dzongkha
Monetary Unit: Ngultrum, Indian rupee

Bhutan

- ⊛ National Capital
- • Other City

1:6,053,000

0   25   50   75 mi

0   25   50   75 km

Lambert Conformal Conic Projection

Bhutan: Map Index

Cities and Towns

Chhuka	A2
Geylegphug	B3
Lhuntshi	A2
Lingshi	A2
Louri	C2
Paro	A2
Phuntsholing	A3
Punakha	A2
Sarbhang	B3
Shamgong	B2
Tashigang	C2

Thimphu, *capital*	A2
Tongsa	B2

Other Features

Chomo Lhari, *mt.*	A1
Dangme, *river*	C2
Duars, *plain*	A3
Himalayas, *mts.*	B1
Kula Kangri, *mt.*	B1
Kuru, *river*	C2
Lhobrak, *river*	B2
Sankosh, *river*	B2
Tongsa, *river*	B2
Wong, *river*	A2

India:
Map Index

Internal Divisions
Andaman and Nicobar
 Islands (territory) F6
Andhra Pradesh (state).....C5
Arunachal Pradesh (state) F3
Assam (state).........F3
Bihar (state).........E3
Chandigarh (territory).....C2
Chhattisgarh (state).....D4
Dadra and Nagar
 Haveli (territory).....B4
Daman and Diu (territory).....B4
Delhi (territory).....C3
Goa (state).........B5
Gujarat (state).........B4
Haryana (state).........C3
Himachal Pradesh (state) C2
Jammu and Kashmir (state).....C2

Jharkhand (state) E4
Karnataka (state).....C6
Kerala (state).........C6
Lakshadweep (territory).....B6
Madhya Pradesh (state).....C4
Maharashtra (state).....B5
Manipur (state).........F4
Meghalaya (state).....F3
Mizoram (state).........F4
Nagaland (state).....F3
Orissa (state).........D4
Pondicherry (territory).....C6
Punjab (state).........C2
Rajasthan (state).....B3
Sikkim (state).........E3
Tamil Nadu (state).....C6
Tripura (state).........F4
Uttar Pradesh (state).....C3
Uttaranchal (state).....C3
West Bengal (state).....E4

Cities and Towns
Agartala F4
Agra.........C3
Ahmadabad.....B4
Aizawl.........F4
Ajmer.........B3
Akola.........C4
Alampur.........Inset II
Aligarh.........C3
Allahabad.........D3
Alleppey (Alappuzha).....C7
Amdanga.........Inset II
Amravati.........C4
Amritsar.........B2
Andheri.........Inset I
Ara.........D3
Asansol.........E4
Aurangabad.....C5
Baidyabati.........Inset II
Bally.........Inset II

Bamangachi.........Inset II
Bananga.........F7
Bandra.........Inset I
Bangalore.........C6
Bansbaria.........Inset II
Barakpur.........Inset II
Baranagar.........Inset II
Barasat.........Inset II
Bareilly.........C3
Bargachia.........Inset II
Bauria.........Inset II
Behala.........Inset II
Belapurpada.........Inset I
Belgaum.........B5
Bellary.........C5
Bhadrakh.........E4
Bhadreswar.........Inset II
Bhagalpur.........E3
Bhamapur.........D5
Bhandup.........Inset I
Bharatpur.........C3

Bhatapara.........D4
Bhatpara.........Inset II
Bhavnagar.........B4
Bhayandar.........Inset I
Bhimpur.........Inset II
Bhiwandi.........Inset I
Bhopal.........C4
Bhubaneswar.........E4
Bhuj.........A4
Bihar.........E3
Bijapur.........C5
Bikaner.........B3
Bilaspur.........D4
Bishnupur.........Inset II
Borivli.........Inset I
Buj-Buj.........Inset II
Burdwan.........E4
Burhanpur.........C4
Chandannagar.........Inset II
Chandigarh.........C2
Chandrapur.........C5

Chembur.........Inset I
Chene.........Inset I
Chennai (Madras).....D6
Cherrapunji.........F3
Chirner.........Inset I
Cochin (Kochi).....C7
Coimbatore.........C6
Cuddalore.........C6
Cuttack.........E4
Daman.........B4
Darbhanga.........E3
Darjiling.........E3
Dehra Dun.........C2
Delhi.........C3
Dhulagarh.........Inset II
Dibrugarh.........F3
Dispur.........F3
Diu.........B4
Dum-Dum.........Inset II
Dumjor.........Inset II
Faizabad.........D3

Gandhinagar.........B4
Ganganagar.........B3
Gangtok.........E3
Garden Reach.........Inset II
Garulia.........Inset II
Gauhati.........F3
Gaya.........E4
Ghatkopar.........Inset I
Gorakhpur.........D3
Gulbarga.........C5
Guntur.........D5
Gwalior.........C3
Halisahar.........Inset II
Haora.........E4, Inset II
Hisabpur.........Inset II
Hubli-Dharwar.........C5
Hugli-Chunchura.........Inset II
Hyderabad.........C5
Imphal.........F4
Indore.........C4
Itanagar.........F3
Jabalpur.........C4
Jagadpur.........D5
Jaipur.........C3
Jammu.........B2
Jamnagar.........B4
Jamshedpur.........E4
Janai.........Inset II
Jejur.........Inset II
Jhansi.........C3
Jodhpur.........B3
Joka.........Inset II
Jullundur.........C2
Junagadh.........B4
Kakinada.........D5
Kalwa.........Inset I
Kaman.........Inset I
Kamarhati.........Inset II
Kanchipuram.........C6
Kanchrapara.........Inset II
Kanpur.........D3
Kansaripara.........Inset II
Kasinathpur.........Inset II
Kathgodam.........C3
Kharagpur.........E4
Kohima.........F3
Kolhapur.........B5
Kolkata (Calcutta).........E4, Inset II
Kolshet.........Inset I
Konnagar.........Inset II
Kota.........C3
Kozhikode.........C6
Kurla.........Inset I
Kurnool.........C5
Lakhpat.........A4
Lucknow.........D3
Ludhiana.........C2
Madurai.........C7
Malad.........Inset I
Malegaon.........B4
Mangalore.........B6
Mathura.........C3
Meerut.........C3
Moradabad.........C3
Mulund.........Inset I
Mumbai (Bombay).........B5, Inset I
Mumbra.........Inset I
Mysore.........C6
Nagpur.........C4
Naihati.........Inset II
Nalikul.........Inset II
Nanded.........C5
Nangi.........Inset I
Nanole.........Inset I
Nasik.........B4
Nellore.........C6
New Delhi, *capital*.........C3
Nizamabad.........C5
Ongole.........C5
Panaji.........B5
Panihati.........Inset II
Patiala.........C2
Patna.........E3
Paye.........Inset I
Polba.........Inset II
Pondicherry.........C6
Port Blair.........F6
Pune.........B5
Raipur.........D4
Rajkot.........B4
Rajpur.........Inset II
Ramanbati.........Inset II
Ranchi.........E4
Raurkela.........D4
Rishra.........Inset II
Saharanpur Panipat.........C3
Salem.........C6
Sambalpur.........D4
Sankrail.........D4
Sasaram.........D4
Sheva.........Inset I
Shillong.........F3
Sholapur.........C5
Shrirampur.........Inset II
Silvassi.........B4
Simla.........C2
Singur.........Inset II
Sonarpur.........Inset II
South Dum-Dum.........Inset II
Srinagar.........B2
Sugandha.........Inset II
Surat.........B4
Thane.........Inset I
Thanjavur.........C6
Tiruchchirappalli.........C6
Titagarh.........Inset II
Trivandrum
 (Thiruvananthapuram).........C7

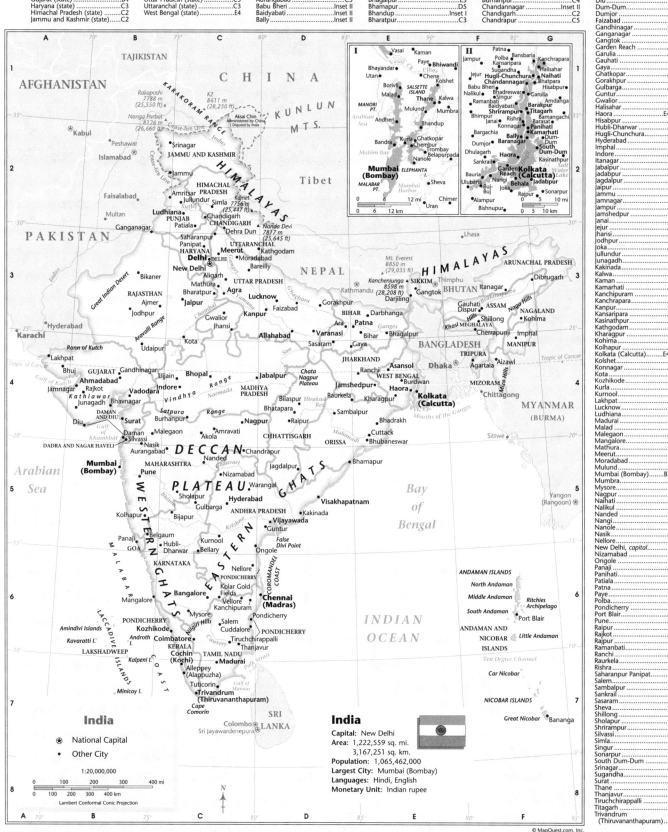

India

⊛ National Capital
• Other City

1:20,000,000

0 100 200 300 400 mi
0 100 200 300 400 km
Lambert Conformal Conic Projection

India
Capital: New Delhi
Area: 1,222,559 sq. mi.
 3,167,251 sq. km.
Population: 1,065,462,000
Largest City: Mumbai (Bombay)
Languages: Hindi, English
Monetary Unit: Indian rupee

© MapQuest.com, Inc.

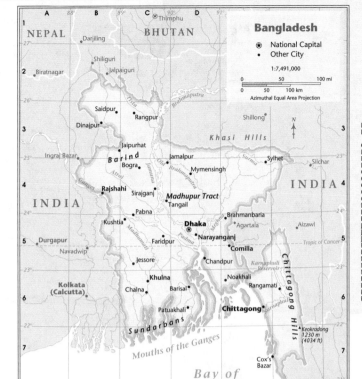

Bangladesh

⊛ National Capital
• Other City

1:7,491,000

0 — 50 — 100 mi
0 — 50 — 100 km
Azimuthal Equal Area Projection

© MapQuest.com, Inc.

Bangladesh

Capital: Dhaka
Area: 57,295 sq. mi.
148,433 sq. km.
Population: 146,736,000
Largest City: Dhaka
Language: Bengali
Monetary Unit: Taka

Bangladesh:
Map Index

Cities and Towns
Barisal D6
Bogra C4
Brahmanbaria E5
Chalna C6
Chandpur D5
Chittagong E6
Comilla E7
Cox's Bazar E7
Dhaka, capital D5
Dinajpur B3
Faridpur C5
Jaipurhat C3
Jamalpur C4
Jessore C5
Khulna C5
Kushtia C5
Mymensingh D4
Narayanganj D5
Noakhali E6
Pabna C4
Patuakhali D6
Rajshahi B4
Rangamati F6

Rangpur C3
Saidpur B3
Sirajganj C4
Sylhet E4
Tangail C4

Other Features
Atrai, river B4
Barind, region B4
Bengal, bay D7
Brahmaputra, river D3
Chittagong Hills, region F5
Ganges, river B4
Jamuna, river C4
Karnaphuli, reservoir F6
Karnaphuli, river E6
Keokradong, mt. F7
Madhumati, river C5
Madhupur Tract, region D4
Meghna, river D5
Mouths of the Ganges,
delta C7
Old Brahmaputra, river C4
Padma, river D5
Sundarbans, region C7
Surma, river E3
Tista, river C2

India: Map Index
Trombay ....Inset I
Tuticorin C7
Udaipur B4
Ujjain C4
Ulubaria ....Inset II
Uran ....Inset I
Utan ....Inset I
Vadodara B4
Varanasi D3
Vasai ....Inset I
Vellore C6
Vijayawada D5
Visakhapatnam D5
Warangal C5

Other Features
Amindivi, islands B6
Andaman, islands F6
Androth, island B6
Arabian, sea ....A5, Inset I
Aravalli, range B3
Bengal, bay E5
Bhima, river C5
Brahmaputra, river F3
Car Nicobar, island F7
Cauvery, river C6
Chambal, river C4
Chata Nagpur, plateau D4
Comorin, cape C7
Coromandel, coast D6
Deccan, plateau C5
Eastern Ghats, mts. C6
Elephanta, island ....Inset I
False Divi, point D5
Ganges, river E3
Ghaghara, river D3
Godavari, river C5
Great Indian, desert B3
Great Nicobar, island F7
Himalayas, mts. C2, E3
Hirakud, reservoir D4
Hugli, river ....Inset II
Indus, river C2
Kalpeni, island B7
Kamet, mt. C2
Kanchenjunga, mt. E3
Karakoram, range C1
Kathiawar, peninsula B4
Kavaratti, island B6
Khambhat, gulf B4
Khasi, hills F3
Kolar, gold fields C6
Krishna, river C5
Kutch, gulf A4
Laccadive, islands B6
Little Andaman, island F6
Mahanadi, river D4
Mahim, bay ....Inset I
Malabar, coast B6
Malabar, point ....Inset I
Mannar, gulf C7
Manori, point ....Inset I
Middle Andaman, island F6
Minicoy, island B7
Mizo, hills F4
Mouths of the Ganges, delta ..E4
Mumbai, harbor ....Inset I
Naga, hills F3
Nanda Devi, mt. C2
Narmada, river C4
Nicobar, islands F7
Nilgiri, hills C6
North Andaman, island F6
Palk, strait C7
Rann of Kutch, mud flat B4
Ritchies, archipelago F6
Salsette, island ....Inset I
Salt Water, lake ....Inset II
Satpura, range C4
Son, river D4
South Andaman, island F6
Sutlej, river C2
Ten Degree, channel F7
Ulhas, river ....Inset I
Vasai, creek ....Inset I
Vindhya, range C4
Western Ghats, mts. B5
Yamuna, river C3

Pakistan

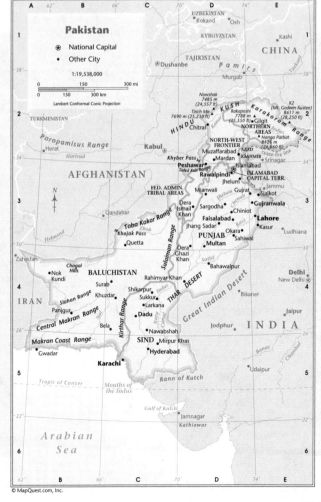

Pakistan

Capital: Islamabad
Area: 339,697 sq. mi.
880,044 sq. km.
Population: 153,578,000
Largest City: Karachi
Languages: Urdu, English
Monetary Unit: Pakistani rupee

Pakistan

⊛ National Capital
• Other City

1:19,538,000

0 — 150 — 300 mi
0 — 150 — 300 km
Lambert Conformal Conic Projection

Pakistan:
Map Index

Internal Divisions
Azad Kashmir Province D2
Baluchistan Province B4
Federally Administrated
Tribal Areas C3
Islamabad Capital Territory D3
Northern Areas D2
North-West Frontier Province ..D3
Punjab Province D3
Sind Province C5

Cities and Towns
Bahawalpur D4
Bela C4
Chiniot D3
Chitral D2
Dadu C4
Dera Ghazi Khan D3
Dera Ismail Khan D3
Faisalabad D3
Gilgit E2
Gujranwala E3
Gujrat E3
Gwadar B5
Hyderabad C5
Islamabad, capital D3
Jhang Sadar D3
Jhelum D3
Karachi C5
Kasur E3
Khuzdar C4
Lahore E3
Larkana C4
Mardan D2
Mianwali D3
Mirpur Khas C4
Multan D3
Muzaffarabad D2
Nawabshah C4
Nok Kundi B4

Okara D3
Panjgur B4
Peshawar D3
Quetta C3
Rahimyar Khan D4
Rawalpindi D3
Sahiwal D3
Sargodha D3
Shikarpur C4
Sialkot E3
Sukkur C4
Surab C4

Other Features
Arabian, sea B6
Central Makran, range B4
Chagai, hills B4
Chenab, river D3
Hindu Kush, mts. D2
Indus, river C4, E2
Jhelum, river D3
Karakoram, range E2
Khojak, pass C3
Khyber, pass D2
Kirthar, range C4
Konar, river D2
K2 (Godwin Austen), mt. E2
Makran Coast, range B5
Mouths of the Indus, delta C5
Nal, river B4
Nanga Parbat, mt. E2
Nara, canal C4
Nowshak, mt. D2
Rakaposhi, mt. E2
Ravi, river D3
Safed Koh, range D3
Siahan, range B4
Sulaiman, range C4
Sutlej, river D4
Thar, desert C4
Tirich Mir, mt. D2
Toba Kakar, range C3
Zhob, river C3

© MapQuest.com, Inc.

Afghanistan: Map Index

Cities and Towns

Asadabad	C2
Baghlan	B1
Balkh	B1
Bamian	B2
Baraki Barak	B2
Chaghcharan	B2
Charikar	B1
Farah	A2
Feyzabad	C1
Gardez	B2
Ghazni	B2
Herat	A2
Jalalabad	C2
Kabul, capital.	B2
Khowst	B2
Konduz	B1
Kowt-e Ashrow	B2
Lashkar Gah	A2
Mazar-e Sharif	B1
Meymaneh	A1
Qalat	B2
Qaleh-ye Now	A2
Qaleh-ye Panjeh	C1
Qandahar	B2
Samangan	B2
Sar-e Pol	B1
Sheberghan	B1
Shindand	A2
Taloqan	B1
Tarin Kowt	B2
Zaranj	A2
Zareh Sharan	B2

Other Features

Amu Darya, river	B1
Arghandab, river	B2
Farah, river	A2
Fuladi, mt.	B2
Gowd-e Zereh, lake	A3
Hamun-e Saberi, lake	A2
Harirud, river	A2
Helmand, river	A2
Hindu Kush, range	B1
Kabul, river	B2
Khojak, pass	B2
Khyber, pass	C2
Konar, river	C1
Konduz, river	B1
Morghab, river	A1
Nowshak, mt.	C1
Panj, river	C1
Paropamisus, range	A2
Registan, region	A2
Shibar, pass	B2
Vakhan, region	C1

Afghanistan

Capital: Kabul
Area: 251,825 sq. mi.
1,638,490 sq. km. ...653,396 sq. km.

Area: 251,825 sq. mi.
652,396 sq. km.
Population: 23,897,000
Largest City: Kabul
Languages: Pashto, Dari Persian
Monetary Unit: Afghani

Afghanistan

⊛ National Capital
• Other City

1:10,870,000

0 50 100 150 mi
0 50 100 150 km

Lambert Conformal Conic Projection

© MapQuest.com, Inc.

Iran

Capital: Tehran
Area: 632,457 sq. mi.
1,638,490 sq. km.
Population: 68,920,000
Largest City: Tehran
Languages: Persian, Turkic, Luri, Kurdish
Monetary Unit: Iranian rial

Iran: Map Index

Cities and Towns

Abadan	B3
Ahvaz	B3
Arak	B3
Ardabil	B2
Bakhtaran	B3
Bam	D4
Bandar Beheshti	E4
Bandar-e Abbas	D4
Bandar-e Anzali	B2
Bandar-e Bushehr	C4
Bandar-e Khomeyni	C3
Bandar-e Torkeman	C2
Birjand	D3
Dezful	B3
Esfahan	C3
Hamadan	B3
Ilam	B3
Iranshahr	E4
Jask	D4
Karaj	C2
Kashan	C3
Kerman	D3
Khorramabad	B3
Khorramshahr	B3
Khvoy	A2
Mashhad	D2
Neyshabur	D2
Orumiyeh (Urmia)	A2
Qazvin	B2
Qom	C3
Rasht	B2
Sabzevar	D2
Sanandaj	B2
Sari	C2
Shahr-e Kord	C3
Shiraz	C4
Sirjan	D4
Tabriz	B2
Tehran, capital	C2
Yasuj	C3
Yazd	C3
Zabol	E3
Zahedan	E4
Zanjan	B2

Other Features

Aras, river	B2
Atrak, river	D2
Azerbaijan, region	B2
Bakhtiari, region	B3
Baluchistan, region	E4
Caspian, sea	C2
Damavand, mt.	C2
Dasht-e Kavir, desert	D3
Dasht-e Lut, desert	D3
Elburz, mts.	C2
Halil, river	D4
Hamun-e Jaz Murian, lake	D4
Hashtadan, region	E3
Hormuz, strait	D4
Karun, river	B3
Kavir-e Namak, desert	D3
Kerman, region	D4
Kharg, island	C4
Khorasan, region	D2
Khuzestan, region	B3
Kopet, mts.	D2
Kul, river	D4
Larestan, region	C4
Mand, river	C4
Mazandaran, region	C2
Oman, gulf	D5
Persian, gulf	C4
Qareh, river	B3
Qeshm, island	D4
Shatt al-Arab, river	B3
Urmia, lake	B2
Yazd, region	C3
Zagros, mts.	B3

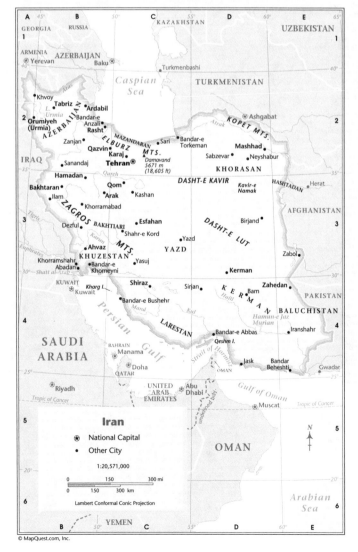

Iran

⊛ National Capital
• Other City

1:20,571,000

0 150 300 mi
0 150 300 km

Lambert Conformal Conic Projection

© MapQuest.com, Inc.

Turkmenistan: Map Index

Cities and Towns

Ashgabat, capital	C3
Bakhardok	C2
Bayramaly	D3
Büzmeyin	C2
Chardzhou	D2
Cheleken	A2
Dashhowuz	D2
Ensanguly	A3
Gazanjyk	B2
Gumdag	B2
Gushgy	D3
Gyzylarbat	B2
Kerki	D3
Mary	C3
Nebitdag	B2

Other Features

Amu Darya, river	D2
Caspian, sea	A2
Etrek, river	B3
Garabil, plateau	D3
Garabogazköl, lake	A2
Gushgy, river	D3
Kara-Kum, canal	D3
Kara-Kum, desert	C2
Kopet, mts.	B2
Murgab, river	D3
Sarygamysh Koli, lake	B2
Sumbar, river	B2
Tedzhen, river	C3
Turan, lowland	C2
Tedzhen	C3
Turkmenbashi	A2

Turkmenistan

Capital: Ashgabat
Area: 188,417 sq. mi.
488,127 sq. km.
Population: 4,867,000
Largest City: Ashgabat
Languages: Turkmen, Russian, Uzbek
Monetary Unit: Manat

Turkmenistan

⊛ National Capital
• Other City

1:16,929,000

0 100 200 mi
0 100 200 km

Lambert Conformal Conic Projection

© MapQuest.com, Inc.

Kazakhstan

Capital: Astana (Aqmola)
Area: 1,049,200 sq. mi.
2,718,135 sq. km.
Population: 15,433,000
Largest City: Almaty (Alma-Ata)
Language: Kazakh
Monetary Unit: Tenge

Kazakhstan: Map Index

Cities and Towns

Beyneu	B2
Ekibastuz	D1
Embi	B2
Esil	C1
Kokshetau	C1
Leninsk	C2
Lepsi	D2
Oral	B1
Öskemen (Ust-Kamenogorsk)	E1
Pavlodar	D1
Petropavl	C1
Qaraghandy (Karaganda)	D2
Qostanay	C1
Qyzylorda	C2
Rudnyy	C1
Saryshaghan	D2
Semey (Semipalatinsk)	E1
Shalqar	B2
Shymkent (Chimkent)	C2
Taldyqorghan	D2
Temirtau	D1
Zaysan	E2
Zhambyl (Dzhambul)	D2
Zhezqazgham	C2

Cities and Towns

Astana (Aqmola), *capital*	D1
Almaty (Alma-Ata)	D2
Aqtau	B2
Aqtobe	B1
Aral	C2
Arqalyq	C1
Atbasar	C1
Atyrau	B2
Ayagöz	E2
Balkhash	D2

Other Features

Alakol, *lake*	E2
Aral, *sea*	B2
Balkhash, *lake*	D2
Betpak Dala, *plain*	C2
Caspian, *depression*	B2
Caspian, *sea*	A2
Ili, *river*	D2
Irtysh, *river*	D1
Ishim, *river*	C1
Kazakh Upland *region*	C2
Khan-Tengri, *mt.*	E2
Muyun Kum, *desert*	D2
Syrdarya, *river*	C2
Tengiz, *lake*	C1
Tobol, *river*	C1
Torghay, *plateau*	C1
Ural, *river*	B2
Ustyurt, *plateau*	B2
Zaysan, *lake*	E2

Kazakhstan
⊛ National Capital
• Other City
1:26,667,000
0 125 250 mi
0 125 250 km
Lambert Conformal Conic Projection

© MapQuest.com, Inc.

Uzbekistan
⊛ National Capital
• Other City
1:14,725,000
0 40 80 mi
0 40 80 km
Lambert Conformal Conic Projection

© MapQuest.com, Inc.

Uzbekistan

Capital: Tashkent
Area: 172,700 sq. mi.
447,409 sq. km.
Population: 26,093,000
Largest City: Tashkent
Languages: Uzbek, Russian
Monetary Unit: Sum

Uzbekistan: Map Index

Cities and Towns

Andizhan	D2
Bukhara	B3
Farghona	D2
Gulistan	C2
Jizzakh	C2
Khujayli	A2
Muynoq	A2
Namangan	D2
Nawoiy	C2
Nukus	A2
Olmaliq	C2
Qarshi	C3
Qunghirot	A2
Ququon	D2
Samarqand	C3
Tashkent, *capital*	C2
Termiz	C3
Uchquduq	B2
Urganch	B2
Zarafshon	B2

Other Features

Amu Darya, *river*	B2
Aral, *sea*	A2
Chirchiq, *river*	C2
Fergana, *valley*	D2
Kyzylkum, *desert*	B2
Syrdarya, *river*	D2
Turan, *lowland*	A2
Ustyurt, *plateau*	A2
Zeravshan, *river*	B2

Kyrgyzstan: Map Index

Cities and Towns

At-Bashy	D2
Balykchy	E1
Bishkek, *capital*	D1
Cholpon-Ata	E1
Jalal-Abad	C2
Jangy-Bazar	B2
Karakol	F1
Kara-Say	F2
Kyzyl-Kyya	C2
Naryn	E2
Osh	C2
Özgön	C2
Sary Tash	C3
Songköl	D2
Sülüktü	A3
Talas	C1
Tash Kömür	C2
Tokmok	D1
Toktogul	C2

Other Features

Alay, *mts.*	C3
Chatkal, *river*	B2
Chu, *river*	D1
Jengish Chokusu, *mt.*	G1
Kyzyl-Suu, *river*	C3
Naryn, *river*	E2
Tien Shan, *mts.*	E2
Toxkan, *river*	E2
Ysyk-Köl, *lake*	E1

Kyrgyzstan

Capital: Bishkek
Area: 76,642 sq. mi.
198,554 sq. km.
Population: 5,138,000
Largest City: Bishkek
Language: Kirghiz
Monetary Unit: Som

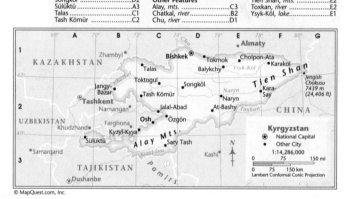

Kyrgyzstan
⊛ National Capital
• Other City
1:14,286,000
0 75 150 mi
0 75 150 km
Lambert Conformal Conic Projection

© MapQuest.com, Inc.

Tajikistan

Capital: Dushanbe
Area: 55,300 sq. mi.
143,264 sq. km.
Population: 6,245,000
Largest City: Dushanbe
Language: Tajik
Monetary Unit: Somoni

Tajikistan: Map Index

Cities and Towns

Dangara	A1
Dushanbe, *capital*	A1
Jirgatol	B1
Kalai Khum	B1
Kansay	A1
Khorugh	B2
Khudzhand	A1
Konibodom	B1
Kulob	A2
Morghob	B1
Navabad	A1
Norak	A1
Panj	A2
Panjakent	A2
Qurghonteppa	A2
Tursunzoda	A1
Uroteppa	A1
Zarafobod	A1

Other Features

Alay, *mts.*	B1
Bartang, *river*	B1
Darya, *river*	A2
Imeni Ismail Samani, *mt.*	B1
Kofarnihon, *river*	A2
Morghob, *river*	B1
Oqsu, *river*	C2
Pamirs, *mts.*	B2
Panj, *river*	B1
Pyandzh, *river*	B1
Qarokul, *lake*	B1
Surkhob, *river*	B1
Syrdarya, *river*	A1, B1
Turkeston, *mts.*	A1
Vahsh, *river*	A1
Zeravshan, *river*	A1
Zeravshan, *mts.*	A1

Tajikistan
⊛ National Capital
• Other City
1:7,622,000
0 40 80 mi
0 40 80 km
Lambert Conformal Conic Projection

© MapQuest.com, Inc.

Iraq:
Map Index

Cities and Towns
Amarah, al-	C2
Baghdad, capital	B2
Baqubah	B2
Basra	C2
Dahuk	B1
Diwaniyah, ad-	C2
Fallujah, al-	B2
Hadithah, al-	B2
Hillah, al-	B2
Irbil	B1
Karbala	B2
Khanaqin	C2
Kirkuk	B1
Kut, al-	C2
Mosul	B1
Najaf, an-	B2
Nasiriyah, an-	C2
Qayyarah, al-	B1
Ramadi, ar-	B2
Rutbah, ar-	B2
Samarra	B2
Samawah, as-	C2
Sulaymaniyah, as-	C1
Tall Afar	B1
Tikrit	B2
Umm Qasr	C2

Other Features
Babylon, ruins	B2
Diyala, river	C2
Euphrates, river	C2
Great Zab, river	B1
Haji Ibrahim, mt.	B1
Little Zab, river	B1
Mesopotamia, region	B2
Milh, lake	B2
Persian, gulf	C3
Shatt al-Arab, river	C2
Syrian, desert	B2
Tigris, river	B1

Iraq

Capital: Baghdad
Area: 167,975 sq. mi.
    435,169 sq. km.
Population: 25,175,000
Largest City: Baghdad
Language: Arabic
Monetary Unit: Iraqi dinar

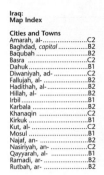

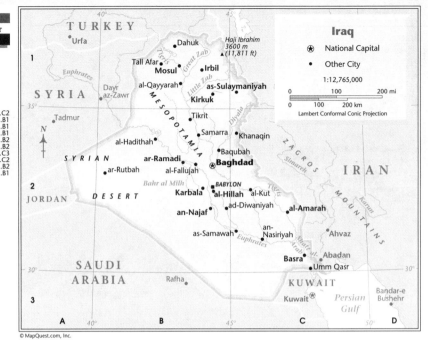

Kuwait

Capital: Kuwait
Area: 6,880 sq. mi.
    17,924 sq. km.
Population: 2,521,000
Largest City: Kuwait
Language: Arabic
Monetary Unit: Kuwaiti dinar

Kuwait:
Map Index

Cities and Towns
Abdali	B1
Ahmadi, al-	C2
Fuhayhil, al-	C2
Hawalli	C2
Jahrah, al-	B2
Khiran, al-	C3
Kuwait, capital	B2
Qasr as-Sabiyah	B2
Rawdatayn, ar-	B2
Sulaybikhat, as-	B2
Wafrah, al-	B3

Other Features
Bubiyan, island	C2
Faylakah, island	C2
Kuwait, bay	B2
Persian, gulf	C2
Wadi al-Batin, river	A2
Warbah, island	C1

Saudi Arabia

Capital: Riyadh
Area: 865,000 sq. mi.
    2,240,933 sq. km.
Population: 24,217,000
Largest City: Riyadh
Language: Arabic
Monetary Unit: Riyal

Saudi Arabia:
Map Index

Cities and Towns
Abha	B2
Badanah	B1
Buqayq	C1
Buraydah	B1
Dammam, ad-	C1
Dhahran	C1
Hail	B1
Harad	C1
Hillah, al-	B2
Hufuf, al-	C1
Jawf, al-	A1
Jeddah	A2
Jizan	B2
Jubayl, al-	C1
Khamis Mushayt	B2
Kharj, al-	B1
Mecca	A2
Medina	A1
Najran	B2
Qalat Bishah	B2
Qunfudhah, al-	A2
Rafha	B1
Ras al-Khafji	C1
Ras Tanura	C1
Riyadh, capital	B1
Sulayyil, as-	B2
Tabuk	A1
Taif, at-	B2
Turayf	A1
Unayzah	B1
Wajh, al-	A1
Yanbu al-Bahr	A1

Other Features
Asir, region	B2
Dahna, ad-, desert	B1
Farasan, islands	B2
Hasa, al-, region	C1
Hijaz, al-, region	A1
Jabal Tuwayq, mts.	B2
Nafud, an-, desert	B1
Najd, region	B1
Persian, gulf	C1
Red, sea	A1
Rub al-Khali (Empty Quarter), desert	C2
Sabkhat Matti, salt flat	C2
Sawda, mt.	B2
Syrian, desert	A1
Umm as-Samim, salt flat	C2
Wadi al-Hamd, river	A1

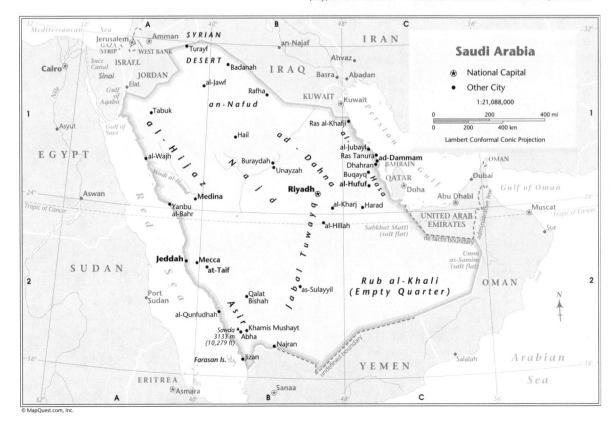

Bahrain and Qatar

⊛ National Capital
• Other City

1:2,842,000

0   10   20 mi
0 10 20 km
Transverse Mercator
Projection

© MapQuest.com, Inc.

Bahrain and Qatar:
Map Index

Bahrain
Cities and Towns
Askar B1
Mamtalah, al- B2
Manama, capital B1
Mina Salman B1

Other Features
Bahrain, gulf A2
Hawar, islands B2
Jiddah, island A1
Muharraq, al-, island B1
Ras al-Barr, cape B2
Sitrah, island B1
Umm an-Nasan, island.......A1

Qatar
Cities and Towns
Doha, capital D3
Dukhan B3
Jumayliyah, al- C2
Khawr, al- D2
Ruways, ar- C1
Umm Bab B3
Umm Said (Musayid)..........D4
Wakrah, al- D3

Other Features
Dawhat as-Salwa, bay B3
Ras Laffan, cape D2
Ras Rakan, cape C1
Tuwayyir al-Hamir, hill........C4

Bahrain

Capital: Manama
Area: 268 sq. mi.
       694 sq. km.
Population: 724,000
Largest City: Manama
Language: Arabic
Monetary Unit: Bahraini dinar

Qatar

Capital: Doha
Area: 4,412 sq. mi.
       11,430 sq. km.
Population: 610,000
Largest City: Doha
Language: Arabic
Monetary Unit: Qatari rial

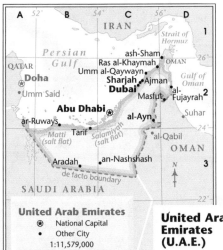

United Arab Emirates

⊛ National Capital
• Other City

1:11,579,000

0   50   100   150 mi
0 50 100 150 km
Lambert Conformal Conic Projection

© MapQuest.com, Inc.

United Arab
Emirates
(U.A.E.)

Capital: Abu Dhabi
Area: 30,000 sq. mi.
       77,720 sq. km.
Population: 2,995,000
Largest City: Abu Dhabi
Language: Arabic
Monetary Unit: Dirham

United Arab Emirates:
Map Index

Cities and Towns
Abu Dhabi, capital C2
Ajman C2
Aradah B3
Ayn, al- C2
Dubai C2
Fujayrah, al- D2
Masfut D2
Nashshash, an- C3
Ras al-Khaymah C2

Ruways, ar- B2
Sham, ash- D1
Sharjah C2
Tarif B2
Umm al-Qaywayn C2

Other Features
Hormuz, strait D1
Matti, salt flat B3
Oman, gulf D2
Persian, gulf B1
Salamiyah, salt flat C3

Yemen:
Map Index

Cities and Towns
Aden B2
Ahwar B2
Amran A1
Ataq B2
Balhaf B2
Bayda, al- B2
Dhamar A2
Ghaydah, al- C1
Habarut C1
Hadiboh C2
Hajjah A1
Hawf C1
Hazm, al- A1
Hudaydah, al- A2
Ibb A2
Lahij A2
Madinat ash-Shab A2
Marib B1
Maydi A1

Mocha (Mukha, al-) A2
Mukalla, al- B2
Qalansiyah C2
Qishn C1
Rida B2
Sadah A1
Sanaa, capital A1
Sanaw C1
Sayhut C1
Saywun B1
Shabwah B1
Taizz A2
Zabid A2

Other Features
Abd al-Kuri, island.............C2
Aden, gulf B2
Arabian, sea C2
Bab al-Mandab, strait A2
Hadhramaut, district B1
Jabal an-Nabi Shuayb, mt...A1
Jabal Zuqar, island A2
Kamaran, island A1
Perim, island A2
Ras al-Kalb, cape B2
Ras Fartak, cape C1
Red, sea A2
Socotra, island C2
The Brothers, islands.........C2
Wadi al-Masilah, river B1

Yemen

Capital: Sanaa
Area: 205,356 sq. mi.
       532,010 sq. km.
Population: 20,010,000
Largest City: Sanaa
Language: Arabic
Monetary Unit: Yemeni rial

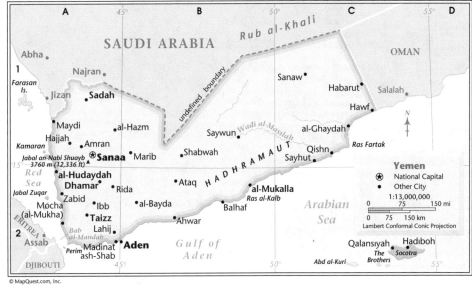

Yemen

⊛ National Capital
• Other City

1:13,000,000

0   75   150 mi
0   75   150 km
Lambert Conformal Conic Projection

© MapQuest.com, Inc.

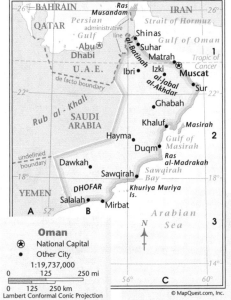

Oman

⊛ National Capital
• Other City

1:19,737,000

0   125   250 mi
0   125   250 km
Lambert Conformal Conic Projection

© MapQuest.com, Inc.

Oman:
Map Index

Cities and Towns
Dawkah B2
Duqm C2
Ghabah C2
Hayma C2
Ibri C1
Izki C1
Khaluf C2
Matrah C1

Mirbat B3
Muscat, capital C1
Salalah B3
Sawqirah C2
Shinas C1
Suhar C1
Sur C1

Other Features
Arabian, sea C3
Batinah, al-, region C1
Dhofar, region B3
Hormuz, strait C1
Jabal al-Akhdar, al-, mts....C1
Khuriya Muriya, islands.....C3
Masirah, gulf C2
Masirah, island C2
Oman, gulf C1
Persian, gulf B1
Ras al-Madrakah, cape.......C2
Ras Musandam, cape C1
Sawqirah, bay C2

Oman

Capital: Muscat
Area: 118,150 sq. mi.
       305,829 sq. km.
Population: 2,851,000
Largest City: Muscat
Language: Arabic
Monetary Unit: Rial Omani

Lebanon

Capital: Beirut
Area: 3,950 sq. mi.
10,233 sq. km.
Population: 3,653,000
Largest City: Beirut
Languages: Arabic, French
Monetary Unit: Lebanese pound

Lebanon: Map Index

Cities and Towns
Amyun A1
Baalbek B1
Babda A2
Batrun, al- A1
Beirut, *capital* A2
Bint Jubayl A2
Bsharri B1
Damur, ad- A2
Duma A1
Halba B1
Hirmil, al- B1
Jazzin A2
Jubayl A1
Juniyah A2
Marj Uyun A2
Nabatiyah at-Tahta, an- A2
Qubayyat, al- B1
Rashayya A2
Riyaq B2
Sidon (Sayda) A2
Sur (Tyre) A2
Tripoli (Tarabulus) A1
Zahlah A2

Other Features
Anti-Lebanon, *mts.* B1
Awwali, *river* A2
Bekaa, *valley* A2
Byblos, *ruins* A1
Hermon, *mt.* A2
Ibrahim, *river* A1
Kebir, *river* A1
Litani, *river* A2
Orontes, *river* B1
Qurnat as-Sawda, *mt.* B1

© MapQuest.com, Inc.

Jordan: Map Index

Cities and Towns
Amman, *capital* A2
Aqabah, al- A3
Azraq ash-Shishan B2
Bair B2
Irbid A1
Jafr, al- B2
Jarash A1
Karak, al- A2
Maan A2
Madaba A2
Mafraq, al- B1
Mudawwarah, al- B3
Qatranah, al- B2
Ramtha, ar- B1
Ras an-Naqb A2
Salt, as- A1
Tafilah, at- A2
Zarqa, az- B1

Other Features
Aqaba, *gulf* A3
Arabah, al-, *river* A2
Dead Sea, *lake* A2
Jabal Ramm, *mt.* A3
Jordan, *river* A2
Petra, *ruins* A2
Syrian, *desert* B1
Wadi as-Sirhan, *depression*..B2

Jordan

Capital: Amman
Area: 34,342 sq. mi.
88,969 sq. km.
Population: 5,473,000
Largest City: Amman
Language: Arabic
Monetary Unit: Jordanian dinar

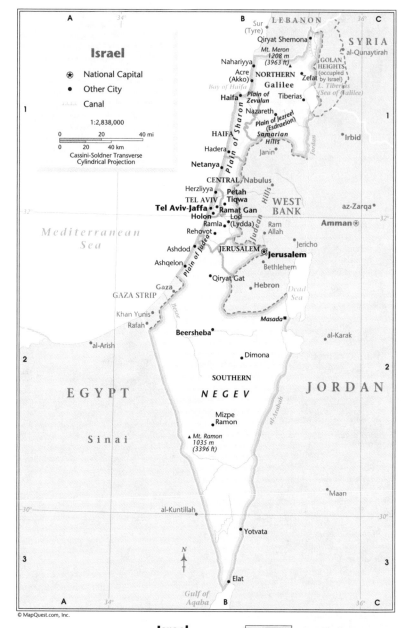

Israel

⊛ National Capital
● Other City
Canal

1:2,838,000

Cassini-Soldner Transverse
Cylindrical Projection

© MapQuest.com, Inc.

Israel

Capital: Jerusalem
Area: 7,992 sq. mi.
20,705 sq. km.
Population: 6,433,000
Largest City: Jerusalem
Languages: Hebrew, Arabic
Monetary Unit: Israeli shekel

Israel: Map Index

Districts
Central B1
Haifa B1
Jerusalem B2
Northern B1
Southern B2
Tel Aviv B1

Cities and Towns
Acre (Akko) B1
Ashdod B2
Ashqelon B2
Beersheba B2
Dimona B2
Elat B3
Hadera B1
Haifa B1
Herzliyya B1
Holon B1
Jerusalem, *capital* B2
Lod (Lydda) B2
Mizpe Ramon B2
Nahariyya B1
Nazareth B1
Netanya B1
Petah Tiqwa B2
Qiryat Gat B2
Qiryat Shemona B1
Ramat Gan B1
Ramla B2
Rehovot B2
Tel Aviv-Jaffa B1
Tiberias B1
Yotvata B3
Zefat B1

Other Features
Aqaba, *gulf* B3
Arabah, al-, *river* B2
Besor, *river* B2
Dead, *sea* B2
Galilee, *region* B1
Haifa, *bay* B1
Jezreel (Esdraelon), *plain* ...B1
Jordan, *river* B1
Judea, *plain* B2
Masada, *ruins* B2
Meron, *mt.* B1
Negev, *region* B2
Ramon, *mt.* B2
Samarian, *hills* B1
Sharon, *plain* B1
Tiberias (Galilee), *lake* B1
Zevulun, *plain* B1

Jordan

⊛ National Capital
● Other City

1:3,250,000

0   50   100 mi
0   50   100 km

Lambert Conformal Conic Projection

© MapQuest.com, Inc.

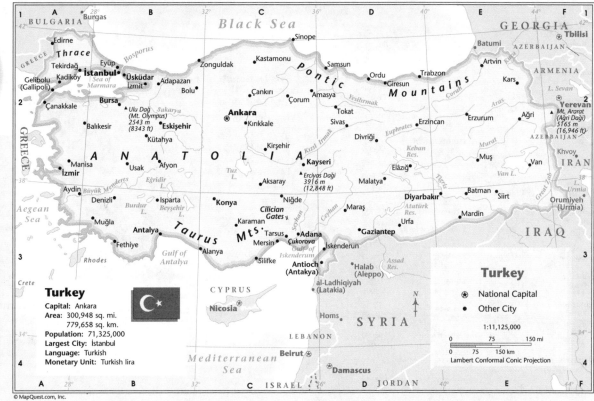

BULGARIA Burgas
GREECE Edirne
Thrace Tekirdağ
Gelibolu (Gallipoli) Kadıköy İstanbul Eyüp Üsküdar
Sea of Marmara İzmit Adapazarı Bolu
Çanakkale Bursa
GREECE Balıkesir Ulu Dağ (Mt. Olympus) 2543 m (8343 ft) Eskişehir Sakarya
Kütahya
Manisa Usak Afyon
İzmir
Aydın Büyük Menderes Denizli Eğridir L. Burdur L. Isparta Beyşehir L. Konya
Aegean Sea Muğla
Antalya Taurus Mts. Fethiye Gulf of Antalya Alanya
Rhodes Silifke
Crete
CYPRUS
Nicosia

Black Sea
Sinope Kastamonu Samsun Ordu Giresun Trabzon Artvin
Zonguldak Pontic Mountains
Çankırı Çorum Amasya Tokat Sivas Erzincan Erzurum Ağrı
Ankara Kırıkkale Yeşilırmak Euphrates Keban Res. Murat
Kırşehir Kızıl Irmak Elâzığ Muş Van
Kayseri Divriği Atatürk Res.
ANATOLIA Erciyas Dağı 3916 m (12,848 ft) Malatya Diyarbakır Batman Siirt Mardin
Aksaray Niğde Maraş Urfa Gaziantep
Cilician Gates Tarsus Ceyhan Çukurova Adana İskenderun
Karaman Mersin Gulf of İskenderun
Silifke Antioch (Antakya) Halab (Aleppo) Assad Res.
al-Ladhiqiyah (Latakia)
Homs **SYRIA**
LEBANON
Mediterranean Sea Beirut Damascus
ISRAEL JORDAN

GEORGIA Batumi Tbilisi
AZERBAIJAN Artvin
ARMENIA Kars
L. Sevan Yerevan Mt. Ararat (Ağrı Dağı) 5165 m (16,946 ft)
AZERBAIJAN Khvoy
IRAN Van L. Orumiyeh (Urmia)
IRAQ

Turkey
Capital: Ankara
Area: 300,948 sq. mi.
779,658 sq. km.
Population: 71,325,000
Largest City: İstanbul
Language: Turkish
Monetary Unit: Turkish lira

Turkey
⊛ National Capital
• Other City
1:11,125,000
0   75   150 mi
0   75   150 km
Lambert Conformal Conic Projection

Turkey: Map Index

Cities and Towns
Adana C3
Adapazarı B2
Afyon B2
Ağrı E2
Aksaray C2
Alanya C3
Amasya C2
Ankara, capital C2
Antalya B3
Antioch (Antakya) ...D3
Artvin E2
Aydın A3
Balıkesir A2
Batman E3
Bolu B2
Bursa B2
Çanakkale A2
Çankırı C2
Çorum C2
Denizli B3
Divriği D2
Diyarbakır E3
Edirne A2
Elâzığ D2
Erzincan D2
Erzurum E2
Eskişehir B2
Eyüp B2
Fethiye B3
Gaziantep D3
Gelibolu (Gallipoli) .A2
Giresun D2
İskenderun D3
Isparta B3
İstanbul B2
İzmir A2
İzmit B2
Kadıköy A2
Karaman C3
Kars E2
Kastamonu C2
Kayseri C2
Kırıkkale C2
Kırşehir C2
Konya C3
Kütahya B2
Malatya D2

Manisa A2
Maraş D3
Mardin E3
Mersin C3
Muğla B3
Muş E2
Niğde C3
Ordu D2
Samsun D2
Siirt E3
Silifke C3
Sinope C2
Sivas D2
Tarsus C3
Tekirdağ A2
Thrace A2
Tokat D2
Trabzon D2
Urfa D3
Usak B2
Üsküdar B2
Van E2
Zonguldak B2

Other Features
Aegean, sea A3
Anatolia, region C2
Antalya, gulf B3
Ararat (Ağrı Dağı), mt. .F2
Aras, river E2
Atatürk, reservoir ..D3
Beyşehir, lake B3
Black, sea C1
Bosporus, strait B2
Burdur, lake B3
Büyük Menderes, rivers .A3
Ceyhan, river C3
Cilician Gates, pass .C3
Çoruh, river E2
Çukurova, region C3
Eğridir, lake B2
Erciyas Dağı, mt. ...C2
Euphrates, river D2
Great Zab, river E3
İskenderun, gulf C3
Keban, reservoir D2
Kızıl Irmak, river ..C2
Kura, river E2
Marmara, sea B2
Mediterranean, sea ..B4

Murat, river E2
Pontic, mts. C2
Sakarya, river B2
Seyhan, river C3
Taurus, mts. B3
Tigris, river E2
Tuz, lake C2
Ulu Dağ (Mt. Olympus), mt. .B2
Van, lake E2
Yesilirmak, river ...D2

© MapQuest.com, Inc.

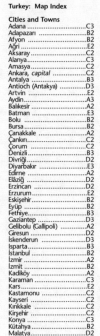

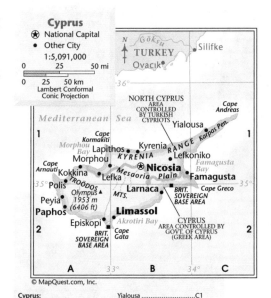

Cyprus
⊛ National Capital
• Other City
1:5,091,000
0   25   50 mi
0   25   50 km
Lambert Conformal Conic Projection

Göksu Silifke
TURKEY Ovacık
NORTH CYPRUS AREA CONTROLLED BY TURKISH CYPRIOTS
Mediterranean Sea
Cape Kormakiti Yialousa Cape Andreas
Morphou Bay Lapithos Kyrenia Karpas Pen. RANGE
Cape Arnauti Morphou KYRENIA Lefkoniko Famagusta Bay
Kokkina Nicosia Mesaoria Plain Famagusta
Polis Lefka TROODOS Larnaca Cape Greco
Peyia Olympus 1953 m (6406 ft) MTS. BRIT. SOVEREIGN BASE AREA
Paphos Limassol Akrotiri Bay CYPRUS AREA CONTROLLED BY GOVT. OF CYPRUS (GREEK AREA)
Episkopi Cape Gata
BRIT. SOVEREIGN BASE AREA

© MapQuest.com, Inc.

Cyprus: Map Index

Cities and Towns
Episkopi A2
Famagusta B1
Kokkina A1
Kyrenia B1
Lapithos B1
Larnaca B2
Lefka A1
Lefkoniko B1
Limassol B2
Morphou A1
Nicosia, capital B1
Paphos A2
Peyia A2
Polis A1

Yialousa C1

Other Features
Akrotiri, bay B2
Andreas, cape C1
Arnauti, cape A1
British Sovereign Base Area A2, B2
Famagusta, bay C1
Gata, cape B2
Greco, cape C2
Karpas, peninsula ...C1
Kormakiti, cape A1
Kyrenia, range B1
Mesaoria, plain B1
Morphou, bay A1
Olympus, mt. A2
Troödos, mts. A2

Cyprus

Capital: Nicosia
Area: 3,572 sq. mi.
9,254 sq. km.
Population: 802,000
Largest City: Nicosia
Languages: Greek, Turkish
Monetary Unit: Cypriot pound, Turkish lira

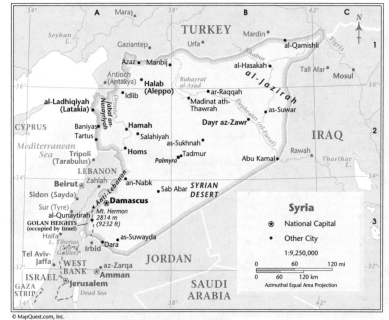

Maraş
TURKEY Mardin
Seyhan L. Gaziantep Urfa al-Qamishli Tigris
Azaz Manbij al-Hasakah Tall Afar Mosul
Antioch (Antakya) Khabur al-Jazirah
Halab (Aleppo) Buhayrat al-Asad ar-Raqqah as-Suwar
al-Ladhiqiyah (Latakia) Idlib Madinat ath-Thawrah Euphrates
Baniyas Jabal an-Nusayriyah Hamah Dayr az-Zawr IRAQ
CYPRUS Tartus Salahiyah as-Sukhnah Rawah
Mediterranean Sea Homs Tadmur Tharthar
Tripoli (Tarabulus) Palmyra Abu Kamal
LEBANON Beirut Zahlah an-Nabk Sab Abar SYRIAN DESERT
Sidon (Sayda) Anti-Lebanon Damascus
Sur (Tyre) al-Qunaytirah Mt. Hermon 2814 m (9232 ft) as-Suwayda
GOLAN HEIGHTS (occupied by Israel) Haifa L. Tiberias (Sea of Galilee) Irbid Dara
Tel Aviv-Jaffa WEST BANK az-Zarqa JORDAN
ISRAEL Jerusalem Amman SAUDI ARABIA
GAZA STRIP Dead Sea

Syria
⊛ National Capital
• Other City
1:9,250,000
0   60   120 mi
0   60   120 km
Azimuthal Equal Area Projection

© MapQuest.com, Inc.

Syria: Map Index

Cities and Towns
Abu Kamal B2
Azaz A1
Baniyas A2
Damascus, capital ...A3
Dara A3
Dayr az-Zawr B2
Halab (Aleppo) A1
Hamah A2
Hasakah, al- B1
Homs A2
Idlib A2
Ladhiqiyah, al- (Latakia) ...A2
Madinat ath-Thawrah .B2
Manbij A1
Nabk, an- A2
Qamishli, al- B1

Qunaytirah, al- A3
Raqqah, ar- B2
Sab Abar A3
Salahiyah A3
Sukhnah, as- B2
Suwar, as- B2
Suwayda, as- A3
Tadmur B2
Tartus A2

Other Features
Anti-Lebanon, mts. ..A3
Buhayrat al-Asad, lake .B1
Euphrates (al-Furat), river .B2
Golan Heights, occupied territory .A3
Hermon, mt. A3
Jabal an-Nusayriyah, mts. .A2
Jazirah, al-, region .B1
Khabur, river B1

Mediterranean, sea ..A2
Orontes, river A2
Palmyra, ruins B2
Syrian, desert B3
Tigris, river C1

Syria
Capital: Damascus
Area: 71,498 sq. mi.
185,228 sq. km.
Population: 17,800,000
Largest City: Damascus
Language: Arabic
Monetary Unit: Syrian pound

MAJOR CITIES

Albania
Tirana — 299,000

Andorra
Andorra la Vella — 21,000

Armenia (metro)
Yerevan — 1,420,000

Austria (metro)
Vienna — 2,066,000

Azerbaijan (metro)
Baku — 1,964,000

Belarus (metro)
Minsk — 1,664,000

Belgium (metro)
Brussels — 1,134,000
Antwerp — 447,000

Bosnia and Herzegovina
Sarajevo — 552,000

Bulgaria (metro)
Sofia — 1,187,000

Croatia (metro)
Zagreb — 1,081,000

Czech Republic (metro)
Prague — 1,202,000

Denmark (metro)
Copenhagen — 1,332,000

Estonia
Tallinn — 401,000

Finland (metro)
Helsinki — 936,000

France (metro)
Paris — 9,658,000
Lyon — 1,353,000
Marseille — 1,290,000
Lille — 991,000

Georgia (metro)
Tbilisi — 1,406,000

Germany
Berlin (metro) — 3,319,000
Stuttgart (metro) — 2,672,000
Hamburg (metro) — 2,664,000
Munich (metro) — 2,291,000
Bielefeld (metro) — 1,294,000
Karlsruhe (metro) — 977,000
Cologne — 963,000
Bremen (metro) — 880,000
Frankfurt-am-Main — 645,000
Düsseldorf — 569,000

Great Britain (metro)
London — 7,640,000
Birmingham — 2,272,000
Manchester — 2,252,000
Leeds — 1,433,000
Tyneside — 981,000
(Newcastle)
Liverpool — 915,000

Greece (metro)
Athens — 3,120,000
Thessaloniki — 789,000

Hungary (metro)
Budapest — 1,812,000

Iceland
Reykjavík — 175,000

Ireland (metro)
Dublin — 993,000

Italy (metro)
Milan — 4,251,000
Naples — 3,012,000
Rome — 2,651,000
Turin — 1,294,000
Genoa — 890,000
Florence — 778,000

Latvia (metro)
Riga — 756,000

Liechtenstein
Vaduz — 5,000

Lithuania
Vilnius — 579,000
Kaunas — 412,640

Luxembourg
Luxembourg — 82,000

F.Y.R. Macedonia
Skopje — 437,000

Malta (metro)
Valletta — 82,000

Moldova
Chişinău — 662,000

Monaco
Monaco — 34,000

Netherlands (metro)
Amsterdam — 1,105,000
Rotterdam — 1,078,000
The Hague — 442,800

Norway (metro)
Oslo — 787,000

Poland (metro)
Katowice — 3,494,000
Warsaw — 2,282,000
Łódź — 1,053,000
Gdansk — 893,000
Kraków — 859,000

Portugal (metro)
Lisbon — 3,942,000
Porto — 1,940,000

Romania (metro)
Bucharest — 1,998,000

Russia (European) (metro)
Moscow — 8,316,000
St. Petersburg — 4,635,000
Nizh. Novgorod — 1,332,000
Samara — 1,132,000
Ufa — 1,102,000
Kazan — 1,063,000
Rostov-na-Donu — 1,012,000
Volgograd — 1,000,000
Perm — 991,000

San Marino
San Marino — 5,000

Serbia and Montenegro
Belgrade (metro) — 1,687,000

Slovakia
Bratislava — 464,000

Slovenia
Ljubljana — 250,000

Spain (metro)
Madrid — 3,969,000
Barcelona — 2,729,000
Valencia — 754,000
Seville — 685,000

Sweden (metro)
Stockholm — 1,626,000
Göteborg — 778,000

Switzerland (metro)
Zürich — 939,000
Geneva — 464,000
Bern — 316,000

Turkey (European) (metro)
İstanbul — 8,953,000

Ukraine (metro)
Kiev — 2,488,000
Kharkiv — 1,416,000
Dnipropetrovsk — 1,069,000
Donetsk — 1,007,000
Odesa — 931,000

International comparability of city population
data is limited by various data inconsistencies.

© MapQuest.com, Inc.

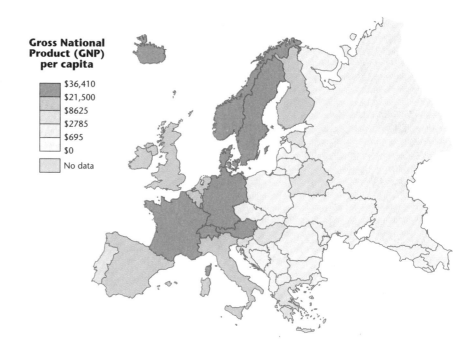

Gross National Product (GNP) per capita

- $36,410
- $21,500
- $8625
- $2785
- $695
- $0
- No data

Vegetation

- Tundra
- Coniferous Forest
- Deciduous Forest
- Mixed Forest
- Midlatitude Scrubland
- Midlatitude Grassland
- Unclassified Highlands or Ice Cap

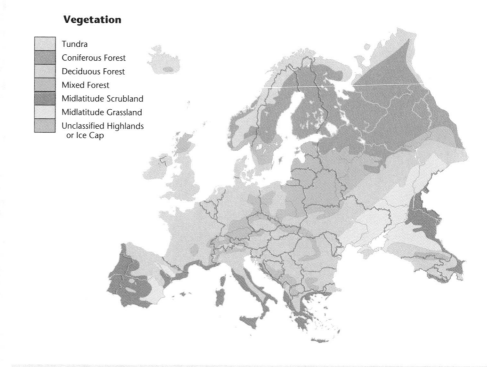

Europe: Population, by nation (in millions)*

| RUSSIA 143.2* | GER. 82.5 | FRANCE 60.1 | GR. BRIT. 59.3 | ITALY 57.4 | UKRAINE 48.5 | SPAIN 41.0 | POLAND 38.6 | ROM. 22.3 | NETH. 16.1 | All other European countries 160.0 |

*Including Asian Russia as well as the more populous European portion of the country.

CLIMATE

Average daily temperature °F range

Average monthly precipitation Inches

High
Low

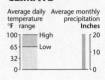
ARKHANGELSK, Russia

ATHENS, Greece

COPENHAGEN, Denmark

DUBLIN, Ireland

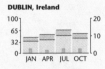
LISBON, Portugal

MOSCOW, Russia

NAPLES, Italy

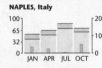
ODESA, Ukraine

PARIS, France

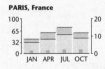
REYKJAVÍK, Iceland

TROMSØ, Norway

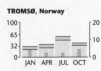
VIENNA, Austria

CITIES

- ⊗ National Capital
- ★ Territorial Capital
- • Other City

ELEVATIONS

Feet	Meters
13,120	4000
6560	2000
1640	500
656	200
0	0
Below sea level	

Population

Persons per sq mi	Persons per sq km
Over 520	Over 200
260–519	100–199
130–259	50–99
25–129	10–49
1–24	1–9
0	0

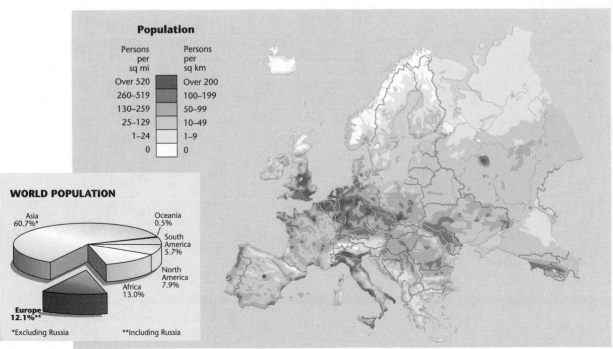

WORLD POPULATION

Asia 60.7%*
Oceania 0.5%
South America 5.7%
North America 7.9%
Africa 13.0%
Europe 12.1%**

*Excluding Russia
**Including Russia

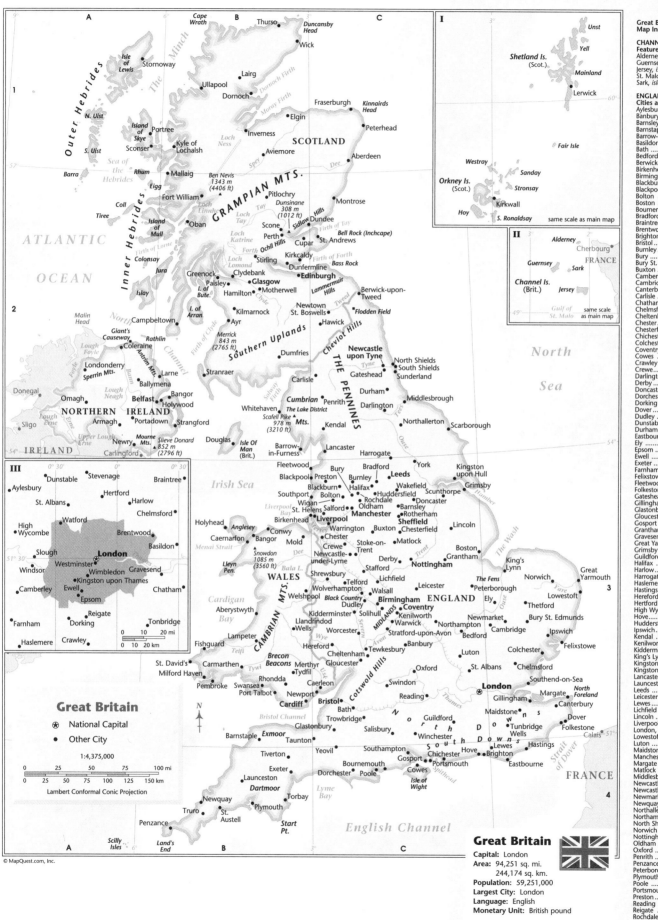

Great Britain

- ⊛ National Capital
- ● Other City

1:4,375,000

0 25 50 75 100 mi
0 25 50 75 100 125 150 km

Lambert Conformal Conic Projection

© MapQuest.com, Inc.

Great Britain
Capital: London
Area: 94,251 sq. mi.
244,174 sq. km.
Population: 59,251,000
Largest City: London
Language: English
Monetary Unit: British pound

Great Britain:
Map Index

CHANNEL ISLANDS
Features
Alderney, island ....Inset II
Guernsey, island ....Inset II
Jersey, island ....Inset II
St. Malo, gulf ....Inset II
Sark, island ....Inset II

ENGLAND
Cities and Towns
Aylesbury ....Inset III
Banbury C3
Barnsley C3
Barnstaple B3
Barrow-in-Furness B2
Basildon ....Inset III
Bath C3
Bedford C3
Berwick-upon-Tweed C2
Birkenhead B3
Birmingham C3
Blackburn C3
Blackpool C3
Bolton C3
Boston C3
Bournemouth C4
Bradford C3
Braintree ....Inset III
Brentwood ....Inset III
Brighton C4
Bristol C3
Burnley C3
Bury C3
Bury St. Edmunds D3
Buxton C3
Camberley ....Inset III
Cambridge D3
Canterbury D3
Carlisle C2
Chatham ....Inset III
Chelmsford ....D3, Inset III
Cheltenham C3
Chester C3
Chesterfield C3
Chichester C4
Colchester D3
Coventry C3
Cowes C4
Crawley ....Inset III
Crewe C3
Darlington C2
Derby C3
Doncaster C3
Dorchester C4
Dorking ....Inset III
Dover D3
Dudley C3
Dunstable ....Inset III
Durham C2
Eastbourne D4
Ely D3
Epsom ....Inset III
Ewell ....Inset III
Exeter B4
Farnham ....Inset III
Felixstowe D3
Fleetwood C3
Folkestone D3
Gateshead C2
Gillingham D3
Glastonbury C3
Gloucester C3
Gosport C4
Grantham C3
Gravesend ....Inset III
Great Yarmouth D3
Grimsby C3
Guildford C3
Halifax C3
Harlow ....Inset III
Harrogate C3
Haslemere ....Inset III
Hastings D4
Hereford C3
Hertford ....Inset III
High Wycombe ....Inset III
Hove C4
Huddersfield C3
Ipswich D3
Kendal C2
Kenilworth C3
Kidderminster C3
King's Lynn D3
Kingston upon Hull C3
Kingston upon Thames ...Inset III
Lancaster C2
Launceston B4
Leeds C3
Leicester C3
Lewes D4
Lichfield C3
Lincoln C3
Liverpool C3
London, capital ....C3, Inset III
Lowestoft D3
Luton C3
Maidstone D3
Manchester.....................C3
Margate D3
Matlock C3
Middlesbrough C2
Newcastle-under-Lyme ...C3
Newcastle upon Tyne C2
Newmarket D3
Newquay B4
Northallerton C2
Northampton C3
North Shields C2
Norwich D3
Nottingham C3
Oldham C3
Oxford C3
Penrith C2
Penzance B4
Peterborough C3
Plymouth B4
Poole C4
Portsmouth.....................C4
Preston C3
Reading C3
Reigate ....Inset III
Rochdale C3
Rotherham C3
St. Albans ....C3, Inset III

Great Britain 🇬🇧
Capital: London
Area: 94,251 sq. mi.
244,174 sq. km.
Population: 59,251,000
Largest City: London
Language: English
Monetary Unit: British pound

Republic of Ireland

Capital: Dublin
Area: 27,137 sq. mi.
70,303 sq. km.
Population: 3,956,000
Largest City: Dublin
Languages: English, Irish
Monetary Unit: Euro

Republic of Ireland: Map Index

Counties

Carlow	C2
Cavan	C2
Clare	B2
Cork	B3
Donegal	B1
Dún Laoghaire-Rathdown	C2
Fingal	C2
Galway	B2
Kerry	B2
Kildare	C2
Kilkenny	C2
Laois	C2
Leitrim	B1
Limerick	B2
Longford	C2
Louth	C2
Mayo	B2
Meath	C2
Monaghan	C1
Offaly	C2
Roscommon	B2
Sligo	B1
South Dublin	C2
Tipperary North Riding	B2
Tipperary South Riding	C2
Waterford	C2
Westmeath	C2
Wexford	C2
Wicklow	C2
Monaghan	C1
Mullingar	C2
Naas	C2
Nenagh	B2
Port Laoise	C2
Roscommon	B2
Roscrea	C2
Rosslare	C2
Shannon	B2
Sligo	B1
Swords	C2
Tipperary	B2
Tralee	B2
Trim	C2
Tuam	B2
Tullamore	C2
Waterford	C2
Westport	B2
Wexford	C2
Wicklow	C2
Youghal	C3

County Boroughs

Cork	B3
Dublin	D2
Galway	B2
Limerick	B2
Waterford	C2

Cities and Towns

Ardara	B1
Arklow	C2
Athlone	C2
Ballina	B1
Bantry	B3
Blarney	B3
Carlingford	C1
Carlow	C2
Carrick-on-Shannon	B2
Cashel	C2
Castlebar	B2
Cavan	C2
Clara	C2
Clifden	A2
Clonmel	C2
Cóbh	B3
Cork	B3
Dingle	A2
Donegal	B1
Drogheda	C2
Dublin, capital	C2
Dundalk	C2
Dungarvan	C2
Dún Laoghaire	C2
Ennis	B2
Ennistymon	B2
Galway	B2
Kildare	C2
Kilkee	B2
Kilkenny	C2
Killarney	B2
Letterkenny	C1
Lifford	C1
Limerick	B2
Longford	C2
Mallow	B2
Maynooth	C2

Other Features

Achill, island	A2
Allen, lake	B1
Aran, islands	B2
Bantry, bay	B3
Barrow, river	C2
Benwee Head, cape	B1
Blackwater, river	B2
Blackwater, river	C1
Boggeragh, mts.	B2
Boyne, river	C2
Caha, mts.	B3
Carlingford, lake	C1
Carnsore, point	C2
Carrantuohill, mt.	B3
Celtic, sea	B3
Clear, cape	B3
Conn, lake	B1
Connaught, province	B2
Connemara, region	B2
Corrib, lake	B2
Derg, lake	B2
Dingle, bay	A2
Donegal, bay	B1
Erne, river	B1
Errigal, mt.	B1
Finn, river	C1
Foyle, inlet	C1
Galway, bay	B2
Grand, canal	C2
Irish, sea	D2
Killala, bay	B1
Knockboy, mt.	B3
Lee, river	B3
Leinster, province	C2
Loop Head, cape	B2
Malin Head, cape	C1
Mask, lake	B2
Maumturk, mts.	B2
Mizen Head, cape	B3
Moher, cliffs	B2
Munster, province	B2
Ree, lake	C2
Royal, canal	C2
Saint George's, channel	C3
Shannon, river	B2
Suir, river	C2
Twelve Pins, mt.	B2
Ulster, province	C1
Wicklow, mts.	C2
Wicklow Head, cape	D2

Great Britain: Map Index

St. Austell	B4
St. Helens	C3
Salford	C3
Salisbury	C3
Scarborough	C2
Scunthorpe	C3
Sheffield	C3
Shrewsbury	C3
Slough	Inset III
Solihull	C4
Southampton	C4
Southend-on-Sea	D3
Southport	C3
South Shields	C2
Stafford	C3
Stevenage	Inset III
Stoke-on-Trent	C3
Stratford-upon-Avon	C3
Sunderland	C3
Swindon	C3
Taunton	C3
Telford	C3
Tewkesbury	C3
Thetford	D3
Tiverton	B4
Tonbridge	Inset III
Torbay	B4
Trowbridge	C3
Truro	B4
Tunbridge Wells	C3
Wakefield	C3
Walsall	C3
Warrington	C3
Warwick	C3
Watford	Inset III
Westminster	Inset III
Whitehaven	B2
Wigan	C3
Winchester	C3
Windsor	Inset III
Wolverhampton	C3
Worcester	C3
Yeovil	C3
York	C3

Other Features

Avon, river	C3
Black Country, region	C3
Bristol, channel	B3
Cheviot, hills	C2
Cotswold, hills	C3
Cumbrian, mts.	B2
Dartmoor, plateau	B4
Dee, river	B3
Dover, strait	D4
English, channel	C4
Exmoor, plateau	B3
Fens, region	D3
Flodden Field, plain	C2
Humber, river	D3
Irish, sea	B3
Lake, district	B2
Land's End, promontory	B4
Liverpool, bay	B3
Lyme, bay	C4
Mersey, river	C3
Midlands, region	C3
North, sea	D2
North Downs, hills	C3
North Foreland, promontory	D3
Ouse, river	C2, D3
Pennines, mts.	C2
Scafell Pike, mt.	B2
Scilly, islands	A4
Severn, river	C3
South Downs, hills	C3
Spithead, channel	C4
Start, point	B4
Tees, river	C2
Thames, river	C3, Inset III
Trent, river	C3
Tweed, river	C2
Tyne, river	C2
Wash, bay	D3
Wight, island	C4
Wye, river	C3
Yare, river	D3

ISLE OF MAN

City

Douglas	B2

NORTHERN IRELAND

Cities and Towns

Armagh	A2
Ballymena	A2
Bangor	B2
Belfast	B2
Coleraine	A2
Holywood	B2
Larne	B2
Londonderry	A2
Newry	A2
Omagh	A2
Portadown	A2
Strangford	B2

Other Features

Antrim, mts.	A2
Bann, river	A2
Erne, river	A2
Foyle, lake	A2
Foyle, river	A2
Giant's Causeway, headland	A2
Irish, sea	B3
Lough Erne, lake	A2
Mourne, mts.	A2
Neagh, lake	A2
North, channel	A2
Rathlin, island	A2
Slieve Donard, mt.	B2
Sperrin, mts.	A2
Upper Lough Erne, lake	A2

SCOTLAND

Cities and Towns

Aberdeen	C1
Aviemore	B1
Ayr	B2
Campbeltown	B2
Clydebank	B2
Cupar	B2
Dornoch	B1
Dumfries	B2
Dundee	B2
Dunfermline	B2
Edinburgh	B2
Elgin	B1
Fort William	B2
Fraserburgh	C1
Glasgow	B2
Greenock	B2
Hamilton	B2
Hawick	C2
Inverness	B1
Kilmarnock	B2
Kirkcaldy	B2
Kirkwall	Inset I
Kyle of Lochalsh	B1
Lairg	B1
Lerwick	Inset I
Mallaig	B1
Montrose	C2
Motherwell	B2
Newtown St. Boswells	C2
Oban	B2
Paisley	B2
Perth	B2
Peterhead	C1
Pitlochry	B2
Portree	A1
St. Andrews	B2
Scone	B2
Sconser	A1
Stirling	B2
Stornoway	A1
Stranraer	B2
Thurso	B1
Ullapool	B1
Wick	B1

Other Features

Arran, island	B2
Barra, island	A2
Bass Rock, islet	C2
Bell Rock (Inchcape), reef	C2
Ben Nevis, mt.	B2
Bute, island	B2
Cheviot, hills	C2
Clyde, estuary	B2
Clyde, river	B2
Coll, island	A2
Colonsay, island	A2
Dee, river	C1
Dornoch, estuary	B1
Duncansby, cape	B1
Dunsinane, mt.	B2
Eigg, island	A2
Fair, island	Inset I
Forth, estuary	B2
Forth, river	B2
Grampian, mts.	B2
Hebrides, sea	A1
Hoy, island	Inset I
Inner Hebrides, islands	A2
Islay, island	A2
Jura, island	B2
Katrine, lake	B2
Kinnairds, cape	C1
Lammermuir, hills	C2
Lewis, island	A1
Linnhe, lake	B2
Lomond, lake	B2
Lorne, estuary	A2
Mainland, island	Inset I
Merrick, mt.	B2
Minch, strait	B1
Moray, estuary	B1
Mull, island	A2
Ness, lake	B1
North Uist, island	A1
Ochil, hills	B2
Orkney, islands	Inset I
Outer Hebrides, islands	A1
Rhum, island	A1
Sanday, island	Inset I
Shetland, islands	Inset I
Sidlaw, hills	B2
Skye, island	A1
Solway, estuary	B2
Southern Uplands, mts.	B2
South Ronaldsay, island	Inset I
South Uist, island	A1
Spey, river	B1
Stronsay, island	Inset I
Tay, estuary	C2
Tay, lake	B2
Tay, river	B2
Tiree, island	A2
Tweed, river	C2
Unst, island	Inset I
Westray, island	Inset I
Wrath, cape	B1
Yell, island	Inset I

WALES

Cities and Towns

Aberystwyth	B3
Bangor	B3
Caerleon	C3
Caernarfon	B3
Cardiff	B3
Carmarthen	B3
Conwy	B3
Fishguard	B3
Holyhead	B3
Lampeter	B3
Llandrindod Wells	B3
Merthyr Tydfil	B3
Milford Haven	B3
Mold	B3
Newport	C3
Pembroke	B3
Port Talbot	B3
Rhondda	B3
St. David's	B3
Swansea	B3
Welshpool	B3

Other Features

Anglesey, island	B3
Bala, lake	B3
Brecon Beacons, mts.	B3
Bristol, channel	B3
Cambrian, mts.	B3
Cardigan, bay	B3
Dee, river	B3
Lleyn, peninsula	B3
Menai, strait	B3
Snowdon, mt.	B3
Teifi, river	B3
Tywi, river	B3
Usk, river	B3
Wye, river	C3

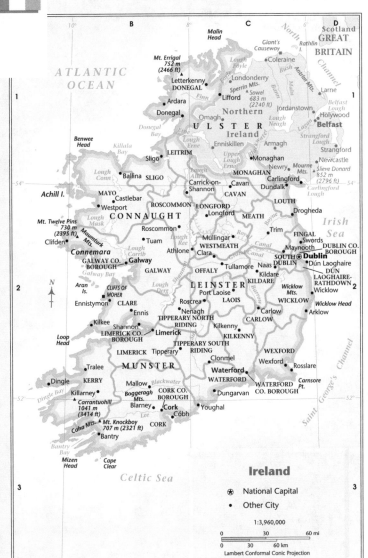

Ireland

⊛ National Capital

• Other City

1:3,960,000

0   30   60 mi
0   30   60 km

Lambert Conformal Conic Projection

Denmark

Capital: Copenhagen
Area: 16,639 sq. mi.
43,080 sq. km.
Population: 5,364,000
Largest City: Copenhagen
Language: Danish
Monetary Unit: Danish krone

Denmark: Map Index

Counties

Århus	C2
Bornholm	E3
Frederiksborg	D2
Fyn	C3
København	D3
Nordjylland	B2
Ribe	B3
Ringkøbing	B2
Roskilde	D3
Sønderjylland	B3
Storstrøm	C4
Vejle	B3
Vestsjælland	C3
Viborg	B2

Cities and Towns

Åbenrå	B3
Ålborg	B1
Århus	C2
Ballerup	D3
Copenhagen, capital	D3
Esbjerg	B3
Fredericia	B3
Frederiksberg	D3
Frederikshavn	C1
Gentofte	D3
Grenå	D2
Greve	D3
Haderslev	B3
Helsingør	D2
Herning	B2
Hillerød	D3
Hirtshals	B1
Hjørring	B1
Holbæk	C3
Holstebro	B2
Horsens	B3
Kalundborg	C3
Kastrup	D3
Køge	D3
Kolding	B3
Næstved	C3
Nakskov	C4
Nyborg	C3
Nykøbing	C4
Odense	C3
Randers	C2
Ribe	B3
Ringkøbing	B2
Rønne	E3
Roskilde	D3
Sandur	Inset
Silkeborg	B2
Skagen	C1
Skive	B2
Slagelse	C3
Sønderborg	B4
Sorø	C3
Svendborg	C3
Thisted	B2
Tórshavn	Inset
Trongisvágur	Inset
Vejle	B3
Vestmanna	Inset
Viborg	B2

Other Features

Ærø, island	C4
Ålborg, bay	B1
Anholt, island	C2
Baltic, sea	D3
Bordoy, island	Inset
Bornholm, island	E3
Eysturoy, island	Inset
Faeroe, islands	Inset
Falster, island	D4
Fanø, island	B3
Fehmarn, strait	C4
Fyn, island	C3
Gudenå, river	B2
Jutland, peninsula	B3
Kattegat, strait	C2
Læsø, island	C1
Langeland, island	C4
Lille, strait	B3
Limfjorden, channel	B2
Lolland, island	C4
Møn, island	D4
Mors, island	B2
North, sea	A3
North Frisian, islands	B4
Norwegian, sea	Inset
Odense, fjord	D3
Øresund, sound	D3
Rømø, island	B3
Samsø, island	C3
Samsø, strait	C3
Sandoy, island	Inset
Sjælland, island	C3
Skagerrak, strait	B1
Skaw, cape	C1
Skjern, river	B3
Storå, river	B2
Store, strait	C3
Streymoy, island	Inset
Suðuroy, island	Inset
Vágar, island	Inset
Varde, river	B3
Yding Skovhøj, hill	B2

Faeroe Islands
same scale as main map

© MapQuest.com, Inc.

Denmark
- ⊛ National Capital
- • Other City

1:4,000,000

0 25 50 mi
0 25 50 km
Lambert Conformal Conic Projection

Netherlands

- ⊛ National Capital
- • Other City
- ⸽⸽⸽ Canal

1:4,400,000

0 25 50 mi
0 25 50 km
Lambert Conformal Conic Projection

Netherlands: Map Index

Provinces

Drenthe	D2
Flevoland	C2
Friesland	C1
Gelderland	D2
Groningen	D1
Limburg	C3
North Brabant	C3
North Holland	B2
Overijssel	D2
South Holland	B2
Utrecht	C2
Zeeland	A3

Cities and Towns

Alkmaar	B2
Almelo	D2
Amersfoort	C2
Amsterdam, capital	B2
Apeldoorn	C2
Arnhem	C3
Assen	D2
Bergen op Zoom	B3
Breda	B3
Delft	B2
Delfzijl	D1
Den Helder	B2
Deventer	D2
Doetinchem	D3
Dordrecht	B3
Edam	C2
Ede	C2
Eindhoven	C3
Emmeloord	C2
Emmen	D2
Enschede	D2
Gouda	B2
Groningen	D1
Haarlem	B2
Heerenveen	C2
Heerlen	C4
Hengelo	D2
Hilversum	C2
Hoogeveen	D2
Hoorn	C2
Leeuwarden	C1
Leiden	B2
Lelystad	C2
Maastricht	C4
Meppel	D2
Middelburg	A3
Nijmegen	C3
Oss	C3
Otterlo	C2
Roermond	D3
Rotterdam	B3
Scheveningen	B2
Schiedam	B3
's Hertogenbosch	C3
Sittard	C4
Sneek	C1
The Hague	B2
Tilburg	C3
Utrecht	C2
Venlo	D3
Vlaardingen	B3
Vlissingen	A3
Weert	C3
Zaandam	B2
Zwolle	D2

Other Features

Ameland, island	C1
Eems, river	D1
Flevoland, polder	C2
IJssel, river	D2
IJsselmeer, sea	C2
Maas, river	C3, D3
Neder Rijn, river	C3
New Waterway, channel	B3
Northeast, polder	C2
North Holland, canal	B2
North Sea, canal	B2
Oosterschelde, channel	A3
Overflakkee, island	B3
Princess Margriet, canal	C1
Schiermonnikoog, island	C1
Schouwen, island	A3
Terschelling, island	C1
Texel, island	B1
Tholen, island	B3
Vaalserberg, mt.	D4
Vlieland, island	B1
Waal, river	C3
Waddenzee, sound	C1
Walcheren, island	A3
Westerschelde, channel	A3
West Frisian, islands	B1
Wilhelmina, canal	B3
Zuid-Willemsvaart, canal	C3

Netherlands

Capital: Amsterdam
Area: 16,033 sq. mi.
41,536 sq. km.
Population: 16,149,000
Largest City: Amsterdam
Language: Dutch
Monetary Unit: Euro

© MapQuest.com, Inc.

North Sea

NETHERLANDS

GERMANY

FLANDERS

WEST FLANDERS

EAST FLANDERS

BRUSSELS CAPITAL REGION

FLEMISH BRABANT

LIMBURG

KEMPENLAND

WALLOON BRABANT

HAINAUT

WALLONIA

NAMUR

LIÈGE

ARDENNES

FRANCE

LUXEMBOURG

Belgium

⊛ National Capital

• Other City

⊔⊔⊔ Canal

1:2,381,000

0   20   40 mi

0   20   40 km

Lambert Conformal Conic Projection

© MapQuest.com, Inc.

Belgium

Capital: Brussels
Area: 11,787 sq. mi.
          30,536 sq. km.
Population: 10,318,000
Largest City: Brussels
Languages: Flemish, French, German
Monetary Unit: Euro

Belgium:
Map Index

Internal Divisions

Antwerp (province)	C1
Brussels Cap. Region	C2
East Flanders (province)	B2
Flanders (region)	C1
Flemish Brabant (province)	C2
Hainaut (province)	B2
Liège (province)	D2
Limburg (province)	D1
Luxembourg (province)	D3
Namur (province)	C2
Walloon Brabant (province)	C2
Wallonia (region)	C2
West Flanders (province)	B1

Cities and Towns

Aalst	C2
Anderlecht	C2
Antwerp	C1
Arlon	D3
Ath	B2
Bastogne	D2
Binche	C2
Brugge	B1
Brussels, capital	C2
Charleroi	C2
Chimay	C2
Dinant	C2
Gembloux	C2
Genk	D2
Ghent	B1
Halle	C2
Hasselt	D2
Ixelles	C2
Knokke	B1
Kortrijk	B2
La Louvière	C2
Leuven	C2
Liège	D2
Limbourg	D2
Malmédy	E2
Mechelen	C1
Mons	B2
Mouscron	B2
Namur	C2
Neufchâteau	D3
Oostende	A1
Poperinge	A2
Roeselare	B2
Schaerbeek	C2
Sint-Niklaas	C1
Sint-Truiden	D2
Spa	D2
Tournai	B2
Turnhout	C1
Uccle	C2
Verviers	D2
Wavre	C2
Ypres	A2
Zeebrugge	B1

Other Features

Albert, canal	C1
Ardennes, plateau	D2
Botrange, mt.	E2
Brugge-Ghent, canal	B1
Dender, river	B2
Kempenland, region	D1
Leie, river	B2
Maas, river	D2
Meuse, river	D2
Oostende-Brugge, canal	B1
Ourthe, river	D2
Rupel, river	C1
Sambre, river	C2
Schelde, river	B2
Semois, river	D3
Senne, river	C2

Liechtenstein

Capital: Vaduz
Area: 62 sq. mi.
          161 sq. km.
Population: 33,145
Largest City: Vaduz
Language: German
Monetary Unit: Swiss franc

Liechtenstein:
Map Index

Cities and Towns

Balzers	B2
Eschen	B1
Gamprin	B1
Malbun	B2
Mauren	B1
Planken	B1
Ruggell	B1
Schaan	B2
Schellenberg	B1
Triesen	B2
Triesenberg	B2
Vaduz, capital	B2

Other Features

Alps, range	A2
Grauspitz, mt.	A2
Rhine, canal	B1, B2
Rhine, river	A1, A2
Samina, river	B2

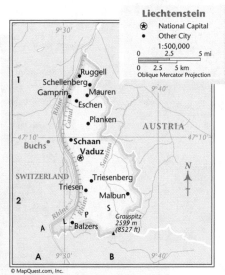

Liechtenstein

⊛ National Capital

• Other City

1:500,000

0   2.5   5 mi

0   2.5   5 km

Oblique Mercator Projection

SWITZERLAND

AUSTRIA

Ruggell
Schellenberg
Gamprin
Mauren
Eschen
Planken
Schaan
Vaduz
Buchs
Triesenberg
Triesen
Malbun
Balzers
Grauspitz 2599 m (8527 ft)

Rhine Canal
Rhine
Samina
ALPS

© MapQuest.com, Inc.

Luxembourg

⊛ National Capital

• Other City

1:1,700,000

0   10   20 mi

0   10   20 km

Azimuthal Equal Area Projection

BELGIUM
Ardennes
Buurgplaatz 559 m (1835 ft)
Troisvierges
Clervaux
Wiltz
Vianden
Diekirch
Ettelbruck
Echternach
Mersch
Larochette
Redange
Bon Pays
Grevenmacher
Luxembourg
GERMANY
Differdange
Remich
Esch-sur-Alzette
Dudelange
FRANCE

Sûre
Clerve
Our
Alzette
Mosel

© MapQuest.com, Inc.

Luxembourg

Capital: Luxembourg
Area: 999 sq. mi.
          2,588 sq. km.
Population: 453,000
Largest City: Luxembourg
Languages: French, German
Monetary Unit: Euro

Luxembourg:
Map Index

Cities and Towns

Clervaux	B1
Diekirch	B2
Differdange	A2
Dudelange	B2
Echternach	B2
Esch-sur-Alzette	A2
Ettelbruck	B2
Grevenmacher	B2
Larochette	B2
Luxembourg, capital	B2
Mersch	B2
Redange	B2
Remich	B2
Troisvierges	B1
Vianden	B2
Wiltz	A2

Other Features

Alzette, river	B2
Ardennes, plateau	A1
Bon Pays, region	B2
Buurgplaatz, mt.	B1
Clerve, river	B1
Mosel, river	B2
Our, river	B1
Sûre, river	A2, B2

France

⊛ National Capital

• Other City

1:5,625,000

0   50   100 mi

0   50   100 km

Lambert Conformal Conic Projection

© MapQuest.com, Inc.

Same scale as main map

CORSICA
CORSE

Calvi • **Bastia**

Ajaccio

Porto-
Vecchio

II

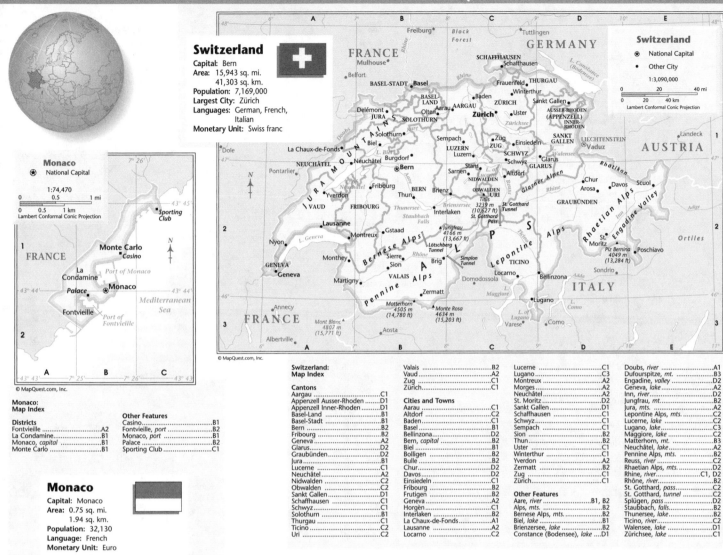

Switzerland

Capital: Bern
Area: 15,943 sq. mi.
41,303 sq. km.
Population: 7,169,000
Largest City: Zürich
Languages: German, French, Italian
Monetary Unit: Swiss franc

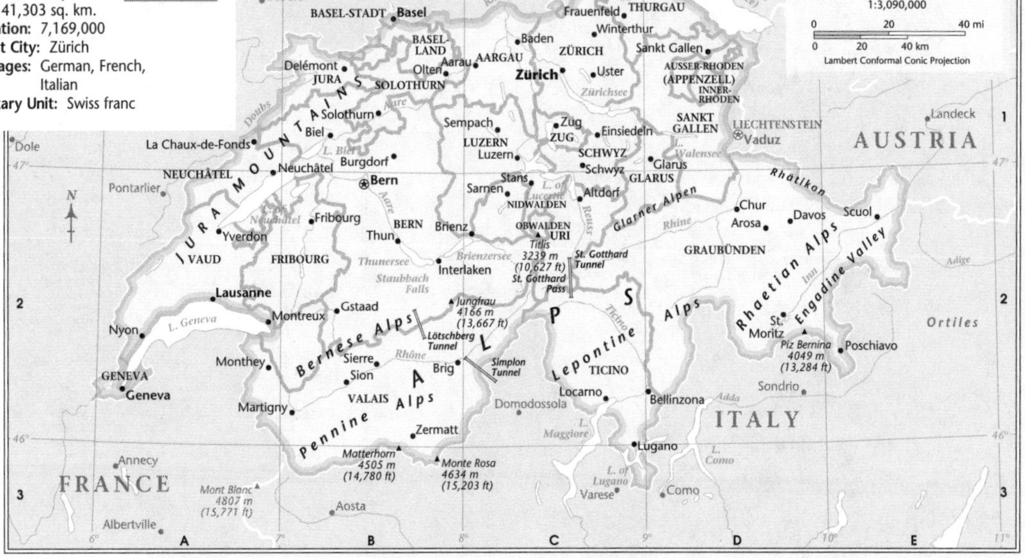

Switzerland
National Capital
Other City
1:3,090,000
0 20 40 mi
0 20 40 km
Lambert Conformal Conic Projection
FRANCE
GERMANY
AUSTRIA
ITALY
LIECHTENSTEIN
Freiburg
Black Forest
Tuttlingen
Mulhouse
Belfort
SCHAFFHAUSEN
Schaffhausen
L. Constance (Bodensee)
Rhine
BASEL-STADT
Basel
BASEL-LAND
Frauenfeld
THURGAU
Winterthur
Baden
ZÜRICH
Sankt Gallen
AARGAU
Aarau
Olten
Delémont
JURA
SOLOTHURN
Zürich
Uster
Zürichsee
AUSSER-RHODEN (APPENZELL) INNER-RHODEN
Solothurn
Biel
L. Biel
Sempach
Zug
ZUG
Einsiedeln
SANKT GALLEN
Vaduz
Landeck
Dole
La Chaux-de-Fonds
JURA MOUNTAINS
Doubs
LUZERN
Luzern
SCHWYZ
Schwyz
Walensee
Glarus
GLARUS
NEUCHÂTEL
Neuchâtel
Burgdorf
Bern
Pontarlier
Sarnen
Stans
NIDWALDEN
Altdorf
Glarner Alpen
Rhaetikon
Chur
Davos
Scuol
Arosa
Yverdon
Fribourg
BERN
Brienz
OBWALDEN
URI
Titlis 3239 m (10,627 ft)
VAUD
FRIBOURG
Thun
Thunersee
Interlaken
Brienzersee
St. Gotthard Tunnel
St. Gotthard Pass
GRAUBÜNDEN
Rhaetian Alps
Engadine Valley
Staubbach Falls
Lausanne
Montreux
Gstaad
Jungfrau 4166 m (13,667 ft)
Lötschberg Tunnel
Inn
Adige
Ortiles
St. Moritz
Piz Bernina 4049 m (13,284 ft)
Poschiavo
Nyon
L. Geneva
Bernese Alps
ALPS
Lepontine Alps
Monthey
Sierre
Rhône
Brig
Simplon Tunnel
TICINO
Sion
VALAIS
Locarno
Bellinzona
Sondrio
GENEVA
Geneva
Martigny
Pennine Alps
Domodossola
Adda
Zermatt
L. Maggiore
Lugano
L. Como
Annecy
Matterhorn 4505 m (14,780 ft)
Monte Rosa 4634 m (15,203 ft)
L. of Lugano
Varese
Como
Mont Blanc 4807 m (15,771 ft)
Aosta
Albertville
A B C D E
1 2 3

© MapQuest.com, Inc.

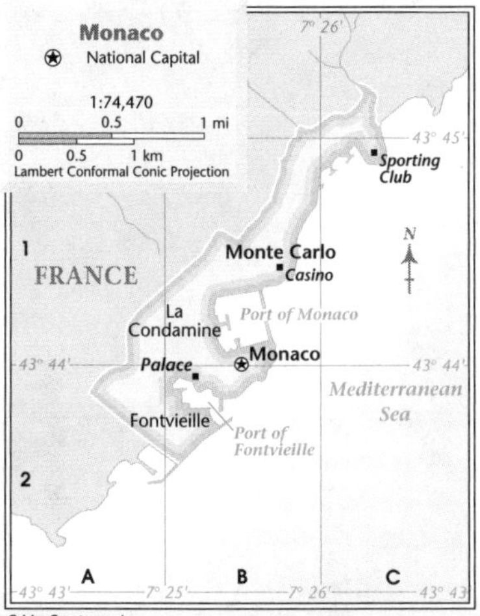

Monaco
National Capital
1:74,470
0 0.5 1 mi
0 0.5 1 km
Lambert Conformal Conic Projection
7° 26'
43° 45'
Sporting Club
Monte Carlo
Casino
FRANCE
Port of Monaco
La Condamine
Monaco
Palace
43° 44'
Mediterranean Sea
Fontvieille
Port of Fontvieille
43° 43'
7° 25'
A B C
1 2

© MapQuest.com, Inc.

Switzerland: Map Index

Cantons
- Aargau C1
- Appenzell Ausser-Rhoden D1
- Appenzell Inner-Rhoden D1
- Basel-Land B1
- Basel-Stadt B1
- Bern B2
- Fribourg B2
- Geneva A2
- Glarus D2
- Graubünden D2
- Jura B1
- Lucerne C1
- Neuchâtel A2
- Nidwalden C2
- Obwalden C2
- Sankt Gallen D1
- Schaffhausen C1
- Schwyz C1
- Solothurn B1
- Thurgau C1
- Ticino C2
- Uri C2
- Valais B2
- Vaud A2
- Zug C1
- Zürich C1

Cities and Towns
- Aarau C1
- Altdorf C2
- Baden C1
- Basel B1
- Bellinzona D2
- Bern, *capital* B2
- Biel B1
- Bolligen B2
- Bulle B2
- Chur D2
- Davos D2
- Einsiedeln C1
- Fribourg B2
- Frutigen B2
- Geneva A2
- Horgèn C1
- Interlaken B2
- La Chaux-de-Fonds A1
- Lausanne A2
- Locarno C2
- Lucerne C1
- Lugano C3
- Montreux A2
- Morges A2
- Neuchâtel A2
- St. Moritz D2
- Sankt Gallen D1
- Schaffhausen C1
- Schwyz C1
- Sempach C1
- Sion B2
- Thun B2
- Uster C1
- Winterthur C1
- Yverdon A2
- Zermatt B2
- Zug C1
- Zürich C1

Other Features
- Aare, *river* B1, B2
- Alps, *mts.* B2
- Bernese Alps, *mts.* B2
- Biel, *lake* B1
- Brienzersee, *lake* B2
- Constance (Bodensee), *lake* D1
- Doubs, *river* A1
- Dufourspitze, *mt.* B3
- Engadine, *valley* D2
- Geneva, *lake* A2
- Inn, *river* D2
- Jungfrau, *mt.* B2
- Jura, *mts.* A2
- Lepontine Alps, *mts.* C2
- Lucerne, *lake* C2
- Lugano, *lake* C3
- Maggiore, *lake* C2
- Matterhorn, *mt.* B3
- Neuchâtel, *lake* A2
- Pennine Alps, *mts.* B2
- Reuss, *river* C2
- Rhaetian Alps, *mts.* D2
- Rhine, *river* C1, D2
- Rhône, *river* B2
- St. Gotthard, *pass* C2
- St. Gotthard, *tunnel* C2
- Splügen, *pass* D2
- Staubbach, *falls* B2
- Thunersee, *lake* B2
- Ticino, *river* C2
- Walensee, *lake* D1
- Zürichsee, *lake* C1

Monaco: Map Index

Districts
- Fontvieille A2
- La Condamine B1
- Monaco, *capital* B1
- Monte Carlo B1

Other Features
- Casino B1
- Fontvieille, *port* B2
- Monaco, *port* B1
- Palace B2
- Sporting Club C1

Monaco

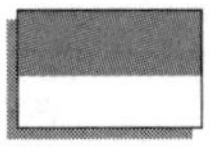

Capital: Monaco
Area: 0.75 sq. mi.
1.94 sq. km.
Population: 32,130
Language: French
Monetary Unit: Euro

France

Capital: Paris
Area: 210,026 sq. mi.
544,109 sq. km.
Population: 60,144,000
Largest City: Paris
Language: French
Monetary Unit: Euro

France: Map Index

Regions
- Alsace D2
- Aquitaine B4
- Auvergne C4
- Basse-Normandie B2
- Bourgogne C3
- Bretagne B2
- Centre C3
- Champagne-Ardenne D2
- Corse ....Inset I
- Franche-Comté D3
- Haute-Normandie C2
- Île-de-France C2
- Languedoc-Roussillon C5
- Limousin C4
- Lorraine D2
- Midi-Pyrénées C5
- Nord-Pas-de-Calais C1
- Pays De La Loire B3
- Picardie C2
- Poitou-Charentes C3
- Provence-Alpes-Côte-d'Azur D4
- Rhône-Alpes D4

Cities and Towns
- Abbeville C1
- Agen C4
- Aix-en-Provence D5
- Aix-les-Bains D4
- Ajaccio ....Inset I
- Albi C5
- Alençon C2
- Alès D4
- Amiens C2
- Angers B3
- Angoulême C4
- Annecy D4
- Arachon B4
- Argenteuil ....Inset II
- Arles D5
- Arpajon ....Inset II
- Arras C1
- Auch C5
- Aurillac C4
- Auxerre C3
- Avignon D5
- Ballancourt-sur-Essonne ....Inset II
- Bar-le-Duc D2
- Bastia ....Inset I
- Bayeux B2
- Bayonne B5
- Beauvais C2
- Belfort D3
- Bergerac C4
- Besançon D3
- Béziers C5
- Biarritz B5
- Blois C3
- Bondy ....Inset II
- Bordeaux B4
- Boulogne-Billancourt ....Inset II
- Boulogne-sur-Mer C1
- Bourg-en-Bresse D3
- Bourges C3
- Brest A2
- Briançon D4
- Brive-la-Gallarde C4
- Caen B2
- Cahors C4
- Calais C1
- Calvi ....Inset I
- Cambrai C1
- Cannes D5
- Carcassonne C5
- Carnac B3
- Châlons-sur-Marne D2
- Chambéry D4
- Chamonix-Mont-Blanc D4
- Chantilly C2
- Charleville Mézières D2
- Chartres C2
- Châteauroux C3
- Châtellerault C3
- Chaumont D2
- Chelles ....Inset II
- Cherbourg B2
- Chevreuse ....Inset II
- Choisy-le Roi ....Inset II
- Cholet B3
- Clermont-Ferrand C4
- Clichy ....Inset II
- Cluny D3
- Cognac B4
- Colmar D2
- Compiègne C2
- Conflans-Sainte-Honorine ....Inset II
- Corbeil-Essonnes ....Inset II
- Coubert ....Inset II
- Créteil ....Inset II
- Dammartin-en-Goële ....Inset II
- Deauville C2
- Dieppe C2
- Digne D4
- Dijon D3
- Dôle D3
- Domont ....Inset II
- Douai C1
- Draguignan D5
- Dreux C2
- Dunkirk (Dunkerque) C1
- Épinal D2
- Étrechy ....Inset II
- Évreux C2
- Évry ....Inset II
- Foix C5
- Fontainebleau C2
- Fréjus D5
- Gap D4
- Gentilly ....Inset II
- Grenoble D4
- Guéret C3
- Laon C2
- La Rochelle B3
- La-Roche-sur-Yon B3
- Laval B2
- Le Creusot D3
- Le Havre C2
- Le Mans C2
- Lens C1
- Le Puy C4
- Les Ulis ....Inset II
- Levallois-Perret ....Inset II
- Lille C1
- Limoges C4
- Limours ....Inset II
- L'Isle-Adam ....Inset II
- Lorient B3
- Lourdes B5
- Louvres ....Inset II
- Luzarches ....Inset II
- Lyon D4
- Mâcon D3
- Maisons-Laffitte ....Inset II
- Marseille D5
- Massy ....Inset II
- Maurepas ....Inset II
- Melun ....Inset II
- Mende C4
- Mennecy ....Inset II
- Metz D2
- Meulan ....Inset II
- Montargis C2
- Montauban C4
- Montélimar D4
- Montluçon C3
- Montpellier C5
- Montreuil ....Inset II
- Mont-Saint-Michel B2
- Morlaix B2
- Mulhouse D3
- Nancy D2
- Nanterre ....Inset II
- Nantes B3
- Narbonne C5
- Nevers C3
- Nice D5
- Nîmes D5
- Niort B3
- Orléans C3
- Ozoir-la-Ferrière ....Inset II
- Palaiseau ....Inset II
- Paris, *capital* ....C2, Inset II
- Pau B5
- Périgueux C4
- Perpignan C5
- Poissy ....Inset II
- Poitiers C3
- Pontchartrain ....Inset II
- Pontoise ....Inset II
- Porto-Vecchio ....Inset I
- Privas D4
- Quimper A2
- Reims D2
- Rennes B2
- Roanne D3
- Rochefort B4
- Rodez C4
- Roubaix C1
- Rouen C2
- Saint-Brieuc B2
- Saint-Cloud ....Inset II
- Saint-Denis ....Inset II
- Saint-Dizier D2
- Saintes B4
- Saint-Étienne D4
- Saint-Germain-en-Laye ....Inset II
- Saint-Lô B2
- Saint-Malo B2
- Saint-Nazaire B3
- Saint-Tropez D5
- Sarcelles ....Inset II
- Saumur B3
- Savigny-sur-Orge ....Inset II
- Sedan D2
- Sevran ....Inset II
- Sèvres ....Inset II
- Soissons C2
- Strasbourg D2
- Tarbes C5
- Taverny ....Inset II
- Toulon D5
- Toulouse C5
- Tourcoing C1
- Tours C3
- Trouville C2
- Troyes D2
- Valence D4
- Valenciennes C1
- Vannes B3
- Verdun D2
- Versailles ....C2, Inset II
- Vesoul D3
- Vichy C3
- Vierzon C3
- Villeneuve-Saint-Georges ....Inset II
- Vincennes ....Inset II

Other Features
- Adour, *river* B5
- Aisne, *river* D2
- Allier, *river* C3
- Alps, *range* D4
- Ardennes, *region* D1
- Argonne, *forest* D2
- Aube, *river* D3
- Belfort, *gap* D3
- Belle, *island* B3
- Biscay, *bay* B4
- Blanc, *mt.* D4
- Cévennes, *mts.* C4
- Charente, *river* B4
- Corsica, *island* ....Inset I
- Cotentin, *peninsula* B2
- Dordogne, *river* C4
- Dover, *strait* C1
- Durance, *river* D5
- English, *channel* B2
- Garonne, *river* C4
- Geneva, *lake* D3
- Gironde, *river* B4
- Hague, *cape* B2
- Isère, *river* D4
- Jura, *mts.* D3
- Landes, *region* B5
- Lion, *gulf* D5
- Little St. Bernard, *pass* D4
- Loire, *river* C3
- Lot, *river* C4
- Maritime Alps, *range* D4
- Marne, *river* ....C2, Inset II
- Massif Central, *plateau* C4
- Meuse, *river* D2
- Moselle, *river* D2
- Oise, *river* ....C2, Inset II
- Oléron, *island* B4
- Omaha, *beach* B2
- Orne, *river* B2
- Pyrenees, *range* C5
- Rance, *river* B2
- Raz, *point* A3
- Ré, *island* B3
- Rhine, *river* D2
- Rhône, *river* D4
- Saint-Malo, *gulf* B2
- Sambre, *river* C1
- Saône, *river* D3
- Seine, *river* ....C2, Inset II
- Somme, *river* C2
- Utah, *beach* B2
- Vienne, *river* C3
- Vignemale, *mt.* B5
- Vilaine, *river* B3
- Vosges, *mts.* D2
- Yeu, *island* B3
- Yonne, *river* C2

Portugal: Map Index

Districts
Aveiro A2
Beja A4
Braga A2
Bragança B2
Castelo Branco B3
Coimbra A2
Évora B3
Faro A4
Guarda B2
Leiria A3
Lisbon A3
Oporto (Porto) A2
Portalegre B3
Santarém A3
Setúbal A3
Viana do Castelo A2
Vila Real B2
Viseu B2

Cities and Towns
Abrantes A3
Almada A3
Amadora A3
Aveiro A2
Barreiro A3
Beja B3
Braga A2
Bragança B2
Caidasm da Rainha A3
Castelo Branco B3
Chaves B2
Coimbra A2
Covilhã B2
Elvas B3
Estoril A3
Évora B3
Faro B4
Figueira da Foz A2
Grândola A3
Guarda B2
Guimarães A2
Lagos A4
Leiria A3

Leixões A2
Lisbon, capital A3
Mafra A3
Moura B3
Odemira A4
Oeiras A3
Oporto (Porto) A2
Peniche A3
Portalegre B3
Portimão A4
Queluz A3
Santarém A3
Setúbal A3
Sines A4
Valença A1
Viana do Castelo A2
Vila do Conde A2
Vila Nova de Gaia A2
Vila Real B2
Vila Real
de Santo Antonio B4
Viseu B2

Other Features
Algarve, region A4
Cádiz, gulf B4
Carvoeiro, cape A3
Chança, river B4
Douro, river B2
Espichel, cape A3
Estrela, mt. B2
Estrela, mts. B2
Guadiana, river B3
Lima, river A2
Minho, river A1
Mondego, cape A2
Mondego, river B2
Roca, cape A3
Sado, river A3
São Vicente, cape A4
Seda, river B3
Setúbal, bay A3
Sor, river B3
Sorraia, river A3
Tagus, river A3
Tâmega, river B2
Zêzere, river A3

Portugal

Capital: Lisbon
Area: 35,672 sq. mi.
  92,415 sq. km.
Population: 10,062,000
Largest City: Lisbon
Language: Portuguese
Monetary Unit: Euro

Portugal
⊛ National Capital
• Other City
1:4,678,000
0   25   50 mi
0   25   50 km
Lambert Conformal Conic Projection
© MapQuest.com, Inc.

Malta
Capital: Valletta
Area: 122 sq. mi.
  316 sq. km.
Population: 394,000
Largest City: Valletta
Languages: Maltese, English
Monetary Unit: Maltese lira

Malta
⊛ National Capital
• Other City
1:650,000
0   4   8 mi
0   4   8 km
Transverse Mercator Projection
© MapQuest.com, Inc.

Malta: Map Index

Cities and Towns
Birkirkara B2
Birzebbuga C3
Dingli B2
Mellieha B2
Nadur B1
Qormi B2
Rabat B2
San Pawl il-Bahar B2
Siggiewi B2
Sliema C2
Valletta, capital C2
Victoria A1
Zabbar C2
Zebbug A1
Zurrieq B2

Other Features
Comino, island B1
Cominotto, island B1
Filfla, island B3
Gozo, island A1
Grand, harbor C2
Malta, island B2
Marsaxlokk, bay C3
Mellieha, bay B2
North Comino, channel B1
Saint Paul's, bay B2
South Comino, channel B2

Gibraltar

Area: 2.25 sq. mi.
  5.83 sq. km.
Population: 27,776
Language: English
Monetary Unit: Gibraltar pound

Gibraltar: Map Index

Features
Catalan, bay A2
Detached, mole A2
Eastern, beach A2
Fortress Headquarters A3
Gibraltar, bay A2
Gibraltar, harbor A2
Gibraltar, strait A4
Governor's Residence A2
Great Europa, point A4
Highest point A3
Little, bay A4
Mediterranean, sea A3
North, mole A2
North Front, airfield A1
Rosia, bay A3
Saint Michael's, cave A3
Sandy, bay A3
Signal, hill A2
South, mole A3
The Rock, prom. A2

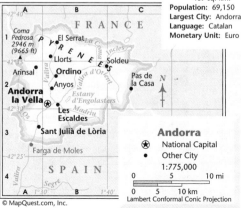

Gibraltar
1:82,200
0   0.5   1 mi
0   0.5   1 km
Miller Cylindrical Projection
© MapQuest.com, Inc.

Andorra
Capital: Andorra la Vella
Area: 181 sq. mi.
  469 sq. km.
Population: 69,150
Largest City: Andorra la Vella
Language: Catalan
Monetary Unit: Euro

Andorra
⊛ National Capital
• Other City
1:775,000
0   5   10 mi
0   5   10 km
Lambert Conformal Conic Projection
© MapQuest.com, Inc.

Andorra: Map Index

Cities and Towns
Andorra la Vella, capital B2
Anyos B2
Arinsal A2
El Serrat B1
Les Escaldes B2
Llorts B1
Ordino B2
Pas de la Casa C2
Sant Julià de Lòria A3
Soldeu B2

Other Features
Coma Pedrosa, mt. A1
Estany d'Engolasters, lake B2
Incles, river C1
La Coma, river B1
Madriu, river B3
Os, river A3
Pyrenees, range A1
Valira, river B2
Valira d'Orient, river B2

Spain:
Map Index

Regions

Andalusia D4
Aragón F2
Asturias C1
Balearic Islands G3
Basque Country E1
Canary Islands ....Inset I
Cantabria D1
Castile-La Mancha E3
Castile-León D1, E1
Catalonia G2
Estremadura C3
Galicia C1
La Rioja E1
Madrid E2
Murcia F4
Navarra F1
Valencia F2, F3

Cities and Towns

Águilas F4
Albacete F3
Alcalá de Henares ......Inset II
Alcañiz F2
Alcázar de San Juan E3
Alcira F3
Alcobendas ....Inset II
Alcorcón ....E2, Inset II
Alcoy F3
Algeciras D4
Alicante F3
Almadén D3
Almansa F3
Almendralejo C3
Almería E4
Antequera D4
Aranda de Duero E2
Aranjuez E2
Astorga C1
Ávila D2
Avilés D1
Badajoz C3
Badalona H2
Baracaldo E1
Barcelona H2

Baza E4
Béjar D2
Benavente D1
Benidorm F3
Bilbao E1
Burgos E1
Cáceres C3
Cádiz C4
Calatayud F2
Cartagena F4
Castellón de la Plana F3
Ceuta D5
Cieza F3
Ciudadela H2
Ciudad Real E3
Ciudad Rodrigo C2
Córdoba D4
Cornellá de Llobregat G2
Coslada ....Inset II
Cuenca E2
Don Benito D3
Dos Hermanas D4
Écija D4
Elche F3
El Ferrol B1
Figueras H1
Fuenlabrada ....Inset II
Gerona H2
Getafe ....E2, Inset II
Gijón D1
Granada E4
Guadalajara E2
Guecho E1
Guernica y Luno E1
Hellín F3
Hospitalet H2
Huelva C4
Huesca F1
Ibiza G3
Jaén E4
Jerez de la Frontera C4
La Coruña B1
La Laguna ....Inset I
La Roda E3
Las Palmas ....Inset I
Leganés ....Inset II
León D1
Lérida G2

Linares E3
Logroño E1
Loja D4
Lorca F4
Lucena D4
Lugo C1
Madrid, capital ......E2, Inset II
Mahón J3
Málaga D4
Marbella D4
Mataró H2
Medina del Campo D2
Mérida C3
Mieres D1
Miranda de Ebro E1
Monforte C1
Morón de la Frontera D4
Móstoles ....Inset II
Murcia F4
Orense C1
Oviedo D1
Palencia D1
Palma H3
Pamplona F1
Plasencia C2
Ponferrada C1
Pontevedra B1
Puertollano D3
Reinosa D1
Reus G2
Sabadell H2
Sagunto F3
Salamanca D2
San Baudilio de Llobregat ..G2
San Fernando C4
San Sebastián F1
Santa Coloma de
  Gramanet H2
Santa Cruz de Tenerife ..Inset I
Santander E1
Santiago de Compostela B1
Segovia D2
Seville D4
Soria E2
Talavera de la Reina D3
Tarragona G2
Tarrasa G2
Telde ....Inset I

Teruel F2
Toledo D3
Tomelloso E3
Torrejón de Ardoz ....Inset II
Torrelavega D1
Torrente F3
Tortosa G2
Úbeda E3
Valdepeñas E3
Valencia F3
Valladolid D2
Vich H2
Vigo B1
Villarreal de los Infantes F3
Vitoria E1
Yecla F3
Zafra C3
Zamora D2
Zaragoza F2

Other Features

Alarcón, reservoir E3
Alboran, sea E4
Alcántara, reservoir C3
Almendra, reservoir C2
Aneto, mt. G1
Balearic, islands G3
Balearic, sea G2
Béticos, mts. D4
Biscay, bay D1
Brava, coast H2
Buendía, reservoir E2
Cabrera, island H3
Cádiz, gulf. C4
Canaray, islands ....Inset I
Cantábrica, mts. C1
Cijara, reservoir D3
Duero, river D2
Ebro, river F1
Esla, river D2
Finisterre, cape B1
Formentera, island G3
Fuerteventura, island ......Inset I
Gata, cape E4
Gibraltar, strait D5
Gomera, island ....Inset I
Gran Canaria, island ......Inset I
Gredos, mts. D2

Guadalquivir, river D4
Guadarrama, mts. D2
Guadiana, river C3
Hierro, island ....Inset I
Ibérico, mts. E1
Ibiza, island G3
Jarama, river ....Inset II
Júcar, river F3
Lanzarote, island ....Inset I
La Palma, island ....Inset I
Majorca, island H3
Mediterranean, sea E4
Mequinenza, reservoir F2
Meseta, plateau D3
Miño, river B1
Minorca, island H2
Morena, mts. D3
Mulhacén, mt. E4
Nao, cape G3
Nevada, mts. E4
Orellana, reservoir D3
Ortegal, cape C1
Palos, cape F4
Pyrenees, mts. F1
Ricobayo, reservoir D2
Segura, river E3
Sol, coast D4
Tagus, river C3
Tenerife, island ....Inset I
Toledo, mts. D3
Tormes, river D2
Tortosa, cape G2
Valdecañas, reservoir D3
Valencia, gulf. G3
Zújar, reservoir D3

Spain

Capital: Madrid
Area: 194,898 sq. mi.
    504,917 sq. km.
Population: 41,060,000
Largest City: Madrid
Language: Spanish
Monetary Unit: Euro

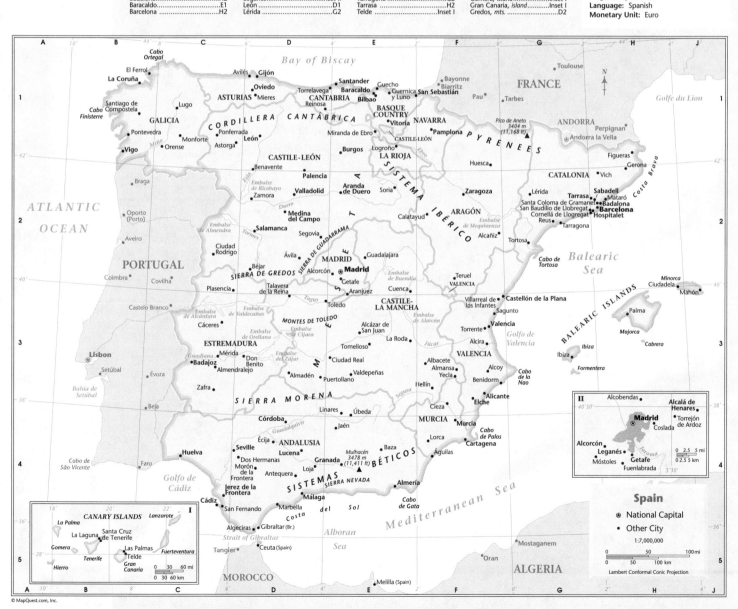

© MapQuest.com, Inc.

Italy

⊛ National Capital

• Other City

1:5,614,000

0   50   100   150 mi

0 50 100 150 km

Lambert Conformal Conic Projection

Italy
Capital: Rome
Area: 116,333 sq. mi.
301,381 sq. km.
Population: 57,423,000
Largest City: Rome
Language: Italian
Monetary Unit: Euro

Austria
⊛ National Capital
• Other City
1:4,714,000
0   25   50 mi
0   25   50 km
Lambert Conformal Conic Projection

© MapQuest.com, Inc.

Austria

Capital: Vienna
Area: 32,378 sq. mi.
83,881 sq. km.
Population: 8,116,000
Largest City: Vienna
Language: German
Monetary Unit: Euro

Austria:
Map Index

Provinces

Burgenland	E3
Carinthia	C4
Lower Austria	D2
Salzburg	C3
Styria	D3
Tirol	B3, C4
Upper Austria	C2
Vienna	E2
Vorarlberg	A3

Cities and Towns

Amstetten	D2
Baden	E2
Bad Ischl	C3
Braunau	C2
Feldkirch	A3
Fürstenfeld	E3
Gmünd	D2
Graz	D3
Hieflau	D3
Innsbruck	B3
Kapfenberg	D3
Klagenfurt	D4
Köflach	D3
Kufstein	C3
Lech	B3
Leoben	D3
Lienz	C4
Linz	D2
Mistelbach	E2
Salzburg	C3
Sankt Pölten	D2
Steyr	D2
Stockerau	E2
Vienna, capital	E2
Villach	C4
Vöcklabruck	C2
Wels	C2
Wiener Neustadt	E3
Wolfsberg	D4

Other Features

Alps, range	B3
Bavarian Alps, range	B3
Brenner, pass	B3
Carnic Alps, range	C4
Constance, lake	A3
Danube, river	D2
Drava, river	C4
Enns, river	D3
Grossglockner, mt.	C3
Hohe Tauern, mts.	C3
Inn, river	B3, C2
Karawanken, range	D4
Mur, river	D3
Mürz, river	D3
Neusiedler, lake	E3
Niedere Tauern, range	D3
Ötztal Alps, range	B4
Salzach, river	C3
Salzburg Alps, range	C3
Semmering, pass	D3
Traun, river	D2
Ybbs, river	D2
Zillertal Alps, range	B3

Italy:
Map Index

Regions

Abruzzi	C2
Apulia	C2
Basilicata	C2
Calabria	D3
Campania	C2
Emilia-Romagna	B1
Friuli-Venezia Giulia	C1
Latium	C2
Liguria	B1
Lombardy	B1
Marche	C2
Molise	C2
Piedmont	A1
Puglia	C2
Sardinia	B3
Sicily	C3
Trentino-Alto Adige	B1
Tuscany	B2
Umbria	C2
Valle d'Aosta	A1
Veneto	B1

Cities and Towns

Agrigento	C3
Alessandria	B1
Alghero	B2
Ancona	C2
Aosta	A1
Aquileia	C1
Arezzo	B2
Ascoli Piceno	C2
Asti	B1
Avellino	C2
Bari	D2
Barletta	C2
Belluno	C1
Benevento	C2
Bergamo	B1
Bologna	B1
Bolzano	B1
Brescia	B1
Brindisi	D2
Cagliari	B3
Caltanissetta	C3
Campobasso	C2
Canossa	B1
Capua	C2
Carbonia	B3
Caserta	C2
Castel Gandolfo	C2
Catania	C3
Catanzaro	D3
Cefalù	C3
Chieti	C2
Chioggia	C1
Civitavecchia	B2
Como	B1
Cortina d'Ampezzo	C1
Cortona	B2
Cosenza	D3
Cremona	B1
Crotone	D3
Cuneo	A1
Enna	C3
Faenza	B1
Ferrara	B1
Florence	B2
Foggia	C2
Forlì	C1
Frosinone	C2
Gaeta	C2
Gela	C3
Genoa	B1
Gorizia	C1
Grosseto	B2
Isernia	C2
L'Aquila	C2
La Spezia	B1
Latina	C2
Lecce	D2
Livorno	B2
Lucca	B2
Macerata	C2
Manfredonia	C2
Mantova	B1
Mantua (Mantova)	B1
Marsala	C3
Matera	D2
Merano	B1
Messina	C3
Milan	B1
Modena	B1
Monopoli	D2
Montepulciano	B2
Monza	B1
Naples	C2
Novara	B1
Nuoro	B2
Olbia	B2
Oristano	B3
Otranto	D2
Padova	B1
Padua (Padova)	B1
Palermo	C3
Parma	B1
Pavia	B1
Perugia	C2
Pesaro	C2
Pescara	C2
Pisa	B2
Pistoia	B2
Piacenza	B1
Potenza	C2
Prato	B2
Ragusa	C3
Ravenna	C1
Reggio di Calabria	C3
Reggio nell'Emilia	B1
Rieti	C2
Rimini	C1
Rome, capital	C2
Rovigo	B1
Salerno	C2
San Gimignano	B2
San Remo	A2
San Severo	C2
Sassari	B2
Savona	B1
Siena	B2
Siracusa	C3
Sondrio	B1
Sorrento	C2
Spoleto	C2
Syracuse (Siracusa)	C3
Taranto	D2
Teramo	C2
Termoli	C2
Terni	C2
Torre del Greco	C2
Trapani	C3
Trento	B1
Treviso	C1
Trieste	C1
Turin	A1
Udine	C1
Venice	C1
Ventimiglia	A2
Vercelli	B1
Verona	B1
Vicenza	B1
Viterbo	C2

Other Features

Adige, river	B1
Adriatic, sea	C2
Alps, mts.	A1, B1
Apennines, range	B2
Arno, river	B2
Asinara, island	B2
Blanc, mt.	A1
Bolsena, lake	B2
Botte Donato, mt.	D3
Bracciano, lake	C2
Brenner, pass	B1
Cagliari, gulf	B3
Campagna di Roma, region	C2
Caprara, point	C2
Capri, island	C2
Carbonara, cape	B3
Cervati, mt.	C2
Cimone, mt.	B1
Como, lake	B1
Corno, mt.	C2
Dolomites, range	B1
Egadi, islands	C3
Elba, island	B2
Etna, mt.	C3
Garda, lake	B1
Gennargentu, mts.	B2
Genoa, gulf	B1
Giglio, island	B2
Ionian, sea	D3
Ischia, island	C2
Ligurian, sea	B2
Lipari, islands	C3
Lombardy, plain	B1
Lugano, lake	B1
Maggiore, lake	B1
Maremma, region	B2
Mediterranean, sea	C3
Messina, strait	C3
Montalto, mt.	C3
Montecristo, island	B2
Naples, bay	C2
Oglio, river	B1
Pantelleria, island	C3
Passero, cape	C3
Pianosa, island	B2
Piave, river	C1
Po, river	A1, B1
Pontine, islands	C2
Pontine, marshes	C2
Rosa, mt.	A1
Salerno, gulf	C2
Sangro, river	C2
San Pietro, island	B3
Santa Maria di Leuca, cape	D3
Sant'Antioco, island	B3
San Vito, cape	C3
Sardinia, island	B2
Sicily, island	C3
Sicily, strait	B3
Spartivento, cape	D3
Stromboli, island	C3
Taranto, gulf	D2
Testa del Gargano, point	D2
Teulada, cape	B3
Tiber, river	C2
Tirso, river	B2
Trasimeno, lake	C2
Tyrrhenian, sea	B2
Ustica, island	C3
Venice, gulf	C1
Vesuvius, volcano	C2

Vatican City

Area: 108.7 acres
Population: 911
Languages: Italian, Latin
Monetary Unit: Euro

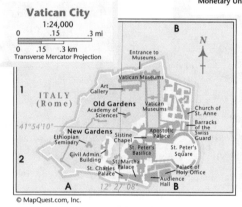

Vatican City
1:24,000
0   .15   .3 mi
0   .15   .3 km
Transverse Mercator Projection

© MapQuest.com, Inc.

Vatican City:
Map Index

Features

Academy of Sciences	B1
Apostolic Palace	B2
Art Gallery	B1
Audience Hall	B2
Barracks of the Swiss Guard	B1
Church of St. Anne	B1
Civil Administration Building	A2
Entrance to Museums	A1
Ethiopian Seminary	A2
New Gardens	A1
Old Gardens	A1
Palace of Holy Office	B2
St. Charles Palace	B2
St. Martha Palace	B2
St. Peter's Basilica	B2
St. Peter's Square	B2
Sistine Chapel	B2
Vatican Museums	B1

San Marino

Capital: San Marino
Area: 24 sq. mi.
62 sq. km.
Population: 28,119
Largest City: San Marino
Language: Italian
Monetary Unit: Euro

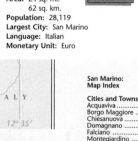

San Marino
⊛ National Capital
• Other City
1:280,000
0   2   4 mi
0   2   4 km
Gauss-Krüger Projection

© MapQuest.com, Inc.

San Marino:
Map Index

Cities and Towns

Acquaviva	A1
Borgo Maggiore	B1
Chiesanuova	B2
Domagnano	B1
Falciano	C1
Montegiardino	B2
San Marino, capital	B2
Serravalle	B1

Other Features

Ausa, river	C1
Marano, river	A1
San Marino, river	A1
Titano, mt.	B1

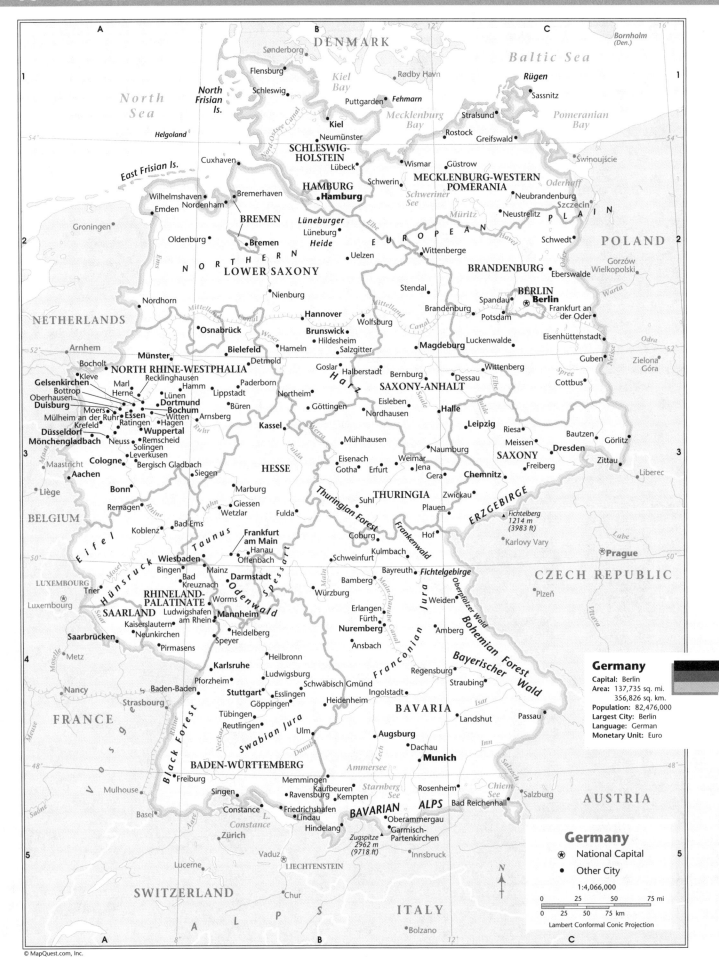

Germany
Capital: Berlin
Area: 137,735 sq. mi.
356,826 sq. km.
Population: 82,476,000
Largest City: Berlin
Language: German
Monetary Unit: Euro

Germany
⊛ National Capital
● Other City

1:4,066,000

0   25   50   75 mi
0 25 50 75 km

Lambert Conformal Conic Projection

© MapQuest.com, Inc.

Poland

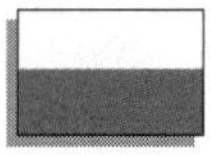

Capital: Warsaw
Area: 120,727 sq. mi.
312,764 sq. km.
Population: 38,587,000
Largest City: Warsaw
Language: Polish
Monetary Unit: Zloty

Poland:
Map Index

Cities and Towns
Biała Podlaska ... F2
Białystok ... F2
Bielsko-Biała ... D4
Bydgoszcz ... C2
Bytom ... D3
Chełm ... F3
Chojnice ... C2
Chorzów ... D3
Ciechánow ... E2
Częstochowa ... D3
Darłowo ... C1
Elbląg ... D1
Ełk ... F2
Gdańsk ... D1
Gdynia ... D1
Gliwice ... D3
Głogów ... C3
Gorzów Wielkopolski ... B2
Grudziądz ... D2
Hel ... D1
Jelenia Góra ... B3
Katowice ... D3
Kielce ... E3
Kołobrzeg ... B1
Konin ... D2
Koszalin ... C1
Kraków ... D3
Krosnow ... E4
Kutno ... D2
Legnica ... C3
Leszno ... C3
Łódź ... D3
Łomża ... F2
Lublin ... F3
Nowy Sącz ... E4
Nysa ... C3
Olsztyn ... E2
Opole ... C3
Ostrołęka ... E2
Piła ... C2
Piotrków Trybunalski ... D3
Płock ... D2
Poznań ... C2
Przemyśl ... F4
Puck ... D1
Puławy ... E3
Radom ... E3
Ruda Śląka ... D3
Rybnik ... D3
Rzeszów ... F3
Sczcecinek ... C2
Siedlce ... F2
Sieradz ... D3
Skierniewice ... E3
Słupsk ... C1
Sosnowiec ... D3
Suwałki ... F1
Świnoujście ... B2
Szczecin ... B2
Tarnobrzeg ... E3
Tarnów ... E3
Toruń ... D2
Tychy ... D3
Ustka ... C1
Wałbrzych ... C3
Warsaw, *capital* ... E2
Władysławowo ... D1
Włocławek ... D2
Wodzisław Śląski ... D3
Wrocław ... C3
Zabrze ... D3
Zakopane ... D4
Zamość ... F3
Zielona Góra ... B3

Other Features
Baltic, *sea* ... B1
Beskid, *mts.* ... D4
Bug, *river* ... E2, F3
Carpathian, *mts.* ... E4
Frisches Haff, *bay* ... D1
Gdańsk, *gulf* ... D1
High Tatra, *mts.* ... D4
Mamry, *lake* ... E1
Narew, *river* ... E2
Neisse, *river* ... B3
Noteć, *river* ... C2, D2
Oder, *river* ... B2, C3
Pilica, *river* ... E3
Pomeranian, *bay* ... B1
Rysy, *mt.* ... E4
San, *river* ... F3
Silesia, *region* ... C3
Śniardwy, *lake* ... E2
Sudeten, *mts.* ... B3
Vistula, *river* ... D2, E3
Warta, *river* ... B2, C2
Wieprz, *river* ... F3

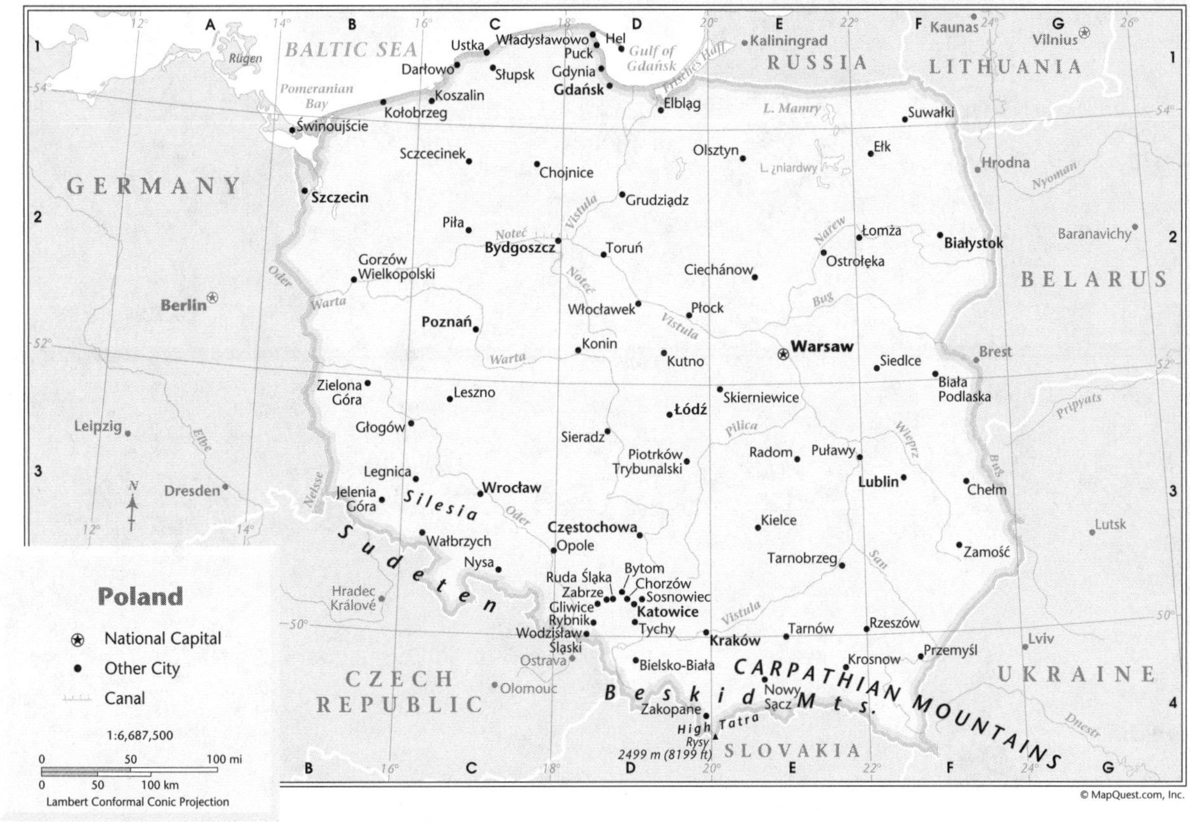

© MapQuest.com, Inc.

Germany:
Map Index

States
Baden-Württemberg ... B4
Bavaria ... B4
Berlin ... C2
Brandenburg ... C2
Bremen ... B2
Hamburg ... B2
Hesse ... B3
Lower Saxony ... B2
Mecklenburg-Western Pomerania ... C2
North Rhine-Westphalia ... A3
Rhineland-Palatinate ... A4
Saarland ... A4
Saxony ... C3
Saxony-Anhalt ... B3
Schleswig-Holstein ... B2
Thuringia ... B3

Cities and Towns
Aachen ... A3
Amberg ... B4
Ansbach ... B4
Arnsberg ... B3
Augsburg ... B4
Bad Ems ... A3
Baden-Baden ... B4
Bad Kreuznach ... A4
Bad Reichenhall ... C5
Bamberg ... B4
Bautzen ... C3
Bayreuth ... B4
Bergisch Gladbach ... A3
Berlin, *capital* ... C2
Bernburg ... B3
Bielefeld ... B2
Bingen ... A4
Bocholt ... A3
Bochum ... A3
Bonn ... A3
Bottrop ... A3
Brandenburg ... C2
Bremen ... B2
Bremerhaven ... B2
Brunswick ... B2
Büren ... B3
Chemnitz ... C3
Coburg ... B3
Cologne ... A3
Constance ... B5
Cottbus ... C3
Cuxhaven ... B2
Dachau ... B4
Darmstadt ... B4
Dessau ... C3
Detmold ... B3
Dortmund ... A3
Dresden ... C3
Duisburg ... A3
Düsseldorf ... A3
Eberswalde ... C2
Eisenach ... B3
Eisenhüttenstadt ... C2
Eisleben ... B3
Emden ... A2
Erfurt ... B3
Erlangen ... B4
Essen ... A3
Esslingen ... B4
Flensburg ... B1
Frankfurt am Main ... B3
Frankfurt an der Oder ... C2
Freiberg ... C3
Freiburg ... A5
Friedrichshafen ... B5
Fulda ... B3
Fürth ... B4
Garmisch-Partenkirchen ... B5
Gelsenkirchen ... A3
Gera ... C3
Giessen ... B3
Göppingen ... B4
Görlitz ... C3
Goslar ... B3
Gotha ... B3
Göttingen ... B3
Greifswald ... C1
Guben ... C3
Güstrow ... C2
Hagen ... A3
Halberstadt ... B3
Halle ... B3
Hamburg ... B2
Hameln ... B2
Hamm ... A3
Hanau ... B3
Hannover ... B2
Heidelberg ... B4
Heidenheim ... B4
Heilbronn ... B4
Herne ... A3
Hildesheim ... B2
Hindelang ... B5
Hof ... B3
Ingolstadt ... B4
Jena ... B3
Kaiserslautern ... A4
Karlsruhe ... B4
Kassel ... B3
Kaufbeuren ... B5
Kempten ... B5
Kiel ... B1
Kleve ... A3
Koblenz ... A3
Krefeld ... A3
Kulmbach ... B3
Landshut ... C4
Leipzig ... C3
Leverkusen ... A3
Lindau ... B5
Lippstadt ... B3
Lübeck ... B2
Luckenwalde ... C2
Ludwigsburg ... B4
Ludwigshafen am Rhein ... B4
Lüneburg ... B2
Lünen ... A3
Magdeburg ... B2
Mainz ... B4
Mannheim ... B4
Marburg ... B3
Marl ... A3
Meissen ... C3
Memmingen ... B5
Moers ... A3
Mönchengladbach ... A3
Mühlhausen ... B3
Mülheim an der Ruhr ... A3
Munich ... B4
Münster ... A3
Naumburg ... B3
Neubrandenburg ... C2
Neumünster ... B1
Neunkirchen ... A4
Neuss ... A3
Neustrelitz ... C2
Nienburg ... B2
Nordenham ... B2
Nordhausen ... B3
Nordhorn ... A2
Northeim ... B3
Nuremberg ... B4
Oberammergau ... B5
Oberhausen ... A3
Offenbach ... B3
Oldenburg ... B2
Osnabrück ... B2
Paderborn ... B3
Passau ... C4
Pforzheim ... B4
Pirmasens ... A4
Plauen ... C3
Potsdam ... C2
Puttgarden ... B1
Ratingen ... A3
Ravensburg ... B5
Recklinghausen ... A3
Regensburg ... C4
Remagen ... A3
Remscheid ... A3
Reutlingen ... B4
Riesa ... C3
Rosenheim ... C5
Rostock ... C1
Saarbrücken ... A4
Salzgitter ... B2
Sassnitz ... C1
Schleswig ... B1
Schwäbisch Gmünd ... B4
Schwedt ... C2
Schweinfurt ... B3
Schwerin ... B2
Siegen ... B3
Singen ... B5
Solingen ... A3
Spandau ... C2
Speyer ... B4
Stendal ... B2
Stralsund ... C1
Straubing ... C4
Stuttgart ... B4
Suhl ... B3
Trier ... A4
Tübingen ... B4
Uelzen ... B2
Ulm ... B4
Weiden ... C4
Weimar ... B3
Wetzlar ... B3
Wiesbaden ... B3
Wilhelmshaven ... B2
Wismar ... B2
Witten ... A3
Wittenberg ... C3
Wittenberge ... B2
Wolfsburg ... B2
Worms ... B4
Wuppertal ... A3
Würzburg ... B4
Zittau ... C3
Zwickau ... C3

Other Features
Ammersee, *lake* ... B4
Baltic, *sea* ... C1
Bavarian Alps, *mts.* ... B5
Bayerischer Wald, *mts.* ... C4
Black, *forest* ... A4
Bohemian, *forest* ... C4
Chiem, *lake* ... C5
Constance, *lake* ... B5
Danube, *river* ... B4
East Frisian, *islands* ... A2
Eifel, *plateau* ... A3
Elbe, *river* ... B2, C3
Ems, *river* ... A2
Erzgebirge, *mts.* ... C3
Fehmarn, *island* ... B1
Fichtelberg, *mt.* ... C3
Fichtelgebirge, *mts.* ... B4
Franconian Jura, *mts* ... B4
Frankenwald, *mts.* ... B3
Fulda, *river* ... B3
Harz, *mts.* ... B3
Havel, *river* ... C2
Helgoland, *island* ... A1
Hünsruck, *mts.* ... A4
Inn, *river* ... C4
Isar, *river* ... C4
Kiel, *bay* ... B1
Lahn, *river* ... B3
Lech, *river* ... B4
Lüneburger Heide, *region* ... B2
Main, *river* ... B4
Main-Danube, *canal* ... B4
Mecklenburg, *bay* ... B1
Mittelland, *canal* ... B2
Mosel, *river* ... A4
Mulde, *river* ... C3
Müritz, *lake* ... C2
Neckar, *river* ... B4
Neisse, *river* ... C3
Nord-Ostsee, *canal* ... B1
North, *sea* ... A1
Northern European, *plain* ... B2
North Frisian, *islands* ... B1
Oberpfälzer Wald, *mts.* ... C4
Odenwald, *forest* ... B4
Oder, *river* ... C2
Oderhaff, *lake* ... C2
Pomeranian, *bay* ... C1
Rhine, *river* ... A3, A4
Rügen, *island* ... C1
Ruhr, *river* ... B3
Saale, *river* ... B3
Saar, *river* ... A4
Salzach, *river* ... C4
Schweriner, *lake* ... B2
Spessart, *mts.* ... B4
Spree, *river* ... C3
Starnberg, *lake* ... B5
Swabian Jura, *mts.* ... B4
Taunus, *mts.* ... B3
Thuringian, *forest* ... B3
Werra, *river* ... B3
Weser, *river* ... B2
Zugspitze, *mt.* ... B5

© MapQuest.com, Inc.

Czech Republic:
Map Index

Administrative Regions
Brněský C4
Budějovický B3
Jihlavský B3
Karlovarský A2
Královehradecký B2
Liberecký B2
Olomoucký C3
Ostravský D3
Prague City B2
Pardubický C3
Plzeňský A3
Středočeský B3
Ustecký A2
Zlínský D3

Cities and Towns
Břeclav C4
Brno C3
České Budějovice B4
Cheb A2
Děčín B2
Frýdek-Místek D3
Havířov D3
Hradec Králové B2
Jihlava B3
Karlovy Vary A2
Karviná D3
Kladno B2
Klatovy A3
Kolín B2
Liberec B2
Most A2
Olomouc C3
Opava C3
Ostrava D3
Pardubice B2
Plzeň A3
Prague, capital B2
Přerov C3
Prostějov C3
Strakonice A3
Šumperk C3
Svitavy C3
Tábor B3
Trutnov B2
Ústí nad Labem B2
Zlín C3
Znojmo C4

Other Features
Berounka, river A3
Bohemia, region A3
Bohemian, forest A3
Bohemian-Moravian, heights B3
Carpathian, mts. C4
Dyje, river B4
Erzgebirge, mts. A2
Labe, Elbe, river B2
Morava, river C3
Moravia, region C3
Odra, Oder, river C3
Sázava, river B3
Silesia, region B2
Sněžka, mt. B2
Šudeten, mts. B2
Šumava, mts. A3
Vltava, river B3

Czech Republic

Capital: Prague
Area: 30,449 sq. mi.
78,883 sq. km.
Population: 10,236,000
Largest City: Prague
Language: Czech
Monetary Unit: Czech koruna

Slovakia

Capital: Bratislava
Area: 18,933 sq. mi.
49,049 sq. km.
Population: 5,402,000
Largest City: Bratislava
Language: Slovak
Monetary Unit: Slovak koruna

Slovakia:
Map Index

Regions
Banskobystrický C2
Bratislavský A2
Košický C2
Nitriansky B2
Prešovský C2
Trenčiansky A2
Trnavský A2
Žilinský B2

Cities and Towns
Banská Bystrica B2
Bardejov C2
Bratislava, capital A2
Humenné C2
Komárno B3
Košice C2
Levice B2
Liptovský Mikuláš B2
Lučenec B2
Martin B2
Michalovce C2
Nitra B2
Nové Zamky B3
Piešťany A2
Poprad C2
Považská Bystrica B2
Prešov C2
Prievidza B2
Ružomberok B2
Spišská Nová Ves C2
Trenčín A2
Trnava A2
Žilina B2
Zvolen B2

Other Features
Biele Karpaty, mts. A2
Carpathian, mts. A2
Danube, river A3
Gerlachovka, mt. C2
Hornád, river C2
Hron, river B2
Ipeľ, river B2
Laborec, river C2
Male Karpaty, mts. A2
Morava, river A2
Ondava, river C2
Slaná, river C2
Slovenskérudohorie, mts. B2
Tatra, range B2
Váh, river A2

© MapQuest.com, Inc.

Romania:
Map Index

Cities and Towns
Alba Iulia B2
Alexandria C4
Arad A2
Bacău D2
Baia Mare B2
Bîrlad D2
Bistrița C2
Botoșani D2
Brăila D3
Brașov C3
Bucharest, capital D3
Buzău D3
Călărași D3
Cernavodă E3
Cluj-Napoca B2
Constanța E3
Craiova B3
Dej B2
Deva B3
Dorohoi D2
Drobeta-Turnu Severin B3
Făgăraș C3
Fetești D3
Focșani D3
Galați E3
Giurgiu C4
Hunedoara B3
Iași D2
Lugoj A3
Lupeni B3
Medgidia E3
Mediaș C2
Miercurea Ciuc C2
Oltenița D3
Onești D2
Oradea A2
Petrila B3
Petroșani B3
Piatra Neamț D2
Pitești C3
Ploiești D3
Rădăuți C2
Reghin C2
Reșița A3
Rîmnicu Vîlcea C3
Roman D2
Salonta A2
Satu Mare B2
Sfîntu Gheorghe C3
Sibiu C3
Sighetul Marmației B2

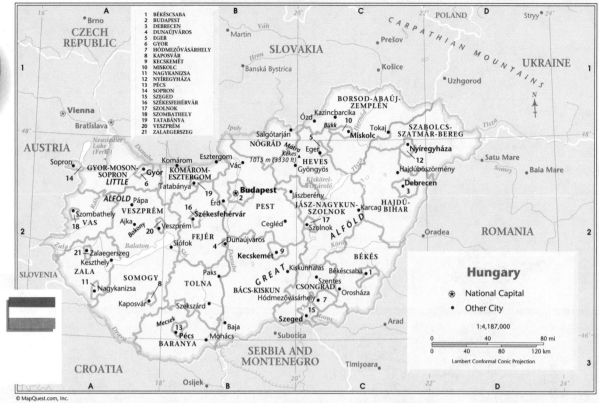

Hungary

Capital: Budapest
Area: 35,919 sq. mi.
 93,054 sq. km.
Population: 9,877,000
Largest City: Budapest
Language: Hungarian
Monetary Unit: Forint

Map labels: CZECH REPUBLIC, Brno, SLOVAKIA, Martin, Prešov, POLAND, Strry, UKRAINE, CARPATHIAN MOUNTAINS, Uzhgorod, Banská Bystrica, Košice, Váh, Hron, Ipoly, AUSTRIA, Vienna, Bratislava, Neusiedler Lake (Fertő), Sopron, GYŐR-MOSON-SOPRON, LITTLE, ALFÖLD, Rába, Szombathely, VAS, Ajka, Pápa, Komárom, Győr, Tatabánya, KOMÁROM-ESZTERGOM, Esztergom, Vác, Érd, Budapest, Bakony, VESZPRÉM, Veszprém, Balaton, Siófok, FEJÉR, Székesfehérvár, PEST, Ózd, Kazincbarcika, BORSOD-ABAÚJ-ZEMPLÉN, Bükk, Tokaj, Miskolc, Salgótarján, NÓGRÁD, Mátra, Kékes 1015 m (3330 ft), Eger, HEVES, Gyöngyös, SZABOLCS-SZATMÁR-BEREG, Tisza, Nyíregyháza, Hajdúböszörmény, Debrecen, Satu Mare, Baia Mare, Somes, Jászberény, Kiskörei-víztároló, JÁSZ-NAGYKUN-SZOLNOK, Karcag, HAJDÚ-BIHAR, Oradea, ROMANIA, SLOVENIA, Zala, Zalaegerszeg, Keszthely, ZALA, Nagykanizsa, SOMOGY, Kaposvár, Dunaújváros, Kecskemét, Paks, TOLNA, Szekszárd, GREAT, BÁCS-KISKUN, Kiskunhalas, Hódmezővásárhely, CSONGRÁD, Szentes, Orosháza, Békéscsaba, BÉKÉS, Körös, Arad, Maros, Mecsek, Pécs, Mohács, BARANYA, Drava, Baja, Subotica, CROATIA, SERBIA AND MONTENEGRO, Timişoara, Osijek

Hungary
⊛ National Capital
• Other City
1:4,187,000
0 40 80 mi
0 40 80 120 km
Lambert Conformal Conic Projection

© MapQuest.com, Inc.

Hungary:
Map Index

Counties

Bács-Kiskun	B2
Baranya	B3
Békés	C2
Békéscsaba	C2
Borsod-Abaúj-Zemplén	C1
Budapest (city)	B2
Csongrád	C2
Debrecen	C2
Dunaújváros	B2
Eger	C2
Fejér	B2
Győr	A2
Győr-Moson- Sopron	A2
Hajdú-Bihar	C2
Heves	C2
Hódmezővásárhely	C2
Jász-Nagykun-Szolnok	C2
Kaposvár	A2
Kecskemét	B2
Komárom-Esztergom	B2
Miskolc	C1
Nagykanizsa	A2
Nógrád	B2
Nyíregyháza	C2
Pécs	B2
Pest	B2
Somogy	A2
Sopron	A2
Szabolcs- Szatmár-Bereg	C1
Szeged	C2
Székesfehérvár	B2
Szolnok	C2
Szombathely	A2
Tatabánya	B2

Tolna	B2
Vas	A2
Veszprém	A2
Zala	A
Zalaegerszeg	A2

Cities and Towns

Ajka	A2
Baja	B2
Békéscsaba	C2
Budapest, *capital*	B2
Cegléd	B2
Debrecen	C2
Dunaújváros	B2
Eger	C2
Érd	B2
Esztergom	B2
Gyöngyös	B2
Győr	A2

Hajdúböszörmény	C2
Hódmezővásárhely	C2
Jászberény	B2
Kaposvár	A2
Karcag	C2
Kazincbarcika	C1
Kecskemét	B2
Keszthely	A2
Kiskunhalas	B2
Komárom	B2
Miskolc	C1
Mohács	B2
Nagykanizsa	A2
Nyíregyháza	C2
Orosháza	C2
Ózd	C1
Paks	B2
Pápa	A2
Pécs	B2

Salgótarján	B1
Siófok	B2
Sopron	A2
Szeged	C2
Székesfehérvár	B2
Szekszárd	B2
Szentes	C2
Szolnok	C2
Szombathely	A2
Tatabánya	B2
Tokaj	C1
Vác	B2
Veszprém	A2
Zalaegerszeg	A2

Other Features

Bakony, *mts.*	A2
Balaton, *lake*	A2
Bükk, *mts.*	C1

Danube, *river*	A2, B2
Drava, *river*	A2
Great Alföld, *plain*	B2
Hernád, *river*	C1
Ipoly, *river*	B1
Kékes, *mt.*	B2
Kiskörei-víztároló, *lake*	C2
Körös, *river*	C2
Little Alföld, *plain*	A2
Maros, *river*	B2
Mátra, *mts.*	B2
Mecsek, *mts.*	B2
Neusiedler (Fertő), *lake*	A2
Rába, *river*	A2
Sió, *river*	B2
Tisza, *river*	C2
Zala, *river*	A2

Romania

Capital: Bucharest
Area: 91,699 sq. mi.
 267,174 sq. km.
Population: 22,334,000
Largest City: Bucharest
Language: Romanian
Monetary Unit: Leu

Map labels: SLOVAKIA, Mukacheve, UKRAINE, Chernovtsi, Dnestr, Miskolc, CARPATHIAN MOUNTAINS, Siret, Rădăuți, Dorohoi, Botoşani, Bălți, Debrecen, Satu Mare, Sighetul Marmaţiei, Suceava, HUNGARY, Baia Mare, Zalău, Somes, Dej, Bistriţa, Tirgu Neamţ, MOLDAVIA, Iaşi, MOLDOVA, Chişinău, Kecskemét, Oradea, Apuseni Mts., Bihor Mts., Cluj-Napoca, Reghin, Piatra Neamţ, Bicaz Res., Romani, Vaslui, Odessa, Békéscsaba, Salonta, Tisza, Turda, Tirgu-Mureş, Bacău, Orosháza, Hódmezővásárhely, Arad, Alba Iulia, Mureş, Sighişoara, Miercurea Ciuc, Tirgu Ocna, Bîrlad, UKRAINE, Szeged, Subotica, Kikinda, Deva, Mediaş, Oneşti, Prut, Tecuci, Timişoara, Hunedoara, Sibiu, Făgăraş, Sfintu Gheorghe, Focşani, Bolgrad, Lugoj, BANAT, Petrila, Moldoveanu 2543 m (8343 ft), Braşov, Galaţi, Reni, Kiliya, Novi Sad, Reşiţa, Lupeni, Petroşani, TRANSYLVANIAN ALPS, Buzău, Brăila, Izmail, Zrenjanin, Tirgu Jiu, Rîmnicu Vîlcea, Tirgovişte, Ploieşti, Tulcea, Mouths of the Danube, Vršac, Iron Gate Res., Jiu, WALACHIA, Pitești, Argeş, Ialomiţa, Slobozia, Black Sea, Serbia, Drobeta-Turnu Severin, Slatina, Bucharest, Fetești, Cernavodă, Medgidia, SERBIA AND MONTENEGRO, Olt, Craiova, Olteniţa, Călăraşi, Constanţa, DOBRUJA, L. Razelm, Danube, Alexandria, Turnu Măgurele, Giurgiu, Ruse, Vidin, BULGARIA, Dobrich

Romania
⊛ National Capital
• Other City
1:5,750,000
0 40 80 mi
0 40 80 km
Lambert Conformal Conic Projection

© MapQuest.com, Inc.

Sighişoara	C2
Siret	D2
Slatina	C3
Slobozia	D3
Suceava	D2
Tecuci	D3
Timişoara	A3
Tîrgovişte	C3
Tirgu Jiu	B3
Tirgu-Mureş	C2
Tirgu Neamţ	D2
Tirgu Ocna	D2
Tulcea	E3
Turda	B2
Turnu Măgurele	C4
Vaslui	D2
Zalău	B2

Other Features

Apuseni, *mts.*	B2
Argeş, *river*	C3
Banat, *region*	A3
Bicaz, *reservoir*	D2
Bihor, *mts.*	B2
Bistriţa, *river*	C2
Carpathian, *mts.*	B1
Danube, *river*	B3, D3, E3
Dobruja, *region*	E4
Ialomiţa, *river*	D3
Iron Gate, *reservoir*	B3
Jiu, *river*	B3
Moldavia, *region*	D2
Moldoveanu, *mt.*	C3
Mouths of the Danube, *delta*	E3
Mureş, *river*	B2
Olt, *river*	C3
Prut, *river*	D2
Razelm, *lake*	E3
Siret, *river*	D2
Someş, *river*	B2
Transylvanian Alps, *mts.*	B3
Walachia, *region*	B3

Part of Russia extends onto the continent of Asia.

Russia

⊛ National Capital
• Other City

1:44,857,000

Russia

Capital: Moscow
Area: 6,592,800 sq. mi.
17,079,793 sq. km.
Population: 143,246,000
Largest City: Moscow
Language: Russian
Monetary Unit: Ruble

INTERNAL DIVISIONS
1 ADYGEYA
2 KARACHAYEVO-CHERKESIYA
3 KABARDINO-BALKARIYA
4 NORTH OSSETIA-ALANIYA
5 INGUSHETIYA
6 CHECHNYA
7 MORDOVIYA
8 CHUVASHIYA
9 MARIY-EL
10 TATARSTAN
11 UDMURTIYA
12 KOMI-PERMYAT AUT. OKRUG

© MapQuest.com, Inc.

**Russia:
Map Index**

Internal Divisions
Adygeya (republic) D5
Aginskiy Buryat (autonomous
okrug) G4
Altay (republic) F4
Bashkortostan (republic)........D4
Buryatiya (republic) G4
Chechnya (republic) D5
Chukotka (autonomous okrug) ..J3
Chuvashiya (republic).............D4
Dagestan (republic) D5
Evenkiya (autonomous okrug)..F3
Ingushetiya (republic) D5
Kabardino-Balkariya (republic)..D5
Kalmykiya (republic) D5
Karachayevo-Cherkesiya
(republic) D5
Kareliya (republic) C3
Khakasiya (republic) F4
Khanty-Mansiya
(autonomous okrug) E3
Komi (republic) D3
Komi-Permyat
(autonomous okrug) D3
Koryakiya (autonomous okrug) ..J3
Mariy-El (republic) D4
Mordoviya (republic) D4
Nenetsiya (autonomous okrug) ..D3
North Ossetia Alaniya (republic)..D5
Tatarstan (republic) D4
Tyva (autonomous okrug)........F2
Tyva (republic) F4
Udmurtiya (republic) D4
Ust-Ordynskiy Buryat (autonomous
okrug) G5
Sakha (Yakutiya) (republic) H3
Yamalo-Nenesiya
(autonomous okrug) E3
Yevrey (autonomous oblast) ...H5

Cities and Towns
Abakan F4
Achinsk F4
Aginskoye G4
Aldan H4
Anadyr J3
Angarsk G4
Apatity C3
Arkhangelsk D3
Astrakhan D5
Barabinsk E4
Barnaul F4
Belomorsk C3
Berezniki D4
Birobizhan H5
Biysk F4
Blagoveshchensk D4
Blagoveshchensk H4
Bodaybo G4
Bratsk G4
Bryansk C4
Cheboksary D4
Chelyabinsk E4
Cherepovets C4
Cherskiy J3
Chita G4
Dikson F2
Dudinka F3
Elista D5
Gorno-Altaysk F4
Groznyy D5
Igarka F3
Inta E3
Ishim E4
Ivanovo D4
Izhevsk D4
Kaliningrad C4
Kamensk-Uralskiy E4
Kansk F4
Kazan D4
Kemerovo F4
Khabarovsk H5
Khanty-Mansiysk E3

Khatanga G2
Kirensk G4
Kirov D4
Kolpashevo F4
Komsomol'sk-na-Amure H4
Kotlas D3
Krasnodar C5
Krasnoyarsk F4
Kudymkar D4
Kurgan E4
Kursk C4
Kyzyl F4
Lensk G3
Lesosibirsk F4
Lipetsk C4
Magadan I4
Magadachi H4
Magnitogorsk D4
Makhachkala D5
Mirnyy G3
Mogocha G4
Moscow, capital C4
Murmansk C3
Naberezhnyye Chelny D4
Nakhodka H5
Naryan-Mar D3
Nikolayevsk-na-Amure I4
Nizhnevartovsk E3
Nizhny Novgorod D4
Nizhny Tagil D4
Nordvik G2
Norilsk F3
Novgorod C4
Novokuznetsk F4
Novosibirsk F4
Okha I4
Okhotsk I4
Omsk E4
Orenburg D4
Orsk D4
Palana I4
Pechora D3
Penza D4
Perm D4

Petropavlovsk-Kamchatskiy......I4
Petrozavodsk C3
Pevek J3
Prokopyevsk F4
Provid)niya K3
Pskov C4
Rostov-na-Donu C5
Rubtsovsk F4
Ryazan C4
St. Petersburg C4
Salekhard E3
Samara D4
Saransk D4
Saratov D4
Serov E4
Skovorodino H4
Smolensk C4
Sochi C5
Sovetskaya Gavan I5
Stavropol D5
Surgut E3
Susuman I3
Svobodnyy H4
Syktyvkar D3
Tara E4
Tiksi H2
Tobolsk E4
Tolyatti D4
Tomsk F4
Tula C4
Tulun G4
Tynda H4
Tyumen E4
Ufa D4
Ukhta D3
Ulan-Ude G4
Ussuriysk H5
Ust-Ilimsk G4
Ust-Kamchatsk J4
Ust-Kut G4
Ust-Ordynskiy G4
Verkhoyansk H3
Vilyuysk H3

Vladivostok H5
Volgograd D5
Vologda C4
Vorkuta E3
Voronezh C4
Yakutsk H3
Yaroslavl C4
Yekaterinburg E4
Yoshkar-Ola D4
Yuzhno-Sakhalinsk I5
Zyryanka I3

Other Features
Aldan, river H4
Amur, river H4
Anadyr, gulf K3
Angara, river F4
Azov, sea C5
Baltic, sea B4
Barents, sea C2
Baykal, lake G4
Bering, sea K4
Bering, strait K3
Black, sea C5
Caspian, sea D6
Caucasus, mts. D5
Central Russian, upland C4
Central Siberian, plateau G3
Central, range I4
Chelyuskin, cape G2
Cherskiy, range H3
Chukchi, peninsula K3
Chukchi, range J3
Chukchi, sea K2
Dnepr, river C4
Dzhugdzhur, range H4
East Siberian, sea J2
Franz Josef Land, islands D1
Gyda, peninsula E2
Indigirka, river I3
Irtysh, river E4
Kamchatka, peninsula J4
Kara, sea E2

Kola, peninsula C3
Kolyma, range J3
Kolyma, river I3
Koryak, range J3
Kuril, islands I5
Ladoga, lake C3
Laptev, sea H2
Lena, river H3
Lower Tunguska, river F3
New Siberian, islands I2
North Siberian, lowland G2
Northern Dvina, river D3
Northern European, plain C4
Novaya Zemlya, islands D2
Ob, river E3
Oka, river D4
Okhotsk, sea I4
Olenek, river G3
Onega, lake C3
Pechora, river D3
Sakhalin, island I4
Sayan, mts. F4
Severnaya Zemlya, islands F1
Shelikhov, gulf I3
Siberia, region G3
Sikhote Alin, range H5
Stanovoy, range H4
Tatar, strait I4
Taymyr, peninsula G2
Ural, mts. D4
Ural, river D5
Verkhoyansk, range H3
Vilyuy, river G3
Volga, river D5
West Siberian, plain E3
White, sea C3
Wrangel, island J2
Yamal, peninsula E3
Yenisey, river F3
Zhelaniya, cape E2

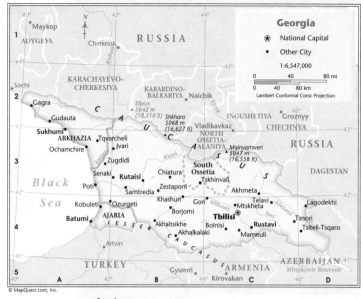

Armenia

Capital: Yerevan
Area: 11,500 sq. mi.
29,793 sq. km.
Population: 3,061,000
Largest City: Yerevan
Language: Armenian
Monetary Unit: Dram

Armenia:
Map Index

Cities and Towns
Alaverdi	B1
Ararat	B3
Artashat	B3
Artik	A2
Artsvashen	C2
Dilijan	B2
Ejmiatsin	B2
Gavarr	C2
Goris	D3
Gyumri	A2
Hoktemberyan	B2
Hrazdan	B2
Ijevan	C2
Kafan	D3
Kirovakan	B2
Martuni	C2
Meghri	D4
Sisian	D3
Sotk	C2
Stepanavan	B2
Tashir	B1
Vardenis	C2
Vayk	C3
Yerevan, capital	B2

Other Features
Akhuryan, river	A2
Aragats, mt.	B2
Aras, river	B2
Arpa, river	B2
Debed, river	B2
Hrazdan, river	B2
Lesser Caucasus, mts.	B1
Sevan, lake	C2
Vorotan, river	C3

Georgia:
Map Index

Cities and Towns
Akhalkalaki	B4
Akhaltsikhe	B4
Akhmeta	C3
Batumi	A4
Bolnisi	C4
Borjomi	B4
Chiatura	B3
Gagra	A2
Gori	C4
Gudauta	A2
Jvari	B3
Khashuri	B4
Kobuleti	A4
Kutaisi	B3
Lagodekhi	D4
Marneuli	C4
Mtskheta	C4
Ochamchire	A3
Ozurgeti	A4
Poti	A3
Rustavi	C4
Samtredia	B3
Senaki	A3
Sukhumi	A3
Tbilisi, capital	C4
Telavi	C4
Tqvarcheli	A3
Tsiteli-Tsqaro	D4
Tskhinvali	B3
Tsnori	C4
Zestaponi	B3
Zugdidi	A3

Other Features
Abkhazia, autonomous republic	A3
Ajaria, autonomous republic	A4
Alazani, river	C4
Caucasus, mts.	A2
Enguri, river	A3
Iori, river	C4
Lesser Caucasus, mts.	B4
Mqinvartsveri, mt.	C3
Mtkvari, river	C4
Rioni, river	B3
Shkhara, mt.	B3
South Ossetia, region	B3

Georgia

Capital: Tbilisi
Area: 26,900 sq. mi.
69,689 sq. km.
Population: 5,126,000
Largest City: Tbilisi
Language: Georgian
Monetary Unit: Lari

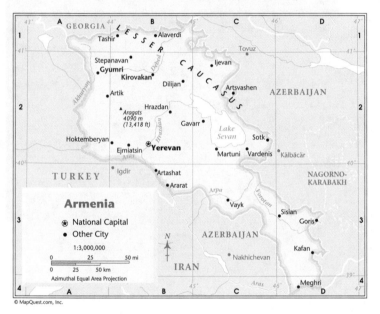

© MapQuest.com, Inc.

Azerbaijan

Capital: Baku
Area: 33,400 sq. mi.
86,528 sq. km.
Population: 8,370,000
Largest City: Baku
Language: Azerbaijani
Monetary Unit: Azerbaijani manat

Azerbaijan:
Map Index

Cities and Towns
Ağcabädi	B2
Ağdam	B3
Ağstafa	A2
Älät	C3
Ali Bayramli	C3
Astara	C3
Baku, capital	C2
Balakän	B2
Bärdä	B2
Biläsuvar	C3
Gäncä	B2
Göyçay	B2
Kälbäcär	B2
Länkäran	B2
Mingäçevir	B2
Nakhichevan	A3
Quba	C2
Şahbuz	A3
Şaki	B2
Salyan	C3
Sumqayit	C2
Tovuz	A2
Xaçmaz	C2
Xankändi	B3
Yevlax	B2
Zaqatala	B2

Other Features
Abşeron, peninsula	C2
Aras, river	B3
Bazardüzü Daği, mt.	B2
Caucasus, range	A1
Karabakh, canal	C2
Kür, river	A2, C2
Kür-Aras, lowland	B2
Lesser Caucasus, range	A2
Mingäçevir, reservoir	B2
Nagorno-Karabakh, autonomous region	B2
Samur, river	B2
Talish, mts.	C3

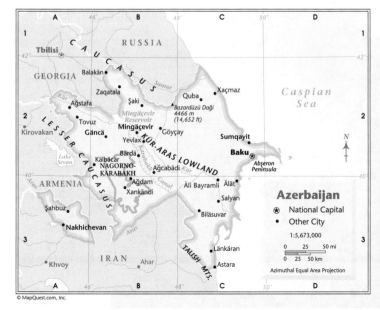

© MapQuest.com, Inc.

Estonia:
Map Index

Cities and Towns
Haapsalu B2
Kärdla B1
Keila C1
Kohtla-Järve D1
Kunda D1
Kuressaare B2
Mustvee D2
Narva E1
Paldiski C1
Pärnu C2
Rapla C1
Tallinn, *capital* C1
Tapa C1
Tartu D2
Tõrva C2
Türi C2

Valga D3
Viljandi C2
Virtsu B2
Võru D3

Other Features
Baltic, *sea* A1
Finland, *gulf* C1
Hiiumaa, *island* B2
Irbe, *strait* A3
Munamägi, *mt.* D3
Narva, *river* D1
Pärnu, *river* C2
Pedja, *river* D2
Peipus, *lake* D2
Pskov, *lake* D3
Riga, *gulf* B3
Saaremaa, *island* B2
Vörts Järv, *lake* D2

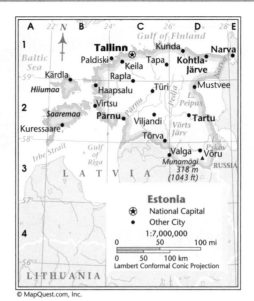

Estonia

Capital: Tallinn
Area: 17,413 sq. mi.
45,111 sq. km.
Population: 1,323,000
Largest City: Tallinn
Language: Estonian
Monetary Unit: Kroon

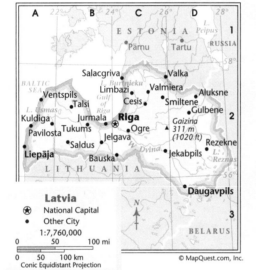

Latvia

Capital: Riga
Area: 24,900 sq. mi.
64,508 sq. km.
Population: 2,307,000
Largest City: Riga
Language: Latvian
Monetary Unit: Lat

Latvia:
Map Index

Cities and Towns
Aluksne D2
Bauska C2
Cesis C2
Daugavpils D3
Gulbene D2
Jekabpils C2
Jelgava B2
Jurmala B2
Kuldiga A2
Liepāja A2
Limbazi C2
Ogre C2
Pavilosta A2
Rezekne D2
Riga, *capital* C2
Salacgriva C2
Saldus B2
Smiltene C2
Talsi B2
Tukums B2
Valka C2
Valmiera C2
Ventspils A2

Other Features
Baltic, *sea* A2
Burtnieku, *lake* C2
Gaizina, *mt.* C2
Reznas, *lake* D2
Riga, *gulf* B2
Usmas, *lake* B2
Western Dvina, *river* C2

Lithuania

Capital: Vilnius
Area: 25,213 sq. mi.
65,319 sq. km.
Population: 3,444,000
Largest City: Vilnius
Language: Lithuanian
Monetary Unit: Litas

Lithuania:
Map Index

Cities and Towns
Alytus C2
Biržai C1
Druskininkai B2
Jonava C2
Jurbarkas B2
Kaunas B2
Kėdainiai B2
Klaipėda A2
Kretinga A2
Kuršėnai B1
Marijampolė B2
Mažeikiai B1
Naujoji Akmenė B1
Palanga A2
Panevėžys C2
Radviliškis B2
Šiauliai B2
Šilalė B2

Šilutė A2
Tauragė B2
Telšiai B2
Ukmergė C2
Utena C2
Vilkaviškis B2
Vilnius, *capital* C2

Other Features
Baltic, *sea* A2
Courland, *lagoon* A2
Dubysa, *river* B2
Juozapines, *mt.* C2
Jura, *river* A2
Merkys, *river* C2
Minija, *river* A2
Mūša, *river* B1
Nemunas, *river* A2, C2
Neris, *river* C2
Nevėžis, *river* B2
Šventoji, *river* C2
Venta, *river* B1

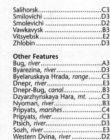

Belarus

Capital: Minsk
Area: 80,134 sq. mi.
207,601 sq. km.
Population: 9,895,000
Largest City: Minsk
Languages: Belarussian, Russian
Monetary Unit: Belarusian ruble

Belarus:
Map Index

Cities and Towns
Asipovichy D3
Babruysk D3
Baranavichy C3
Brest A3
Homyel E3
Hrodna A3
Krychaw E3
Lida B3
Mahilyow E3
Maladzyechna C2
Mazyr D3
Minsk, *capital* C3
Orsha E2
Pastavy C2
Pinsk C3
Polotsk D2
Rechytsa E3

Salihorsk C3
Smilovichi D3
Smolevichi D2
Vawkavysk B3
Vitsyebsk E2
Zhlobin D3

Other Features
Bug, *river* A3
Byarezina, *river* D3
Byelaruskaya Hrada, *range* C3
Dnepr, *river* E3
Dnepr-Bug, *canal* C3
Dzyarzhynskaya Hara, *mt.* C3
Nyoman, *river* B3
Pripyats, *marshes* C4
Pripyats, *river* C3
Ptsich, *river* D3
Sozh, *river* E3
Western Dvina, *river* D2

Ukraine:
Map Index

Cities and Towns
Balaklava C4
Belaya Tserkov C2
Berdyansk D3
Cherkassy C2
Chernivtsi B2
Chernigov C1
Chornobyl' C2
Dneprodzerzhinsk D2
Dnipropetrovsk D2
Donetsk D2
Feodosiya D3

Gorlovka D2
Ivano-Frankovsk A2
Izmail B3
Kachovka C3
Kerch D3
Kharkiv D1
Kherson C3
Khmelnytskyy B2
Khust A2
Kiev, *capital* C1
Kirovograd C2
Konotop C1
Korosten B1
Kotovsk B2
Kovel A1

Kramatorsk D2
Kremenchug C2
Kryvyi Rih C2
Lisichansk D2
Luhansk D2
Lutsk B1
Lviv A2
Makeyevka D2
Mariupol D3
Melitopol D3
Mogilev Podolskiy B2
Mykolaiv C2
Nikopol C2
Odesa C3
Pervomaysk C2

Poltava C2
Priluki C1
Rovno B1
Sevastopol C4
Shostka C1
Simferopol C4
Sumy C1
Ternopol B2
Uman C2
Uzhgorod A2
Vinnitsa B2
Yalta C4
Yevpatoriya C3
Zaporizhzhia D2
Zhitomir B1

Other Features
Azov, *sea* D3
Black, *sea* C3
Bug, *river* B2
Carpathian, *mts.* A2
Crimean, *mts.* C4
Crimean, *peninsula* C3
Desna, *river* C1
Dneprodzerzhinsk, *reservoir* .. C2
Dnieper, *river* C1,C3
Dniester, *river* B2
Donets, *basin* D2
Donets, *river* D2
Kakhovka, *reservoir* C3

Karkinit, *bay* C3
Kerch, *strait* D3
Kiev, *reservoir* C1
Kremenchug, *reservoir* C2
Pripyat, *river* A1
Prut, *river* B2
Psel, *river* C1
Sluch, *river* B1
Southern Bug, *river* B2
Taganrog, *gulf* D3
Tisza, *river* A2
Volyno-Podol'skaya
Vozvyshennost, *uplands* B2
Vorskla, *river* C1

Ukraine

Capital: Kiev
Area: 233,100 sq. mi.
603,886 sq. km.
Population: 48,523,000
Largest City: Kiev
Languages: Ukrainian, Russian
Monetary Unit: Hryvnia

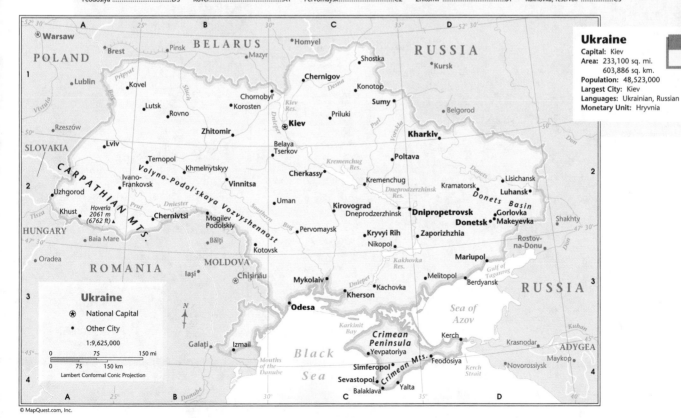

Slovenia

Capital: Ljubljana
Area: 7,821 sq. mi.
20,262 sq. km.
Population: 1,984,000
Largest City: Ljubljana
Languages: Slovenian, Serbo-Croatian
Monetary Unit: Tolar

Slovenia: Map Index

Cities and Towns

Celje	C2
Idrija	B2
Jesenice	B2
Kočevje	B3
Koper	A3
Kranj	B2
Krško	C3
Ljubljana, capital	B2
Maribor	C2
Murska Sobota	D2
Nova Gorica	A3
Novo Mesto	C3
Postojna	B3
Ptuj	C2

Other Features

Adriatic, sea	A3
Drava, river	C2
Julian Alps, mts.	A2
Krka, river	B3
Kupa, river	B3
Mura, river	C2
Sava, river	B2
Savinja, river	B2
Trieste, gulf	A3
Triglav, mt.	A2

© MapQuest.com, Inc.

Croatia

Capital: Zagreb
Area: 21,829 sq. mi.
56,552 sq. km.
Population: 4,428,000
Largest City: Zagreb
Language: Serbo-Croatian
Monetary Unit: Kuna

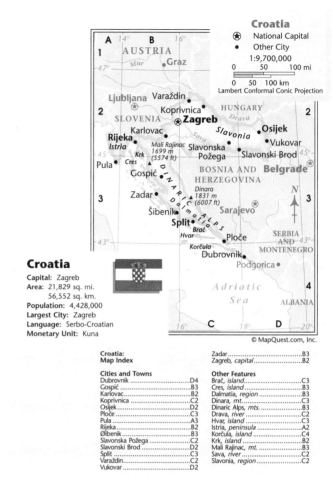

© MapQuest.com, Inc.

Croatia: Map Index

Cities and Towns

Dubrovnik	D4	Zadar	B3	
Gospić	B3	Zagreb, capital	B2	
Karlovac	B2			
Koprivnica	C2	**Other Features**		
Osijek	D2	Brač, island	C3	
Ploče	C3	Cres, island	B3	
Pula	A3	Dalmatia, region	B3	
Rijeka	B2	Dinara, mt.	C3	
Ølbenik	B3	Dinaric Alps, mts.	B3	
Slavonska Požega	C2	Drava, river	C2	
Slavonski Brod	D2	Hvar, island	C3	
Split	C3	Istria, peninsula	A2	
Varaždin	C2	Korčula, island	C4	
Vukovar	D2	Krk, island	B2	
		Mali Rajinac, mt.	B3	
		Sava, river	C2	
		Slavonia, region	C2	

Bosnia and Hercegovina: Map Index

Cities and Towns

Banja Luka	B1
Bihać	A1
Bijeljina	C1
Bosanska Gradiška	B1
Bosanska Krupa	A1
Brčko	B1
Bugojno	B1
Derventa	B1
Doboj	B1
Foča	B2
Gacko	B2
Goražde	B2
Gračanica	B1
Jajce	B1
Livno	B2
Mostar	B2
Pale	B2
Prijedor	A1
Sanski Most	A1
Sarajevo, capital	B2
Srebrenica	C1
Teslić	B1
Trebinje	B2
Tuzla	B1
Zavidovići	B1
Zenica	B1
Zvornik	C1

Other Features

Bosna, river	B1
Dinara, mt.	A2
Dinaric Alps, mts.	A1
Drina, river	C1
Neretva, river	B2
Sava, river	B1
Una, river	A1
Vrbas, river	B1

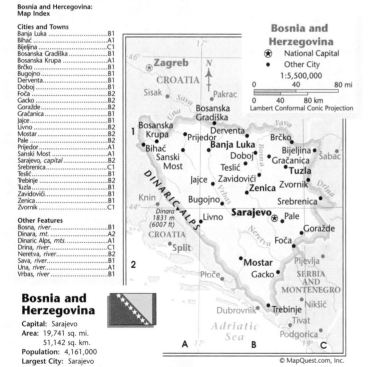

© MapQuest.com, Inc.

Bosnia and Herzegovina

Capital: Sarajevo
Area: 19,741 sq. mi.
51,142 sq. km.
Population: 4,161,000
Largest City: Sarajevo
Language: Serbo-Croatian
Monetary Unit: Marka

F.Y.R. Macedonia

Capital: Skopje
Area: 9,928 sq. mi.
25,720 sq. km.
Population: 2,056,000
Largest City: Skopje
Languages: Macedonian, Albanian, Serbo-Croatian, Turkish
Monetary Unit: Denar

F.Y.R. Macedonia: Map Index

Cities and Towns

Bitola	B2
Blatec	C2
Debar	A2
Gevgelija	C2
Kavadarci	C2
Kičevo	A2
Kočani	C2
Kruševo	B2
Kumanovo	B1
Ohrid	A2
Prilep	B2
Skopje, capital	B2
Štip	C2
Struga	A2
Strumica	C2
Tetovo	A1
Titov Veles	B2

Other Features

Belasica, mts.	C2
Bregalnica, river	C2
Crna, river	B2
Crna Gora, mts.	B1
Doiran, lake	C2
Jakupica, mts.	B2
Korab, mt.	A2
Kožuf, mts.	C2
Nidže, mts.	B3
Ogražden, mts.	C2
Ohrid, lake	A3
Prespa, lake	B3
Treska, river	B2
Vardar, river	C2

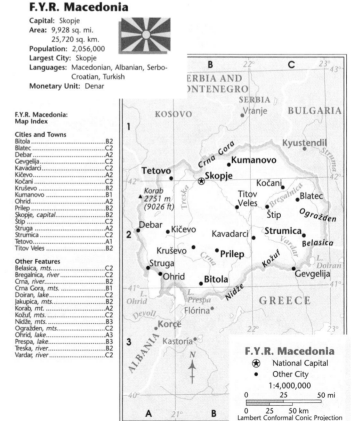

© MapQuest.com, Inc.

Albania

⊛ National Capital
• Other City

1:3,750,000

0   15   30 mi
0   15   30 km

Lambert Conformal
Conic Projection

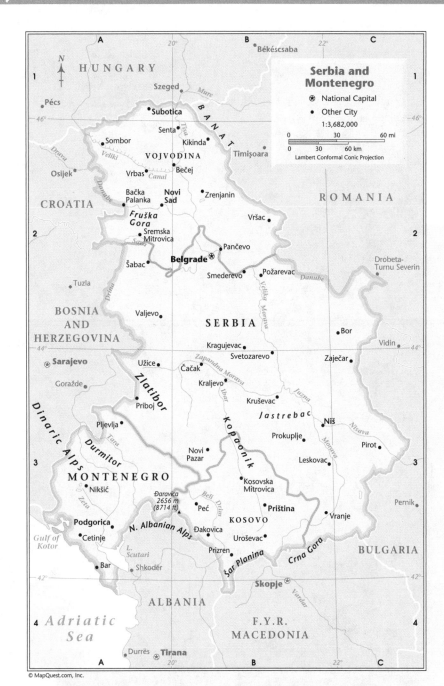

Serbia and Montenegro

⊛ National Capital
• Other City

1:3,682,000

0   30   60 mi
0   30   60 km

Lambert Conformal Conic Projection

**Albania:
Map Index**

Cities and Towns

Berat	A3
Durrës	A2
Elbasan	B2
Ersekë	B3
Fier	A3
Gjirokastër	B3
Kavajë	A2
Korçë	B3
Krujë	A2
Kukës	B1
Laç	A2
Lushnjë	A3
Peshkopi	B2
Pogradec	B3
Pukë	A1
Sarandë	A4
Shëngjin	A2
Shkodër	A1
Tirana, capital	A2
Vlorë	A3

Other Features

Adriatic, sea	A2
Buene, river	A2
Devoll, river	B3

Drin, river	A1
Erzen, river	A2
Ionian, sea	A4
Korab, mt.	B2
Mat, river	B2
North Albanian Alps, range	A1
Ohrid, lake	B2
Osum, river	B3
Otranto, strait	A3
Prespa, lake	C3
Scutari, lake	A1
Seman, river	A3
Shkumbin, river	A2
Vijosë, river	A3

Albania

Capital: Tirana
Area: 11,100 sq. mi.
  28,756 sq. km.
Population: 3,166,000
Largest City: Tirana
Languages: Albanian, Greek
Monetary Unit: Lek

**Serbia and Montenegro:
Map Index**

Internal Divisions

Kosovo (province)	B3
Montenegro (republic)	A3
Serbia (republic)	B2
Vojvodina (province)	A2

Cities and Towns

Bačka Palanka	A2
Bar	A3
Bečej	B2
Belgrade, capital	B2
Bor	C2
Čačak	B3
Cetinje	A3
Đakovica	A3
Kikinda	B2
Kosovska Mitrovica	B2
Kragujevac	B2
Kraljevo	B3
Kruševac	B3
Leskovac	B3
Nikšić	A3
Niš	B3
Novi Pazar	B3
Novi Sad	B2
Pančevo	B2
Peć	A3
Pirot	C3
Pljevlja	A3
Podgorica	A3

Požarevac	B2
Priboj	A3
Priština	B3
Prizren	B3
Prokuplje	B3
Šabac	A2
Senta	B2
Smederevo	B2
Sombor	A2
Sremska Mitrovica	A2
Subotica	A1
Svetozarevo	B3
Uroševac	B3
Užice	A3
Valjevo	A2
Vranje	B3
Vrbas	A2
Vršac	B2
Zaječar	C3
Zrenjanin	B2

Other Features

Adriatic, sea	A4
Balkan, mts.	C3
Beli Drim, river	B3
Crna Gora, mts.	B3
Danube, river	A2, B2
Đaravica, mt.	B3
Dinaric Alps, mts.	A3
Drina, river	A2
Durmitor, mts.	A3
Fruška Gora, mts.	B2
Ibar, river	B3

Jastrebac, mts.	B3
Južna, river	B3
Kopaonik, mts.	B3
Kotor, gulf	A3
Morava, river	B3
Nišava, river	C3
North Albanian Alps, mts.	A3
Šar Planina, mts.	B3
Sava, river	A2
Scutari, lake	A3
Tara, river	A3
Tisa, river	B2
Velika Morava, river	B2
Veliki, canal	A2
Zapandna Morava, river	A3
Zeta, river	A3
Zlatibor, mts.	A3

Serbia and Montenegro

Capital: Belgrade
Area: 39,449 sq. mi.
  102,199 sq. km.
Population: 10,527,000
Largest City: Belgrade
Language: Serbo-Croatian
Monetary Unit: New Yugoslav dinar, euro

© MapQuest.com, Inc.

Moldova

⊛ National Capital
● Other City

1:4,800,000

0   35   70 mi
0   35   70 km

Lambert Conformal Conic Projection

© MapQuest.com, Inc.

Moldova

Capital: Chişinău
Area: 13,012 sq. mi.
    33,710 sq. km.
Population: 4,267,000
Largest City: Chişinău
Languages: Moldovan, Russian
Monetary Unit: Moldovan leu

Moldova:
Map Index

Cities and Towns
Bălţi A2
Basarabeasca B2
Bender (Tighina) B2
Briceni A1
Cahul B3
Căuşeni B2
Chişinău, *capital* B2
Comrat B2
Dubăsari B2
Făleşti A2
Floreşti B2
Leova B2
Orhei B2
Rîbniţa B2
Rîşcani A2
Soroca B1
Tiraspol B2
Ungheni A2

Other Features
Botna, *river* B2
Bugeac, *region* B3
Codri, *region* A3
Cogalnic, *river* B2
Dnestr, *river* B2
Ialpug, *river* B2
Prut, *river* A1, B3
Raut, *river* B2

Bulgaria:
Map Index

Administrative Regions
Blagoevgrad B4
Burgas F3
Dobrich F2
Gabrovo D3
Haskovo D4
Jambol E3
Kardzhali D4
Kjustendil A3
Lovech C3
Montana B2
Pazardzhik C3
Pernik A3
Pleven C2
Plovdiv C3
Razgrad E2
Ruse D2
Shumen F2
Silistra F2
Sliven E3
Smoljan C4
Sofia B3
Sofia City B3
Stara Zagora D3
Targovishte E2
Varna F2
Veliko Tarnovo D2
Vidin A2
Vraca B2

Cities and Towns
Asenovgrad C3
Aytos F3
Blagoevgrad B4
Burgas F3
Dimitrovgrad D3
Dobrich F2
Elkhovo E3
Gabrovo D3
Haskovo D4
Jambol E3
Kardzhali D4
Kazanlŭk D3
Kjustendil A3
Kozloduy B2
Lom B2
Lovech C2
Madan C4
Montana B2
Oryakhovo B2
Panagyurishte C3
Pazardzhik C3
Pernik B3
Petrich B4

Pleven C2
Plovdiv C3
Primorsko F3
Razgrad E2
Ruse D2
Samokov B3
Shumen E2
Silistra F1
Sliven E3
Smoljan C4
Sofia, *capital* B3
Stara Zagora D3
Svilengrad E4
Svishtov D2
Targovishte E2
Varna F2
Veliko Tarnovo D2
Vidin A2
Vratsa B2

Other Features
Arda, *river* C4
Balkan, *mts.* B2
Danube, *river* B2
Golyama Kamchiya, *river* .. E2
Iskŭr, *river* C2
Kamchiya, *river* F2
Luda Kamchiya, *river.* E3
Ludogorie, *region* E2
Maritsa, *river* D3
Mesta, *river* B4
Musala, *mt.* B3
Ogosta, *river* B2
Osŭm, *river* C3
Rhodope, *mts.* C4
Rila, *mts.* B3
Sredna Gora, *mts.* C3
Struma, *river* A3
Stryama, *river* C3
Thrace, *region* D4
Thracian, *plain* C3
Tundzha, *river* E3
Yantra, *river* D2

Bulgaria

Capital: Sofia
Area: 42,855 sq. mi.
    111,023 sq. km.
Population: 7,897,000
Largest City: Sofia
Language: Bulgarian
Monetary Unit: Lev

Bulgaria

⊛ National Capital
● Other City

1:3,210,000

0   25   50   75 mi
0   25   50   75 km

Lambert Conformal Conic Projection

© MapQuest.com, Inc.

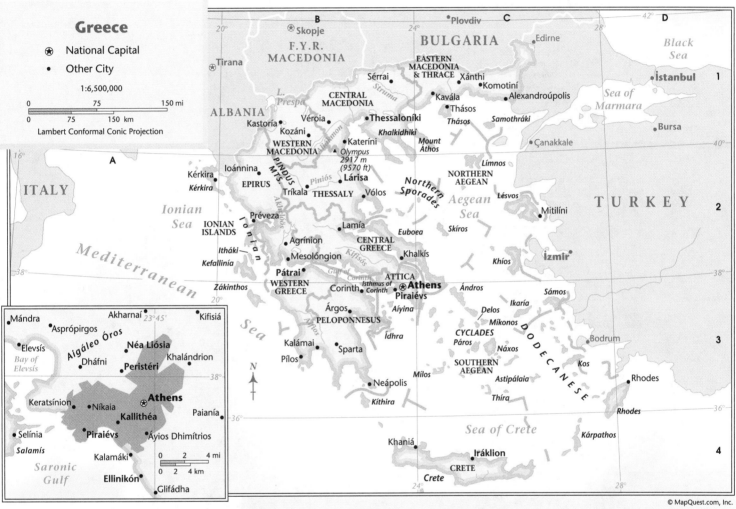

Greece

⊛ National Capital

• Other City

1:6,500,000

| 0 | 75 | 150 mi |
| 0 | 75 | 150 km |

Lambert Conformal Conic Projection

© MapQuest.com, Inc.

**Greece:
Map Index**

Regions

Attica	B2
Central Greece	B2
Central Macedonia	B1
Crete	C4
Eastern Macedonia and Thrace	C1
Epirus	B2
Ionian Islands	B2
Northern Aegean	C2
Peloponnesus	B3
Southern Aegean	C3
Thessaly	B2
Western Greece	B3
Western Macedonia	B1

Cities and Towns

Agrínion	B2
Akharnaí	Inset
Alexandroúpolis	C1
Argos	B3
Asprópirgos	Inset
Athens, capital	B3, Inset
Áyios Dhimítrios	Inset
Corinth	B3
Dháfni	Inset
Elevsís	Inset
Ellinikón	Inset
Glifádha	Inset
Ioánnina	B2
Iráklion	C4
Kalámai	B3

Kalamáki	Inset
Kallithéa	Inset
Kastoría	B1
Kateríni	B1
Kavála	C1
Keratsínion	Inset
Kérkira	A2
Khalándrion	Inset
Khalkís	B2
Khaniá	B4
Kifisiá	Inset
Komotiní	C1
Kozáni	B1
Lamía	B2
Lárisa	B2
Mándra	Inset
Mesolóngion	B2
Mitilíni	C2
Néa Liósia	Inset
Neápolis	B3
Níkaia	Inset
Paianía	Inset
Pátrai	B2
Peristéri	Inset
Pílos	B3
Piraiévs	B3, Inset
Préveza	B2
Rhodes	D3
Selínia	Inset
Sérrai	B1
Sparta	B3
Thásos	C1
Thessaloníki	B1
Tríkala	B2
Véroia	B1

Vólos	B2
Xánthi	C1

Other Features

Aegean, sea	C2
Aigáleo, mts.	Inset
Aíyina, sea	B3
Akhelóos, river	B2
Alfíos, river	B3
Aliákmon, river	B1
Ándros, island	C3
Astipálaia, island	C3
Áthos, mt.	C1
Corinth, gulf	B2
Corinth, isthmus	B3
Crete, island	C4
Crete, sea	C4
Cyclades, islands	C3
Delos, island	C3
Dodecanese, islands	C3
Elevsís, bay	Inset
Euboea, island	B2
Idhra, island	B3
Ikaría, island	C3
Ionian, islands	B2
Ionian, sea	A2
Itháki, island	B2
Kárpathos, island	C4
Kefallinía, island	B2
Kérkira, island	A2
Khalkidhikí, peninsula	B1
Khíos, island	C2
Kifissós, river	B2
Kíthira, island	B3
Kos, island	C3

Lésvos, island	C2
Límnos, island	C2
Míkonos, island	C3
Mílos, island	C3
Náxos, island	C3
Northern Sporades, islands	B2
Olympus, mt.	B1
Páros, island	C3
Pindus, mts.	B2
Piniós, river	B2
Prespa, lake	B1
Rhodes, island	D3
Salamís, island	Inset
Sámos, island	C3
Samothráki, island	C1
Saronic, gulf	Inset
Skíros, island	C2
Struma, river	B1
Thásos, island	C1
Thíra, island	C3
Zákinthos, island	B3

Greece

Capital: Athens
Area: 50,949 sq. mi.
131,992 sq. km.
Population: 10,976,000
Largest City: Athens
Language: Greek
Monetary Unit: Euro

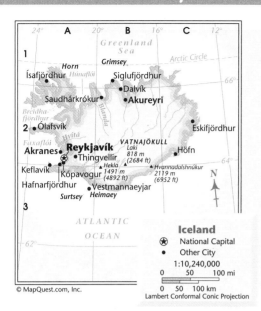

Iceland

Capital: Reykjavík
Area: 36,699 sq. mi.
95,075 sq. km.
Population: 290,000
Largest City: Reykjavík
Language: Icelandic
Monetary Unit: Icelandic króna

Iceland: Map Index

Cities and Towns

Akranes	A2
Akureyri	B2
Dalvík	B2
Eskifjördhur	C2
Hafnarfjördhur	A3
Höfn	C2
Ísafjördhur	A1
Keflavík	A3
Kópavogur	A2
Ólafsvík	A2
Reykjavík, capital	A2
Saudhárkrókur	B2
Siglufjördhur	B1
Thingvellir	A2
Vestmannaeyjar	A3

Other Features

Blanda, river	B2
Breidhafjördhur, fjord	A2
Faxaflói, bay	A2
Greenland, sea	B1
Grimsey, island	B1
Heimaey, island	A3
Hekla, volcano	B3
Horn, cape	A1
Húnaflói, bay	A2
Hvannadalshnúkur, mt.	B3
Hvítá, river	A2
Laki, volcano	B2
Surtsey, island	A3
Vatnajökull, ice cap	B2

Norway

Capital: Oslo
Area: 125,050 sq. mi.
323,964 sq. km.
Population: 4,533,000
Largest City: Oslo
Language: Norwegian
Monetary Unit: Norwegian krone

Norway: Map Index

Cities and Towns

Ålesund	B3
Alta	E1
Arendal	B4
Bergen	B3
Bodø	C2
Drammen	C4
Dumbås	B3
Egersund	B4
Florø	A3
Fredrikstad	C4
Gjøvik	C3
Hamar	C3
Hammerfest	E1
Harstad	D2
Haugesund	B4
Kinsarvik	B3
Kirkenes	F2
Kristiansand	B4
Kristiansund	B3
Lakselv	F1
Leikanger	B3
Lillehammer	C3
Mo	C2
Molde	B3
Mosjøen	C2
Moss	C4
Namsos	C3
Narvik	D2
Oslo, capital	C3
Skien	B4
Stavanger	B4
Steinkjer	C3
Tromsø	D2
Trondheim	C3
Vadsø	F1

Other Features

Barents, sea	E1
Boknafjord, fjord	B4
Dovrefjell, mts.	B3
Finnmark, plateau	E2
Glåma, river	C3
Glittertinden, mt.	B3
Hallingdal, valley	B3
Hardangerfjord, fjord	B4
Hardangervidda, plateau	B3
Jotunheimen, mts.	B3
Lofoten, islands	C2
Mjøsa, lake	C3
North, cape	F1
North, sea	A3
Norwegian, sea	A2
Oslofjord, fjord	C4
Skagerrak, strait	B4
Sognafjord, fjord	B3
Tana, river	F1
Trondheimsfjord, fjord	B3
Vesterålen, islands	C2

Finland: Map Index

Internal Divisions
Eastern Finland (province) C2
Lapland (province) C1
Oulu (province) C1
Southern Finland (province) C2
Western Finland (province) B2
Central Finland (region) C2
Central Ostrobothnia (region) B2
Etelä-Savo (region) C2
Häme (region) B2
Itä-Uusimaa (region) C2
Kainuu (region) C2
Kymenlaakso (region) C2
North Karelia (region) C2
Northern Ostrobothnia
(region) B2
Ostrobothnia (region) B2
Päijät Häme (region) C2
Pirkanmaa (region) B2
Satakunta (region) B2
Savo (region) C2
South Karelia (region) C2
South Ostrobothnia (region) B2
South-West Finland (region) B2
Uusimaa (region) B2

Cities and Towns
Espoo B2
Hämeenlinna B2
Hangö B3
Helsinki, capital B2
Hyvinkää B2
Iisalmi C2
Imatra C2
Ivalo C1
Jakobstad B2
Jämsä C2
Joensuu C2
Jyväskylä C2
Kajaani C2
Kemi B1
Kemijärvi C1
Kokkola B2
Kolari B1
Kotka C2
Kouvola C2
Kuopio C2
Lahti C2
Lappeenranta C2
Lieksa D2
Mariehamn (Maarianhamina) A2
Mikkeli C2
Muonio B1
Oulu C1
Pori B2
Raahe B2
Rauma B2
Rovaniemi C1
Salo B2
Savonlinna C2
Seinäjoki B2
Tampere B2
Tornio B1
Turku B2
Vaasa B2
Vantaa C2
Varkaus C2
Ylivieska B2

Other Features
Åland, islands B2
Baltic, sea B3
Bothnia, gulf B2
Finland, gulf C3
Haltiatunturi, mt. B1
Iijoki, river C1
Inari, lake C1
Kemijoki, river C1
Kivi, lake C2
Lapland, region B1
Lokka, reservoir C1
Muoniojoki, river B1
Näsi, lake B2
Oulu, lake C2
Oulujoki, river C2
Ounasjoki, river B1
Päijänne, lake C2
Pielinen, lake C2
Saimaa, lake C2
Tenojoki, river C1
Torniojoki, river B1
Ylikitka, lake C1

Finland
- National Capital
- Other City

1:10,000,000

0   50   100   150 mi
0 50 100 150 200 km
Lambert Conformal Conic Projection

Finland
Capital: Helsinki
Area: 130,559 sq. mi.
338,236 sq. km.
Population: 5,207,000
Largest City: Helsinki
Languages: Finnish, Swedish
Monetary Unit: Euro

Sweden
- National Capital
- Other City

1:11,333,000

0   50   100   150 mi
0 50 100 150 km
Lambert Conformal Conic Projection

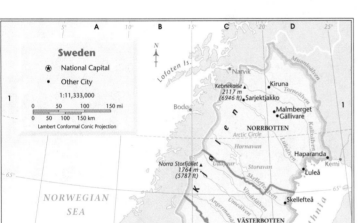

Sweden
Capital: Stockholm
Area: 173,732 sq. mi.
450,083 sq. km.
Population: 8,876,000
Largest City: Stockholm
Language: Swedish
Monetary Unit: Swedish krona

Sweden: Map Index

Counties
Blekinge C3
Dalarna B2
Gävleborg C2
Gotland C3
Halland B3
Jämtland B2
Jönköping B3
Kalmar C3
Kronoberg B3
Malmöhus B3
Norrbotten C1
Örebro B3
Östergötland C3
Skåne B3
Södermanland C3
Stockholm C3
Uppsala C2
Värmland B3
Västerbotten C2
Västernorrland C2
Västmanland C3
Västra Götaland B3

Cities and Towns
Borås B3
Eskilstuna C3
Falun C2
Gällivare D1
Gävle C2
Göteborg B3
Halmstad B3
Haparanda D1
Härnösand C2
Helsingborg B3
Hudiksvall C2
Jönköping B3
Kalmar C3
Karlskrona C3
Karlstad B3
Kiruna D1
Kristianstad B3
Kristinehamn B3
Linköping C3
Luleå D1
Lund B3
Malmberget D1
Malmö B3
Norrköping C3
Örebro B3
Örnsköldsvik C2
Orrefors C3
Östersund B2
Sarjektjakko C1
Skellefteå D2
Söderhamn C2
Stockholm, capital C3
Sundsvall C2
Trollhättan B3
Uddevalla B3
Umeå D2
Uppsala C3

Västerås C3
Växjö B3
Visby C3

Other Features
Ångermanälven, river C2
Baltic, sea C3
Bothnia, gulf D2
Dalälven, river C2
Faxälven, river C2
Göta, canal B3
Gotland, island C3
Hornavan, lake C1
Indalsälven, river B2
Kalixälven, river D1
Kattegat, strait B3
Kebnekaise, mt. C1
Kjölen, mts. C1
Klarälven, river B2
Ljusnanälven, river B2
Luleälven, river D1
Mälaren, lake C3
Muonioälven, river D1
Norra Storfjället, mt. C1
Öland, island B3
Öresund, sound B3
Osterdalälven, river B2
Skagerrak, strait A3
Skellefteälven, river C1
Småland, region B3
Storavan, lake C1
Storsjön, lake B2
Torneälven, river D1
Uddjaur, lake C1
Umeälven, river C1
Vänern, lake B3
Vättern, lake B3
Vindelälven, river C2

© MapQuest.com, Inc.

MAJOR CITIES

Algeria	(metro)
Algiers	2,761,000
Oran	693,000
Constantine	492,000
Angola	(metro)
Luanda	2,697,000
Benin	
Cotonou	750,000
Porto-Novo	225,000
Botswana	
Gaborone	225,000
Burkina Faso	(metro)
Ouagadougou	831,000
Burundi	
Bujumbura	346,440
Cameroon	(metro)
Douala	1,642,000
Yaoundé	1,420,000
Cape Verde	
Praia	82,000
Central African Republic	
Bangui	666,000
Chad	(metro)
N'Djamena	735,000
Comoros	(metro)
Moroni	49,000
Congo, Democratic Republic of the	(metro)
Kinshasa	5,054,000
Lubumbashi	965,000
Congo, Republic of the	
Brazzaville (metro)	1,306,000
Côte d'Ivoire	(metro)
Abidjan	3,956,000
Yamoussoukro	107,000
Djibouti	(metro)
Djibouti	542,000
Egypt	(metro)
Cairo	9,462,000
Alexandria	3,506,000
Shubra al-Khaymah	937,000
Equatorial Guinea	
Malabo	33,000
Eritrea	
Asmara	503,000
Ethiopia	(metro)
Addis Ababa	2,645,000
Gabon	
Libreville	573,000
The Gambia	
Banjul	418,000
Ghana	(metro)
Accra	1,868,000
Guinea	(metro)
Conakry	1,232,000
Guinea-Bissau	
Bissau	292,000
Kenya	(metro)
Nairobi	2,243,000
Mombasa	462,000

Lesotho	
Maseru	271,000
Liberia	(metro)
Monrovia	491,000
Libya	(metro)
Tripoli	1,733,000
Benghazi	829,000
Madagascar	(metro)
Antananarivo	1,603,000
Malawi	
Blantyre	2,000,000
Lilongwe	523,000
Mali	(metro)
Bamako	1,161,000
Mauritania	
Nouakchott	626,000
Mauritius	
Port Louis	176,000
Morocco	(metro)
Casablanca	3,357,000
Rabat	1,616,000
Fez	907,000
Marrakech	822,000
Mozambique	(metro)
Maputo	1,094,000
Namibia	
Windhoek	216,000
Niger	(metro)
Niamey	775,000
Nigeria	(metro)
Lagos	8,665,000
Ibadan	1,549,000
Ogbomosho	809,000
Abuja	420,000
Rwanda	
Kigali	412,000
São Tomé & Príncipe	
São Tomé	67,000
Senegal	(metro)
Dakar	2,078,000
Seychelles	(metro)
Victoria	30,000
Sierra Leone	(metro)
Freetown	800,000
Somalia	(metro)
Mogadishu	1,157,000
South Africa	(metro)
Johannesburg	2,950,000
Cape Town	2,930,000
Durban	2,391,000
Pretoria	1,590,000
Port Elizabeth	1,006,000
Bloemfontein	364,000
Sudan	(metro)
Khartoum	2,853,000
Omdurman	1,271,000
Swaziland	
Mbabane	80,000
Tanzania	(metro)
Dar es-Salaam	2,115,000
Dodoma	180,000
Togo	
Lomé	600,000
Tunisia	(metro)
Tunis	1,927,000
Uganda	(metro)
Kampala	1,274,000
Western Sahara	
el-Aaiún	207,000
Zambia	(metro)
Lusaka	1,653,000
Zimbabwe	(metro)
Harare	1,791,000
Bulawayo	824,000

International comparability of city population data is limited by various data inconsistencies.

© MapQuest.com, Inc.

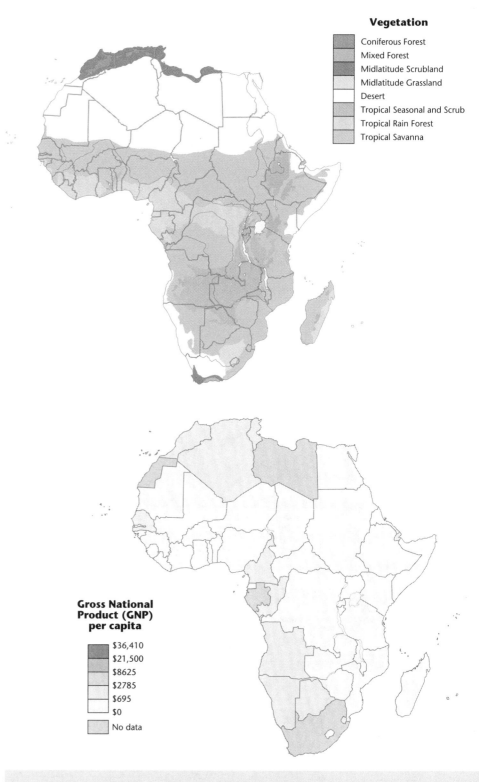

Vegetation

- Coniferous Forest
- Mixed Forest
- Midlatitude Scrubland
- Midlatitude Grassland
- Desert
- Tropical Seasonal and Scrub
- Tropical Rain Forest
- Tropical Savanna

Gross National Product (GNP) per capita

- $36,410
- $21,500
- $8625
- $2785
- $695
- $0
- No data

Africa: Population, by nation (in millions)

NIGERIA	EGYPT	ETHIOPIA	CONGO, DEM. REP.	S. AFR.	TANZ.	SUDAN	KENYA	ALGERIA	MOROC.	All other African countries
124.0	71.9	70.7	52.8	40.0	37.0	33.6	32.0	31.8	30.6	333.0

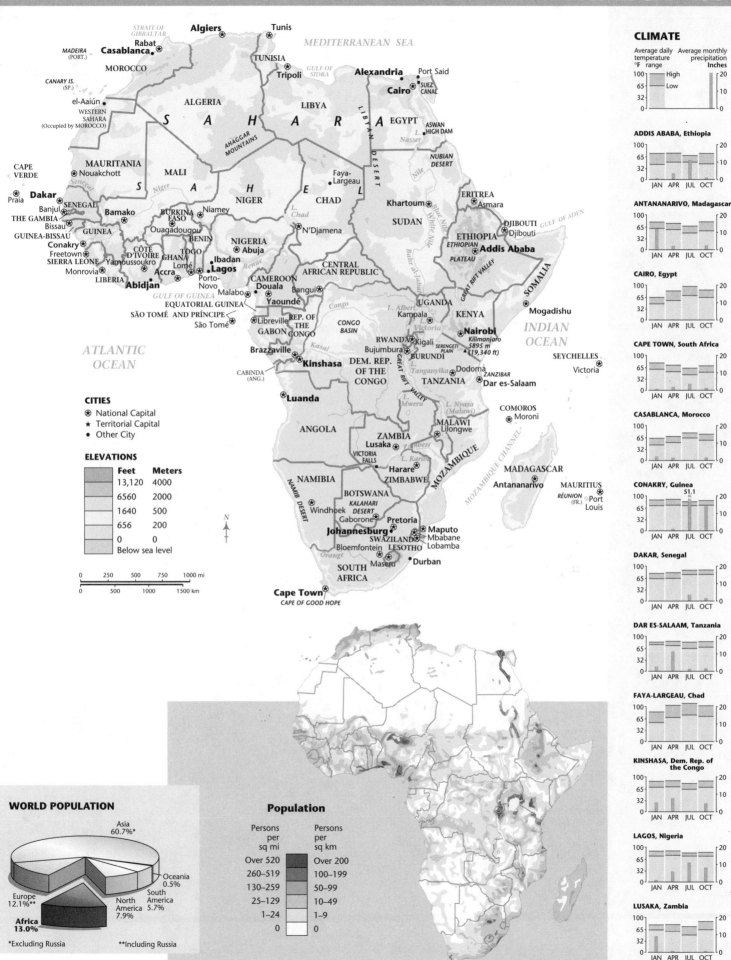

CITIES

⊛ National Capital
★ Territorial Capital
• Other City

ELEVATIONS

Feet	Meters
13,120	4000
6560	2000
1640	500
656	200
0	0
	Below sea level

CLIMATE

Average daily
temperature
°F range

Average monthly
precipitation
Inches

High
Low

ADDIS ABABA, Ethiopia
ANTANANARIVO, Madagascar
CAIRO, Egypt
CAPE TOWN, South Africa
CASABLANCA, Morocco
CONAKRY, Guinea
DAKAR, Senegal
DAR ES-SALAAM, Tanzania
FAYA-LARGEAU, Chad
KINSHASA, Dem. Rep. of the Congo
LAGOS, Nigeria
LUSAKA, Zambia

WORLD POPULATION

Asia 60.7%*
Oceania 0.5%
Europe 12.1%**
North America 7.9%
South America 5.7%
Africa 13.0%

*Excluding Russia
**Including Russia

Population

Persons per sq mi	Persons per sq km
Over 520	Over 200
260–519	100–199
130–259	50–99
25–129	10–49
1–24	1–9
0	0

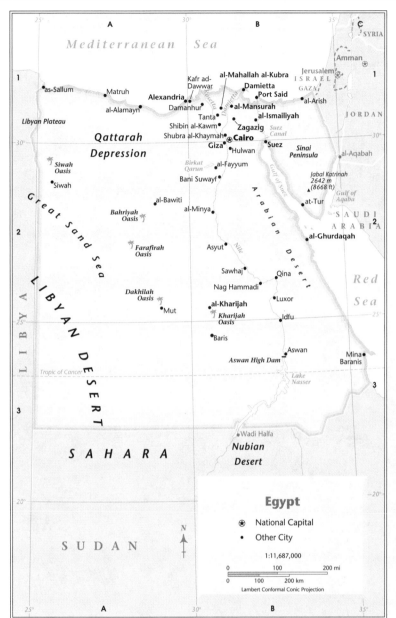

Egypt

Capital: Cairo
Area: 385,229 sq. mi.
1,998,003 sq. km.
Population: 71,931,000
Largest City: Cairo
Language: Arabic
Monetary Unit: Egyptian pound

Egypt: Map Index

Cities and Towns

Alamayn, al- A1
Alexandria A1
Arish, al- B1
Aswan B3
Asyut B2
Bani Suwayf B2
Baris B3
Bawiti, al- A2
Cairo, capital B1
Damanhur B1
Damietta B1
Fayyum, al- B2
Ghurdaqah, al- B2
Giza B2
Hulwan B2
Idfu B3
Ismailiyah, al- B1
Kafr ad-Dawwar B1
Kharijah, al- B2
Luxor B2
Mahallah al-Kubra, al- B1
Mansurah, al- B1
Matruh A1
Mina Baranis C3
Minya, al- B2
Mut A2
Nag Hammadi B2
Port Said B1
Qina B2
Sallum, as- A1
Sawhaj B2
Shibin al-Kawm B1
Shubra al-Khaymah B1
Siwah A2
Suez B2
Tanta B1
Tur, at- B2
Zagazig B1

Other Features

Aqaba, gulf B2
Arabian, desert B2
Aswan High, dam B3
Bahriyah, oasis A2
Birkat Qarun, lake B2
Dakhilah, oasis A2
Damietta, river B1
Farafirah, oasis A2
Great Sand Sea, desert............A2
Jabal Katrinah, mt. B2
Kharijah, oasis B2
Libyan, desert A2
Libyan, plateau A1
Nasser, lake B3
Nile, river B2
Qattarah, depression A2
Red, sea C2
Rosetta, river B1
Sahara, desert A3
Sinai, peninsula B2
Siwah, oasis A2
Suez, canal B1
Suez, gulf B2

Egypt
⊛ National Capital
• Other City
1:11,687,000
0   100   200 mi
0 100 200 km
Lambert Conformal Conic Projection

© MapQuest.com, Inc.

Libya

Capital: Tripoli
Area: 679,359 sq. mi.
1,759,997 sq. km.
Population: 5,551,000
Largest City: Tripoli
Language: Arabic
Monetary Unit: Libyan dinar

Libya: Map Index

Cities and Towns

Ajdabiya D1
Awbari B2
Bani Walid B1
Bayda, al- D1
Benghazi D1
Birak B2
Darnah D1
Ghadamis A1
Gharyan B1
Ghat B3
Jaghbub, al- D2
Jalu D2
Jawf, al- D3
Khums, al- B1
Marj, al- D1
Marsa al-Burayqah C1
Misurata C1
Murzuq B2
Qaryah ash-Sharqiyah, al- B1
Qatrun, al- B3
Sabha B2
Surt C1
Tobruk D1
Tripoli, capital B1
Uwaynat, al- B2
Waddan C2
Yafran B1
Zillah C2
Zuwarah B1

Other Features

Bette, mt. C3
Cyrenaica, region.....................D2
Fezzan, region C2
Hamra, al-, plateau B1
Haruj al-Aswad, al-, hills C2
Jabal Akakus, mts. B2
Jabal al-Uwaynat, mt. D3
Libyan, desert D2
Sahara, desert C1
Sidra, gulf C1
Tripolitania, region B1

Libya
⊛ National Capital
• Other City
1:20,200,000
0   100   200 mi
0 100 200 km
Lambert Conformal Conic Projection

© MapQuest.com, Inc.

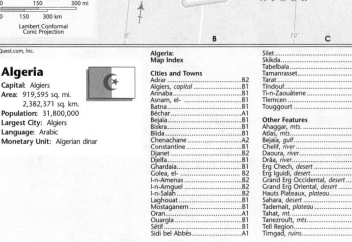

Algeria

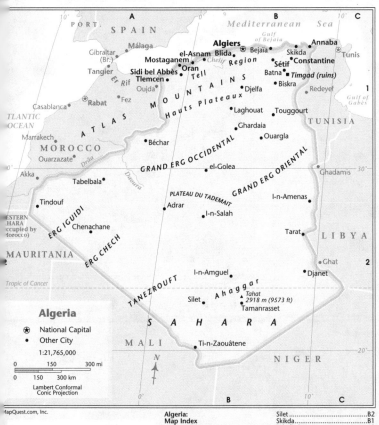

Capital: Algiers
Area: 919,595 sq. mi.
2,382,371 sq. km.
Population: 31,800,000
Largest City: Algiers
Language: Arabic
Monetary Unit: Algerian dinar

Algeria:
Map Index

Cities and Towns
Adrar B2
Algiers, *capital* B1
Annaba B1
Asnam, el- B1
Batna B1
Béchar A1
Bejaïa B1
Biskra B1
Blida B1
Chenachane A2
Constantine B1
Djanet B2
Djelfa B1
Ghardaïa B1
Golea, el- B2
I-n-Amenas B2
I-n-Amguel B2
I-n-Salah B2
Laghouat B1
Mostaganem B1
Oran A1
Ouargla B1
Sétif B1
Sidi bel Abbès A1

Silet B2
Skikda B1
Tabelbala A2
Tamanrasset B2
Tarat B2
Tindouf A2
Ti-n-Zaouâtene B2
Tlemcen A1
Touggourt B1

Other Features
Ahaggar, *mts.* B2
Atlas, *mts.* A1
Bejaïa, *gulf* B1
Chelif, *river* B1
Daoura, *river* A1
Drâa, *river* A1
Erg Chech, *desert* A2
Erg Iguidi, *desert* A2
Grand Erg Occidental, *desert* B1
Grand Erg Oriental, *desert* B2
Hauts Plateaux, *plateau* B1
Sahara, *desert* B2
Tademait, *plateau* B2
Tahat, *mt.* B2
Tanezrouft, *mts.* A2
Tell Region B1
Timgad, *ruins* B1

Tunisia

Capital: Tunis
Area: 63,378 sq. mi.
164,192 sq. km.
Population: 9,832,000
Largest City: Tunis
Language: Arabic
Monetary Unit: Tunisian dinar

Tunisia:
Map Index

Cities and Towns
Ariana C1
Béja B1
Bizerte B1
Gabès C3
Gafsa B2
Hammamat, al- C1
Houmt Souk C3
Kasserine B2
Kebili B3
Kef, el- B1
La Goulette C1
Mahdia C2
Menzel Bourguiba B1

Monastir C2
Nabeul C1
Nefta A3
Qayrawan, al- C2
Sfax C2
Sidi Bou Zid B2
Siliana B1
Sousse C2
Sukhayrah, as- B2
Tataouine C3
Tozeur B3
Tunis, *capital* C1
Zaghouan C1
Zarzis C3

Other Features
Atlas, *mts.* A1
Bon, *cape* C1
Carthage, *ruin* C1
Djerba, *island* C3
Djerid, *salt marsh* B3
Gabès, *gulf* C2
Galite, *island* B1
Grand Erg Oriental, *dune* B3
Hammamet, *gulf* C1
Kerkennah, *islands* C2
Majardah, *river* B1
Mediterranean, *sea* A1
Rharsa, *salt marsh* A2
Sahara, *desert* B4
Tabassah, *mts.* A1
Tunis, *gulf* C1

Morocco

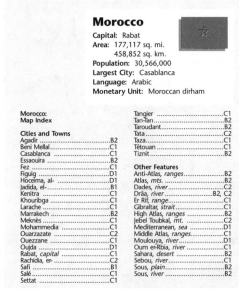

Capital: Rabat
Area: 177,117 sq. mi.
458,852 sq. km.
Population: 30,566,000
Largest City: Casablanca
Language: Arabic
Monetary Unit: Moroccan dirham

Morocco:
Map Index

Cities and Towns
Agadir B2
Beni Mellal C1
Casablanca C1
Essaouira B2
Fez C1
Figuig D1
Hoceima, al- D1
Jadida, el- B1
Kenitra C1
Khouribga C1
Larache C1
Marrakech B2
Meknès C1
Mohammedia C1
Ouarzazate C1
Ouezzane C1
Oujda D1
Rabat, *capital* C1
Rachidia, er- C2
Safi B1
Salé C1
Settat C1

Tangier C1
Tan-Tan B2
Taroudant B2
Tata C2
Taza C1
Tétouan C1
Tiznit B2

Other Features
Anti-Atlas, *ranges* B2
Atlas, *mts.* B2
Dades, *river* C2
Drâa, *river* B2, C2
Er Rif, *range* C1
Gibraltar, *strait* C1
High Atlas, *ranges* C1
Jebel Toubkal, *mt.* B2
Mediterranean, *sea* D1
Middle Atlas, *ranges* C1
Moulouya, *river* C1
Oum er-Rbia, *river* B2
Sahara, *desert* B2
Sebou, *river* C1
Sous, *plain* B2
Sous, *river* B2

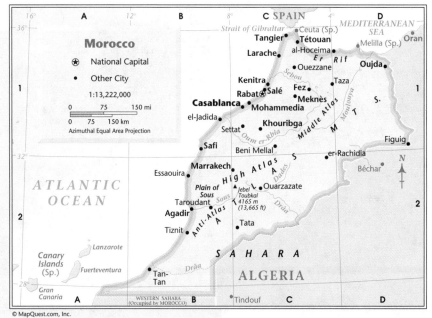

© MapQuest.com, Inc.

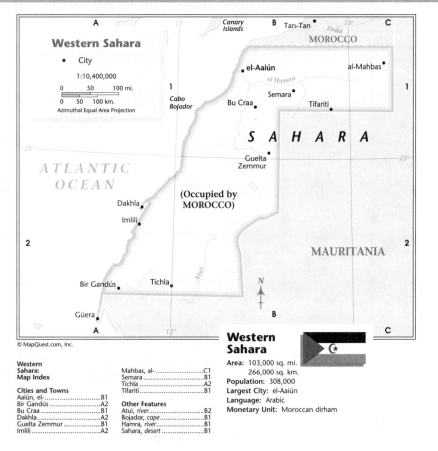

Western Sahara

- City

1:10,400,000

0 50 100 mi.
0 50 100 km.

Azimuthal Equal Area Projection

© MapQuest.com, Inc.

Cape Verde

⊛ National Capital
• Other City

1:6,110,000

0 40 80 mi.
0 40 80 km.

Lambert Conformal Conic Projection

© MapQuest.com, Inc.

Western Sahara

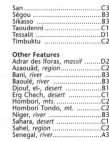

Area: 103,000 sq. mi.
266,000 sq. km.
Population: 308,000
Largest City: el-Aaiún
Language: Arabic
Monetary Unit: Moroccan dirham

Western Sahara:
Map Index

Cities and Towns
Aaiún, el-..................B1
Bir Gandús..............A2
Bu Craa..................B1
Dakhla....................A2
Guelta Zemmur........B1
Imlili......................A2

Mahbas, al-..............C1
Semara....................B1
Tichla......................A2
Tifariti....................B1

Other Features
Atui, river................B2
Bojador, cape..........B1
Hamra, river............B1
Sahara, desert..........B1

Cape Verde

Capital: Praia
Area: 1,557 sq. mi.
4,034 sq. km.
Population: 463,000
Largest City: Praia
Language: Portuguese
Monetary Unit: Escudo

Cape Verde:
Map Index

Cities and Towns
Curral Velho................D3
Mindelo......................B2
Pedra Lume.................D2

Pôrto Inglês................C3
Praia, capital..............C4
Ribeira Brava..............B2
Ribeira Grande............A1
Sal Rei......................D2
Santa Maria................D2
São Filipe..................B4
Tarrafal......................C3

Other Features
Boa Vista, island..........D2
Brava, island..............B4
Fogo, island................B4
Leeward Group............B3
Maio, island................C3
Pico do Cano, volcano..B4
Sal, island..................D2
Santa Luzia, island......B2
Santo Antão, island......A1
São Nicolau, island......B2
São Tiago, island..........C3
São Vicente, island......A2
Windward Group..........B2

Mali:
Map Index

Cities and Towns
Ansongo....................D2
Bafoulabé..................A3
Bamako, capital..........B3
Bougouni..................B3
Bourem....................C2
Djenné......................C3
Gao..........................D2
Goundam..................C2
Kayes........................A3
Kidal........................D2
Kita..........................B3
Koulikoro..................B3
Koutiala....................B3
Ménaka....................D2
Mopti........................C3
Niono........................B3
Nioro du Sahel............B2

San..........................C3
Ségou........................B3
Sikasso......................B3
Taoudenni..................C1
Tessalit......................D1
Timbuktu..................C2

Other Features
Adrar des Iforas, massif..D2
Azaouâd, region..........C2
Bani, river..................B3
Baoulé, river..............B3
Djouf, el-, desert..........B1
Erg Chech, desert........C1
Hombori, mts..............C2
Hombori Tondo, mt......C2
Niger, river................B3
Sahara, desert............C1
Sahel, region..............C2
Senegal, river............A3

Mali

Capital: Bamako
Area: 482,077 sq. mi.
1,248,904 sq. km.
Population: 13,007,000
Largest City: Bamako
Language: French
Monetary Unit: CFA franc

Mauritania

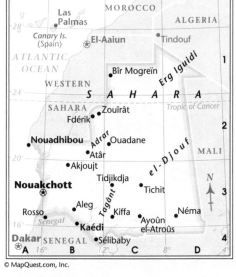

Capital: Nouakchott
Area: 398,000 sq. mi.
1,031,088 sq. km.
Population: 2,893,000
Largest City: Nouakchott
Languages: Arabic, Wolof
Monetary Unit: Ouguiya

Mauritania

⊛ National Capital
• Other City

1:2,350,000

0 150 300 mi.
0 150 300 km.

Lambert Conformal Conic Projection

© MapQuest.com, Inc.

Mali

⊛ National Capital
• Other City

1:21,265,000

0 200 400 mi.
0 200 400 km.

Lambert Conformal Conic Projection

© MapQuest.com, Inc.

Mauritania:
Map Index

Cities and Towns
Akjoujt......................B3
Aleg..........................B3
Atâr..........................B2
Ayoûn el-Atroûs..........C3
Bîr Mogreïn................C1
Fdérik........................B2
Kaédi........................B3
Kiffa..........................C3
Néma........................D3
Nouadhibou................A2
Nouakchott, capital......A3

Ouadane....................C2
Rosso........................B3
Sélibaby....................B4
Tichit........................C3
Tidjikdja....................C3
Zouïrât......................B2

Other Features
Adrar, region..............B2
Djouf, el-, desert..........C2
Erg Iguidi, desert........D1
Sahara, desert............C1
Senegal, river............B3
Tagânt, region............C3

**Niger:
Map Index**

Cities and Towns
Agadès B2
Arlit B2
Bilma C2
Birni Nkonni B3
Diffa C3
Djado C1
Dogondoutchi A3
Dosso A3
Gaya A3
Gouré C3
Maradi B3
Nguigmi C3
Niamey, *capital* A3
Tahoua B3
Téra A3
Tessaoua B3
Tillabéry A3
Zinder B3

Other Features
Air, *mts.* B2
Bagzane, *mt.* B2
Chad, *lake* C3
Dallol Bosso, *river* A3
Dillia, *river* C2
Djado, *plateau* C1
Erg du Ténéré, *desert* B2
Grand Erg de Bilma,
   desert C2
Gréboun, *mt.* B1
Komadugu Yobe, *river* C3
Manga, *region* C2
Niger, *river* A3
Sahara, *desert* A1
Sahel, *region* A3
Talak, *region* B2
Ténéré, *desert* C1

Niger

Capital: Niamey
Area: 497,000 sq. mi.
   1,287,565 sq. km.
Population: 11,972,000
Largest City: Niamey
Language: French
Monetary Unit: CFA franc

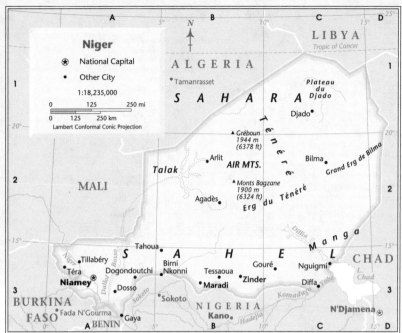

© MapQuest.com, Inc.

**Chad:
Map Index**

Cities and Towns
Abéché C4
Abou Deïa B5
Am Timan C5
Aozou B2
Ati B4
Bardaï B2
Berdoba C4
Biltine C4
Bol A4
Bongor A5
Bousso B5
Doba B5
Fada C3
Faya-Largeau B3
Koro Toro B4
Laï A5
Mao A4
Massenya B5
Melfi B5
Mongo B4
Moundou B5
N'Djamena, *capital* A5
Pala A5
Sarh B5
Zouar B2

Other Features
Bahr Salamat, *river* B5
Batha, *river* C4
Bodélé, *depression* B3
Chad, *lake* A4
Chari, *river* A5
Emi Koussi, *mt.* B3
Ennedi, *plateau* C3
Enneri Ke, *river* B3
Ghazal, *river* B4
Grand Erg de Bilma,
   desert A3
Logone, *river* A5
Ouadi Maba, *river* C4
Sahara, *desert* A2
Tibesti, *massif* B2

Chad

Capital: N'Djamena
Area: 495,755 sq. mi.
   1,248,339 sq. km.
Population: 8,598,000
Largest City: N'Djamena
Languages: French, Arabic
Monetary Unit: CFA franc

**Sudan:
Map Index**

Cities and Towns
Atbarah C2
Babanusah B3
Damazin, ad- C3
Dunqulah C1
Fashir, al- B2
Halaib D1
Juba C4
Junaynah, al- A2
Kaduqli B3
Kassala D2
Khartoum, *capital* C2
Khartoum North C2
Khashm al-Qirbah C2
Kuraymah C1
Kusti C2
Malakal C3
Nuhud, an- B2
Nyala B2
Omdurman C2
Pibor Post C3
Port Sudan D1
Qadarif, al- C2
Rumbek B3
Sannar C2
Ubayyid, al- C2
Wadi Halfa C1
Wad Madani C2
Waw B3
Yambio B4

Other Features
Akobo, *river* C3
Atbarah, *river* C2

Bahr al-Arab, *river* B3
Bahr al-Ghazal, *river* C3
Bahr al-Jabal, *river* C3
Blue Nile, *river* C2
Kangen, *river* C3
Kinyeti, *mt.* C4
Libyan, *desert* B1
Lol, *river* B3
Nasser, *lake* C1
Nile, *river* C1, C2
Nuba, *mts.* C3
Nubian, *desert* C1
Red, *sea* D1
Red Sea, *hills* D1
Sobat, *river* C3
Sudd, *region* B3
Sue, *river* B3
Wadi al-Malik, *river* B2
Wadi Howar, *river* B2
White Nile, *river* C3

Sudan

Capital: Khartoum
Area: 966,757 sq. mi.
   2,530,459 sq. km.
Population: 33,610,000
Largest City: Khartoum
Language: Arabic
Monetary Unit: Sudanese dinar

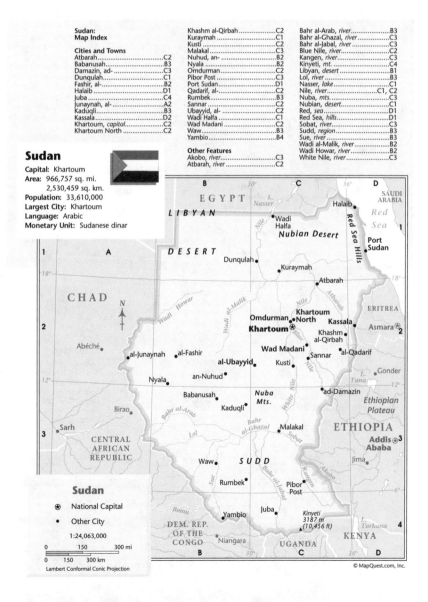

© MapQuest.com, Inc.

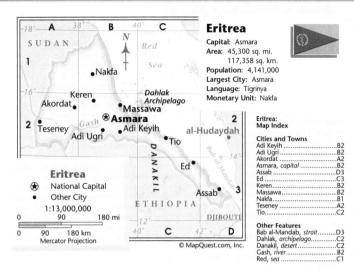

Eritrea

Capital: Asmara
Area: 45,300 sq. mi.
117,358 sq. km.
Population: 4,141,000
Largest City: Asmara
Language: Tigrinya
Monetary Unit: Nakfa

Eritrea

★ National Capital
• Other City
1:13,000,000
0   90   180 mi
0   90   180 km
Mercator Projection

© MapQuest.com, Inc.

Eritrea: Map Index

Cities and Towns
Adi Keyih	B2
Adi Ugri	B2
Akordat	A2
Asmara, capital	B2
Assab	D3
Ed	C3
Keren	B2
Massawa	B2
Nakfa	B1
Teseney	A2
Tio	C2

Other Features
Bab al-Mandab, strait	D3
Dahlak, archipelago	C2
Danakil, desert	C2
Gash, river	B2
Red, sea	C1

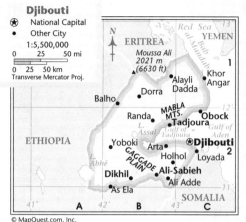

Djibouti

★ National Capital
• Other City
1:5,500,000
0   25   50 mi
0   25   50 km
Transverse Mercator Proj.

© MapQuest.com, Inc.

Djibouti: Map Index

Cities and Towns
Alayli Dadda	B1
Ali Adde	B2
Ali-Sabieh	B2
Arta	B2
As Ela	B2
Balho	B1
Dikhil	B2
Djibouti, capital	C2
Dorra	B1
Holhol	B2
Khor Angar	C1
Loyada	C2
Obock	C2
Randa	B2
Tadjoura	B2
Yoboki	B2

Other Features
Abhé, lake	A2
Aden, gulf	C2
Assal, lake	B2
Bab al-Mandab, strait	C1
Gaggade, plain	B2
Mabla, mts.	B2
Moussa Ali, mt.	B1
Red, sea	C1
Tadjoura, gulf	B2

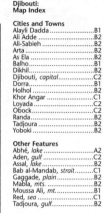

Djibouti

Capital: Djibouti
Area: 8,950 sq. mi.
23,187 sq. km.
Population: 703,000
Largest City: Djibouti
Languages: Cushitic languages
Monetary Unit: Djiboutian franc

© MapQuest.com, Inc.

Ethiopia

★ National Capital
• Other City
1:15,053,000
0   100   200 mi
0   100   200 km
Mercator Projection

Ethiopia

Capital: Addis Ababa
Area: 437,794 sq. mi.
1,134,181 sq. km.
Population: 70,678,000
Largest City: Addis Ababa
Language: Amharic
Monetary Unit: Birr

Ethiopia: Map Index

Cities and Towns
Addis Ababa, capital	C2
Adwa	C1
Arba Minch	B3
Asela	C3
Asosa	B2
Awasa	C3
Bahir Dar	B2
Debre Birhan	C2
Debre Markos	B2
Degeh Bur	D2
Dese	C2
Dire Dawa	D2
Goba	C3
Gonder	B1
Gore	B2
Harer	D2
Imi	D3
Jima	B3
Mekele	C1
Nazret	C2
Negele	C3
Nekemte	B2
Shewa Gimira	B3
Weldiya	C2
Werder	D3

Other Features
Abaya, lake	B3
Abhe, lake	C2
Akobo, river	A3
Atbara, river	B1
Awash, river	C2
Baro, river	B2
Blue Nile, river	B2
Choke, mts.	B2
Dawa, river	C3
Denakil, desert	C1
Dinder, river	B1
Ethiopian, plateau	C2
Genale, river	C3
Great Rift, valley	C3
Ogaden, region	D3
Omo, river	B3
Provisional Administrative Line	D3
Ras Dashen, mt.	C1
Tana, lake	B1
Tekeze, river	B1
Turkana, lake	B3
Wabe Gestro, river	C3
Wabe Shebele, river	D3
Ziway, lake	C3

Somalia: Map Index

Cities and Towns
Baraawe	A3
Baydhabo	A3
Beledweyne	B3
Benderbeyla	C2
Berbera	B1
Boosaaso	B1
Burco	B2
Ceerigaabo	B1
Dhuusamareeb	B2
Eyl	B2
Gaalkacyo	B2
Garoowe	B2
Hargeysa	A2
Hobyo	B2
Jamaame	A3
Jawhar	B3
Jilib	A3
Kismayu	A4
Luuq	A3
Marka	A3
Mogadishu, capital	B3
Qardho	B2
Xuddur	A3

Other Features
Aden, gulf	B1
Gees Gwardafuy, cape	C1
Juba, river	A3
Nugaal, valley	B2
Raas Xaafun, cape	C1
Surud Ad, mt.	B1
Webi Shabeelle, river	B3

Somalia

Capital: Mogadishu
Area: 246,300 sq. mi.
638,083 sq. km.
Population: 9,890,000
Largest City: Mogadishu
Language: Somali, Arabic
Monetary Unit: Somali shilling

Somalia

★ National Capital
• Other City
1:22,100,000
0   150   300 mi
0   150   300 km
Miller Cylindrical Projection

© MapQuest.com, Inc.

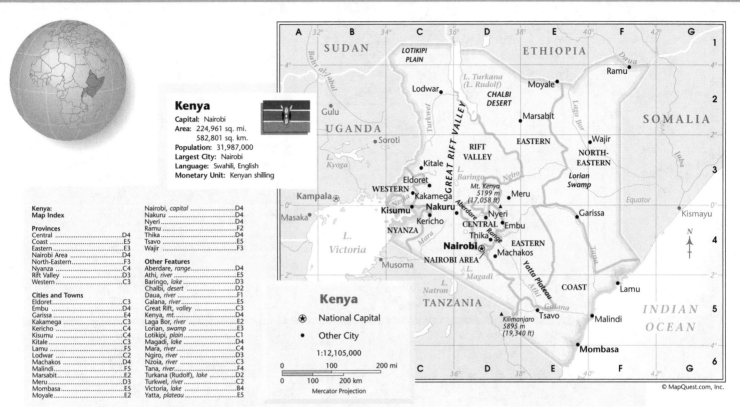

Kenya

Capital: Nairobi
Area: 224,961 sq. mi.
      582,801 sq. km.
Population: 31,987,000
Largest City: Nairobi
Language: Swahili, English
Monetary Unit: Kenyan shilling

Kenya:
Map Index

Provinces
Central D4
Coast E5
Eastern E3
Nairobi Area D4
North-Eastern F3
Nyanza C4
Rift Valley D3
Western C3

Cities and Towns
Eldoret C3
Embu D4
Garissa E4
Kakamega C3
Kericho C4
Kisumu C4
Kitale C3
Lamu F5
Lodwar C2
Machakos D4
Malindi F5
Marsabit E2
Meru D3
Mombasa E5
Moyale E2

Nairobi, *capital* D4
Nakuru D4
Nyeri D4
Ramu F2
Thika D4
Tsavo E5
Wajir F3

Other Features
Aberdare, *range* D4
Athi, *river* E5
Baringo, *lake* D3
Chalbi, *desert* D2
Daua, *river* F1
Galana, *river* E5
Great Rift, *valley* C3
Kenya, *mt.* D4
Laga Bor, *river* E2
Lorian, *swamp* E3
Lotikipi, *plain* C1
Magadi, *lake* D4
Mara, *river* C4
Ngiro, *river* D3
Nzoia, *river* C3
Tana, *river* F4
Turkana (Rudolf), *lake* ..D2
Turkwel, *river* C2
Victoria, *lake* B4
Yatta, *plateau* E5

Kenya
⊛ National Capital
● Other City

1:12,105,000

0 — 100 — 200 mi
0 — 100 — 200 km
Mercator Projection

© MapQuest.com, Inc.

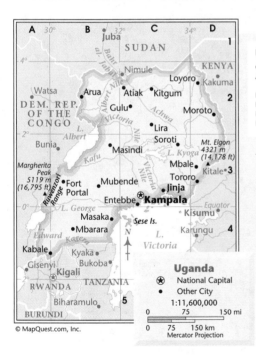

Uganda

Capital: Kampala
Area: 93,070 sq. mi.
      241,114 sq. km.
Population: 25,827,000
Largest City: Kampala
Language: English
Monetary Unit: Ugandan shilling

Uganda:
Map Index

Cities and Towns
Arua B2
Atiak C2
Entebbe C3
Fort Portal B3
Gulu C2
Jinja C3
Kabale A4
Kampala, *capital* C3
Kitgum C2
Lira C2
Loyoro D2
Masaka B4
Masindi B3
Mbale D3
Mbarara B4
Moroto D2

Mubende B3
Soroti C3
Tororo D3

Other Features
Achwa, *river* C2
Albert, *lake* B3
Albert Nile, *river* B2
Bahr al-Jabal, *river* B2
Edward, *lake* A4
Elgon, *mt.* D3
George, *lake* B4
Kafu, *river* B3
Kagera, *river* B4
Kyoga, *lake* C3
Margherita, *peak* A3
Ruwenzori, *range* B3
Sese, *islands* C4
Victoria, *lake* C4
Victoria Nile, *river* B2,C3

Uganda
⊛ National Capital
● Other City

1:11,600,000

0 — 75 — 150 mi
0 — 75 — 150 km
Mercator Projection

© MapQuest.com, Inc.

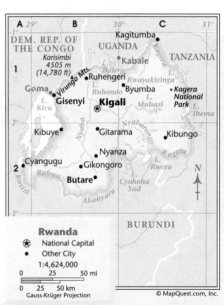

Rwanda
⊛ National Capital
● Other City

1:4,624,000

0 — 25 — 50 mi
0 — 25 — 50 km
Gauss-Krüger Projection

© MapQuest.com, Inc.

Rwanda

Capital: Kigali
Area: 10,169 sq. mi.
      26,345 sq. km.
Population: 8,387,000
Largest City: Kigali
Languages: French, Kinyarwanda
Monetary Unit: Rwandan franc

Rwanda:
Map Index

Cities and Towns
Butare B2
Byumba C1
Cyangugu A2
Gikongoro B2
Gisenyi B1
Gitarama B2
Kagitumba C1
Kibungo C2
Kibuye B1
Kigali, *capital* B1
Nyanza B2
Ruhengeri B1

Bulera, *lake* B1
Cyohoha Sud, *lake* C2
Ihema, *lake* C2
Kagera National Park C1
Kagera, *river* C1, C2
Karisimbi, *mt.* B1
Kivu, *lake* B1
Muhazi, *lake* C1
Nyaba, *river* B2
Nyabarongo, *river* C2
Ruhondo, *lake* B1
Ruhwa, *river* B2
Ruzizi, *river* A2
Rwayakizinga, *lake* C1
Rweru, *lake* C2
Virunga, *mts.* B1

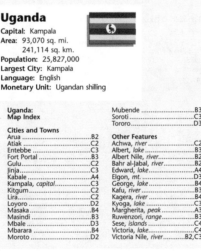

Burundi
⊛ National Capital
● Other City

1:6,548,000

0 — 50 — 100 mi
0 — 50 — 100 km
Conic Equidistant Projection

© MapQuest.com, Inc.

Burundi

Capital: Bujumbura
Area: 10,740 sq. mi.
      27,824 sq. km.
Population: 6,825,000
Largest City: Bujumbura
Languages: French, Kirundi
Monetary Unit: Burundi franc

Burundi:
Map Index

Cities and Towns
Bubanza B2
Bujumbura, *capital* B2
Bururi B2
Cankuzo C2
Gitega B2
Karuzi B2
Makamba B3
Muramvya B2
Muyinga C1
Ngozi B1

Rutana B2
Ruyigi C2

Other Features
Heha, *mt.* B2
Kagera, *river* C1
Malagarasi, *river* C2
Ruvubu, *river* C2
Ruzizi, *river* A1
Tanganyika, *lake* B2

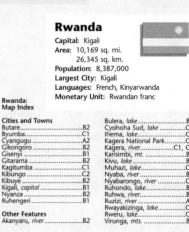

Senegal

Capital: Dakar
Area: 75,951 sq. mi.
196,764 sq. km.
Population: 10,095,000
Largest City: Dakar
Language: French
Monetary Unit: CFA franc

Senegal:
Map Index

Cities and Towns
Bakel	C2
Bignona	A3
Dakar, *capital*	A2
Dara	B2
Dialakoto	C3
Diourbel	A2
Fatick	A2
Goudiri	C2
Haïré Lao	B1
Kaffrine	B2
Kaolack	A2
Kédougou	C3
Kolda	B3
Koungheul	B2
Linguère	B2
Louga	A2
Mamâri	C2
Matam	C2
Mbaké	A2
Mbour	A2
Nioro du Rip	B3
Payar	B2
Richard-Toll	B1
Rufisque	A2
Saint-Louis	A1
Saraya	D3
Sédhiou	B3
Tambacounda	C3
Thiès	A2
Tivaouane	A2
Vélingara	B2
Vélingara	B3
Ziguinchor	A3

Other Features
Casamance, *region*	B3
Casamance, *river*	B3
Falémé, *river*	C3
Ferlo, *river*	C2
Gambia, *river*	C3
Guiers, *lake*	B1
Koulountou, *river*	C3
Mboune, *river*	C2
Niéri Ko, *river*	C2
Sahel, *region*	C2
Saloum, *river*	B2
Sandougou, *river*	B3
Senegal, *river*	B1, C2
Siné, *river*	B2
Soungrougrou, *river*	B3
Vert, *cape*	A2

© MapQuest.com, Inc.

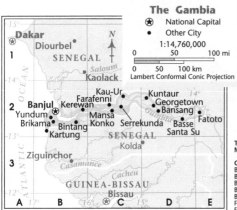

The Gambia

Capital: Banjul
Area: 4,127 sq. mi.
10,692 sq. km.
Population: 1,426,000
Largest City: Banjul
Language: English
Monetary Unit: Dalasi

The Gambia:
Map Index

Cities and Towns
Banjul, *capital*	B2
Bansang	D2
Basse Santa Su	D2
Bintang	B2
Brikama	B2
Farafenni	C2
Fatoto	E2
Georgetown	D2
Kartung	B2
Kau-Ur	C2
Kerewan	B2
Kuntaur	D2
Mansa Konko	C2
Serrekunda	B2
Yundum	B2

Other Feature
Gambia, *river*	D2

© MapQuest.com, Inc.

Guinea-Bissau

Capital: Bissau
Area: 13,948 sq. mi.
36,135 sq. km.
Population: 1,493,000
Largest City: Bissau
Language: Portuguese
Monetary Unit: CFA franc

Guinea-Bissau:
Map Index

Cities and Towns
Bafatá	C1
Bambadinca	C1
Barro	B1
Bissau, *capital*	B2
Bissorã	B1
Bolama	B2
Buba	C2
Bubaque	B2
Bula	B1
Cacheu	A1
Cacine	A1
Canchungo	A1
Catió	B2
Farim	B1
Fulacunda	B2
Gabú	C1
Ondame	B2
Pirada	C1
Quebo	C2
Quinhámel	B2
São Domingos	A1

Other Features
Bijagós, *islands*	A2
Cacheu, *river*	B1
Corubal, *river*	D1
Gêba, *river*	C1

Guinea:
Map Index

Cities and Towns
Beyla	D3
Conakry, *capital*	B3
Coyah	B3
Dabola	C2
Fria	B2
Guéckédou	C3
Kailahun	C3
Kali	C1
Kamsar	A2
Kankan	D2
Kérouané	D3
Kindia	B2
Kissidougou	C3
Kouroussa	C2
Labé	B2
Lélouma	B2
Macenta	D3
Mamou	B2
Niagassola	D1
Nzérékoré	D4
Siguiri	D2
Tougué	C2
Yomou	D4

Other Features
Bafing, *river*	C2
Futa Jallon, *plateau*	B1
Gambia, *river*	B2
Los, *islands*	A3
Milo, *river*	D3
Niger, *river*	C2
Nimba, *mts.*	D4
Tinkissa, *river*	C2

Guinea

Capital: Conakry
Area: 94,926 sq. mi.
245,922 sq. km.
Population: 8,480,000
Largest City: Conakry
Language: French
Monetary Unit: Guinean franc

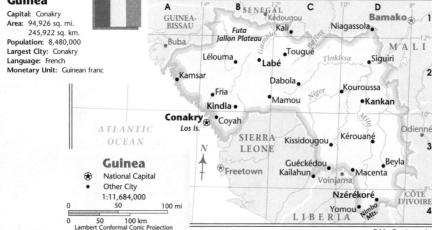

© MapQuest.com, Inc.

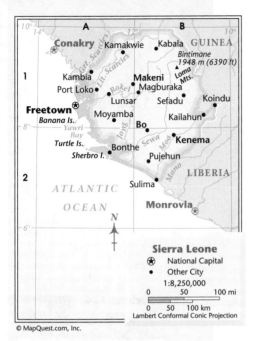

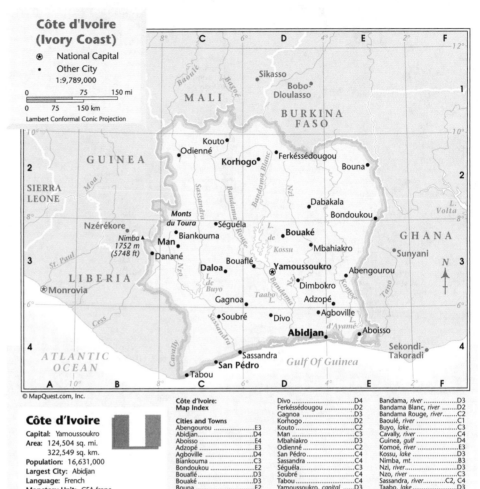

Côte d'Ivoire (Ivory Coast)

⊛ National Capital
• Other City
1:9,789,000

0   75   150 mi
0   75   150 km
Lambert Conformal Conic Projection

© MapQuest.com, Inc.

Sierra Leone

⊛ National Capital
• Other City
1:8,250,000

0   50   100 mi
0   50   100 km
Lambert Conformal Conic Projection

© MapQuest.com, Inc.

Sierra Leone

Capital: Freetown
Area: 27,699 sq. mi.
    71,759 sq. km.
Population: 4,971,000
Largest City: Freetown
Language: English
Monetary Unit: Leone

Sierra Leone: Map Index

Cities and Towns

Bo	B2
Bonthe	A2
Freetown, *capital*	A1
Kabala	B1
Kailahun	B1
Kamakwie	A1
Kambia	A1
Kenema	B2
Koindu	B1
Lunsar	A1
Magburaka	B1
Makeni	B1
Moyamba	A1
Port Loko	A1
Pujehun	B2
Sefadu	B1
Sulima	B2

Other Features

Banana, *islands*	A1
Bintimane, *mt.*	B1
Great Scarcies, *river*	A1
Jong, *river*	A2
Little Scarcies, *river*	A1
Loma, *mts.*	B1
Mano, *river*	B2
Moa, *river*	B2
Rokel, *river*	A1
Sewa, *river*	B2
Sherbro, *island*	A2
Turtle, *islands*	A2
Yawri, *bay*	A2

Côte d'Ivoire

Capital: Yamoussoukro
Area: 124,504 sq. mi.
    322,549 sq. km.
Population: 16,631,000
Largest City: Abidjan
Language: French
Monetary Unit: CFA franc

Côte d'Ivoire: Map Index

Cities and Towns

Abengourou	E3
Abidjan	D4
Aboisso	E4
Adzopé	E3
Agboville	D4
Biankouma	C3
Bondoukou	E2
Bouaflé	D3
Bouaké	D3
Bouna	E2
Dabakala	D2
Daloa	C3
Danané	B3
Dimbokro	D3
Divo	D4
Ferkéssédougou	D2
Gagnoa	D3
Korhogo	D2
Kouto	C2
Man	C3
Mbahiakro	D3
Odienné	C2
San Pédro	C4
Sassandra	C4
Séguéla	C3
Soubré	C4
Tabou	C4
Yamoussoukro, *capital*	D3

Other Features

Ayamé, *lake*	E4
Bagoé, *river*	C1
Bandama, *river*	D3
Bandama Blanc, *river*	D2
Bandama Rouge, *river*	C1
Baoulé, *river*	C1
Buyo, *lake*	C3
Cavally, *river*	C4
Guinea, *gulf*	D4
Komoé, *river*	E3
Kossu, *lake*	D3
Nimba, *mt.*	B3
Nzi, *river*	D3
Nzo, *river*	C3
Sassandra, *river*	C2, C4
Taabo, *lake*	D3
Tano, *river*	E3
Toura, *mts.*	C2

Liberia

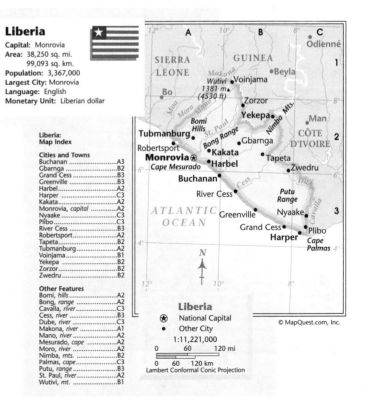

Capital: Monrovia
Area: 38,250 sq. mi.
    99,093 sq. km.
Population: 3,367,000
Largest City: Monrovia
Language: English
Monetary Unit: Liberian dollar

Liberia: Map Index

Cities and Towns

Buchanan	A3
Gbarnga	B2
Grand Cess	B3
Greenville	B3
Harbel	A2
Harper	C3
Kakata	A2
Monrovia, *capital*	A2
Nyaake	C3
Plíbo	C3
River Cess	B3
Robertsport	A2
Tapeta	B2
Tubmanburg	A2
Voinjama	B1
Yekepa	B2
Zorzor	B2
Zwedru	B2

Other Features

Bomi, *hills*	A2
Bong, *range*	A2
Cavalla, *river*	C3
Cess, *river*	B3
Dube, *river*	C3
Makona, *river*	A1
Mano, *river*	A2
Mesurado, *cape*	A2
Moro, *river*	A2
Nimba, *mts.*	B2
Palmas, *cape*	C3
Putu, *range*	B3
St. Paul, *river*	A2
Wutivi, *mt.*	B1

Liberia

⊛ National Capital
• Other City
1:11,221,000

0   60   120 mi
0   60   120 km
Lambert Conformal Conic Projection

© MapQuest.com, Inc.

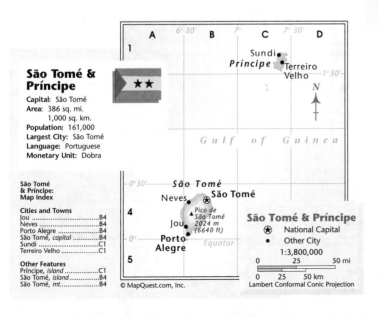

São Tomé & Príncipe

Capital: São Tomé
Area: 386 sq. mi.
    1,000 sq. km.
Population: 161,000
Largest City: São Tomé
Language: Portuguese
Monetary Unit: Dobra

São Tomé & Príncipe: Map Index

Cities and Towns

Jou	B4
Neves	B4
Porto Alegre	B4
São Tomé, *capital*	B4
Sundi	C1
Terreiro Velho	C1

Other Features

Príncipe, *island*	C1
São Tomé, *island*	B4
São Tomé, *mt.*	B4

São Tomé & Príncipe

⊛ National Capital
• Other City
1:3,800,000

0   25   50 mi
0   25   50 km
Lambert Conformal Conic Projection

© MapQuest.com, Inc.

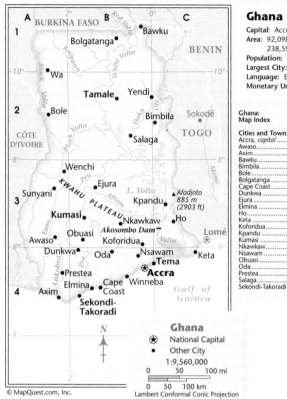

Ghana

Capital: Accra
Area: 92,098 sq. mi.
238,596 sq. km.
Population: 20,922,000
Largest City: Accra
Language: English
Monetary Unit: Cedi

Ghana:
Map Index

Cities and Towns
Accra, capital B4
Awaso A3
Axim A4
Bawku B1
Bimbila C2
Bole A2
Bolgatanga B1
Cape Coast B4
Dunkwa B4
Ejura B3
Elmina B4
Ho C3
Keta C4
Koforidua B3
Kpandu C3
Kumasi B3
Nkawkaw B3
Nsawam B4
Obuasi B3
Oda B4
Prestea A4
Salaga B2
Sekondi-Takoradi B4

Sunyani A3
Tamale B2
Tema C4
Wa A1
Wenchi A3
Winneba B4
Yendi B2

Other Features
Afadjoto, mt. C3
Afram, river B3
Akosombo, dam C3
Ankobra, river A4
Black Volta, river A2
Daka, river B2
Guinea, gulf C4
Kulpawn, river B1
Kwahu, plateau B3
Oti, river C2
Pra, river B4
Pru, river B3
Red Volta, river B1
Tano, river A3
Volta, lake C3
Volta, river C3
White Volta, river B1

Ghana

⊛ National Capital
• Other City
1:9,560,000

0   50   100 mi
0   50   100 km
Lambert Conformal Conic Projection

© MapQuest.com, Inc.

Burkina Faso

⊛ National Capital
• Other City
1:14,785,000

0   100   200 mi
0   100   200 km
Lambert Conformal Conic Projection

© MapQuest.com, Inc.

Burkina Faso

Capital: Ouagadougou
Area: 105,946 sq. mi.
274,472 sq. km.
Population: 13,002,000
Largest City: Ouagadougou
Language: French
Monetary Unit: CFA franc

Burkina Faso:
Map Index

Cities and Towns
Bobo-Dioulasso B3
Dédougou C2
Dori D1
Gaoua C3
Koudougou C2
Léo C3
Ouagadougou, capital D2
Ouahigouya C2
Tenkodogo D3

Other Features
Black Volta, river B3
Red Volta, river D3
Sirba, river D2
Téna Kourou, mt. B3
White Volta, river D2

Benin

⊛ National Capital
• Other City
1:14,800,000

0   100   200 mi
0   100   200 km
Lambert Conformal Conic Projection

© MapQuest.com, Inc.

Benin

Capital: Porto-Novo
Area: 43,500 sq. mi.
112,694 sq. km.
Population: 6,736,000
Largest City: Cotonou
Language: French
Monetary Unit: CFA franc

Benin:
Map Index

Cities and Towns
Abomey A4
Bassila A3
Cotonou B4
Djougou A3
Kandi B2
Lokossa A4
Malanville B2
Natitingou A2
Nikki B3
Ouidah B4
Parakou B3
Pobé B4

Porto-Novo, capital B4
Savalou A3
Savé B3
Segbana B2
Tchaourou B3

Other Features
Alibori, river B2
Chaîne de l'Atacora, mts. A2
Couffo, river B4
Guinea, gulf A4
Mékrou, river B2
Mono, river A4
Niger, river B1
Ouémé, river B3
Sota, river B2

Togo

Capital: Lomé
Area: 21,925 sq. mi.
56,801 sq. km.
Population: 4,909,000
Largest City: Lomé
Language: French
Monetary Unit: CFA franc

Togo:
Map Index

Cities and Towns
Amlamé B3
Aného B3
Anié B3
Atakpamé B3
Badou B3
Bafilo B2
Bassar B2
Blitta B2
Dapaong B1
Kanté B2
Kara B2
Kpalimé B3
Kpémé B3
Lomé, capital B3
Mango B1
Niamtougou B2
Sokodé B2
Sotouboua B3
Tablgbo B3
Tchamba B3
Tsévié B3

Other Features
Agou, mt. B3
Benin, bight B4
Mono, river B2
Oti, river B1

Togo

⊛ National Capital
• Other City
1:8,600,000

0   50   100 mi
0   50   100 km
Lambert Conformal Conic Projection

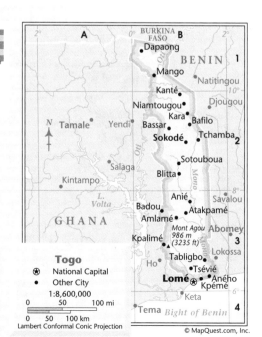

© MapQuest.com, Inc.

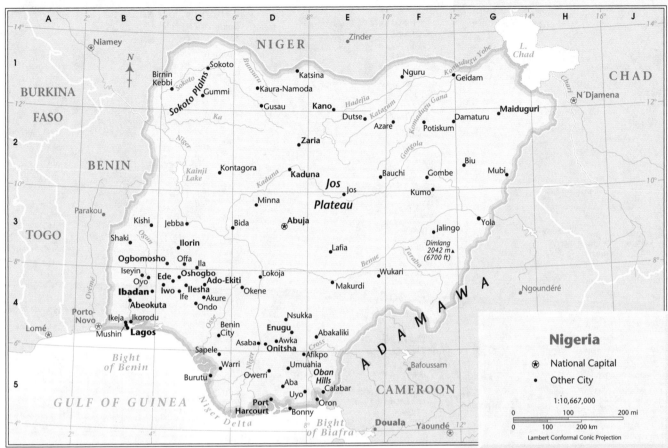

Nigeria

⊛ National Capital
• Other City

1:10,667,000

0 — 100 — 200 mi
0 — 100 — 200 km

Lambert Conformal Conic Projection

© MapQuest.com, Inc.

Nigeria

Capital: Abuja
Area: 356,669 sq. mi.
924,013 sq. km.
Population: 124,009,000
Largest City: Lagos
Language: English
Monetary Unit: Naira

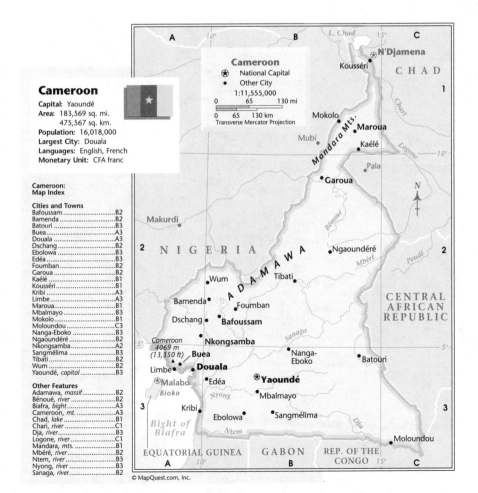

Cameroon

⊛ National Capital
• Other City

1:11,555,000

0 — 65 — 130 mi
0 — 65 — 130 km

Transverse Mercator Projection

Cameroon

Capital: Yaoundé
Area: 183,569 sq. mi.
475,567 sq. km.
Population: 16,018,000
Largest City: Douala
Languages: English, French
Monetary Unit: CFA franc

© MapQuest.com, Inc.

Cameroon:
Map Index

Cities and Towns
Bafoussam B2
Bamenda B2
Batouri B3
Buea A3
Douala A3
Dschang B2
Ebolowa B3
Edéa B3
Foumban B2
Garoua B2
Kaélé B1
Kousséri B1
Kribi A3
Limbe A3
Maroua B1
Mbalmayo B3
Mokolo B1
Moloundou C3
Nanga-Eboko B3
Ngaoundéré B2
Nkongsamba A2
Sangmélima B3
Tibati B2
Wum B2
Yaoundé, capital B3

Other Features
Adamawa, massif B2
Bénoué, river B2
Biafra, bight A3
Cameroon, mt. A3
Chad, lake B1
Chari, river C1
Dja, river B3
Logone, river C1
Mandara, mts. B1
Mbéré, river B3
Ntem, river B3
Nyong, river B2
Sanaga, river B2

Nigeria:
Map Index

Cities and Towns
Aba D5
Abakaliki E4
Abeokuta B4
Abuja, capital D3
Ado-Ekiti C4
Afikpo D5
Akure C4
Asaba D4
Awka D4
Azare F2
Bauchi E2
Benin City C4
Bida D3
Birnin Kebbi C1
Biu G2
Bonny D5
Burutu C5
Calabar E5
Damaturu F2
Dutse E2
Ede C4
Enugu D4
Geidam F1
Gombe F2
Gummi C1
Gusau D1
Ibadan B4
Ife B4
Ikeja B4
Ikorodu B4
Ila C3
Ilesha C4
Ilorin C3
Iseyin B4
Iwo C4
Jalingo F3
Jebba C3
Jos E3
Kaduna D2
Kano E1
Katsina D1
Kaura-Namoda D1
Kishi B3
Kontagora C2
Kumo F2
Lafia E3
Lagos B4
Lokoja D4
Maiduguri G2

Makurdi E4
Minna D3
Mubi G2
Mushin B4
Nguru F1
Nsukka D4
Offa C3
Ogbomosho C3
Okene D4
Ondo C4
Onitsha D4
Oron E5
Oshogbo C4
Owerri D5
Oyo B4
Port Harcourt D5
Potiskum F2
Sapele C5
Shaki B3
Sokoto C1
Umuahia D5
Uyo D5
Warri C5
Wukarl E4
Yola G3
Zaria D2

Other Features
Adamawa, massif E5
Benin, bight B5
Benue, river E3
Bunsuru, river D1
Chad, lake G1
Cross, river E4
Dimlang, mt. F3
Gongola, river F2
Guinea, gulf B5
Hadejia, river E1
Jos, plateau E2
Ka, river C2
Kaduna, river D2
Kainji, lake C2
Katagum, river E2
Komadugu Gana, river ...F2
Komadugu Yobe, river ...F1
Niger, delta C5
Niger, river C2, D5
Oban, hills E5
Ogun, river B3
Osse, river C4
Sokoto, plains C1
Sokoto, river C1
Taraba, river F3

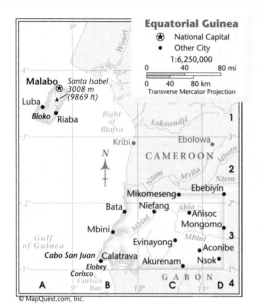

Equatorial Guinea

⊛ National Capital
● Other City

1:6,250,000

0   40   80 mi
0   40   80 km
Transverse Mercator Projection

© MapQuest.com, Inc.

Equatorial Guinea

Capital: Malabo
Area: 10,831 sq. mi.
28,060 sq. km.
Population: 494,000
Largest City: Malabo
Language: Spanish
Monetary Unit: CFA franc

Equatorial Guinea:
Map Index

Cities and Towns
Aconibe C3
Akurenam C3
Añisoc C3
Bata B3
Calatrava B3
Ebebiyín D2
Evinayong C3
Luba A1
Malabo, *capital* A1
Mbini B3
Mikomeseng C2
Mongomo D3

Niefang C3
Nsok D3
Riaba A1

Other Features
Abia, *river* C3
Biafra, *bight* B1
Bioko, *island* A1
Corisco, *bay* B4
Corisco, *island* B4
Elobey, *islands* B3
Guinea, *gulf* A3
Mbini, *river* C3
Mboro, *river* D4
San Juan, *cape* B3
Santa Isabel, *peak* A1

Gabon

Capital: Libreville
Area: 103,347 sq. mi.
267,738 sq. km.
Population: 1,329,000
Largest City: Libreville
Language: French
Monetary Unit: CFA franc

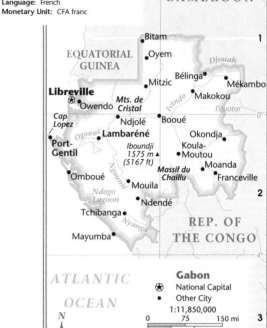

Gabon

⊛ National Capital
● Other City

1:11,850,000

0   75   150 mi
0   75   150 km
Azimuthal Equal Area Projection

© MapQuest.com, Inc.

Gabon:
Map Index

Cities and Towns
Bélinga B1
Bitam A1
Booué A2
Franceville B2
Koula-Moutou B2
Lambaréné A2
Libreville, *capital* A1
Makokou B1
Mayumba A2
Mékambo B1
Mitzic A1
Moanda B2
Mouila A2
Ndendé A2
Ndjolé A2

Okondja B2
Omboué A2
Owendo A1
Oyem A1
Port-Gentil A2
Tchibanga A2

Other Features
Chaillu, *mts.* B2
Cristal, *mts.* A1
Djouah, *river* B1
Iboundji, *mt.* A2
Ivindo, *river* B1
Lopez, *cape* A2
Ndogo, *lagoon* A2
Ngounié, *river* A2
Nyanga, *river* A2
Ogooué, *river* A2

Republic of the Congo

⊛ National Capital
● Other City

1:18,000,000

0   100   200 mi
0   100   200 km
Azimuthal Equal Area Projection

© MapQuest.com, Inc.

Republic of the Congo

Capital: Brazzaville
Area: 132,047 sq. mi.
342,091 sq. km.
Population: 3,724,000
Largest City: Brazzaville
Language: French
Monetary Unit: CFA franc

Republic of the Congo:
Map Index

Cities and Towns
Bétou E2
Brazzaville, *capital* C6
Djambala C5
Ewo C4
Impfondo D3
Kinkala C6
Loubomo B6
Makoua C4
Mossendjo B5
Ouesso D3
Owando C4
Pointe-Noire A6

Sembé C3
Sibiti B5

Other Features
Alima, *river* D4
Batéké, *plateau* C5
Congo, *basin* D3
Congo, *river* D4
Ivindo, *river* B3
Lékéti, *mts.* C5
Lengoué, *river* C3
Mayombé, *massif* B5
Niari, *river* B5
Nyanga, *river* A5
Sangha, *river* D2
Ubangi, *river* E2

Central African Republic (C.A.R.)

Capital: Bangui
Area: 240,324 sq. mi.
622,601 sq. km.
Population: 3,865,000
Largest City: Bangui
Language: French
Monetary Unit: CFA franc

Central African Republic:
Map Index

Cities and Towns
Bambari B2
Bangassou B3
Bangui, *capital* A3
Batangafo A2
Berbérati A3
Birao B1
Bossangoa A2
Bouar A2
Bria B2
Kaga Bandoro A2
Mobaye B3
Ndélé B2
Nola A3
Obo C2
Yalinga B2

Other Features
Chari, *river* A2
Chinko, *river* B2
Gribingui, *river* A2
Kadei, *river* A3
Kotto, *river* B2
Lobaye, *river* A2
Mambéré, *river* A2
Massif des Bongos, *range* B2
Mpoko, *river* A2
Ouaka, *river* B2
Ouarra, *river* C2
Ouham, *river* A2
Pendé, *river* A2
Toussoro, *mt.* B2
Ubangi, *river* A3

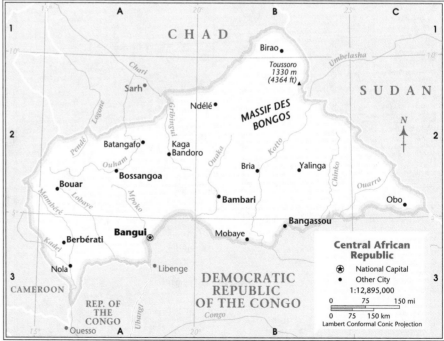

Central African Republic

⊛ National Capital
● Other City

1:12,895,000

0   75   150 mi
0   75   150 km
Lambert Conformal Conic Projection

© MapQuest.com, Inc.

Democratic Republic of the Congo

Capital: Kinshasa
Area: 905,446 sq. mi.
2,345,715 sq. km.
Population: 52,771,000
Largest City: Kinshasa
Language: French
Monetary Unit: Congolese franc

Democratic Republic of the Congo

⊛ National Capital
• Other City

1:20,235,000

0 150 300 mi
0 150 300 km
Mercator Conic Projection

© MapQuest.com, Inc.

Democratic Republic of the Congo:
Map Index

Regions
Bandundu B2
Bas-Congo A2
Équateur B1
Kasai-Occidental B2
Kasai-Oriental B2
Katanga C3
Kinshasa B2
Maniema C2
Nord-Kivu C2
Orientale C1
Sud-Kivu C2

Cities and Towns
Banana A2
Bandundu B2
Boende B2
Bolobo B2
Boma A2
Bondo B1
Bukavu C2
Bumba B1
Bunia C1
Buta C1
Dilolo B3
Gemena B1
Goma C2
Ikela B2
Ilebo B2
Inga A2
Isiro C1
Kabalo C2
Kahemba B2
Kalemie C2
Kamina C3
Kananga B2
Kikwit B2
Kindu C2
Kinshasa, *capital* A2
Kisangani C1
Kolwezi C3

Likasi C3
Lisala B1
Lodja B2
Lubumbashi C3
Lusambo B2
Manono C2
Matadi A2
Mbandaka A2
Mbanza-Ngungu A2
Mbuji-Mayi B2
Moba C2
Mwene-Ditu B2
Tshikapa B2
Uvira C2
Watsa C1
Yangambi C1

Other Features
Albert, *lake* C1
Aruwimi, *river* C1
Bomu, *river* B1
Congo, *river* B1
Congo Basin, *region* .B1
Edward, *lake* C2
Kasai, *river* B2
Katanga, *plateau* B3
Kivu, *lake* C2
Kwa, *river* B2
Kwango, *river* B2
Lomami, *river* C2
Lualaba, *river* C2
Luapula, *river* C3
Lukuga, *river* C2
Luvua, *river* C2
Mai-Ndombe, *lake* ...B2
Margherita, *peak* C1
Mitumba, *mts.* C2
Mweru, *lake* C3
Sankuru, *river* B2
Tanganyika, *lake* C2
Tshuapa, *river* B2
Tumba, *lake* B2
Ubangi, *river* B1
Uele, *river* C1
Upemba, *lake* C3

Zambia

⊛ National Capital
• Other City

1:14,541,000

0 100 200 mi
0 100 200 km
Lambert Conformal Conic Projection

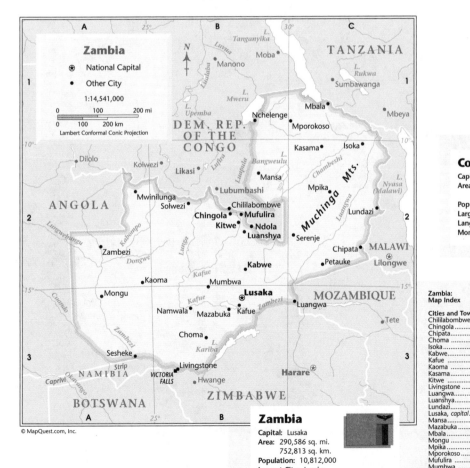

© MapQuest.com, Inc.

Zambia

Capital: Lusaka
Area: 290,586 sq. mi.
752,813 sq. km.
Population: 10,812,000
Largest City: Lusaka
Language: English
Monetary Unit: Zambian kwacha

Comoros

⊛ National Capital
★ Territorial Capital
• Other City

1: 5,278,000

0 30 60 mi
0 30 60 km
Lambert Conformal Conic Projection

© MapQuest.com, Inc.

Comoros

Capital: Moroni
Area: 719 sq. mi.
1,863 sq. km.
Population: 768,000
Largest City: Moroni
Languages: Arabic, French
Monetary Unit: Comoran franc

Comoros:
Map Index

Cities and Towns
Chingoni C2
Dzaoudzi, *territorial capital* C2
Fomboni A2
Foumbouni A1
M'Beni A1
Mitsamiouli A1
Moroni, *national capital* A1
M'Ramani B2
Mutsamudu B2
Sima B2

Other Features
Kartala, *mt.* A1
Mayotte, *island* C2
Mozambique, *channel* B2
Mwali (Mohéli), *island* A2
Njazidja (Grande Comore),
island A1
Nzwani (Anjouan), *island* ..B2

Zambia:
Map Index

Cities and Towns
Chililabombwe B2
Chingola B2
Chipata C2
Choma B3
Isoka C2
Kabwe B2
Kafue B3
Kaoma A2
Kasama C2
Kitwe B2
Livingstone B3
Luangwa C3
Luanshya B2
Lundazi C2
Lusaka, *capital* B3
Mansa B2
Mazabuka B3
Mbala C1
Mongu A3
Mpika C2
Mporokoso C1
Mufulira B2
Mumbwa B3
Mwinilunga A2

Namwala B3
Nchelenge B1
Ndola B2
Petauke C2
Serenje C2
Sesheke A3
Solwezi B2
Zambezi A2

Other Features
Bangweulu, *lake* B2
Chambeshi, *river* C2
Cuando, *river* A3
Dongwe, *river* A2
Kabompo, *river* A2
Kafue, *river* B2
Kariba, *lake* B3
Luangwa, *river* C2
Lunga, *river* B2
Lungwebungu, *river* ..A2
Luvua, *river* B1
Muchinga, *mts.* C2
Mweru, *lake* B1
Tanganyika, *lake* C1
Victoria, *falls* B3
Zambezi, *river* A3, B3

Tanzania

⊛ National Capital

• Other City

1:11,000,000

| 0 | 100 | 200 mi |
| 0 | 100 | 200 km |

Lambert Conformal Conic Projection

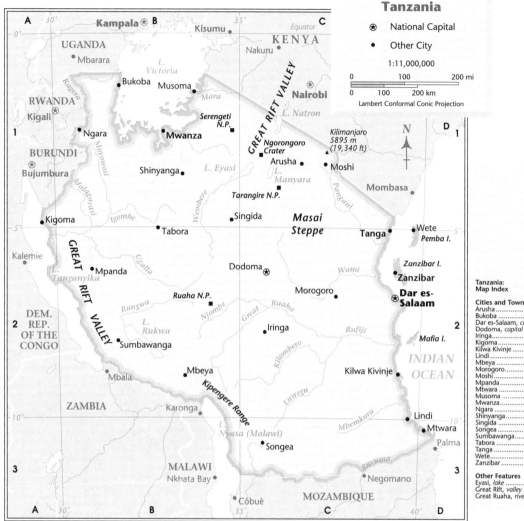

© MapQuest.com, Inc.

Tanzania

Capital: Dar es-Salaam, Dodoma
Area: 364,017 sq. mi.
943,049 sq. km.
Population: 36,977,000
Largest City: Dar es-Salaam
Languages: Swahili, English
Monetary Unit: Tanzanian shilling

Tanzania:
Map Index

Cities and Towns

Arusha	C1
Bukoba	B1
Dar es-Salaam, capital	C2
Dodoma, capital	C2
Iringa	C2
Kigoma	A1
Kilwa Kivinje	C2
Lindi	C2
Mbeya	B2
Morogoro	C2
Moshi	C1
Mpanda	B2
Mtwara	D3
Musoma	B1
Mwanza	B1
Ngara	B1
Shinyanga	B1
Singida	B1
Songea	C3
Sumbawanga	B2
Tabora	B2
Tanga	C2
Wete	C2
Zanzibar	C2

Other Features

Eyasi, lake	B1
Great Rift, valley	B2, C1
Great Ruaha, river	C2
Igombe, river	B1
Kagera, river	B1
Kilimanjaro, mt.	C1
Kilombero, river	C2
Kipengere, range	B2
Luwegu, river	C2
Mafia, island	C2
Malagarasi, river	B1
Manyara, lake	C1
Mara, river	B1
Masai, steppe	C1
Mbemkuru, river	C3
Moyowosi, river	B1
Natron, lake	C1
Ngorongoro, crater	C1
Njombe, river	B2
Nyasa (Malawi), lake	B3
Pangani, river	C1
Pemba, island	C2
Ruaha Natl. Park	B2
Rufiji, river	C2
Rukwa, lake	B2
Rungwa, river	B2
Ruvuma, river	C3
Serengeti Natl. Park	B1
Tanganyika, lake	A2
Tarangire Natl. Park	C1
Ugalla, river	B2
Victoria, lake	B1
Wami, river	C2
Wembere, river	B1
Zanzibar, island	C2

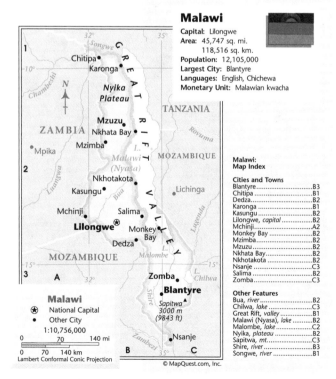

© MapQuest.com, Inc.

Malawi

Capital: Lilongwe
Area: 45,747 sq. mi.
118,516 sq. km.
Population: 12,105,000
Largest City: Blantyre
Languages: English, Chichewa
Monetary Unit: Malawian kwacha

Malawi

⊛ National Capital

• Other City

1:10,756,000

| 0 | 70 | 140 mi |
| 0 | 70 | 140 km |

Lambert Conformal Conic Projection

Malawi:
Map Index

Cities and Towns

Blantyre	B3
Chitipa	B1
Dedza	B2
Karonga	B1
Kasungu	B2
Lilongwe, capital	B2
Mchinji	A2
Monkey Bay	B2
Mzimba	B2
Mzuzu	B2
Nkhata Bay	B2
Nkhotakota	B2
Nsanje	C3
Salima	B2
Zomba	C3

Other Features

Bua, river	B2
Chilwa, lake	C3
Great Rift, valley	B1
Malawi (Nyasa), lake	B2
Malombe, lake	C2
Nyika, plateau	B1
Sapitwa, mt.	C3
Shire, river	B3
Songwe, river	B1

Mozambique

Capital: Maputo
Area: 313,661 sq. mi.
812,593 sq. km.
Population: 18,863,000
Largest City: Maputo
Language: Portuguese
Monetary Unit: Metical

Mozambique:
Map Index

Cities and Towns

Angoche	C3
Beira	B3
Chimoio	B3
Chinde	C3
Cuamba	B2
Inhambane	B5
Lichinga	B2
Maputo, capital	B5
Moçambique	D2
Mocímbo da Praia	D1
Nacala	D2
Nampula	D2
Pebane	C3
Pemba	D2
Quelimane	C3
Tete	B3
Vilanculos	B5
Xai-Xai	B5

Other Features

Binga, mt.	B3
Búzi, river	B4
Cabora Bassa, dam	B3
Cabora Bassa, lake	A2
Changane, river	B4
Chilwa, lake	B3
Chire, river	B3
Lebombo, mts.	A4
Limpopo, river	B4
Lúrio, river	C2
Lugenda, river	C2
Mozambique, channel	C3
Namuli, highlands	C2
Nyasa (Malawi), lake	B2
Rovuma, river	C1
Save, river	B4
Zambezi, river	B3

Mozambique

⊛ National Capital

• Other City

1:25,181,000

| 0 | 150 | 300 mi |
| 0 | 150 | 300 km |

Modified Lambert Conformal Conic Projection

© MapQuest.com, Inc.

Mauritius

⊛ National Capital
● Other City

1:1,635,000

0   10   20 mi
0   10   20 km
Transverse Mercator Projection

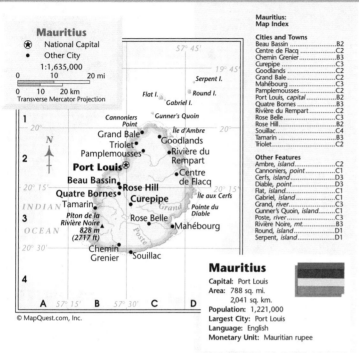

© MapQuest.com, Inc.

Mauritius:
Map Index

Cities and Towns
Beau Bassin B2
Centre de Flacq C2
Chemin Grenier B3
Curepipe C3
Goodlands C2
Grand Bale C2
Mahébourg C3
Pamplemousses C2
Port Louis, capital B2
Quatre Bornes B3
Rivière du Rempart C2
Rose Belle C3
Rose Hill B2
Souillac C4
Tamarin B3
Triolet C2

Other Features
Ambre, island C2
Cannoniers, point C1
Cerfs, island D3
Diable, point D3
Flat, island C1
Gabriel, island C1
Grand, river C3
Gunner's Quoin, island ...C1
Poste, river C3
Rivière Noire, mt. B3
Round, island D1
Serpent, island D1

Mauritius

Capital: Port Louis
Area: 788 sq. mi.
  2,041 sq. km.
Population: 1,221,000
Largest City: Port Louis
Language: English
Monetary Unit: Mauritian rupee

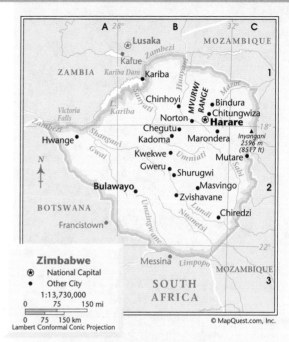

© MapQuest.com, Inc.

Zimbabwe

⊛ National Capital
● Other City

1:13,730,000

0   75   150 mi
0   75   150 km
Lambert Conformal Conic Projection

Zimbabwe

Capital: Harare
Area: 150,872 sq. mi.
  390,860 sq. km.
Population: 12,891,000
Largest City: Harare
Language: English
Monetary Unit: Zimbabwean dollar

Zimbabwe:
Map Index

Cities and Towns
Bindura B1
Bulawayo B2
Chegutu B2
Chinhoyi B1
Chiredzi B2
Chitungwiza B1
Gweru B2
Harare, capital B1
Hwange A2

Kadoma B2
Kariba B1
Kwekwe B2
Marondera B2
Masvingo B2
Mutare C2
Norton B1
Shurugwi B2
Zvishavane B2

Other Features
Gwai, river A2
Hunyani, river B1
Inyangani, mt. C2
Kariba, lake A1
Limpopo, river B3
Lundi, river B2
Mazoe, river B1
Mvurwi, range B1
Nuanetsi, river B2
Sabi, river C2
Sanyati, river B1
Shangani, river A2
Umniati, river B2
Umzingwani, river B2
Victoria, falls A1
Zambezi, river A1, B1

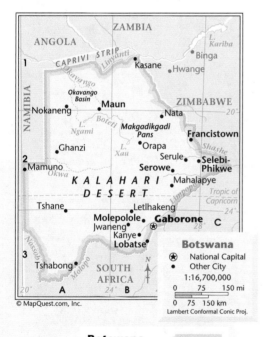

© MapQuest.com, Inc.

Botswana

⊛ National Capital
● Other City

1:16,700,000

0   75   150 mi
0   75   150 km
Lambert Conformal Conic Proj.

Botswana

Capital: Gaborone
Area: 224,607 sq. mi.
  581,883 sq. km.
Population: 1,785,000
Largest City: Gaborone
Language: English
Monetary Unit: Pula

Botswana:
Map Index

Cities and Towns
Francistown B2
Gaborone, capital. B3
Ghanzi A2
Jwaneng B3
Kanye B3
Kasane B1
Letlhakeng B3
Lobatse B3
Mahalapye B2
Mamuno A2
Maun A1
Molepolole B3
Nata B1
Nokaneng A1
Orapa B2
Selebi-Phikwe C2
Serowe B2
Serule B2

Tshabong A3
Tshane A3

Other Features
Boteti, river A2
Kalahari, desert A3
Limpopo, river B2
Linvanti, river A1
Makgadikgadi,
  salt pans B2
Molopo, river A3
Ngami, lake A2
Nossob, river A3
Okavango, basin A1
Okavango, river A1
Okwa, river A2
Shashe, river C2
Xau, lake B2

Madagascar

⊛ National Capital
● Other City

1:17,474,000

0   100   200 mi
0   100   200 km
Lambert Conformal Conic Projection

© MapQuest.com, Inc.

Madagascar

Capital: Antananarivo
Area: 226,658 sq. mi.
  587,197 sq. km.
Population: 17,404,000
Largest City: Antananarivo
Languages: Malagasy, French
Monetary Unit: Malagasy franc

Madagascar:
Map Index

Cities and Towns
Ambatolampy B2
Ambatondrazaka B2
Ambositra B3
Ampanihy A3
Andoany B1
Antalaha C1
Antananarivo, capital B2
Antsirabe B2
Antsiranana B1
Antsohihy B1
Farafangana B3
Fianarantsoa B3
Ihosy B3
Mahajanga A2
Maintirano A2
Manakara B3
Marovoay B2
Morombe A3
Morondava A3
Toamasina B2
Tôlanaro B3

Toliara A3
Tsiroanomandidy B2

Other Features
Alaotra, lake B2
Ambre, cape B1
Ankaratra, mts. B2
Bemaraha, plateau A2
Betsiboka, river B2
Kinkony, lake A2
L'Isalo, mts. B3
Mahajamba, river B2
Mangoky, river A3
Maromokotro, mt. B1
Menarandra, river A3
Mozambique, channel A2
Nosy Be, island B1
Nosy Sainte Marie, island .B2
Onilahy, river A3
Saint-André, cape A2
Sainte-Marie, cape B4
Sofia, river B2
Tsaratanana, mts. B1
Tsiribihina, river A2

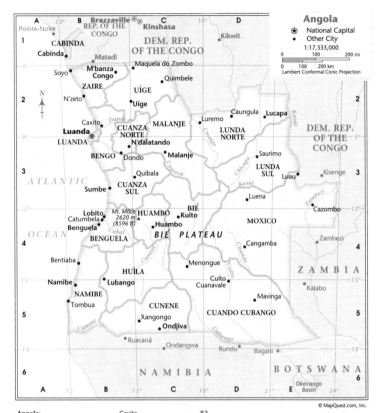

© MapQuest.com, Inc.

Angola

Capital: Luanda
Area: 481,354 sq. mi.
1,247,031 sq. km.
Population: 13,625,000
Largest City: Luanda
Language: Portuguese
Monetary Unit: Kwanza

Angola:
Map Index

Provinces

Bengo	B3
Benguela	B4
Bié	C4
Cabinda	B1
Cuando Cubango	D5
Cuanza Norte	B2
Cuanza Sul	B3
Cunene	C5
Huambo	C4
Huíla	B4
Luanda	B3
Lunda Norte	D2
Lunda Sul	D3
Malanje	C2
Moxico	D4
Namibe	B5
Uíge	C2
Zaire	B2

Cities and Towns

Benguela	B4
Bentiaba	B4
Cabinda	B1
Cangamba	D4
Catumbela	B4
Caungula	D2
Caxito	B2
Cazombo	E3
Cuíto Cuanavale	D5
Dondo	B3
Huambo	C4
Kuito	C4
Lobito	B4
Luanda, capital	B2
Luau	E3
Lubango	B5
Lucapa	D2
Luena	D3
Luremo	C2
Malanje	C2
Maquela do Zombo	C2
Mavinga	D5
M'banza Congo	B2
Menongue	C4
Namibe	B5
N'dalatando	B3
N'zeto	B2
Ondjiva	C5
Quibala	C3
Quimbele	C2
Saurimo	D3
Soyo	B2
Sumbe	B3
Tombua	B5
Uíge	C2
Xangongo	C5

Other Features

Bié, plateau	C4
Chicapa, river	D3
Cuando, river	D4
Cuango, river	D2
Cuanza, river	C3
Cubal, river	B4
Cubango, river	D5
Cuito, river	D4
Cunene, river	B5, C4
Dande, river	B2
Kasai, river	D3
Môco, mt.	C4
Zambezi, river	E3

Seychelles

Capital: Victoria
Area: 176 sq. mi.
456 sq. km.
Population: 80,469
Largest City: Victoria
Languages: English, French
Monetary Unit: Seychelles rupee

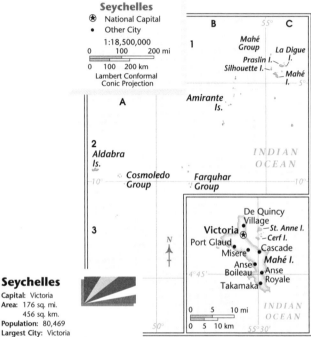

© MapQuest.com, Inc.

Seychelles:
Map Index

Cities and Towns

Anse Boileau	Inset
Anse Royale	Inset
Cascade	Inset
De Quincy Village	Inset
Misere	Inset
Port Glaud	Inset
Takamaka	Inset
Victoria, capital	Inset

Other Features

Aldabra, islands	A2
Amirante, islands	B2
Cerf, island	Inset
Cosmoledo, island group	A2
Farquhar, island group	B2
La Digue, island	C1
Mahé, island	C1, Inset
Mahé, island group	B1
Praslin, island	C1
St. Anne, island	Inset
Silhouette, island	C1

Namibia

Capital: Windhoek
Area: 318,146 sq. mi.
824,212 sq. km.
Population: 1,987,000
Largest City: Windhoek
Language: English, Afrikaans
Monetary Unit: Namibian dollar,
South African rand

Namibia:
Map Index

Cities and Towns

Bethanien	C4
Gobabis	C2
Grootfontein	C1
Karasburg	C4
Karibib	B2
Katima Mulilo	E1
Keetmanshoop	C4
Khorixas	B2
Lüderitz	B4
Maltahöhe	B3
Mariental	C3
Okahandja	B2
Okakarara	B2
Omaruru	B2
Ondangwa	B1
Opuwo	A1
Oranjemund	B4
Oshakati	B1
Otavi	C1
Otjiwarongo	B2
Outjo	B2
Rehoboth	C3
Rundu	C1

Swakopmund	B2
Tsumeb	C1
Tsumkwe	D1
Walvis Bay	B2
Windhoek, capital	C2

Other Features

Auob, river	C3
Brandberg, mt.	B2
Caprivi, strip	D1
Eiseb, river	D2
Etosha, pan	B1
Fish, river	C4
Kalahari, desert	C3
Kaoko Veld, mts.	A1
Kaukau Veld, region	C2
Kunene, river	A1
Linyanti, river	E1
Namib, desert	A1, B3
Nossob, river	C3
Okavango, river	C1
Omatako, river	C1
Orange, river	C4
Ruacana, falls	B1
Skeleton, coast	A1
Ugab, river	B2
Zambezi, river	E1

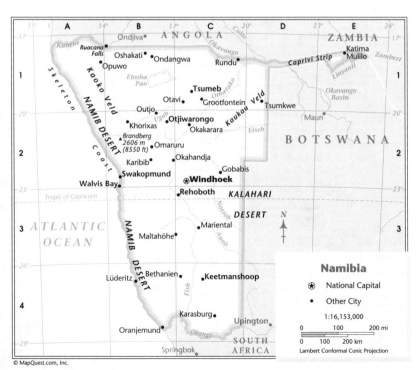

© MapQuest.com, Inc.

Namibia

⊛ National Capital
• Other City

1:16,153,000

0   100   200 mi
0   100   200 km

Lambert Conformal Conic Projection

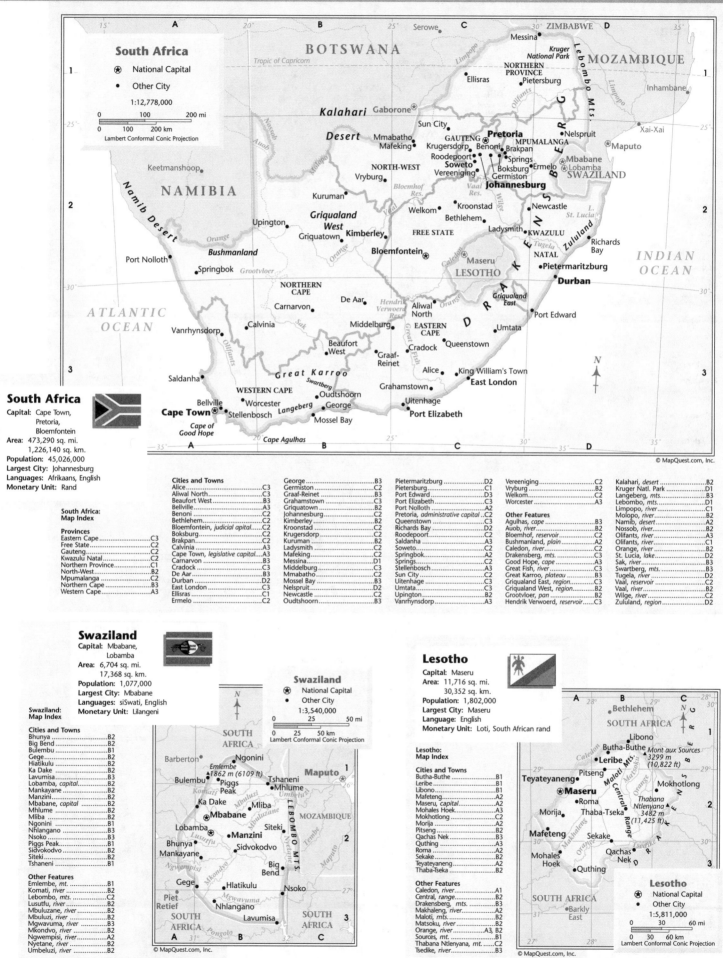

© MapQuest.com, Inc.

South Africa

Capital: Cape Town,
Pretoria,
Bloemfontein
Area: 473,290 sq. mi.
1,226,140 sq. km.
Population: 45,026,000
Largest City: Johannesburg
Languages: Afrikaans, English
Monetary Unit: Rand

South Africa: Map Index

Provinces

Eastern Cape	C3
Free State	C2
Gauteng	C2
Kwazulu Natal	C2
Northern Province	C1
North-West	B2
Mpumalanga	C2
Northern Cape	B3
Western Cape	A3

Cities and Towns

Alice	C3
Aliwal North	C3
Beaufort West	B3
Bellville	A3
Benoni	C2
Bethlehem	C2
Bloemfontein, *judicial apital*	C2
Boksburg	C2
Brakpan	C2
Calvinia	A3
Cape Town, *legislative capital*	A3
Carnarvon	B3
Cradock	C3
De Aar	B3
Durban	D2
East London	C3
Ellisras	C1
Ermelo	C2

George	B3
Germiston	C2
Graaf-Reinet	B3
Grahamstown	C3
Griquatown	B2
Johannesburg	C2
Kimberley	B2
Kroonstad	C2
Krugersdorp	C2
Kuruman	B2
Ladysmith	C2
Mafeking	B2
Messina	D1
Middelburg	C3
Mmabatho	B2
Mossel Bay	B3
Nelspruit	C2
Newcastle	C2
Oudtshoorn	B3

Pietermaritzburg	D2
Pietersburg	C1
Port Edward	D3
Port Elizabeth	C3
Port Nolloth	A2
Pretoria, *administrative capital*	C2
Queenstown	C3
Richards Bay	D2
Roodepoort	C2
Saldanha	A3
Soweto	C2
Springbok	A2
Springs	C2
Stellenbosch	A3
Sun City	C2
Uitenhage	C3
Umtata	C3
Upington	B2
Vanrhynsdorp	A3

Vereeniging	C2
Vryburg	B2
Welkom	C2
Worcester	A3

Other Features

Agulhas, *cape*	B3
Auob, *river*	B2
Bloemhof, *reservoir*	C2
Bushmanland, *plain*	A2
Caledon, *river*	C2
Drakensberg, *mts.*	C3
Good Hope, *cape*	A3
Great Fish, *river*	C3
Great Karroo, *plateau*	B3
Griqualand East, *region*	C3
Griqualand West, *region*	B2
Grootvloer, *pan*	B2
Hendrik Verhoeurd, *reservoir*	C3

Kalahari, *desert*	B2
Kruger Natl. Park	D1
Langeberg, *mts.*	B3
Lebombo, *mts.*	D1
Limpopo, *river*	C1
Molopo, *river*	B2
Namib, *desert*	A2
Nossob, *river*	B2
Olifants, *river*	A3
Olifants, *river*	C1
Orange, *river*	B2
St. Lucia, *lake*	D2
Sak, *river*	B3
Swartberg, *mts.*	B3
Tugela, *river*	D2
Vaal, *reservoir*	C2
Vaal, *river*	B2
Wilge, *river*	C2
Zululand, *region*	D2

Swaziland

Capital: Mbabane,
Lobamba
Area: 6,704 sq. mi.
17,368 sq. km.
Population: 1,077,000
Largest City: Mbabane
Languages: siSwati, English
Monetary Unit: Lilangeni

Swaziland: Map Index

Cities and Towns

Bhunya	B2
Big Bend	B2
Bulembu	B1
Gege	B2
Hiatikulu	B2
Ka Dake	B2
Lavumisa	B3
Lobamba, *capital*	B2
Mankayane	B2
Manzini	B2
Mbabane, *capital*	B2
Mhlume	B2
Mliba	B2
Ngonini	B1
Nhlangano	B3
Nsoko	B3
Piggs Peak	B1
Sidvokodvo	B2
Siteki	B2
Tshaneni	B1

Other Features

Emlembe, *mt.*	B1
Komati, *river*	B2
Lebombo, *mts.*	C2
Lusutfu, *river*	B2
Mbuluzane, *river*	B2
Mbuluzi, *river*	B2
Mgwavuma, *river*	B3
Mkondvo, *river*	B2
Ngwempisi, *river*	A2
Nyetane, *river*	B2
Umbeluzi, *river*	B2

Swaziland

⊛ National Capital
• Other City

1:3,540,000

0   25   50 mi
0   25   50 km
Lambert Conformal Conic Projection

© MapQuest.com, Inc.

Lesotho

Capital: Maseru
Area: 11,716 sq. mi.
30,352 sq. km.
Population: 1,802,000
Largest City: Maseru
Language: English
Monetary Unit: Loti, South African rand

Lesotho: Map Index

Cities and Towns

Butha-Buthe	B1
Leribe	B1
Libono	B1
Mafeteng	A2
Maseru, *capital*	A2
Mohales Hoek	A3
Mokhotlong	C2
Morija	A2
Pitseng	B2
Qachas Nek	B3
Quthing	A3
Roma	A2
Sekake	B2
Teyateyaneng	A2
Thaba-Tseka	B2

Other Features

Caledon, *river*	A1
Central, *range*	B2
Drakensberg, *mts.*	B3
Makhaleng, *river*	A2
Maloti, *mts.*	B2
Matsoku, *river*	B2
Orange, *river*	A3, B2
Sources, *mt.*	B1
Thabana Ntlenyana, *mt.*	B2
Tsedike, *river*	B3

Lesotho

⊛ National Capital
• Other City

1:5,811,000

0   30   60 mi
0   30   60 km
Lambert Conformal Conic Projection

MAJOR CITIES

Argentina (metro)
Buenos Aires 12,024,000
Córdoba 1,368,000
Rosario 1,279,000
Mendoza 934,000
San Miguel de
Tucumán 792,000

Bolivia (metro)
La Paz 1,499,000
Santa Cruz 1,062,000
Sucre 183,000

Brazil (metro)
São Paulo 17,962,000
Rio de Janeiro 10,652,000
Belo Horizonte 4,224,000
Pôrto Alegre 3,757,000
Recife 3,346,000
Salvador 3,238,000
Fortaleza 3,066,000
Curitiba 2,562,000
Brasília 2,073,000
Campinas 1,895,000
Belém 1,658,000
Manaus 1,467,000

Chile (metro)
Santiago 5,551,000
Puente Alto 501,000

Colombia (metro)
Bogotá 6,957,000
Medellín 2,866,000
Cali 2,233,000
Barranquilla 1,683,000
Cartagena 845,000

Ecuador (metro)
Guayaquil 2,118,000
Quito 1,660,000

Falkland Islands
Stanley 1,200

French Guiana
Cayenne 53,000

Guyana
Georgetown 280,000

Paraguay (metro)
Asunción 1,302,000

Peru (metro)
Lima 7,594,000
Arequipa 710,100
Callao 424,290

Suriname
Paramaribo 240,000

Uruguay (metro)
Montevideo 1,329,000

Venezuela (metro)
Caracas 3,177,000
Maracaibo 1,901,000
Valencia 1,893,000
Maracay 1,100,000
Barquisimeto 923,000
Ciudad Guayana 799,000

International comparability of city population
data is limited by various data inconsistencies.

Map Labels

CARIBBEAN SEA

Barranquilla
Cartagena
Maracaibo
Barquisimeto
Valencia
Maracay
Caracas Cumaná
Maturín
Ciudad
Bolívar
Ciudad Guayana
Cúcuta
San Cristóbal
L. Maracaibo
VENEZUELA
Georgetown
GUYANA
Paramaribo
SURINAME
FRENCH GUIANA (FR.)
Cayenne
ATLANTIC OCEAN
Bucaramanga
Medellín
Manizales
Pereira
Ibagué
Bogotá
Cali
COLOMBIA
GUIANA HIGHLANDS
Pasto
Quito
ECUADOR
Guayaquil
Chimborazo 6267 m (20,561 ft)
Cuenca
Iquitos
Negro
Ilha Marajó
Belém
AMAZON
Manaus
Amazon
SELVAS
Fortaleza
Teresina
Natal
PERU
Piura
Chiclayo
Trujillo
Chimbote
BASIN
Purus
Juruá
Tapajós
Xingu
BRAZIL
Pucallpa
Huascarán 6768 m (22,205 ft)
Pôrto Velho
Madeira
Recife
Maceió
Huancayo
Callao Lima
Ica
Cuzco
BOLIVIA
La Paz
Arequipa
Oruro
Cochabamba
Santa Cruz
MATO GROSSO
Cuiabá
PLATEAU
Goiânia
Brasília
BRAZILIAN
Salvador
São Francisco
HIGHLANDS
Uberlândia
Belo Horizonte
Vitória
Arica
Sucre
Potosí
GRAN CHACO
Campo Grande
Campinas
Santos
Rio de Janeiro
Iquique
PACIFIC OCEAN
ATACAMA DESERT
Antofagasta
Salta
PARAGUAY
Asunción
Ciudad del Este
Curitiba
São Paulo
Isla San Ambrosio (CHILE)
Isla San Félix (CHILE)
San Miguel de Tucumán
Ojos del Salado 6880 m (22,572 ft)
Santiago del Estero
Resistencia
Encarnación
Pôrto Alegre
Aconcagua 6960 m (22,834 ft)
Córdoba
San Juan
Mendoza
Santa Fe
Salto
Paysandú
URUGUAY
ATLANTIC OCEAN
CHILE
Islas Juan Fernández (CHILE)
Valparaíso
Santiago
Rancagua
Rosario
Buenos Aires
Montevideo
Río de la Plata
Talca
Concepción
Temuco
ARGENTINA
Neuquén
Bahía Blanca
Mar del Plata
Puerto Montt
Chiloé
Península Valdés
Archipiélago de los Chonos
Península Taitao
Comodoro Rivadavia
PATAGONIA
ANDES
PAMPAS
Falkland Is. (Islas Malvinas) (BR.)
Stanley
Strait of Magellan
Punta Arenas
Tierra del Fuego
Ushuaia
Cape Horn

CITIES

⊛ National Capital
★ Territorial Capital
● Other City

ELEVATIONS

Feet	Meters
13,120	4000
6560	2000
1640	500
656	200
0	0
Below sea level	

0 250 500 750 1000 mi
0 250 500 750 1000 1250 1500 km

N

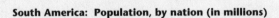

South America: Population, by nation (in millions)

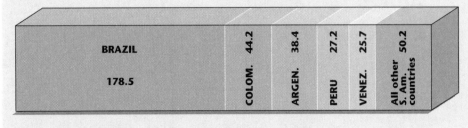

BRAZIL 178.5	COLOM. 44.2	ARGEN. 38.4	PERU 27.2	VENEZ. 25.7	All other S. Am. countries 50.2

© MapQuest.com, Inc.

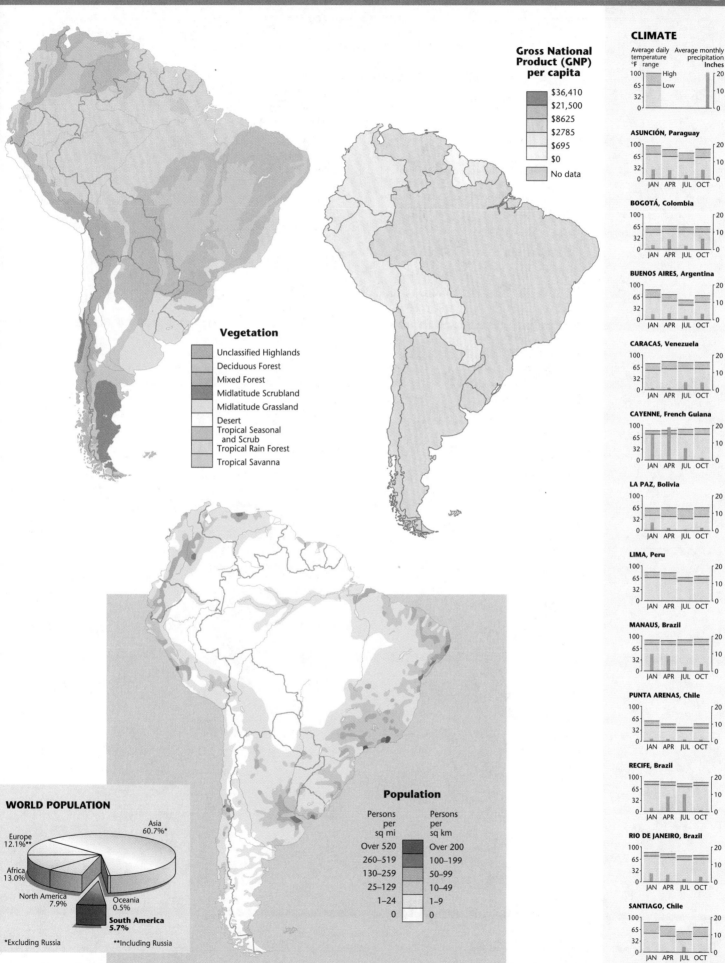

Gross National Product (GNP) per capita

- $36,410
- $21,500
- $8625
- $2785
- $695
- $0
- No data

Vegetation

- Unclassified Highlands
- Deciduous Forest
- Mixed Forest
- Midlatitude Scrubland
- Midlatitude Grassland
- Desert
- Tropical Seasonal and Scrub
- Tropical Rain Forest
- Tropical Savanna

CLIMATE

Average daily temperature °F range

Average monthly precipitation Inches

High
Low

ASUNCIÓN, Paraguay

BOGOTÁ, Colombia

BUENOS AIRES, Argentina

CARACAS, Venezuela

CAYENNE, French Guiana

LA PAZ, Bolivia

LIMA, Peru

MANAUS, Brazil

PUNTA ARENAS, Chile

RECIFE, Brazil

RIO DE JANEIRO, Brazil

SANTIAGO, Chile

WORLD POPULATION

Europe 12.1%**

Asia 60.7%*

Africa 13.0%

North America 7.9%

Oceania 0.5%

South America 5.7%

*Excluding Russia   **Including Russia

Population

Persons per sq mi	Persons per sq km
Over 520	Over 200
260–519	100–199
130–259	50–99
25–129	10–49
1–24	1–9
0	0

A   B   BOLIVIA   C   D   E

PARAGUAY

BRAZIL

Tropic of Capricorn

Tropic of Capricorn

Chuquicamata

Antofagasta

JUJUY   Embarcación   Concepción

ATACAMA DESERT

San Salvador
de Jujuy

Llullaillaco
6723 m
(22,057 ft)

Salta   FORMOSA   Asunción

SALTA   CHACO   BRAZIL

San Miguel
de Tucumán   SANTIAGO
DEL
ESTERO   CHACO   Formosa   Foz do Iguaçu

Ojos del Salado
6880 m
(22,572 ft)   TUCUMÁN   Presidencia Roque Sáenz Peña   Iguaçu
Falls   Curitiba

CATAMARCA   Resistencia   MISIONES

PACIFIC   Santiago
del Estero   Corrientes   Posadas

OCEAN   Catamarca   CORRIENTES

La Rioja   Reconquista   Santa Maria

La Serena   LA RIOJA   Curuzú Cuatiá

CÓRDOBA   SANTA FE   ENTRE
RÍOS   Pôrto Alegre

SAN JUAN   San
Francisco   Santa Fe   Concordia

Mercedario
6770 m
(22,211 ft)   Córdoba   Champaquí
2850 m
(9350 ft)   Paraná   Pelotas

San Juan   Villa
María

Aconcagua
6960 m
(22,834 ft)   Mendoza   Rosario   Negro

Santiago   Godoy Cruz   San Luis   Río
Cuarto   San Nicolás   URUGUAY

Tupungato
6800 m
(22,310 ft)   SAN
LUIS   DISTRITO FEDERAL

San
Rafael   Buenos Aires   Avellaneda   Montevideo

MENDOZA   Lanús

CHILE   Lomas de
Zamora   La
Plata

Domuyo
4709 m
(15,450 ft)   LA PAMPA   BUENOS AIRES   Cabo
San Antonio

Concepción   Santa Rosa   Olavarría   Tandil

NEUQUÉN

Mar del Plata

Neuquén   Bahía Blanca   Necochea

Lanín
3776 m
(12,389 ft)

RÍO NEGRO   San Antonio
Oeste   ATLANTIC

San Carlos
de Bariloche   Viedma   Punta Rasa   OCEAN

Puerto Montt   Golfo
San Matías

Chiloé   Península Valdés

CHUBUT   Rawson

Esquel

Coihaique   Comodoro Rivadavia

Golfo San Jorge

Peninsula
Taitao   Cabo Tres Puntas

SANTA CRUZ   Puerto Deseado

Fitzroy
3375 m
(11,073 ft)

Calafate   Puerto Santa Cruz

Bahía
Grande   West
Falkland I.   East
Falkland I.

Río Gallegos   Stanley

Punta Dungeness   Falkland Islands
(Islas Malvinas)
(Br.)
(claimed by Argentina)

Strait of Magellan

Punta Arenas   TIERRA
DEL
FUEGO   Isla de
los Estados

Ushuaia

Cape Horn   Beagle
Channel

A   B   C   D   E   F

Argentina

⊛ National Capital

★ Territorial Capital

● Other City

1:17,760,000

0   200   400 mi

0   200   400 km

Modified Chamberlain Trimetric Projection

© MapQuest.com, Inc.

Argentina

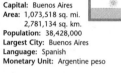

Capital: Buenos Aires
Area: 1,073,518 sq. mi.
2,781,134 sq. km.
Population: 38,428,000
Largest City: Buenos Aires
Language: Spanish
Monetary Unit: Argentine peso

Argentina: Map Index

Provinces

Buenos Aires	C4
Catamarca	B2
Chaco	C2
Chubut	B5
Córdoba	C3
Corrientes	D2
Distrito Federal	D3
Entre Ríos	D3
Formosa	D1
Jujuy	B1
La Pampa	B4
La Rioja	B2
Mendoza	B3
Misiones	E2
Neuquén	B4
Río Negro	B5
Salta	B1
San Juan	B3
San Luis	B3
Santa Cruz	A6
Santa Fe	C2
Santiago del Estero	C2
Tierra del Fuego	B7
Tucumán	B2

Cities and Towns

Avellaneda	D3
Bahía Blanca	C4
Buenos Aires, *capital*	D3
Calafate	A7
Catamarca	B2
Comodoro Rivadavia	B6
Concordia	D3
Córdoba	C3
Corrientes	D2
Curuzú Cuatiá	D2
Embarcación	C1
Esquel	A5
Formosa	D2
Godoy Cruz	B3
Lanús	D3

La Plata	D4
La Rioja	B2
Lomas de Zamora	D4
Mar del Plata	D4
Mendoza	B3
Necochea	D4
Neuquén	B4
Olavarría	C4
Paraná	C3
Posadas	D2
Presidencia Roque Sáenz Peña	C2
Puerto Deseado	B6
Puerto Santa Cruz	B7
Rawson	B5
Reconquista	D2
Resistencia	D2
Río Cuarto	C3
Río Gallegos	B7
Rosario	C3
Salta	B1
San Antonio Oeste	B5
San Carlos de Bariloche	A5
San Francisco	C3
San Juan	B3
San Luis	B3
San Miguel de Tucumán	B2
San Nicolás	C3
San Rafael	B3
San Salvador de Jujuy	B1
Santa Fe	C3
Santa Rosa	C4
Santiago del Estero	C2
Tandil	D4
Ushuaia	B7
Viedma	C5
Villa María	C3

Other Features

Aconcagua, *mt.*	A3
Andes, *mts.*	A6–B1
Argentino, *lake*	A7
Atuel, *river*	B4
Beagle, *channel*	B7
Bermejo, *river*	C2

Blanca, *bay*	C4
Buenos Aires, *lake*	A6
Cardiel, *lake*	A6
Champaquí, *mt.*	C3
Chico, *river*	B6
Chubut, *river*	A5
Colorado, *river*	B4
Córdoba, *range*	B3
Desaguadero, *river*	B2
Deseado, *river*	B6
Domuyo, *volcano*	A4
Dungeness, *point*	B7
Estados, *island*	C7
Fitzroy, *mt.*	A6
Gallegos, *river*	A7
Gran Chaco, *region*	C1
Grande, *bay*	B7
Iguaçu, *falls*	E2
Iguaçu, *river*	E2
Lanín, *volcano*	A4
Llullaillaco, *volcano*	B1
Magellan, *strait*	B7
Mar Chiquita, *lake*	C3
Mercedario, *mt.*	B3
Negro, *river*	B4
Ojos del Salado, *mt.*	B2
Pampas, *plain*	C4
Paraguay, *river*	D2
Paraná, *river*	D2
Patagonia, *region*	A6
Pilcomayo, *river*	C1
Plata, Río de la, *estuary*	D4
Rasa, *point*	C5
Salado, *river*	B3
Salado, *river*	C2
San Antonio, *cape*	D4
San Jorge, *gulf*	B6
San Martín, *lake*	A6
San Matías, *gulf*	C5
Santa Cruz, *river*	A7
Tres Puntas, *cape*	B6
Tupungato, *mt.*	B3
Uruguay, *river*	D3
Valdés, *peninsula*	C5
Viedma, *lake*	A6

Paraguay

Paraguay

★ National Capital
• Other City

1:10,375,000

0   50   100 mi
0   50   100 km
Conic Equidistant Projection

Paraguay

Capital: Asunción
Area: 157,048 sq. mi.
406,752 sq. km.
Population: 5,878,000
Largest City: Asunción
Language: Spanish
Monetary Unit: Guarani

Paraguay: Map Index

Departments

Alto Paraguay	C2
Alto Paraná	E4
Amambay	E3
Asunción	D4
Boquerón	B3
Caaguazú	D4
Caazapá	D5
Canendiyú	E4
Central	D4
Concepción	D3
Cordillera	D4
Guairá	D4
Itapúa	E5
Misiones	D5
Ñeembucú	C5
Paraguarí	D5
Presidente Hayes	C4
San Pedro	D4

Cities and Towns

Abaí	E4
Asunción, *capital*	D4
Caacupé	D4
Caaguazú	E4
Caazapá	D5
Capitán Pablo Lagerenza	B1
Ciudad del Este	E4
Concepción	D3
Coronel Oviedo	D4
Doctor Pedro P. Peña	A3
Encarnación	E5

Filadelfia	B3
Fuerte Olimpo	D2
General Eugenio A. Garay	A2
Mariscal Estigarribia	B3
Paraguarí	D4
Pedro Juan Caballero	E3
Pilar	C5
Pozo Colorado	C3
Puerto Bahía	C2
Puerto Pinasco	D3
Salto del Guairá	E4
San Juan Bautista	D5
San Lorenzo	D4
San Pedro	D4
Villa Hayes	D4
Villarrica	D4

Other Features

Acaray, *river*	E4
Amambay, *mts.*	E3
Apa, *river*	D3
Chaco Boreal, *region*	B2
Gran Chaco, *region*	B3
Iguazú, *falls*	E4
Itaipú, *reservoir*	E4
Jejuí-Guazú, *river*	D4
Montelindo, *river*	C3
Paraguay, *river*	C2, C5
Paraná, *river*	C5, E5
Pilcomayo, *river*	B3, C4
Tebicuary, *river*	D5
Verde, *river*	C3
Ypané, *river*	D3
Ypoá, *lake*	D4

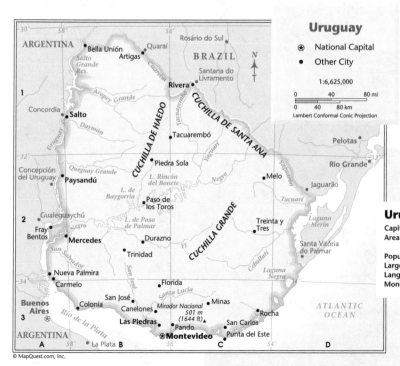

© MapQuest.com, Inc.

Uruguay

★ National Capital
• Other City

1:6,625,000

0   40   80 mi
0   40   80 km
Lambert Conformal Conic Projection

Uruguay

Capital: Montevideo
Area: 68,037 sq. mi.
176,215 sq. km.
Population: 3,415,000
Largest City: Montevideo
Language: Spanish
Monetary Unit: Uruguayan peso

Uruguay: Map Index

Cities and Towns

Artigas	B1
Bella Unión	B1
Canelones	B3
Carmelo	A2
Colonia	B3
Durazno	B2
Florida	B3
Fray Bentos	A2
Las Piedras	B3
Melo	C2
Mercedes	A2
Minas	C3
Montevideo, *capital*	B3
Nueva Palmira	A2
Pando	C3
Paso de los Toros	B2
Paysandú	A2
Piedra Sola	B2
Punta del Este	C3
Rivera	C1
Rocha	C3
Salto	B1
San Carlos	C3
San José	B3
Tacuarembó	C1
Treinta y Tres	C2
Trinidad	B2

Other Features

Arapey Grande, *river*	B1
Baygorria, *lake*	B2
Cebollatí, *river*	C2
Cuareim, *river*	B1
Daymán, *river*	B1
Grande, *range*	C2
Haedo, *range*	B2
Merín, *lagoon*	D2
Mirador Nacional, *mt.*	C3
Negra, *lagoon*	D2
Negro, *river*	C2
Plata, Río de la, *river*	B3
Queguay Grande, *river*	B2
Rincón del Bonete, *lake*	B2
Salto Grande, *reservoir*	B1
San José, *river*	B2
San Salvador, *river*	A2
Santa Ana, *range*	C1
Santa Lucía, *river*	B3
Tacuarembó, *river*	B1
Tacuarí, *river*	D2
Uruguay, *river*	A1
Yaguarí, *river*	C1
Yaguarón, *river*	D2
Yi, *river*	C2

Chile

Capital: Santiago
Area: 292,135 sq. mi.
756,826 sq. km.
Population: 15,805,000
Largest City: Santiago
Language: Spanish
Monetary Unit: Chilean peso

Chile:
Map Index

Regions
Aisén del General Carlos
Ibáñez del Campo B8
Antofagasta C2
Atacama B3
Bío-Bío B6
Coquimbo B4
El Libertador General
Bernardo O'Higgins B4
La Araucanía B6
Los Lagos B7
Magallanes y Antártica
Chilena B9
Maule B5, B6
Región Metropolitana B4,
Inset
Tarapacá C1
Valparaíso ....B4, Inset

Cities and Towns
Aguada de Cachinal C2
Aguas Blancas C2
Algarrobo ....Inset

Altamira C3
Ancud B7
Angol B6
Antofagasta B2
Arica B1
Balmaceda B8
Calama C2
Casablanca ....Inset
Castro B7
Cerro Castillo B9
Chaitén B7
Chañaral B3
Chiapa C1

Altamira C3
Ancud B7
Angol B6
Antofagasta B2
Arica B1
Balmaceda B8
Calama C2
Casablanca ....Inset
Castro B7
Cerro Castillo B9
Chaitén B7
Chañaral B3
Chiapa C1

Chile Chico B8
Chillán B6
Chuquicamata C2
Cochrane B8
Coihaique B8
Colina ....Inset
Collaguasi C2
Concepción B6
Conchalí ....Inset
Constitución B5
Copiapó B3
Coquimbo B3
Curicó B4

El Tabo ....Inset
El Trebolar ....Inset
Freirina B3
Gatico B2
Illapel B4
Iquique B2
Lampa ....Inset
La Serena B3
La Unión B6
Lebu B6
Linares B5
Los Andes B4
Los Ángeles B6
Maipú ....Inset
Mamiña C2
Melipilla ....Inset
Nuñoa ....Inset
Osorno B7
Ovalle B4
Parral B6
Pisagua B1
Porvenir B9
Potrerillos C3
Puente Alto ....Inset
Puerto Aisén B8
Puerto Cisnes B7
Puerto Montt B7
Puerto Natales B9
Puerto Varas B7
Puerto Williams C9
Punta Arenas B9
Punta Delgada B9
Putre C1
Quellón B7
Quillota B4
Quilpué ....Inset
Rancagua ....Inset
Rungue ....Inset
San Antonio ....B4, Inset
San Bernardo ....Inset
San Félix B3
San Fernando B4
San Pedro de Atacama C2
Santa Inés ....Inset
Santiago, capital ....B4, Inset
Socompa C2
Talagante ....Inset
Talca B5
Talcahuano B6
Taltal B3
Temuco B6
Tilomonte C2
Tocopilla B2
Tomé B6
Unión C2
Valdivia B6
Vallenar B4
Valparaíso ....B4, Inset
Victoria B6
Viña del Mar ....B4, Inset

Other Features
Aconcagua, river B4
Ancud, gulf B7
Andes, mts. B8, C4
Atacama, desert C2
Bascuñán, cape B3
Bío-Bío, river B6
Brunswick, peninsula B9
Buenos Aires, lake B8
Campana, island A8
Chiloé, island B7
Chonos, archipelago B7
Cochrane, lake B8
Concepción, bay B6
Copiapó, river B3
Corcovado, gulf B7
Desolación, island B9
Domeyko, mts. C3
Dungeness, point C9
Duque de York, island A9
Elqui, river B3
Fitzroy, mt. B8
Galera, point B6
Horn, cape C9
Hoste, island C9
Imperial, river B6
Lanín, volcano B6
Lengua de Vaca, point B4
Llanquihue, lake B7
Llullaillaco, volcano C2
Loa, river B2
Madre de Dios, island A9
Magdalena, island B7
Magellan, strait B9
Maipo, river ....B4, Inset
Maule, river B5
Navarino, island C9
Occidental, mts. C1
Ojos del Salado, mt. C3
Ollagüe, volcano C2
Penas, gulf B8
Rapel, river B4
Reina Adelaida, archipelago ..B9
San Martín, lake B8
San Valentín, mt. B8
Santa Inés, island B9
Taitao, peninsula A8
Tierra del Fuego, island C9
Toltén, river B6
Wellington, island A8

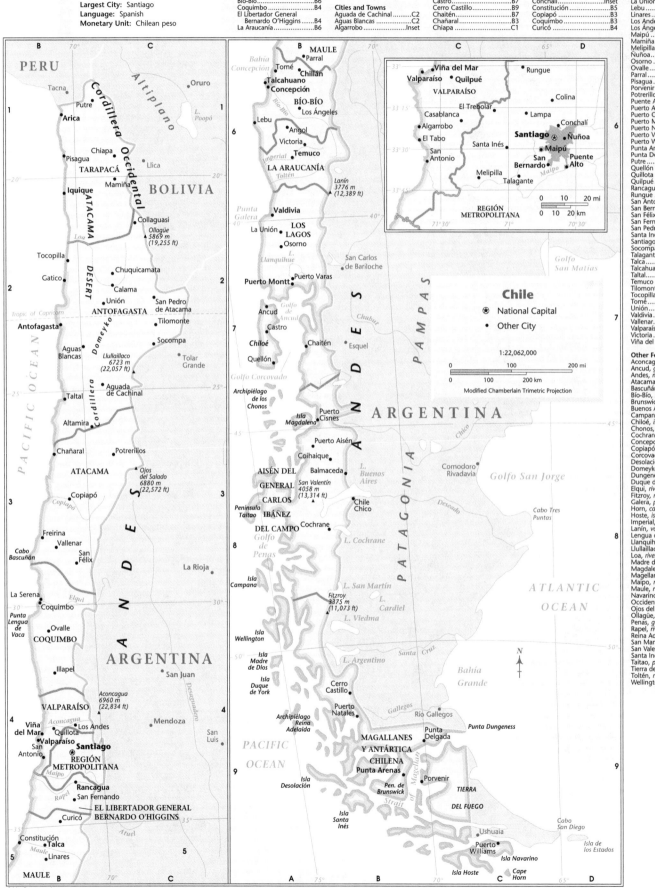

© MapQuest.com, Inc.

Peru

Capital: Lima
Area: 496,225 sq. mi.
1,285,216 sq. km.
Population: 27,167,000
Largest City: Lima
Languages: Spanish, Quechua
Monetary Unit: Nuevo sol

Peru:
Map Index

Cities and Towns

Abancay	C3
Arequipa	C4
Ayacucho	C3
Cajamarca	B2
Callao	B3
Cerro de Pasco	B3
Chachapoyas	B2
Chiclayo	B2
Chimbote	B2
Chincha Alta	B3
Cuzco	C3
Huacho	B3
Huancavelica	B3
Huancayo	B3
Huánuco	B2
Huaraz	B2
Ica	B3
Ilo	C4
Iquitos	C1
Juliaca	C4
La Oroya	B3
Lima, capital	B3
Mollendo	C4
Moquegua	C4
Moyobamba	B2
Nazca	C3
Pacasmayo	B2
Paita	A2
Patavilca	B3
Pisco	B3
Piura	A2
Pucallpa	C2
Puerto Maldonado	D3
Puno	C4
Salaverry	B2
San Juan	B4
Sicuani	C3
Sullana	A1
Tacna	C4
Talara	A1
Tarapoto	B2
Tingo María	B2
Trujillo	B2
Tumbes	A1
Yurimaguas	B2

Other Features

Amazon, river	C1
Andes, mts.	B1, C3
Apurímac, river	C3
Central, mts.	B2
Colca, river	C4
Coropuna, mt.	C4
Guayaquil, gulf	A1
Huallaga, river	B2
Huascarán, mt.	B2
La Montaña, region	C2
Machupicchu, ruins	C3
Madre de Dios, river	C3
Mantaro, river	B3
Marañón, river	B1, B2
Napo, river	C1
Negra, point	A2
Occidental, mts.	B2, C4
Oriental, mts.	B2, C3
Pastaza, river	B1
Purús, river	C3
Putumayo, river	C1
Santiago, river	B1
Sechura, desert	A2
Tambo, river	C3
Tambo, river	C4
Tigre, river	B1
Titicaca, lake	D4
Ucayali, river	C2
Urubamba, river	C3
Vilcabamba, mts.	C3
Yavarí, river	C1

Peru map

COLOMBIA

Equator

ECUADOR

Quito

Guayaquil

Golfo de Guayaquil

Cuenca

Tumbes
Talara
Sullana
Paita
Piura
Desierto de Sechura
Punta Negra

Chiclayo
Pacasmayo
Cajamarca
Trujillo
Salaverry
Chimbote
Huaraz
Patavilca
Huacho
Callao
Lima

PACIFIC OCEAN

Chachapoyas
Yurimaguas
Moyobamba
Tarapoto

Iquitos

SELVAS

BRAZIL

Cruzeiro do Sul

Pucallpa

Huascarán 6768 m (22,205 ft)
Tingo María
Huánuco
Cerro de Pasco
La Oroya
Huancayo
Huancavelica
Ayacucho
Chincha Alta
Pisco
Ica
Nazca
San Juan
Coropuna 6425 m (21,079 ft)

Machupicchu
Cuzco
Abancay
Sicuani
Juliaca
Puno

Rio Branco

Puerto Maldonado

L. Titicaca
La Paz

Arequipa
Mollendo
Ilo
Tacna
Moquegua

BOLIVIA
CHILE
Arica

Cordillera Occidental · Cordillera Central · Cordillera Oriental · La Montaña · Cordillera de Vilcabamba · Cordillera Oriental · Cordillera Occidental · ANDES

Peru
⊛ National Capital
• Other City
1:15,900,000
0 100 200 mi
0 100 200 km
Transverse Mercator Projection

© MapQuest.com, Inc.

Bolivia:
Map Index

Departments

Beni	A2
Chuquisaca	B4
Cochabamba	A3
La Paz	A2
Oruro	A3
Pando	A2
Potosí	A4
Santa Cruz	B3
Tarija	B4

Cities and Towns

Aiquile	A3
Camiri	B4
Cobija	A2
Cochabamba	A3
Fortín Ravelo	B3
Guaqui	A3
La Paz, capital	A3
Llallagua	A3
Magdalena	B2
Mojos	A3
Montero	B3
Oruro	A3
Potosí	A3
Puerto Suárez	C3
Riberalta	A2
Roboré	C3
San Borja	A2
San Cristóbal	B2
San Ignacio	B3
San José de Chiquitos	B3
San Matías	C3
Santa Ana	A2
Santa Cruz	B3
Santa Rosa del Palmar	B3
Sucre, capital	A3
Tarija	B4
Tarvo	B2
Trinidad	B2
Tupiza	A4
Uyuni	A4
Villazón	A4
Yacuiba	B4

Other Features

Abuná, river	A2
Altiplano, plateau	A3
Beni, river	A2
Chaparé, river	A3
Cordillera Central, mts.	A3
Cordillera Occidental, mts.	A3
Cordillera Oriental, mts.	A3
Cordillera Real, mts.	A3
Desaguadero, river	A3
Gran Chaco, region	B4
Grande, river	B3
Guaporé, river	B2
Ichilo, river	B3
Illampu, mt.	A3
Illimani, mt.	A3
Iténez, river	B2
Madre de Dios, river	A2
Mamoré, river	A2
Ollagüe, volcano	A4
Paraguá, river	B2
Paraguay, river	C4
Pilaya, river	B4
Pilcomayo, river	B3
Poopó, lake	A3
Sajama, mt.	A3
Salar de Uyuni, salt flat	A4
San Luis, lake	B2
San Pablo, river	B3
Titicaca, lake	A3
Yata, river	A2
Yungas, region	A3

Bolivia

Capital: La Paz, Sucre
Area: 424,164 sq. mi.
1,098,871 sq. km.
Population: 8,808,000
Largest City: La Paz
Languages: Spanish, Quechua, Aymara
Monetary Unit: Boliviano

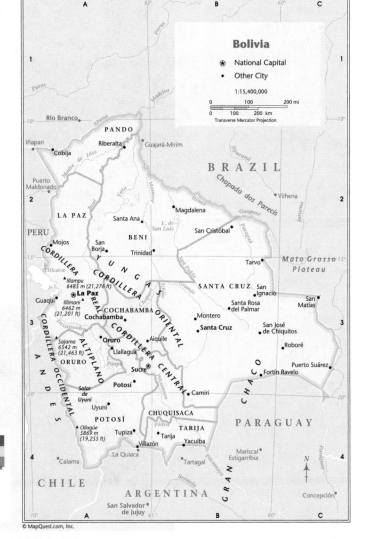

Bolivia map

Iñapari
Cobija
PANDO
Riberalta
Guajará-Mirim
Puerto Maldonado
Rio Branco
PERU
LA PAZ
BENI
Mojos
San Borja
San Ignacio?
Trinidad
Santa Ana
L. de San Luis
Magdalena
San Cristóbal
BRAZIL
Chapada dos Parecis
Vilhena
Mato Grosso Plateau
Tarvo
SANTA CRUZ
San Ignacio
Santa Rosa del Palmar
San Matías
Montero
San José de Chiquitos
Roboré
Santa Cruz
Puerto Suárez
Fortín Ravelo
Camiri
Illampu 6485 m (21,276 ft)
La Paz
Guaqui
Illimani 6462 m (21,201 ft)
Cochabamba
Aiquile
COCHABAMBA
Sajama 6542 m (21,463 ft)
Oruro
Llallagua
ORURO
Poopó
Sucre
Potosí
POTOSÍ
Salar de Uyuni
Uyuni
Ollagüe 5869 m (19,255 ft)
Tupiza
Villazón
La Quiaca
Calama
CHILE
CHUQUISACA
Tarija
TARIJA
Yacuiba
PARAGUAY
GRAN CHACO
Mariscal Estigarribia
Tartagal
ARGENTINA
San Salvador de Jujuy
Concepción

CORDILLERA REAL · CORDILLERA OCCIDENTAL · CORDILLERA CENTRAL · CORDILLERA ORIENTAL · ALTIPLANO · YUNGAS · ANDES

Bolivia
⊛ National Capital
• Other City
1:15,400,000
0 100 200 mi
0 100 200 km
Transverse Mercator Projection

© MapQuest.com, Inc.

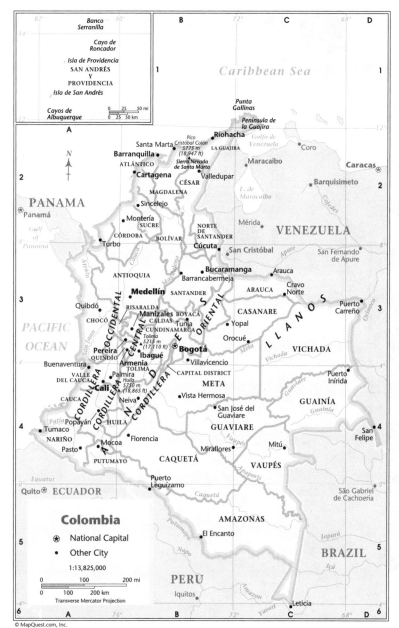

Banco Serranilla
Cayo de Roncador
Isla de Providencia
SAN ANDRÉS Y PROVIDENCIA
Isla de San Andrés
Cayos de Albuquerque

0 25 50 mi
0 25 50 km

Caribbean Sea

PANAMA
⊛ Panamá
Gulf of Panama

PACIFIC OCEAN

Punta Gallinas
Peninsula de la Guajira
Ríohacha
LA GUAJIRA
Golfo de Venezuela
Coro
Santa Marta
Pico Cristóbal Colón 5775 m (18,947 ft)
Barranquilla
ATLÁNTICO
Sierra Nevada de Santa Marta
Maracaibo
Caracas
Cartagena
CÉSAR
Valledupar
L. de Maracaibo
MAGDALENA
Barquisimeto
Sincelejo
Mérida
VENEZUELA
Montería
SUCRE
NORTE DE SANTANDER
CÓRDOBA
BOLÍVAR
Turbo
Cúcuta
San Cristóbal
Apure
San Fernando de Apure
ANTIOQUIA
Bucaramanga
Barrancabermeja
Arauca
ARAUCA
Cravo Norte
Medellín
SANTANDER
Puerto Carreño
Quibdó
RISARALDA
CASANARE
Orinoco
Manizales
BOYACÁ
CALDAS
Tunja
Yopal
CHOCÓ
CUNDINAMARCA
LLANOS
Tolima 5215 m (17,110 ft)
Orocué
VICHADA
Pereira
⊛ **Bogotá**
QUINDÍO
Ibagué
Villavicencio
Armenia
CAPITAL DISTRICT
Puerto Inírida
TOLIMA
META
Buenaventura
Palmira
VALLE DEL CAUCA
Huila 5750 m (18,865 ft)
Vista Hermosa
Cali
Neiva
CAUCA
San José del Guaviare
GUAINÍA
Patía
HUILA
GUAVIARE
San Felipe
Popayán
Mocoa
Florencia
Miraflores
Mitú
NARIÑO
Tumaco
Pasto
PUTUMAYO
CAQUETÁ
VAUPÉS
Equator
Quito ⊛ ECUADOR
Puerto Leguízamo
Apaporis
São Gabriel de Cachoeira
AMAZONAS
El Encanto
BRAZIL
PERU
Iquitos
Leticia
Yavarí

Colombia
⊛ National Capital
• Other City

1:13,825,000

0 100 200 mi
0 100 200 km
Transverse Mercator Projection

© MapQuest.com, Inc.

Colombia

Capital: Bogotá
Area: 440,831 sq. mi.
1,142,049 sq. km.
Population: 44,222,000
Largest City: Bogotá
Language: Spanish
Monetary Unit: Colombian peso

Colombia:
Map Index

Internal Divisions
Amazonas (commissary)...........B5
Antioquia (dept.)......................B3
Arauca (intendency).................C3
Atlántico (dept.).......................B2
Bolívar (dept.).........................B2
Boyacá (dept.).........................B3
Caldas (dept.)..........................B3
Capital District.........................B4
Caquetá (dept.)........................B4
Casanare (intendency).............C3
Cauca (dept.)...........................A4
César (dept.)............................B2
Chocó (dept.)...........................A3
Córdoba (dept.)........................B2
Cundinamarca (dept.)...............B3
Guainía (commissary)..............C4
Guaviare (commissary).............B4
Huila (dept.).............................A4
La Guajira (dept.).....................B2
Magdalena (dept.)....................B2
Meta (dept.).............................B4
Nariño (dept.)...........................A4
Norte de Santander (dept.)......B2
Putumayo (intendency)............A4
Quindío (dept.).........................A4
Risaralda (dept.)......................B3
San Andrés y Providencia
(intendency)........................Inset
Santander (dept.).....................B3
Sucre (dept.)............................B2
Tolima (dept.)...........................B4
Valle del Cauca (dept.)............A4
Vaupés (commissary)...............C4
Vichada (commissary)..............C4

Cities and Towns
Arauca C3
Armenia B3
Barrancabermeja B3
Barranquilla B2
Bogotá, *capital* B3
Bucaramanga B3
Buenaventura A4
Cali A4
Cartagena B2
Cravo Norte C3
Cúcuta B3
El Encanto B5
Florencia B4
Ibagué B3
Leticia C6
Manizales B3
Medellín B3
Miraflores B4
Mitú C4

Mocoa A4
Montería B2
Neiva B4
Orocué C3
Palmira A4
Pasto A4
Pereira B3
Popayán A4
Puerto Carreño D3
Puerto Inírida D4
Puerto Leguízamo B5
Quibdó A3
Ríohacha B2
San Felipe D4
San José del Guaviare B4
Santa Marta B2
Sincelejo B2
Tumaco A4
Tunja B3
Turbo A2
Valledupar B2
Villavicencio B3
Vista Hermosa B4
Yopal B3

Other Features
Albuquerque, *cays*................Inset
Amazon, *river*........................C5
Andes, *range*........................A4
Apaporis, *river*......................C4
Atrato, *river*...........................A3
Caquetá, *river*.......................B5
Cauca, *river*..........................B3
Cordillera Central, *range*......A4
Cordillera Occidental,
range..................................A4
Cordillera Oriental, *range* B4
Cristóbal Colón, *peak*...........B2
Gallinas, *point*......................C1
Guainía, *river*........................C4
Guajira, *peninsula* C1
Guaviare, *river*......................C4
Huila, *mt.*..............................A4
Llanos, *prairie*......................C3
Magdalena, *river*...................B3
Meta, *river*............................C3
Orinoco, *river*........................D3
Patía, *river*............................A4
Providencia, *island*...............Inset
Putumayo, *river*....................B5
Roncador, *cay*.......................Inset
San Andrés, *island*...............Inset
San Juan, *river*.....................A3
Serranilla, *bank*....................Inset
Sierra Nevada de Santa
Marta, *mts.*.........................B2
Tolima, *mt.*............................B3
Vaupés, *river*........................B4
Vichada, *river*.......................C3

Venezuela:
Map Index

Internal Divisions
Amazonas (territory) C3
Anzoátegui (state) D2
Apure (state)............................C2
Aragua (state)..........................C2
Barinas (state).........................C2
Bolívar (state) D2
Carabobo (state) C2
Cojedes (state).........................C2
Delta Amacuro (territory) D1
Dependencias Federales..........C1
Distrito Federal.........................C1
Falcón (state)...........................B1
Guárico (state)..........................C2
Lara (state)...............................B1
Mérida (state)...........................B2
Miranda (state).........................C1
Monagas (state).......................D2
Nueva Esparta (state)..............D1
Portuguesa (state)....................C2
Sucre (state).............................D1
Táchira (state)..........................B2
Trujillo (state)...........................B2
Yaracuy (state).........................C1
Zulia (state)..............................B2

Cities and Towns
Acarigua C2
Anaco.......................................D2
Barcelona D1
Barinas B2
Barquisimeto C1
Baruta C1
Cabimas B1
Calabozo C2
Canaima D2
Caracas, *capital*.....................C1
Carora C1
Carúpano D1
Ciudad Bolívar D2
Ciudad Guayana.......................D2
Coro C1
Cumaná D1
El Tigre D2
Guanare C2
Güiria D1
La Asunción D1
La Guaira Maiquetía C1
Los Teques C1
Maiquetía C1
Maracaibo B1
Maracay C2
Maturín D2
Mérida B2

Petare C1
Puerto Ayacucho C2
Puerto Cabello.........................C1
Puerto La Cruz.........................D1
Punto Fijo B1
San Cristóbal...........................B2
San Felipe C1
San Fernando de Apure C2
San Juan de Los Morros C2
Santa Elena de Uairén.............D3
Trujillo......................................B2
Tucupita...................................D2
Valencia C1
Valera B2

Other Features
Angel, *falls*............................D2
Apure, *river*...........................C2
Arauca, *river*.........................C2
Bolívar, *mt.*...........................B2
Caroni, *river*..........................D2
Casiquiare, *river*....................C3
Caura, *river*...........................D2
Cojedes, *river*........................C2
Guri, *reservoir*......................D2
Guiana, *highlands* D2
La Tortuga, *island* C1
Llanos, *plain*.........................B2

Maracaibo, *lake*....................B2
Margarita, *island*...................D1
Mérida, *mts.*.........................B2
Meta, *river*............................C2
Neblina, *mt.*..........................C3
Negro, *river*...........................B3
Orinoco, *river*....................C3, D2
Pacaraima, *mts.*....................D3
Paria, *gulf*.............................D1
Parima, *mts.*.........................D3
Roraima, *mt.*.........................D2
Venezuela, *gulf*.....................B1

Venezuela

Capital: Caracas
Area: 352,144 sq. mi.
912,050 sq. km.
Population: 25,699,000
Largest City: Caracas
Language: Spanish
Monetary Unit: Bolívar

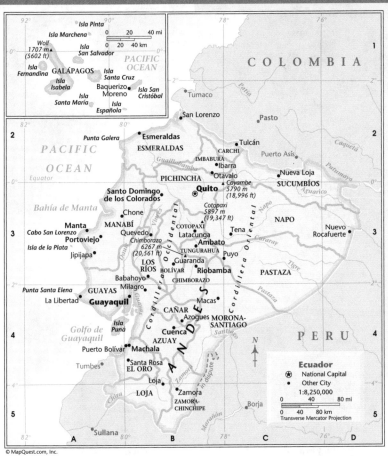

Ecuador

Capital: Quito
Area: 105,037 sq. mi.
272,117 sq. km.
Population: 13,003,000
Largest City: Guayaquil
Language: Spanish
Monetary Unit: U.S. dollar

Ecuador:
Map Index

Provinces
Azuay B4
Bolívar B3
Cañar B4
Carchi C2
Chimborazo B3
Cotopaxi B3
El Oro B4
Esmeraldas B2
Galápagos ....Inset
Guayas A4
Imbabura B2
Loja B5
Los Ríos A3
Manabí C4
Morona-Santiago C3
Napo C3
Pastaza C3
Pichincha B2
Sucumbíos C3
Tungurahua B3
Zamora-Chinchipe B5

Cities and Towns
Ambato B3
Azogues B4
Babahoyo B3
Baquerizo Moreno ....Inset
Chone A3
Cuenca B4

Esmeraldas B2
Guaranda B3
Guayaquil B4
Ibarra B2
Jipijapa A3
La Libertad A4
Latacunga B3
Loja B5
Macas B4
Machala B4
Manta A3
Milagro B4
Nueva Loja C2
Nuevo Rocafuerte D3
Otavalo B2
Portoviejo A3
Puerto Bolívar B4
Puyo C3
Quevedo B3
Quito, *capital* B3
Riobamba B3
San Lorenzo B2
Santa Rosa B4
Santo Domingo
de los Colorados B3
Tena C3
Tulcán C2
Zamora B5

Other Features
Aguarico, *river* C3
Andes, *mts.* B4
Cayambe, *mt.* C3

Chimborazo, *mt.* B3
Chira, *river* A5
Cordillera Occidental, *mts.* ...B4
Cordillera Oriental, *mts.* C4
Cotopaxi, *mt.* B3
Curaray, *river* C3
Daule, *river* B3
Española, *island* ....Inset
Fernandina, *island* ....Inset
Galera, *point* A2
Guaillabamba, *river* B2
Guayaquil, *gulf* A4
Guayas, *river* B4
Isabela, *island* ....Inset
Manta, *bay* A3
Marchena, *rna.* ....Inset
Napo, *river* C3
Pastaza, *river* C4
Pinta, *island* ....Inset
Plata, *island* A3
Puná, *island* A4
Putumayo, *river* D2
San Cristóbal, *island* ....Inset
San Lorenzo, *cape* A3
San Salvador, *island* ....Inset
Santa Cruz, *island* ....Inset
Santa Elena, *point* A4
Santa María, *island* ....Inset
Santiago, *river* B4
Tigre, *river* C3
Vinces, *river* B3
Wolf, *mt.* ....Inset
Zamora, *river* B4

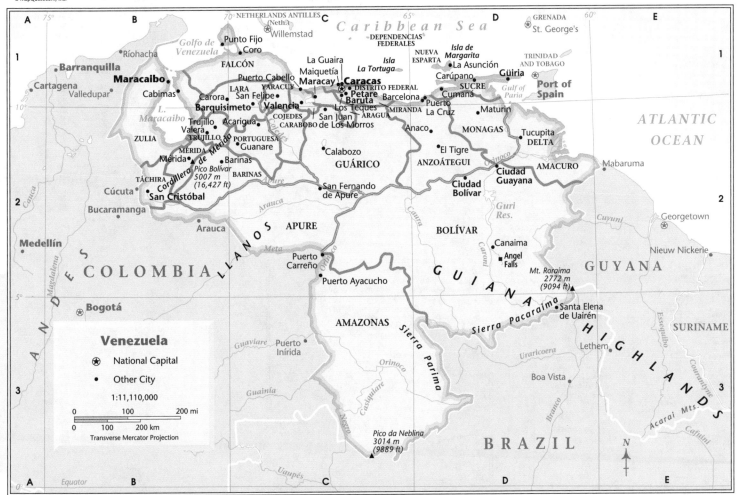

© MapQuest.com, Inc.

Guyana

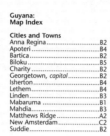

Capital: Georgetown
Area: 83,000 sq. mi.
 214,969 sq. km.
Population: 765,000
Largest City: Georgetown
Language: English
Monetary Unit: Guyanese dollar

Guyana
★ National Capital
● Other City
1:10,660,000
0   75   150 mi
0   75   150 km
Transverse Mercator Projection

© MapQuest.com, Inc.

Guyana:
Map Index

Cities and Towns
Anna Regina....................B2
Apoteri.............................B4
Bartica............................B2
Biloku.............................B5
Charity............................B2
Georgetown, *capital*........B2
Isherton...........................B4
Lethem............................B4
Linden.............................B3
Mabaruma........................B1
Mahdia............................B3
Matthews Ridge.................A2
New Amsterdam................C2
Suddie.............................B2

Other Features
Acarai, *mts.*....................B5
Barama, *river*..................B2
Berbice, *river*..................B3
Courantyne, *river*.............B3
Cuyuni, *river*...................A2
Demerara, *river*...............B3
Essequibo, *river*...........B3, B5
Kaieteur, *falls*.................B3
Kanuku, *mts.*...................B4
Mazaruni, *river*................A2
Merume, *mts.*..................A2
New, *river*.......................C4
Pakaraima, *mts.*...............A3
Potaro, *river*....................B3
Rawa, *river*.....................B4
Roraima, *mt.*...................A3
Takutu, *river*...................B4

Suriname

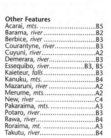

Capital: Paramaribo
Area: 63,037 sq. mi.
 163,265 sq. km.
Population: 436,000
Largest City: Paramaribo
Language: Dutch
Monetary Unit: Surinamese guilder

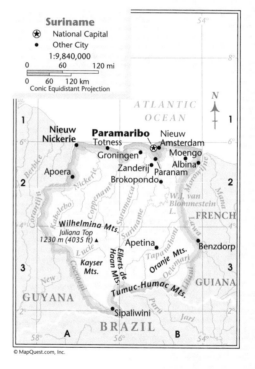

Suriname
★ National Capital
● Other City
1:9,840,000
0   60   120 mi
0   60   120 km
Conic Equidistant Projection

© MapQuest.com, Inc.

Suriname:
Map Index

Cities and Towns
Albina...............................B2
Apetina............................B3
Apoera.............................A2
Benzdorp.........................B3
Brokopondo......................B2
Groningen.........................B2
Moengo............................B2
Nieuw Amsterdam.............B2
Nieuw Nickerie..................A2
Paramaribo, *capital*.........B2
Paranam..........................B2
Sipaliwini.........................A3
Totness............................A2
Zanderij...........................B2

Other Features
Coeroeni, *river*................A3
Coppename, *river*.............A2
Corantijn, *river*................A2
Ellerts de Haan, *mts.*........A3
Juliana Top, *mt.*...............A3
Kabelebo, *river*................A3
Kayser, *mts.*...................A3
Lawa, *river*.....................B2
Litani, *river*.....................B3
Lucie, *river*.....................A3
Marowijne, *river*...............B2
Nickerie, *river*.................A2
Oelemari, *river*................B3
Oranje, *mts.*...................B3
Saramacca, *river*.............B2
Suriname, *river*................B3
Tapanahoni, *river*.............B3
Tumuc-Humac, *mts.*.........B3
Wilhelmina, *mts.*..............A2
W.J. van Blommestein, *lake*....B2

French Guiana

Capital: Cayenne
Area: 35,135 sq. mi.
 91,000 sq. km.
Population: 178,000
Largest City: Cayenne
Language: French
Monetary Unit: Euro, French franc

French Guiana:
Map Index

Cities and Towns
Apatou.............................A1
Cacao.............................B1
Camopi............................B2
Cayenne, *capital*.............B1
Grand Santi......................A1
Iracoubo..........................B1
Kaw................................B1
Kourou............................B1
Mana..............................B1
Maripasoula......................A2
Ouanary..........................C1
Régina............................B1
Rémire............................B1
Saint-Élie.........................B1
Saint-Georges..................C2
Saint-Laurent du Maroni......A1
Saül...............................B2

Other Features
Camopi, *river*..................B2
Devil's, *island*.................B1
Lawa, *river*.....................A2
Litani, *river*.....................A2
Mana, *river*....................B1
Maroni, *river*...................A1
Oyapock, *river*................B2
Salut, *islands*.................B1
Tampok, *river*.................B2
Tumuc-Humac, *mts.*.........A2

French Guiana
★ Territorial Capital
● Other City
1:8,410,000
0   50   100 mi
0   50   100 km
Conic Equidistant Projection

© MapQuest.com, Inc.

Brazil:
Map Index

States and Federal District

Acre A2
Alagoas E2
Amapá C1
Amazonas B2
Bahia D3
Ceará E2
Espírito Santo D3
Federal District D3
Goiás D3
Maranhão D2
Mato Grosso C3
Mato Grosso do Sul C4
Minas Gerais D3
Pará C2
Paraíba E2
Paraná C4
Pernambuco E2
Piauí D2
Rio de Janeiro ....D4, Inset I
Rio Grande do Norte E2
Rio Grande do Sul C4
Rondônia B3
Roraima B1
Santa Catarina C4
São Paulo ....C4, Inset II
Sergipe E3
Tocantins D3

Cities and Towns

Alagoinhas E3
Altamira C2
Anápolis D3
Aracaju E3
Bacabal D2
Bauru D4
Belém D2
Belford Roxo ....Inset I
Belo Horizonte D3
Boa Vista B1
Bom Jesus da Lapa D3
Brasília, capital D3

Cáceres C3
Cachimbo C2
Campina Grande E2
Campinas D4
Campo Grande C4
Campos D4
Campos Elísios ....Inset I
Carapicuíba ....Inset II
Corumbá C3
Cotia ....Inset II
Cruzeiro do Sul A2
Cubatão ....Inset II
Cuiabá C3
Curitiba D4
Diadema ....Inset II
Dourados C4
Duque de Caxias ....Inset I
Feira de Santana E3
Floriano D2
Florianópolis D4
Fortaleza E2
Foz do Iguaçu C4
Goiânia D3
Governador Valadares D3
Guajara Mirim B3
Guarujá ....Inset II
Guarulhos ....Inset II
Ilhéus E3
Imbariê ....Inset I
Imperatriz D2
Inhomirim ....Inset I
Ipiíba ....Inset I
Itabira D3
Itabuna E3
Itaipu ....Inset I
Itajaí D4
Itapecerica da Serra ....Inset II
Itapeva ....Inset II
Itaquaquecetuba ....Inset II
Jaboatão E2
Jacare-Acanga C2
Japeri ....Inset I
Jí Paraná B3
João Pessoa E2
Joinville D4

Juàzeiro D2
Juàzeiro do Norte E2
Juiz de Fora D4
Jundiaí D4
Lajes C4
Londrina C4
Macapá C1
Maceió E2
Majé ....Inset I
Manaus C2
Maraba D2
Mariana D3
Mauá ....Inset II
Mogi das Cruzes ....Inset II
Monjolo ....Inset I
Montes Claros D3
Mozzoro E2
Natal E2
Neves ....Inset I
Nilópolis ....Inset I
Niterói ....D4, Inset I
Nova Iguaçu ....Inset I
Olinda E2
Osasco ....Inset II
Palmas D3
Paranaguá D4
Parnaíba D2
Passo Fundo C4
Paulo Afonso E2
Pelotas C5
Petrólina D2
Petrópolis ....D4, Inset I
Piracicaba D4
Poá ....Inset II
Pôrto Alegre C5
Pôrto Velho B2
Queimados ....Inset I
Randonopolis C3
Recife E2
Ribeirão Pires ....Inset II
Ribeirão Prêto D4
Rio Branco B2
Rio de Janeiro ....D4, Inset I
Rio Grande C5
Rio Verde D3

Salvador E3
Santa Maria C4
Santana do Livramento C5
Santarém C2
Santo André ....Inset II
Santos ....D4, Inset II
São Bernardo do Campo .....Inset II
São Caetano do Sul ....Inset II
São Gonçalo ....Inset I
São João de Meriti ....Inset I
São José do Rio Prêto D4
São Luís D2
São Paulo ....D4, Inset II
São Vicente ....Inset II
Sobral D2
Sorocaba D4
Suzano ....Inset II
Taboão da Serra ....Inset II
Tefé B2
Teresina D2
Tubarão D4
Uberaba D3
Uberlândia D3
Vicente de Carvalho ....Inset II
Vitória D4
Vitória da Conquista D3
Volta Redonda D4

Other Features

Acaraí, range C1
Açúcar, mt. ....Inset I
Amazon, basin B2
Amazon, river B2
Araguaia, river C3
Aripuanã, river B2
Baleia, point E3
Bandeira, mt. D4
Billings, reservoir ....Inset II
Branco, river B1
Brazilian, highlands D3
Caviana, island D1
Chapada dos Parecis, range C3
Corcovado, mt. ....Inset I
Corumbau, point E3
Furnas, reservoir D4

Geral, range C4
Grande, river D3
Guandu, river ....Inset I
Guaporé, river B3
Guiana, highlands B1
Içá, river B2
Iguaçu, falls C4
Itaipu, reservoir C4
Japurá, river B2
Jari, river C1
Javari, river A2
Juruá, river B2
Juruena, river C3
Madeira, river B2
Mantiqueira, range D4
Mar, range D4
Marajó, island D2
Mato Grosso, plateau C3
Mexiana, island D1
Neblina, mt. B1
Negro, river B2
Orgãos, range ....Inset I
Pantanal, lowland C4
Pará, river C2
Paraguai, river C3
Paraná, river C4
Parima, range B1
Parnaíba, river D2
Patos, lagoon C5
Paulo Afonso, falls E2
Pedra Açú, mt. ....Inset I
Purus, river B2
Roncador, range C3
São Francisco, river D3
Selvas, region B2
Sobradinho, reservoir D2
Tapajós, river C2
Taquari, river C3
Teles Pires, river C2
Tietê, river ....Inset II
Tocantins, river D2
Tucuruí, reservoir D2
Tumucumaque, range C1
Uruguai, river C4
Xingu, river C3

Brazil

Capital: Brasília
Area: 3,286,470 sq. mi.
  8,514,171 sq. km.
Population: 178,470,000
Largest City: São Paulo
Language: Portuguese
Monetary Unit: Real

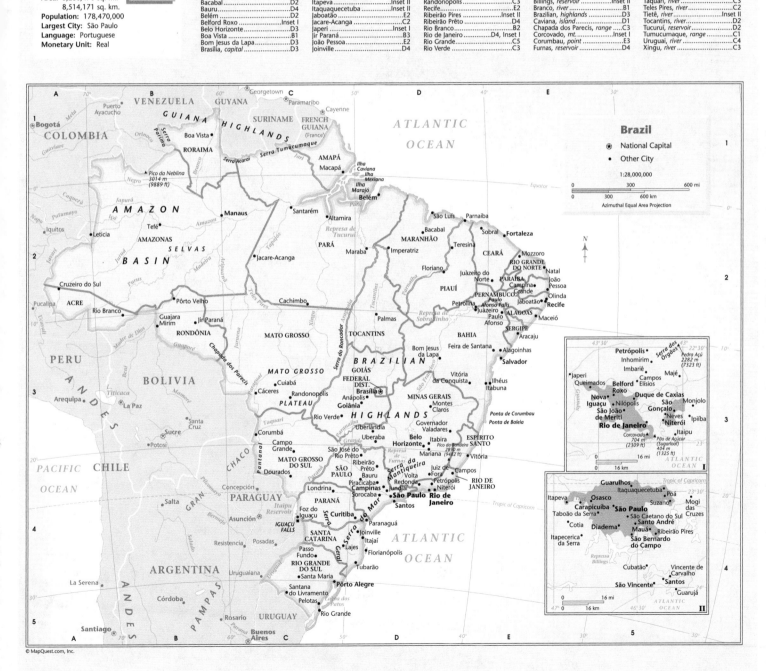

MAJOR CITIES

Antigua & Barbuda
St. John's — 24,000

Bahamas
Nassau — 220,000

Barbados
Bridgetown — 136,000

Belize
Belize City — 49,000
Belmopan — 9,000

Canada (metro)
Toronto — 4,752,000
Montréal — 3,480,000
Vancouver — 2,049,000
Ottawa — 1,094,000
Calgary — 953,000
Edmonton — 944,000

Costa Rica (metro)
San José — 983,000

Cuba (metro)
Havana — 2,268,000

Dominica
Roseau — 26,000

Dominican Republic (metro)
Santo Domingo — 2,629,000
Santiago de los
Caballeros — 804,000

El Salvador (metro)
San Salvador — 1,381,000

Grenada
St. George's — 36,000

Guatemala (metro)
Guatemala — 3,366,000

Haiti (metro)
Port-au-Prince — 1,838,000

Honduras (metro)
Tegucigalpa — 980,000

Jamaica (metro)
Kingston — 672,000

Mexico (metro)
Mexico City — 18,268,000
Guadalajara — 3,697,000
Monterrey — 3,267,000
Puebla — 1,888,000
Toluca — 1,455,000
Tijuana — 1,297,000
Ciudad Juarez — 1,239,000

Nicaragua (metro)
Managua — 1,039,000

Panama (metro)
Panamá — 1,202,000

Puerto Rico (metro)
San Juan — 1,404,000

St. Kitts & Nevis
Basseterre — 12,000

St. Lucia
Castries — 57,000

St. Vincent & Grenadines
Kingstown — 28,000

Trinidad & Tobago
Port of Spain — 54,000

United States
New York — 8,084,316
Los Angeles — 3,798,981
Chicago — 2,886,251
Houston — 2,009,834
Philadelphia — 1,492,231
Phoenix — 1,371,960
San Diego — 1,259,532
Washington, D.C. — 570,898

International comparability of city population
data is limited by various data inconsistencies.

CITIES

⊛ National Capital
★ Territorial Capital
• Other City

ELEVATIONS

Feet	Meters
13,120	4000
6560	2000
1640	500
656	200
0	0
Below sea level	

N

0 250 500 750 1000 mi
0 500 1000 1500 km

North America: Population, by nation (in millions)

UNITED STATES	MEXICO	CANADA	GUATEM.	CUBA	All other N. Am. countries
288.4	103.4	31.5	12.3	11.3	56.5

© MapQuest.com, Inc.

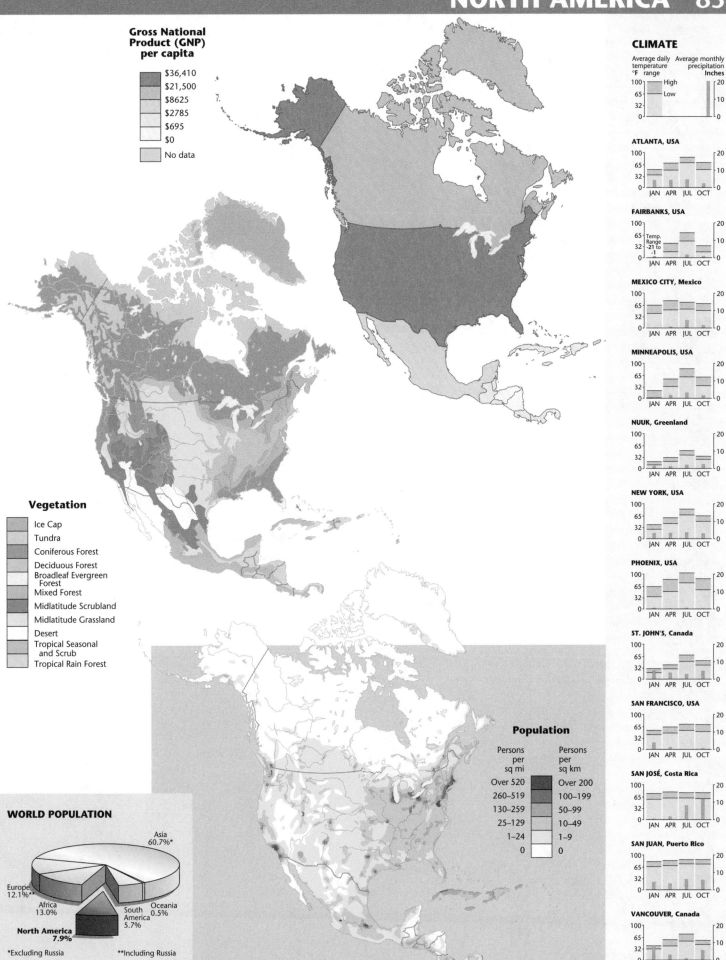

Gross National Product (GNP) per capita

- $36,410
- $21,500
- $8625
- $2785
- $695
- $0
- No data

Vegetation

- Ice Cap
- Tundra
- Coniferous Forest
- Deciduous Forest
- Broadleaf Evergreen Forest
- Mixed Forest
- Midlatitude Scrubland
- Midlatitude Grassland
- Desert
- Tropical Seasonal and Scrub
- Tropical Rain Forest

CLIMATE

Average daily temperature °F range   Average monthly precipitation Inches

High
Low

ATLANTA, USA

FAIRBANKS, USA
Temp. Range -21 to -1

MEXICO CITY, Mexico

MINNEAPOLIS, USA

NUUK, Greenland

NEW YORK, USA

PHOENIX, USA

ST. JOHN'S, Canada

SAN FRANCISCO, USA

SAN JOSÉ, Costa Rica

SAN JUAN, Puerto Rico

VANCOUVER, Canada

Population

Persons per sq mi	Persons per sq km
Over 520	Over 200
260–519	100–199
130–259	50–99
25–129	10–49
1–24	1–9
0	0

WORLD POPULATION

Asia 60.7%*

Europe 12.1%**

Africa 13.0%

South America 5.7%

Oceania 0.5%

North America 7.9%

*Excluding Russia   **Including Russia

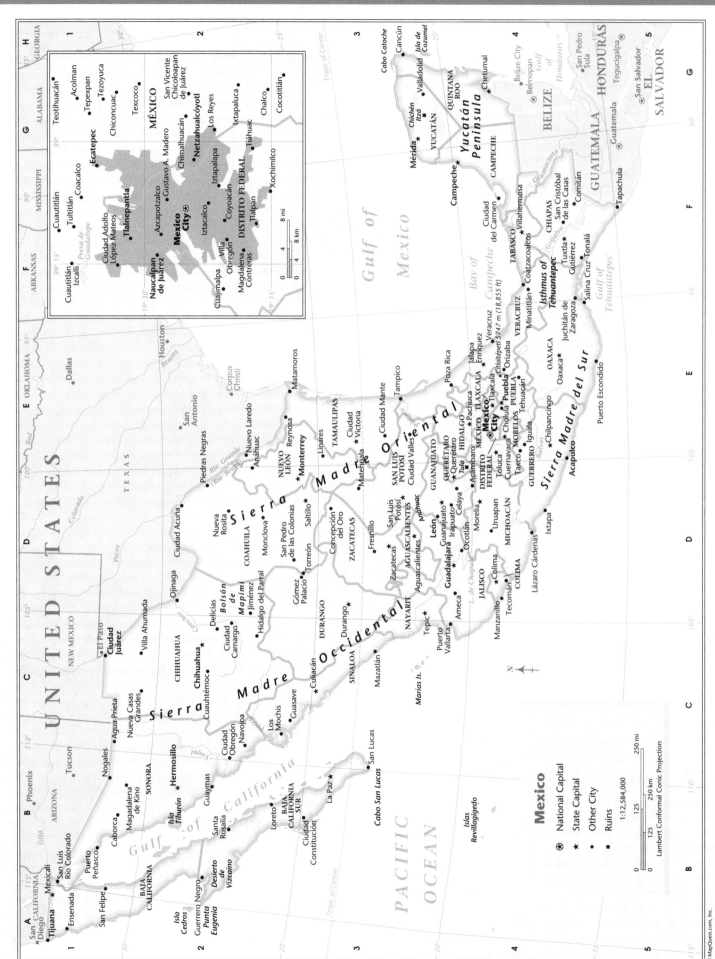

Mexico

⊗ National Capital
★ State Capital
• Other City
■ Ruins

1:12,584,000

Lambert Conformal Conic Projection

0 125 250 mi
0 125 250 km

© MapQuest.com, Inc.

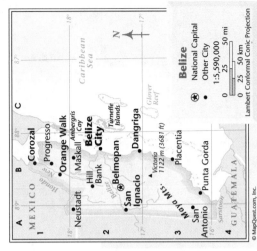

Belize

Belize

National Capital
Other City
1:5,590,000
0 25 50 mi
0 25 50 km
Lambert Conformal Conic Projection

Caribbean Sea

Corozal
Progresso
Orange Walk
Maskall
Ambergris Cay
Turneffe Islands
Glover Reef
Hill Bank
Belize City
Neustadt
Belmopan
Dangriga
San Ignacio
San Antonio
Placentia
Punta Gorda
▲ Victoria 1122 m (3681 ft)
Maya Mts.
New
Hondo
Sarstoon
MEXICO
GUATEMALA

© MapQuest.com, Inc.

Belize

Capital: Belmopan
Area: 8,867 sq. mi.
   22,972 sq. km.
Population: 256,000
Largest City: Belize City
Language: English
Monetary Unit: Belizean dollar

Belize:
Map Index

Cities and Towns

Belize City	B2
Belmopan, capital	B2
Corozal	B1
Dangriga	B2
Hill Bank	B2
Maskall	B2
Neustadt	B1
Orange Walk	B1
Placentia	B3
Progresso	B1
Punta Gorda	B3
San Antonio	A3
San Ignacio	A2

Other Features

Ambergris Cay, *island*	C2
Belize, *river*	B2
Glover, *reef*	C3
Hondo, *river*	A1
Maya, *mts.*	A3
New, *river*	A1
Sarstoon, *river*	A4
Turneffe, *islands*	C2
Victoria, *peak*	B3

Guatemala (map)

Guatemala

National Capital
Other City
1:8,150,000
0 50 100 mi
0 50 100 km
Lambert Conformal Conic Projection

MEXICO
BELIZE
Belize City
Belmopan
Gulf of Honduras
Paxbán
L. Petén-Itzá
Tikal
Flores
La Libertad
San Luis
Puerto Barrios
Santo Tomás de Castilla
Lago de Izabal
San Pedro Sula
Cobán
Chinajá
de Juárez
Zacapa
Santa Rosa de Copán
HONDURAS
Salamá
Huehuetenango
Guatemala City
Antigua
Quetzaltenango
Jutiapa
Escuintla
Santa Ana
San Salvador
EL SALVADOR
Mazatenango
▲ Tacaná 4093 m (13,428 ft)
Tajumulco ▲ 4220 m (13,845 ft)
Sierra Madre
L. de Atitlán
Champerico
San José
PACIFIC OCEAN
Comitán
San Pedro
Usumacinta
Chixoy
Pasión
Motagua

© MapQuest.com, Inc.

Guatemala

Capital: Guatemala City
Area: 42,042 sq. mi.
   108,917 sq. km.
Population: 12,347,000
Largest City: Guatemala City
Language: Spanish
Monetary Unit: Quetzal, U.S. dollar

Guatemala:
Map Index

Cities and Towns

Antigua	C5
Champerico	C5
Chinajá	C4
Cobán	C4
Escuintla	C5
Flores	D3
Guatemala City, *capital*	B4
Huehuetenango	B4
Jutiapa	D5
La Libertad	C3
Mazatenango	C5
Paxbán	C2
Puerto Barrios	E4
Quetzaltenango	B5
Salamá	C4
San José	C6
San Luis	D3
Santo Tomás de Castilla	E4
Tikal	D2
Zacapa	D5

Other Features

Atitlán, *lake*	B5
Chixoy, *river*	C4
Honduras, *gulf*	E3
Izabal, *lake*	E4
Motagua, *river*	D4
Pasión, *river*	C3
Paz, *river*	C6
Petén-Itzá, *lake*	D3
San Pedro, *river*	D4
Sierra Madre, *mts.*	C5
Suchiate, *river*	A5
Tacaná, *volcano*	A4
Tajumulco, *volcano*	B4
Usumacinta, *river*	C3

Mexico

Mexico

Capital: Mexico City
Area: 756,066 sq. mi.
   1,958,720 sq. km.
Population: 103,457,000
Largest City: Mexico City
Language: Spanish
Monetary Unit: Mexican peso

Mexico:
Map Index

States

Aguascalientes	D3
Baja California	A1
Baja California Sur	B2
Campeche	Inset
Chiapas	Inset
Chihuahua	C2
Coahuila	D2
Colima	D4
Distrito Federal	E4, Inset
Durango	D2
Guanajuato	D3
Guerrero	D4
Hidalgo	E3
Jalisco	D4
México	E4, Inset
Michoacán	D4
Morelos	Inset
Nayarit	C3
Nuevo León	D2
Oaxaca	E4
Puebla	E4
Querétaro	D3
Quintana Roo	G4
San Luis Potosí	D3
Sinaloa	B1
Sonora	B1
Tabasco	Inset
Tamaulipas	E3
Tlaxcala	E4
Veracruz	E4
Yucatán	G3
Zacatecas	D3

Cities and Towns

Acámbaro	D4
Acapulco	Inset
Agua Prieta	C1
Aguascalientes, *state capital*	D3
Ameca	D3
Anáhuac	D2
Azcapotzalco	Inset
Caborca	B1
Campeche, *state capital*	F4
Cancún	G3
Celaya	D3
Chalco	Inset
Chetumal, *state capital*	G4
Chiconcuac	Inset
Chihuahua, *state capital*	C2
Chilpancingo, *state capital*	E4
Chimalhuacán	Inset
Cholula	E4
Ciudad Acuña	D2
Ciudad Adolfo López Mateos	Inset
Ciudad Camargo	D2
Ciudad Constitución	B3
Ciudad del Carmen	F4
Ciudad Juárez	C1
Ciudad Mante	E3
Ciudad Obregón	C2
Ciudad Victoria, *state capital*	E3
Coacalco	Inset
Coatzacoalcos	F4
Cocotitlán	Inset
Comitán	F4
Concepción del Oro	D3
Coyoacán	Inset
Cuajimalpa	Inset
Cuautitlán	Inset
Cuautitlán Izcalli	Inset
Cuauhtémoc	C2
Cuernavaca, *state capital*	E4
Culiacán, *state capital*	C3
Delicias	D2
Durango, *state capital*	D3
Ecatepec	Inset
Ensenada	A1
Fresnillo	D3
Gómez Palacio	D2
Guadalajara, *state capital*	D3
Guanajuato, *state capital*	D3
Guasave	C2
Guaymas	B2
Guerrero Negro	B2
Gustavo A. Madero	Inset
Hermosillo, *state capital*	B2
Hidalgo del Parral	C2
Iguala	D4
Irapuato	D3
Ixtapaluca	Inset
Iztacalco	Inset
Iztapalapa	Inset
Jiménez	D2
Jalapa Enríquez, *state capital*	E4
Juchitán de Zaragoza	F4
La Paz, *state capital*	B3
Lázaro Cárdenas	D4
León	D3
Linares	E3
Loreto	C2
Los Mochis	C2
Los Reyes	Inset
Magdalena de Kino	B1
Magdalena Contreras	Inset
Manzanillo	D4
Matamoros	E2
Matehuala	D3
Mazatlán	C3
Mérida, *state capital*	G3
Mexicali, *state capital*	A1
Mexico City, *national capital*	E4, Inset
Minatitlán	F4
Monclova	D2
Monterrey, *state capital*	D2
Morelia, *state capital*	D4
Naucalpan de Juárez	Inset
Navojoa	C2
Netzahualcóyotl	Inset
Nogales	B1
Nueva Casas Grandes	C1
Nueva Rosita	D2
Nuevo Laredo	E2
Oaxaca, *state capital*	E4
Ocotlán	D3
Orizaba	E4
Pachuca, *state capital*	E3
Piedras Negras	D2
Poza Rica	E3
Puebla, *state capital*	E4
Puerto Escondido	E4
Puerto Peñasco	B1
Puerto Vallarta	C3
Querétaro, *state capital*	D3
Reynosa	E2
Salina Cruz	E4
Saltillo, *state capital*	D2
San Cristóbal de las Casas	F4
San Felipe	B1
San Lucas	C3
San Luis Potosí, *state capital*	D3
San Luis Río Colorado	B1
San Pedro de las Colonias	D2
Santa Rosalía	B2
San Vicente Chicoloapan	Inset
Tampico	E3
Tapachula	F5
Taxco	E4
Tecomán	D4
Tehuacán	E4
Tehuantepec	F4
Tepexpan	Inset
Tepic, *state capital*	D3
Texcoco	Inset
Tezoyuca	Inset
Tijuana	A1
Tlalpan	Inset
Tlalnepantla	Inset
Tlaxcala, *state capital*	E4
Toluca, *state capital*	E4
Tonalá	F4
Torreón	D2
Tultitlán	Inset
Tuxtla Gutiérrez, *state capital*	F4
Uruapan	D4
Valladolid	G3
Veracruz	E4
Villa Ahumada	C1
Villahermosa, *state capital*	F4
Villa Obregón	Inset
Xochimilco	Inset
Zacatecas, *state capital*	D3

Other Features

Anáhuac, *depression*	D3
Balsas, *river*	E4
Bolsón de Mapimí, *depression*	D2
California, *gulf*	B1
Campeche, *bay*	F4
Catoche, *cape*	G3
Cedros, *island*	A2
Chapala, *lake*	D3
Chichén Itzá, *ruins*	G3
Citlaltépetl, *mt.*	E4
Conchos, *river*	C2
Cozumel, *island*	G3
Eugenia, *point*	A2
Fuerte, *river*	C2
Grijalva, *river*	F4
Guadalupe, *reservoir*	Inset
Marías, *islands*	C3
Pánuco, *river*	E3
Revillagigedo, *islands*	B4
Rio Grande (Río Bravo), *river*	D2
San Lucas, *cape*	B3
Sierra Madre del Sur, *mts.*	D4
Sierra Madre Occidental, *mts.*	C2
Sierra Madre Oriental, *mts.*	D2
Tehuantepec, *gulf*	F4
Tehuantepec, *isthmus*	F4
Tiburón, *island*	B2
Tula, *ruins*	D3
Usumacinta, *river*	F4
Vizcaíno, *desert*	B2
Yaqui, *river*	C3
Yucatán, *peninsula*	G4

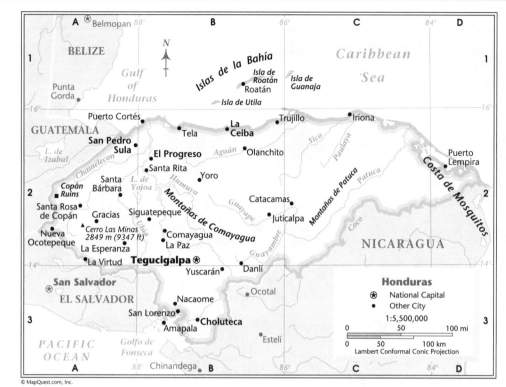

© MapQuest.com, Inc.

Honduras

Capital: Tegucigalpa
Area: 43,277 sq. mi.
  112,117 sq. km.
Population: 6,941,000
Largest City: Tegucigalpa
Language: Spanish
Monetary Unit: Lempira

Honduras: Map Index

Cities and Towns

Amapala	B3
Catacamas	C2
Choluteca	B3
Comayagua	B2
Danlí	B3
El Progreso	B2
Gracias	A2
Iriona	C2
Juticalpa	B2
La Ceiba	B2
La Esperanza	A2
La Paz	B2
La Virtud	A2
Nacaome	B3
Nueva Ocotepeque	A2
Olanchito	B2
Puerto Cortés	B2
Puerto Lempira	D2
Roatán	B1
San Lorenzo	B3
San Pedro Sula	A2
Santa Bárbara	A2
Santa Rita	A2
Santa Rosa de Copán	A2
Siguatepeque	B2
Tegucigalpa, capital	B2
Tela	B2
Trujillo	B2
Yoro	B2
Yuscarán	B3

Other Features

Aguán, river	B2
Bahía, islands	B1
Caribbean, sea	C1
Chamelecon, river	A2
Coco, river	C2
Comayagua, mts.	B2
Copán, ruins	A2
Fonseca, gulf	B3
Guanaja, island	C1
Guayambre, river	B2
Guayape, river	B2
Honduras, gulf	A1
Humuya, river	B2
Las Minas, mt.	A2
Mosquitos, coast	D2
Patuca, mts.	C2
Patuca, river	C2
Paulaya, river	C2
Roatán, island	B1
Sico, river	C2
Ulúa, river	A2
Utila, island	B1
Yojoa, lake	B2

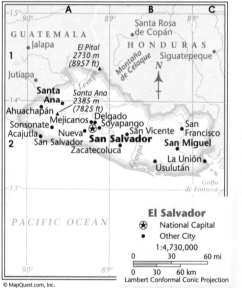

© MapQuest.com, Inc.

El Salvador

Capital: San Salvador
Area: 8,124 sq. mi.
  21,047 sq. km.
Population: 6,515,000
Largest City: San Salvador
Language: Spanish
Monetary Unit: U.S. dollar

El Salvador: Map Index

Cities and Towns

Acajutla	A2
Ahuachapán	A2
Delgado	A2
La Unión	C2
Mejicanos	A2
Nueva San Salvador	A2
San Francisco	B2
San Miguel	B2
San Salvador, capital	A2
Santa Ana	A2
San Vicente	A2
Sonsonate	A2
Soyapango	A2
Usulután	B2
Zacatecoluca	B2

Other Features

El Pital, mt.	A1
Fonseca, gulf	C2
Lempa, river	A1, B2
Santa Ana, volcano	A2

Costa Rica: Map Index

Cities and Towns

Alajuela	B2
Cartago	C3
Colorado	C2
Golfito	C4
Heredia	B2
La Cruz	A1
Liberia	A2
Limón	C3
Los Chiles	B1
Puerto Jiménez	C4
Puerto Quepos	B3
Puntarenas	B3
San José, capital	B3
Santa Cruz	A2

Other Features

Arenal, lake	B2
Central, range	C3
Chirripó, mt.	C3
Chirripó, river	C2
Coronado, bay	C4
Dulce, gulf	C4
Frío, river	B2
General, river	C3
Grande, river	B3
Guanacaste, range	A2
Irazú, volcano	C3
Nicoya, gulf	B3
Papagayo, gulf	A2
Pirris, river	B3
Reventazón, river	C3
San Carlos, river	B2
San Juan, river	B2
Sarapiquí river	B2
Sixaola, river	C3
Talamanca, range	C3
Tempisque, river	A2

Costa Rica

Capital: San José
Area: 19,730 sq. mi.
  51,114 sq. km.
Population: 4,173,000
Largest City: San José
Language: Spanish
Monetary Unit: Colón

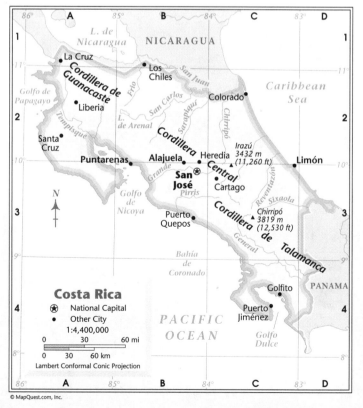

© MapQuest.com, Inc.

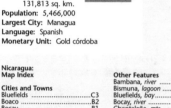

Nicaragua

Capital: Managua
Area: 50,880 sq. mi.
131,813 sq. km.
Population: 5,466,000
Largest City: Managua
Language: Spanish
Monetary Unit: Gold córdoba

Nicaragua:
Map Index

Cities and Towns
Bluefields	C3
Boaco	B2
Bocay	B1
Chinandega	A2
Colonia Nueva Guínea	B3
Corinto	A2
Diriamba	A2
Estelí	A2
Granada	A3
Jinotega	B2
Jinotepe	A3
Juigalpa	B2
La Rosita	B2
León	A2
Managua, *capital*	A2
Masaya	A3
Matagalpa	B2
Nagarote	A2
Ocotal	A2
Prinzapolka	C2
Puerto Cabezas	C1
Puerto Sandino	A2
Rama	B2
Río Blanco	B2
Río Grande	B2
Rivas	B3
San Carlos	B3
San Juan del Norte	C3
San Juan del Sur	B3
Siuna	B2
Somoto	A2
Waspam	C1
Wiwili	B2

Other Features
Bambana, *river*	B2
Bismuna, *lagoon*	C1
Bluefields, *bay*	C3
Bocay, *river*	B2
Chontaleña, *mts.*	B2
Coco, *river*	A2, C1
Cosigüina, *mt.*	A2
Cosigüina, *point*	A2
Dariense, *mts.*	B2
Escondido, *river*	B2
Fonseca, *gulf*	A2
Gracias a Dios, *cape*	C1
Grande de Matagalpa, *river*	B2
Huapí, *mts.*	B2
Isabelia, *mts.*	B2
Kurinwás, *river*	B2
Maíz, *islands*	C2
Managua, *lake*	A2
Mico, *river*	B2
Miskitos, *cays*	C1
Mogotón, *mt.*	A2
Mosquitos, *coast*	C3
Nicaragua, *lake*	B3
Ometepe, *island*	B3
Perlas, *lagoon*	C2
Perlas, *point*	C2
Prinzapolka, *river*	B2
San Juan, *river*	B3
San Juan del Norte, *bay*	C3
Siquia, *river*	B2
Solentiname, *island*	B3
Tipitapa, *river*	A2
Tuma, *river*	B2
Wawa, *river*	B1
Zapatera, *island*	B3

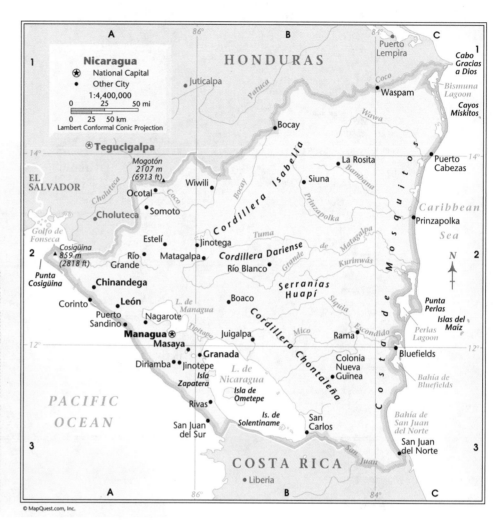

© MapQuest.com, Inc.

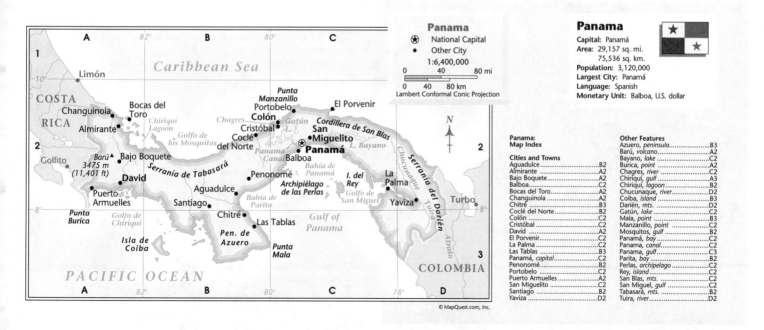

Panama

Capital: Panamá
Area: 29,157 sq. mi.
75,536 sq. km.
Population: 3,120,000
Largest City: Panamá
Language: Spanish
Monetary Unit: Balboa, U.S. dollar

Panama:
Map Index

Cities and Towns
Aguadulce	B2
Almirante	A2
Bajo Boquete	A2
Balboa	C2
Bocas del Toro	A2
Changuinola	A2
Chitré	B3
Coclé del Norte	B2
Colón	C2
Cristóbal	C2
David	A2
El Porvenir	C2
La Palma	C2
Las Tablas	B3
Panamá, *capital*	C2
Penonomé	B2
Portobelo	C2
Puerto Armuelles	A2
San Miguelito	B2
Santiago	B2
Yaviza	D2

Other Features
Azuero, *peninsula*	B3
Barú, *volcano*	A2
Bayano, *lake*	C2
Burica, *point*	A2
Chagres, *river*	C2
Chiriquí, *gulf*	A3
Chiriquí, *lagoon*	A2
Chucunaque, *river*	D2
Coiba, *island*	B3
Darién, *mts.*	D2
Gatún, *lake*	C2
Mala, *point*	B3
Manzanillo, *point*	C2
Mosquitos, *gulf*	B2
Panamá, *bay*	C2
Panamá, *canal*	C2
Panama, *gulf*	C3
Parita, *bay*	B2
Perlas, *archipelago*	C2
Rey, *island*	C2
San Blas, *mts.*	C2
San Miguel, *gulf*	C2
Tabasará, *mts.*	B2
Tuira, *river*	D2

© MapQuest.com, Inc.

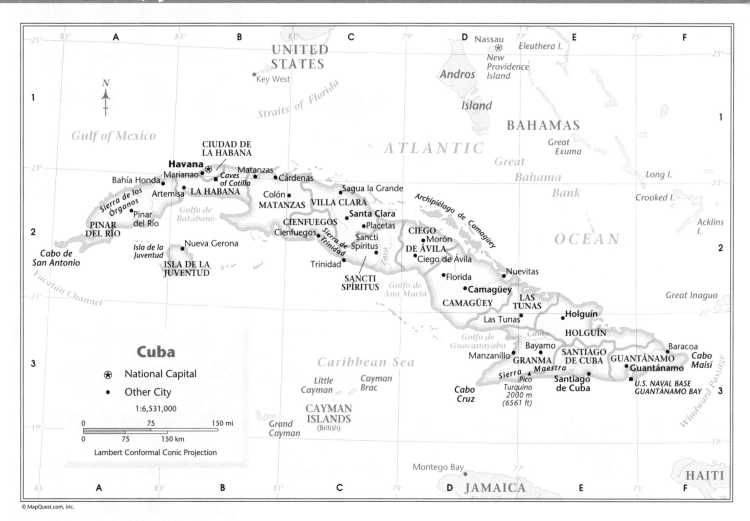

© MapQuest.com, Inc.

Cuba

Capital: Havana
Area: 42,804 sq. mi.
110,890 sq. km.
Population: 11,300,000
Largest City: Havana
Language: Spanish
Monetary Unit: Cuban peso

Cuba:
Map Index

Provinces
Camagüey.................................D2
Ciego de Ávila D2
Cienfuegos..............................C2
Ciudad de La Habana B1
Granma E3
Guantánamo E3
Holguín E3
Isla de la Juventud
(special municipality)............B2
La Habana................................B2
Las Tunas.................................E2
Matanzas..................................B2
Pinar del Río............................A2
Sancti Spíritus C2
Santiago de Cuba.....................E3
Villa Clara................................C2

Cities and Towns
Artemisa...................................B2
Bahía Honda.............................A2
Baracoa....................................F3
Bayamo....................................E3
Camagüey.................................D2
Cárdenas..................................B1
Ciego de Ávila D2
Cienfuegos...............................C2
Colón.......................................C2
Florida.....................................D2
Guantánamo E3
Havana, *capital* B1
Holguín E3
Las Tunas.................................E3

Manzanillo...............................D3
Marianao..................................B1
Matanzas..................................B1
Morón......................................D2
Nueva Gerona..........................B2
Nuevitas...................................D2
Pinar del Río............................A2
Placetas...................................C2
Sagua la Grande.......................C2
Sancti Spíritus C2
Santa Clara..............................C2
Santiago de Cuba.....................E3
Trinidad...................................C2

Other Features
Ana María, *gulf* D2
Batabanó, *gulf* B2
Camagüey, *archipelago* D2
Cauto, *river* E3
Cotilla, *caves* B2
Cruz, *cape* D3
Florida, *straits* B1
Guacanayabo, *gulf* D3
Juventud, *island* B2
Maestra, *mts.* D3
Maisí, *cape* F3
Mexico, *gulf* A1
Organos, *mts.* A2
San Antonio, *cape* A2
Trinidad, *mts.* E3
Turquino, *mt.* E3
U.S. Naval Base
Guantánamo Bay E3
Windward, *passage* F3
Yucatán, *channel* A2
Zaza, *river* C2

Jamaica

Capital: Kingston
Area: 4,244 sq. mi.
10,995 sq. km.
Population: 2,651,000
Largest City: Kingston
Language: English
Monetary Unit: Jamaican dollar

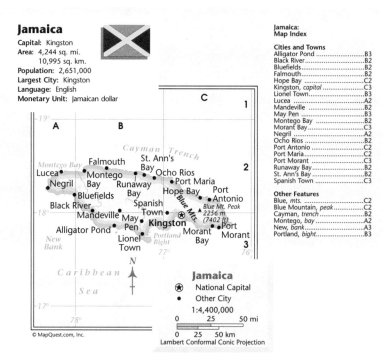

© MapQuest.com, Inc.

Jamaica:
Map Index

Cities and Towns
Alligator Pond B3
Black River..............................B2
Bluefields................................B2
Falmouth.................................B2
Hope Bay.................................C2
Kingston, *capital* C3
Lionel Town.............................B3
Lucea.......................................A2
Mandeville B2
May Pen B3
Montego Bay B2
Morant Bay..............................C3
Negril......................................A2
Ocho Rios................................B2
Port Antonio............................C2
Port Maria...............................C2
Port Morant.............................C3
Runaway Bay...........................B2
St. Ann's Bay...........................B2
Spanish Town..........................C3

Other Features
Blue, *mts.* C2
Blue Mountain, *peak* C2
Cayman, *trench* B2
Montego, *bay* A2
New, *bank* A3
Portland, *bight* B3

Bonao B2
Cabrera C1
Comendador A2
Cotuí B1
Dajabón A1
El Macao D2
El Seibo C2
Hato Mayor C2
Higüey D2
Jimaní A2
La Romana D2
La Vega B1
Luperón B1
Mao A1
Miches C2
Moca B1
Monte Cristi A1
Monte Plata C2
Nagua C1
Neiba A2
Oviedo A3
Pedernales A3
Pedro Santana A2
Puerto Plata B1
Sabana de la Mar C1
Sabaneta A1
Salcedo B1
Samaná C1
San Cristóbal B2
San Francisco de Macorís B1
San José de las Matas A2
San Juan A2
San Pedro de Macorís C2
Santiago B1
Santo Domingo, capital B2
Sousúa B1

Dominican Republic:
Map Index

Provinces
Azua B2
Bahoruco A2
Barahona A2
Dajabón A1
Distrito Nacional B2
Duarte C1
El Seibo C2
Espaillat B1
Hato Mayor C2
Independencia A2
La Altagracia D2
La Estrelleta A1
La Romana D2
La Vega B2
María Trinidad Sánchez B1
Monseñor Nouel B2
Monte Cristi A1
Monte Plata C2
Pedernales A3
Peravia B2
Puerto Plata B1
Salcedo C1
Samaná C1
Sánchez Ramírez B2
San Cristóbal B2
San Juan A2
San Pedro de Macorís C2
Santiago B1
Santiago Rodríguez A1
Valverde B1

Cities and Towns
Azua B2
Baní B2
Barahona A2

Other Features
Bahoruco, mts. A2
Beata, cape A3
Beata, island A3
Calderas, bay B2
Camú, river B1
Central, range B1
Cibao, valley A1
Duarte, mt. B2
Engaño, cape D2
Enriquillo, lake A2
Mona, passage D2
Neiba, mts. A2
Ocoa, bay B2
Oriental, range C2
Ozama, river B2
Samaná, bay C1
Samaná, cape C1
Saona, island D2
Septentrional, range A1
Soco, river C2
Yaque del Norte, river A1
Yaque del Sur, river A2
Yuna, river B2

Dominican Republic

Capital: Santo Domingo
Area: 18,704 sq. mi.
48,456 sq. km.
Population: 8,745,000
Largest City: Santo Domingo
Language: Spanish
Monetary Unit: Dominican peso

© MapQuest.com, Inc.

Dominican Republic
⊛ National Capital
• Other City
1:3,778,000
0   20   40 mi
0   20   40 km
Transverse Mercator Projection

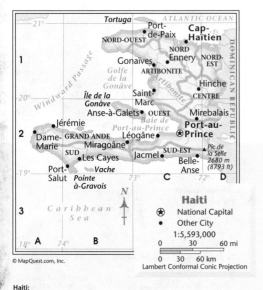

Haiti

Capital: Port-au-Prince
Area: 10,695 sq. mi.
27,614 sq. km.
Population: 8,326,000
Largest City: Port-au-Prince
Languages: French, Creole
Monetary Unit: Gourde

Haiti
⊛ National Capital
• Other City
1:5,593,000
0   30   60 mi
0   30   60 km
Lambert Conformal Conic Projection

© MapQuest.com, Inc.

Haiti:
Map Index

Departments
Artibonite C1
Centre D1
Grand Ande B2
Nord C1
Nord-Est D1
Nord-Ouest B1
Ouest C2
Sud B2
Sud-Est C2

Cities and Towns
Anse-à-Galets C2
Belle-Anse C2
Cap-Haïtien C1
Dame-Marie A2
Ennery C1
Gonaïves C1
Hinche C1
Jacmel C2
Jérémie A2
Léogâne C2
Les Cayes B2
Miragoâne B2
Mirebalais C2
Port-au-Prince, capital C2
Port-de-Paix C1
Port-Salut B2
Saint-Marc C1

Other Features
Artibonite, river C1
Gonâve, gulf B1
Gonâve, island B2
Gravois, point B3
Pic de la Selle, mt. D2
Port-au-Prince, bay C2
Tortuga, island C1
Vache, island B2
Windward, passage B1

The Bahamas

Capital: Nassau
Area: 5,382 sq. mi.
13,943 sq. km.
Population: 314,000
Largest City: Nassau
Languages: English, Creole
Monetary Unit: Bahamian dollar

Turks and Caicos Is.

Capital: Grand Turk
Area: 193 sq. mi.
500 sq. km.
Population: 19,350
Largest City: Grand Turk
Language: English
Monetary Unit: U.S. Dollar

Bahamas and
Turks & Caicos Islands:
Map Index

Bahamas

Cities and Towns
Alice Town B2
Arthur's Town B3
Freeport A2
Kemps Bay B3
Marsh Harbour B2
Matthew Town C4
Nassau, capital B2
Nicholls' Town A2
Sandy Point B2

Other Features
Acklins, island C4
Andros, island A3
Cat, island B3
Crooked, island C4
Crooked Island, passage C4
Eleuthera, island B2
Exuma, sound B3
Grand Bahama, island A2
Great Abaco, island B2
Great Bahama, bank A3

Great Exuma, island B3
Great Inagua, island C4
Harbour, island B2
Little Inagua, island C4
Long, island C3
Mayaguana, island C4
Mayaguana, passage C4
New Providence, island B3
Northeast Providence,
    channel B2
Rum, cay C3
Samana, cay C3
San Salvador, island C3
Water, cay A3

Turks & Caicos Islands

Cities and Towns
Cockburn Harbour D4
Grand Turk, capital D4

Other Features
Ambergris, cay D4
Caicos, islands D4
Grand Turk, island D4
Providenciales, island C4
Salt, cay D4
Turks, islands D4

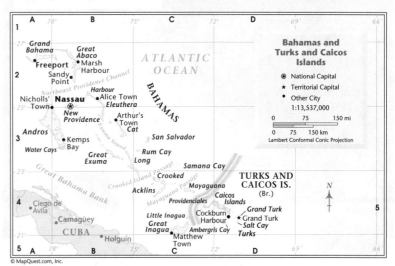

Bahamas and
Turks and Caicos
Islands
⊛ National Capital
★ Territorial Capital
• Other City
1:13,537,000
0   75   150 mi
0   75   150 km
Lambert Conformal Conic Projection

© MapQuest.com, Inc.

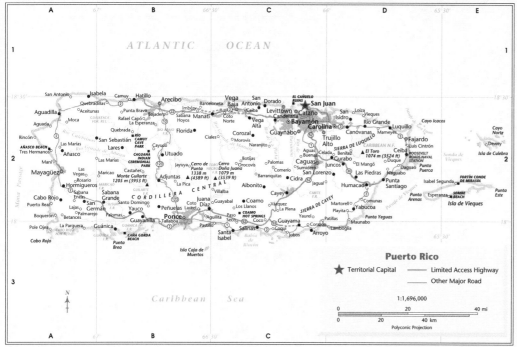

Puerto Rico

Capital: San Juan
Area: 3,492 sq. mi.
9,047 sq. km.
Population: 3,879,000
Largest City: San Juan
Languages: Spanish, English
Monetary Unit: U.S. dollar

Puerto Rico

Territorial Capital

Limited Access Highway

Other Major Road

1:1,696,000

0   20   40 km
0   20   40 mi

Polyconic Projection

© MapQuest.com, Inc.

Puerto Rico: Map Index

Cities and Towns

Adjuntas	B2
Aguada	A2
Aguadilla	A2
Aguas Buenas	C2
Aguilita	B2
Aibonito	C2
Añasco	A2
Arecibo	B2
Arroyo	C3
Bajadero	B2
Barceloneta	B2
Barranquitas	C2
Bayamón	C2
Cabo Rojo	A2
Caguas	C2
Camuy	B2
Candelaria	C2
Canóvanas	D2
Carolina	D2
Cataño	C2
Cayey	C2
Ceiba	D2
Ceiba	D2
Celada	D2
Ciales	C2
Cidra	C2
Coamo	C2
Coco	C2
Comerío	C2
Coquí	C3
Corazón	C3
Corozal	C2
Coto Laurel	B2
Dorado	C2
Fajardo	D2
Florida	B3
Guánica	C3
Guayama	C3
Guayanilla	B2
Guaynabo	C2
Gurabo	D2
Hatillo	B2
Hormigueros	A2
Humacao	D2
Imbéry	B2
Isabela	A1
Jayuya	B2
Jobos	C3
Juana Díaz	C2
Juncos	D2
Lajas	A2
Lares	B2
Las Piedras	D2
Levittown	C2
Loíza	D2
Luquillo	D2
Manatí	B2
Martorell	D2
Maunabo	D2
Mayagüez	A2
Moca	A2
Naguabo	D2
Pastillo	C3
Patillas	D2
Peñuelas	B2
Ponce	B2
Puerto Real	A2
Punta Santiago	D2

Quebradillas	B2
Río Grande	D2
Sabana Grande	B2
Salinas	C3
San Antonio	B2
San Germán	A2
San Isidro	D2
San Juan, capital	C2
San Lorenzo	D2
San Sebastián	B2
Santa Isabel	C3
Santo Domingo	B2
Trujillo Alto	B2
Utuado	B2
Vega Alta	C2
Vega Baja	C2
Vieques	D2
Villalba	C2
Yabucoa	D2
Yauco	B2

Other Features

Añasco, beach	A2
Arenas, point	D2
Bayamón, river	C2
Brea, point	B3
Cabo Rojo Natl. Wildlife Refuge	A3
Caguana Indian Ceremonial Park	B2
Caja de Muertos, island	B3
Caña Gorda, beach	B3
Caribbean, sea	B3
Caribbean Natl. Forest	D2
Carite Forest Reserve	C2
Coamo Hot Springs	C2
Cordillera Central, mts.	B2
Culebra, island	E2
Culebrinas, river	A2
Doña Juana, mt.	C2
El Cañuelo, ruins	C2
El Toro, mt.	D2
Este, point	E2
Fortín Conde de Mirasol, fort	E2
Grande de Añasco, river	A2
Grande de Manatí, river	C2
Guajataca Forest Reserve	B2
Guánica Forest Reserve	B3
Guilarte, mt.	B2
Guilarte Forest Reserve	B2
Icacos, key	D2
La Plata, river	C2
Maricao Forest Reserve	B2
Mona, passage	A2
Norte, key	E2
Puerca, point	D2
Punta, mt.	B2
Rincón, bay	C3
Río Abajo Forest Reserve	B2
Río Camuy Cave Park	B2
Rojo, cape	A3
Roosevelt Roads Naval Station	D2
San Juan, passage	D2
Sierra de Cayey, mts.	C2
Sierra de Luquillo, mts.	D2
Sombe, beach	D2
Susua Forest Reserve	B2
Toro Negro Forest Reserve	C2
Vieques, island	E2
Vieques, passage	D2
Vieques, sound	E2
Yeguas, point	D2

Antigua & Barbuda

National Capital

Other City

1:1,480,000

0   10   20 mi
0   10   20 km

Transverse Mercator Projection

© MapQuest.com, Inc.

Antigua and Barbuda

Capital: St. John's
Area: 171 sq. mi.
443 sq. km.
Population: 67,897
Largest City: St. John's
Language: English
Monetary Unit: East Caribbean dollar

Antigua and Barbuda: Map Index

Cities and Towns

Bolands	D5
Cedar Grove	E5
Codrington	E2
Falmouth	E5
Freetown	E5
Old Road	D5
St. John's, capital	D5

Other Features

Antigua, island	D4
Barbuda, island	E3
Boggy, peak	D5
Cobb, cove	E1
Codrington, lagoon	D1
Goat, point	D1
Gravenor, bay	E2
Palmetto, point	D2
Redonda, island	A6
Shirley, cape	E6
Spanish, point	E2
Willoughby, bay	E5

St. Kitts & Nevis

National Capital

Other City

1:670,000

0   4   8 mi
0   4   8 km

Transverse Mercator Projection

St. Kitts & Nevis: Map Index

Cities and Towns

Basseterre, capital	B2
Bath	C3
Cayon	B1
Charlestown	C3
Cotton Ground	C2
Dieppe Bay Town	B1
Fig Tree	C3
Newcastle	C2
Old Road Town	B1
St. Paul's	A1
Sandy Point Town	A1
Zion	C3

Other Features

Great Salt, pond	C2
Nag's Head, cape	C2
Narrows, strait	C2
Nevis, island	C3
St. Kitts (St. Christopher), island	B2

St. Kitts & Nevis

Capital: Basseterre
Area: 104 sq. mi.
269 sq. km.
Population: 38,763
Largest City: Basseterre
Language: English
Monetary Unit: East Caribbean dollar

Dominica: Map Index

Cities and Towns

Berekua	B4
Castle Bruce	B2
Colihaut	A2
Glanvillia	A2
La Plaine	B3
Laudat	B3
Marigot	B2
Massacre	B3
Pointe Michel	B3
Pont Cassé	B3
Portsmouth	A2
Rosalie	B3
Roseau, capital	B3
Saint Joseph	A3
Salibia	B2
Salisbury	A2
Soufrière	B4
Vieille Case	B1
Wesley	B2

Other Features

Boiling, lake	B3
Dominica, passage	A1
Grand, bay	B4
Layou, river	B3
Morne Diablotin, mt.	B2
Roseau, river	B3
Toulaman, river	B2

Dominica

Capital: Roseau
Area: 290 sq. mi.
751 sq. km.
Population: 69,655
Largest City: Roseau
Language: English
Monetary Unit: East Caribbean dollar

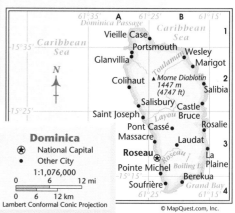

Dominica

National Capital

Other City

1:1,076,000

0   6   12 mi
0   6   12 km

Lambert Conformal Conic Projection

© MapQuest.com, Inc.

St. Lucia

Capital: Castries
Area: 238 sq. mi.
617 sq. km.
Population: 149,000
Largest City: Castries
Language: English
Monetary Unit: East Caribbean dollar

St. Lucia:
Map Index

Cities and Towns
Canaries.............................A2
Castries, *capital*................B1
Choiseul.............................A3
Dauphin.............................B1
Dennery.............................B2
Desruisseau.......................B3
Grand Anse........................B2
Gros Islet...........................B1
Laborie..............................B3
La Croix Maingot.................A2
Micoud..............................B3
Mon Repos.........................B2

Other Features
Canelles, *river*..................B3
Cul de Sac, *river*..............B2
Fond d'Or, *river*................B2
Gimie, *mt.*.......................A2
Maria, *islands*..................B3
Moule à Chique, *cape*......B3
Point, *cape*......................B1
Saint Lucia, *channel*.........B1
Saint Vincent, *passage*......B4
Soufrière, *volcano*............A2

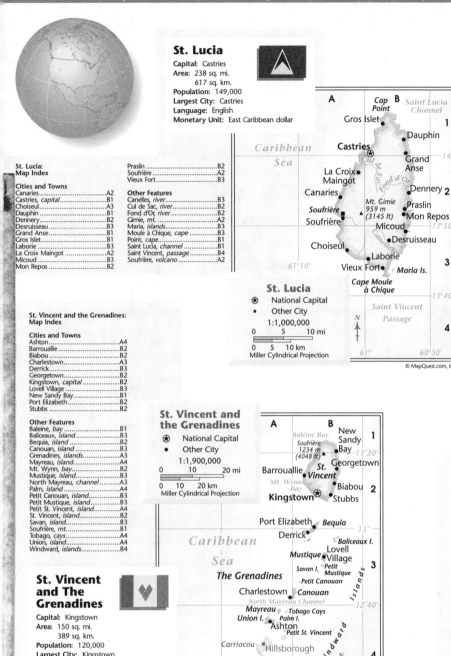

St. Lucia
⊛ National Capital
• Other City
1:1,000,000
0   5   10 mi
0   5   10 km
Miller Cylindrical Projection

© MapQuest.com, Inc.

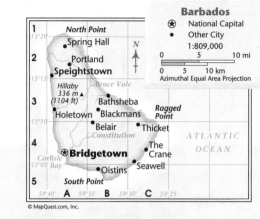

Barbados
⊛ National Capital
• Other City
1:809,000
0   5   10 mi
0   5   10 km
Azimuthal Equal Area Projection

© MapQuest.com, Inc.

Barbados

Capital: Bridgetown
Area: 166 sq. mi.
430 sq. km.
Population: 270,000
Largest City: Bridgetown
Language: English
Monetary Unit: Barbadian dollar

Barbados:
Map Index

Cities and Towns
Bathsheba...........................B3
Belair.................................B4
Blackmans..........................B3
Bridgetown, *capital*..........A4
Holetown............................A3
Oistins...............................B5
Portland.............................A2
Seawell...............................C4
Speightstown......................A2
Spring Hall.........................A2
The Crane...........................C4
Thicket...............................C4

Other Features
Bruce Vale, *river*..............B3
Carlisle, *bay*....................A4
Constitution, *river*............B4
Hillaby, *mt.*.....................A3
North, *point*.....................A1
Ragged, *point*..................C3
South, *point*.....................B5

St. Vincent and the Grenadines:
Map Index

Cities and Towns
Ashton...............................A4
Barrouallie.........................B2
Biabou...............................B2
Charlestown........................A3
Derrick...............................B3
Georgetown........................B2
Kingstown, *capital*............B2
Lovell Village......................B3
New Sandy Bay....................B1
Port Elizabeth.....................B2
Stubbs...............................B2

Other Features
Baleine, *bay*.....................B1
Baliceaux, *island*..............B3
Bequia, *island*..................B2
Canouan, *island*...............B3
Grenadines, *islands*..........A3
Mayreau, *island*...............A4
Mt. Wynn, *bay*.................B2
Mustique, *island*..............B3
North Mayreau, *channel*....A3
Palm, *island*....................A4
Petit Canouan, *island*.......B3
Petit Mustique, *island*......B3
Petit St. Vincent, *island*....A4
St. Vincent, *island*............B2
Savan, *island*...................B3
Soufrière, *mt.*..................B1
Tobago, *cays*...................A4
Union, *island*...................A4
Windward, *islands*............B4

St. Vincent and The Grenadines

Capital: Kingstown
Area: 150 sq. mi.
389 sq. km.
Population: 120,000
Largest City: Kingstown
Languages: English, French patois
Monetary Unit: East Caribbean dollar

St. Vincent and the Grenadines
⊛ National Capital
• Other City
1:1,900,000
0   10   20 mi
0   10   20 km
Miller Cylindrical Projection

© MapQuest.com, Inc.

Trinidad & Tobago

Capital: Port of Spain
Area: 1,980 sq. mi.
5,130 sq. km.
Population: 1,303,000
Largest City: Port of Spain
Language: English
Monetary Unit: Trinidad and Tobago dollar

Trinidad & Tobago:
Map Index

Cities and Towns
Arima.................................A2
Canaan...............................B1
Chaguanas..........................A2
Charlotteville......................B1
Couva................................A2
Fullarton............................A2
Guayaguayare.....................A2
Matelot..............................A2
Moruga..............................A2
Pierreville...........................A2
Plymouth............................B1
Point Fortin........................A2
Port of Spain, *capital*........A2
Princes Town.......................A2
Rio Claro............................A2
St. Augustine......................A2
San Fernando......................A2
San Francique......................A2
Sangre Grande....................A2
Scarborough.......................B1
Siparia...............................A2
Toco..................................B2

Other Features
El Cerro del Aripo, *mt.*......A2
Paria, *gulf*.......................A2
Pitch, *lake*.......................A2
Tobago, *island*.................B1
Trinidad, *island*................A2

Trinidad & Tobago
⊛ National Capital
• Other City
1:2,700,000
0   15   30 mi
0   15   30 km
Azimuthal Equal Area Projection

© MapQuest.com, Inc.

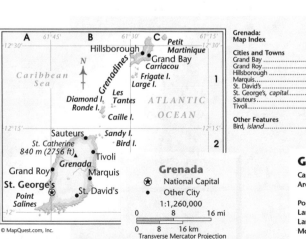

Grenada:
Map Index

Cities and Towns
Grand Bay...........................C1
Grand Roy...........................B2
Hillsborough.......................C1
Marquis..............................B2
St. David's...........................B2
St. George's, *capital*..........A2
Sauteurs.............................B2
Tivoli.................................B2

Other Features
Bird, *island*......................B2

Caille, *island*....................B1
Carriacou, *island*..............C1
Diamond, *island*...............B1
Frigate, *island*..................C1
Grenada, *island*................B2
Grenadines, *island*
group.............................B1, C1
Large, *island*....................C1
Les Tantes, *island*.............B1
Petit Martinique, *island*.....C1
Ronde, *island*...................B1
St. Catherine, *mt.*.............B2
Salines, *point*...................A2
Sandy, *island*...................B2

Grenada

Capital: St. George's
Area: 133 sq. mi.
345 sq. km.
Population: 89,258
Largest City: St. George's
Language: English
Monetary Unit: East Caribbean dollar

Grenada
⊛ National Capital
• Other City
1:1,260,000
0   8   16 mi
0   8   16 km
Transverse Mercator Projection

© MapQuest.com, Inc.

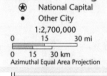

© MapQuest.com, Inc.

Canada:
Map Index

ALBERTA
Cities and Towns
Banff E3
Calgary E3
Edmonton, capital E3
Fort McMurray F3
Grande Prairie E3
High Level F3
Lethbridge F4
Medicine Hat F4
Peace River E3
Red Deer E3
Whitecourt E3
Other Features
Athabasca, river F3
Peace, river E3

BRITISH COLUMBIA
Cities and Towns
Dawson Creek E3
Fort Nelson E3
Fort St. John E3
Kamloops E4
Kelowna E4
Kitimat D3
Masset D4
Nanaimo E4
Ocean Falls E3
Port Hardy E3
Prince George E3
Prince Rupert D3
Trail E4
Vancouver, capital E4
Victoria, capital E3
Williams Lake E3
Other Features
Coast, mts. D3
Fraser, river E3
Queen Charlotte, islands D3
Robson, mt. E3
Rocky, mts. E3
Vancouver, island E4
Waddington, mt. E4

MANITOBA
Cities and Towns
Brandon H4
Brochet F3
Churchill G3
Dauphin G3
Flin Flon G3
Lynn Lake F3
Thompson H4
Winnipeg, capital H4
York Factory H3
Other Features
Churchill, river G3
Hudson, bay H3
Manitoba, lake G3
Nelson, river H3
Saskatchewan, river G3
Southern Indian, lake G3
Winnipeg, lake H3
Winnipegosis, lake G3

NEW BRUNSWICK
Cities and Towns
Fredericton, capital L4
Moncton L3
Saint John L4
Other Feature
Fundy, bay L4

NEWFOUNDLAND AND LABRADOR
Cities and Towns
Cartwright M3
Corner Brook M4
Gander M4
Grand Falls M4
Happy Valley-Goose Bay L3
Hebron L3
Labrador City L3
Marystown M4

Nain E3
St. John's, capital E4
Other Features
Hamilton, inlet L3
Labrador, region L3
Labrador, sea M3
Smallwood, reservoir L3

NORTHWEST TERRITORIES
Cities and Towns
Arviat H2
Déline E2
Fort McPherson D2
Fort Simpson E2
Fort Smith F2
Holman Island F2
Inuvik D2
Sachs Harbour E1
Yellowknife, capital F2
Other Features
Amundsen, gulf E1
Banks, island E1
Beaufort, sea D1
Great Bear, lake E2
Great Slave, lake F2
Inuvik, region D2
Mackenzie, gulf D2
Mackenzie, mts. D2
Mackenzie, river E2
M'Clure, strait E1
Melville, island F1
Slave, river F2
Viscount Melville, sound F1

NUNAVUT
Cities and Towns
Arctic Bay J1
Baker Lake H2

Cambridge Bay G2
Grise Fiord J1
Iqaluit, capital L2
Kugluktuk F2
Pangnirtung L2
Pond Inlet K1
Rankin Inlet H2
Repulse Bay J2
Resolute H1
Other Features
Amadjuak, lake K2
Axel Heiberg, island H1
Back, river G2
Baffin, bay L1
Baffin, island K1
Baffin, region J1
Bathurst, island H1
Belcher, islands K3
Boothia, peninsula J2
Boothia, gulf H1
Brodeur, peninsula J1
Coats, island J2
Cumberland, sound L2
Davis, strait M2
Devon, island J1
Dubawnt, lake G2
Ellesmere, island K1
Foxe, basin K2
Foxe, channel J2
Home, bay L2
Hudson, bay J2
Hudson, strait K2
James, bay J3
Jones, sound J1
Keewatin, region H2
King William, island H2
Kitikmeot, region G2
Mansel, island J2
Melville, peninsula J2
Nettilling, lake L2
Ottawa, islands J3
Parry, channel F1

Prince Charles, island K2
Prince of Wales, island H1
Queen Elizabeth, islands G2
Queen Maud, gulf G2
Smith, sound L2
Somerset, island H1
Southampton, island J2
Victoria, island G1

NOVA SCOTIA
Cities and Towns
Halifax, capital L4
Sydney M4
Yarmouth L4
Other Features
Cabot, strait M4
Fundy, bay L4
Sable, cape L4

ONTARIO
Cities and Towns
Cornwall K4
Fort Frances H4
Geraldton J4
Hamilton J4
Kapuskasing K4
Kingston K4
Kirkland Lake K4
Kitchener J4
London J4
Moosonee J3
Nipigon J3
North Bay K4
Ottawa, national capital K4
Peterborough K4
Rouyn-Noranda K4
Sandy Lake H3
Sarnia J4
Sault Ste. Marie J4
Sudbury J4
Thunder Bay J4
Timmins K4
Toronto, capital K4
Windsor J4

Winisk J3
Other Features
Akimiski, island J3
Albany, river J3
Erie, lake J4
Hudson, bay J3
Huron, lake J4
James, bay J3
Nipigon, lake J3
Ontario, lake K4
Ottawa, river K4
Superior, lake J4
Woods, lake H4

PRINCE EDWARD ISLAND
Cities and Towns
Charlottetown, capital L4

QUÉBEC
Cities and Towns
Bae-Comeau L4
Chibougamau K4
Chicoutimi K4
Chisasibi K3
Gagnon L3
Gaspé L4
Havre-St-Pierre L3
Inukjuak K3
Kuujjuaq L3
Matagami K4
Montréal K4
Port-Cartier L3
Puvirnituq K3
Québec, capital K4
Rimouski L4
Rouyn-Noranda K4
Schefferville L3
Sept-Îles L4
Shawinigan K4
Sherbrooke K4
Trois-Rivières K4
Val-d'Or K4
Waskaganish K3

Other Features
Anticosti, island L4
Caniapiscau, river L3
Feuilles, river K3
Hudson, bay J2
Hudson, strait K3
James, bay J3
Minto, lake K3
Mistassini, lake K3
Ottawa, river K4
St. Lawrence, gulf L4
St. Lawrence, river K4
Ungava, bay L3
Ungava, peninsula K2

SASKATCHEWAN
Cities and Towns
Estevan G4
La Loche G3
Moose Jaw G3
Prince Albert G3
Regina, capital G3
Saskatoon G3
Uranium City G3
Other Features
Athabasca, lake G3
Churchill, river G3
Great Plains, plain G3
Reindeer, lake G3
Saskatchewan, river G3
Wollaston, lake G3

YUKON TERRITORY
Cities and Towns
Dawson D2
Faro D2
Mayo D2
Watson Lake E2
Whitehorse, capital D2
Other Features
Beaufort, sea D1
Logan, mt. C2
St. Elias, mt. C2
Yukon, river D2

Canada
Capital: Ottawa
Area: 3,855,101 sq. mi.
9,984,670 sq. km.
Population: 30,007,094
Largest City: Toronto
Languages: English, French
Monetary Unit: Canadian dollar

New Brunswick
Capital: Fredericton
Area: 28,150 sq. mi.
72,908 sq. km.
Population: 729,498
Largest City: Saint John

Newfoundland and Labrador
Capital: St. John's
Area: 156,453 sq. mi.
405,212 sq. km.
Population: 512,930
Largest City: St. John's

Prince Edward Island
Capital: Charlottetown
Area: 2,185 sq. mi.
5,660 sq. km.
Population: 135,294
Largest City: Charlottetown

Ontario
Capital: Toronto
Area: 415,598 sq. mi.
1,076,395 sq. km.
Population: 11,410,046
Largest City: Toronto

Alberta
Capital: Edmonton
Area: 255,541 sq. mi.
661,848 sq. km.
Population: 2,974,807
Largest City: Edmonton

British Columbia
Capital: Victoria
Area: 364,764 sq. mi.
944,735 sq. km.
Population: 3,907,738
Largest City: Vancouver

Manitoba
Capital: Winnipeg
Area: 250,116 sq. mi.
647,797 sq. km.
Population: 1,119,583
Largest City: Winnipeg

Northwest Territories
Capital: Yellowknife
Area: 519,734 sq. mi.
1,346,106 sq. km.
Population: 37,360
Largest City: Yellowknife

Nova Scotia
Capital: Halifax
Area: 21,345 sq. mi.
55,284 sq. km.
Population: 908,007
Largest City: Halifax

Nunavut
Capital: Iqaluit
Area: 808,185 sq. mi.
2,093,190 sq. km.
Population: 26,745
Largest City: Iqaluit

Québec
Capital: Québec
Area: 595,391 sq. mi.
1,542,056 sq. km.
Population: 7,237,479
Largest City: Montréal

Saskatchewan
Capital: Regina
Area: 251,366 sq. mi.
651,036 sq. km.
Population: 978,933
Largest City: Saskatoon

Yukon Territory
Capital: Whitehorse
Area: 186,272 sq. mi.
482,443 sq. km.
Population: 28,674
Largest City: Whitehorse

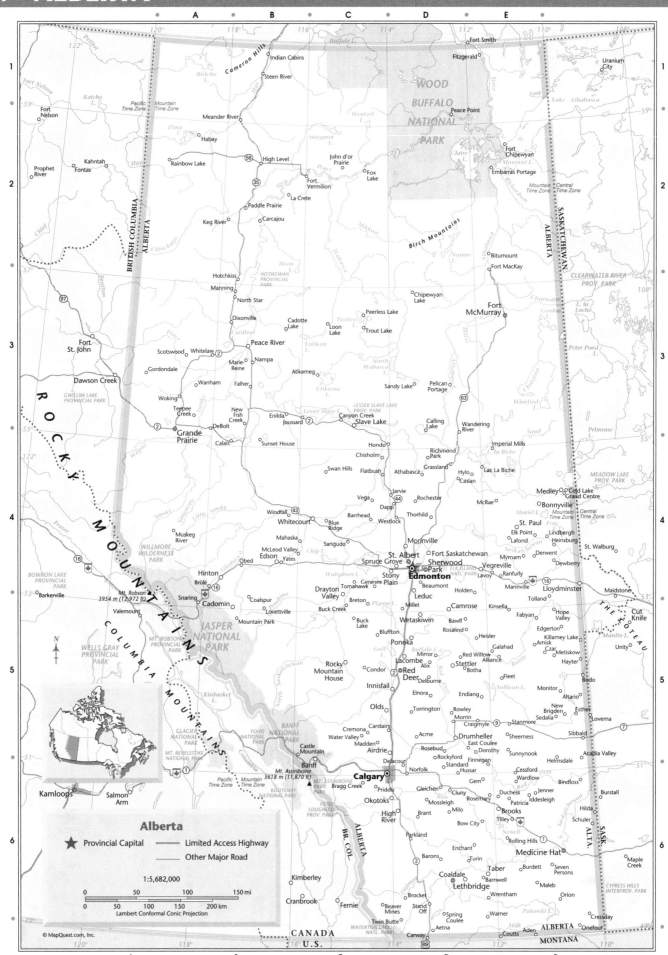

Alberta

★ Provincial Capital
— Limited Access Highway
— Other Major Road

1:5,682,000

0 50   100   150 mi

0 50 100 150 200 km

Lambert Conformal Conic Projection

© MapQuest.com, Inc.

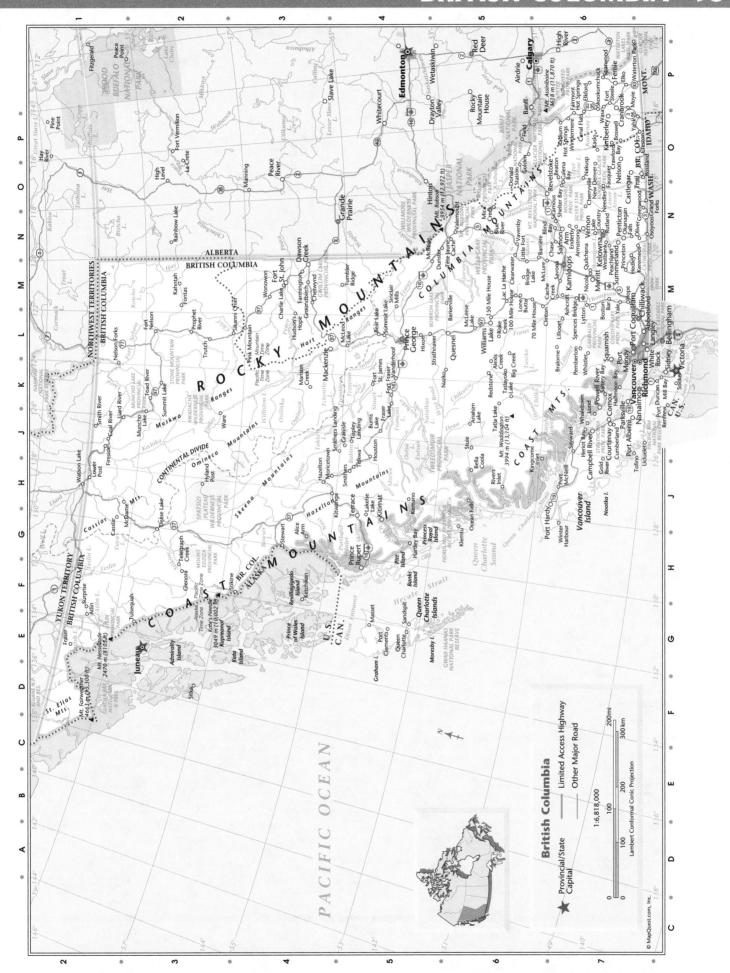

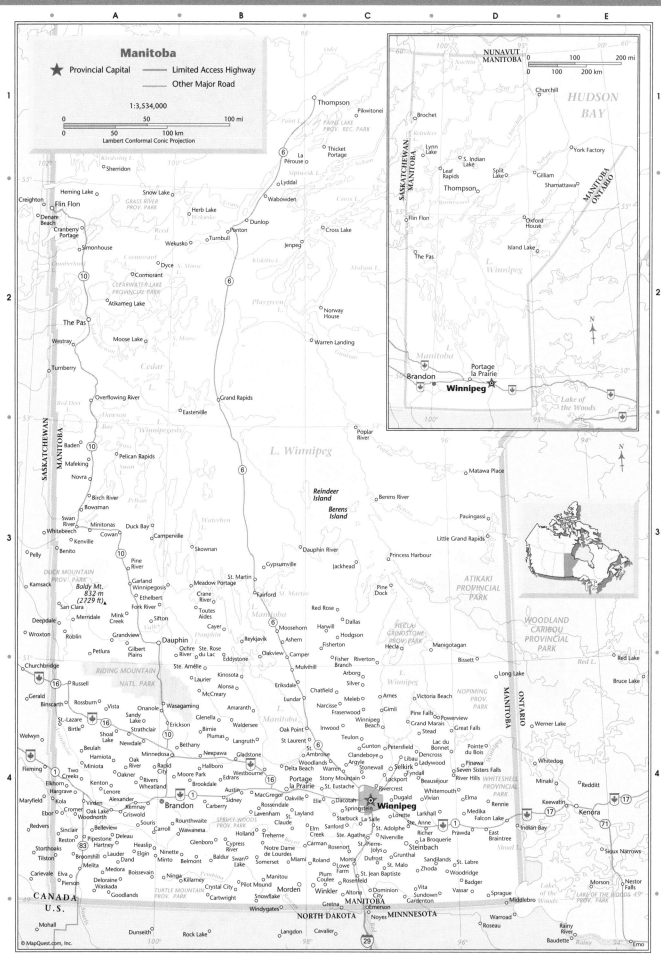

Manitoba

★ Provincial Capital

━━━ Limited Access Highway

━━━ Other Major Road

1:3,534,000

0   50   100 mi

0   50   100 km

Lambert Conformal Conic Projection

NUNAVUT
MANITOBA

0   100   200 mi
0   100   200 km

HUDSON BAY

Churchill

Brochet

SASKATCHEWAN MANITOBA

Lynn Lake
Leaf Rapids
S. Indian Lake
Split Lake
York Factory
Gilliam
Shamattawa

Thompson

Flin Flon

The Pas

Oxford House

Island Lake

L. Winnipeg

MANITOBA ONTARIO

Brandon
Portage la Prairie
Winnipeg

Lake of the Woods

N

Thompson

Pikwitonei

PAINT LAKE PROV. REC. PARK

La Pérouse

Thicket Portage

Brochet

Sherridon

Snow Lake

Heming Lake

Creighton
Flin Flon

Denare Beach
Cranberry Portage

Simonhouse

GRASS RIVER PROV. PARK

Herb Lake

Wekusko

Dunlop

Lyddal

Wabowden

Cross Lake

Jenpeg

Ponton
Turnbull

Dyce
Cormorant
N. Moose L.

CLEARWATER LAKE PROVINCIAL PARK

Atikameg Lake

The Pas

Westray
Turnberry

Moose Lake

Cedar L.

Overflowing River

Easterville

Grand Rapids

Poplar River

L. Winnipeg

Matawa Place

Baden

Mafeking

Novra

Pelican Rapids

Birch River
Bowsman

Swan River
Minitonas
Whitebeech
Cowan
Kenville
Benito

Duck Bay
Camperville

Skownan

Reindeer Island

Berens Island

Berens River

Pauingassi

Little Grand Rapids

Princess Harbour

ATIKAKI PROVINCIAL PARK

WOODLAND CARIBOU PROVINCIAL PARK

Pelly

Pine River

Garland
Winnipegosis
Ethelbert
Fork River

Meadow Portage
Crane River
Toutes Aides

Dauphin River

Gypsumville

St. Martin

Fairford

Dauphin River

Jackhead

Red Rose

Dallas

Harwill
Hodgson

Pine Dock

Kamsack

Baldy Mt. 832 m (2729 ft)

San Clara

Deepdale
Wroxton

Merridale
Mink Creek

Sifton

Cayer

Grandview

Roblin
Petlura
Gilbert Plains

Dauphin

Ochre River
Ste. Rose du Lac
Eddystone

Reykjavik

Oakview
Camper

Mooseorn
Ashern

Fisherton

Fisher Branch

Riverton

Bissett

Manigotagan

Hecla

HECLA GRINDSTONE PROV. PARK

L. Winnipeg

Red Lake

Bruce Lake

Churchbridge

Gerald
Binscarth
St.-Lazare
Birtle

Russell

Vista

Rossburn

Sandy Lake
Strathclair

Wasagaming

RIDING MOUNTAIN NATL. PARK

Onanole

Glenella

Laurier
Alonsa

McCreary

Amaranth

Kinosota

Eriksdale

Chatfield

Lundar

Narcisse

Silver

Arborg

Long Lake

Red Lake

Arnes

Meleb
Fraserwood

Gimli

Pine Falls
Powerview

Victoria Beach

NOPIMING PROV. PARK

Werner Lake

MANITOBA ONTARIO

Welwyn

Fleming

Two Creeks

Beulah
Hamiota
Miniota

Oakner

Elkhorn
Hargrave
Maryfield
Kola

Kenton
Lenore

Rivers
Wheatland

Oak River
Rapid City

Minnedosa

Bethany

Neepawa

Birnie
Plumas

Langruth

Glenboro

Shoal Lake
Newdale

Strathclair

Erickson

Gladstone

St. Ambroise
Woodlands

Delta Beach

Oak Point

St Laurent

Inwood

Teulon

Gunton

Petersfield

Clandeboye
Argyle
Stonewall

Libau
Ladywood

Beausejour

Lac du Bonnet

Dencross

Pinawa

Pointe du Bois

Seven Sisters Falls

River Hills

Whitedog

Minaki

Redditt

Winnipeg Beach

Grand Marais
Stead

Great Falls

WHITESHELL PROVINCIAL PARK

Keewatin

Kenora

Portage la Prairie

Austin
MacGregor
Oakville

St. Eustache

Elie
Dacotah

Winnipeg

Rivercrest

Dugald
Vivian
Elma

Medika
Falcon Lake

Rennie

East Braintree

Indian Bay

Brandon

Carberry

Sidney

Lavenham
St. Claude

Layland

Starbuck
Sanford

La Salle

St. Adolphe

Ste. Anne
Richer

Prawda

Keewatin

Kenora

Maryfield
Kola
Virden
Cromer
Oak Lake
Woodnorth

Alexander
Kemnay
Griswold

Souris

Rounthwaite
Wawanesa

Carroll

Glenboro

Treherne

Holland

Elm Creek

Carman

Rosenort

St-Pierre-Jolys

Niverville

La Broquerie

Grunthal

Sandilands

St. Labre

Woodridge

Badger

Sprague

Ebor
Redvers

Sinclair
Belleview

Pipestone
Hartney
Deleau

Heaslip

Ninette
Minto
Elgin

Baldur

Belmont

Somerset

Miami

Roland

Morris
Lowe Farm

Dufrost

St. Malo
Zhoda

Vita
Sundown
Gardenton

Badger

Storthoaks
Tilston

Broomhill
Lauder
Dand

Medora

Boissevain

Ninga
Killarney

Crystal City

Pilot Mound

Manitou

Plum Coulee

St. Jean Baptiste

Grunthal

Dominion City

Vassar

Sprague

Carievale
Elva
Pierson

Deloraine
Waskada

Goodlands

Cartwright

Snowflake

TURTLE MOUNTAIN PROV. PARK

Winkler
Morden

Gretna

MANITOBA

Emerson

Middlebro

LAKE OF THE WOODS PROV. PARK

Mohall

CANADA
U.S.

Dunseith

Rock Lake

Langdon

Cavalier

NORTH DAKOTA

Noyes

MINNNESOTA

Warroad
Roseau

Rainy River

Baudette

Emo

© MapQuest.com, Inc.

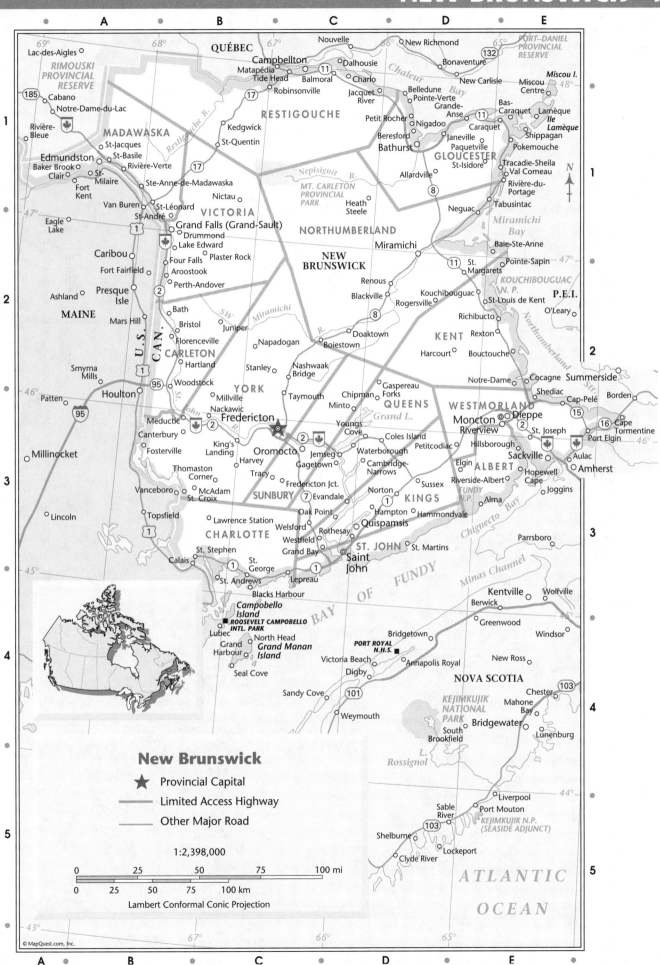

New Brunswick

★ Provincial Capital

— Limited Access Highway

— Other Major Road

1:2,398,000

0   25   50   75   100 mi

0   25   50   75   100 km

Lambert Conformal Conic Projection

© MapQuest.com, Inc.

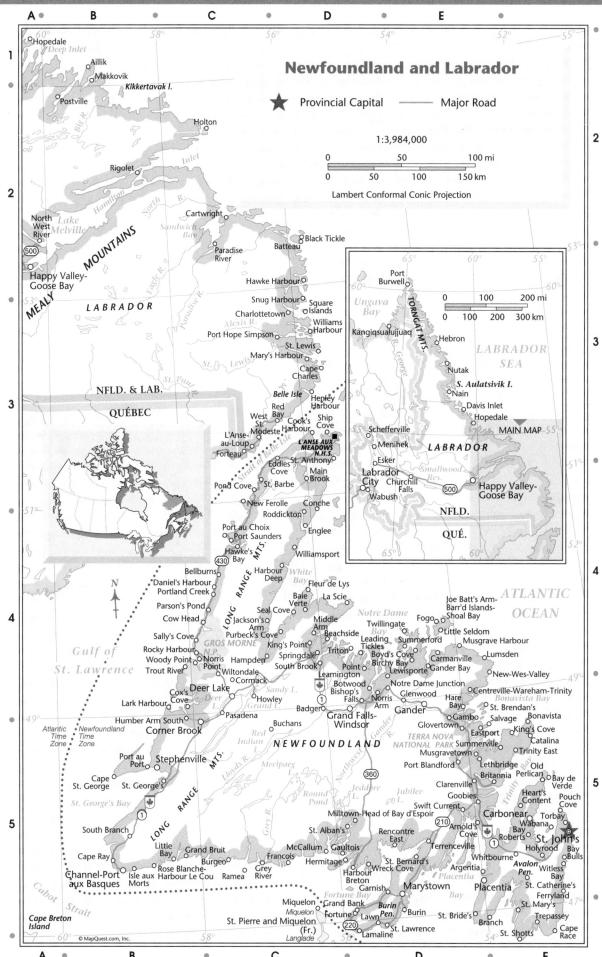

Newfoundland and Labrador

★ Provincial Capital —— Major Road

1:3,984,000

0 ___ 50 ___ 100 mi
0 __ 50 __ 100 __ 150 km

Lambert Conformal Conic Projection

0 __ 100 __ 200 mi
0 __ 100 __ 200 __ 300 km

Hopedale
Deep Inlet
Aillik
Makkovik
Kikkertavak I.
Postville
Holton
Rigolet
Hamilton Inlet
Cartwright
Lake Melville
Sandwich Bay
Paradise River
Black Tickle
Batteau
North West River
Hwy. 500 (500)
Happy Valley-Goose Bay
MEALY MOUNTAINS
LABRADOR
North R.
Eagle R.
Paradise R.
Hawke Harbour
Snug Harbour
Charlottetown
Square Islands
Williams Harbour
Port Hope Simpson
St. Lewis
Mary's Harbour
Alexis R.
Cape Charles
Belle Isle
Henley Harbour
Red Bay
West St. Modeste
Cook's Harbour
Ship Cove
L'Anse-au-Loup
Forteau
L'ANSE AUX MEADOWS N.H.S.
Eddies Cove
St. Anthony
Main Brook
Pond Cove
St. Barbe
New Ferolle
Conche
Roddickton
Englee
Port au Choix
Port Saunders
Williamsport
Hawke's Bay
(430)
LONG RANGE MTS.
White Bay
Harbour Deep
Fleur de Lys
Bellburns
Daniel's Harbour
Portland Creek
Baie Verte
La Scie
Parson's Pond
Seal Cove
Cow Head
Jackson's Arm
Middle Arm
Beachside
Sally's Cove
Purbeck's Cove
King's Point
Rocky Harbour
GROS MORNE N.P.
Norris Point
Hampden
Springdale
Triton
Leading Tickles
Woody Point
Trout River
Wiltondale
South Brook
Cormack
Sandy L.
Botwood
Bishop's Falls
Howley
Badger
Deer L.
Grand L.
Leamington
(1)
Deer Lake
Cox's Cove
Lark Harbour
Pasadena
Buchans
Humber Arm South
Corner Brook
Red Indian L.
NEWFOUNDLAND
Atlantic Time Zone
Newfoundland Time Zone
Gulf of St. Lawrence
Port au Port
Stephenville
LONG RANGE MTS.
Lloyds R.
Meelpaeg L.
Cape St. George
St. George's
St. George's Bay
(1)
South Branch
Little Bay
Grand Bruit
Cape Ray
Rose Blanche-Harbour Le Cou
Isle aux Morts
Burgeo
Ramea
Grey River
Channel-Port aux Basques
Cabot Strait
Cape Breton Island
© MapQuest.com, Inc.

Port Burwell
Ungava Bay
TORNGAT MTS.
Hebron
LABRADOR SEA
Kangiqsualujjuaq
Nutak
S. Aulatsivik I.
Nain
George R.
Davis Inlet
Hopedale
Schefferville
MAIN MAP
Menihek
LABRADOR
Esker
Labrador City
Churchill Falls
Smallwood Res.
Wabush
(500)
Happy Valley-Goose Bay
NFLD.
QUÉ.

NFLD. & LAB.
QUÉBEC

White Bay
Fleur de Lys
La Scie
Joe Batt's Arm-Barr'd Islands-Shoal Bay
ATLANTIC OCEAN
Middle Arm
Fogo
Notre Dame Bay
Twillingate
Little Seldom
Musgrave Harbour
Summerford
Carmanville
Lumsden
King's Point
Boyd's Cove
Gander Bay
New-Wes-Valley
Springdale
Birchy Bay
Lewisporte
Centreville-Wareham-Trinity
Leamington
Notre Dame Junction
Bonavista Bay
Glenwood
Hare Bay
St. Brendan's
Norris Arm
Gander
Gambo
Salvage
Bonavista
Grand Falls-Windsor
Glovertown
Eastport
King's Cove
TERRA NOVA NATIONAL PARK
Summerville
Catalina
Trinity East
Musgravetown
Lethbridge
Port Blandford
Old Perlican
Britannia
Bay de Verde
Clarenville
Goobies
Heart's Content
Pouch Cove
Milltown-Head of Bay d'Espoir
Swift Current
Arnold's Cove
(210)
Carbonear
Torbay
Wabana
Bay Roberts
St. Alban's
Rencontre East
Terrenceville
Whitbourne
(1)
St. John's
Holyrood
Bay Bulls
McCallum
Gaultois
St. Bernard's
Argentia
Witless Bay
Hermitage
Wreck Cove
Avalon Pen.
Francois
Harbour Breton
Garnish
Marystown
Placentia
St. Catherine's
Ferryland
Fortune Bay
Burin Pen.
Placentia Bay
Miquelon
Grand Bank
Fortune
Lawn
Burin
St. Bride's
Branch
St. Mary's
Trepassey
St. Pierre and Miquelon (Fr.)
(220)
Lamaline
St. Lawrence
St. Shotts
Cape Race
Langlade
Buchans
Grey R.
Round Pond
Jubilee L.
Jeddore L.
Northwest Gander R.
(360)
Gander R.
Bonavista Bay
Trinity Bay

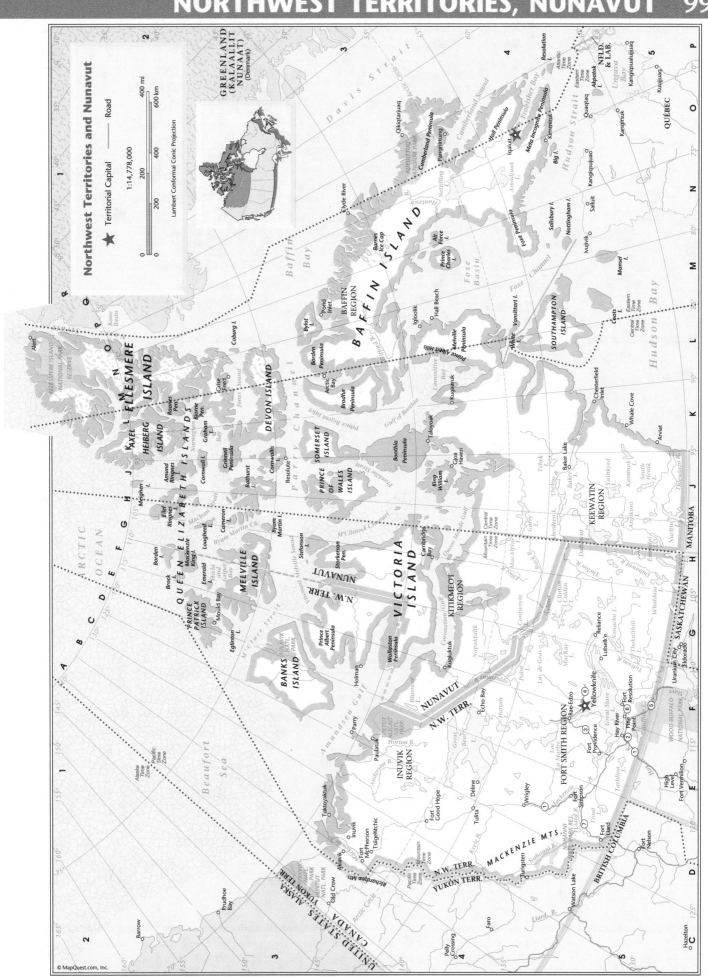

Northwest Territories and Nunavut

1:14,778,000

Lambert Conformal Conic Projection

★ Territorial Capital — Road

© MapQuest.com, Inc.

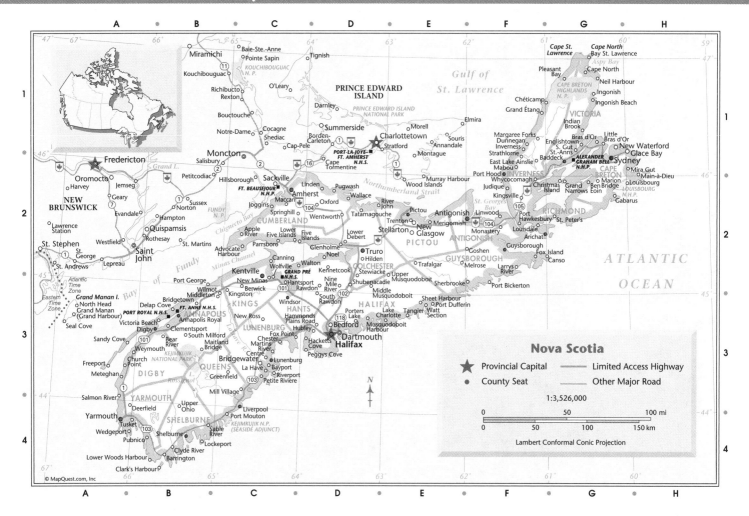

Nova Scotia

★ Provincial Capital — Limited Access Highway
● County Seat — Other Major Road

1:3,526,000

0   50   100 mi
0   50   100   150 km

Lambert Conformal Conic Projection

© MapQuest.com, Inc

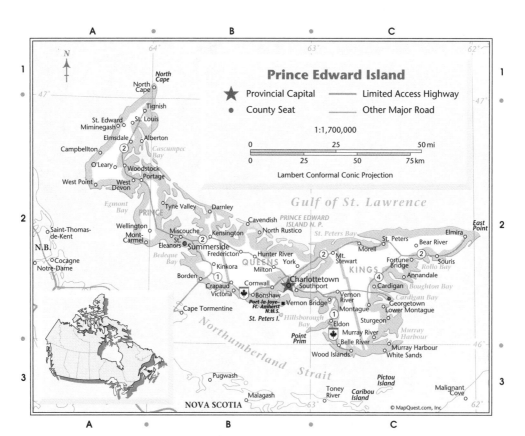

Prince Edward Island

★ Provincial Capital — Limited Access Highway
● County Seat — Other Major Road

1:1,700,000

0   25   50 mi
0   25   50   75 km

Lambert Conformal Conic Projection

© MapQuest.com, Inc

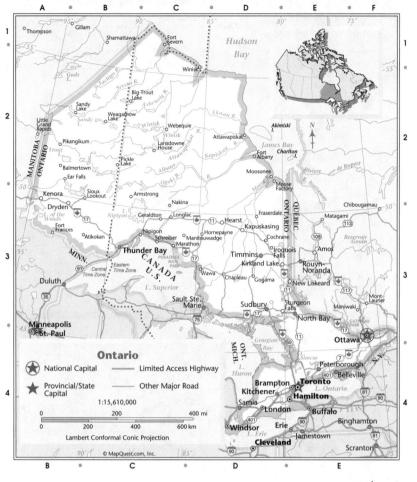

Ontario

Legend:
- ⬡ National Capital
- ★ Provincial/State Capital
- Limited Access Highway
- Other Major Road

1:15,610,000

0 — 200 — 400 mi
0 — 200 — 400 — 600 km

Lambert Conformal Conic Projection

© MapQuest.com, Inc.

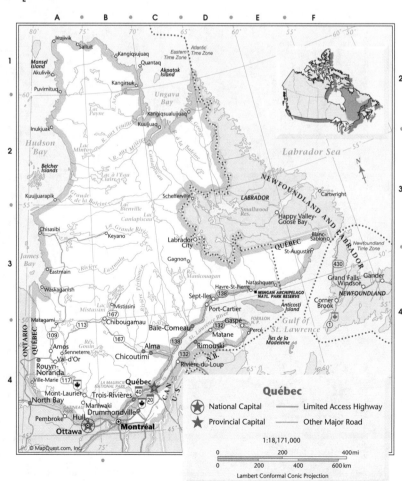

Québec

Legend:
- ⬡ National Capital
- ★ Provincial Capital
- Limited Access Highway
- Other Major Road

1:18,171,000

0 — 200 — 400mi
0 — 200 — 400 — 600 km

Lambert Conformal Conic Projection

© MapQuest.com, Inc

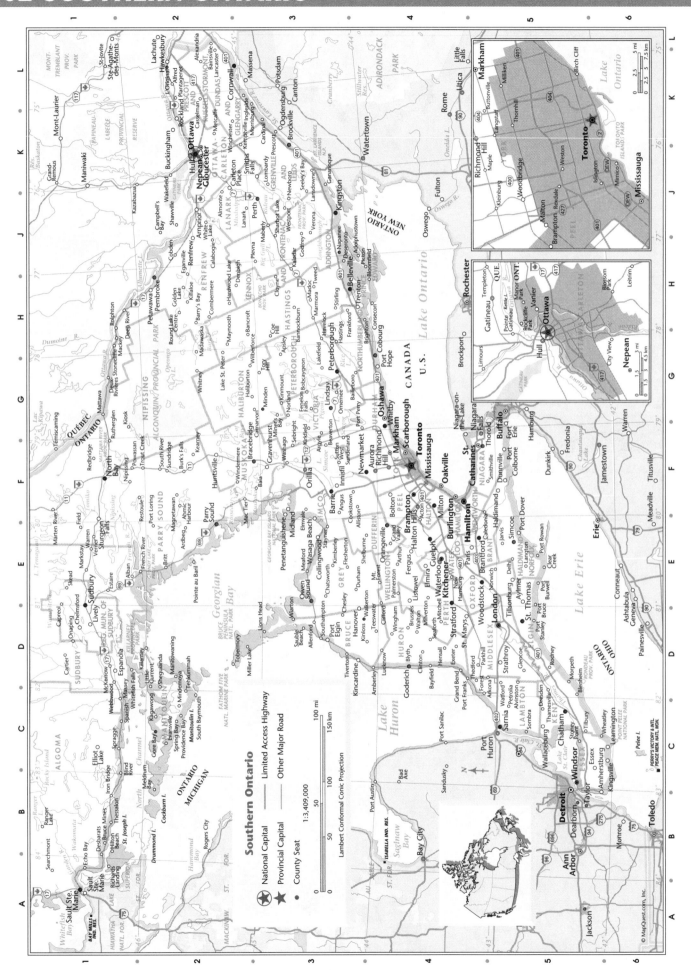

Southern Ontario

⊛ National Capital
★ Provincial Capital
• County Seat

1:3,409,000

Limited Access Highway
Other Major Road

Lambert Conformal Conic Projection

© MapQuest.com, Inc.

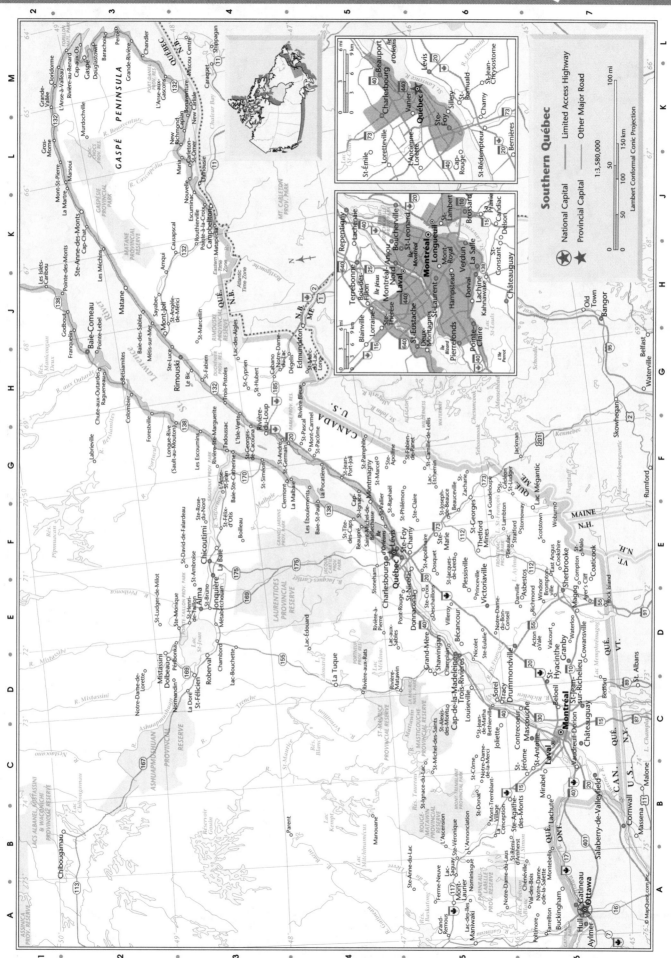

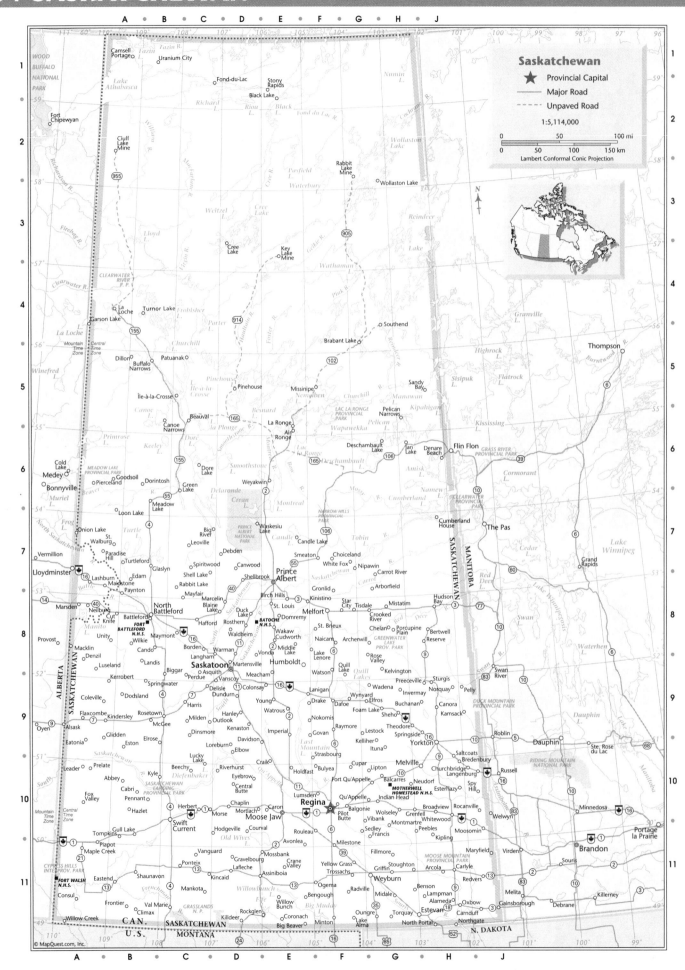

Saskatchewan

★ Provincial Capital
— Major Road
-- Unpaved Road

1:5,114,000

0   50   100 mi
0   50   100   150 km
Lambert Conformal Conic Projection

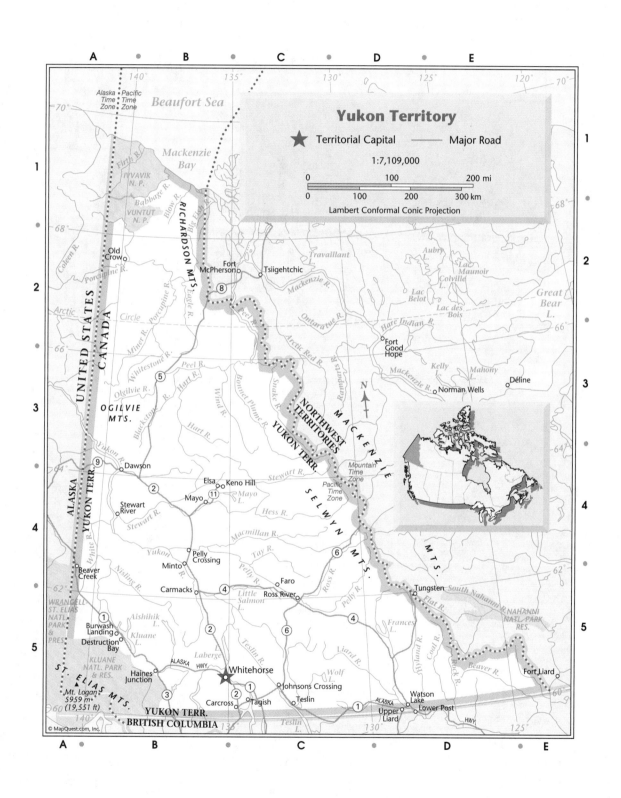

Yukon Territory

★ Territorial Capital ——— Major Road

1:7,109,000

0   100   200 mi

0   100   200   300 km

Lambert Conformal Conic Projection

Beaufort Sea

Alaska Time Zone · Pacific Time Zone

Mackenzie Bay

IVVAVIK N. P.

VUNTUT N. P.

Firth R.

Babbage R.

Blow R.

RICHARDSON MTS.

Big Fish R.

Eagle R.

Old Crow

Fort McPherson

Tsiigehtchic

Travaillant

Aubry L.

Lac Maunoir

Colville L.

Lac Belot

Lac des Bois

Great Bear L.

Coleen R.

Porcupine R.

Porcupine R.

UNITED STATES

CANADA

Arctic Circle

Miner R.

Whitestone R.

Ogilvie R.

Peel R.

Hart R.

OGILVIE MTS.

Wind R.

Bonnet Plume R.

Snake R.

Arctic Red R.

Mackenzie R.

Rampart R.

Ontaratue R.

Hare Indian R.

Fort Good Hope

Mackenzie R.

Norman Wells

Kelly L.

Mahony L.

Déline

NORTHWEST TERRITORIES

YUKON TERR.

M A C K E N Z I E

Mountain Time Zone

Pacific Time Zone

S E L W Y N   M T S.

M T S.

ALASKA

YUKON TERR.

White R.

Yukon R.

Dawson

Elsa   Keno Hill

Mayo

Stewart River

Stewart R.

Hess R.

Macmillan R.

Yukon R.

Pelly Crossing

Minto

Nisling R.

Carmacks

Little Salmon

Ross River

Faro

Pelly R.

Ross R.

Tungsten

South Nahanni R.

NAHANNI NATL. PARK RES.

Flat R.

Hyland R.

Coal R.

Rock R.

Beaver R.

Beaver Creek

WRANGELL ST. ELIAS NATL. PARK & PRES.

Aishihik L.

Kluane L.

Burwash Landing

Destruction Bay

KLUANE NATL. PARK & RES.

ST. ELIAS MTS.

Mt. Logan 5959 m* (19,551 ft)

Haines Junction

ALASKA HWY.

L. Laberge

Teslin R.

Whitehorse

Carcross

Tagish

Johnsons Crossing

Teslin

Wolf L.

Frances L.

Watson Lake

Lower Post

Upper Liard

Fort Liard

ALASKA HWY.

YUKON TERR.

BRITISH COLUMBIA

Liard R.

Teslin L.

© MapQuest.com, Inc.

140° 135° 130° 125° 120°

70° 68° 66° 64° 62° 60°

1   2   3   4   5

A   B   C   D   E

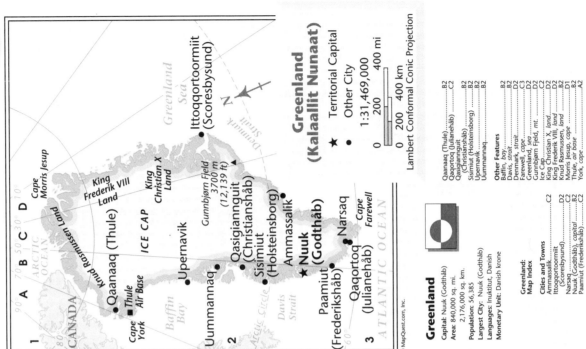

Greenland (Kalaallit Nunaat)

★ Territorial Capital
● Other City

1:31,469,000

0   200   400 km
0   200   400 mi

Lambert Conformal Conic Projection

Greenland

Capital: Nuuk (Godthåb)
Area: 840,000 sq. mi.
2,176,000 sq. km.
Population: 56,385
Largest City: Nuuk (Godthåb)
Languages: Inuktitut, Danish
Monetary Unit: Danish krone

Greenland: Map Index

Cities and Towns

Ammassalik C2
Ittoqqortoormiit
(Scoresbysund) D2
Narsaq C2
Nuuk (Godthåb), *capital* .. C2
Paamiut (Frederikshåb) C2

Qaanaaq (Thule) B2
Qaqortoq (Julianehåb) C2
Qasigiannguit
(Christianshåb) B2
Sisimiut (Holsteinsborg) B2
Upernavik B2
Uummannaq B2

Other Features

Baffin, *bay* B2
Davis, *strait* B2
Denmark, *strait* D2
Farewell, *cape* C3
Greenland, *sea* D2
Gunnbjørn Field, *mt.* C2
Ice Cap D2
King Christian X, *land* D2
King Frederik VIII, *land* B1
Knud Rasmussen, *land* B2
Morris Jesup, *cape* B2
Thule, *air base* B2
York, *cape* A2

Arctic Regions

⊛ National Capital
● Other City

1:43,520,000

0   400   800 km
0   400   800 mi

Polar Equal Area Projection

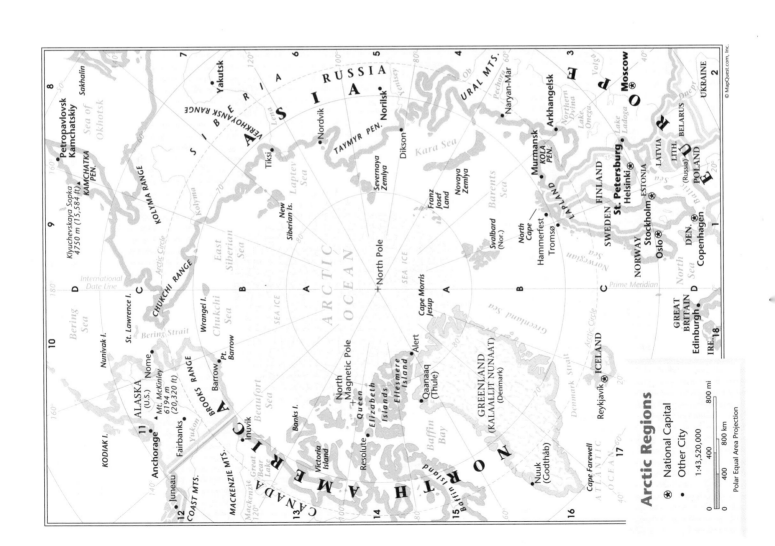

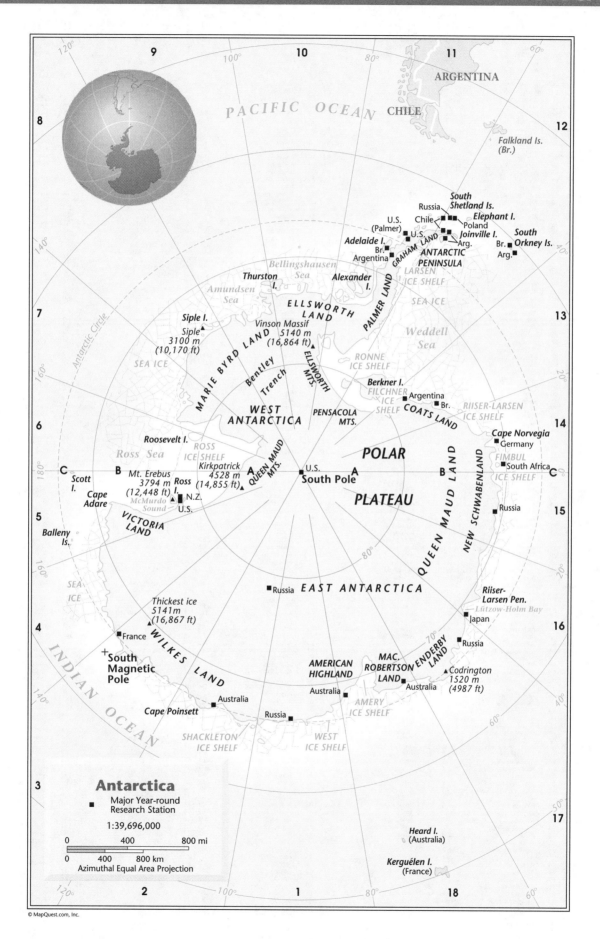

PACIFIC OCEAN

CHILE

ARGENTINA

Falkland Is.
(Br.)

South
Shetland Is.
Russia
Chile
U.S.
(Palmer)
Poland
Elephant I.
Joinville I.
Arg.
South
Orkney Is.
Br.
Arg.
Adelaide I.
Br.
Argentina
U.S.
ANTARCTIC
PENINSULA

Bellingshausen
Sea

Thurston
I.

Amundsen
Sea

Alexander
I.

PALMER LAND
GRAHAM LAND

LARSEN
ICE SHELF

SEA ICE

ELLSWORTH
LAND

Weddell
Sea

Antarctic Circle

Siple I.
Siple
3100 m
(10,170 ft)

SEA ICE

Vinson Massif
5140 m
(16,864 ft)

RONNE
ICE SHELF

Berkner I.
FILCHNER
ICE
SHELF

Argentina
Br.

RIISER-LARSEN
ICE SHELF

MARIE BYRD LAND

Bentley
Trench

ELLSWORTH MTS.

WEST
ANTARCTICA

PENSACOLA
MTS.

COATS LAND

Cape Norvegia
Germany

Roosevelt I.

Ross Sea

ROSS
ICE SHELF

Kirkpatrick
4528 m
(14,855 ft)

QUEEN MAUD MTS.

U.S.
South Pole

POLAR

QUEEN MAUD LAND

NEW SCHWABENLAND

FIMBUL
ICE SHELF
South Africa

C   B
Scott
I.
Cape
Adare

Mt. Erebus
3794 m
(12,448 ft)
McMurdo
Sound

Ross
I.
N.Z.
U.S.

PLATEAU

B   C

Russia

Balleny
Is.

VICTORIA
LAND

SEA
ICE

Russia

EAST ANTARCTICA

Riiser-
Larsen Pen.

Lützow-Holm Bay

Japan

Thickest ice
5141m
(16,867 ft)

Russia

France

+ South
Magnetic
Pole

WILKES LAND

AMERICAN
HIGHLAND

MAC.
ROBERTSON
LAND

ENDERBY LAND

Codrington
1520 m
(4987 ft)

Australia

Australia

INDIAN OCEAN

Cape Poinsett

Australia

Russia

SHACKLETON
ICE SHELF

WEST
ICE SHELF

AMERY
ICE SHELF

Antarctica

■ Major Year-round
Research Station

1:39,696,000

| 0 | 400 | 800 mi |

| 0 | 400 | 800 km |

Azimuthal Equal Area Projection

Heard I.
(Australia)

Kerguélen I.
(France)

A

Key Page
Aachen A3 40
Aaiún, el- B1 58
Aalst C2 33
Aarau C1 35
Aare, *river* B1, B2 35
Aba D5 65
Abadan B3 22
Abaí E4 75
Abakaliki E4 65
Abakan D6 44
Abancay C3 77
Abaya, *lake* B3 60
Abbeville C1 34
Abbey B10 104
Abbotsford L6 95
Abdali B1 24
Abéché C4 59
Abemama, *island* A1 17
Abengourou E3 63
Åbenrå B3 32
Abeokuta B4 65
Aberdeen Inset 10
Aberdeen C1 30
Aberdeen, *lake* H4 99
Aberdeen, S. Dak. D1 126
Aberystwyth B3 30
Abha B2 24
Abhe, *lake* C2 60
Abia, *river* C3 66
Abidjan D4 63
Abilene, Tex. D2 126
Abkhazia, autonomous republic A3 45
Aboisso E4 63
Abomey A4 64
Abou Deïa B5 59
Abrantes A3 36
Abruzzi C2 38
Abşeron, *peninsula* C2 45
Abu Dhabi, *capital* C2 25
Abu Kamal B2 27
Abuja, *capital* D3 65
Abuná, *river* A2 77
Acadia Valley E5 94
Acajutla A2 86
Acámbaro D4 84
Acapulco E4 84
Acarai, *mts.* B5 80
Acaray, *river* E4 75
Acarigua C2 79
Accra, *capital* B4 64
Achill, *island* A2 31
Achinsk D6 44
Achwa, *river* C2 61
Acklins, *island* C4 89
Acme D5 94
Acolman Inset 84
Aconcagua, *mt.* A3 74
Aconcagua, *river* B4 76
Aconibe C3 66
Acquaviva A1 39
Acre A2 81
Acre (Akko) B1 26
Acton E4 102
Acton Vale D6 103
Açúcar, *mt.* Inset I 81
Adamawa, *massif* B2, E5 65
Adams, *lake* N5 95
Adana C3 27
Adapazarı B2 27
Adare, *cape* B5 107
Addis Ababa, *capital* C2 60
Addu, *atoll* A5 19
Adelaide, *island* C11 107
Adelaide, S.A., *capital* C3, Inset II 14
Aden B2 25
Aden E6 94
Aden, *gulf* B1, C2 60
Adi Keyih B2 60
Adi Ugri B2 60
Adige, *river* B1 38
Adirondack, *mts.*, N.Y. F1 126
Adjuntas B2 90
Admiralty, *islands* A2 15
Ado-Ekiti C4 65
Adolphustown H3 102
Adour, *river* B5 34
Adrar B2 57
Adrar des Iforas, *massif* D2 58
Adriatic, *sea* C2 38
Advocate Harbour C2 100
Adwa C1 60
Adygeya, republic E4 44
Adzopé E3 63
Aegean, *sea* C2 51
Ærø, *island* C4 32
Aetna D6 94
Afadjoto, *mt.* C3 64
Afghanistan **22**
Afikpo D5 65
Afram, *river* B3 64
Afyon B2 27
Agadès B2 59
Agadir B2 57
Agartala F4 20
Agboville D4 63
Ağcabädi B2 45
Ağdam B3 45
Agen C4 34
Aginskiy Buryat, autonomous okrug D7 44
Aginskoye D7 44
Agou, *mt.* B3 64
Agra C3 20
Ağri E2 27
Agrigento C3 38
Agrínion B2 51
Ağstafa A2 45
Agua Prieta C1 84
Aguada A2 90
Aguadilla A2 90
Aguadulce B2 87
Aguán, *river* B2 86
Aguarico, *river* C3 79
Aguas Blancas C2 76
Aguas Buenas C2 90
Aguascalientes, *state capital* D3 84
Águilas F4 37
Aguilita B2 90
Agung, *mt.* C2 13
Agusan, *river* C4 12
Ahmadabad B4 20
Ahmadi, al- C2 24
Ahmic Harbour F2 102
Ahuachapán A2 86
Ahvaz B3 22
Ahwar B2 25
Aibonito C2 90
Aigáleo, *mts.* Inset 51
Ailinglapalap, *island* B2 16
Aillik B1 98
Ailuk, *island* B1 16
Aiquile A3 77
Air Force, *island* O3 99
Air Ronge E5 104
Aïr, *mts.* B2 59
Airdrie C5 94
Aishihik, *lake* B5 105
Aisne, *river* D2 34
Aiwo A2 16
Aix-en-Provence D5 34
Aix-les-Bains D4 34
Aíyina, *island* B3 51
Aizawl F4 20
Aizuwakamatsu C2 8
Ajaccio Inset I 34
Ajaria, autonomous republic A4 45
Ajdabiya D1 56
Ajka A2 43
Ajman C2 25
Ajmer B3 20
Akanyaru, *river* B2 61
Akashi B3 8
Akhalkalaki B4 45
Akhaltsikhe B4 45
Akharnaí Inset 51
Akhelóös, *river* B2 51
Akhmeta C3 45
Akhuryan, *river* A2 45
Akita D2 8
Akjoujt B3 58
Aklavik A3 99
Akobo, *river* A3 60
Akola C4 20
Akordat A2 60
Akosombo, *dam* C3 64
Akpatok, *island* P4 99
Akranes A2 52
Akron, Ohio E1 126
Aksaray C2 27
Aksu B1 10
Akulivik A1 101
Akure C4 65
Akurenam C3 66
Akureyri B2 52
Akuseki, *island* A4 8
Alabama E2 126
Alagoas E2 81
Alagoinhas E3 81
Alajuela B2 86
Alakol, *lake* E2 23
Alamayn, al- A1 56
Alameda H11 104
Alampur Inset II 20
Åland, *islands* B2 53
Alanya C3 27
Alarcón, *reservoir* E3 37
Alaska Inset I 126
Alaska, *gulf*, Alaska Inset I 126
Alaska, *range*, Alaska Inset I 126
Älät C3 45
Alaverdi B1 45
Alay, *mts.* B1, C3 23
Alayli Dadda B1 60
Alazani, *river* C4 45
Alba Iulia B2 43
Albacete F3 37
Alban E1 102
Albania **49**
Albany, *capital*, N.Y. F1 126
Albany, Ga. E2 126
Albany, *river* C2 101
Albany, W.A. A3 14
Albert Nile, *river* B2 61
Albert, *canal* C1 33
Albert, *lake* B3 61
Alberton A2 100
Albi C5 34
Albina B2 80
Alboran, *sea* E4 37
Ålborg B1 32
Ålborg, *bay* C2 32
Albuquerque, *cays* Inset 78
Albuquerque, N. Mex. C2 126
Albury, N.S.W. D3 14
Alcalá de Henares Inset II 37
Alcañiz F2 37
Alcántara, *reservoir* C3 37
Alcázar de San Juan E3 37
Alcira F3 37
Alcobendas Inset II 37
Alcorcón E2, Inset II 37
Alcoy F3 37
Aldabra, *islands* A2 70
Aldan D8 44
Aldan, *river* D8 44
Alderney, *island* Inset II 30
Aleg B3 58
Alençon C2 34
Alert Q1 99
Alès D4 34
Alessandria B1 38
Ålesund B3 52
Aleutian *islands*, Alaska Inset I 126
Alexander A4 96
Alexander, *island* B11 107
Alexandra A4 15
Alexandria C4 43
Alexandria A1 56
Alexandria L2 102
Alexandria, La. D2 126
Alexandroúpolis C1 51
Alexis Creek L5 95
Alexis, *river* C3 98
Alfios, *river* B3 51
Alfred L2 102
Algarrobo Inset 76
Algarve, *region* A4 36
Algeciras D4 37
Algeria **57**
Alghero B2 38
Algiers, *capital* B1 57
Ali Adde B2 60
Äli Bayramli C3 45
Ali Sabieh B2 60
Aliákmon, *river* B1 51
Alibori, *river* B2 64
Alicante F3 37
Alice C3 71
Alice Arm H3 95
Alice Springs, N.T. C2 14
Alice Town B2 89
Aligarh C3 20
Alima, *river* D4 66
Aliwal North C3 71
Alix D5 94
Alkmaar B2 32
Allahabad D3 20
Allardville D1 97
Allen, *lake* B1 31
Allenford D3 102
Allentown, Pa. F1 126
Alleppey (Alappuzah) C7 20
Alliance E5 94
Allier, *river* C3 34
Alligator Pond B3 88
Alliston F3 102
Allumette, *lake* H2 102
Alma E3 97
Alma E3 103
Almada A3 36
Almadén D3 37
Almansa F3 37
Almaty (Alma-Ata) D2 23
Almendralejo C3 37
Almelo D2 32
Almendra, *reservoir* C2 37
Almería E4 37
Almirante A2 87
Almonte J2 102
Alonsa B4 96
Alor Setar A1 13
Alor, *island* D2 13
Alotau B3 15
Alpena, Mich. E1 126
Alps, *mts.* 29
Alsace D2 34
Alsask A9 104
Alta E1 52
Altai, *mts.* B1 10
Altamira C2 81
Altamira C3 76
Altario E5 94
Altay B1 10
Altay B2 11
Altay, republic F4 44
Altdorf C2 35
Altiplano, *plateau* A3 77
Altona C4 96
Altun, *range* B2 10
Aluksne D2 46
Alvinston D5 102
Alytus C2 46
Alzette, *river* B2 33
Am Timan C5 59
Amadjuak, *lake* O4 99
Amadora A3 36
Amagasaki B3 8
Amahai D2 13
Amakusa, *islands* A3 8
Amambay, *mts.* E3 75
Amami, *island* Inset II 8
Amapá C1 81
Amapala B3 86
Amarah, al- C2 24
Amaranth B4 96
Amarillo, Tex. C2 126
Amasya C2 27
Amazon, *basin* B2 81
Amazon, *river* B2 81
Amazonas B2 81
Ambato B3 79
Ambatolampy B2 69
Ambatondrazaka B2 69
Amberg B4 40
Ambergris Cay, *island* C2 85
Ambergris, *cay* D4 89
Amberley D3 102
Ambon D2 13
Ambositra B3 69
Ambre, *cape* B1 69
Ambrym, *island* C3 18
Amdanga Inset II 20
Ameca D3 84
Ameland, *island* C1 32
American Samoa **18**
Amersfoort C2 32
Amery Ice Shelf, *glacier* C18 107
Amherst C2 100
Amherstburg B5 102
Amiens C2 34
Amindivi, *islands* B6 20
Amirante, *islands* B2 70
Amisk E5 94
Amisk, *lake* H6 104
Amlamé B3 64
Amman, *capital* A2 26
Ammassalik C2 106
Ammersee, *lake* B4 40
Amos A4 101
Ampanihy A3 69
Amparai C4 19
Amqui J3 103
Amran A1 25
Amravati C4 20
Amritsar B2 20
Amsterdam, *capital* B2 32
Amstetten D2 39
Amu Darya, *river* B1, D2 22
Amund Ringnes, *island* J1 99
Amundsen, *gulf* C2 99
Amundsen, *sea* B9 107
Amur, *river* D8 44
Amyun A1 26
Ana María, *gulf* D2 88
Anabar C1 16
Anaco D2 79
Anadyr C10 44
Anadyr, *gulf* C11 44
Anahim Lake K5 95
Anáhuac D2 84
Anápolis D3 81
Añasco A2 90
Añasco, *beach* A2 90
Anatolia, *region* B2 27
Anatom, *island* C5 18
Anchorage, Alaska Inset I 126
Ancona C2 38
Ancud B7 76
Ancud, *gulf* B7 76
Andalusia D4 37
Andaman, *islands* F6 20
Andaman, *sea* B3 12
Anderlecht C2 33
Anderson, *river* C3 99
Andes, *mts.* 73
Andheri Inset I 20
Andizhan D2 23
Andoany B1 69
Andong C4 9
Andorra **36**
Andorra la Vella, *capital* B2 36
Andreas, *cape* C1 27
Andros, *island* A3 89
Ándros, *island* C3 51
Androth, *island* B6 20
Anécho B3 64
Anelghowhat C5 18
Anetan B1 16
Aneto, *mt.* G1 37
Angara, *river* D6 44
Angarsk D7 44
Angaur B4 17
Angel, *falls* D2 79
Angeles B3 12
Ångermanälven, *river* C2 53
Angers B3 34
Angikuni, *lake* H4 99
Angkor Thom, *ruins* B2 11
Angkor Wat, *ruins* B2 11
Anglesey, *island* B3 30
Angoche C3 68
Angol B6 76
Angola **70**
Angoulême C4 34
Angus F3 102
Anholt, *island* C2 32
Anhui E2 10
Anibare B2 16
Anié B3 64
Añisoc C3 66
Anjou J5 103
Anju A3 9
Ankang D2 10
Ankara, *capital* C2 27
Ankaratra, *mts.* B2 69
Ankobra, *river* A4 64
Ann Arbor, Mich. E1 126
Anna Regina B2 80
Annaba B1 57
Annam, *mts.* A2 11
Annandale C2 100
Annapolis Royal B3 100
Annapolis, *capital*, Md. F2 126
Annapurna, *mt.* B2 19
Annecy D4 34
Anqing E2 10
Ansbach B4 40
Anse Boileau Inset 70
Anse Royale Inset 70
Anse-à-Galets C2 89
Anshan F1 10
Ansongo D2 58
Antalaha C1 69
Antalya B3 27
Antalya, *gulf* B3 27
Antananarivo, *capital* B2 69
Antarctic, *peninsula* C12 107
Antarctica **107**
Antequera D4 37
Anti-Atlas, *ranges* B2 57
Anti-Lebanon, *mts.* B1 26
Anticosti, *island* D4 101
Antigonish F2 100
Antigua C5 85
Antigua, *island* D4 90
Antigua and Barbuda **90**
Antioch (Antakya) D3 27
Antofagasta B2 76
Antrim, *mts.* A2 30
Antsirabe B2 69
Antsiranana B1 69
Antsohihy B1 69
Antwerp C1 33
Anuradhapura B3 19
Anyang E2 10
Anyang B4 9
Anyos B2 36
Aoa C1 18
Aoba, *island* B2 18
Aomori D1 8
Aoral, *mt.* C3 11
Aosta A1 38
Aozou B2 59
Apa, *river* D3 75
Apaporis, *river* C4 78
Apatity C3 44
Apatou A1 80
Apeldoorn C2 32
Apennines, *range* B1 38
Apetina B3 80
Api, *mt.* A2 19
Apia, *capital* C2 18
Apo, *volcano* C5 12
Apoera A2 80
Apolima, *island* B2 18
Apolima, *strait* B2 18
Apoteri B4 80
Appalachian, *mts.* E2 126
Apple River C2 100
Apsley G3 102
Apulia C2 38
Apure, *river* C2 79
Apurímac, *river* C3 77
Apuseni, *mts.* B2 43
Aqaba, *gulf* A3, B3 26
Aqabah, al- A3 26
Aqtau B2 23
Aqtobe B1 23
Aquileia C1 38
Aquitaine B4 34
Ara D3 20
Arabah, al-, *river* A2, B2 26
Arabian, *desert* B2 56
Arabian, *sea* A5, Inset I 20
Aracaju E3 81
Arachon B4 34
Arad A2 43
Aradah B3 25
Arafura, *sea* E2 13
Aragats, *mt.* B2 45
Aragón F2 37
Araguaia, *river* C3 81
Arak B3 22
Arakabesan, *island* B3 17
Arakan Yoma, *mts.* B2 12
Aral C2 23
Aral, *sea* A2, B2 23
Aran, *islands* B2 31
Aranda de Duero E2 37
Aranjuez E2 37
Aranyaprathet C3 12
Arapey Grande, *river* B1 75
Ararat B3 45
Ararat (Ağri Daği), *mt.* F2 27
Aras, *river* E2 27
Arauca C3 78
Arauca, *river* C2 79
Aravalli, *range* B3 20
Arawa B2 15
Arba Minch B3 60
Arborfield G7 104
Arborg C4 96
Archerwill G8 104
Arcola H11 104
Arctic Bay L2 99
Arctic Red River B3 99
Arda, *river* C4 50
Ardabil B2 22
Ardara B1 31
Ardbeg E2 102
Ardennes, *plateau* D2 33
Ardennes, *region* D1 34
Arecibo B2 90
Arekalong, *peninsula* C2 17
Arenal, *lake* B2 86
Arenas, *point* D2 90
Arendal B4 52
Arequipa C4 77
Arezzo B2 38
Argenteuil Inset II 34
Argentia D5 98
Argentina **74**
Argentino, *lake* A7 74
Argeş, *river* C3 43
Arghandab, *river* B2 22
Argonne, *forest* D2 34
Árgos B3 51
Argyle C4 96
Argyle F3 102
Århus C2 32
Ari, *atoll* A3 19
Ariana C1 57
Arica B1 76
Arichat F2 100
Arima A2 91
Arinsal A2 36
Aripuanã, *river* C2 81
Arish, al- B1 56
Arizona B2 126
Arkansas D2 126
Arkansas, *river* D2 126
Arkhangelsk C4 44
Arklow C2 31
Arkona D4 102
Arles D5 34
Arlit B2 59
Arlon D3 33
Armagh A2 30
Armenia **45**
Armenia B3 78
Armidale, N.S.W. E3 14
Armstrong N6 95
Armstrong C2 101
Arnaud, *river* B2 101
Arnes C4 96
Arnhem C3 32
Arnhem Land, *region* C1 14
Arnhem, *cape* C1 14
Arno, *island* C2 16
Arno, *river* B2 38
Arnold's Cove D5 98
Arnprior J2 102
Arnsberg B3 40
Aroostook B2 97
Arorae, *island* A2 17
Arpa, *river* C3 45
Arpajon Inset II 34
Arqalyq C1 23
Arran, *island* B2 30
Arras C1 34
Arroyo C3 90
Arta B2 60
Artashat B3 45
Artemisa B2 88
Arthur E4 102
Arthur's Town B3 89
Artibonite, *river* C1 89
Artigas B1 75
Artik A2 45
Artsvashen C2 45
Artvin E2 27
Aru, *islands* E2 13
Arua B2 61
Aruba, *island* 82
Arun, *river* D2 19
Arusha C1 68
Aruvi, *river* B3 19
Aruwimi, *river* C1 67
Arvayheer C2 11
As Ela B2 60
Asaba D4 65
Asadabad C2 22
Asahi Dake, *mt.* Inset I 8
Asahikawa Inset I 8
Asama, *mt.* C2 8
Asansol E4 20
Asau A2 18
Asbestos E6 103
Ascoli Piceno C2 38
Asela C3 60
Asenovgrad C3 50
Ashburton B3 15
Ashburton, *river* A2 14
Ashcroft M6 95
Ashdod B2 26
Ashern B3 96
Asheville, N.C. E2 126
Asheweig, *river* C2 101
Ashgabat, *capital* C3 22
Ashikaga C2 8
Ashizuri, *cape* B3 8
Ashmore and Cartier, *islands* B1 14
Ashqelon B2 26
Ashton A4 91
Ashuapmushuan, *river* C2 103
Asinara, *island* B2 38
Asipovichy D3 47
Asir, *region* B2 24
Askar B1 25
Asmara, *capital* B2 60
Asnam, el- B1 57
Aso, *mt.* A3 8
Asosa B2 60
Aspiring, *mt.* A3 15
Aspropirgos Inset 51
Asquith C8 104
Assab D3 60
Assal, *lake* B2 60
Assen D2 32
Assiniboia D11 104
Assiniboine, *mt.* P6 95
Assiniboine, *river* A4 96
Astana (Akmola), *capital* D1 23
Astara C3 45
Asti B1 38
Astipálaia, *island* C3 51
Astorga C1 37
Astrakhan E4 44
Astrolabe, *reefs* C2 18
Asturias C1 37
Asunción, *capital* D4 75
Aswan B3 56
Aswan High, *dam* B3 56
Asyut B2 56
At-Bashy D2 23
Atacama, *desert* C2 76
Atakpamé B3 64
Ataq B2 25
Atâr B2 58
Atatürk, *reservoir* D3 27
Atbara, *river* B1 60
Atbarah C2 59
Atbarah, *river* C2 59
Atbasar C1 23
Ath B2 33
Athabasca D4 94
Athabasca, *lake* A1 104
Athabasca, *river* B4, D3, E2 94
Athens, *capital* B3, Inset 51
Athens, Ga. E2 126
Athi, *river* E5 61
Athlone C2 31
Áthos, *mt.* C1 51
Ati B4 59
Atiak C2 61
Atikameg C3 94
Atikameg Lake A2 96
Atikokan B3 101
Atitlán, *lake* B5 85
Atlanta, *capital*, Ga. E2 126
Atlantic City, N.J. F2 126
Atlas, *mts.* A1, B2 57
Atlin F1 95
Atlin, *lake* F1 95
Atrai, *river* B4 21
Atrak, *river* D2 22
Atrato, *river* A3 78
Attapu D4 11
Attawapiskat D2 101
Attawapiskat, *river* C2 101
Atuel, *river* B4 74
Atyrau B2 23
Aua C1 18
Aube, *river* D3 34
Auch C5 34
Auckland B2 15
Augsburg B4 40
Augusta, *capital*, Maine G1 126
Augusta, Ga. E2 126
Auki B1 16
Aulac E3 97
Aunuu, *island* C1 18
Auob, *river* C3 70
Aur, *island* C2 16
Aurangabad C5 20
Aurillac C4 34
Aurora F3 102
Ausa, *river* C1 39
Austin B4 96
Austin, *capital*, Tex. D2 126
Australia **14**
Australian Alps, *mts.* D3 14
Australian Capital Territory D3 14
Austria **39**
Auvergne C4 34
Auxerre C3 34
Avalon, *peninsula* E5 98
Aveiro A2 36
Avellaneda D3 74
Avellino C2 38
Aviemore B1 30
Avignon D5 34
Ávila D2 37
Avilés D1 37
Avon, *islands* A2 18
Avon, *river* C3 30
Avonlea E10 104
Awaji B3 8

Key Page
Awaji, *island* B3 8
Awasa C3 60
Awash, *river* C2 60
Awaso A3 64
Awbari B2 56
Awka D4 65
Awwali, *river* A2 26
Axel Heiberg, *island* K1 99
Axim A4 64
Ayacucho C3 77
Ayagöz E2 23
Aydin A3 27
Ayer Chawan, *island* A1 13
Ayer's Cliff D6 103
Áyios Dhimítrios Inset 51
Aylesbury Inset III 30
Aylmer E5 102
Aylmer A6 103
Aylmer, *lake* G4 99
Aylmer, *lake* E6 103
Ayn, al- C2 25
Ayoûn el-Atroûs C3 58
Ayr B2 30
Aytos F3 50
Azaouâd, *region* C2 58
Azare F2 65
Azaz A1 27
Azcapotzalco Inset 84
Azerbaijan **45**
Azerbaijan, *region* B2 22
Azogues B4 79
Azores, *islands* 5
Azov, *sea* D3 47
Azraq ash-Shishan B2 26
Azua B2 89
Azuero, *peninsula* B3 87

B

Ba, *river* B3 11
Baalbek B1 26
Bab al-Mandab, *strait* C1 60
Babahoyo B3 79
Babanusah B3 59
Babar, *island* D2 13
Babbage, *river* B1 105
Babda A2 26
Babelthuap, *island* C3 17
Babine, *lake* J4 95
Babine, *river* J3 95
Babruysk D3 47
Babu Bheri Inset II 20
Babuyan, *channel* B2 12
Babuyan, *islands* B2 12
Babylon, *ruins* B2 24
Bac Lieu A5 11
Bacabal D2 81
Bacău D2 43
Back, *river* H3 99
Bačka Palanka A2 49
Bacolod B4 12
Bad Ems A3 40
Bad Ischl C3 39
Bad Kreuznach A4 40
Bad Reichenhall C5 40
Badajoz C3 37
Badalona H2 37
Badanah B1 24
Badas A2 13
Baddeck G1 100
Baden C1 35
Baden E2 39
Baden A3 96
Baden-Baden B4 40
Baden-Württemberg B4 40
Badger D4 96
Badger C5 98
Badou B3 64
Bafatá C1 62
Baffin, *bay* L1 92
Baffin, *island* M2 99
Baffin, *region* N2 99
Bafilo B2 64
Bafing, *river* C2 62
Bafoulabé A3 58
Bafoussam B2 65
Baghdad, *capital* B2 24
Baghlan B1 22
Baglung B2 19
Bagmati, *river* C2 19
Bagoé, *river* C1 63
Baguio B2 12
Bagzane, *mt.* B2 59
Bahamas **89**
Bahawalpur D4 21
Bahia D3 81
Bahía Blanca C4 74
Bahía Honda A2 88
Bahía, *islands* B1 86
Bahir Dar B2 60
Bahoruco, *mts.* A2 89
Bahr al-Arab, *river* B3 59
Bahr al-Ghazal, *river* C3 59
Bahr al-Jabal, *river* C3 59
Bahr Salamat, *river* B5 59
Bahrain **25**
Bahrain, *gulf* A2 25
Baia Mare B2 43
Baicheng E1 10
Baidyabati Inset II 20
Baie Verte C4 98
Baie-Comeau H2 103
Baie-des-Sables J3 103
Baie-St-Paul F4 103
Baie-Ste-Anne E1 97
Baie-Ste-Catherine G3 103
Bailieboro G3 102
Bainsville L2 102
Bair B2 26
Baiti B1 16
Baja B2 43
Baja California A1 84
Baja California Sur B2 84
Bajadero B2 90
Bajo Boquete A2 87
Bakel C2 62
Baker Brook A1 97
Baker Lake J4 99
Bakersfield, Calif. B2 126
Bakhardok C2 22
Bakhtaran B3 22
Bakhtiari, *region* B3 22
Bakony, *mts.* A2 43
Baku, *capital* C2 45
Bala F2 102
Bala, *lake* B3 30
Balabac, *island* A5 12
Balabac, *strait* A5 12
Balakän B2 45
Balaklava C4 47
Balaton, *lake* A2 43
Balboa C2 87
Balcarres G10 104
Baldur B4 96
Baldy, *mt.* A3 96
Balearic, *islands* G3 37
Balearic, *sea* G2 37
Baleia, *point* E3 81
Baleine, *river* C2 101
Balgonie F10 104
Balhaf B2 25
Balho B1 60
Bali, *island* C2 13
Baliceaux, *island* B3 91
Balıkesir A2 27
Balikpapan C2 13
Balkan, *mts.* B2 50
Balkh B1 22
Balkhash D2 23
Balkhash, *lake* D2 23
Ballancourt-sur-Essonne Inset II 34
Ballarat, Vic. D3 14
Balleny, *islands* C5 107
Ballerup D3 32
Ballina B1 31
Bally Inset II 20
Ballymena A2 30
Balmaceda B8 76
Balmertown B2 101
Balmoral C1 97
Balsas, *river* E4 84
Bălţi A2 50
Baltic, *sea* 29
Baltimore, Md. F2 126
Baluchistan, *region* E4 22
Balykchy E1 23
Balzers B2 33
Bam D4 22
Bamako, *capital* B3 58
Bamangachi Inset II 20
Bambadinca C1 62
Bambana, *river* B2 87
Bambari B2 66
Bamberg B4 40
Bamenda B2 65
Bamian B2 22
Ban Houayxay A1 11
Ban Phai C2 12
Banaba, *island* A2 17
Banana A2 67
Banana, *islands* A1 63
Bananga F7 20
Banat, *region* A3 43
Banbury C3 30
Bancroft H2 102
Banda Aceh A1 13
Banda, *sea* D2 13
Bandama Blanc, *river* D2 63
Bandama Rouge, *river* C2 63
Bandama, *river* D3 63
Bandar Beheshti E4 22
Bandar Lampung B2 13
Bandar Seri Begawan, *capital* B2 13
Bandar-e Abbas D4 22
Bandar-e Anzali B2 22
Bandar-e Bushehr C4 22
Bandar-e Khomeyni B3 22
Bandar-e Torkeman C2 22
Bandeira, *mt.* D4 81
Bandra Inset I 20
Bandundu B2 67
Bandung B2 13
Banff C5 94
Bangalore C6 20
Bangar C2 13
Bangassou B3 66
Banggi, *island* D1 13
Banghiang, *river* C3 11
Bangka, *island* B2 13
Bangkok, *capital* B3 12
Bangladesh **21**
Bangor B2 30
Bangor B3 30
Bangor, Maine G1 126
Bangui, *capital* A3 66
Bangweulu, *lake* B2 67
Baní B2 89
Bani Suwayf B2 56
Bani Walid B1 56
Bani, *river* B3 58
Baniyas A2 27
Banja Luka B1 48
Banjarmasin C2 13
Banjul, *capital* B2 62
Banks, *island* G4 95
Banks, *island* D2 99
Banks, *islands* B1 18
Banks, *peninsula* B3 15
Bann, *river* A2 30
Bannockburn H3 102
Bansang D2 62
Bansbaria Inset II 20
Banská Bystrica B2 42
Bantry B3 31
Bantry, *bay* B3 31
Baoding E2 10
Baoshan C3 10
Baotou E1 10
Baoulé, *river* B3 58
Baqubah B2 24
Baquerizo Moreno Inset 79
Bar A3 49
Bar-le-Duc D2 34
Baraawe A3 60
Barabinsk D5 44
Baracaldo E1 37
Barachois M3 103
Baracoa F3 88
Barahona A2 89
Baraki Barak B2 22
Barakpur Inset II 20
Baram, *river* D2 13
Barama, *river* B2 80
Baranagar Inset II 20
Baranavichy C3 47
Barasat Inset II 20
Barbados **91**
Barbuda, *island* E3 90
Barcelona D1 79
Barcelona H2 37
Barceloneta B2 90
Bärdä B2 45
Bardaï B2 59
Bardejov C2 42
Bareilly C3 20
Barents, *sea* B3 44
Bargachia Inset II 20
Bari D2 38
Baril, *lake* E2 94
Barinas B2 79
Barind, *region* B4 21
Baris B3 56
Barisal D6 21
Bark, *lake* H2 102
Barkerville M4 95
Barkly, *tableland* C1 14
Barletta D2 38
Barnaul D6 44
Barnes, *ice cap* O3 99
Barnsley C3 30
Barnstaple B3 30
Barnwell D6 94
Baro, *river* B2 60
Barons D6 94
Barquisimeto C1 79
Barra, *island* A2 30
Barrancabermeja B3 78
Barranquilla B2 78
Barranquitas C2 90
Barreiro A3 36
Barrhead C4 94
Barrie F3 102
Barrière M5 95
Barrington B4 100
Barro B1 62
Barrouallie B2 91
Barrow, Alaska Inset I 126
Barrow, *river* C2 31
Barrow-in-Furness B2 30
Barry's Bay H2 102
Bartang, *river* B1 23
Bartica B2 80
Barú, *volcano* A2 87
Baruta C1 79
Baruun-Urt D2 11
Bas-Caraquet E1 97
Basarabeasca B2 50
Basel B1 35
Bashi, *channel* B1 12
Basilan B5 12
Basilan, *island* B5 12
Basildon Inset III 30
Basilicata C2 38
Baskatong, *reservoir* A5 103
Basque Country E1 37
Basra C2 24
Bass Rock, *islet* C2 30
Bass, *strait* D3 14
Bassar B2 64
Basse Santa Su D2 62
Basse-Normandie B2 34
Bassein B3 12
Basseterre, *capital* B2 90
Bassila A3 64
Bastia Inset I 34
Bastogne D2 33
Bata B3 66
Bataan, *peninsula* B3 12
Batabanó, *gulf* B2 88
Batan, *islands* B1 12
Batang C3 10
Batang Duri C2 13
Batangafo A2 66
Batangas B3 12
Batdambang B3 11
Bate, *bay* Inset IV 14
Batéké, *plateau* C5 66
Bath C3 90
Bath C3 30
Bath B2 97
Batha, *river* C4 59
Bathsheba B3 91
Bathurst D1 97
Bathurst, *island* J1 99
Batin, Wadi al-, *river* A2 24
Batinah, al-, *region* C1 25
Batman E3 27
Batna B1 57
Baton Rouge, *capital*, La. D2 126
Batouri B3 65
Batrun, al- A1 26
Batteau D2 98
Batticaloa C4 19
Battle, *river* A7 104
Battleford B8 104
Batu Pahat B2 13
Batumi A4 45
Baubau D2 13
Bauchi E2 65
Bauria Inset II 20
Bauru D4 81
Bauska C2 46
Bautzen C3 40
Bavaria B4 40
Bavarian Alps, *mts.* B5 40
Bawiti, al- A2 56
Bawku B1 64
Bawlf D5 94
Bay Bulls E5 98
Bay de Verde E5 98
Bay Roberts E5 98
Bay St. Lawrence G1 100
Bayamo E3 88
Bayamón C2 90
Bayamón, *river* C2 90
Bayan Har, *range* C2 10
Bayanhongor C2 11
Bayda, al- B2 25
Bayda, al- D1 56
Baydhabo A3 60
Bayerischer Wald, *mts.* C4 40
Bayeux B2 34
Bayfield D4 102
Baygorria, *lake* B2 75
Baykal, *lake* D7 44
Bayonne B5 34
Bayport C3 100
Bayramaly D3 22
Bayreuth B4 40
Bays, *lake* F2 102
Baza E4 37
Bazardüzü Daği, *mt.* B2 45
Bazin, *river* A4 103
Beachside D4 98
Beagle, *channel* B7 74
Bear Lake L4 95
Bear River C2 100
Beata, *cape* A3 89
Beata, *island* A3 89
Beaton O6 95
Beau Bassin B2 69
Beauceville F5 103
Beaufort West B3 71
Beaufort, *sea* B1 105
Beaulac E6 103
Beaumont D4 94
Beaumont, Tex. D2 126
Beauport L5 103
Beaupré F4 103
Beauséjour C4 96
Beauvais C2 34
Beauval C5 104
Beaver Creek A4 105
Beaver Harbour E3 100
Beaver Hill, *lake* D2 96
Beaver Mines C6 94
Beaver, *river* A6 104
Beaver, *river* D5 105
Beaverton F3 102
Bécancour D5 103
Bečej B2 49
Béchar A1 57
Bedeque, *bay* B2 100
Bedford C3 30
Bedford D3 100
Bedford D6 103
Bedok B1 13
Beechy C10 104
Beersheba B2 26
Behala Inset II 20
Bei'an F1 10
Beihai D3 10
Beijing, *capital* E2 10
Beira B3 68
Beirut, *capital* A2 26
Beja B3 36
Béja B1 57
Bejaïa B1 57
Bejaïa, *gulf* B1 57
Béjar D2 37
Bekaa, *valley* A2 26
Békéscsaba C2 43
Bela C4 21
Belair B4 91
Belapurpada Inset I 20
Belarus **47**
Belasica, *mts.* C2 48
Belaya Tserkov C2 47
Beledweyne B3 60
Belém D2 81
Bélep, *islands* C2 18
Belfast B2 30
Belford Roxo Inset I 81
Belfort D3 34
Belfort, *gap* D3 34
Belgaum B5 20
Belgium **33**
Belgrade, *capital* B2 49
Beli Drim, *river* B3 49
Bélinga B1 66
Belitung, *island* B2 13
Belize **85**
Belize City B2 85
Belize, *river* B2 85
Bella Coola J5 95
Bella Unión B1 75
Bellary C5 20
Belburns C4 98
Belle Isle, *strait* C3 98
Belle River C3 100
Belle, *island* B3 34
Belle, *island* C3 98
Belle-Anse C2 89
Belledune D1 97
Belleview A4 96
Belleville H3 102
Bellingham L7 95
Bellingham, Wash. A1 126
Bellingshausen, *sea* B10 107
Bellinzona D2 35
Bellona, *island* A2 16
Belluno C1 38
Bellville A3 71
Belmont B4 96
Belmopan, *capital* B2 85
Belo Horizonte D3 81
Beloeil C6 103
Belomorsk C3 44
Bemaraha, *plateau* A2 69
Bemidji, Minn. D1 126
Ben Eoin G2 100
Ben Nevis, *mt.* B2 30
Benavente D1 37
Bend, Oreg. A1 126
Bender (Tighina) B2 50
Benderbeyla C2 60
Bendigo, Vic. D3 14
Benevento C2 38
Bengal, *bay* E5 20
Bengbu E2 10
Benghazi D1 56
Bengkulu B2 13
Bengough E11 104
Benguela B4 70
Beni Mellal C1 57
Beni, *river* A2 77
Benidorm F3 37
Benin **64**
Benin City C4 65
Benin, *bight* B5 65
Benito A3 96
Benoit's Cove B5 98
Benoni C2 71
Bénoué, *river* B2 65
Benson G11 104
Bentiaba B4 70
Benue, *river* E3 65
Benxi F1 10
Benzdorp B3 80
Beqa, *island* B3 17
Bequia, *island* B2 91
Berat A3 49
Berbera B1 60
Berbérati A3 66
Berbice, *river* B3 80
Berdoba C4 59
Berdyansk D3 47
Berekua B4 90
Berens River C3 96
Berens, *island* C3 96
Berens, *river* C3 96
Beresford D1 97
Berezniki D4 44
Bergamo B1 38
Bergen B3 52
Bergen op Zoom B3 32
Bergerac C4 34
Bergisch Gladbach A3 40
Bering, *sea* Inset I 126
Bering, *strait* C11 44
Berkner, *island* B12 107
Berlin, *capital* C2 40
Bermejo, *river* C2 74
Bermuda, *island* 82
Bern, *capital* B2 35
Bernburg B3 40
Bernese Alps, *mts.* B2 35
Bernières K6 103
Berounka, *river* A3 42
Bertwell H8 104
Berwick C2 100
Berwick-upon-Tweed C2 30
Besançon D3 34
Beskid, *mts.* D4 41
Besnard, *lake* D5 104
Besor, *river* B2 26
Bethanien C4 70
Bethany B4 96
Bethel, Alaska Inset I 126
Bethierville C5 103
Bethlehem C2 71
Béticos, *mts.* E4 37
Bétou E2 66
Betsiamites H3 103
Betsiamites, *river* G2 103
Betsiboka, *river* B2 69
Bette, *mt.* C3 56
Beulah A4 96
Beyla D3 62
Beyneu B2 23
Beyşehir, *lake* B3 27
Béziers C5 34
Bhadrakh E4 20
Bhadreswar Inset II 20
Bhagalpur E3 20
Bhairahawa B2 19
Bhaktapur C2 19
Bhamapur D5 20
Bhamo C1 12
Bhandup Inset I 20
Bharatpur C3 20
Bhatapara D4 20
Bhatpara Inset II 20
Bhavnagar B4 20
Bhayandar Inset I 20
Bheri, *river* B2 19
Bhima, *river* C5 20
Bhimpur Inset II 20
Bhiwandi Inset I 20
Bhopal C4 20
Bhubaneswar E4 20
Bhuj A4 20
Bhunya B2 71
Bhutan **19**
Biabou B2 91
Biafra, *bight* A3 65
Biak, *island* E2 13
Biała Podlaska F2 41
Białystok F2 41
Biankouma C3 63
Biarritz B5 34
Bicaz, *reservoir* D2 43
Biche, *lake* E4 94
Bida D3 65
Bié, *plateau* C4 70
Biel B1 35
Biel, *lake* B1 35
Biele Karpaty, *mts.* A2 42
Bielefeld B2 40
Bielsko-Biała D4 41
Bien Hoa B4 11
Bienville, *lake* B2 101
Big Beaver E11 104
Big Bend B2 71
Big Creek L5 95
Big Fish, *river* B1 105
Big Gull, *lake* J3 102
Big Muddy, *lake* F11 104
Big River C7 104
Big Trout Lake C2 101
Big, *island* O4 99
Big, *river* B2 98
Biggar C8 104
Bignona A3 62
Bigstone, *river* D1 96
Bihać A1 48
Bihar E3 20
Bihor, *mts.* B2 43
Bijagós, *islands* A2 62
Bijapur C5 20
Bijeljina C1 48
Bikaner B3 20
Bikar, *island* C1 16
Bikini, *island* B1 16
Bilaspur D4 20
Biläsuvar C3 45
Bilauktaung, *range* B3, C3 12
Bilbao E1 37
Billings, Mont. C1 126
Billings, *reservoir* Inset II 81
Bilma C2 59
Biloku B5 80
Biloxi, Miss. E2 126
Biltine C4 59
Bimbila C2 64
Binche C2 33
Bindloss E6 94
Bindura B1 69
Binga, *mt.* B3 68
Bingen A4 40
Binscarth A4 96
Bint Jubayl A2 26
Bintang B2 62
Bintimane, *mt.* B1 63
Bío-Bío, *river* B6 76
Bioko, *island* A1 66
Bir Gandús A2 58
Bir Morgrein C1 58
Birak B2 56
Birao B1 66
Biratnagar D3 19
Birch Cliff K5 102
Birch Hills E7 104
Birch River A3 96
Birch, *mts.* D2 94
Birchy Bay D4 98
Bird, *island* B2 91
Birendranagar B2 19
Birganj C2 19
Birjand D3 22
Birkat Qarun, *lake* B2 56
Birkenhead B3 30
Birkirkara B2 36
Bîrlad D2 43
Birmingham C3 30
Birmingham, Ala. E2 126
Birni Nkonni B3 59
Birnie B4 96
Birnin Kebbi C1 65
Birobizhan E8 44
Birtle A4 96
Biržai C1 46
Birzebbuga C3 36
Biscay, *bay* B4 34
Bishkek, *capital* D1 23
Bishnupur Inset II 20
Bishop's Falls D4 98
Biskra B1 57
Bislig C4 12
Bismarck, *archipelago* A2 15
Bismarck, *capital*, N. Dak. C1 126
Bismarck, *range* A2 15
Bismarck, *sea* A2 15
Bismuna, *lagoon* C1 87
Bison, *lake* B2 94
Bissau, *capital* B2 62
Bissett D3 96
Bissorã B1 62
Bistcho, *lake* A1 94
Bistriţa C2 43
Bistriţa, *river* C2 43
Bitam A1 66
Bitola B2 48
Bitumount E2 94
Biu G2 65
Biwa, *lake* B3 8
Biysk D6 44
Bizard, *island* H5 103
Bizerte B1 57
Bjorne, *peninsula* L1 99
Black (Da), *river* A2 11
Black Country, *region* C3 30
Black Lake E1 104
Black River B2 88
Black Tickle D2 98
Black Volta, *river* A2, B3 64
Black, *forest* A4 40
Black, *hills*, S. Dak. C1 126
Black, *lake* E1 104
Black, *sea* 29
Blackburn C3 30
Blackmans B3 91
Blackpool C3 30
Blacks Harbour C3 97
Blackstone, *river* B3 105
Blackville D2 97
Blackwater, *river* B2, C1 31
Blagoevgrad B4 50
Blagoveshchensk D4 44
Blagoveshchensk D8 44
Blaine Lake D8 104
Blainville H5 103
Blanc, *mt.* D4 34
Blanc, *reservoir* C4 103
Blanc-Sablon E3 101
Blanca, *bay* C4 74
Blanda, *river* B2 52
Blantyre B3 68
Blarney B3 31
Blatec C2 48
Blenheim B3 15
Blenheim D5 102
Blida B1 57
Bligh Water, *sound* B2 17
Blind Bay N6 95
Blind River C1 102
Blitta B2 64
Bloemfontein, *judicial capital* C2 71
Blois C3 34
Bloodvein, *river* C3 96
Bloomfield H4 102
Bloomington, Ind. E2 126
Blossom Park H6 102
Blow, *river* B1 105
Blue Mountain, *peak* C2 88
Blue Nile, *river* C2 59
Blue Ridge C4 94
Blue River N5 95
Blue, *mts.* E3 14
Blue, *mts.* C2 88
Bluefields B2 88
Bluefields C3 87

Key Page
Bluenose, *lake* E3 99
Bluffton C5 94
Blyth D4 102
Bo B2 63
Bo Hai, *gulf* E2 10
Boa Vista B1 81
Boa Vista, *island* D2 58
Boaco B2 87
Bobcaygeon G3 102
Bobo-Dioulasso B3 64
Bocas del Toro A2 87
Bocay B1 87
Bocay, *river* B2 87
Bocholt A3 40
Bochum A3 40
Bodaybo D7 44
Bodo E5 94
Bodø C2 52
Boende B2 67
Boggeragh, *mts.* B2 31
Boggy, *peak* D5 90
Bogor B2 13
Bogotá, *capital* B3 78
Bogra C4 21
Bohemia, *region* A3 42
Bohemian, *forest* A3 42
Bohemian-Moravian, *heights* B3 42
Bohol, *island* C4 12
Bohol, *sea* C4 12
Boiestown C2 97
Boilleau F3 103
Bois-des-Filion H5 103
Boise, *capital*, Idaho B1 126
Boissevain A4 96
Boknafjord, *fjord* B4 52
Boksburg C2 71
Bol A4 59
Bolama B2 62
Bolands D5 90
Bole A2 64
Bolgatanga B1 64
Bolívar, *mt.* B2 79
Bolivia **77**
Bolligen B2 35
Bolnisi C4 45
Bolobo B2 67
Bologna B1 38
Bolovens, *plateau* D4 11
Bolsena, *lake* B2 38
Bolsón de Mapimí, *depression* D2 84
Bolton C3 30
Bolton F4 102
Bolu B2 27
Bolzano B1 38
Bom Jesus da Lapa D3 81
Boma A2 67
Bombay B5, Inset I 20
Bomu, *river* C1 67
Bon Pays, *region* B2 33
Bon, *cape* C1 57
Bonaire, *island* 82
Bonao B2 89
Bonaventure L3 103
Bonaventure, *river* L3 103
Bonavista E5 98
Bonavista, *bay* E5 98
Bondo B1 67
Bondoukou E2 63
Bondy Inset II 34
Bongor A5 59
Bonin, *islands* Inset III 8
Bonn A3 40
Bonnet Plume, *river* C3 105
Bonny D5 65
Bonnyville E4 94
Bonshaw B2 100
Bonthe A2 63
Bööntsagaan, *lake* B2 11
Boosaaso B1 60
Boothia, *gulf* K2 99
Boothia, *peninsula* K2 99
Booué A2 66
Bor C2 49
Borås B3 53
Bordeaux B4 34
Borden B2 100
Borden C8 104
Borden, *island* F1 99
Borden, *peninsula* M2 99
Bordoy, *island* Inset 32
Borgo Maggiore B1 39
Borivli Inset I 20
Borjomi B4 45
Borneo, *island* C1 13
Bornholm, *island* E3 32
Bosanska Gradiška B1 48
Bosanska Krupa A1 48
Bosna, *river* B1 48
Bosnia ř Hercegovina **48**
Boso, *peninsula* D3 8
Bosporus, *strait* B2 27
Bossangoa A2 66
Bosten, *lake* B1 10
Boston C3 30
Boston Bar M6 95
Boston, *capital*, Mass. F1 126
Boswell O6 95
Botany, *bay* Inset IV 14
Boteti, *river* A2 69
Botha D5 94
Bothnia, *gulf* B2, D2 53
Botna, *river* B2 50
Botoşani D2 43
Botrange, *mt.* E2 33
Botswana **69**
Botte Donato, *mt.* D3 38
Bottrop A3 40
Botwood D4 98
Bouaflé D3 63
Bouaké D3 63
Bouar A2 66
Boucherville J5 103
Bouctouche E2 97
Bougainville, *island* B2 15
Boughton, *bay* C2 100
Bougouni B3 58
Boulder, Colo. C2 126
Boulogne-Billancourt Inset II 34
Boulogne-sur-Mer C1 34
Bouna E2 63
Bourail C2 18
Bourem C2 58
Bourg-en-Bresse D3 34
Bourges C3 34
Bourgogne C3 34
Bourke, N.S.W. D3 14
Bournemouth C4 30
Bousso B5 59
Bow City D6 94
Bow, *river* D6 94
Bow, *river* E6 104
Bowen, Qld. D2 14
Bowling Green, Ky. E2 126
Bowser, *lake* H3 95
Bowsman A3 96
Boyd's Cove D4 98
Boyne, *river* C2 31
Boyne, *river* B4 96
Bozeman, Mont. B1 126
Brabant Lake G4 104
Brač, *island* C3 48
Bracciano, *lake* C2 38
Bracebridge F2 102
Bradford C3 30
Braga A2 36
Bragança B2 36
Bragg Creek C6 94
Brahmanbaria E5 21
Brahmaputra, *river* F3 20
Brăila D3 43
Braintree Inset III 30
Brakpan C2 71
Bralorne L6 95
Bramalea H5 102
Brampton F4 102
Branch E5 98
Branco, *river* B1 81
Brandberg, *mt.* B2 70
Brandenburg C2 40
Brandon B4, C2 96
Brant D6 94
Brantford E4 102
Bras d'Or G1 100
Brasília, *capital* D3 81
Braşov C3 43
Bratislava, *capital* A2 42
Bratsk D7 44
Braunau C2 39
Brava, *coast* H2 37
Brava, *island* B4 58
Brazil **81**
Brazilian, *highlands* D3 81
Brazzaville, *capital* C6 66
Brčko B1 48
Brea, *point* B3 90
Břeclav C4 42
Brecon Beacons, *mts.* C3 30
Breda B3 32
Bredenbury H10 104
Bregalnica, *river* C2 48
Breidhafjördhur, *fjord* A2 52
Bremen B2 40
Bremerhaven B2 40
Brenner, *pass* B3 39
Brentwood Inset III 30
Brescia B1 38
Brest A3 47
Brest A2 34
Bretagne B2 34
Breton C4 94
Bria B2 66
Briançon D4 34
Briceni A1 50
Bridge Lake M5 95
Bridgeport, Conn. F1 126
Bridgetown B3 100
Bridgetown, *capital* A4 91
Bridgewater C3 100
Brienzersee, *lake* B2 35
Brighton C4 30
Brighton H3 102
Brikama B2 62
Brindisi D2 38
Brisbane, Qld., *capital* E2, Inset III 14
Brisbane, *river* Inset III 14
Bristol C3 30
Bristol B2 97
Bristol, *channel* B3 30
Britannia E5 98
Britt E2 102
Brive-la-Gallarde C4 34
Brno C3 42
Broadview H10 104
Brochet C1 96
Brock, *island* F1 99
Brocket D6 94
Brockville K3 102
Brodfur, *peninsula* L2 99
Broken Hill, N.S.W. D3 14
Brokopondo B2 80
Brolin C3 30
Bromptonville E6 103
Brookdale B4 96
Brooks E6 94
Brooks *range*, Alaska Inset I 126
Broome, W.A. B1 14
Broomhill A4 96
Brossard J6 103
Brownsville, Tex. D3 126
Bruce Mines B1 102
Bruce Peninsula N.P. B2 102
Brugge B1 33
Brugge-Ghent, *canal* B1 33
Brûlé B4 94
Brunei **13**
Brunei, *bay* C1 13
Brunei, *river* B2 13
Brunswick B2 40
Brunswick, Ga. E2 126
Brunswick, *peninsula* B9 76
Brussels D4 102
Brussels, *capital* C2 33
Bryan, Tex. D2 126
Bryansk D3 44
Bsharri B1 26
Bu Craa B1 58
Bua, *river* B2 68
Buada B2 16
Buala A1 16
Buba C2 62
Bubanza B2 61
Bubaque B2 62
Bubiyan, *island* C2 24
Bucaramanga B3 78
Buchanan A3 63
Buchanan H9 104
Buchans C5 98
Bucharest, *capital* D3 43
Buck Creek C4 94
Buck Lake C5 94
Buckingham A6 103
Budapest, *capital* B2 43
Buea A3 65
Buenaventura A4 78
Buendía, *reservoir* E2 37
Buene, *river* A2 49
Buenos Aires, *capital* D3 74
Buenos Aires, *lake* A6 74
Buffalo Narrows B5 104
Buffalo, *lake* D5 94
Buffalo, *lake* E4 99
Buffalo, N.Y. F1 126
Bug, *river* E2, F3 41
Bugeac, *region* B3 50
Bugojno B1 48
Buhayrat al-Asad, *lake* B1 27
Buj-Buj Inset II 20
Bujumbura, *capital* B2 61
Buka, *island* B2 15
Bukavu C2 67
Bukhara B3 23
Bukit Pagon, *mt.* C3 13
Bukit Panjang B1 13
Bukit Timah B1 13
Bükk, *mts.* C1 43
Bukoba B1 68
Bula B1 62
Bulawayo B2 69
Bulembu B1 71
Bulgan C2 11
Bulgaria **50**
Bulle B2 35
Bulyea F10 104
Bumba B1 67
Bunbury, W.A. A3 14
Bundaberg, Qld. E2 14
Bungo, *channel* B3 8
Bunia C1 67
Bunsuru, *river* D1 65
Buon Me Thuot B4 11
Buqayq C1 24
Buraydah B1 24
Burco B2 60
Burdekin, *river* D1 14
Burdett E6 94
Burdur, *lake* B3 27
Burdwan E4 20
Büren B3 40
Burgas F3 50
Burgeo C5 98
Burgos E1 37
Burhanpur C4 20
Burica, *point* A2 87
Burin D5 98
Burin, *peninsula* D5 98
Buriram C3 12
Burk's Falls F2 102
Burke, *channel* J5 95
Burkina Faso **64**
Burlington F4 102
Burlington, Vt. F1 126
Burma (Myanmar) **12**
Burnley C3 30
Burns Lake K4 95
Burntwood, *lake* A1 96
Burntwood, *river* B1, C1, D2 96
Bursa B2 27
Burtnieku, *lake* C2 46
Buru, *island* D2 13
Burundi **61**
Bururi B2 61
Burutu C5 65
Burwash Landing B5 105
Bury C3 30
Bury St. Edmunds D3 30
Buryatiya, *republic* D7 44
Bushmanland, *plain* A4 71
Buta C1 67
Butare B2 61
Bute, *island* B2 30
Butha-Buthe B1 71
Butte, Mont. B1 126
Buttonville K5 102
Butuan C4 12
Butwal B2 19
Buurgplaatz, *mt.* B1 33
Buxton C3 30
Buyant-Uhaa D3 11
Buyo, *lake* C3 63
Büyük Menderes, *lake* A3 27
Buzău D3 43
Búzi, *river* B4 68
Büzmeyin C2 22
Byam Martin, *channel* G1 99
Byam Martin, *island* H1 99
Byarezina, *river* D3 47
Byblos, *ruins* A1 26
Bydgoszcz C2 41
Byelaruskaya Hrada, *range* C3 47
Bylot, *island* N2 99
Bytom D3 41
Byumba C1 61

C

Ca Mau A5 11
Ca, *river* A2 11
Caacupé D4 75
Caaguazú E4 75
Caazapá D5 75
Cabanatuan B3 12
Cabano H4 103
Cabimas B1 79
Cabinda B1 70
Cabo Rojo A2 90
Cabora Bassa, *dam* B2 68
Cabora Bassa, *lake* A2 68
Caborca B1 84
Cabrera C1 89
Cabrera, *island* H3 37
Cabri B10 104
Čačak B3 49
Cacao B1 80
Cáceres C3 81
Cáceres C3 37
Cache Creek M6 95
Cacheu A1 62
Cacheu, *river* B1 62
Cachimbo C2 81
Cacine B2 62
Cacouna G4 103
Cadiz B4 12
Cádiz C4 37
Cádiz, *gulf* C4 37
Cadomin B4 94
Cadotte Lake B3 94
Caen B2 34
Caerleon C3 30
Caernarfon B3 30
Cagayan de Oro C4 12
Cagayan Sulu, *island* A5 12
Cagayan, *islands* B4 12
Cagayan, *river* B2 12
Cagliari B3 38
Cagliari, *gulf* B3 38
Caguas C2 90
Caha, *mts.* B3 31
Cahors C4 34
Cahul B3 50
Caicos, *islands* D4 89
Caidasm da Rainha A3 36
Caille, *island* B1 91
Cairns, Qld. D1 14
Cairo, *capital* B1 56
Cairo, Ill. E2 126
Caja de Muertos, *island* B3 90
Cajamarca B2 77
Calabar E5 65
Calabogie J2 102
Calabozo C2 79
Calabria D3 38
Calafate A7 74
Calais C1 34
Calais B3 94
Calais B3 97
Calama C2 76
Calamian, *islands* A3 12
Calapan B3 12
Călăraşi D3 43
Calatayud F2 37
Calatrava B3 66
Calbayog C3 12
Calcutta E4, Inset II 20
Caledon, *river* A1, C2 71
Caledonia F4 102
Calgary C5 94
Cali A4 78
California B2 126
California, *gulf* B1 84
Callao B3 77
Calling Lake D3 94
Caltanissetta C3 38
Calvi Inset I 34
Calvinia A3 71
Cam Ranh B4 11
Camagüey D2 88
Camagüey, *archipelago* D2 88
Camberley Inset III 30
Cambodia **11**
Cambrai C1 34
Cambrian, *mts.* B3 30
Cambridge D3 30
Cambridge Bay G3 99
Cambridge-Narrows D3 97
Cameron, *hills* B1 94
Cameron, *island* H1 99
Cameroon **65**
Cameroon, *mt.* A3 65
Camiri B4 77
Camopi B2 80
Camopi, *river* B2 80
Campana, *island* A8 76
Campania C2 38
Campbell River K6 95
Campbellton C1 97
Campbellton A2 100
Campbellton K4 103
Campbelltown, N.S.W. Inset IV 14
Campbelltown, S.A. Inset II 14
Campbeltown B2 30
Campeche, *bay* F4 84
Campeche, *state capital* F4 84
Camper B3 96
Camperville A3 96
Campina Grande E2 81
Campinas D4 81
Campo Grande C4 81
Campobasso C2 38
Campobello, *island* C4 97
Campos D4 81
Campos Elísios Inset I 81
Camrose D4 94
Camsell Portage A1 104
Camú, *river* B1 89
Camuy B2 90
Can Tho A4 11
Caña Gorda, *beach* B3 90
Canaan B1 91
Canada **92**
Canaima D2 79
Çanakkale A2 27
Canal Flats P6 95
Canaray, *islands* Inset I 37
Canaries A2 91
Canary, *islands* 55
Canaveral, *cape*, Fla. E3 126
Canberra, A.C.T., *natl. capital* D3 14
Canchungo A1 62
Cancún G3 84
Candelaria C2 90
Candiac J6 103
Candle Lake E7 104
Cando B8 104
Canelles, *river* B3 91
Canelones B3 75
Cangamba D4 70
Cangzhou E2 10
Caniapiscau, *lake* C3 101
Caniapiscau, *river* C2 101
Çankırı C2 27
Cankuzo C2 61
Cannes D5 34
Canning C2 100
Canning, *river* Inset I 14
Canoe Narrows B5 104
Canoe, *lake* B5 104
Canora H9 104
Canossa B1 38
Canouan, *island* B3 91
Canóvanas D2 90
Canso G2 100
Cantabria D1 37
Cantábrica, *mts.* C1 37
Canterbury D3 30
Canterbury B3 97
Canterbury, *bight* B3 15
Canterbury, *plains* B3 15
Canton, *island* B2 17
Canwood D7 104
Canyon Creek C3 94
Cao Bang B1 11
Cap-aux-Os M3 103
Cap-Chat K2 103
Cap-de-la-Madeleine D5 103
Cap-Haïtien C1 89
Cap-Pelé E2 97
Cap-Rouge K6 103
Cap-St-Ignace F4 103
Cape Charles D3 98
Cape Coast B4 64
Cape Girardeau, Mo. E2 126
Cape North G1 100
Cape Race E5 98
Cape Ray B5 98
Cape St. George B5 98
Cape Tormentine E2 97
Cape Town, *legislative capital* A3 71
Cape Verde **58**
Cape York, *peninsula* D1 14
Capitán Pablo Lagerenza B1 75
Caplan L3 103
Caprara, *point* B2 38
Capreol D1 102
Capri, *island* C2 38
Capua C2 38
Caquetá, *river* B5 78
Car Nicobar, *island* F7 20
Caracas, *capital* C1 79
Caramoan, *peninsula* B3 12
Carapicuíba Inset II 81
Caraquet E1 97
Carberry B4 96
Carbonara, *cape* B3 38
Carbonear E5 98
Carbonia B3 38
Carcajou B2 94
Carcassonne C5 34
Carcross C5 105
Cardamom, *mts.* A3 11
Cárdenas B1 88
Cardiel, *lake* A6 74
Cardiff B3 30
Cardigan C2 100
Cardigan, *bay* B3 30
Cardigan, *bay* C2 100
Cardinal K3 102
Cardinal, *lake* B3 94
Caribbean, *sea* 82
Carievale A4 96
Carleton K3 103
Carleton Place J2 102
Carlingford C1 31
Carlingford, *lake* C1 31
Carlisle C2 30
Carlisle, *bay* A4 91
Carlow C2 31
Carlsbad, N. Mex. C2 126
Carlyle H11 104
Carmacks B4 105
Carman B4 96
Carmanville D4 98
Carmarthen B3 30
Carmelo A2 75
Carnac B3 34
Carnarvon B3 71
Carnarvon G2 102
Carnarvon, W.A. A2 14
Carnduff J11 104
Carnic Alps, *range* C4 39
Carnsore, *point* C2 31
Carolina D2 90
Caroline, *island* D2 17
Caroline, *islands* B2 15
Caron E10 104
Caroni, *river* D2 79
Carora C1 79
Carpathian, *mts.* 43
Carpentaria, *gulf* C1 14
Carrantuohill, *mt.* B3 31
Carriacou, *island* C1 91
Carrick-onShannon B2 31
Carroll A4 96
Carrot River G7 104
Carson City, *capital*, Nev. B2 126
Carstairs C5 94
Cartagena B2 78
Cartagena F4 37
Cartago C3 86
Carthage, *ruin* C1 57
Cartier D1 102
Cartwright B4 96
Cartwright C2 98
Carúpano D1 79
Carvoeiro, *cape* A3 36
Carway D6 94
Casa Grande, Ariz. B2 126
Casablanca Inset 76
Casablanca C1 57
Casamance, *region* B3 62
Casamance, *river* B3 62
Cascade Inset 70
Cascade, *range* A1 126
Cascapedia, *river* K3 103
Cascumpec, *bay* B2 100
Caserta C2 38
Cashel C2 31
Casiquiare, *river* C3 79
Caslan D4 94
Casper, Wyo. C1 126
Caspian, *depression* B2 23
Caspian, *sea* 7
Casselman K2 102
Cassiar H1 95
Cassiar, *mts.* G1 95
Castel Gandolfo C2 38
Castellón de la Plana F3 37
Castelo Branco B3 36
Castile and León D1, E1 37
Castile-la Mancha E3 37
Castle Bruce B2 90
Castle Mountain C5 94
Castlebar B2 31
Castlegar O6 95
Castries, *capital* B1 91
Castro B7 76
Cat, *island* B3 89
Catacamas C2 86
Catalina E5 98
Catalonia G2 37
Catamarca B2 74
Catanduanes, *island* C3 12
Catania C3 38
Cataño C2 90
Catanzaro D3 38
Catió B2 62
Catoche, *cape* G3 84
Catumbela B4 70
Cauca, *river* B3 78
Caucasus, *mts.* A1, A2 45
Caungula D2 70
Caura, *river* D2 79
Causapscal J3 103
Căuşeni B2 50
Cauto, *river* E3 88
Cauvery, *river* C6 20
Cavalla, *river* C3 63
Cavally, *river* C4 63
Cavan C2 31
Cavendish B2 100
Caviana, *island* D1 81
Caxito B2 70
Cayambe, *mt.* C3 79
Cayenne, *capital* B1 80
Cayer B3 96
Cayey C2 90
Cayman, *trench* B2 88
Cayman, *islands* 82
Cayon B1 90
Cazombo E3 70
Ceará E2 81
Cebollatí, *river* C2 75
Cebu B4 12
Cebu, *island* B4 12
Cedar City, Utah B2 126
Cedar Grove E5 90
Cedar Rapids, Iowa D1 126
Cedar, *lake* A2 96
Cedros, *island* A2 84
Ceduna, S.A. C3 14
Ceerigaabo B1 60
Cefalù C3 38
Cegléd B2 43
Ceiba C2 90
Ceiba D2 90
Celada D2 90
Celaya D3 84
Celebes (Sulawesi), *island* D2 13
Celebes, *sea* D1 13
Celje C2 48
Celtic, *sea* B3 31
Central African Republic **66**
Central Butte D10 104
Central Makran, *range* B4 21
Central Siberian, *plateau* C7 44
Centre C3 34
Centre C3 100
Centre de Flacq C2 69
Centreville E4 98
Ceram, *island* D2 13
Ceram, *sea* D2 13
Cerf, *island* Inset 70
Cernavodă E3 43
Cerro Castillo B9 76
Cerro de Pasco B3 77
Cervati, *mt.* C2 38
Çesis C2 46
České Budějovice B4 42
Cess, *river* B3 63
Cessford E6 94
Cetinje A3 49
Ceuta D5 37
Cévennes, *mts.* C4 34
Ceyhan, *river* D3 27
Chachapoyas B2 77
Chaco Boreal, *region* B2 75
Chad **59**
Chad, *lake* A4, C3 59
Chaeryŏng, *river* A3 9
Chagai, *hills* B4 21
Chaghcharan B2 22
Chagres, *river* C2 87
Chaguanas A2 91
Chaitén B7 76
Chaiyaphum C3 12
Chalco Inset 84
Chaleur, *bay* D1 97
Chalna C6 21
Châlons-sur-Marne D2 34
Chambal, *river* C3 20
Chambéry D4 34
Chambeshi, *river* C2 67
Chambord D3 103
Chamelecon, *river* A2 86
Chamonix-Mont-Blanc D4 34
Champagne Castle, *mt.* C2 72
Champagne-Ardenne D2 34
Champaquí, *mt.* C3 74
Champasak C4 11
Champerico B5 85

Key Page
Champlain D5 103
Chañaral B3 76
Chança, *river* B4 36
Chandannagar Inset II 20
Chandigarh C2 20
Chandler M3 103
Chandpur D5 21
Chandrapur C5 20
Chang (Yangtze), *river* D2, E2 10
Changane, *river* B4 68
Changchun F1 10
Changde E3 10
Changhua B1 9
Changi B1 13
Changjin B2 9
Changjin, *river* B2 9
Changsha E3 10
Changuinola A2 87
Changyŏn A3 9
Changzhi E2 10
Changzhou F2 10
Channel *islands*, Calif. A2 126
Channel-Port aux Basques B5 98
Chantilly C2 34
Chao Phraya, *river* B3 12
Chapada dos Parecis, *range* C3 81
Chapala, *lake* D3 84
Chaparé, *river* A3 77
Chapleau D3 101
Chaplin D10 104
Chardzhou D2 22
Charente, *river* B4 34
Chari, *river* A5 59
Charikar B1 22
Charity B2 80
Charleroi C2 33
Charles A1 96
Charlesbourg E5, Inset 103
Charleston, *capital*, W. Va. E2 126
Charleston, S.C. F2 126
Charlestown C3 90
Charlestown A3 91
Charleville Mézières D2 34
Charleville, Qld. D2 14
Charlie Lake M3 95
Charlo C1 97
Charlotte, N.C. E2 126
Charlottetown C3 98
Charlottetown B2 100
Charlotteville B1 91
Charny E5, K6 103
Charters Towers, Qld. D2 14
Chartres C2 34
Chase N6 95
Châteauguay C6, H6 103
Châteauroux C3 34
Châtellerault C3 34
Chatfield C4 96
Chatham Inset III 30
Chatham C5 102
Chatham, *sound* G4 95
Chatkal, *river* B2 23
Chatsworth E3 102
Chattanooga, Tenn. E2 126
Chau Doc A4 11
Chaumont D2 34
Chaves B2 36
Cheb A2 42
Cheboksary D4 44
Chech'ŏn C4 9
Chechnya, republic E4 44
Cheduba, *island* B2 12
Chegutu B2 69
Cheju Inset 9
Cheju, *island* Inset 9
Cheju, *strait* Inset 9
Chek Keng Inset 10
Chelan G8 104
Cheleken A2 22
Chelif, *river* B1 57
Chelles Inset II 34
Chełm F3 41
Chelmsford D3, Inset III 30
Cheltenham C3 30
Chelyabinsk D5 44
Chelyuskin, *cape* B7 44
Chembur Inset I 20
Chemin Grenier B3 69
Chemnitz C3 40
Chenab, *river* D3 21
Chenachane A2 57
Chene Inset I 20
Chénéville A6 103
Chengde E1 10
Chengdu D2 10
Chennai (Madras) D6 20
Cherbourg B2 34
Cherepovets D3 44
Cherkassy C2 47
Chernigov C1 47
Chernivtsi B2 47
Cherrapunji F3 20
Cherryville N6 95
Cherskiy C10 44
Cherskiy, *range* C8 44
Chesapeake, *bay* F2 126
Chesley D3 102
Chester C3 30
Chester C3 100
Chesterfield C3 30
Chesterfield Inlet K4 99
Chesterfield, *islands* A2 18
Cheticamp G1 100
Chetumal, *state capital* G4 84
Chetwynd M3 95
Cheviot, *hills* C2 30
Chevreuse Inset II 34
Cheyenne, *capital*, Wyo. C1 126
Chhukha A2 19
Chi, *river* C2 12
Chiai B2 9
Chiang Mai B2 12
Chiang Rai B2 12
Chiapa C1 76
Chiapas F4 84
Chiatura B3 45
Chiba D3 8
Chibougamau B2 103
Chibougamau, *lake* B2 103
Chicago, Ill. E1 126
Chicapa, *river* D3 70
Chichén Itzá, *ruins* G3 84
Chichester C4 30
Chichi, *island* Inset III 8
Chiclayo B2 77
Chico, *river* B6 74
Chiconcuac Inset 84
Chicoutimi E3 103
Chief, *river* L2 95
Chiem, *lake* C5 40
Chiesanuova B2 39
Chieti C2 38
Chifeng E1 10
Chignecto, *bay* C2 100
Chihuahua, *state capital* C2 84
Chilcotin, *river* K5 95
Chile 76
Chile Chico B8 76
Chililabombwe B2 67
Chilko, *lake* K5 95
Chillán B6 76
Chilliwack M6 95
Chiloé, *island* B7 76
Chilpancingo, *state capital* E4 84
Chilung B1 9
Chilwa, *lake* B2, C3 68
Chimalhuacán Inset 84
Chimay C2 33
Chimborazo, *mt.* B3 79
Chimbote B2 77
Chimoio B3 68
Chin, *hills* B2 12
China 10
Chinajá C4 85
Chinandega A2 87
Chincha Alta B3 77
Chinchaga, *river* A2 94
Chinde C3 68
Chindwin, *river* B1 12
Chingola B2 67
Chingoni C2 67
Chinhae C5 9
Chinhoyi B1 69
Chiniot D3 21
Chinju C5 9
Chinko, *river* B2 66
Chioggia C1 38
Chip, *lake* C4 94
Chipata C2 67
Chipewyan Lake D3 94
Chipman D2 97
Chira, *river* A5 79
Chirchiq, *river* C2 23
Chire, *river* B3 68
Chiredzi B2 69
Chiriquí, *gulf* A3 87
Chiriquí, *lagoon* B2 87
Chirner Inset I 20
Chirripó, *mt.* C3 86
Chirripó, *river* C2 86
Chisasibi A3 101
Chisholm C4 94
Chişinău, *capital* B2 50
Chita D7 44
Chitipa B1 68
Chitose Inset I 8
Chitral D2 21
Chitré B3 87
Chittagong E6 21
Chitungwiza B1 69
Chixoy, *river* C4 85
Choa Chu Kang A1 13
Choiceland F7 104
Choiseul A3 91
Choiseul, *island* A1 16
Choisy-le Roi Inset II 34
Chojnice C2 41
Choke, *mts.* B2 60
Cholet B3 34
Cholpon-Ata E1 23
Cholula E4 84
Choluteca B3 86
Choma B3 67
Chomo Lhari, *mt.* A1 19
Chon Buri B3 12
Chone A3 79
Ch'ŏngch'ŏn, *river* A3 9
Ch'ŏngjin C2 9
Ch'ŏngju B4 9
Chŏngju A3 9
Chongqing D3 10
Chŏnju B5 9
Chonos, *archipelago* B7 76
Chontaleña, *mts.* B2 87
Chornobyl' C1 47
Chorzów D3 41
Choshui, *river* B2 9
Choybalsan D2 11
Christchurch B3 15
Christina, *river* E3 94
Christmas Island G2 100
Chu, *river* D1 23
Chubut, *river* A5 74
Chucunaque, *river* D2 87
Chugoku, *mts.* B3 8
Chukchi, *peninsula* C11 44
Chukchi, *range* C10 44
Chukchi, *sea* B11 44
Chukotka,
autonomous okrug C10 44
Chumphon B4 12
Chunan B1 9
Ch'unch'ŏn B4 9
Chung Hau Inset 10
Chungho B1 9
Ch'ungju B4 9
Chungli B1 9
Chungqing, Ind. Mun. D3 10
Chungyang, *range* B2 9
Chuquicamata C2 76
Chur D2 35
Church Point A3 100
Churchbridge A4 96
Churchbridge J10 104
Churchill D1 96
Churchill Falls D3 98
Churchill, *lake* B4 104
Churchill, *river* D1 96
Churia, *mts.* B2 19
Chute-aux-Outardes H2 103
Chuuk, *islands* C2 15
Chuvashiya, republic D4 44
Ciales C2 90
Cibao, *valley* A1 89
Cicia, *island* C2 17
Cidra C2 90
Ciechánow E2 41
Ciego de Ávila D2 88
Cienfuegos C2 88
Cieza F3 37
Cijara, *reservoir* D3 37
Cikobia, *island* C1 17
Cilacap B2 13
Cilician Gates, *pass* C3 27
Cimone, *mt.* B1 38
Cincinnati, Ohio E2 126
Cirebon B2 13
Citlaltépetl, *mt.* E4 84
City View G6 102
Ciudad Acuña D2 84
Ciudad Bolívar D2 79
Ciudad Camargo C2 84
Ciudad Constitución B3 84
Ciudad del Carmen F4 84
Ciudad del Este E4 75
Ciudad Guayana D2 79
Ciudad Juárez C1 84
Ciudad Mante E3 84
Ciudad Obregón C2 84
Ciudad Real E3 37
Ciudad Rodrigo C2 37
Ciudad Valles E3 84
Ciudad Victoria,
state capital E3 84
Ciudadela H2 37
Civitavecchia B2 38
Clair A1 97
Claire, *lake* D2 94
Clandeboye C4 96
Clara C2 31
Clarenville D5 98
Clark's Harbour B4 100
Clarksville, Tenn. E2 126
Clear Creek E5 102
Clear, *cape* B3 31
Clearwater M5 95
Clearwater, *river* E3 94
Clementsport B3 100
Clermont F4 103
Clermont-Ferrand C4 34
Clervaux B1 33
Clerve, *river* B2 33
Cleveland, Ohio E1 126
Clichy Inset II 34
Clifden A2 31
Clifford E4 102
Climax B11 104
Clinton M5 95
Clinton D4 102
Clinton Colden, *lake* G4 99
Cloncurry, Qld. D2 14
Clonmel C2 31
Cloridorme M2 103
Clovis, N. Mex. C2 126
Cloyne H3 102
Cluff Lake Mine A2 104
Cluj-Napoca B2 43
Cluny D3 34
Cluny D6 94
Clutha, *river* A4 15
Clyde River B4 100
Clyde River P2 99
Clyde, *estuary* B2 30
Clyde, *river* B2 30
Clydebank B2 30
Coacalco Inset 84
Coahuila D2 84
Coal River J1 95
Coal, *river* D5 105
Coaldale D6 94
Coalspur B4 94
Coamo C2 90
Coast, *mts.* F2, J5 95
Coast, *ranges* A1, A2 126
Coaticook E6 103
Coats Land, *region* B13 107
Coats, *island* M4 99
Coatzacoalcos F4 84
Cobán C4 85
Cobden J2 102
Cóbh B3 31
Cobham, *river* D2 96
Cobija A2 77
Cobourg G4 102
Coburg B3 40
Coburg, *island* N1 99
Cocagne E2 97
Cochabamba A3 77
Cochin (Kochi) C7 20
Cochrane B8 76
Cochrane D3 101
Cochrane, *lake* B8 76
Cochrane, *river* H2 104
Cockburn Harbour D4 89
Cockburn, *island* B2 102
Coclé del Norte B2 87
Coco C2 90
Coco, *islands* B3 12
Coco, *river* A2, C1 87
Cocos, *islands* 5
Cocotitlán Inset 84
Cod, *cape*, Mass. G1 126
Codri, *region* A3 50
Codrington E2 90
Codrington, *mt.* C17 107
Cody, Wyo. C1 126
Coe Hill H3 102
Coeroeni, *river* A3 80
Coeur d'Alene, Idaho B1 126
Cogalnic, *river* B2 50
Cognac B4 34
Coiba, *island* B3 87
Coihaique B8 76
Coimbatore C6 20
Coimbra A2 36
Cojedes, *river* C2 79
Colca, *river* C4 77
Colchester D3 30
Cold Lake E4 94
Coleraine A2 30
Coles Island D3 97
Coleville A9 104
Colihaut A2 90
Colima, *state capital* D4 84
Colina Inset 76
Coll, *island* A2 30
Collaguasi C2 76
Collingwood B3 15
Collingwood E3 102
Colmar D2 34
Cologne A3 40
Colombia 78
Colombier H3 103
Colombo, *capital* A5 19
Colón C2 87
Colón C2 88
Colonia A2 15
Colonia B3 75
Colonia Nueva Guinea B3 87
Colonsay E9 104
Colonsay, *island* A2 30
Colorado C2 86
Colorado C2 126
Colorado Springs, Colo. C2 126
Colorado, *plateau* B2 126
Colorado, *river* B4 74
Colorado, *river* B2 126
Columbia, *capital*, S.C. E2 126
Columbia, *mts.* M4 95
Columbia, *plateau* B1 126
Columbia, *river* B1 126
Columbus, *capital*, Ohio E2 126
Columbus, Ga. E2 126
Coma Pedrosa, *mt.* A1 36
Comayagua B2 86
Comayagua, *mts.* B2 86
Combermere H2 102
Comendador A2 89
Comerío C2 90
Comilla E5 21
Comino, *island* B1 36
Cominotto, *island* B1 36
Comitán F4 84
Committee, *bay* L3 99
Como B1 38
Como, *lake* B1 38
Comodoro Rivadavia B6 74
Comorin, *cape* C7 20
Comoros 67
Comox K6 95
Compiègne C2 34
Compton E6 103
Comrat B2 50
Con Son, *islands* B5 11
Conakry, *capital* B3 62
Concepción B6 76
Concepción D3 75
Concepción del Oro D3 84
Conchalí Inset 76
Conche D4 98
Conchos, *river* C2 84
Concord, *capital*, N.H. F1 126
Concordia D3 74
Condor C5 94
Congo, Dem Rep of 67
Congo, Rep of 66
Congo, *basin* D3 66
Congo, *river* D4 66
Congo, *river* B1 67
Conn, *lake* B1 31
Connecticut F1 126
Connemara, *region* B2 31
Consecon H4 102
Constance B5 40
Constance (Bodensee), *lake* D1 35
Constanţa E3 43
Constantine B1 57
Constitución B5 76
Consul A11 104
Contrecoeur C6 103
Contwoyto, *lake* G3 99
Conwy B3 30
Coober Pedy, S.A. C2 14
Cook's Harbour D3 98
Cook, *mt.* B3 15
Cook, *strait* B3 15
Cookshire E6 103
Cookstown F3 102
Coos Bay, Oreg. A1 126
Copán, *ruins* A2 86
Copenhagen, *capital* D3 32
Copiapó B3 76
Copiapó, *river* B3 76
Coppename, *river* A2 80
Coppermine, *river* F3 99
Coquí C3 90
Coquimbo B3 76
Coral, *sea* E1 14
Corantijn, *river* A2 80
Corazón C3 90
Corbeil-Essonnes Inset II 34
Corcovado, *gulf* B7 76
Corcovado, *mt.* Inset I 81
Córdoba C3 74
Córdoba D4 37
Córdoba, *range* B3 74
Corinth B3 51
Corinth, *gulf* B3 51
Corinth, *isthmus* B3 51
Corinto A2 87
Corisco, *bay* B4 66
Corisco, *island* B4 66
Cork B3 31
Cormack C4 98
Cormoran, *reef* B2 17
Cormorant A2 96
Cormorant, *lake* A2 96
Cornellá de Llogregat G2 37
Corner Brook C5 98
Corno, *mt.* C2 38
Cornwall B2 100
Cornwall L2 102
Cornwall, *island* K1 99
Cornwallis, *island* J1 99
Coro C1 79
Coromandel, *peninsula* C2 15
Coronach E11 104
Coronado, *bay* B3 86
Coronation, *gulf* F3 99
Coronel Oviedo D4 75
Coropuna, *mt.* C4 77
Corozal B1 85
Corozal C2 90
Corpus Christi, Tex. D3 126
Corregidor, *island* B3 12
Corrib, *lake* B2 31
Corrientes D2 74
Corse Inset I 34
Corsica, *island* Inset I 34
Cortina d'Ampezzo C1 38
Cortona B2 38
Corubal, *river* D1 62
Çoruh, *river* E2 27
Çorum C2 27
Corumbá C3 81
Corumbau, *point* E3 81
Corvallis, Oreg. A1 126
Cosenza D3 38
Coslada Inset II 37
Cosmoledo, *island group* A2 70
Costa Rica 86
Cotabato C5 12
Côte d'Ivoire 63
Cotentin, *peninsula* B2 34
Cotia Inset II 81
Coto Laurel B2 90
Cotonou B4 64
Cotopaxi, *mt.* B3 79
Cotswold, *hills* C3 30
Cottbus C3 40
Cotton Ground C2 90
Cotuí B1 89
Coubert Inset II 34
Couffo, *river* B4 64
Courantyne, *river* B3 80
Courland, *lagoon* A2 46
Courtenay K6 95
Courval D10 104
Coutts E6 94
Couva A2 91
Coventry C3 30
Covilhã B2 36
Cow Head C4 98
Cowan A3 96
Cowansville D6 103
Cowes C4 30
Cox's Bazar E7 21
Cox's Cove B4 98
Coyah B3 62
Coyoacán Inset 84
Cozumel, *island* G3 84
Cradock C3 71
Craigmyle D5 94
Craik E9 104
Craiova B3 43
Cranberry Portage A2 96
Cranbrook P6 95
Crane River B3 96
Crane Valley E11 104
Crapaud B2 100
Cravo Norte C3 78
Crawford Bay O6 95
Crawley Inset III 30
Crean, *lake* D6 104
Cree Lake D3 104
Cree, *river* E2 104
Cremona B1 38
Cremona C5 94
Cres, *island* B3 48
Cressday E6 94
Creston O6 95
Crete, *island* C4 51
Crete, *sea* C4 51
Créteil Inset II 34
Crewe C3 30
Crimean, *mts.* C4 47
Crimean, *peninsula* C3 47
Cristal, *mts.* A1 66
Cristóbal C2 87
Cristóbal Colón, *peak* B2 78
Crna Gora, *mts.* B3 49
Crna, *river* B2 48
Croatia 48
Crocker, *range* D2 13
Cromer A4 96
Crooked River G8 104
Crooked, *island* C4 89
Crooked, *river* L4 95
Cross Lake C2 96
Cross, *river* E4 65
Crotone D3 38
Cruz, *cape* D3 88
Cruzeiro do Sul A2 81
Crystal City B4 96
Cu Lao Thu, *island* B4 11
Cuajimalpa Inset 84
Cuamba C2 68
Cuando, *river* D4 70
Cuango, *river* D2 70
Cuanza, *river* C3 70
Cuareim, *river* B1 75
Cuauhtémoc C2 84
Cuautitlán Inset 84
Cuautitlán Izcalli Inset 84
Cuba 88
Cubal, *river* B4 70
Cubango, *river* D5 70
Cubatão Inset II 81
Cúcuta B3 78
Cuddalore C6 20
Cudworth E8 104
Cuenca B4 79
Cuenca E2 37
Cuernavaca, *state capital* E4 84
Cuiabá C3 81
Cuíto Cuanavale D5 70
Cuito, *river* D4 70
Cukorova, *region* C3 27
Culebra, *island* E2 90
Culebrinas, *river* A2 90
Culiacán, *state capital* C3 84
Cumaná D1 79
Cumberland K6 95
Cumberland House H7 104
Cumberland, *lake* H6 104
Cumberland, *peninsula* P3 99
Cumberland, *sound* P3 99
Cumbrian, *mts.* B2 30
Cunene, *river* B5, C4 70
Cuneo A1 38
Cupar B2 30
Cupar F10 104
Curaçao, *island* 82
Curaray, *river* C3 79
Curepipe C3 69
Curicó B4 76
Curitiba D4 81
Curral Velho D3 58
Curuzú Cuatiá D2 74
Cut Knife A8 104
Cuttack E4 20
Cuxhaven B2 40
Cuyo, *islands* B4 12
Cuyuni, *river* A2 80
Cuzco C3 77
Cyangugu A2 61
Cyclades, *islands* C3 51
Cypress River B4 96
Cyprus 27
Czar E5 94
Czech Republic 42
Częstochowa D3 41

D

Da Lat B4 11
Da Nang B3 11
Dabakala D2 63
Dabola C2 62
Dachang D3 10
Dachau B4 40
Dacotah C4 96
Dades, *river* C2 57
Dadu C4 21
Dafoe F9 104
Dagestan, republic E4 44
Dagupan B2 12
Dahlak, *archipelago* C2 60
Dahna, ad-, *desert* B1 24
Dahuk B1 24
Dajabón A1 89
Daka, *river* B2 64
Dakar, *capital* A2 62
Dakhla A2 58
Đakovica B3 49
Dalälven, *river* C2 53
Dalandzadgad C3 11
Dalhousie C1 97
Dalhousie K3 103
Dali D2 10
Dalian F2 10
Dallas C3 96
Dallas, Tex. D2 126
Dallol Bosso, *river* A3 59
Dalmatia, *region* B3 48
Daloa C3 63
Dalvík B2 52
Daly, *river* C1 14
Daman B4 20
Damanhur B1 56
Damascus, *capital* A3 27
Damaturu F2 65
Damavand, *mt.* C2 22
Damazin, ad- C3 59
Dame-Marie A2 89
Damietta B1 56
Damietta, *river* B1 56
Dammam, ad- C1 24
Dammartin-en-Goële Inset II 34
Dampier, W.A. A2 14
Damur, ad- A2 26
Danakil, *desert* C2 60
Danané B3 63
Dand A4 96
Dande, *river* B2 70
Dandeldhura A2 19
Dandong F1 10
Dangara A1 23
Dangme, *river* C2 19
Dangrek, *mts.* C3 12
Dangriga B2 85
Daniel's Harbour C4 98
Danjiangkou E2 10
Danlí B2 86
Danube, *river* 29
Danville D6 103
Danville, Va. F2 126
Dao Phu Quoc, *island* A4 11
Dapaong B1 64
Dapp D4 94
Daqing F1 10
Dar es-Salaam, *capital* C2 68
Dara A3 27
Dara B2 62
Đaravica, *mt.* B3 49
Darbhanga E3 20
Darhan C2 11
Darién, *mts.* D2 87
Dariense, *mts.* B2 87
Darjiling E3 20
Darling, *range* A3 14
Darling, *river* D3 14
Darlington C2 30
Darłowo C1 41
Darmstadt B4 40
Darnah D1 56
Darnley B2 100
Dartmoor, *plateau* B4 30
Dartmouth D3 100
Daru A2 15
Darwin, N.T., *capital* C1 14
Dashhowuz C2 22
Dasht-e Kavir, *desert* D3 22
Dasht-e Lut, *desert* D3 22
Datong E1 10
Daua, *river* F1 61
Daugavpils D3 46
Daule, *river* B3 79
Dauphin B1 91
Dauphin A3 96
Dauphin River B3 96
Dauphin, *lake* B3 96
Davao C5 12
Davao, *gulf* C5 12

Key Page
Davenport, Iowa D1 126
David A2 87
Davidson D9 104
Davis Inlet E3 98
Davis, *strait* M2 92
Davos D2 35
Dawa, *river* C3 60
Dawhat asSalwa, *bay* B3 25
Dawkah B2 25
Dawna, *range* B2 12
Dawson B3 105
Dawson Creek M3 95
Dawson, *bay* A2 96
Daymán, *river* B1 75
Dayr az-Zawr B2 27
Dayton, Ohio E2 126
Daytona Beach, Fla. E3 126
De Aar B3 71
De Quincy Village Inset 70
Dead Sea, *lake* A2 26
Dead, *sea* B2 26
Dean, *channel* J5 95
Dean, *river* K5 95
Dease Lake G2 95
Death, *valley*, Calif. B2 126
Deauville C2 34
Debar A2 48
Debden D7 104
Debed, *river* B2 45
DeBolt A3 94
Debre Birhan C2 60
Debre Markos B2 60
Debrecen C2 43
Decatur, Ill. E2 126
Deccan, *plateau* C5 20
Děčín B2 42
Dédougou C2 64
Dedza B2 68
Dee, *river* B3, C1 30
Deep River H1 102
Deep, *inlet* B1 98
Deepdale A3 96
Deer Lake C4 98
Deerfield A4 100
Degeh Bur D2 60
Dégelis H4 103
Dehiwala-Mt. Lavinia A5 19
Dehra Dun C2 20
Dej B2 43
Del Rio, Tex. C3 126
Delacour D5 94
Delap Cove B3 100
Delaronde, *lake* C6 104
Delaware F2 126
Delburne D5 94
Deleau A4 96
Delft B2 32
Delft, *island* A2 19
Delfzijl D1 32
Delgado A2 86
Delhi C3 20
Delhi E5 102
Delicias C2 84
Déline D3 99
Delisle C9 104
Deloraine A4 96
Delos, *island* C3 51
Delson J6 103
Delta Beach B4 96
Demerara, *river* B3 80
Den Helder B2 32
Denakil, *desert* C1 60
Denare Beach H6 104
Denbigh H2 102
Dencross C4 96
Dender, *river* B2 33
Denigomodu A2 16
Denmark 32
Denmark, *strait* D2 106
Dennery B2 91
Denpasar C2 13
D'Entrecasteaux, *islands* B2 15
D'Entrecasteaux, *reefs* C1 18
Denver, *capital*, Colo. C2 126
Denzil A8 104
Dera Ghazi Khan D3 21
Dera Ismail Khan D3 21
Derby C3 30
Derg, *lake* B2 31
Derrick B3 91
Derventa B1 48
Derwent E4 94
Des Moines, *capital*, Iowa D1 126
Desaguadero, *river* B2 74
Desaguadero, *river* A3 77
Desberats B1 102
Deschaillons D5 103
Deschambault Lake G6 104
Dese C2 60
Deseado, *river* B6 74
Deseronto H3 102
Desna, *river* C1 47
Desolación, *island* B9 76
Desruisseau B3 91
Dessau C3 40
Destruction Bay B5 105
Detmold B3 40
Detroit, Mich. E1 126
Deux Rivieres G1 102
Deux-Montagnes H5 103
Deva B3 43
Deventer D2 32
Devil's, *island* B1 80
Devoll, *river* B3 49
Devon, *island* L1 99
Devonport, Tas. D4 14
Dewberry E4 94
Dezful B3 22
Dháfni Inset 51
Dhahran C1 24
Dhaka, *capital* D5 21
Dhamar A2 25
Dhangarhi A2 19
Dhankuta D2 19
Dharan D3 19
Dhaulagiri, *mt.* B2 19
Dhofar, *region* B3 25
Dhulagarh Inset II 20
Dhuusamareeb B2 60
Diadema Inset II 81
Dialakoto C3 62
Diamond, *island* B1 91
Dibrugarh F3 20
Diefenbaker, *lake* C10 104
Diekirch B2 33
Dien Bien Phu A2 11
Dieppe C2 34
Dieppe E2 97
Dieppe Bay Town B1 90
Diffa C3 59
Differdange A2 33
Digby B3 100
Digne D4 34
Digul, *river* E2 13
Dijon D3 34
Dikhil B2 60
Dikson B6 44
Dili, *capital* B1 15
Dilijan B2 45
Dillon B5 104
Dilolo B3 67
Dimbokro D3 63
Dimitrovgrad D3 50
Dimlang, *mt.* F3 65
Dimona B2 26
Dinagat, *island* C4 12
Dinajpur B3 21
Dinant C2 33
Dinara, *mt.* A2, C3 48
Dinaric Alps, *mts.* A1, B3 48
Dinder, *river* B1 60
Dingle A2 31
Dingle, *bay* A2 31
Dingli B2 36
Dinsmore C9 104
Diourbel A2 62
Dipolog B4 12
Dire Dawa D2 60
Diriamba A3 87
Dispur F3 20
Diu B4 20
Diuata, *mts.* C4 12
Divo D4 63
Divriği D2 27
Diwaniyah, ad- C2 24
Dixon Entrance, *channel* F4 95
Dixonville B3 94
Diyala, *river* C2 24
Diyarbakır E3 27
Dja, *river* B3 65
Djado C1 59
Djambala C5 66
Djanet B2 57
Djelfa B1 57
Djenné C3 58
Djerba, *island* C3 57
Djibouti 60
Djibouti, *capital* C2 60
Djouah, *river* B1 66
Djouf, el-, *desert* B1, C3 58
Djougou A3 64
Dnepr-Bug, *canal* B3 47
Dneprodzerzhinsk C2 47
Dnieper, *river* C1, E3 47
Dniester, *river* B2 47
Dnipropetrovsk D2 47
Doaktown C2 97
Doba B5 59
Doboj B1 48
Dobrich F2 50
Dobruja, *region* E3 43
Doctor Pedro P. Peña A3 75
Dodecanese, *islands* C3 51
Dodge City, Kans. C2 126
Dodoma, *capital* C2 68
Dodsland B9 104
Doetinchem D3 32
Dogo, *island* B2 8
Dogondoutchi A3 59
Doha, *capital* D3 25
Doiran, *lake* C2 48
Dolbeau D3 103
Dôle D3 34
Dolomites, *range* B1 38
Domagnano B1 39
Domeyko, *mts.* C3 76
Dominica 90
Dominica, *passage* A1 90
Dominican Republic 89
Dominion City C4 96
Domont Inset II 34
Domremy E8 104
Domuyo, *volcano* A4 74
Don Benito D3 37
Doña Juana, *mt.* C2 90
Donald Station O5 95
Doncaster C3 30
Dondo B3 70
Donegal B1 31
Donegal, *bay* B1 31
Donets, *basin* D2 47
Donetsk D2 47
Dong Hoi B3 11
Dong Nai, *river* B4 11
Dongting, *lake* E3 10
Dongwe, *river* A2 67
Donnacona E5 103
Dor, *lake* C6 104
Dorado C2 90
Dorchester C4 30
Dordogne, *river* C4 34
Dordrecht B3 32
Dore Lake C6 104
Dörgön, *lake* B2 11
Dori D1 64
Dorintosh B6 104
Dorking Inset III 30
Dornoch B1 30
Dorohoi D2 43
Dorothy D5 94
Dorra B1 60
Dortmund A3 40
Dorval H6 103
Dos Hermanas D4 37
Dosquet E5 103
Dosso A3 59
Dothan, Ala. E2 126
Douai C1 34
Douala A3 65
Doubs, *river* A1 35
Douglas B2 30
Douglas, *channel* H4 95
Douglastown M3 103
Dourados C4 81
Douro, *river* B2 36
Dover D3 30
Dover, *capital*, Del. F2 126
Dover, *strait* D4 30
Dovrefjell, *mts.* B3 52
Dozen, *island* B2 8
Drâa, *river* A1, B2, C2 57
Draguignan D5 34
Drake E9 104
Drakensberg, *mts.* B3, C3 71
Drammen C4 52
Drava, *river* A2 43
Drayton Valley C4 94
Dresden C3 40
Dresden C5 102
Dreux C2 34
Drin, *river* A1 49
Drina, *river* A2 49
Drobeta-Turnu Severin B3 43
Drogheda C2 31
Drumheller D5 94
Drummond B2 97
Drummondville D6 103
Druskininkai B2 46
Dryden B3 101
Dschang B2 65
Duars, *plain* A3 19
Duarte, *mt.* B1 89
Dubai C2 25
Dubăsari B2 50
Dubawnt, *lake* H4 99
Dubawnt, *river* H4 99
Dubbo, N.S.W. D3 14
Dube, *river* C3 63
Dublin, *capital* C2 31
Dubrovnik D4 48
Dubuque, Iowa D1 126
Dubysa, *river* B2 46
Duchess E6 94
Duck Bay A3 96
Duck Lake D8 104
Dudelange B2 33
Dudinka C6 44
Dudley C3 30
Duero, *river* D2 37
Dufourspitze, *mt.* B3 35
Dufrost C4 96
Dugald C4 96
Duisburg A3 40
Dukhan B3 25
Dulce, *gulf* C4 86
Duluth, Minn. D1 126
Dum-Dum Inset II 20
Duma A1 26
Dumaguete B4 12
Dumbås B3 52
Dumfries B2 30
Dumjor Inset II 20
Dún Laoghaire C2 31
Dunaújváros B2 43
Duncan L7 95
Duncansby, *cape* B1 30
Dund-Us B2 11
Dundalk C2 31
Dundee C2 30
Dundurn D9 104
Dunedin B4 15
Dunfermline B2 30
Dungarvan C2 31
Dunkirk (Dunkerque) C1 34
Dunkwa B4 64
Dunlop B2 96
Dunnegan F1 100
Dunnville F5 102
Dunqulah C1 59
Dunsinane, *mt.* B2 30
Dunstable Inset III 30
Dunster N4 95
Duqm C2 25
Duque de Caxias Inset I 81
Duque de York, *island* A9 76
Durance, *river* D5 34
Durango, Colo. C2 126
Durango, *state capital* D3 84
Durazno B2 75
Durban D2 71
Durham C2 30
Durham E3 102
Durham, N.C. F2 126
Durmitor, *mts.* A3 49
Durrës A2 49
Dushanbe, *capital* A1 23
Düsseldorf A3 40
Dutse E2 65
Dyce A2 96
Dyje, *river* B4 42
Dzaoudzi, territorial *capital* C2 67
Dzavhan, *river* B2 11
Dzhugdzhur, *range* D8 44
Dzungaria, *desert basin* B1 10
Dzyarzhynskaya Hara, *mt.* C3 47

E

Eagle, *river* B2 98
Eagle, *river* B2 105
Ear Falls B2 101
East Angus E6 103
East Antarctica B1 107
East Braintree D4 96
East China, *sea* 7
East Coast Bays B2 15
East Coulee D5 94
East Frisian, *islands* A2 40
East Lake Ainslie F1 100
East London C3 71
East Point C2 100
East Siberian, *sea* B10 44
East Timor 15
East York K5 102
East, *cape* C2 15
Eastbourne D4 30
Eastend B11 104
Eastern Ghats, *mts.* C6 20
Easterville B2 96
Eastmain A3 101
Eastmain, *river* B3 101
Eastport E5 98
Eatonia A9 104
Eau Claire, Wis. D1 126
Eauripik, *atoll* B2 15
Ebebiyín D2 66
Eberswalde C2 40
Ebolowa B3 65
Ebon, *island* B3 16
Ebor A4 96
Ebro, *river* F1 37
Ecatepec Inset 84
Echo Bay E3 99
Echo Bay A1 102
Echternach B2 33
Écija D4 37
Ecuador 79
Ed C3 60
Edam C2 32
Edam B7 104
Eddies Cove C3 98
Eddystone B3 96
Ede C4 65
Ede C2 32
Edéa B3 65
Edgerton E5 94
Edinburgh B2 30
Edirne A2 27
Edmonton, *capital* D4 94
Edmundston A1 97
Edmundston H4 103
Édouard, *lake* D4 103
Edrans B4 96
Edson B4 94
Edward, *lake* A4 61
Edwards *plateau*, Tex. C2 126
Eems, *river* D1 32
Éfaté, *island* C3 18
Egadi, *islands* C3 38
Eganville H2 102
Eger C2 43
Egersund B4 52
Eglinton, *island* E1 99
Egmont, *bay* A2 100
Egmont, *cape* B2 15
Egmont, *mt.* B2 15
Eğridir, *lake* B2 27
Egypt 56
Eifel, *plateau* A3 40
Eigg, *island* A2 30
Eindhoven C3 32
Einsiedeln C1 35
Eiseb, *river* D2 70
Eisenach B3 40
Eisenhüttenstadt C2 40
Eisleben B3 40
Ejmiatsin B2 45
Ejura B3 64
Ekibastuz D1 23
Ekwan, *river* D2 101
El Cañuelo, *ruins* C2 90
El Cerro del Aripo, *mt.* A2 91
El Encanto B5 78
El Ferrol B1 37
El Macao D2 89
El Paso, Tex. C2 126
El Pital, *mt.* A1 86
El Porvenir C2 87
El Progreso B2 86
El Salvador 86
El Seibo C2 89
El Serrat B1 36
El Tabo Inset 76
El Tigre D2 79
El Toro, *mt.* D2 90
El Trebolar Inset 76
Elat B3 26
Elâzığ D2 27
Elba, *island* B2 38
Elbasan B2 49
Elbe, *river* B2, C3 40
Elbert *mt.*, Colo. C2 126
Elbląg D1 41
Elbow D9 104
Elburz, *mts.* C2 22
Elche F3 37
Eldon C2 100
Eldoret C3 61
Elephant, *island* C12 107
Elephanta, *island* Inset I 20
Eleuthera, *island* B2 89
Elevsís Inset 51
Elfros G9 104
Elgin B1 30
Elgin A4 96
Elgin D3 97
Elgon, *mt.* D3 61
Eli Malk, *island* B3 17
Elie C4 96
Elista E4 44
Elk F2 41
Elk Point E4 94
Elkford P6 95
Elkhorn A4 96
Elkhovo E3 50
Elko P6 95
Elko, Nev. B1 126
Ellef Ringnes, *island* H1 99
Ellerts de Haan, *mts.* A3 80
Ellesmere, *island* M1 99
Ellice, *river* G3 99
Ellinikón Inset 51
Elliot Lake C1 102
Ellisras C1 71
Ellsworth Land, *region* B10 107
Ellsworth, *mts.* B10 107
Elm Creek C4 96
Elma D4 96
Elmina B4 64
Elmira C2 100
Elmira E4 102
Elmsdale A2 100
Elmvale F3 102
Elnora D5 94
Elqui, *river* B3 76
Elrose B9 104
Elsa B4 105
Elva A4 96
Elvas B3 36
Ely D3 30
Ely, Nev. B2 126
Embarcación C1 74
Embarras Portage E2 94
Embi B2 23
Embu D4 61
Emden A2 40
Emerald, *island* F1 99
Emerald, Qld. D2 14
Emerson C4 96
Emi Koussi, *mt.* B3 59
Emilia-Romagna B1 38
Emlembe, *mt.* B1 71
Emmeloord C2 32
Emmen D2 33
Emporia, Kans. D2 126
Ems, *river* A2 40
Encarnación E5 75
Enchant D6 94
Ende D2 13
Enderbury, *island* B2 17
Enderby N6 95
Enderby Land, *region* C17 107
Endiang D5 94
Enewetak, *island* A1 16
Engadine, *valley* D2 35
Engaño, *cape* D2 89
Enggano, *island* B2 13
Englee C4 98
English, *channel* C4 30
Englishtown G1 100
Enguri, *river* A3 45
Enid, Okla. D2 126
Enilda B3 94
Enna C3 38
Ennadai, *lake* H4 99
Ennery C1 89
Ennis B2 31
Ennistymon B2 31
Enns, *river* D3 39
Enriquillo, *lake* A2 89
Enschede D2 32
Ensenada A1 84
Ensenguly A3 22
Entebbe C3 61
Enugu D4 65
Épi, *island* C3 18
Épinal D2 34
Episkopi A2 27
Epsom Inset III 30
Equatorial, *channel* A5 19
Equatorial Guinea 66
Er Rif, *range* C1 57
Erciyes Daği, *mt.* C2 27
Érd B2 43
Erdenet C2 11
Erebus, *mt.* B5 107
Erenhot E1 10
Erfurt B3 40
Erg Chech, *desert* C1 58
Erg Iguidi, *desert* D1 58
Erickson B4 96
Erie, *lake* E5 102
Erie, Pa. E1 126
Eriksdale B4 96
Erimo, *cape* Inset I 8
Eritrea 60
Erlangen B4 40
Ermelo C2 71
Erne, *river* A2 30
Errigal, *mt.* B1 31
Erromango, *island* C4 18
Ersekë B3 49
Erzen, *river* A2 49
Erzgebirge, *mts.* C3 40
Erzincan D2 27
Erzurum E2 27
Esbjerg B3 32
Esch-sur-Alzette B2 33
Eschen B1 33
Escondido, *river* B2 87
Escuintla C5 85
Escuminac K3 103
Esfahan C3 22
Esil C1 23
Esker D3 98
Eskifjördhur C2 52
Eskilstuna C3 53
Eskimo Point K4 99
Eskişehir B2 27
Esla, *river* D2 37
Esmeraldas B2 79
Espanola D1 102
Española, *island* Inset 79
Esperance, W.A. B3 14
Espichel, *cape* A3 36
Espírito Santo D3 81
Espiritu Santo, *island* B2 18
Espoo B2 53
Esquel A5 74
Essaouira B2 57
Essen A3 40
Essequibo, *river* B3, B5 80
Essex C5 102
Esslingen B4 40
Estados, *island* C7 74
Estaire E1 102
Estany d'Engolasters, *lake* B2 36
Este, *point* E2 90
Estelí A2 87
Esterhazy H10 104
Estevan G11 104
Esther E5 94
Eston B9 104
Estonia 46
Estoril A3 36
Estrela, *mts.* B2 36
Esztergom B2 43
Etchemin, *river* L6 103
Ethelbert A3 96
Ethiopia 60
Ethiopia, *plateau* C2 60
Etna, *mt.* C3 38
Etobicoke J5 102
Etosha, *pan* B1 70
Etrechy Inset II 34
Etrek, *river* B3 22
Ettelbruck B2 33
'Eua, *island* C4 17
Euboea, *island* B2 51
Eugene, Oreg. A1 126
Eugenia, *point* A2 84
Euphrates, *river* C2 24
Eureka, Calif. A1 126
Eutsuk, *lake* J4 95
Evandale C3 97
Evansville C2 102
Evansville, Ind. E2 126
Evenkiya,
autonomous okrug C6 44
Everest, *mt.* C2 19
Everett, Wash. A1 126
Evinayong C3 66
Évora B3 36
Évreux C2 34
Évry Inset II 34
Ewa B1 16
Ewell Inset III 30
Ewo C4 66
Exeter B4 30
Exeter D4 102
Exmoor, *plateau* B3 30
Extremadura C3 37
Exuma, *sound* B3 89
Eyasi, *lake* B1 68
Eyebrow D10 104
Eyl B2 60
Eyre, *lake* C2 14
Eyre, *peninsula* C3 14
Eysturoy, *island* Inset 32

F

Fabyan E5 94
Fada C3 59
Fadiffolu, *atoll* A2 19
Faenza B1 38
Faeroe, *islands* Inset 32
Fagamalo B1 18
Făgăras C3 43
Fagasa B1 18
Fagatogo B1 18
Fair, *island* Inset I 30
Fairbanks, Alaska Inset I 126
Fairford B3 96
Fairmont Hot Springs P6 95
Fairweather, *mt.* D1 95
Faisalabad D3 21
Faizabad D3 20
Fajardo D2 90
Fakfak E2 13
Falciano C1 39
Falcon Lake D4 96
Falelatai B2 18
Falelima A2 18
Falémé, *river* C3 62
Faleniu B1 18
Fălești A2 50
Falher B3 94
Falkland, *islands* C7 74
Fallujah, al- B2 24
Falmouth B2 88
Falmouth E5 90
False Divi, *point* D5 20
Falster, *island* D4 32
Falun C2 53
Famagusta B1 27
Fan Si Pan, *mt.* A1 11
Fangliao B2 9
Fanø, *island* B3 32
Farafangana B3 69
Farafenni C2 62
Farah A2 22
Farah, *river* A2 22
Faraulep, *atoll* B2 15
Farewell, *cape* B3 15
Farewell, *cape* C3 106
Farghona D2 23
Fargo, N. Dak. D1 126
Faridpur C5 21
Farim B1 62
Farmington M3 95
Farmington, N. Mex. C2 126
Farnham Inset III 30
Faro B4 36
Faro C4 105
Farquhar, *island group* B2 70
Farrellton A6 103
Fashir, al- B2 59
Fatick A2 62
Fatoto E2 62
Fauquier N6 95
Faxaflói, *bay* A2 52
Faxälven, *river* C2 53
Faya-Largeau B3 59
Faylakah, *island* C2 24
Fayyum, al- B2 56
Fdérik B2 58
Fehmarn, *island* B1 40
Fehmarn, *strait* C4 32
Feira de Santana E3 81
Feldkirch A3 39
Felidu, *atoll* A3 19
Felixstowe D3 30
Fen, *river* E2 10
Fenelon Falls G3 102
Fengshan B2 9
Fengyüan B1 9
Feni, *islands* B2 15
Fens, *region* D3 30
Feodosiya D3 47
Fergana, *valley* D2 23
Fergus E4 102
Ferkéssédougou D2 63
Ferlo, *river* B2 62
Ferme-Neuve A5 103
Fernandina, *island* Inset 79
Fernie P6 95
Ferrara B1 38
Ferryland E5 98
Fethiye B3 27
Feuilles, *river* B2 101
Feyzabad C1 22
Fez C1 57
Fianarantsoa B3 69

Key Page
Fichtelberg, *mt.* C3 40
Fichtelgebirge, *mts.* B4 40
Field O5 95
Field E1 102
Fier A3 49
Fife, *lake* E11 104
Fig Tree C3 90
Figueira da Foz A2 36
Figueres H1 37
Figuig D1 57
Fiji 17
Filadelfia B3 75
Filchner Ice Shelf *glacier* B12 107
Filfla, *island* B3 36
Fillmore G11 104
Fimbul Ice Shelf, *glacier* B14 107
Finisterre, *cape* B1 37
Finland 53
Finland, *gulf* C3 53
Finlay, *river* J2 95
Finn, *river* C1 31
Finnegan D5 94
Finnmark, *plateau* E2 52
Fireside J1 95
Firth, *river* A1 105
Fish, *river* C4 70
Fisher Branch C3 96
Fisherton C3 96
Fishguard B3 30
Fitzgerald E1 94
Fitzroy, *mt.* B8 76
Fitzroy, *river* B1 14
Five Islands C2 100
Flagstaff, Ariz. B2 126
Flat, *island* C1 69
Flatbush C4 94
Flaxcombe A9 104
Fleet E5 94
Fleetwood C3 30
Fleming A4 96
Flensburg B1 40
Flesherton E3 102
Fleur de Lys C4 98
Flevoland, *polder* C2 32
Flin Flon A2, C2 96
Flinders, *range* C3 14
Flinders, *river* D1 14
Flint, *island* D3 17
Flint, Mich. E1 126
Flodden Field, *plain* C2 30
Florence B2 38
Florence, S.C. F2 126
Florenceville B2 97
Florencia B4 78
Flores D3 85
Flores, *island* D2 13
Flores, *sea* C2 13
Florești B2 50
Floriano D2 81
Florianópolis D4 81
Florida B3 75
Florida D2 88
Florida B2 90
Florida E3 126
Florida Keys, Fla. E3 126
Florida, *straits* B1 88
Florø A3 52
Fly, *river* A2 15
Foam Lake G9 104
Foča B2 48
Focșani D3 43
Foggia C2 38
Fogo D4 98
Fogo, *island* B4 58
Foix C5 34
Folkestone D3 30
Fomboni A2 67
Fond du Lac, *river* F2 104
Fond-du-Lac C1 104
Fonseca, *gulf* B3, C2 86
Fontainebleau C2 34
Fontas M2 95
Fontvieille A2 35
Fonuafo'ou (Falcon), *island* B3 17
Fonualei, *island* C2 17
Forest D4 102
Forestville G3 103
Fork River A3 96
Forli C1 38
Formentera, *island* G3 37
Formosa D2 74
Fort Albany D2 101
Fort Chipewyan E2 94
Fort Collins, Colo. C1 126
Fort Erie G5 102
Fort Frances B3 101
Fort Fraser K4 95
Fort Good Hope C3 99
Fort Lauderdale, Fla. E3 126
Fort Liard D4 99
Fort MacKay E2 94
Fort McMurray E3 94
Fort McPherson B3 99
Fort Myers, Fla. E3 126
Fort Nelson L2 95
Fort Nelson, *river* L1 95
Fort Norman C4 99
Fort Portal B3 61
Fort Providence E4 99
Fort Qu'Appelle G10 104
Fort Resolution F4 99
Fort Saskatchewan D4 94
Fort Severn C1 101
Fort Simpson D4 99
Fort Smith, Ark. D2 126
Fort Smith, *region* E4 99
Fort St. James K4 95
Fort St. John M3 95
Fort Steele P6 95
Fort Stockton, Tex. C2 126
Fort Vermilion C2 94
Fort Wayne, Ind. E1 126
Fort William B2 30
Fort Worth, Tex. D2 126
Fortaleza E2 81
Forteau C3 98
Forth, *estuary* C2 30

Key Page
Forth, *river* B2 30
Fortín Conde de Mirasol, *fort* E2 90
Fortín Ravelo B3 77
Fortune D5 98
Fortune Bridge C2 100
Fortune, *bay* D5 98
Foster, *river* E4 104
Fosterville B3 97
Foumban B2 65
Foumbouni A1 67
Four Falls B2 97
Foveaux, *strait* A4 15
Fox Island F2 100
Fox Lake C2 94
Fox Valley A10 104
Foxe, *basin* N3 99
Foxe, *channel* M3 99
Foxe, *peninsula* N4 99
Foyle, *inlet* C1 31
Foyle, *lake* A2 30
Foyle, *river* A2 30
Foz do Iguaçu C4 81
France 34
Frances, *lake* D5 105
Franceville B2 66
Franche-Comté D3 34
Francis G10 104
Francistown B2 69
Francois C5 98
François, *lake* K4 95
Franconian Jura, *mts.* B4 40
Frankenwald, *mts.* B3 40
Frankford H3 102
Frankfort, *capital*, Ky. E2 126
Frankfurt am Main B3 40
Frankfurt an der Oder C2 40
Franklin, *strait* J2 99
Franquelin J2 103
Franz Josef Land, *islands* A4 44
Fraser E1 95
Fraser Lake K4 95
Fraser, *river* L5, M4 95
Fraserburgh C1 30
Fraserdale D2 101
Fraserwood C4 96
Fray Bentos A2 75
Fredericia B3 32
Fredericton C3 97
Fredericton B2 100
Fredericton Jct. C3 97
Frederiksberg D3 32
Frederikshavn C1 32
Fredrikstad C4 52
Freeport A2 89
Freeport A3 100
Freetown E5 90
Freetown, *capital* A1 63
Freiberg C3 40
Freiburg A5 40
Freirina B3 76
Fréjus D5 34
Fremantle, W.A. A3, Inset I 14
French Guiana 80
French River E1 102
Frenchman, *river* B11 104
Fresnillo D3 84
Fresno, Calif. B2 126
Fria B2 62
Fribourg B2 35
Friedrichshafen B5 40
Frigate, *island* C1 91
Frisches Haff, *bay* D1 41
Friuli-Venezia Giulia C1 38
Frobisher, *lake* C4 104
Frog, *lake* E4 94
Frome, *lake* D2 14
Frontier B11 104
Frosinone C2 38
Fruška Gora, *mts.* A2 49
Frutigen B2 35
Frýdek-Místek D3 42
Fua'amotu B4 17
Fuenlabrada Inset II 37
Fuerte Olimpo D2 75
Fuerte, *river* C2 84
Fuerteventura, *island* Inset I 37
Fuhayhil, al- C2 24
Fujayrah, al- D2 25
Fuji, *mt.* C3 8
Fujian E3 10
Fujisawa C3 8
Fukue A3 8
Fukue, *island* A3 8
Fukui C2 8
Fukuoka A3 8
Fukushima D2 8
Fukuyama B3 8
Fulacunda B2 62
Fuladi, *mt.* B2 22
Fulda B3 40
Fulda, *river* B3 40
Fullarton A2 91
Funabashi D3 8
Funafuti, *capital* C3 16
Funafuti, *island* C3 16
Fundy, *bay* A3 100
Furnas, *reservoir* D4 81
Fürstenfeld E3 39
Fürth B4 40
Fushun F1 10
Futa Jallon, *plateau* B1 62
Futuna, *island* C4 18
Fuxin F1 10
Fuzhou E3 10
Fyn, *island* C3 32

G

Gaalkacyo B2 60
Gabarus G2 100
Gabès C3 57
Gabès, *gulf* C2 57
Gaborone, *capital* B3 69
Gabon 66
Gabriel, *island* C1 69
Gabrovo D3 50
Gabú C1 62

Key Page
Gacko B2 48
Gaeta C2 38
Gafsa B2 57
Gagetown C3 97
Gagnoa D3 63
Gagnon C3 101
Gagra A2 45
Gainesville, Fla. E3 126
Gainsborough J11 104
Gairdner, *lake* C3 14
Gaizina, *mt.* C2 46
Galahad E5 94
Galana, *river* E5 61
Galápagos, *islands* Inset 79
Galați E3 43
Galena Bay O6 95
Galicia C1 37
Galilee, *region* B1 26
Galle B5 19
Gallegos, *river* A7 74
Gallinas, *point* C1 78
Gällivare D1 53
Galoa B3 17
Galveston, Tex. D3 126
Galway B2 31
Galway, *bay* B2 31
Gam, *river* A1 11
Gambia, The 62
Gambia, *river* B2, C3, D2 62
Gambo D5 98
Gamprin B1 33
Gan, *river* E3 10
Gananoque J3 102
Găncă B2 45
Gander D5 98
Gander Bay D4 98
Gandhinagar B4 20
Ganganagar B3 20
Ganges, *river* E3 20
Gangtok E3 20
Gansu C1, D2 10
Ganzhou E3 10
Gao D2 58
Gaoua C3 64
Gap D4 34
Garabil, *plateau* D3 22
Garabogazköl, *lake* A2 22
Garda, *lake* B1 38
Garden Hill D2 96
Garden Reach Inset II 20
Garden, *island* Inset I 14
Garden, *river* A1 102
Gardenton C4 96
Gardez B2 22
Gardner, *canal* H4 95
Gardner, *island* B2 17
Garissa E4 61
Garland A3 96
Garmisch-Partenkirchen B5 40
Garnish D5 98
Garonne, *river* C4 34
Garoowe B2 60
Garoua B2 65
Garry, *lake* H3 99
Garson Lake A4 104
Garulia Inset II 20
Gary, Ind. E1 126
Gascoyne *river* A2 14
Gash, *river* B2 60
Gaspé M3 103
Gaspé, *peninsula* L3 103
Gaspereau Forks D2 97
Gatal, *cape* E4 37
Gateshead C2 30
Gatico B2 76
Gatineau A6 103
Gatineau Park A6 103
Gatineau, *river* A4, A5 103
Gatún, *lake* C2 87
Gau, *island* B3 17
Gauhati F3 20
Gaultois D5 98
Gavarr C2 45
Gävle C2 53
Gaya E4 20
Gaya A3 59
Gazanjyk B2 22
Gazelle, *peninsula* B2 15
Gaziantep D3 27
Gbarnga B2 63
Gdańsk D1 41
Gdańsk, *gulf* D1 41
Gdynia D1 41
Gêba, *river* C1 62
Geelong, Vic. D3 14
Gege B2 71
Geidam F1 65
Geikie, *river* F3 104
Gejiu D3 10
Gela C3 38
Gelibolu (Gallipoli) A2 27
Gelsenkirchen A3 40
Gem D6 94
Gembloux C2 33
Gemena B1 67
General Eugenio A. Garay A2 75
General Santos C5 12
General, *river* C3 86
Genesee C4 94
Geneva A2 35
Geneva, *lake* A2 35
Genk D2 33
Gennargentu, *mts.* B2 38
Genoa B1 38
Genoa, *gulf* B1 38
Gentilly Inset II 34
Gentofte D3 32
George B3 71
George Town A2 13
George, *river* C2 101
Georgetown B2 91
Georgetown D2 62
Georgetown C2 100
Georgetown, *capital* B2 80
Georgia 45
Georgia E2 126
Georgian, *bay* E2 102
Gera C3 40

Key Page
Geral, *range* C4 81
Gerald A4 96
Geraldton C3 101
Geraldton, W.A. A2 14
Gerlachovka, *mt.* C2 42
Germany 40
Germiston C2 71
Gerona H2 37
Getafe E2, Inset II 37
Gevgelija C2 48
Geylegphug B3 19
Ghabah C2 25
Ghadamis A1 56
Ghaghara, *river* D3 20
Ghana 64
Ghanzi A2 69
Ghardaia B1 57
Gharyan B1 56
Ghat B3 56
Ghatkopar Inset I 20
Ghaydah, al- C1 25
Ghazal, *river* B4 59
Ghazni B2 22
Ghent B1 33
Ghurdaqah, al- B2 56
Giant's Causeway, *headland* A2 30
Gibraltar 36
Gibraltar, *strait* D5 37
Gibson, *desert* B2 14
Giessen B3 40
Gifford, *river* M2 99
Gifu C3 8
Giglio, *island* B2 38
Gijón D1 37
Gikongoro B2 61
Gilbert Plains A3 96
Gilbert, *islands* A1 17
Gilbert, *river* D1 14
Gilgit E2 21
Gilliam D1 96
Gillingham D3 30
Gimie, *mt.* A2 91
Gimli C4 96
Giresun D2 27
Gironde, *river* B4 34
Gisborne C2 15
Gisenyi B1 61
Gitarama B2 61
Gitega B2 61
Giurgiu C4 43
Giza B2 56
Gizo A1 16
Gjirokastër B3 49
Gjoa Haven J3 99
Gjøvik C3 52
Glace Bay H1 100
Gladstone B4 96
Gladstone, Qld. E2 14
Glåma, *river* C3 52
Glanvillia A2 90
Glasgow B2 30
Glasgow, Mont. C1 126
Glaslyn B7 104
Glastonbury C3 30
Gleichen D6 94
Glen Margaret D3 100
Glenboro B4 96
Glencoe D5 102
Glenella B4 96
Glenholme D2 100
Glenora G2 95
Glenwood D5 98
Glidden A9 104
Glifádha Inset 51
Glittertinden, *mt.* B3 52
Gliwice D3 41
Głogów C3 41
Gloucester C3 30
Gloucester K2 102
Glover, *reef* C3 85
Glovertown D5 98
Gmünd D2 39
Goba C3 60
Gobabis C2 70
Gobi, *desert* D1 10
Godavari, *river* C5 20
Godbout J2 103
Goderich D4 102
Godfrey J3 102
Godoy Cruz B3 74
Gods, *lake* D2 96
Gogama D3 101
Goiânia D3 81
Goiás D3 81
Golan Heights, *occ. terr.* A3 27
Gold Coast, Qld. E2 14
Gold River J6 95
Golden O5 95
Golden Lake H2 102
Golea, el- B2 57
Golfito C4 86
Golmud C2 10
Golyama Kamchiya, *river* E2 50
Goma C2 67
Gombe F2 65
Gomera, *island* Inset I 37
Gómez Palacio D2 84
Gonaïves C1 89
Gonâve, *gulf* B1 89
Gonâve, *island* B2 89
Gonder B1 60
Gongola, *river* F2 65
Goobies E5 98
Good Hope, *cape* A3 71
Goodlands C2 69
Goodlands A4 96
Goodsoil A6 104
Göppingen B4 40
Gorakhpur D3 20
Goražde B2 48
Gordon, *lake* E3 94
Gordondale A3 94
Gore B2 60
Gore Bay C2 102
Gori C4 45
Goris D3 45
Gorizia C1 38
Görlitz C3 40

Key Page
Gorlovka D2 47
Gorno-Altay, *republic* D6 44
Gorno-Altaysk D6 44
Goroka A2 15
Gorontalo D1 13
Gorzów Wielkopolski B2 41
Gosford, N.S.W. E3 14
Goshen F2 100
Goslar B3 40
Gospić B3 48
Gosport C4 30
Göta, *canal* B3 53
Göteborg och Bohus B3 53
Gotha B3 40
Gotland, *island* C3 53
Gotsu B3 8
Göttingen B3 40
Gouda B2 32
Goudiri C2 62
Gouin, *reservoir* B3 103
Goundam C2 58
Gouré C3 59
Govan E9 104
Governador Valadares D3 81
Gowd-e Zereh, *lake* A3 22
Göyçay B2 45
Gozo, *island* A1 36
Graaf-Reinet B3 71
Gračanica B1 48
Gracias A2 86
Grafton, N.S.W. E2 14
Graham Land, *region* C11 107
Graham, *island* F4 95
Graham, *island* K1 99
Grahamstown C3 71
Grampian, *mts.* B2 30
Gran Canaria, *island* Inset I 37
Gran Chaco, *region* B3 75
Granada B3 87
Granada E4 37
Granby D6 103
Grand Anse B1 91
Grand Bahama, *island* A2 89
Grand Bale C2 69
Grand Bank D5 98
Grand Bay C1 91
Grand Bay C3 97
Grand Bend D4 102
Grand Bruit B5 98
Grand Canyon, Ariz. B2 126
Grand Centre E4 94
Grand Cess B3 63
Grand Erg Occidental, *desert* B1 57
Grand Erg Oriental, *desert* B2 57
Grand Falls B1 97
Grand Falls-Windsor D5 98
Grand Forks N6 95
Grand Forks, N. Dak. D1 126
Grand Island, Nebr. D1 126
Grand Junction, Colo. C2 126
Grand Manan, *island* C4 97
Grand Marais C4 96
Grand Narrows G2 100
Grand Pré C2 100
Grand Rapids B2 96
Grand Rapids, Mich. E1 126
Grand Roy B2 91
Grand Santi A1 80
Grand Turk, *capital* D4 89
Grand Turk, *island* D4 89
Grand Valley E4 102
Grand, *canal* C2 31
Grand, *harbor* C2 36
Grand, *lake* D2 97
Grand, *lake* C4 98
Grand, *river* C3 69
Grand-Etang F1 100
Grand-Mère D5 103
Grand-Remous A5 103
Grande Baleine, *river* A2 101
Grande de Añasco, *river* A2 90
Grande de Manatí, *river* C2 90
Grande de Matagalpa, *river* B2 87
Grande Prairie A3 94
Grande, *bay* B7 74
Grande, *range* C2 75
Grande, *river* B3 77
Grande, *river* D3 81
Grande, *river* B3 86
Grande-Anse D1 97
Grande-Rivière M3 103
Grande-Vallée M2 103
Grândola A3 36
Grandview A3 96
Granisle J4 95
Grantham C3 30
Granville Lake A1 96
Gras, *lake* F4 99
Grass, *river* A3, B2 96
Grassland D4 94
Grauspitz, *mt.* B2 33
Gravelbourg D11 104
Gravenhurst F3 102
Gravesend Inset III 30
Gravois, *point* B3 89
Graz D3 39
Great Abaco, *island* B2 89
Great Alföld, *plain* B2 43
Great Artesian, *basin* D2 14
Great Australian, *bight* B3 14
Great Bahama, *bank* B4 89
Great Barrier, *island* C2 15
Great Barrier, *reef* D1 14
Great *basin*, Nev. B2 126
Great Bear, *lake* D3 99
Great Britain 30
Great Dividing, *range* D1, D3 14
Great Exuma, *island* B3 89
Great Falls C4 96
Great Falls, Mont. B1 126
Great Fish, *river* C3 71
Great Inagua, *island* C4 89
Great Indian, *desert* B3 20
Great Karroo, *plateau* B3 71
Great Nicobar, *island* F7 20
Great Rift, *valley* 55
Great Ruaha, *river* C2 68

Key Page
Great Salt, *lake*, Utah B1 126
Great Sand Sea, *desert* A2 56
Great Sandy, *desert* B2 14
Great Scarcies, *river* A1 63
Great Sea, *reef* B1 17
Great Slave, *lake* F4 99
Great Victoria, *desert* B2 14
Great Wall of China D2 10
Great Yarmouth D3 30
Great Zab, *river* B1 24
Great, *plains* C1 126
Greater Hinggan, *range* F1 10
Greater Sunda, *islands* B2 13
Gréboun, *mt.* B1 59
Gredos, *mts.* D2 37
Greece 51
Greeley, Colo. C1 126
Greely, *fjord* L1 99
Green Bay, Wis. E1 126
Green Lake C6 104
Green, *islands* B2 15
Greenland 106
Greenland, *sea* D2 106
Greenock B2 30
Greensboro, N.C. F2 126
Greenville B3 63
Greenville, S.C. E2 126
Greenwood N6 95
Greifswald C1 40
Grenå C2 32
Grenada 91
Grenada, *island* B2 91
Grenadines, *islands* A3, B1, C1 91
Grenfell H10 104
Grenoble D4 34
Gretna C4 96
Greve D3 32
Grevenmacher B2 33
Grey River C5 98
Grey, *range* D2 14
Greymouth B3 15
Gribingui, *river* A2 66
Griffin G11 104
Griffith, N.S.W. D3 14
Grijalva, *river* F4 84
Grimsby C3 30
Grimsey, *island* B1 52
Grinnell, *peninsula* J1 99
Griqualand East, *region* C3 71
Griqualand West, *region* B2 71
Griquatown B2 71
Grise Ford M1 99
Griswold A4 96
Groningen B2 80
Groningen D1 32
Gronlid F7 104
Groote Eylandt, *island* C1 14
Grootfontein C1 70
Grootvloer, *pan* B2 71
Gros Islet B1 91
Gros Morne Natl. Park C4 98
Gros-Morne L2 103
Grosseto B2 38
Grossglockner, *mt.* C3 39
Groundbirch M3 95
Groznyy E4 44
Grudziądz D2 41
Grunthal C4 96
Guacanayabo, *gulf* D3 88
Guadalajara E2 37
Guadalajara, *state capital* D3 84
Guadalcanal, *island* A1 16
Guadalquivir, *river* D4 37
Guadalupe, *reservoir* Inset 84
Guadarrama, *mts.* D2 37
Guadeloupe, *island* 82
Guadiana, *river* C3 37
Guaillabamba, *river* B2 79
Guainía, *river* C4 78
Guajara Mirim B3 81
Guajira, *peninsula* C1 78
Guam, *island* 5
Guanacaste, *range* A2 86
Guanaja, *island* B1 86
Guanajuato, *state capital* D3 84
Guanare C2 79
Guandu, *river* Inset I 81
Guangdong E3 10
Guangxi Zhuang D3 10
Guangzhou E3 10
Guánica B2 90
Guantánamo E3 88
Guaporé, *river* B3 81
Guaqui A3 77
Guaranda B3 79
Guarda B2 36
Guarujá Inset II 81
Guarulhos Inset II 81
Guasave C2 84
Guatemala 85
Guatemala City, *capital* C5 85
Guaviare, *river* C4 78
Guayaguayare A2 91
Guayama C3 90
Guayambre, *river* B2 86
Guayanilla B2 90
Guayape, *river* B2 86
Guayaquil B4 79
Guayaquil, *gulf* A4 79
Guayas, *river* B4 79
Guaymas B2 84
Guaynabo C2 90
Guben C3 40
Gudauta A2 45
Gudenå, *river* B2 32
Guecho E1 37
Guéckédou C3 62
Guelph E4 102
Guelta Zemmur B1 58
Guéret C3 34
Guernica Y Luno E1 37
Guernsey, *island* Inset II 30
Guerrero D4 84
Guerrero Negro B2 84
Guiana, *highlands* D2 79
Guiers, *lake* B1 62
Guilarte, *mt.* B2 90
Guildford C3 30

Key Page
Guilin E3 10
Guimarães A2 36
Guinea 62
Guinea, *gulf* 55
Guinea-Bissau 62
Güiria D1 79
Guiyang D3 10
Guizhou D3 10
Gujranwala E3 21
Gujrat E3 21
Gulbarga C5 20
Gulbene D2 46
Gulf Coastal, *plain* D3 126
Gulistan C2 23
Gull Lake B10 104
Gull, *lake* C5 94
Gulu C2 61
Gumdag B2 22
Gummi C1 65
Gunisao, *river* C2 96
Gunnbjørn Fjeld, *mt.* D2 106
Gunton C4 96
Guntur D5 20
Gurabo D2 90
Guri, *reservoir* D2 79
Gusau D1 65
Gushgy D3 22
Gushgy, *river* D3 22
Gushikawa Inset II 8
Gustavo A. Madero Inset 84
Güstrow C2 40
Guyana 80
Guysborough F2 100
Gwadar B5 21
Gwai, *river* A2 69
Gwalior C3 20
Gweru B2 69
Gyda, *peninsula* B5 44
Gympie, Qld. E2 14
Gyöngyös B2 43
Győr A2 43
Gypsumville B3 96
Gyumri A2 45
Gyzylarbat B2 22

H

Ha Giang A1 11
Ha'apai, *island group* B3 17
Haapsalu B2 46
Haarlem B2 32
Habarut C1 25
Habay A2 94
Haboro Inset I 8
Hachijo, *island* C3 8
Hachinohe D1 8
Hachioji C3 8
Haddummati, *atoll* A4 19
Hadejia, *river* E1 65
Hadera B1 26
Haderslev B3 33
Hadhramaut, *district* B1 25
Hadithah, al- B2 24
Haedo, *range* B2 75
Haeju A3 9
Hafford C8 104
Hafnarfjördhur A3 52
Hagen A3 40
Hague, *cape* B2 34
Haha, *island* Inset III 8
Haifa B1 26
Haifa, *bay* B1 26
Haikou E4 10
Hail B1 24
Hailar E1 10
Hainan D4 10
Haines Junction B5 105
Haiphong B2 11
Hairé Lao B1 62
Haiti 89
Hajdúböszörmény C2 43
Haji Ibrahim, *mt.* B1 24
Hajjah A1 25
Haka B2 12
Hakodate D1, Inset I 8
Halab (Aleppo) A1 27
Halaib D1 59
Halba B1 26
Halberstadt B3 40
Haldimand F5 102
Halfmoon Bay L6 95
Haliburton G2 102
Halifax C3 30
Halifax, *capital* D3 100
Halil, *river* D4 22
Halisahar Inset II 20
Hall Beach M3 99
Hall, *peninsula* P4 99
Halla-san, *mt.* Inset 9
Hallboro B4 96
Halle C2 33
Halle B3 40
Hallingdal, *valley* B3 52
Halmahera, *island* D1 13
Halmstad B3 53
Haltiatunturi, mt B1 53
Halton Hills F4 102
Hamadan B3 22
Hamah A2 27
Hamamatsu C3 8
Hamar C3 52
Hambantota C5 19
Hamburg B2 40
Hämeenlinna B2 53
Hameln B2 40
Hamersley, *range* A2 14
Hamgyŏng, *mts.* C2 9
Hamhŭng B3 9
Hami C1 10
Hamilton C2 15
Hamilton B2 30
Hamilton F4 102
Hamilton, *inlet* B2 98
Hamiota A4 96
Hamm A3 40
Hammamat, al- C1 57
Hammamet, *gulf* C1 57
Hammerfest E1 52
Hammonds Plains D3 100
Hammondvale D3 97
Hampden C4 98
Hampstead J5 103
Hampton D3 97
Hamun-e Jaz Murian, *lake* D4 22
Hamun-e Saberi, *lake* A2 22
Han, *river* E2 10
Han, *river* B4 9
Hanau B3 40
Handan E2 10
Hangayn, *mts.* B2 11
Hangö B3 53
Hangzhou F2 10
Hanley D9 104
Hannibal, Mo. D2 126
Hannover B2 40
Hanoi, *capital* A2 11
Hanover D3 102
Hantzsch, *river* O3 99
Hanzhong D2 10
Haora E4, Inset II 20
Haparanda D1 53
Happy Valley-Goose Bay A2, E4 98
Har Us, *lake* B2 11
Harad C1 24
Harare, *capital* B1 69
Harbel A2 63
Harbin F1 10
Harbour Breton D5 98
Harbour Deep C4 98
Harbour, *island* B2 89
Harcourt D2 97
Hardangerfjord, *fjord* B4 52
Hardangervidda, *plateau* B3 52
Hardwood Lake H2 102
Hare Bay D5 98
Harer D2 60
Hargeysa A2 60
Hargrave A4 96
Harirud, *river* A2 22
Harlow Inset III 30
Härnösand C2 53
Harper C3 63
Harris C9 104
Harrisburg, *capital*, Pa. F1 126
Harrogate C2 30
Harstad D2 52
Hart, *ranges* L3 95
Hart, *river* B3 105
Hartford, *capital*, Conn. F1 126
Hartland B2 97
Hartley Bay H4 95
Hartney A4 96
Harvey C3 97
Harwill C3 96
Harz, *mts.* B3 40
Hasa, al-, *region* C1 24
Hasakah, al- B1 27
Hashtadan, *region* E3 22
Haslemere Inset III 30
Hasselt D2 33
Hastings C2 15
Hastings D4 30
Hastings H3 102
Hat Yai B5 12
Hatillo B2 90
Hato Mayor C2 89
Hatteras *cape*, N.C. F2 126
Hattiesburg, Miss. E2 126
Haugesund B4 52
Haultain, *river* D4 104
Haute-Normandie C2 34
Havana, *capital* B1 88
Havel, *river* C2 40
Havelock H3 102
Havířov D3 42
Havre, Mont. C1 126
Havre-St-Pierre D3 101
Hawaii Inset II 126
Hawaii *island*, Hawaii Inset II 126
Hawalli C2 24
Hawar, *islands* B2 25
Hawea, *lake* A3 15
Hawf C1 25
Hawick C2 30
Hawke Harbour D2 98
Hawke's Bay C4 98
Hawke, *bay* C2 15
Hawkesbury L2 102
Hay River E4 99
Hay, *river* A2, B1 94
Hayes, *river* D1, D2 96
Hayma C2 25
Hayter E5 94
Hazelton J3 95
Hazelton, *mts.* H3 95
Hazlet B10 104
Hazm, al- A1 25
Hearst D3 101
Heart's Content E5 98
Heaslip A4 96
Heath Steele C1 97
Hebei E2 10
Hebrides, *sea* A1 30
Hebron E3 98
Hecate, *strait* G4 95
Hecla C3 96
Hecla and Griper, *bay* F1 99
Hedley M6 95
Heerenveen C2 32
Heerlen C4 32
Hefei E2 10
Hegang G1 10
Heha, *mt.* B2 61
Heidelberg B4 40
Heidenheim B4 40
Heilbronn B4 40
Heilong (Amur), *river* F1 10
Heilongjiang F1 10
Heimaey, *island* A3 52
Heinsburg E4 94
Heisler D5 94
Hekla, *volcano* B3 52
Hel D1 41
Helen, *reef* Inset 17
Helena, *capital*, Mont. B1 126
Helgoland, *island* A1 40
Hellin F3 37
Helmand, *river* A2 22
Helmsdale E5 94
Helsingborg B3 53
Helsingør D2 32
Helsinki, *capital* B2 53
Heming Lake A2 96
Henan E2 10
Henashi, *cape* C1 8
Hengch'un B2 9
Hengelo D2 32
Hengyang E3 10
Henley Harbour D3 98
Hensall D4 102
Henzada B3 12
Herat A2 22
Herb Lake B2 96
Herbert C10 104
Heredia B2 86
Hereford C3 30
Heriot Bay K6 95
Hermitage-Sandyville D5 98
Hermon, *mt.* A3 27
Hermosillo, *state capital* B2 84
Hernád, *river* C1 43
Herne A3 40
Herning B2 32
Hertford Inset III 30
Herzliyya B1 26
Hess, *river* C4 105
Hesse B3 40
Hetauda C2 19
Hiatikulu B2 71
Hibbing, Minn. D1 126
Hicks Bay C2 15
Hidaka, *mts.* Inset I 8
Hidalgo E3 84
Hidalgo del Parral C2 84
Hieflau D3 39
Hierro, *island* Inset I 37
Higashiosaka B3 8
High Atlas, *ranges* B2 57
High Level B2 94
High River D6 94
High Tatra, *mts.* D4 41
High Wycombe Inset III 30
Highrock A1 96
Highrock, *lake* A1 96
Higüey D2 89
Hiiumaa, *island* B2 46
Hijaz, al-, *region* A1 24
Hilda E6 94
Hilden D2 100
Hildesheim B2 40
Hill Bank B2 85
Hillaby, *mt.* A3 91
Hillah, al- B2 24
Hillerød D3 32
Hillsborough C1 91
Hillsborough E3 97
Hillsborough, *bay* B2 100
Hilo, Hawaii Inset II 126
Hilton Beach B1 102
Hilversum C2 32
Himalayas, *mts.* 7
Himeji B3 8
Hinche C1 89
Hindelang B5 40
Hindu Kush, *range* B1 21
Hino, *cape* B3 8
Hinton B4 94
Hirakata B3 8
Hirakud, *reservoir* D4 20
Hirara Inset II 8
Hirmil, al- B1 26
Hirosake D1 8
Hiroshima B3 8
Hirtshals B1 32
Hisabpur Inset II 20
Hitachi D2 8
Hixon L4 95
Hjørring B1 32
Hkakabo Razi, *mt.* C1 12
Ho C3 64
Ho Chi Minh City B4 11
Hoa Binh A2 11
Hobart, Tas., *capital* D4 14
Hobsons, *bay* Inset V 14
Hobyo B2 60
Hoceima, al- D1 57
Hodgeville D10 104
Hodgson C3 96
Hódmezővásárhely C2 43
Hoeryŏng C1 9
Hof B3 40
Höfn C2 52
Hohe Tauern, *mts.* C3 39
Hohhot E1 10
Hokkaido, *island* D1, Inset I 8
Hoktemberyan B2 45
Holbæk C3 32
Holden D4 94
Holdfast E10 104
Holetown A3 91
Holguín E3 88
Holhol B2 60
Holland B4 96
Holman E2 99
Holon B1 26
Holstebro B2 32
Holton C2 98
Holyhead B3 30
Holyrood E5 98
Holywood B2 30
Homathko, *river* K5 95
Hombori Tondo, *mt.* C2 58
Hombori, *mts.* C2 58
Homer, Alaska Inset I 126
Homo, *bay* B2 18
Homs A2 27
Homyel E3 47
Hon Gai B2 11
Hondo C3 94
Hondo, *river* B1 85
Honduras 86
Honduras, *gulf* A1 86
Hong Kong, S.A.R. E3 10
Hong Kong, *island* Inset 10
Hongze, *lake* E2 10
Honiara, *capital* A1 16
Honolulu, *capital*,
Hawaii Inset II 126
Honshu, *island* C2 8
Hoogeveen D2 32
Hoorn C2 32
Hope M6 95
Hope Bay C2 88
Hope Valley E5 94
Hopedale A1 98
Hopedale E3 98
Hopewell Cape E3 97
Horgèn C1 35
Hormigueros A2 90
Hormuz, *strait* D4 22
Horn, *cape* C9 76
Horn, *cape* A1 52
Hornád, *river* C2 42
Hornavan, *lake* C1 53
Hornepayne D3 101
Horsburgh, *atoll* A2 19
Horse, *river* D3 94
Horsens B3 32
Horton, *river* D3 99
Hospitalet H2 37
Hoste, *island* C9 76
Hot Springs, Ark. D2 126
Hotan A2 10
Hotchkiss B2 94
Hottah, *lake* E3 99
Houghton, Mich. E1 126
Houmt Souk C3 57
Houston J4 95
Houston, Tex. D3 126
Hovd, *river* B2 11
Hove C4 30
Hoverla, *mt.* A2 47
Hövsgöl, *lake* C1 11
Howley C4 98
Hoy, *island* Inset I 30
Hradec Králové B2 42
Hrazdan B2 45
Hrazdan, *river* B2 45
Hrodna A3 47
Hron, *river* B2 42
Hsinchu B1 9
Hsinchuang B1 9
Hsintien B1 9
Hsinying B2 9
Hua Hin B3 12
Huacho B3 77
Huai, *river* E2 10
Huainan E2 10
Hualien B2 9
Huallaga, *river* B2 77
Huambo C4 70
Huancavelica B3 77
Huancayo B3 77
Huang (Yellow), *river* D2, E2 10
Huánuco B2 77
Huapí, *mts.* B2 87
Huaraz B2 77
Huascarán, *mt.* B2 77
Hubbards C3 100
Hubei E2 10
Hubley D3 100
Hubli-Dharwar C5 20
Hudaydah, al- A2 25
Huddersfield C3 30
Hudiksvall C2 53
Hudson Bay H8 104
Hudson's Hope M3 95
Hudson, *bay* J3 92
Hudson, *strait* O4 99
Hue B3 11
Huehuetenango B4 85
Huelva C4 37
Huesca F1 37
Hufuf, al- C1 24
Hugli, *river* Inset II 20
Hugli-Chunchura Inset II 20
Hŭich'ŏn B2 9
Huila, *mt.* A4 78
Hŭksan Chedo, *islands* A5 9
Hull A6 103
Hulun, *lake* E1 10
Hulwan B2 56
Humacao D2 90
Humber, *river* D3 30
Humboldt E8 104
Humenné C2 42
Humuya, *river* B2 86
Húnaflói, *bay* A2 52
Hunan E3 10
Hunedoara B3 43
Hungary 43
Hŭngnam B3 9
Hünsruck, *mts.* A4 40
Hunter River B2 100
Huntington, W. Va. E2 126
Huntsville F2 102
Huntsville, Ala. E2 126
Hunyani, *river* B1 69
Huon, *islands* B1 18
Huon, *peninsula* A2 15
Huron, *lake* E1 126
Hussar D5 94
Hutchinson, Kans. D2 126
Hvannadalshnúkur, *mt.* B3 52
Hvar, *island* C3 48
Hvítá, *river* A2 52
Hwange A2 69
Hyargas, *lake* B2 11
Hyderabad C5 20
Hyderabad C5 21
Hyesan C2 9
Hyland Post H2 95
Hyland, *river* D5 105
Hylo D4 94
Hyvinkää B2 53

I

Ialomița, *river* D3 43
Ialpug, *river* B2 50
Iași D2 43
Ibadan B4 65
Ibagué B3 78
Ibar, *river* B3 49
Ibaraki B3 8
Ibarra B2 79
Ibb A2 25
Ibérico, *mts.* F2 37
Ibiza G4 37
Ibiza, *island* G3 37
Iboundji, *mt.* A2 66
Ibrahim, *river* A1 26
Ibri C1 25
Ica B3 77
Içá, *river* B2 81
Icacos, *key* D2 90
Ice Cap C2 106
Iceland 52
Ich'ŏn B3 9
Ichihara D3 8
Ichikawa D3 8
Ichilo, *river* B3 77
Ichinomiya C3 8
Idaho B1 126
Idaho Falls, Idaho B1 126
Iddesleigh E6 94
Idfu B3 56
Ídhra, *island* B3 51
Idlib A2 27
Idrija B2 48
Ife C4 65
Igarka C6 44
Igloolik M3 99
Igombe, *river* B1 68
Iguaçu, *falls* C4 81
Iguaçu, *river* E2 74
Iguala E4 84
Iguazú, *falls* E4 75
Ih Bogd Uul, *mt.* C3 11
Ihavandiffulu, *atoll* A1 19
Ihosy B3 69
Ilan B1 9
Iijoki, *river* C1 53
Iisalmi C2 53
Ijevan C2 45
IJssel, *river* D2 32
IJsselmeer, *sea* C2 32
Ijuw C2 16
Ikaría, *island* C3 51
Ikeja B4 65
Ikela B2 67
Iki, *island* A3 8
Ikorodu B4 65
Ila C3 65
Ilam D3 19
Ilam B3 22
Île-à-la-Crosse C5 104
Île-de-France C2 34
Ilebo B2 67
Ilesha C4 65
Ilford D1 96
Ilhéus E3 81
Ili, *river* D2 23
Iligan C4 12
Illampu, *mt.* A3 77
Illapel B4 76
Illimani, *mt.* A3 77
Illinois E1 126
Illo C4 77
Iloilo B4 12
Ilorin C3 65
Imatra C2 53
Imbarié Inset I 81
Imbéry B2 90
Imeni Ismail Samani, *peak.* B1 23
Imi D3 60
Imjin, *river* B3 9
Imlili A2 58
Imperatriz D2 81
Imperial E9 104
Imperial Mills E4 94
Imperial, *river* B6 76
Impfondo D3 66
Imphal F4 20
Inari, *lake* C1 53
Inch'ŏn B4 9
Incles, *river* C1 36
Indalsälven, *river* B2 53
India 20
Indian Bay D4 96
Indian Brook G1 100
Indian Cabins B1 94
Indian Harbour D3 100
Indian Head G10 104
Indiana E1 126
Indianapolis, *capital*, Ind. E2 126
Indigirka, *river* C9 44
Indispensable, *reefs* B2 16
Indonesia 13
Indore C4 20
Indus, *river* C4, E2 21
Ingleside K3 102
Ingolstadt B4 40
Ingonish G1 100
Ingonish Beach G1 100
Ingushetiya, republic E4 44
Inhambane B5 68
Inhomirim Inset I 81
Inland, *sea* B3 8
Inn, *river* B3, C2 39
Inner Hebrides, *islands* A2 30
Inner Mongolia E1 10
Innisfail D5 94
Innisfil F3 102
Innsbruck B3 39
Inta C5 44
Interlaken B2 35
International Falls, Minn. D1 126
Inthanon, *mt.* B2 12
Inukjuak A2 101
Inuvik B3 99
Inuvik, *region* C3 99
Invercargill A4 15
Invermay G9 104
Inverness B1 30
Inverness F1 100
Inwood C4 96
Inyangani, *mt.* C2 69
Ioánnina B2 51
Ionian, *islands* B2 51
Ionian, *sea* A2 51
Iori, *river* C4 45
Iowa D1 126
Ipel', *river* B2 42
Ipiíba Inset I 81
Ipoh A2 13
Ipoly, *river* B1 43
Ipswich D3 30
Iqaluit, *capital*, Nunivut P4 99
Iquique B2 76
Iquitos C1 77
Iracoubo B1 80
Iráklion C4 51
Iran 22
Iranshahr E4 22
Irapuato D3 84
Iraq 24
Irazú, *volcano* C3 86
Irbe, *strait* A3 46
Irbid A1 26
Irbil B1 24
Ireland 31
Iri B5 9
Irian Jaya, *region* E2 13
Iringa C2 68
Iriomote, *island* Inset II 8
Iriona C2 86
Irish, *sea* B3 30
Irkutsk D7 44
Iron Bridge B1 102
Iron Gate Reservoir B3 43
Iroquois Falls D3 101
Irrawaddy, *river* B2 12
Irtysh, *river* D1 23
Irtysh, *river* D5 44
Isabela A1 90
Isabela, *island* Inset 79
Isabelia, *mts.* B2 87
Ísafjördhur A1 52
Isangel C4 18
Isar, *river* C4 40
Ischia, *island* C2 38
Ise C3 8
Ise, *bay* C3 8
Isère, *river* D4 34
Isernia C2 38
Iseyin B4 65
Isherton B4 80
Ishigaki, *island* Inset II 8
Ishikari, *river* Inset I 8
Ishim D5 44
Ishim, *river* C1 23
Ishinomaki D2 8
Ishinomaki, *bay* D2 8
Ishizuchi, *mt.* B3 8
Isiro C1 67
Iskenderun D3 27
Iskŭr, *river* C2 50
Islamabad, *capital* D3 21
Island Lake D2 96
Island, *lake* D2 96
Islay, *island* A2 30
Isle aux Morts B5 98
Islington J6 102
Ismailiyah, al- B1 56
Isoka C2 67
Isparta B3 27
Israel 26
İstanbul B2 27
Istria, *peninsula* A2 48
Italy 38
İzmir A2 27
İzmit B2 27
Itabira D3 81
Itabuna E3 81
Itaipu Inset I 81
Itaipú, *reservoir* E4 75
Itajaí D4 81
Itanagar F3 20
Itapecerica da Serra Inset II 81
Itapeva Inset II 81
Itaquaquecetuba Inset II 81
Iténez, *river* B2 77
Itháki, *island* B2 51
Ittoqqortoormiit
(Scoresbysund) D2 106
Ituna G9 104
Ivalo C1 53
Ivano-Frankivsk A2 47
Ivanovo D3 44
Ivindo, *river* B1 66
Ivujivik A1 101
Iwaki D2 8
Iwakuni B3 8
Iwo C4 65
Iwo Jima, *island* Inset III 8
Ixelles C2 33
Ixtapa D4 84
Ixtapaluca Inset 84
Izabal, *lake* E4 85
Izhevsk D4 44
Izki C1 25
Izmail B3 47
Iztacalco Inset 84
Iztapalapa Inset 84
Izu, *islands* C3 8
Izu, *peninsula* C3 8
Izuhara A3 8

J

Jabal al-Akhdar, al-, *mts.* C1 25
Jabal al-Uwaynat, *mt.* D3 56
Jabal an-Nabi Shuayb, *mt.* A1 25
Jabal an-Nusayriyah, *mts.* A2 27
Jabal Katrinah, *mt.* B2 56
Jabal Ramm, *mt.* A3 26
Jabal Tuwayq, *mts.* B2 24
Jabal Zuqar, *island* A2 25
Jabalpur C4 20
Jaboatão E2 81
Jacare-Acanga C2 81
Jackhead C3 96
Jackson's Arm C4 98
Jackson, *capital*, Miss. D2 126
Jackson, port Inset IV 14
Jackson, Wyo. B1 126
Jacksonville, Fla. E2 126
Jacmel C2 89
Jacques-Cartier, *river* E4 103
Jacquet River C1 97
Jadabpur Inset II 20
Jadida, el- B1 57
Jaén E4 37

	Key	Page
Jaffna	B2	19
Jafr, al-	B2	26
Jagdalpur	D5	20
Jaghbub, al-	D2	56
Jahrah, al-	B2	24
Jamaica		**88**
Jaipur	C3	20
Jaipurhat	B3	21
Jajce	B1	48
Jakarta, *capital*	B2	13
Jakobstad	B2	53
Jakupica, *mts.*	B2	48
Jalal-Abad	C2	23
Jalalabad	C2	22
Jalapa Enríquez, *state capital*	E4	84
Jalingo	F3	65
Jalisco	D4	84
Jalu	D2	56
Jaluit, *island*	B2	16
Jamaame	A3	60
Jamalpur	C4	21
Jambi	B2	13
James, *bay*	J3	92
Jammu	B2	20
Jamnagar	B4	20
Jampur	Inset II	20
Jämsä	C2	53
Jamshedpur	E4	20
Jamuna, *river*	C4	21
Jan Lake	H6	104
Jan Mayen, *island*		5
Janai	Inset II	20
Janakpur	C3	19
Janeville	D1	97
Jangy-Bazar	B2	23
Japan		**8**
Japan, *sea*	B2	8
Japanese Alps, *mts.*	C3	8
Japeri	Inset I	81
Japurá, *river*	B2	81
Jarama, *river*	Inset II	37
Jarash	A1	26
Jari, *river*	C1	81
Jarvie	D4	94
Jarvis	E5	102
Jask	D4	22
Jastrebac, *mts.*	B3	49
Jászberény	B2	43
Java, *island*	C2	13
Java, *sea*	C2	13
Javari, *river*	A2	81
Jawf, al-	A1	24
Jawf, al-	D3	56
Jawhar	B3	60
Jaya, *mt.*	E2	13
Jayapura	F2	13
Jayuya	B2	90
Jazirah, al-, *region*	B1	27
Jazzin	A2	26
Jebba	C3	65
Jebel Toubkal, *mt.*	C2	57
Jeddah	A2	24
Jeddore, *lake*	D5	98
Jefferson City, *capital*, Mo.	D2	126
Jejuí-Guazú, *river*	D4	75
Jejur	Inset II	20
Jekabpils	C2	46
Jelenia Góra	B3	41
Jelgava	B2	46
Jemseg	C3	97
Jena	B3	40
Jengish Chokusu, *mt.*	G1	23
Jenner	E6	94
Jenpeg	B2	96
Jérémie	A2	89
Jerez de la Frontera	C4	37
Jersey, *island*	Inset II	30
Jerudong	B2	13
Jerusalem, *capital*	B2	26
Jesenice	B2	48
Jessore	C5	21
Jésus, *island*	J5	103
Jetait	A1	96
Jhang Sadar	D3	21
Jhansi	C3	20
Jhelum	D3	21
Jhelum, *river*	D3	21
Ji'an	E3	10
Jiamusi	G1	10
Jiangsu	E2	10
Jiangxi	E3	10
Jiddah, *island*	A1	25
Jihlava	B3	42
Jilib	A3	60
Jilin	F1	10
Jilin	F1	10
Jima	B3	60
Jimaní	A2	89
Jiménez	D2	84
Jinan	E2	10
Jingdezhen	E3	10
Jining	E2	10
Jinja	C3	61
Jinotega	B2	87
Jinotepe	A3	87
Jinsha (Yangtze), *river*	C2	10
Jinzhou	F1	10
Jipijapa	A3	79
Jir Paraná	B3	81
Jirgatol	B1	23
Jiu, *river*	B3	43
Jiujiang	E3	10
Jixi	G1	10
Jizan	B2	24
Jizzakh	C2	23
João Pessoa	E2	81
Jobos	C3	90
Jodhpur	B3	20
Joe Batt's Arm	D4	98
Joensuu	C2	53
Joetsu	C2	8
Joggins	C2	100
Johannesburg	C2	71
John Dɒr Prairie	C2	94
Johnsons Crossing	C5	105
Johor Baharu	B2	13
Johor, *strait*	B1	13
Joinville	D4	81
Joinville, *island*	C12	107
Joka	Inset II	20
Joliet, Ill.	E1	126
Joliette	C5	103
Jolo	B5	12
Jolo, *island*	B5	12
Jonava	C2	46
Jones, *sound*	L1	99
Jonesboro, Ark.	D2	126
Jong, *river*	A2	63
Jönköping	B3	53
Jonquière	E3	103
Joplin, Mo.	D2	126
Jordan		**26**
Jordan, *river*	A2	26
Jos	E3	65
Jos, *plateau*	E2	65
Jotunheimen, *mts.*	B3	52
Jou	B4	63
Joussard	C3	94
Juan de Fuca, *strait*	L7	95
Juana Díaz	B2	90
Juàzeiro	D2	81
Juàzeiro do Norte	E2	81
Juba	C4	59
Juba, *river*	A3	60
Jubayl	A1	26
Jubayl, al-	C1	24
Jubilee, *lake*	D5	98
Júcar, *river*	F3	37
Juchitán de Zaragoza	F4	84
Judique	F2	100
Juigalpa	B2	87
Juiz de Fora	D4	81
Juliaca	C4	77
Julian Alps, *mts.*	A2	48
Juliana Top, *mt.*	A3	80
Jullundur	C2	20
Jumayliyah, al-	C2	25
Jumla	B2	19
Junagadh	B4	20
Junaynah, al-	A2	59
Juncos	D2	90
Jundiai	D4	81
Juneau, *capital*, Alaska	Inset I	126
Jungfrau, *mt.*	B2	35
Juniper	B2	97
Juniyah	A2	26
Juozapines, *mt.*	C2	46
Jura, *island*	B2	30
Jura, *mts.*	A2	35
Jura, *river*	A2	46
Jurbarkas	B2	46
Jurmala	B2	46
Jurong	A1	13
Juruá, *river*	B2	81
Juruena, *river*	C3	81
Jutiapa	D5	85
Juticalpa	B2	86
Jutland, *peninsula*	B3	32
Juventud, *island*	B2	88
Južna, *river*	B3	49
Jvari	B3	45
Jwaneng	B3	69
Jyväskylä	C2	53

K

	Key	Page
K2 (Godwin Austen), *mt.*	A2	10
Ka Dake	B2	71
Ka, *river*	C2	65
Kabala	B1	63
Kabale	A4	61
Kabalo	C2	67
Kabardino-Balkariya, republic	E4	44
Kabelebo, *river*	A2	80
Kabompo, *river*	A2	67
Kabul, *capital*	B2	22
Kabul, *river*	B2	22
Kabwe	B2	67
Kachovka	C3	47
Kadavu, *island*	B3	17
Kadei, *river*	A3	66
Kadoma	B2	69
Kaduna	D2	65
Kaduna, *river*	D2	65
Kaduqli	B3	59
Kaédi	B3	58
Kaélé	B1	65
Kaeo	B2	15
Kaesŏng	B4	9
Kafan	D3	45
Kaffrine	B2	62
Kafr ad-Dawwar	B1	56
Kafu, *river*	B3	61
Kafue	B3	67
Kafue, *river*	B2	67
Kaga Bandoro	A2	66
Kagawong	C2	102
Kagera, *river*	B4, C1, C2	61
Kagitumba	C1	61
Kagoshima	A4	8
Kahayan, *river*	C2	13
Kahemba	B2	67
Kahnawake	H6	103
Kahntah	M2	95
Kahoolawe *island*, Hawaii	Inset II	126
Kai, *islands*	E2	13
Kaieteur, *falls*	B3	80
Kaifeng	E2	10
Kaikoura	B3	15
Kailahun	C3	62
Kailahun	B1	63
Kainji, *lake*	C2	65
Kaiserslautern	A4	40
Kaitaia	B2	15
Kajaani	C2	53
Kakamega	C3	61
Kakata	A2	63
Kakeroma, *island*	Inset II	8
Kakhovka, *reservoir*	C3	47
Kakinada	D5	20
Kaladar	H3	102
Kalahari, *desert*	A2	69
Kalámai	B3	51
Kalamáki	Inset	51
Kälbäcär	B2	45
Kalemie	C2	67
Kalgoorlie-Boulder, W.A.	B3	14
Kali	C1	62
Kali, *river*	B2	19
Kalimantan, *region*	C2	13
Kaliningrad	D3	44
Kalixälven, *river*	D1	53
Kallithéa	Inset	51
Kalmar	C3	53
Kalmykiya, republic	E4	44
Kalpeni, *island*	B7	20
Kalu, *river*	B5	19
Kalundborg	C3	32
Kalutara	A5	19
Kalwa	Inset I	20
Kamakwie	A1	63
Kaman	Inset I	20
Kamaran, *island*	A1	25
Kamarhati	Inset II	20
Kambia	A1	63
Kamchatka, *peninsula*	D10	44
Kamchiya, *river*	F2	50
Kamensk-Uralsky	D5	44
Kamet, *mt.*	C2	20
Kamina	C3	67
Kaminak, *lake*	J4	99
Kamloops	M6	95
Kampala, *capital*	C3	61
Kampong Cham	D4	11
Kampong Chhnang	C3	11
Kampong Saom	B5	11
Kampong Thum	C3	11
Kampot	C5	11
Kamsack	J9	104
Kamsar	A2	62
Kamui, *cape*	Inset I	8
Kananga	B2	67
Kanazawa	C2	8
Kanchenjunga, *mt.*	D2	19
Kanchipuram	C6	20
Kanchrapara	Inset II	20
Kandi	B2	64
Kandy	B4	19
Kane, *basin*	P1	99
Kangaroo, *island*	C3	14
Kangen, *river*	C3	59
Kanggye	B2	9
Kanghwa, *bay*	A4	9
Kangiqsualujjuaq	C2	101
Kangiqsujuaq	B1	101
Kangirsuk	B1	101
Kangnŭng	C4	9
Kangshan	B2	9
Kankan	D2	62
Kano	E1	65
Kanpur	D3	20
Kansaripara	Inset II	20
Kansas	D2	126
Kansas City, Kans.	D2	126
Kansas City, Mo.	D2	126
Kansay	A1	23
Kansk	D6	44
Kanté	B2	64
Kanuku, *mts.*	B4	80
Kanye	B3	69
Kaohsiung	B2	9
Kaoko Veld, *mts.*	A1	70
Kaolack	A2	62
Kaoma	A2	67
Kaop'ing, *river*	B2	9
Kapfenberg	D3	39
Kapingamarangi, *atoll*	C2	15
Kapiskau, *river*	D2	101
Kaposvár	A2	43
Kapuskasing	D3	101
Kara	B2	64
Kara, *sea*	B5	44
Kara-Kum, *canal*	D3	22
Kara-Kum, *desert*	C2	22
KaraŠay	F2	23
Karabakh, *canal*	B2	45
Karachayevo-Cherkesiya, republic	E4	44
Karachi	C5	21
Karaj	C2	22
Karak, al-	A2	26
Karakol	F1	23
Karakoram, *range*	C1	20
Karaman	C3	27
Karasburg	C4	70
Karawanken, *range*	D4	39
Karbala	B2	24
Karcag	C2	43
Kardiva, *channel*	A2	19
Kärdla	B1	46
Kareliya, republic	C3	44
Kariba	B1	69
Kariba, *lake*	A1	69
Karibib	B2	70
Karisimbi, *mt.*	B1	61
Karkar, *island*	A2	15
Karkinit, *bay*	C3	47
Karlovac	B2	48
Karlovy Vary	A2	42
Karlskrona	C3	53
Karlsruhe	B4	40
Karlstad	B3	53
Karnali, *river*	B2	19
Karnaphuli, *reservoir*	F6	21
Karnaphuli, *river*	E6	21
Karonga	B1	68
Karpas, *peninsula*	C1	27
Kárpathos, *island*	C4	51
Kars	E2	27
Kartala, *mt.*	A1	67
Kartung	B2	62
Karun, *river*	B3	22
Karuzi	C2	61
Karviná	D3	42
Kasai, *river*	B2	67
Kasama	C2	67
Kasane	B1	69
Kasba, *lake*	H4	99
Kashan	C3	22
Kashi	A2	10
Kashiwa	D3	8
Kasinathpur	Inset II	20
Kaslo	O6	95
Kassala	D2	59
Kassel	B3	40
Kasserine	B2	57
Kastamonu	C2	27
Kastoría	B1	51
Kastrup	D3	32
Kasugai	C3	8
Kasungu	B2	68
Kasur	E3	21
Katagum, *river*	E2	65
Katanga, *plateau*	B3	67
Kateríni	B1	51
Kate's Needle, *mt.*	F2	95
Katherine, N.T.	C1	14
Kathgodam	C3	20
Kathiawar, *peninsula*	B4	20
Kathmandu, *capital*	C2	19
Katowice	D3	41
Katrine, *lake*	B2	30
Katsina	D1	65
Kattegat, *strait*	C2	32
Kau-Ur	C2	62
Kauai *island*, Hawaii	Inset II	126
Kaufbeuren	B5	40
Kaukau Veld, *region*	C2	70
Kaunas	B2	46
Kaura-Namoda	D1	65
Kavadarci	C2	48
Kavajë	A2	49
Kavála	C1	51
Kavaratti, *island*	B6	20
Kavieng	B2	15
Kavir-e Namak, *desert*	D3	22
Kaw	B1	80
Kawagoe	C3	8
Kawaguchi	C3	8
Kawasaki	C3	8
Kawhia	B2	15
Kawthaung	C4	12
Kayangel, *islands*	C1	17
Kayes	A3	58
Kayser, *mts.*	A3	80
Kayseri	C2	27
Kazakh Upland, *region*	C2	23
Kazakhstan		**23**
Kazan	D4	44
Kazanlŭk	D3	50
Kazincbarcika	C1	43
Kearney	F2	102
Kearney, Nebr.	D1	126
Keban, *reservoir*	D2	27
Kebili	B3	57
Kebir, *river*	B1	26
Kebnekaise, *mt.*	C1	53
Kechika, *river*	J2	95
Kecskemét	B2	43
Kėdainiai	B2	46
Kedgwick	B1	97
Kediri	C2	13
Kédougou	C3	62
Keele, *river*	C4	99
Keeley, *lake*	B6	104
Keetmanshoop	C4	70
Keewatin, *region*	J4	99
Kef, el-	B1	57
Kefallinía, *island*	B2	51
Keflavík	A3	52
Keg River	B2	94
Keila	C1	46
Kékes, *mt.*	C2	43
Kelang	A2	13
Kelani, *river*	B4	19
Kelliher	G9	104
Kelowna	N6	95
Kelsey	C1	96
Keluang	B2	13
Kelvington	G8	104
Kemano	J4	95
Kemerovo	D6	44
Kemi	B1	53
Kemijärvi	C1	53
Kemijoki, *river*	C1	53
Kemnay	A4	96
Kempenland, *region*	D1	33
Kemps Bay	B3	89
Kempt, *lake*	B4	103
Kempten	B5	40
Kemptville	K2	102
Kenaston	D9	104
Kendal	C2	30
Kendari	D2	13
Kenema	B2	63
Keng Tung	C2	12
Kenilworth	C3	30
Kenitra	C1	57
Kennetcook	D2	100
Keno	B4	105
Kenora	B3	101
Kensington	B2	100
Kenton	A4	96
Kentucky	E2	126
Kentville	C2	100
Kenville	A3	96
Kenya		**61**
Kenya, *mt.*	D4	61
Keokradong, *mt.*	F7	21
Kerangan Nyatan	B3	13
Keratsínion	Inset	51
Kerch	D3	47
Kerch, *strait*	D3	47
Kerema	A2	15
Keremeos	N6	95
Keren	B2	60
Kerewan	B2	62
Kerguelen, *islands*		5
Kericho	C4	61
Kerinci, *mt.*	B2	13
Kerkennah, *islands*	C2	57
Kerki	D3	22
Kérkira	A2	51
Kérkira, *island*	A2	51
Kerman	D3	22
Kerman, *region*	D4	22
Kérouané	D3	62
Kerrobert	A9	104
Kerulen, *river*	D2	11
Keszthely	A2	43
Keta	C4	64
Ketchikan, Alaska	Inset I	126
Key Lake Mine	E3	104
Key West, Fla.	E3	126
Keyano	B3	101
Khabarovsk	E8	44
Khabur, *river*	B1	27
Khakasiya, republic	D6	44
Khalándrion	Inset	51
Khalkidhikí, *peninsula*	B1	51
Khalkís	B2	51
Khaluf	C2	25
Khambhât, *gulf*	B4	20
Khamis Mushayt	B2	24
Khan-Tengri, *mt.*	E2	23
Khanaqin	C2	24
Khaniá	B4	51
Khanka, *lake*	G1	10
Khanty-Mansiya, autonomous okrug	C5	44
Khanty-Mansiysk	C5	44
Kharagpur	E4	20
Kharg, *island*	C4	22
Kharijah, al-	B2	56
Kharijah, *oasis*	B2	56
Kharj, al-	B1	24
Kharkiv	D1	47
Khartoum North	C2	59
Khartoum, *capital*	C2	59
Khashm al-Qirbah	C2	59
Khashuri	B4	45
Khasi, *hills*	F3	20
Khaskovo	D4	50
Khatanga	B7	44
Khawr, al-	D2	25
Kherson	C3	47
Khíos, *island*	C2	51
Khiran, al-	C3	24
Khmelnytskyy	B2	47
Khojak, *pass*	C3	21
Khon Kaen	C2	12
Khor Angar	C1	60
Khorasan, *region*	D2	22
Khorat, *plateau*	C3	12
Khorixas	B2	70
Khorramabad	B3	22
Khorramshahr	B3	22
Khorugh	B2	23
Khouribga	C1	57
Khowst	B2	22
Khudzhand	A1	23
Khujayli	A2	23
Khulna	C6	21
Khums, al-	B1	56
Khuriya Muriya, *islands*	C3	25
Khust	A2	47
Khuzdar	C4	21
Khuzestan, *region*	B3	22
Khvoy	A2	22
Khyber, *pass*	D2	21
Kibungo	C2	61
Kibuye	B2	61
Kičevo	A2	48
Kidal	D2	58
Kidderminster	C3	30
Kiel	B1	40
Kiel, *bay*	B1	40
Kielce	E3	41
Kiev, *capital*	C1	47
Kiev, *reservoir*	C1	47
Kiffa	C3	58
Kifisiá	Inset	51
Kifissós, *river*	B2	51
Kigali, *capital*	B1	61
Kigoma	A1	68
Kii, *channel*	B3	8
Kii, *peninsula*	B3	8
Kikinda	B2	49
Kikkertavak, *island*	B2	98
Kikwit	B2	67
Kilchu	C2	9
Kildare	C2	31
Kilimanjaro, *mt.*	C1	68
Kilinochchi	B2	19
Kilkee	B2	31
Kilkenny	C2	31
Killala, *bay*	B1	31
Killaloe	H2	102
Killarney	B2	31
Killarney	B4	96
Killarney	D1	102
Killarney Lake	E5	94
Killdeer	D11	104
Killeen, Tex.	D2	126
Kilmarnock	B2	30
Kilombero, *river*	C2	68
Kilwa Kivinje	C2	68
Kimbe	B2	15
Kimberley	B2	71
Kimberley	O6	95
Kimberley	E3	102
Kimberley, *plateau*	B1	14
Kimch'aek	C2	9
Kimch'ŏn	C4	9
Kinabalu, *mt.*	D1	13
Kinabatangan, *river*	D2	13
Kinbasket, *lake*	B5	94
Kinbasket, *lake*	O5	95
Kincaid	C11	104
Kincardine	D3	102
Kindersley	A9	104
Kindia	B2	62
Kindu	C2	67
King Leopold, *range*	B1	14
King William, *island*	J3	99
King's Cove	E5	98
King's Landing	B3	97
King's Lynn	D3	30
King's Point	C4	98
Kingcome Inlet	J6	95
Kingman, Ariz.	B2	126
Kingston	C3	100
Kingston	J3	102
Kingston upon Hull	C3	30
Kingston upon Thames	Inset III	30
Kingston, *capital*	C3	88
Kingstown, *capital*	B2	91
Kingsville	F2	100
Kingsville	C5	102
Kinistino	E8	104
Kinkala	C6	66
Kinkora	B2	100
Kinloss	D3	102
Kinmount	G3	102
Kinnairds, *cape*	C1	30
Kinosota	B4	96
Kinsarvik	B3	52
Kinsella	E5	94
Kinshasa, *capital*	A2	67
Kinyeti, *mt.*	C4	59
Kioa, *island*	C2	17
Kiosk	G1	102
Kipengere, *range*	B2	68
Kipling	H10	104
Kirakira	B2	16
Kirensk	D7	44
Kiribati		**17**
Kırıkkale	C2	27
Kiritimati (Christmas), *island*	D1	17
Kirkcaldy	B2	30
Kirkenes	F2	52
Kirkfield	G3	102
Kirkland Lake	D3	101
Kirkpatrick, *mt.*	A5	107
Kirkuk	B1	24
Kirkwall	Inset I	30
Kirov	D4	44
Kirovakan	B2	45
Kirovograd	C2	47
Kirşehir	C2	27
Kirthar, *range*	C4	21
Kiruna	D1	53
Kisangani	C1	67
Kishi	B3	65
Kiskitto, *lake*	B2	96
Kiskörei-víztároló, *lake*	C2	43
Kiskunhalas	B2	43
Kismayo	A4	60
Kissidougou	C3	62
Kississing, *lake*	A1	96
Kisumu	C4	61
Kita	B3	58
Kita, *island*	Inset III	8
Kitakami, *river*	D2	8
Kitakyushu	A3	8
Kitale	C3	61
Kitami	Inset I	8
Kitami, *mts.*	Inset I	8
Kitchener	E4	102
Kitgum	C2	61
Kíthira, *island*	B3	51
Kitikmeot, *region*	G3	99
Kitimat	H4	95
Kitwanga	H3	95
Kitwe	B2	67
Kivi, *lake*	C2	53
Kivu, *lake*	B1	61
Kızıl Irmak, *river*	C2	27
Kjølen, *mts.*	C1	53
Kladno	B2	42
Klagenfurt	D4	39
Klaipėda	A2	46
Klamath Falls, Oreg.	A1	126
Klarälven, *river*	B2	53
Klatovy	A3	42
Kleinburg	J5	102
Klemtu	H5	95
Kleve	A3	40
Kloulklubed	B3	17
Kluane, *lake*	B5	105
Knee, *lake*	D1	96
Knight, *inlet*	K6	95
Knockboy, *mt.*	B3	31
Knokke	B1	33
Knoxville, Tenn.	E2	126
Ko Chang, *island*	C3	12
Ko Kut, *island*	C4	12
Ko Phangan, *island*	B4	12
Ko Samui, *island*	B4	12
Ko Tarutao, *island*	B5	12
Kobe	B3	8
Koblenz	A3	40
Kobuleti	A4	45
Kočani	C2	48
Kočevje	B3	48
Kochi	B3	8
Kodiak, Alaska	Inset I	126
Kofarnihon, *river*	A2	23
Köflach	D3	39
Koforidua	B3	64
Kofu	C3	8
Køge	D3	32
Kohima	F3	20
Kohtla-Järve	D1	46
Koindu	B1	63
Koje-do, *island*	C5	9
Kokkina	A1	27
Kokkola	B2	53
Kokshetau	C1	23
Kola	A4	96
Kola, *peninsula*	C3	44
Kolari	B1	53
Kolda	B3	62
Kolding	B3	32
Kolhapur	B5	20
Kolín	B2	42
Kolkata (Calcutta)	E4, Inset II	20
Kołobrzeg	B1	41
Kolpashevo	D6	44
Kolshet	Inset I	20
Kolumadulu, *atoll*	A3	19
Kolwezi	C3	67
Kolyma, *range*	C10	44
Kolyma, *river*	C9	44
Komadugu Gana, *river*	F2	65
Komadugu Yobe, *river*	F1	65
Komárno	B3	42
Komárom	B2	43
Komati, *river*	B2	71
Komatsu	C2	8
Komi, republic	C4	44
Komi-Permyat, autonomous okrug	D4	44
Komoé, *river*	E3	63
Komotiní	C1	51
Komsomolsk-na-Amure	D8	44
Konar, *river*	D2	21
Konduz	B1	22
Konduz, *river*	B1	22
Koné	C2	18

Key Page
Kong, *river* D4 11
Konibodom B1 23
Konin D2 41
Konnagar Inset II 20
Konotop C1 47
Kontagora C2 65
Kontum B3 11
Konya C3 27
Kootenay, *lake* O6 95
Kootenay, *river* P6 95
Kopaonik, *mts.* B3 49
Kópavogur A2 52
Koper A3 48
Kopet, *mts.* B2, D2 22
Koprivnica C2 48
Korab, *mt.* B2 49
Korab, *mt.* A2 48
Korçë B3 49
Korčula, *island* C4 48
Korea, *bay* A3 9
Korea, *strait* C5 9
Korhogo D2 63
Koriyama D2 8
Korla B1 10
Koro Toro B4 59
Koro, *island* B2 17
Koro, *sea* B2 17
Koror, *capital* B3 17
Koror, *island* C3 17
Körös, *river* C2 43
Korosten B1 47
Kortrijk B2 33
Koryak, *range* C10 44
Koryakiya,
autonomous okrug C10 44
Kosŏng C3 9
Kos, *island* C3 51
Kosciusko, *mt.* D3 14
Koshigaya C3 8
Koshiki, *islands* A4 8
Košice C2 42
Kosovo, province B3 49
Kosrae D2 15
Kosrae, *island* D2 15
Kossol, *passage* C2 17
Kossol, *reef* C2 17
Kossu, *lake* D3 63
Koszalin C1 41
Kota C3 20
Kota Baharu B1 13
Kota Kinabalu D2 13
Kotcho, *lake* M1 95
Kotka C2 53
Kotlas C4 44
Kotor, *gulf* A3 49
Kotovsk B2 47
Kotto, *river* B2 66
Kouchibouguac D2 97
Koudougou C2 64
Koula-Moutou B2 66
Koulikoro B3 58
Koulountou, *river* C3 62
Koumac C2 18
Koungheul B2 62
Kourou B1 80
Kouroussa D2 62
Kousséri B1 65
Koutiala B3 58
Kouto C2 63
Kouvola C2 53
Kovel A1 47
Kowŏn B3 9
Kowloon Inset 10
Kowt-e Ashrow B2 22
Kozáni B1 51
Kozhikode C6 20
Kozloduy B2 50
Kozu, *island* C3 8
Kožuf, *mts.* C2 48
Kpalimé B3 64
Kpandu C3 64
Kpémé B3 64
Kra, *isthmus* B4 12
Kracheh E3 11
Kragujevac B2 49
Krakatau, *island* B2 13
Kraków D3 41
Kraljevo B3 49
Kramatorsk D2 47
Kranj B2 48
Kranji B1 13
Krasnodar E3 44
Krasnoyarsk D6 44
Krefeld A3 40
Kremenchug C2 47
Kretinga A2 46
Kribi A3 65
Krishna, *river* C5 20
Kristiansand B4 52
Kristianstad B3 53
Kristiansund B3 52
Kristinehamn B3 53
Krk, *island* B2 48
Krka, *river* B3 48
Krong Kaoh Kong A4 11
Kroonstad C2 71
Krosno E4 41
Krško C3 48
Krugersdorp C2 71
Krujë A2 49
Kruševac B3 49
Kruševo B2 48
Krychaw E3 47
Kryvyi Rih C2 47
Kuala Abang B2 13
Kuala Belait A2 13
Kuala Lumpur, *capital* A2 13
Kuala Terengganu B2 13
Kuantan B2 13
Kuching C2 13
Kuchino, *island* A4 8
Kudymkar D4 44
Kufstein E3 99
Kugluktuk C3 39
Kuito C4 70
Kukës B1 49
Kul, *river* D4 22
Kula Kangri, *mt.* B1 19
Kuldiga A2 46
Kulmbach B3 40
Kulob A2 23
Kulpawn, *river* B1 64
Kum, *river* B4 9
Kumamoto A3 8
Kumanovo B1 48
Kumasi B3 64
Kume, *island* Inset II 8
Kumo F2 65
Kunda D1 46
Kunene, *river* A1 70
Kunlun, *mts.* B2 10
Kunming D3 10
Kunsan B5 9
Kuntaur D2 62
Kuopio C2 53
Kupa, *river* B3 48
Kupang D3 13
Kür, *river* A2, C2 45
Kür-Aras, *lowland* B2 45
Kura, *river* E2 27
Kurashiki B3 8
Kuraymah C1 59
Kŭrdzhali D4 50
Kure B3 8
Kuressaare B2 46
Kurgan D5 44
Kuril, *islands* E9 44
Kurinwás, *river* B2 87
Kurla Inset I 20
Kurnool C5 20
Kuršėnai B1 46
Kursk D3 44
Kuru, *river* C2 19
Kuruman B2 71
Kurume A3 8
Kurunegala B4 19
Kushiro Inset I 8
Kushtia C5 21
Kusŏng A3 9
Kusti C2 59
Kut, al- C2 24
Kütahya B2 27
Kutaisi B3 45
Kutch, *gulf* A4 20
Kutno D2 41
Kuujjuaq C2 101
Kuujjuarapik A2 101
Kuwait 24
Kuwait, *bay* B2 24
Kuwait, *capital* B2 24
Kwa, *river* B2 67
Kwahu, *plateau* B3 64
Kwajalein, *island* B2 16
Kwangju B5 9
Kwango, *river* B2 67
Kwekwe B2 69
Kyaukpyu B2 12
Kyle B10 104
Kyle of Lochalsh B1 30
Kyoga, *lake* C3 61
Kyŏngju C5 9
Kyoto B3 8
Kyrenia B1 27
Kyrgyzstan 23
Kyrenia, *range* B1 27
Kyushu, *island* A3 8
Kyustendil A3 50
Kyzyl D6 44
Kyzyl-Kyya C2 23
Kyzylsuu, *river* C3 23
Kyzylkum, *desert* B2 23

L

La Asunción D1 79
La Baie F3 103
La Broquerie C4 96
La Ceiba B2 86
La Chaux-de-Fonds A1 35
La Coma, *river* B1 36
La Conception B5 103
La Condamine B1 35
La Coruña B1 37
La Crete B2 94
La Croix Maingot A2 91
La Crosse, Wis. D1 126
La Cruz A1 86
La Digue, *island* C1 70
La Doré D3 103
La Esperanza A2 86
La Goulette C1 57
La Grande, *river* B3 101
La Guadeloupe F6 103
La Guaira Maiquetía C1 79
La Have C3 100
La Laguna Inset I 37
La Libertad A4 79
La Libertad C3 85
La Loche A4 104
La Louvière C2 33
La Malbaie F4 103
La Martre K2 103
La Martre, *lake* E4 99
La Montaña, *region* C2 77
La Oroya B3 77
La Palma C2 87
La Palma, *island* Inset I 37
La Paz B2 86
La Paz, *capital* A3 77
La Paz, *state capital* B3 84
La Pérouse B1 96
La Pérouse, *strait* Inset I 8
La Plaine B3 90
La Plata D4 74
La Plata, *river* C2 90
La Plonge, *lake* C5 104
La Pocatière F4 103
La Prairie J6 103
La Rioja B2 74
La Rioja E1 37
La Rochelle B3 34
La Roda E3 37
La Romana D2 89
La Ronge E5 104
La Ronge, *lake* E6 104
La Rosita B2 87
La Salle C4 96
La Salle J6 103
La Scie D4 98
La Serena B3 76
La Spezia B1 38
La Tortuga, *island* C1 79
La Tuque D4 103
La Unión B7 76
La Unión C2 86
La Vega B1 89
La Virtud A2 86
La-Roche-sur-Yon B3 34
Labasa B2 17
Labé B2 62
Labe (Elbe), *river* B2 42
Labelle C3 100
Laberge, *lake* B5 105
Labi A3 13
Laborec, *river* C2 42
Laborie B3 91
Labrador City D3 98
Labrieville G2 103
Labu C2 13
Labuan, *island* D2 13
Laç A2 49
Lac du Bonnet C4 96
Lac La Biche E4 94
Lac La Hache M5 95
Lac Mégantic F6 103
Lac-aux-Sables D5 103
Lac-Bouchette D3 103
Lac-des-Aigles H4 103
Lac-des-Îles A5 103
Lac-Édouard D4 103
Lac-Etchemin F5 103
Lac-Nominingue A5 103
Lac-Saguay A5 103
Laccadive, *islands* B6 20
Lachenaie J5 103
Lachine H6 103
Lachute B6 103
Lacombe D5 94
Ladhiqiyah, al- (Latakia) A2 27
Ladoga, *lake* C3 44
Ladysmith C2 71
Ladywood C4 96
Lae A2 15
Lae, *island* B2 16
Laem, *mt.* B3 12
Læsø, *island* C1 32
Lafayette, La. D2 126
Lafia E3 65
Lafleche D11 104
Lafond E4 94
Laghouat B1 57
Lagodekhi D4 45
Lagos B4 65
Lagos A4 36
Laguna de Bay, *lake* B3 12
Lahave, *river* C3 100
Lahij A2 25
Lahn, *river* B3 40
Lahore E3 21
Lahti C2 53
Laï B5 59
Lairg B1 30
Lajas A2 90
Lajes C4 81
Lakatoro B3 18
Lake Alma F11 104
Lake Charlotte E3 100
Lake Edward B2 97
Lake Harbour O4 99
Lake Lenore F8 104
Lake St. Peter G2 102
Lake, district B2 30
Lakeba, *island* C3 17
Lakeba, *passage* C3 17
Lakefield G3 102
Lakelse Lake H4 95
Lakhpat A4 20
Laki, *volcano* B2 52
Lakselv F1 52
Lalitpur C2 19
Lamaline D5 98
Lamap B3 18
Lambaréné A2 66
Lambton E6 103
Lamèque E1 97
Lamèque, *island* E1 97
Lami B3 17
Lamía B2 51
Lammermuir, *hills* C2 30
Lamon, *bay* B3 12
Lampa Inset 76
Lampang B2 12
Lampeter B3 30
Lampman H11 104
Lamu F5 61
Lan, *island* B2 9
Lanai *island*, Hawaii Inset II 126
Lanark J2 102
Lancaster C2 30
Lancaster J2 102
L'Ancienne-Lorette K5 103
Land's End, *promontory* B4 30
Lander, Wyo. C1 126
Landes, *region* B5 34
Landis B8 104
Landshut C4 40
Lang Son B1 11
Langeburg, *mts.* B3 71
Langeland, *island* C4 32
Langenburg J10 104
Langham D8 104
Langkawi, *island* A1 13
Langley L6 95
Langruth B4 96
Langstaff K5 102
Langton E5 102
Languedoc-Roussillon C5 34
Lanigan E9 104
Lanín, *volcano* A4 74
Länkäran C3 45
L'Annonciation B5 103
Lansdowne J3 102
Lansdowne House C2 101
L'Anse-à-Valleau M2 103
L'Anse-au-Loup C3 98
L'Anse-aux-Gascons M3 103
L'Anse-St-Jean F3 103
Lansing, *capital*, Mich. E1 126
Lantau, *island* Inset 10
Lanús D3 74
Lanzarote, *island* Inset I 37
Lanzhou D2 10
Lao Cai A1 11
Laoag B2 12
Laoang C3 12
Laon C2 34
Laos 11
Lapithos B1 27
Lapland, *region* B1 53
Lappeenranta C2 53
Laptev, *sea* B8 44
L'Aquila C2 38
Larache C1 57
Laramie, Wyo. C1 126
Laredo, Tex. D3 126
Lares B2 90
Larestan, *region* C4 22
Large, *island* C1 91
Lárisa B2 51
Lark Harbour B4 98
Larkana C4 21
Larkhall C4 96
Larnaca B2 27
Larne B2 30
Larochette B2 33
Larrys River F2 100
Larsen Ice Shelf, *glacier* C12 107
Las Cruces, N. Mex. C2 126
Las Minas, *mt.* A2 86
Las Palmas Inset I 37
Las Piedras D2 90
Las Piedras B3 75
Las Tablas B3 87
Las Tunas E3 88
Las Vegas, N. Mex. C2 126
Las Vegas, Nev. B2 126
L'Ascension B5 103
Lashburn A7 104
Lashio C2 12
Lashkar Gah A2 22
Last Mountain, *lake* E9 104
Latacunga B3 79
Late, *island* C2 17
Latina C2 38
Latium C2 38
Latvia 46
Lau, *island group* C2 17
Laucala, *island* C2 17
Laudat B3 90
Lauder A4 96
Launceston B4 30
Launceston, Tas. D4 14
Laurie River A1 96
Laurier B4 96
Lausanne A2 35
Lautoka A2 17
Laval B2 34
Laval C6, J5 103
Lavenham B4 96
Lavoy E4 94
Lavumisa B3 71
Lawa, *river* A2, B2 80
Lawn D5 98
Lawrence Station B3 97
Lawton, Okla. D2 126
Layland B4 96
Layou, *river* B3 90
Lázaro Cárdenas D4 84
Le Bic H3 103
Le Creusot D3 34
Le Havre C2 34
Le Mans C2 34
Le Puy C4 34
Leader A10 104
Leading Tickles D4 98
Leaf Rapids D1 96
Leamington C5 102
l'Eau Claire, *lake* B2 101
Lebanon 26
Lebanon, *mts.* B1 26
Lebombo, *mts.* C2, D1 71
Lebu B6 76
Lecce D2 38
Lech B3 39
Lech, *river* B4 40
Leduc D4 94
Lee, *river* B3 31
Leeds C3 30
Leeuwarden C1 32
Leeuwin, *cape* A3 14
Leeward Group B3 58
Lefka A1 27
Lefkoniko B1 27
Leganés Inset II 37
Legazpi B3 12
Legnica C3 41
Leicester C3 30
Leichhardt, *river* D1 14
Leiden B2 32
Leie, *river* B2 33
Leikanger B3 52
Leipzig C3 40
Leiria A3 36
Leitrim H6 102
Leixões A2 36
Lékéti, *mts.* C5 66
Lélouma B2 62
Lelystad C2 32
Lempa, *river* A1, B2 86
Lena, *river* C8 44
Leneinsk C2 23
Lenghu C2 10
Lengoué, *river* C3 66
Lenore A4 96
Lens C1 34
Lensk C7 44
Léo C3 64
Leoben D3 39
Léogâne C2 89
León D3 84
León A2 87
León D1 37
Leone B2 18
Leova B2 50
Leoville C7 104
Lepontine Alps, *mts.* C2 35
Lepreau C3 97
Lepsi D2 23
Leribe B1 71
Lérida G2 37
Lerwick Inset I 30
Les Cayes B2 89
Les Éboulements F4 103
Les Escaldes B2 36
Les Escoumins G3 103
Les Islets-Caribou J2 103
Les Méchins K3 103
Les Tantes, *island* B1 91
Les Ulis Inset II 34
Leskovac B3 49
Lesosibirsk D6 44
Lesotho 71
Lesser Caucasus, *mts.* A2, B4 45
Lesser Hinggan, *range* F1 10
Lesser Slave, *lake* C3 94
Lesser Sunda, *islands* C2 13
Lestrock G9 104
Lésvos, *island* C2 51
Leszno C3 41
Lethbridge D6 94
Lethbridge E5 98
Lethem B4 80
Leticia C6 78
Letlhakeng B3 69
Letterkenny C1 31
Leuven C2 33
Levack D1 102
Levallois-Perret Inset II 34
Leveque, *cape* B1 14
Leverkusen A3 40
Levice B2 42
Lévis E5, L6 103
Levittown C2 90
Lewes D4 30
Lewis, *island* A1 30
Lewisporte D4 98
Lewiston, Idaho B1 126
Lewiston, Maine F1 126
Lexington, Ky. E2 126
Leyte, *island* C4 12
Lhasa C3 10
Lhobrak, *river* C2 19
Lhuntshi C2 19
Lianyungang E2 10
Liao, *river* F1 10
Liaoning F1 10
Liaoyang F1 10
Liaoyuan F1 10
Liard River J1 95
Liard, *river* K1 95
Libau C4 96
Liberec B2 42
Liberia 63
Liberia A2 86
Libono B1 71
Libreville, *capital* A1 66
Libya 56
Libyan, *desert* A2, D2 56
Lichfield C3 30
Lichinga B2 68
Lida B3 47
Liechtenstein 33
Liège D2 33
Lieksa D2 53
Lienz C4 39
Liepāja A2 46
Lièvre, *river* A5 103
Lifford C1 31
Lifou, *island* D2 18
Lifuka, *island* C3 17
Liguria B1 38
Ligurian, *sea* B2 38
Lihir, *group* B2 15
Likasi C3 67
Likiep, *island* B1 16
Lille C1 34
Lille, *strait* B3 32
Lillehammer C3 52
Lillooet M6 95
Lillooet, *river* L6 95
Lilongwe, *capital* B2 68
Lima, *capital* B3 77
Lima, *river* A2 36
Limassol B2 27
Limbazi C2 46
Limbe A3 65
Limbourg D2 33
Limerick B2 31
Limfjorden, *channel* B2 32
Límnos, *island* C2 51
Limoges C4 34
Limón C3 86
Limours Inset II 34
Limousin C4 34
Limpopo, *river* C1 71
Linares B5 76
Linares E3 84
Linares E3 37
Lincoln C3 30
Lincoln, *capital*, Nebr. D1 126
Lindau B5 40
Lindbergh E4 94
Linden B3 80
Linden D2 100
Lindi C2 68
Lindsay G3 102
Line, *islands* D1 17
Lingayen, *gulf* B2 12
Lingga, *island* B2 13
Lingshi A2 19
Linguère B2 62
Linköping C3 53
Linnhe, *lake* B2 30
Linvanti, *river* A1 69
Linwood F2 100
Linz D2 39
Lion, *gulf* D5 34
Lionel Town B3 88
Lions Head D3 102
Lipa B3 12
Lipari, *islands* C3 38
Lipetsk D3 44
Lippstadt B3 40
Lipton G10 104
Liptovský Mikuláš B2 42
Lira C2 61
Lisala B1 67
L'Isalo, *mts.* B3 69
Lisbon, *capital* A3 36
Lisichansk D2 47
L'Isle-Adam Inset II 34
L'Isle-Verte G3 103
Lismore, N.S.W. E2 14
Listowel E4 102
Litani, *river* A2 26
Litani, *river* A2, B3 80
Lithuania 46
Little Alföld, *plain* A2 43
Little Andaman, *island* F6 20
Little Bay B5 98
Little Bras d'Or G1 100
Little Current D2 102
Little Fort M5 95
Little Grand Rapids D3 96
Little Inagua, *island* C4 89
Little Rock, *capital*, Ark. D2 126
Little Salmon, *lake* C4 105
Little Scarcies, *river* A1 63
Little Seldom D4 98
Little Smoky, *river* A4 94
Little St. Bernard, *pass* D4 34
Little Zab, *river* B1 24
Liuzhou D3 10
Liverpool C3 30
Liverpool C3 100
Liverpool, *bay* B3 30
Livingstone B3 67
Livno B2 48
Livorno B2 38
Ljubljana, *capital* B2 48
Ljusnanälven, *river* B2 53
Llallagua A3 77
Llandrindod Wells B3 30
Llanos, *plain* C2 79
Llanos, prairie C3 78
Llanquihue, *lake* B7 76
Lleyn, *peninsula* B3 30
Llorts B1 36
Lloyd, *lake* B3 104
Lloydminster E4 94
Lloydminster A7 104
Lloyds, *river* C5 98
Llullaillaco, *volcano* B1 74
Lo Wu Inset 10
Lo, *river* A1 11
Loa, *river* B2 76
Lobamba, *capital* B2 71
Lobatse B3 69
Lobaye, *river* A2 66
Lobito B4 70
Locarno C2 35
Lockeport B4 100
Lockport C4 96
Lod (Lydda) B2 26
Lodja B2 67
Lodwar C2 61
Łódź D3 41
Loei B2 12
Loess, *plateau* D2 10
Lofoten, *islands* C2 52
Logan, *mt.* A5 105
Logan, *river* Inset III 14
Logan, Utah B1 126
Logone, *river* A5 59
Logroño E1 37
Loi-kaw C2 12
Loire, *river* C3 34
Loíza D2 90
Loja B4 79
Loja D4 37
Lokka, *reservoir* C1 53
Lokoja D4 65
Lokossa A4 64
Lol, *river* B3 59
Lolland, *island* C4 32
Lom B2 50
Lomami, *river* C2 67
Lomas de Zamora D4 74
Lomawai A3 17
Lombardy B1 38
Lombardy J3 102
Lombok, *island* C2 13
Lomé, *capital* B3 64
Lomond, *lake* B2 30
Łomża F2 41
London D5 102
London, *capital* C3, Inset III 30
Londonderry A2 30
Londrina C4 81
Lone Butte M5 95
Long Beach, Calif. B2 126
Long *island*, N.Y. F1 126
Long Lake D4 96
Long Range, *mts.* B5, C4 98
Long Xuyen A4 11
Long, *island* C3 89
Longford C2 31
Longlac C3 101
Longreach, Qld. D2 14
Longueuil J5 103
Longview, Tex. D2 126
Loon Lake C3 94
Loon Lake A6 104
Loop Head, *cape* B2 31
Lop Buri B3 12
Lop, *lake* C1 10
Lorca F4 37
Loreburn D9 104
Lorengau A2 15
Loreto B2 84
Lorette C4 96
Loretteville K5 103
Lorient B3 34
L'Original L2 102
Lorne, *estuary* A2 30
Lorraine D2 34
Lorraine H5 103
Los Andes B4 76
Los Ángeles B6 76
Los Angeles, Calif. B2 126
Los Chiles B1 86
Los Mochis C2 84
Los Reyes Inset 84
Los Teques C1 79

Key Page
Lot, *river* C4 34
Louang Namtha A1 11
Loubomo B6 66
Louga A2 62
Lough Erne, *lake* A2 30
Loughborough, *lake* J3 102
Lougheed, *island* G1 99
Louisbourg H2 100
Louisdale F2 100
Louiseville D5 103
Louisiade, *archipelago* B3 15
Louisiana D2 126
Louisville, Ky. E2 126
Lourdes B5 34
Louri C2 19
Louvres Inset II 34
Lovech C2 50
Lovell Village B3 91
Lovettville B4 94
Lowe Farm C4 96
Lower Arrow, *lake* N6 95
Lower Debert D2 100
Lower Five Islands C2 100
Lower Hutt B3 15
Lower Montague C2 100
Lower Post H1 95
Lower Saxony B2 40
Lower Tunguska, *river* C6 44
Lower Woods Harbour B4 100
Lowestoft D3 30
Loyada C2 60
Loyalty, *islands* C2 18
Loyoro D2 61
Lualaba, *river* C2 67
Luanda, *capital* B2 70
Luang Prabang B2 11
Luang Prabang, *range* A3 11
Luang, *mt.* B4 12
Luangwa C3 67
Luangwa, *river* C2 67
Luanshya B2 67
Luapula, *river* B2, C3 67
Luau E3 70
Luba A1 66
Lubango B5 70
Lubbock, Tex. C2 126
Lübeck B2 40
Lubicon, *lake* C3 94
Lublin F3 41
Lubumbashi C3 67
Lucapa D2 70
Lucca B2 38
Lucea A2 88
Lucena B3 12
Lucena D4 37
Lučenec B2 42
Lucern, *lake* C2 35
Lucerne C1 35
Lucie, *river* A3 80
Luckenwalde C2 40
Lucknow D3 20
Lucknow D4 102
Lucky Lake C9 104
Luda Kamchiya, *river* E3 50
Lüderitz B4 70
Ludhiana C2 20
Ludogorie, *region* E2 50
Ludwigsburg B4 40
Ludwigshafen am Rhein B4 40
Luena D3 70
Lugano C3 35
Lugano, *lake* C3 35
Luganville B2 18
Lugenda, *river* C2 68
Lugo C1 37
Lugoj A3 43
Luhansk D2 47
Lukuga, *river* C2 67
Luleå D1 53
Luleälven, *river* D1 53
Lumphat F2 11
Lumsden E4 98
Lumsden F10 104
Lumut A2 13
Lund B3 53
Lund K6 95
Lundar B4 96
Lundazi C2 67
Lundi, *river* B2 69
Lüneburg B2 40
Lünen A3 40
Lunenburg C3 100
Lunga, *river* B2 67
Lungwebungu, *river* A2 67
Lunsar A1 63
Luoyang E2 10
Lupeni B3 43
Luperón B1 89
Luquillo D2 90
Luremo C2 70
Lúrio, *river* C2 68
Lusaka, *capital* B3 67
Lusambo B2 67
Luseland A8 104
Lushnjë A3 49
Lusutfu, *river* B2 71
Luton C3 30
Lutsk B1 47
Lützow-Holm, *bay* C16 107
Luuq A3 60
Luvua, *river* B1, C2 67
Luwegu, *river* C2 68
Luxembourg 33
Luxembourg, *capital* B2 33
Luxor B2 56
Luzarches Inset II 34
Luzhou D3 10
Luzon, *island* B3 12
Luzon, *strait* B2 12
Lviv A2 47
Lyddal B1 96
Lyme, *bay* C4 30
Lynn Lake C1 96
Lyon D4 34
Lytton M6 95

M

Ma, *river* A2 11

Key Page
Maan A2 26
Maas, *river* C3, D3 32
Maastricht C4 32
Mabaruma B1 80
Maberly J3 102
Mabou F1 100
Mac Tier F2 102
MacAlpine, *lake* H3 99
Macao, S.A.R. E3 10
Macapá C1 81
Macas B4 79
Maccan C2 100
Macdonnell, *ranges* C2 14
Macedonia, F.Y.R. 48
Maceió E2 81
Macenta D3 62
Macerata C2 38
Macfarlane, *river* C2 104
Macgregor B4 96
Machakos D4 61
Machala B4 79
Machida C3 8
Machupicchu, *ruins* C3 77
MacKay, *lake* F4 99
Mackay, Qld. D2 14
Mackenzie L3 95
Mackenzie King, *island* F1 99
Mackenzie, *bay* B1 105
Mackenzie, *mts.* C4 99
Mackenzie, *river* B3, D4 99
Mackey H1 102
Macklin A8 104
Maclean, *strait* G1 99
Macmillan, *river* C4 105
Mâcon D3 34
Macon, Ga. E2 126
Madaba A2 26
Madagascar 69
Madan C4 50
Madang A2 15
Madawaska G2 102
Madden C5 94
Madeira, *island* 55
Madeira, *river* B2 81
Madhumati, *river* C5 21
Madhupur Tract, *region* D4 21
Madinat ath-Thawrah B2 27
Madison, *capital*, Wis. E1 126
Madiun C2 13
Madoc H3 102
Madre de Dios, *island* A9 76
Madre de Dios, *river* A2, C3 77
Madrid, *capital* E2, Inset II 37
Madriu, *river* B3 36
Madura, *island* C2 13
Madurai C7 20
Maebashi C2 8
Maestra, *mts.* D3 88
Maéwo, *island* C2 18
Mafeking A3 96
Mafeteng A2 71
Mafia, *island* C2 68
Mafikeng C2 71
Mafra A3 36
Mafraq, al- B1 26
Magadalena de Kino B1 84
Magadan D9 44
Magburaka B1 63
Magdagachi D8 44
Magdalena B2 77
Magdalena Contreras Inset 84
Magdalena, *island* B7 76
Magdalena, *river* B3 78
Magdeburg B2 40
Magelang C2 13
Magellan, *strait* B9 76
Maggiore, *lake* B1 38
Magnetawan F2 102
Magnitogorsk D4 44
Magog D6 103
Mahabharat, *range* B2 19
Mahajamba, *river* B2 69
Mahajanga B2 69
Mahalapye B2 69
Mahallah al-Kubra, al- B1 56
Mahanadi, *river* D4 20
Mahaska C4 94
Mahbas, al- C1 58
Mahdia B3 80
Mahdia C2 57
Mahé, *island* C1, Inset 70
Mahébourg C3 69
Mahilyow E3 47
Mahim, *bay* Inset I 20
Mahón J3 37
Mai-Ndombe, *lake* B2 67
Maidstone D3 30
Maidstone A7 104
Maiduguri G2 65
Main Brook C3 98
Main, *river* B4 40
Main-à-Dieu H1 100
Main-Danube, *canal* B4 40
Maine G1 126
Mainland, *island* Inset I 30
Maintirano A2 69
Mainz B4 40
Maio, *island* C3 58
Maipo, *river* B4, Inset 76
Maipú Inset 76
Maisí, *cape* F3 88
Maisons-Laffitte Inset II 34
Maitland Bridge B3 100
Maíz, *islands* C2 87
Maizuru B3 8
Majardah, *river* B1 57
Majé Inset I 81
Majorca, *island* H3 37
Majuro, *capital* C2 16
Majuro, *island* C2 16
Makamba B3 61
Makassar, *strait* C2 13
Makeni B1 63
Makeyevka D2 47
Makhachkala E4 44
Makhaleng, *river* A2 71
Makin, *island* A1 17
Makkovik B1 98
Makokou B1 66

Key Page
Makona, *river* A1 63
Makoua C4 66
Makran Coast, *range* B5 21
Makung A2 9
Makurdi E4 65
Malabar, *coast* B6 20
Malabo, *capital* A1 66
Malacca, *strait* A1, A2 13
Malad Inset I 20
Maladzyechna C2 47
Málaga D4 37
Malagarasi, *river* B1 68
Malaita, *island* B1 16
Malakal C3 59
Malakula, *island* B3 18
Malang C2 13
Malanje C3 70
Malanville B2 64
Mälaren, *lake* C3 53
Malatya D2 27
Malawi 68
Malay, *peninsula* A1 13
Malaysia 13
Malbaie, *river* F4 103
Malbun B2 33
Malcolm, *atoll* A1 19
Malden, *island* D2 17
Maldives 19
Male Karpaty, *mts.* A2 42
Male, *atoll* A2 19
Male, *capital* A2 19
Maleb E6 94
Malegaon B4 20
Mali 58
Mali Rajinac, *mt.* B3 48
Malindi F5 61
Mallaig B1 30
Mallow B2 31
Malmberget D1 53
Malmédy E2 33
Malmö B3 53
Maloelap, *island* C2 16
Malombe, *lake* C2 68
Maloti, *mts.* B2 71
Malta 36
Maltahöhe B3 70
Malton J5 102
Mamâri C2 62
Mamawi, *lake* E2 94
Mambéré, *river* A2 66
Mamburao B3 12
Mamiña C2 76
Mamoré, *river* A2 77
Mamou B2 62
Mamry, *lake* E1 41
Mamtalah, al- B2 25
Mamuno A2 69
Man C3 63
Mana B1 80
Mana, *river* B1 80
Manado D1 13
Managua, *capital* A2 87
Managua, *lake* A2 87
Manakara B3 69
Manama, *capital* B1 25
Manatí B2 90
Manaus C2 81
Manawan, *lake* G5 104
Manbij A1 27
Manchester C3 30
Manchester, N.H. F1 126
Manchurian, *plain* F1 10
Mand, *river* C4 22
Mandalay C2 12
Mandalgov C2 11
Mandara, *mts.* B1 65
Mandaue B4 12
Mandeville B2 88
Mándra Inset 51
Mandurah, W.A. A3 14
Manfredonia C2 38
Manga, *region* C2 59
Mangalore B6 20
Mango B1 64
Mangoky, *river* A3 69
Manicouagan, *reservoir* C3 101
Manicougan Deux,
reservoir H2 103
Manigotagan C3 96
Manila, *bay* B3 12
Manila, *capital* B3 12
Manisa A2 27
Manito, *lake* A8 104
Manitoba, *lake* B3, B4, D2 96
Manitou B4 96
Manitoulin, *island* C2 102
Manitouwadge C3 101
Manitowaning D2 102
Maniwaki A5 103
Manizales B3 78
Mankato, Minn. D1 126
Mankayane B2 71
Mankota C11 104
Mankulam B2 19
Mannar A3 19
Mannar, *gulf* C7 20
Mannar, *island* A2 19
Mannheim B4 40
Manning B3 94
Mannville E4 94
Mano, *river* A2, B2 63
Manokwari E2 13
Manono C2 67
Manono, *island* B2 18
Manor Park H5 102
Manori, *point* Inset I 20
Manouane B4 103
Manpo B2 9
Mansa B2 67
Mansa Konko C2 62
Mansel, *island* M4 99
Manson Creek K3 95
Mansurah, al- B1 56
Manta A3 79
Manta, *bay* A3 79
Mantaro, *river* B3 77
Mantiqueira, *range* D4 81
Mantova B1 38
Mantua (Mantova) B1 38

Key Page
Manukau B2 15
Manus, *island* A2 15
Manyara, *lake* C1 68
Manzanillo D3 88
Manzanillo D4 84
Manzini B2 71
Mao A1 89
Mao A4 59
Maple J5 102
Maple Creek A11 104
Maputo, *capital* B5 68
Maquela do Zombo C2 70
Mar Chiquita, *lake* C3 74
Mar del Plata D4 74
Mar, *range* D4 81
Mara, *river* C4 61
Maraba D2 81
Maracaibo B1 79
Maracaibo, *lake* B2 79
Maracay C1 79
Maradi B3 59
Marajó, *island* D2 81
Marakei, *island* A1 17
Maramasike, *island* B1 16
Maranhão D2 81
Marano, *river* C1 39
Marañón, *river* B1, B2 77
Maras D3 27
Marathon C3 101
Marbella D4 37
Marburg B3 40
Marcelin D8 104
Marche C2 38
Marchena, *island* Inset 79
Mardan D2 21
Mardin E3 27
Maré, *island* D2 18
Maremma, *region* B2 38
Margaree Forks F1 100
Margaret, *lake* C2 94
Margarita, *island* D1 79
Margate D3 30
Margherita, *peak* A3 61
Maria L3 103
Maria, *islands* B3 91
Mariana D3 81
Marianao B1 88
Marías, *islands* C3 84
Marib B1 25
Maribor C2 48
Marie Byrd Land, *region* B8 107
Marie-Reine B3 94
Mariehamn
(Maarianhamina) A2 53
Mariental C3 70
Marigot B2 90
Marijampolė B2 46
Marinduque, *island* B3 12
Marino C2 18
Marion Bridge G2 100
Maripasoula A2 80
Mariscal Estigarribia B3 75
Maritime Alps, *range* D4 34
Maritsa, *river* D3 50
Mariupol D3 47
Mariy El, *republic* D4 44
Marj Uyun A2 26
Marj, al- D1 56
Marka A3 60
Markham F4, K5 102
Markham, *river* A2 15
Markstay E1 102
Marl A3 40
Marmara, *sea* B2 27
Marmora H3 102
Marne, *river* C2, Inset II 34
Marneuli C4 45
Maromokotro, *mt.* B1 69
Marondera B2 69
Maroni, *river* A1 80
Maros, *river* C2 43
Maroua B1 65
Marovoay B2 69
Marowijne, *river* B2 80
Marquette, Mich. E1 126
Marquis B2 91
Marrakech B2 57
Marsa al-Burayqah C1 56
Marsabit E2 61
Marsala C3 38
Marsaxlokk, *bay* C3 36
Marsden A8 104
Marseille D5 34
Marsh Harbour B2 89
Marshall Is. 16
Marsoui L2 103
Martaban, *gulf* C3 12
Marten River F1 102
Martensville D8 104
Martin B2 42
Martinique, *island* 82
Martins River C3 100
Martorell D2 90
Martuni C2 45
Mary C3 22
Mary's Harbour D3 98
Maryborough, Qld. E2 14
Maryfield A4 96
Maryfield J11 104
Maryland F2 126
Marystown D5 98
Masada, *ruins* B2 26
Masai, *steppe* C1 68
Masaka B4 61
Masan C5 9
Masaya A3 87
Masbate B3 12
Masbate, *island* B3 12
Mascouche C6 103
Maseru, *capital* A2 71
Masfut D2 25
Mashhad D2 22
Masindi B3 61
Masirah, *gulf* C2 25
Masirah, *island* C2 25
Mask, *lake* B2 31
Maskall B2 85
Massachusetts F1 126
Massacre B3 90

Key Page
Massawa B2 60
Massenya B5 59
Masset F4 95
Massey C1 102
Massif Central, *plateau* C4 34
Massif des Bongos, *range* B2 66
Massy Inset II 34
Masuda A3 8
Masvingo B2 69
Mat, *river* B2 49
Matadi A2 67
Matagalpa B2 87
Matagami A4 101
Matale B4 19
Matam C2 62
Matamoros E2 84
Matane J3 103
Matanzas B1 88
Matapédia C1 97
Matapédia K4 103
Matara B6 19
Mataram C2 13
Mataró H2 37
Matautu C2 18
Matawa Place D3 96
Matehuala D3 84
Matelot A2 91
Matera D2 38
Mathura C3 20
Matlock C3 30
Mato Grosso C3 81
Mato Grosso do Sul C4 81
Mato Grosso, *plateau* C3 81
Mátra, *mts.* B2 43
Matrah C1 25
Matruh A1 56
Matsoku, *river* B2 71
Matsudo C3 8
Matsue B3 8
Matsumae D1, Inset I 8
Matsumoto C2 8
Matsuyama B3 8
Mattawa G1 102
Mattawin, *river* C5 103
Matterhorn, *mt.* B3 35
Matthew Town C4 89
Matthews Ridge A2 80
Mauá Inset II 81
Maui, *island*, Hawaii Inset II 126
Maule, *river* B5 76
Maumturk, *mts.* B2 31
Maun A1 69
Mauna Loa, *mt.*, Hawaii Inset II 126
Maunabo D2 90
Mauren B1 33
Maurepas Inset II 34
Mauritania 58
Mauritius 69
Mavinga D5 70
May Pen B3 88
Maya, *mts.* A3 85
Mayaguana, *island* C4 89
Mayaguana, *passage* C4 89
Mayagüez A2 90
Maydi A1 25
Mayfair C7 104
Maymont C8 104
Maymyo C2 12
Maynooth C2 31
Maynooth H2 102
Mayo B4 105
Mayo, *lake* C4 105
Mayombé, *massif* B5 66
Mayon, *volcano* B3 12
Mayotte, *island* C2 67
Mayreau, *island* A4 91
Mayumba A2 66
Mazabuka B3 67
Mazandaran, *region* C2 22
Mazar-e Sharif B1 22
Mazaruni, *river* A2 80
Mazatenango B5 85
Mazatlán C3 84
Mažeikiai B1 46
Mazoe, *river* B1 69
Mazyr D3 47
Mbabane, *capital* B2 71
Mbahiakro D3 63
Mbaké A2 62
Mbala C1 67
Mbale D3 61
Mbalmayo B3 65
Mbandaka B2 67
M'banza Congo B2 70
Mbanza-Ngungu A2 67
Mbarara B4 61
Mbemkuru, *river* C3 68
M'Beni A1 67
Mbéré, *river* B2 65
Mbeya B2 68
Mbini B3 66
Mbini, *river* C3 66
Mboro, *river* D4 66
Mboune, *river* B2 62
Mbour A2 62
Mbuji-Mayi B2 67
Mbuluzane, *river* B2 71
Mbuluzi, *river* B2 71
McAdam B3 97
McAllen, Tex. D3 126
McBride M4 95
McCallum C5 98
McCreary B4 96
McDame H1 95
McGee B9 104
Mchinji A2 68
McKerrow D1 102
McKinley *mt.*, Alaska Inset I 126
McLeese Lake L5 95
McLeod Lake L4 95
McLeod Valley C4 94
M'Clintock, *channel* H2 99
M'Clure, *strait* D2 99
McLure M5 95
McMurdo, *sound* B5 107
McRae E4 94
Meacham E8 104
Meadow Lake B6 104
Meadow Portage B3 96

Key Page
Meaford E3 102
Mealy, *mts.* A3 98
Meander River B1 94
Mecca A2 24
Mechelen C1 33
Mecklenburg, *bay* B1 40
Mecklenburg-
Western Pomerania C2 40
Mecsek, *mts.* B2 43
Medan A1 13
Medellín B3 78
Medford, Oreg. A1 126
Medgidia E3 43
Mediaș C2 43
Medicine Hat E6 94
Medika D4 96
Medina A1 24
Medina del Campo D2 37
Medit B2 13
Mediterranean, *sea* 29
Medley E4 94
Medora A4 96
Meductic B3 97
Meelpaeg, *lake* C5 98
Meerut C3 20
Meghna, *river* D5 21
Meghri D4 45
Meighen, *island* J1 99
Meiktila B2 12
Meissen C3 40
Mejicanos A2 86
Mékambo B1 66
Mekele C1 60
Mékinac, *lake* D4 103
Meknès C1 57
Mekong, *delta* B5 11
Mekong, *river* A1, A4, C4, D3 11
Mékrou, *river* B2 64
Melaka B2 13
Melbourne, Fla. E3 126
Melbourne, Vic., *capital* D3 14
Meldrum Bay B2 102
Meleb C4 96
Melekeok C3 17
Mélèzes, *river* B2 101
Melfi B5 59
Melfort F8 104
Melipilla Inset 76
Melita A4 96
Melitopol D3 47
Mellieha B2 36
Mellieha, *bay* B2 36
Melo C2 75
Melrose E2 100
Melun Inset II 34
Melville H10 104
Melville, *island* C1 14
Melville, *island* F1 99
Melville, *lake* B2 98
Melville, *peninsula* M3 99
Memmingen B5 40
Memphis, Tenn. D2 126
Memphrémagog, *lake* D6 103
Menai, *strait* B3 30
Ménaka D2 58
Mende C4 34
Mendoza B3 74
Meneng B3 16
Menihek D3 98
Mennecy Inset II 34
Menongue C4 70
Mentawai, *islands* A2 13
Menzel Bourguiba B1 57
Meppel D2 32
Mequinenza, *lake* F2 37
Merano B1 38
Merauke F2 13
Mercedario, mt. B3 74
Mercedes A2 75
Mergui C3 12
Mergui, *archipelago* C4 12
Mérida B2 79
Mérida C3 37
Mérida, *mts.* B2 79
Mérida, *state capital* G3 84
Meridian, Miss. E2 126
Merigomish E2 100
Merín, *lagoon* D2 75
Merir, *island* Inset 17
Merkys, *river* C2 46
Meron, *mt.* B1 26
Merredin, W.A. A3 14
Merrick, *mt.* B2 30
Merridale A3 96
Merritt M6 95
Mersch B2 33
Mersey, *river* C3 30
Mersin C3 27
Merthyr Tydfil B3 30
Meru D3 61
Merume, *mts.* A2 80
Mesaoria, *plain* B1 27
Meseta, *plateau* D3 37
Mesolóngion B2 51
Mesopotamia, *region* B2 24
Messina D1 71
Messina C3 38
Messina, *strait* C3 38
Mesta, *river* B4 50
Meta Incognita, *peninsula* P4 99
Meta, *river* C3 78
Métabetchouan E3 103
Metcalfe K2 102
Meteghan A3 100
Métis-sur-Mer J3 103
Metiskow E5 94
Metz D2 34
Meulan Inset II 34
Meuse, *river* D2 33
Mexiana, *island* D1 81
Mexicali, *state capital* A1 84
Mexico 84
Mexico City,
national capital E4, Inset 84
Mexico, *gulf* 82
Meymaneh A1 22
Meyungs B3 17
Mgwavuma, *river* B3 71
Mhlume B2 71

Key Page
Miami B4 96
Miami, Fla. E3 126
Mianwali D3 21
Miaoli B1 9
Mica Creek N5 95
Michalovce C2 42
Miches C2 89
Michigan E1 126
Michigan, *lake* E1 126
Michoacán D4 84
Mico, *river* B2 87
Micoud B3 91
Micronesia 15
Midale G11 104
Middelburg C3 71
Middelburg A3 32
Middle Andaman, *island* F6 20
Middle Arm C4 78
Middle Atlas, *ranges* C1 57
Middle Lake E8 104
Middle Musquodoboit D2 100
Middlebro D4 96
Middlesbrough C2 30
Middleton B3 100
Midi-Pyrénées C5 34
Midland F3 102
Midland, Tex. C2 126
Midlands, *region* C3 30
Miercurea Ciuc C2 43
Mieres D1 37
Mikkeli C2 53
Mikkwa, *river* C2 94
Mikomeseng C2 66
Míkonos, *island* C3 51
Mikura, *island* C3 8
Miladummadulu, *atoll* A1 19
Milagro B4 79
Milan B1 38
Milden C9 104
Mildura, Vic. D3 14
Miles City, Mont. C1 126
Milestone F10 104
Milford Haven B3 30
Milford Sound A3 15
Milh, *lake* B2 24
Mili, *island* C2 16
Milk, *river* E6 94
Mill Bay L7 95
Mill Village C3 100
Miller Lake D2 102
Millet D4 94
Milliken K5 102
Milltown D5 98
Millville B2 97
Milne, *bay* B3 15
Milo D6 94
Milo, *river* D3 62
Mílos, *island* C3 51
Milton B2 100
Milton F4 102
Milverton E4 102
Milwaukee, Wis. E1 126
Mimico J6 102
Miminegash A2 100
Mina Baranis C3 56
Mina Salman B1 25
Minami, *island* Inset III 8
Minas C3 75
Minas Gerais D3 81
Minas, *channel* C2 100
Minatitlán F4 84
Minch, *strait* B1 30
Mindanao, *island* C5 12
Mindelo B2 58
Mindemoya C2 102
Minden G3 102
Mindoro, *island* B3 12
Mindoro, *strait* B3 12
Miner's Bay G3 102
Miner, *river* B3 105
Mingäçevir B2 45
Mingäçevir, *reservoir* B2 45
Minho, *river* A1 36
Minicoy, *island* B7 20
Minija, *river* A2 46
Miniota A4 96
Minitonas A3 96
Mink Creek A3 96
Minna D3 65
Minneapolis, Minn. D1 126
Minnedosa B4 96
Minnesota D1 126
Miño, *river* C1 37
Minorca, *island* H2 37
Minot, N. Dak. C1 126
Minsk, *capital* C3 47
Minto B4 96
Minto C2 97
Minto B4 105
Minto, *lake* B2 101
Minton F11 104
Minya, al- B2 56
Miquelon, *island* M4 92
Mira H1 100
Mirabel B6 103
Mirador Nacional, *mt.* C3 75
Miraflores B4 78
Miragoâne B2 89
Miramichi D1 97
Miramichi, *bay* E1 97
Miranda de Ebro E1 37
Mirbat B3 25
Mirebalais C2 89
Miri D2 13
Mirnyy C7 44
Mirpur Khas C5 21
Mirror D5 94
Miscou, *island* E1 97
Miscouche B2 100
Misere Inset 70
Misery, *mt.* B1 90
Miskolc C1 43
Misool, *island* E2 13
Missinipe F5 104
Mississauga F4, J6 102
Mississippi D2 126
Mississippi, *lake* J2 102
Mississippi, *river* D1 126
Missoula, Mont. B1 126
Missouri D2 126
Missouri, *river* D1 126
Mistassibi, *river* D1 103
Mistassini D3 103
Mistassini, *lake* B3 101
Mistassini, *river* D2 103
Mistatim G8 104
Mistelbach E2 39
Misurata C1 56
Mitchell D4 102
Mitchell, *mt.*, N.C. E2 126
Mitchell, *river* D1 14
Mitchinamécus, *lake* A4 103
Mitilíni C2 51
Mito D2 8
Mitsamiouli A1 67
Mittelland, *canal* B2 40
Mitú C4 78
Mitumba, *mts.* C2 67
Mitzic A1 66
Miyake, *island* C3 8
Miyako D2 8
Miyako, *island* Inset II 8
Miyakonojo A4 8
Miyazaki A4 8
Mizen Head, *cape* B3 31
Mizo, *hills* F4 20
Mizpe Ramon B2 26
Mjøsa, *lake* C3 52
Mkondvo, *river* B2 71
Mliba B2 71
Mmabatho C2 71
Mo C2 52
Moa, *island* D2 13
Moa, *river* B2 63
Moab, Utah C2 126
Moala, *island group* B3 17
Moanda B2 66
Moba C2 67
Mobaye B3 66
Mobile, Ala. E2 126
Moca B1 89
Moca A2 90
Moçambique D2 68
Mocha, (Mukha, al-) A2 25
Mocímboa da Praia D1 68
Môco, *mt.* C4 70
Mocoa A4 78
Modena B1 38
Moengo B2 80
Moers A3 40
Mogadishu, *capital* B3 60
Mogami, *river* D2 8
Mogi das Cruzes Inset II 81
Mogilev Podolskiy B2 47
Mogocha D7 44
Mogotón, *mt.* A2 87
Mohács B2 43
Mohales Hoek A3 71
Mohammedia C1 57
Moher, *cliffs* B2 31
Mojave, *desert*, Calif. B2 126
Mojos A2 77
Mokhotlong C2 71
Mokolo B1 65
Mokpo B5 9
Mold B3 30
Moldavia, *region* D2 43
Molde B3 52
Moldova 50
Moldoveanu, *mt.* C3 43
Molepolole B3 69
Molise C2 38
Mollendo C4 77
Molokai *island*, Hawaii Inset II 126
Molopo, *river* B2 71
Moloundou C3 65
Molson, *lake* C2 96
Molucca, *sea* D2 13
Moluccas, *islands* D2 13
Mombasa E5 61
Mombetsu Inset I 8
Mon Repos B2 91
Møn, *island* D4 32
Mona, *passage* D2 89
Monaco 35
Monaco, *capital* B1 35
Monaghan C1 31
Monastery F2 100
Monastir C2 57
Mönchengladbach A3 40
Monclova D2 84
Moncton E2 97
Mondego, *cape* A2 36
Mondego, *river* B2 36
Monforte C1 37
Mongo B4 59
Mongolia 11
Mongolian, *plateau* C2 11
Mongomo D3 66
Mongu A3 67
Monitor E5 94
Monjolo Inset I 81
Monkey Bay B2 68
Mono, *river* A4, B2 64
Monopoli D2 38
Monrovia, *capital* A2 63
Mons B2 33
Mont-Carmel G4 103
Mont-Joli H3 103
Mont-Laurier A5 103
Mont-Royal J5 103
Mont-Saint-Michel B2 34
Mont-St-Pierre L2 103
Mont-Tremblant-Village B5 103
Montague C2 100
Montalto, *mt.* C3 38
Montana B2 50
Montana B1 126
Montargis C2 34
Montauban C4 34
Monte Carlo B1 35
Monte Cristi A1 89
Monte Plata C2 89
Montebello B6 103
Montecristo, *island* B2 38
Montegiardino B2 39
Montego Bay B2 88
Montélimar D4 34
Montelindo, *river* C3 75
Montenegro, *republic* A3 49
Montepulciano B2 38
Monterey, Calif. A2 126
Montería B2 78
Montero B3 77
Monterrey, *state capital* D2 84
Montes Claros D3 81
Montevideo, *capital* B3 75
Montgomery, *capital*, Ala. E2 126
Montluçon C3 34
Montmagny F5 103
Montmartre G10 104
Montpelier, *capital*, Vt. F1 126
Montpellier C5 34
Montréal C6, J5 103
Montréal, *island* J5 103
Montreal, *lake* E6 104
Montreal, *river* E6 104
Montreuil Inset II 34
Montreux A2 35
Montrose C2 30
Monywa B2 12
Monza B1 38
Moore Park B4 96
Moose Factory D2 101
Moose Jaw E10 104
Moose Lake A2 96
Moose, *river* D2 101
Moosehorn B3 96
Moosomin J10 104
Moosonee D2 101
Mopti C3 58
Moquegua C4 77
Moradabad C3 20
Morant Bay C3 88
Moratuwa A5 19
Morava, *river* A2, C3 42
Morava, *river* B3 49
Moravia, *region* C3 42
Moray, *estuary* B1 30
Morden B4 96
Mordoviya, *republic* E4 44
Moree, N.S.W. D2 14
Morehead A2 15
Morelia, *state capital* D4 84
Morell C2 100
Morelos E4 84
Morena, *mts.* D3 37
Moresby, *island* F5 95
Moreton, *bay* Inset III 14
Morgan City, La. D3 126
Morges A2 35
Morghab, *river* A1 22
Morghob B1 23
Morghob, *river* B1 23
Morice, *lake* J4 95
Moricetown J3 95
Morija A2 71
Morinville D4 94
Morioka D2 8
Morlaix B2 34
Morne Diablotin, *mt.* B2 90
Moro, *gulf* B5 12
Moro, *river* A2 63
Morocco 57
Morogoro C2 68
Morombe A3 69
Morón D2 88
Mörön C2 11
Morón de la Frontera D4 37
Morondava A3 69
Moroni, *national capital* A1 67
Morotai, *island* D1 13
Moroto D2 61
Morpeth D5 102
Morphou A1 27
Morrin D5 94
Morris C4 96
Morrisburg K3 102
Mors, *island* B2 32
Morse C10 104
Mortlach D10 104
Mortlock, *islands* C2 15
Moruga A2 91
Moscow, *capital* D3 44
Mosel, *river* A4 40
Moselle, *river* D2 34
Moshi C1 68
Mosjøen C2 52
Mosquitos, *coast* C3 87
Moss C4 52
Mossbank E11 104
Mossel Bay B3 71
Mossendjo B5 66
Mossleigh D6 94
Mossy, *river* F6 104
Most A2 42
Mostaganem B1 57
Mostar B2 48
Móstoles Inset II 37
Mosul B1 24
Motagua, *river* D4 85
Motherwell B2 30
Mouila A2 66
Mould Bay E1 99
Moule à Chique, *cape* B3 91
Moulmein C3 12
Moulouya, *river* D1 57
Moundou B5 59
Mount Carmel A2 100
Mt. Forest E4 102
Mount Gambier, S.A. D3 14
Mount Hagen A2 15
Mount Isa, Qld. C2 14
Mt. Stewart C2 100
Mountain Park B5 94
Moura B3 36
Mourne, *mts.* A2 30
Mouscron B2 33
Moussa Ali, *mt.* B1 60
Mouths of the Danube, *delta* E3 43
Mouths of the Ganges, *delta* C7 21
Mouths of the Indus, *delta* C5 21
Moyale E2 61
Moyamba A1 63
Moyie P6 95
Moyobamba B2 77
Moyowosi, *river* B1 68
Mozambique 68
Mozambique, *channel* 55
Mozzoro E2 81
Mpanda B2 68
Mpika C2 67
Mpoko, *river* A2 66
Mporokoso C1 67
Mqinvartsveri, *mt.* C3 45
M'Ramani B2 67
Mtkvari, *river* C4 45
Mtskheta C4 45
Mtwara D3 68
Muang Khammouan C3 11
Muang Không C4 11
Muang Khôngxédôn C4 11
Muang Paklay A2 11
Muang Pakxan B2 11
Muang Vangviang B2 11
Muang Xaignabouri A2 11
Muang Xay A1 11
Muang Xépôn D3 11
Muang Xon B1 11
Muar B2 13
Muara C1 13
Mubende B3 61
Mubi G2 65
Muchinga, *mts.* C2 67
Mudanjiang F1 10
Mudawwarah, al- B3 26
Mufulira B2 67
Muğla B3 27
Muharraq, al-, *island* B1 25
Mühlhausen B3 40
Mui Bai Bung, *point* A5 11
Mukalla, al- B2 25
Muko, *island* Inset III 8
Mulaku, *atoll* A3 19
Mulde, *river* C3 40
Mulhacén, *mt.* E4 37
Mülheim an der Ruhr A3 40
Mulhouse D3 34
Mull, *island* A2 30
Mullaittivu B2 19
Mullingar C2 31
Multan D3 21
Mulund Inset I 20
Mulvihill B4 96
Mumbai (Bombay) B5, Inset I 20
Mumbai (Bombay), *harbor* Inset I 20
Mumbra Inset I 20
Mumbwa B3 67
Mun, *river* C3 12
Muna, *island* D2 13
Munamägi, *mt.* D3 46
Muncho Lake K2 95
Munich B4 40
Munsan B4 9
Münster A3 40
Munster, *province* B2 31
Muonio B1 53
Muonioälven, *river* D1 53
Muoniojoki, *river* B1 53
Mur, *river* D3 39
Mura, *river* C2 48
Muramvya B2 61
Murat, *river* E2 27
Murchison, *river* A2 14
Murcia F4 37
Murdochville L3 103
Mureş, *river* B2 43
Murgab, *river* D3 22
Muriel, *lake* E4 94
Murilo, *atoll* C2 15
Müritz, *lake* C2 40
Murmansk C3 44
Muroran D1, Inset I 8
Muroto, *cape* B3 8
Murray Harbour C3 100
Murray River C2 100
Murray, *harbour* C2 100
Murray, *lake* A2 15
Murray, *river* D3 14
Murrumbidgee, *river* D3 14
Murska Sobota D2 48
Mürz, *river* D3 39
Murzuq B2 56
Muş E2 27
Mūša, *river* B1 46
Musala, *mt.* B3 50
Musan C1 9
Muscat, *capital* C1 25
Musgrave Harbour E4 98
Musgrave, *ranges* C2 14
Musgravetown E5 98
Mushin B4 65
Muskeg River A4 94
Muskegon, Mich. E1 126
Muskogee, Okla. D2 126
Muskoka, *lake* F2 102
Muskwa, *ranges* J2 95
Musoma B1 68
Musquodoboit Harbour D3 100
Mussau, *island* A2 15
Mustang B2 19
Mustique, *island* B3 91
Mustvee D2 46
Musu-dan, *point* C2 9
Mut A2 56
Mutare C2 69
Mutsamudu B2 67
Mutsu D1 8
Muyinga C1 61
Muyun Kum, *desert* D2 23
Muzaffarabad D2 21
Muynoq A2 23
Mwali (Mohéli), *island* A2 67
Mwanza B1 68
Mwene-Ditu B2 67
Mweru, *lake* B1, C3 67
Mwinilunga A2 67
My Tho B4 11
Myanmar (Burma) 12
Myingyan B2 12
Myitkyina C1 12
Mykolaiv C3 47
Mymensingh D4 21
Myrnam E4 94
Mysore C6 20
Mzimba B2 68
Mzuzu B2 68

N

Ndalatando B3 70
N'Djamena, *capital* A4 59
N'zeto B2 70
Naas C2 31
Nabatiyah at-Tahta, an- A2 26
Naberezhnyye Chelny D4 44
Nabeul C1 57
Nabk, an- A2 27
Nabouwalu B2 17
Nacala D2 68
Nacaome B3 86
Nackawic B3 97
Nadi A2 17
Nadi, *bay* A2 17
Nadur B1 36
Naduri B2 17
Næstved C3 32
Nafud, an-, *desert* B1 24
Nag Hammadi B2 56
Naga B3 12
Naga, *hills* F3 20
Nagano C2 8
Nagaoka C2 8
Nagarote A2 87
Nagasaki A3 8
Nagorno-Karabakh, autonomous region B2 45
Nagoya C3 8
Nagpur C4 20
Nagua C1 89
Naguabo D2 90
Nagykanizsa A2 43
Naha Inset II 8
Nahanni, *river* C4 99
Nahariyya B1 26
Naicam F8 104
Naihati Inset II 20
Nain E3 98
Nairobi, *capital* D4 61
Najaf, an- B2 24
Najd, *region* B1 24
Najin D1 9
Najran B2 24
Nakadori, *island* A3 8
Nakano, *island* A4 8
Nakfa B1 60
Nakhichevan A3 45
Nakhodka E8 44
Nakhon Phanom C2 12
Nakhon Ratchasima C3 12
Nakhon Sawan B3 12
Nakhon Si Thammarat B4 12
Nakina C2 101
Nakodu B2 17
Nakskov C4 32
Naktong, *river* C5 9
Nakuru D4 61
Nakusp O6 95
Nal, *river* B4 21
Nalikul Inset II 20
Nam Dinh B2 11
Nam Ngum, *reservoir* B2 11
Nam Tok B3 12
Namangan D2 23
Namew, *lake* H6 104
Namib, *desert* A1, B3 70
Namibe B5 70
Namibia 70
Namoluk, *atoll* C2 15
Namonuito, *atoll* C2 15
Nampo A3 9
Nampa B3 94
Nampula C2 68
Namsos C3 52
Namu, *island* B2 16
Namuli, *highlands* C2 68
Namur C2 33
Namur, *lake* D2 94
Namwala B3 67
Nan B2 12
Nan Ling, *mts.* E3 10
Nan, *river* B2 12
Nanaimo L6 95
Nanchang E3 10
Nanchong D2 10
Nancy D2 34
Nanda Devi, *mt.* C2 20
Nanded C5 20
Nanga Parbat, *mt.* E2 21
Nanga-Eboko B3 65
Nangi Inset II 20
Nangnim-sanmaek, *mts.* B3 9
Nanjing E2 10
Nanning D3 10
Nanole Inset I 20
Nantbu B2 9
Nanterre Inset II 34
Nantes B3 34
Nanticoke E5 102
Nanumanga, *island* B2 16
Nanumea, *island* B1 16
Nanyang E2 10
Nao, *cape* G3 37
Napadogan C2 97
Napaktulik, *lake* F3 99
Napanee J3 102
Napier C2 15
Naples C2 38
Naples, *bay* C2 38
Napo, *river* C1 77
Nara B3 8
Nara, *canal* C4 21
Narathiwat B5 12
Narayanganj D5 21
Narayani, *river* B2 19
Narbonne C5 34
Narcisse C4 96
Nares, *strait* O1 99
Narew, *river* E2 41
Narmada, *river* C4 20
Narrogin, W.A. A3 14
Narrows, *strait* C2 90
Narsaq C2 106
Narva E1 46
Narva, *river* D1 46
Narvik D2 52
Naryan-Mar C4 44
Naryn E2 23
Naryn, *river* E2 23
Nashshash, an- C3 25
Nashville, *capital*, Tenn. E2 126
Nashwaak Bridge C2 97
Näsi, *lake* B2 53
Nasik B4 20
Nasiriyah, an- C2 24
Nass, *river* H3 95
Nassau, *capital* B2 89
Nasser, *lake* B3 56
Nata B2 69
Natal E2 81
Natalkuz, *lake* K4 95
Natashquan D3 101
Natitingou A2 64
Natron, *lake* C1 68
Natuna Besar, *island* B1 13
Naucalpan de Juárez Inset 84
Naujoji Akmenė B1 46
Naumburg B3 40
Nauru 16
Navabad A1 23
Navarino, *island* C9 76
Navarra F1 37
Navojoa C2 84
Navua B3 17
Navua, *river* A3 17
Nawabshah C4 21
Nawoiy C2 23
Náxos, *island* C3 51
Nayarit C3 84
Nazareth B1 26
Nazca C3 77
Naze Inset II 8
Nazko L5 95
Nazret C2 60
Nchelenge B1 67
Ndélé B2 66
Ndendé A2 66
Ndjolé A2 66
Ndola B2 67
Néa Liósia Inset 51
Neagh, *lake* A2 30
Neápolis B3 51
Nebitdag B2 22
Neblina, *mt.* B1 81
Nebraska D1 126
Nechako, *river* K4 95
Neckar, *river* B4 40
Necochea D4 74
Neder Rijn, *river* C3 32
Nee Soon B1 13
Needles N6 95
Neepawa B4 96
Nefta A3 57
Negele C3 60
Negev, *region* B2 26
Negombo A4 19
Negra, *lagoon* D2 75
Negra, *point* A2 77
Negril A2 88
Negro, *river* B4 74
Negro, *river* B2 81
Negro, *river* C2 75
Negros, *island* B4 12
Neguac D1 97
Neiafu C2 17
Neiba A2 89
Neiba, *mts.* A2 89
Neijiang D3 10
Neil Harbour G1 100
Neilburg A8 104
Neisse, *river* C3 40
Neiva B4 78
Nekemte B2 60
Nellore C6 20
Nelson B3 15
Nelson O6 95
Nelson Forks L1 95
Nelson House B1 96
Nelson, *river* C1, D1 96
Nelspruit D2 71
Néma D3 58
Nemeiben, *lake* E5 104
Nemunas, *river* A2, C2 46
Nemuro Inset I 8
Nemuro, *strait* Inset I 8
Nenagh B2 31
Nendo, *island* C2 16
Nenetsiya, autonomous okrug C4 44
Nepal 19
Nepalganj B2 19
Nepean G6, K2 102
Nepisiguit, *river* C1 97
Neretva, *river* B2 48
Neris, *river* C2 46
Ness, *lake* B1 30
Nesselrode, *mt.* E1 95
Nestaocano, *river* C2 103
Netanya B1 26
Netherlands 32
Nettilling, *lake* O3 99
Netzahualcóyotl Inset 84
Neubrandenburg C2 40
Neuchâtel A2 35
Neuchâtel, *lake* A2 35
Neudorf G10 104
Neufchâteau D3 33
Neumünster B1 40
Neunkirchen A4 40
Neuquén B4 74
Neusiedler, *lake* E3 39
Neuss A3 40
Neustadt A2 85
Neustrelitz C2 40
Nevada B2 126
Nevada, *mts.* E4 37
Nevers C3 34
Neves B4 63
Neves Inset I 81
Nevėžis, *river* B2 46
Nevis, *island* C3 90

Key Page
New Amsterdam C2 80
New Brigden E5 94
New Britain, island B2 15
New Caledonia, island C2 18
New Carlisle L4 103
New Delhi, capital C3 20
New Denver O6 95
New England, range E3 14
New Ferolle C4 98
New Fish Creek B3 94
New Georgia Group, islands A1 16
New Glasgow E2 100
New Guinea, island A2 15
New Hamburg E4 102
New Hampshire F1 126
New Hanover, island B2 15
New Haven, Conn. F1 126
New Ireland, island B2 15
New Jersey F1 126
New Kowloon Inset 10
New Liskeard E3 101
New Mexico C2 126
New Minas C2 100
New Orleans, La. D3 126
New Plymouth B2 15
New Providence, island B3 89
New Richmond L3 103
New Ross C3 100
New Sandy Bay B1 91
New Schwabenland, region B16 107
New Siberian, islands B9 44
New South Wales D3 14
New Territories, island Inset 10
New Waterford G1 100
New Waterway, channel B3 32
New York F1 126
New York, N.Y. F1 126
New Zealand 15
New, river C4 80
New, river B1 85
Newark, N.J. F1 126
Newboro J3 102
Newcastle C2 90
Newcastle C2 71
Newcastle upon Tyne C2 30
Newcastle, N.S.W. E3 14
Newcastle-under-Lyme C3 30
Newdale A4 96
Newell, lake E6 94
Newman, W.A. A2 14
Newmarket D3 30
Newmarket F3 102
Newport C3 30
Newport News, Va. F2 126
Newquay B4 30
Newry A2 30
Newtown St. Boswells C2 30
Neyagawa B3 8
Neyshabur D2 22
Ngami, lake A2 69
Ngaoundéré B2 65
Ngara B1 68
Ngaramasch B4 17
Ngauruhoe, mt. C2 15
Ngerkeel B3 17
Ngemelis, islands B3 17
Ngermechau C2 17
Ngetbong C2 17
Ngiro, river D3 61
Ngoc Linh, mt. B3 11
Ngonini B1 71
Ngorongoro, crater C1 68
Ngounié, river A2 66
Ngozi B1 61
Nguigmi C3 59
Ngulu, atoll A2 15
Nguru F1 65
Ngwempisi, river A2 71
Nha Trang B4 11
Nhlangano B3 71
Niagara Falls F4 102
Niagara-on-the-Lake F4 102
Niagassola D1 62
Niamey, capital A3 59
Niamtougou B2 64
Niari, river B5 66
Nias, island A1 13
Nibok B2 16
Nicaragua 87
Nicaragua, lake B3 87
Nice D5 34
Nicholls' Town A2 89
Nickerie, river A2 80
Nicobar, islands F7 20
Nicola M6 95
Nicolet D5 103
Nicosia, capital B1 27
Nicoya, gulf B3 86
Nictau B1 97
Nidže, mts. B3 48
Niedere Tauern, range D3 39
Niefang C3 66
Nienburg B2 40
Niéri Ko, river C2 62
Nieuw Amsterdam B2 80
Nieuw Nickerie A2 80
Nigadoo D1 97
Niğde C3 27
Niger 59
Niger, delta C5 65
Niger, river B3 58
Nigeria 65
Nii, island C3 8
Niigata C2 8
Niihama B3 8
Niihau, island, Hawaii Inset II 126
Nijmegen C3 32
Nikaia Inset 51
Nikki B3 64
Nikko C2 8
Nikolayevsk-na-Amure D9 44
Nikopol C2 47
Nikšić A3 49
Nikunau, island A2 17
Nilandu, atoll A3 19
Nile, river B2 56
Nilgiri, hills C6 20
Nilópolis Inset I 81
Nimba, mt. B3 63
Nimba, mts. B2 62
Nîmes D5 34
Nine Mile River D2 100
Ninette B4 96
Ninga B4 96
Ningbo F3 10
Ningxia Hui D2 10
Ninigo, group A2 15
Niono B3 58
Nioro du Rip B3 62
Nioro du Sahel B2 58
Niort B3 34
Nipawin F7 104
Nipigon C3 101
Nipigon, lake C3 101
Nipissing F1 102
Nipissing, lake F1 102
Niš B3 49
Nišava, river C3 49
Nishino, island Inset III 8
Nishinomiya B3 8
Nisling, river B4 105
Niterói D4, Inset I 81
Nitra B2 42
Niuafo'ou, island B1 17
Niuatoputapu, island C1 17
Niulakita, island C4 16
Niutao, island B2 16
Niverville C4 96
Nizamabad C5 20
Nizhnevartosk C5 44
Nizhny Novgorod D4 44
Nizhny Tagil D4 44
Njazidja (Grande Comore), island A1 67
Njombe, river B2 68
Nkawkaw B3 64
Nkhata Bay B2 68
Nkhotakota B2 68
Nkongsamba A2 65
Noakhali E6 21
Nobeoka A3 8
Noel D2 100
Nogales B1 84
Nogales, Ariz. B2 126
Nojima, cape D3 8
Nok Kundi B4 21
Nokaneng A1 69
Nokomis E9 104
Nola A3 66
Nome, Alaska Inset I 126
Nonacho, lake G4 99
Nong Khai C2 11
Nonsan B4 9
Nonthaburi B3 12
Nootka, island J6 95
Norak A1 23
Nord-Ostsee, canal B1 40
Nord-Pas-de-Calais C1 34
Nordenham B2 40
Nordhausen B3 40
Nordhorn A2 40
Nordvik B7 44
Norfolk D5 94
Norfolk, Va. F2 126
Norilsk C6 44
Norland G3 102
Normandin D3 103
Norquay H9 104
Norra Storfjället, mt. C1 53
Norris Arm D4 98
Norris Point C4 98
Norrköping C3 53
Norte, key E2 90
N. Albanian Alps, mts. A1, B3 49
North Andaman, island F6 20
North Battleford B8 104
North Bay F1 102
North Cape B1 100
North Carolina F2 126
North China, plain E2 10
North Comino, channel B1 36
North Dakota C1 126
North Downs, hills C3 30
North Frisian, islands B4 32
North Holland, canal B2 32
North Korea 9
North Magnetic Pole B13 106
North Malosmadulu, atoll A2 19
N. Moose, lake B2 96
North Ossetiya, republic E4 44
North Platte, Nebr. C1 126
North Portal H11 104
North Rhine-Westphalia A3 40
North Rustico B2 100
North Saskatchewan, river D8 104
North Sea, canal B2 32
North Shields C2 30
North Siberian, lowland B6 44
North Star B3 94
North Taranaki, bight B2 15
N. Thompson, river N5 95
North Uist, island A1 30
North Wabasca, lake D3 94
North West River A2 98
North West, cape A2 14
North York K5 102
North, cape F1 52
North, channel A2 30
North, channel B1 102
North, island B2 15
North, river B2 98
North, sea 29
Northallerton C2 30
Northampton C3 30
Northeast, polder C2 32
Northeim B3 40
Northern Divina, river C4 44
Northern European, plain B2 4
Northern Sporades, islands B2 51
Northern Territory C2 14
Northgate H11 104
Northumberland, strait B3, D2 100
Northwest Gander, river D5 98
Norton D3 97
Norvegia, cape B14 107
Norway 52
Norway House C2 96
Norwegian, bay K1 99
Norwegian, sea A2 52
Norwich D3 30
Norwich E4 102
Nossob, river C3 70
Nosy Be, island B1 69
Nosy Sainte Marie, island B2 69
Noteć, river C2, D2 41
Noto, peninsula C2 8
Notre Dame de Lourdes B4 96
Notre Dame Junction D4 98
Notre Dame, bay D4 98
Notre-Dame E2 97
Notre-Dame-de-la-Merci B5 103
Notre-Dame-de-laSalette A6 103
Notre-Dame-de-Lorette D2 103
Notre-Dame-du-Bon-Conseil D5 103
Notre-Dame-du-Lac H4 103
Notre-Dame-du-Laus A5 103
Nottingham C3 30
Nottingham, island N4 99
Nouadhibou A2 58
Nouakchott, capital A3 58
Nouméa, capital C2 18
Nouvelle K3 103
Nova Gorica A3 48
Nova Iguaçu Inset I 81
Novara B1 38
Novaya Zemlya, islands B4 44
Nové Zamky B3 42
Novgorod D3 44
Novi Pazar B3 49
Novi Sad A2 49
Novo Mesto C3 48
Novokuznetsk D6 44
Novosibirsk D6 44
Novra A3 96
Nowshak, mt. D2 21
Nowy Sącz E4 41
Nsanje C3 68
Nsawam B4 64
Nsok D3 66
Nsoko B3 71
Nsukka D4 65
Ntem, river B3 65
Nu'ulua, island D3 18
Nu'utele, island D3 18
Nuba, mts. C3 59
Nubian, desert C1 59
Nueltin, lake J4 99
Nueva Casas Grandes C1 84
Nueva Gerona B2 88
Nueva Loja C2 79
Nueva Ocotepeque A2 86
Nueva Palmira A2 75
Nueva Rosita D2 84
Nueva San Salvador A2 86
Nuevitas D2 88
Nuevo Laredo E2 84
Nuevo León D2 84
Nuevo Rocafuerte D3 79
Nuguria, islands B2 15
Nuhud, an- B2 59
Nui, island B2 16
Nuku'alofa, capital B4 17
Nukufetau, island C2 16
Nukulaelae, island C3 16
Nukuoro, atoll C2 15
Nukus A2 23
Nullarbor, plain B3 14
Numazu C3 8
Ñuñoa Inset 76
Nuoro B2 38
Nuremberg B4 40
Nutak E3 98
Nuuk (Godthåb), capital B2 106
Nuuli B1 18
Nuwara Eliya B5 19
Nyaake C3 63
Nyaba, river B2 61
Nyala B2 59
Nyanga, river A2 66
Nyanza B2 61
Nyasa (Malawi), lake B2, B3 68
Nyborg C3 32
Nyeri D4 61
Nyetane, river B2 71
Nyika, plateau B2 68
Nyíregyháza C2 43
Nykøbing C4 32
Nyoman, river B3 47
Nyong, river B3 65
Nysa C3 41
Nzérékoré D4 62
Nzi, river D3 63
Nzo, river C3 63
Nzoia, river C3 61
Nzwani (Anjouan), island B2 67

O
O'Leary A2 100
Oahu, island, Hawaii Inset II 126
Oak Lake A4 96
Oak Point C4 96
Oak Point C3 97
Oak River A4 96
Oakland, Calif. A2 126
Oakner A4 96
Oakview B3 96
Oakville C4 96
Oakville F4 102
Oamaru B4 15
Oaxaca, state capital E4 84
Ob, river C5 44
Oban B2 30
Obed B4 94
Oberammergau B5 40
Oberhausen A3 40
Oberpfälzer Wald, mts. C4 40
Obi, island D2 13
Obihiro Inset I 8
Obo C2 66
Obock C2 60
Obuasi B3 64
Occidental, mts. B2, C4 77
Ocean Falls J5 95
Ochamchire A3 45
Ochil, hills B2 30
Ocho Rios B2 88
Ochre River B3 96
Ocoa, bay B2 89
Ocotal A2 87
Ocotlán D3 84
Oda B4 64
Odei, river C1 96
Odemira A4 36
Odense C3 32
Odense, fjord C3 32
Odenwald, forest B4 40
Oder, river B2, C3 41
Oderhaff, lake C2 40
Odesa C3 47
Odessa, Tex. C2 126
Odienné C2 63
Oeiras A3 36
Oelemari, river B3 80
Offa C3 65
Offenbach B3 40
Ofu, island A1 18
Ogaden, region D3 60
Ogbomosho C3 65
Ogden, Utah B1 126
Ogema F11 104
Ogilvie, mts. B3 105
Oglio, river B1 38
Ogoki, river C2 101
Ogooué, river A2 66
Ogosta, river B2 50
Ogražden, mts. C2 48
Ogre C2 46
Ogun, river B3 65
Ohio E1 126
Ohio, river E2 126
Ohonua C4 17
Ohrid A2 48
Ohrid, lake B2 49
Øibenik B3 48
Oise, river C2, Inset II 34
Oistins B5 91
Oita A3 8
Ojinaga D2 84
Ojos del Salado, mt. B2 74
Oka, river D4 44
Okahandja B2 70
Okakarara C2 70
Okanagan Falls N6 95
Okanagan, lake N6 95
Okara D3 21
Okavango, basin A1 69
Okavango, river A1 69
Okayama B3 8
Okazaki C3 8
Okeechobee, lake, Fla. E3 126
Okene D4 65
Okha D9 44
Okhotsk D9 44
Okhotsk, sea D9 44
Oki, islands B2 8
Okinawa, island Inset II 8
Okino Erabu, island Inset II 8
Oklahoma D2 126
Oklahoma City, capital, Okla. D2 126
Okondja B2 66
Okotoks C6 94
Okushiri, island C1, Inset I 8
Okwa, river A2 69
Ólafsvík A2 52
Olanchito B2 86
Öland, island C3 53
Olavarría C4 74
Olbia B2 38
Old Brahmaputra, river C4 21
Old Crow B2 105
Old Perlican E5 98
Old Road D5 90
Old Road Town B2 90
Old Wives, lake D10 104
Oldenburg B2 40
Oldham C3 30
Oldman, river D6 94
Olds C5 94
Olenek, river C7 44
Oléron, island B4 34
Olgilvie, river B3 105
Ölgiy A2 11
Olifants, river A3, C1 71
Olinda E2 81
Oliver N6 95
Ollagüe, volcano C2 76
Ollei C2 17
Olmaliq C2 23
Olomouc C3 42
Olongapo B3 12
Olosega, island A1 18
Olsztyn E2 41
Olt, river C3 43
Oltenița D3 43
Olympia, capital, Wash. A1 126
Olympus mt., Wash. A1 126
Olympus, mt. A2 27
Olympus, mt. B1 51
Omagh A2 30
Omaha, beach B2 34
Omaha, Nebr. D1 126
Oman 25
Oman, gulf C1, D2 25
Omaruru B2 70
Omatako, river C1 70
Omboué A2 66
Omdurman C2 59
Omemee G3 102
Ometepe, island B3 87
Omineca, mts. J2 95
Omineca, river K3 95
Omiya C3 8
Omo, river B3 60
Omsk D5 44
Omuta A3 8
Onanole B4 96
Ondame B2 62
Ondangwa B1 70
Ondava, river C2 42
Ondjiva C5 70
Ondo C4 65
Öndörhaan D2 11
Onefour E6 94
Onega, lake C3 44
Onești D2 43
Ongjin A4 9
Ongole C5 20
Onilahy, river A3 69
Onion Lake A7 104
Onitsha D4 65
Ono, island B3 17
Onon, river D2 11
Onota, island A2 17
Onsŏng C1 9
Ontario, lake K4 92
Ontong Java, island A1 16
Oostende A1 33
Oostende-Brugge, canal B1 33
Oosterschelde, channel A3 32
Ootsa, lake J4 95
Opava C3 42
Opeongo, lake G2 102
Opole C3 41
Oporto (Porto) A2 36
Opuwo A1 70
Oqsu, river C2 23
Oradea A2 43
Oral B1 23
Oran A1 57
Orange Walk B1 85
Orange, N.S.W. D3 14
Orange, river A3, B2 71
Orangeville E4 102
Oranje, mts. B3 80
Oranjemund B4 70
Orapa B2 69
Ordino B2 36
Ordu D2 27
Örebro C3 53
Oregon A1 126
Orellana, lake D3 37
Orenburg D4 44
Orense C1 37
Øresund, sound D3 32
Órganos, mts. A2 88
Órgãos, range Inset I 81
Orhei B2 50
Orhon, river C2 11
Oriental, mts. B2, C3 77
Oriental, range C2 89
Orillia F3 102
Orinoco, river C3, D2 79
Orion E6 94
Oristano B3 38
Orizaba E4 84
Orkney, islands Inset I 30
Orlando, Fla. E3 126
Orléans C3 34
Orléans, island F5, L5 103
Ormoc C4 12
Orne, river B2 34
Örnsköldsvik C2 53
Orocué C3 78
Oroluk, atoll C2 15
Oromocto C3 97
Oron E5 65
Orontes, river A2 27
Orosháza C2 43
Orrefors C3 53
Orsha E2 47
Orsk D4 44
Ortegal, cape C1 37
Orumiyeh (Urmia) A2 22
Oruro A3 77
Oryakhovo B2 50
Os, river A3 36
Osaka B3 8
Osasco Inset II 81
Osh C2 23
Oshakati B1 70
Oshawa G4 102
Oshima, peninsula D1, Inset I 8
Oshogbo C4 65
Osijek D2 48
Osilinka, river K3 95
Öskemen (Ust-Kamenogorsk) E1 23
Oslo, capital C3 52
Oslofjord, fjord C4 52
Osnabrück B2 40
Osorno B7 76
Osoyoos N6 95
Oss C3 32
Osse, river C4 65
Österdalälven, river B2 53
Östersund B2 53
Ostrava D3 42
Ostrołęka E2 41
Osum, river B3 49
Osumi, islands A4 8
Osumi, peninsula A4 8
Osumi, strait A4 8
Osŭm, river C3 50
Otaru Inset I 8
Otavalo B2 79
Otavi C1 70
Oti, river B1, C2 64
Otjiwarongo B2 70
Otranto D2 38
Otranto, strait A3 49
Otsu B3 8
Ottawa H5, K2 102
Ottawa, river G1, G5 H5, K2 102
Otterlo C2 32
Ötztal Alps, range B4 39
Ou, mts. D2 8
Ou, river B1 11
Ouadane C2 58
Ouagadougou, capital D2 64
Ouahigouya C2 64
Ouaka, river B2 66
Ouanary C1 80
Ouargla B1 57
Ouarra, river C2 66
Ouarzazate C2 57
Oudtshoorn B3 71
Ouémé, river B3 64
Ouesso D3 66
Ouezzane C1 57
Ouham, river A2 66
Ouidah B4 64
Oujda D1 57
Oulu C1 53
Oulu, lake C2 53
Oulujoki, river C2 53
Oum er-Rbia, river C1 57
Ounasjoki, river B1 53
Oungre G11 104
Our, river B1 33
Ourthe, river D2 33
Ouse, river C2, D3 30
Outarde, river H2 103
Outer Hebrides, islands A1 30
Outjo B2 70
Outlook C9 104
Ouvéa, island C2 18
Ovalau, island B2 17
Ovalle B4 76
Overflakkee, island B3 32
Overflowing River A2 96
Oviedo A3 89
Oviedo D1 37
Owando C4 66
Owen Sound E3 102
Owen Stanley, range A2 15
Owendo A1 66
Owensboro, Ky. E2 126
Owerri D5 65
Oxbow H11 104
Oxford C3 30
Oxford D2 100
Oxford House D1, D2 96
Oxford, lake D2 96
Oyapock, river B2 80
Oyem A1 66
Oyo B4 65
Ozama, river B2 89
Ozark, plateau D2 126
Ózd C1 43
Özgön C2 23
Ozoir-la-Ferrière Inset II 34
Ozurgeti A4 45

P
Pa-an C3 12
Paamiut (Frederikshåb) C2 106
Pabna C4 21
Pacaraima, mts. D3 79
Pacasmayo B2 77
Pachuca, state capital E3 84
Padang B2 13
Paddle Prairie B2 94
Paderborn B3 40
Padma, river D5 21
Padua (Padova) B1 38
Paektu-san, mt. C2 9
Pagadian B5 12
Pago Pago, capital B1 18
Pahang, river B2 13
Paianía Inset 51
Päijänne, lake C2 53
Paint, lake B1 96
Paisley B2 30
Paita A2 77
Pakaraima, mts. A3 80
Pakistan 21
Pakowki, lake E6 94
Paks B2 43
Pakse C4 11
Pala A5 59
Palaiseau Inset II 34
Palana D10 44
Palanga A2 46
Palangkaraya C2 13
Palau 17
Palawan, island A4 12
Paldiski C1 46
Pale B2 48
Palembang B2 13
Palencia D1 37
Palermo C3 38
Palikir, capital C2 15
Palk, strait C7 20
Palliser, cape C3 15
Palm, island A4 91
Palma H3 37
Palmas D3 81
Palmer Land, region B11 107
Palmerston E4 102
Palmerston North C3 15
Palmira A4 78
Palmyra, ruins B2 27
Palos, cape F4 37
Palu C2 13
Pamirs, mts. B2 23
Pamirs, region A2 10
Pampas, plain C4 74
Pamplemousses C2 69
Pamplona F1 37
Panagyurishte C3 50
Panaji B5 20
Panama 87
Panama, canal C2 87
Panamá, capital C2 87
Panama, gulf C3 87
Panay, gulf B4 12
Panay, island B4 12
Pančevo B2 49
Panch'iao B1 9
Pandan, strait A2 13
Pandaruan, river C2 13
Pando C3 75
Panevėžys C2 46
Pangani, river C1 68
Pangkalpinang B2 13
Pangnirtung P3 99
Panihati Inset II 20
Panj A2 23
Panj, river B2 23
Panjakent A1 23
Panjgur B4 21
P'anmunjŏm B4 9
Pantanal, lowland C4 81
Pantelleria, island C3 38
Pánuco, river E3 84
Panzhihua D3 10
Pápa A2 43
Papagayo, gulf A2 86
Paphos A2 27

Key Page
Papua, gulf A2 15
Papua New Guinea 15
Paquetville D1 97
Pará C2 81
Pará, river C2 81
Paradise Hill A7 104
Paradise River C2 98
Paraguá, river B2 77
Paraguai, river C3 81
Paraguarí D4 75
Paraguay 75
Paraguay, river C2, C5 75
Paraíba E2 81
Parakou B3 64
Paramaribo, capital B2 80
Paraná C3 74
Paraná C4 81
Paraná, river D2 74
Paranaguá D4 81
Paranam B2 80
Pardubice B2 42
Parent B4 103
Parepare C2 13
Paria, gulf D1 79
Parima, range B1 81
Paris, capital C2, Inset II 34
Paris E4 102
Parkhill D4 102
Parkland D6 94
Parksville K6 95
Parma B1 38
Parnaiba D2 81
Parnaíba, river D2 81
Pärnu C2 46
Pärnu, river C2 46
Paro A2 19
Paropamisus, range A2 22
Páros, island C3 51
Parral B6 76
Parrsboro C2 100
Parry D2 99
Parry Sound E2 102
Parry, channel J2 99
Parsnip, river L4 95
Parson's Pond C4 98
Pas de la Casa C2 36
Pasadena C5 98
Pasfield, lake E2 104
Pasión, river C3 85
Paso de los Toros B2 75
Paso de Palmar, lake B2 75
Passau C4 40
Passero, cape C3 38
Passo Fundo C4 81
Pastavy C2 47
Pastaza, river B1 77
Pastillo C3 90
Pasto A4 78
Patagonia, region A6 74
Patavilca B3 77
Paterson, N.J. F1 126
Patía, river A4 78
Patiala C2 20
Patillas C2 90
Patna E3 20
Patos, lagoon C5 81
Pátrai B2 51
Patricia E6 94
Pattani B5 12
Patuakhali D6 21
Patuanak C5 104
Patuca, mts. C2 86
Patuca, river C2 86
Pau B5 34
Pauingassi D3 96
Paulatuk D3 99
Paulaya, river C2 86
Paulo Afonso E2 81
Pavaiai B2 18
Pavia B1 38
Pavilosta A2 46
Pavlodar D1 23
Paxbán C2 85
Payar B2 62
Paye Inset I 20
Payne, lake B2 101
Paynton B7 104
Pays De La Loire B3 34
Paysandú A2 75
Paz, river C6 85
Pazardzhik C3 50
Peace Point D1 94
Peace River B3 94
Peace, river A3, C2 94
Peachland N6 95
Pebane C3 68
Peć B3 49
Pechora C4 44
Pechora, river C4 44
Pécs B2 43
Pedernales A2 89
Pedja, river D2 46
Pedra Açú, mt. Inset I 81
Pedra Lume D2 58
Pedro Juan Caballero E3 75
Pedro Santana A1 89
Peebles H10 104
Peel, river B3, C2 105
Peerless Lake C3 94
Pegasus, bay B3 15
Pegu C3 12
Peipus, lake D2 46
Pekalongan B2 13
Pekanbaru B1 13
Pelee, island C6 102
Peleliu, island B4 17
Peleng, island D2 13
Pelican Narrows H5 104
Pelican Portage D3 94
Pelican Rapids A3 96
Pelican, lake G5 104
Pelkan, lake A3 96
Pelly J9 104
Pelly Bay L3 99
Pelly Crossing B4 105
Pelly, river C4, C5 105
Pelotas C5 81
Pematangsiantar A1 13
Pemba D2 68
Pemba, island C2 68
Pemberton L6 95
Pembina, river B4 94
Pembina, river B4 96
Pembroke B3 30
Pembroke H2 102
Penas, gulf B8 76
Pendé, river A2 66
Pendleton, Oreg. B1 126
Penetanguishene F3 102
Pênghu (Pescadores), islands A2 9
Peniche A3 36
Peninsular Malaysia, region B2 13
Pennant B10 104
Pennine Alps, mts. B2 35
Pennines, mts. C2 30
Pennsylvania F1 126
Penonomé B2 87
Penrith C2 30
Pensacola, Fla. E2 126
Pensacola, mts. A11 107
Pentecost, island C2 18
Penticton N6 95
Peñuelas B2 90
Penza D4 44
Penzance B4 30
Peoria, Ill. E1 126
Perak, river A2 13
Percé M3 103
Perdue C8 104
Pereira B3 78
Péribonca, river B3 101
Péribonka D3 103
Périgueux C4 34
Perim, island A2 25
Peristéri Inset 51
Perlas, archipelago C2 87
Perlas, lagoon C2 87
Perm D4 44
Pernambuco E2 81
Pernik B3 50
Perpignan C5 34
Perrot, island G6 103
Persian, gulf C1, C2, C3 24
Perth B2 30
Perth J3 102
Perth, W.A., capital A3, Inset I 14
Perth-Andover B2 97
Peru 77
Perugia C2 38
Pervomaysk C2 47
Pesaro C2 38
Pescadores, channel A2 9
Pescara C2 38
Peshawar D3 21
Peshkopi B2 49
Petah Tiqwa B1 26
Petare C1 79
Petauke C2 67
Petawawa H2 102
Petén-Itzá, lake D3 85
Peterborough C3 30
Peterborough G3 102
Peterhead C1 30
Petersfield C4 96
Petit Canouan, island B3 91
Petit Martinique, island C1 91
Petit Mustique, island B3 91
Petit St. Vincent, island A4 91
Petit-Rocher D1 97
Petitcodiac D3 97
Petite Riviere C3 100
Petlura A3 96
Petra, ruins A2 26
Petrich B4 50
Petrila B3 43
Petrolia C5 102
Petrólina D2 81
Petropavl C1 23
Petropavlovsk-Kamchatskiy D9 44
Petrópolis D4, Inset I 81
Petroşani B3 43
Petrozavodsk C3 44
Pevek C10 44
Peyia A2 27
Pforzheim B4 40
Phan Rang B4 11
Phan Thiet B4 11
Phatthalung B5 12
Phayao B2 12
Phetchabun B2 12
Phetchabun, range B3 12
Phetchaburi B3 12
Phichit B2 12
Philadelphia, Pa. F2 126
Philippine, sea C3 12
Philippine, sea B2 17
Philippines 12
Phitsanulok B2 12
Phnom Penh, capital C4 11
Phnum Tbeng Meanchey C2 11
Phoenix, capital, Ariz. B2 126
Phoenix, island B2 17
Phoenix, islands B2 17
Phôngsali B1 11
Phou Bia, mt. B2 11
Phra Nakhon Si Ayutthaya B3 12
Phuket B5 12
Phumi Samraong B1 11
Phuntsholing A3 19
Pianosa, island B2 38
Piapot A10 104
Piatra Neamţ D2 43
Piauí D2 81
Piave, river C1 38
Pibor Post C3 59
Pic de la Selle, mt. D2 89
Picardie C2 34
Pickle Lake B2 101
Pico do Cano, volcano B4 58
Picton H3 102
Pictou E2 100
Pidurutalagala, mt. B4 19
Piedmont A1 38
Piedra Sola B2 75
Piedras Negras D2 84
Pielinen, lake C2 53
Pierceland A6 104
Pierre, capital, S. Dak. C1 126
Pierrefonds G5 103
Pierreville A2 91
Pierson A4 96
Piešťany A2 42
Pietermaritzburg D2 71
Pietersburg C1 71
Pigeon, lake C4 94
Pigeon, lake G3 102
Piggs Peak B1 71
Pikangikum B2 101
Pikes peak, Colo. C2 126
Pikwitonei C1 96
Piła C2 41
Pilar C5 75
Pilaya, river B4 77
Pilcomayo, river B3, C4 75
Pilica, river E3 41
Pílos B3 51
Pilot Butte F10 104
Pilot Mound B4 96
Pinang, island A2 13
Pinar del Río A2 88
Pinawa D4 96
Pindus, mts. B2 51
Pine Bluff, Ark. D2 126
Pine Dock C3 96
Pine Falls C4 96
Pine Point F4 99
Pine River A3 96
Pinehouse Lake D5 104
Pines, island D2 18
Ping, river B2 12
P'ingtung B2 9
Pingxiang E3 10
Piniós, river B2 51
Pink Mountain L2 95
Pink, river F4 104
Pinsk C3 47
Pinta, island Inset 79
Piotrków Trybunalski D3 41
Pipestone A4 96
Pipmuacan, reservoir F2 103
Piracicaba D4 81
Pirada C1 62
Piraiévs B3, Inset 51
Pirmasens A4 40
Pirot C3 49
Pirris, river B3 86
Pisa B2 38
Pisagua B1 76
Pisco B3 77
Pistoia B2 38
Piteşti C3 43
Pitlochry B2 30
Pitseng B2 71
Pitt, island H4 95
Pittsburgh, Pa. E1 126
Piura A2 77
Placentia B3 85
Placentia D5 98
Placentia, bay D5 98
Placenza B1 38
Placetas C2 88
Planken B1 33
Plantagenet K2 102
Plasencia C2 37
Plaster Rock B2 97
Plata, Río de la, estuary D3 74
Plata, river B3 75
Platte, river, Nebr. C1 126
Plauen C3 40
Playgreen, lake B2 96
Pleasant Bay G1 100
Pleiku B4 11
Plenty, bay C2 15
Plessisville E5 103
Pleven C2 50
Plevna J3 102
Plibo C3 63
Pljevlja A3 49
Ploče C3 48
Płock D2 41
Ploieşti D3 43
Plovdiv C3 50
Plum Coulee C4 96
Plumas B4 96
Plymouth B1 91
Plymouth B4 30
Plzeň A3 42
Po, river A1, B1 38
Poá Inset II 81
Pobé B4 64
Pocatello, Idaho B1 126
Podgorica A3 49
Pogradec B3 49
Pohang C4 9
Pohnpei, island D2 15
Poinsett, cape C2 107
Point Fortin A2 91
Point Leamington D4 98
Point Pedro B2 19
Point Prim B2 100
Point, lake F3 99
Pointe au Baril E2 102
Pointe du Bois D4 96
Pointe Michel B3 90
Pointe Sapin E2 97
Pointe-a-la-Croix K3 103
Pointe-Claire H6 103
Pointe-des-Monts J2 103
Pointe-Lebel H2 103
Pointe-Noire A6 66
Pointe-Verte D1 97
Poisson Blanc, reservoir A6 103
Poissy Inset II 34
Poitiers C3 34
Poitou-Charentes C3 34
Pokemouche E1 97
Pokhara B2 19
Poland 41
Polar, plateau A14 107
Polba Inset II 20
Polis A1 27
Polonnaruwa C4 19
Polotsk D2 47
Poltava C2 47
Poltimore A6 103
Pomeranian, bay C1 40
Ponce B2 90
Pond Cove C3 98
Pond Inlet N2 99
Pondicherry C6 20
Ponferrada C1 37
Ponoka D5 94
Pont Cassé B3 90
Pont-Rouge E5 103
Pontchartrain Inset II 34
Ponteix C11 104
Pontevedra B1 37
Pontianak B2 13
Pontic, mts. D2 27
Pontine, islands C2 38
Pontine, marshes C2 38
Pontoise Inset II 34
Ponton B2 96
Poole C4 30
Poopó, lake A3 77
Popayán A4 78
Poperinge A2 33
Poplar River C3 96
Popomanaseu, mt. B1 16
Popondetta A2 15
Poprad C2 42
Porcupine Plain G8 104
Porcupine, river B2 105
Pori B2 53
Port Alberni K6 95
Port Antonio C2 88
Port au Choix C4 98
Port au Port B5 98
Port Augusta, S.A. C3 14
Port Bickerton F2 100
Port Blair F6 20
Port Blandford D5 98
Port Bruce E5 102
Port Burwell D3 98
Port Burwell E5 102
Port Clements F4 95
Port Colborne F5 102
Port Coquitlam L6 95
Port Dufferin E3 100
Port Elgin E3 97
Port Elgin D3 102
Port Elizabeth B2 91
Port Elizabeth C3 71
Port Franks D4 102
Port George B2 100
Port Glaud Inset 70
Port Harcourt D5 65
Port Hardy J6 95
Port Hawkesbury F2 100
Port Hedland, W.A. A2 14
Port Hood F1 100
Port Hope G4 102
Port Hope Simpson C3 98
Port Laoise C2 31
Port Lincoln, S.A. C3 14
Port Loko A1 63
Port Loring E2 102
Port Louis, capital B2 69
Port Macquarie, N.S.W. E3 14
Port Maria C2 88
Port McNeill J6 95
Port Moody L6 95
Port Morant C3 88
Port Moresby, capital A2 15
Port Mouton C4 100
Port Nolloth A2 71
Port of Spain, capital A2 91
Port Perry G3 102
Port Phillip, bay Inset V 14
Port Pirie, S.A. C3 14
Port Renfrew K7 95
Port Rowan E5 102
Port Said B1 56
Port Saunders C4 98
Port Stanley D5 102
Port Sudan D1 59
Port Talbot B3 30
Port-au-Prince, bay C2 89
Port-au-Prince, capital C2 89
Port-Cartier C3 101
Port-de-Paix C1 89
Port-Gentil A2 66
Port-Salut B2 89
Portadown A2 30
Portage A2 100
Portage la Prairie B4, D2 96
Portalegre B3 36
Porter, lake C4 104
Porters Lake D3 100
Porth Edward D3 71
Portimão A4 36
Portland A2 91
Portland Creek C4 98
Portland, bight B3 88
Portland, inlet G4 95
Portland, Maine F1 126
Portland, Oreg. A1 126
Portneuf, river G3 103
Porto Alegre B4 63
Pôrto Alegre C5 81
Pôrto Inglês C3 58
Pôrto Velho B2 81
Porto-Novo, capital B4 64
Porto-Vecchio Inset I 34
Portobelo C2 87
Portoviejo A3 79
Portree A1 30
Portsmouth C4 30
Portsmouth A2 90
Portsmouth, Va. F2 126
Portugal 36
Porvenir B9 76
Posadas D2 74
Poste, river C3 69
Postojna B3 48
Postville B3 98
Potaro, river B3 80
Potenza C2 38
Poti A3 45
Potiskum F2 65
Potnarvin C4 18
Potosí A3 77
Potrerillos C3 76
Potsdam C2 40
Pottuvil C5 19
Pouch Cove E5 98
Poutasi C3 18
Pouthisat B3 11
Považská Bystrica B2 42
Powassan F1 102
Powell River K6 95
Powerview C4 96
Poyang, lake E3 10
Poza Rica E3 84
Požarevac B2 49
Poznań C2 41
Pozo Colorado C3 75
Pra, river B4 64
Prachuap Khiri Khan B4 12
Prague, capital B2 42
Praia, capital C4 58
Praslin B2 91
Praslin, island C1 70
Prato B2 38
Prawda D4 96
Preeceville H9 104
Prelate A10 104
Preparis, island B3 12
Přerov C3 42
Prescott K3 102
Prescott, Ariz. B2 126
Presidencia Roque Sáenz Peña C2 74
Prešov C2 42
Prespa, lake B3 48
Presque Isle, Maine G1 126
Prestea A4 64
Preston C3 30
Pretoria, administrative capital C2 71
Préveza B2 51
Prey Veng D4 11
Priboj A3 49
Priddis C6 94
Prievidza B2 42
Prijedor A1 48
Prilep B2 48
Priluki C1 47
Primorsko F3 50
Primrose, lake A6 104
Prince Albert E7 104
Prince Albert, hills L3 99
Prince Albert, peninsula E2 99
Prince Charles, island N3 99
Prince George L4 95
Prince of Wales, island J2 99
Prince Patrick, island E1 99
Prince Regent, inlet K2 99
Prince Rupert G4 95
Princes Town A2 91
Princess Harbour C3 96
Princess Margriet, canal C1 32
Princess Royal, island H4 95
Princeton M6 95
Princeville E5 103
Príncipe, island C1 63
Prinzapolka C2 87
Prinzapolka, river B2 87
Pripyats, marshes C4 47
Pripyats, river C3 47
Priština B3 49
Privas D4 34
Prizren B3 49
Progresso B1 85
Prokopyevsk D6 44
Prokuplje B3 49
Prome B2 12
Prophet River L2 95
Prostějov C3 42
Provence-Alpes-Côte-d'Azur D4 34
Providence Bay C2 102
Providence, capital, R.I. F1 126
Providencia, island Inset 78
Providenciales, island C4 89
Provideniya C11 44
Provo, Utah B1 126
Pru, river B3 64
Prut, river B2 47
Przemyśl F4 41
Psel, river C1 47
Pskov D3 44
Pskov, lake D3 46
Ptsich, river D3 47
Ptuj C2 48
Pu'apu'a B2 18
Pubnico B4 100
Pucallpa C2 77
Puck D1 41
Puebla, state capital E4 84
Pueblo, Colo. C2 126
Puente Alto Inset 76
Puerca, point D2 90
Puerto Aisén B8 76
Puerto Armuelles A2 87
Puerto Ayacucho C2 79
Puerto Bahía C2 75
Puerto Barrios E4 85
Puerto Bolívar B4 79
Puerto Cabello C1 79
Puerto Cabezas C1 87
Puerto Carreño D3 78
Puerto Cisnes B7 76
Puerto Cortés B2 86
Puerto Deseado B6 74
Puerto Escondido E4 84
Puerto Inírida D4 78
Puerto Jiménez C4 86
Puerto Leguízamo B5 78
Puerto Lempira D2 86
Puerto Maldonado D3 77
Puerto Montt B7 76
Puerto Natales B9 76
Puerto Peñasco B1 84
Puerto Pinasco D3 75
Puerto Plata B1 89
Puerto Princesa A4 12
Puerto Real A2 90
Puerto Rico 90
Puerto Quepos B3 86
Puerto Sandino A2 87
Puerto Santa Cruz B7 74
Puerto Suárez C3 77
Puerto Vallarta C3 84
Puerto Varas B7 76
Puerto Williams C9 76
Puertollano D3 37
Puglia C2 38
Pugwash D2 100
Pujehun B2 63
Pukatawagan A1 96
Pukch'ŏng C2 9
Pukë A1 49
Pula A3 48
Pulangi, river C5 12
Puławy E3 41
Pulo Anna, island Inset 17
Pulusuk, island C2 15
Puná, island A4 79
Punakha A2 19
Pune B5 20
Punggol B1 13
P'ungsan C2 9
Puno C4 77
Punta, mt. B2 90
Punta Arenas B9 76
Punta del Este C3 75
Punta Delgada B9 76
Punta Gorda B3 85
Punta Santiago D2 90
Puntarenas B3 86
Punto Fijo B1 79
Purari, river A2 15
Purbeck's Cove C4 98
Purus, river B2 81
Pusan C5 9
Putao C1 12
Putre C1 76
Puttalam A3 19
Puttgarden B1 40
Putumayo, river B5 78
Puvirnituq A1 101
Puyo C3 79
Puysegur, point A4 15
Pyandzh, river B1 23
P'yŏnggang B3 9
P'yŏngsŏng A3 9
P'yŏngsan B3 9
P'yŏngyang, capital A3 9
Pyrenees, range C5 34

Q

Qaanaaq (Thule) B2 106
Qachas Nek B3 71
Qadarif, al- C2 59
Qaidam, basin C2 10
Qalat B2 22
Qalat Bishah B2 24
Qaleh-ye Now A2 22
Qaleh-ye Panjeh C1 22
Qamea, island C2 17
Qamishli, al- B1 27
Qandahar B2 22
Qaqortoq (Julianehåb) C2 106
Qaraghandy (Karaganda) D2 23
Qardho B2 60
Qareh, river B1 22
Qarokul, lake B1 23
Qarshi C3 23
Qaryah ash-Sharqiyah, al- B1 56
Qasigiannguit (Christianshåb) B2 106
Qasr as-Sabiyah C2 24
Qatar 25
Qatranah, al- B2 26
Qatrun, al- B3 56
Qattarah, depression A2 56
Qayrawan, al- C2 57
Qayyarah, al- B1 24
Qazvin B2 22
Qelelevu, island C2 17
Qeshm, island D4 22
Qilian, range C2 10
Qin Ling, mts. D2 10
Qina B2 56
Qingdao F2 10
Qinghai C2 10
Qinghai, lake C2 10
Qinhuangdao E2 10
Qiqihar F1 10
Qiryat Gat B2 26
Qiryat Shemona B1 26
Qishn C1 25
Qom C3 22
Qormi B2 36
Qostanay C1 23
Qu'Appelle G10 104
Qu'Appelle, river D10 104
Quang Ngai B3 11
Quantaq C1 101
Quanzhou E3 10
Quatre Bornes B3 69
Quba C2 45
Qubayyat, al- B1 26
Québec, capital E5, L6 103
Quebo C2 62
Quebradillas B2 90
Queen Charlotte F4 95
Queen Charlotte, islands G4 95
Queen Charlotte, sound H5 95
Queen Charlotte, strait H5 95
Queen Elizabeth, islands H1 99
Queen Maud Land, region B16 107
Queen Maud, mts. A5 107
Queen Maude, gulf H3 99
Queensland D2 14
Queenstown B1 13
Queenstown A3 15
Queenstown C3 71
Queenstown, Tas. D4 14
Queguay Grande, river B2 75
Queimados Inset I 81
Quelimane C3 68
Quellón B7 76
Queluz A3 36
Querétaro, state capital D3 84
Quesnel L5 95
Quesnel, lake M5 95
Quetta C3 21
Quetzaltenango B5 85
Quevedo B3 79
Quezon City B3 12
Qui Nhon B4 11

Key Page
Quibala C3 70
Quibdó A3 78
Quilchena M6 95
Quill Lake F8 104
Quill, lakes F8 104
Quillota B4 76
Quilpué Inset 76
Quimbele C2 70
Quimper A2 34
Quinhámel B2 62
Quintana Roo G4 84
Quispamsis D3 97
Quito, capital B3 79
Qunaytirah, al- A3 27
Qunfudhah, al- B2 24
Qunghirot A2 23
Quqon D2 23
Qurghonteppa A2 23
Qurnat asSawda, mt. B1 26
Quthing A3 71
Qyzylorda C2 23

R

Raahe B2 53
Raanes, peninsula L1 99
Raba C2 13
Rába, river A2 43
Rabat B2 36
Rabat, capital C1 57
Rabaul B2 15
Rabbit Lake C7 104
Rabbit Lake Mine G2 104
Rabi, island C2 17
Rach Gia A4 11
Rachidia, er- C2 57
Racine, Wis. E1 126
Rădăuţi C2 43
Radium Hot Springs O6 95
Radom E3 41
Radviliškis B2 46
Radville F11 104
Rae E4 99
Rafha B1 24
Rafter A1 96
Ragged, point C3 91
Ragueneau H2 103
Ragusa C3 38
Rahimyar Khan D4 21
Rainbow Lake A2 94
Rainier mt., Wash. A1 126
Raipur D4 20
Rajang, river C2 13
Rajbiraj C3 19
Rajkot B4 20
Rajpur Inset II 20
Rajshahi B4 21
Rakaposhi, mt. E2 21
Raleigh, capital, N.C. F2 126
Ralik, island chain A1 16
Rama B2 87
Ramadi, ar- B2 24
Ramanbati Inset II 20
Ramat Gan B1 26
Ramea C5 98
Ramla B2 26
Ramon, mt. B2 26
Ramree, island B2 12
Ramtha, ar- B1 26
Ramu F2 61
Ramu, river A2 15
Rancagua B4 76
Rance, river B2 34
Ranchi E4 20
Randa B2 60
Randers C2 32
Randonopolis C3 81
Ranfurly E4 94
Rangamati F6 21
Ranger Lake B1 102
Rangitikei, river C2 15
Rangpur C3 21
Ranong B4 12
Rapel, river B4 76
Rapid City A4 96
Rapid City, S. Dak. C1 126
Rapla C1 46
Rapti, river B2 19
Raqqah, ar- B2 27
Ras al-Khafji C1 24
Ras al-Khaymah C2 25
Ras an-Naqb A2 26
Ras Dashen, mt. C1 60
Ras Musandam, cape C1 25
Ras Tanura C1 24
Rasa, point C5 74
Rashayya A2 26
Rasht B2 22
Ratak, island chain B1 16
Ratchaburi B3 12
Rathlin, island A2 30
Ratingen A3 40
Ratnapura B5 19
Raukumara, range C2 15
Rauma B2 53
Raurkela D4 20
Raut, river B2 50
Ravenna C1 38
Ravensburg B5 40
Ravi, river D3 21
Rawa, river B4 80
Rawalpindi D3 21
Rawdatayn, ar- B2 24
Rawdon D2 100
Rawson B5 74
Raymore F9 104
Rayong B3 12
Rayside-Balfour D1 102
Raz, point A3 34
Razelm, lake E3 43
Razgrad E2 50
Ré, island B3 34
Reading C3 30
Rebun, island Inset I 8
Rechytsa E3 47
Recife E2 81
Recklinghausen A3 40
Reconquista D2 74
Red (Hong), river A2 11
Red Bay C3 98
Red Deer D5 94
Red Deer, lake A2 96
Red Deer, river D5, E6 94
Red Indian, lake C5 98
Red Rose C3 96
Red Sucker, lake E2 96
Red Volta, river B1, D3 64
Red Willow D5 94
Red, river C4 96
Red, river D2 126
Red, sea A1 24
Redange A2 33
Redbridge F1 102
Redding, Calif. A1 126
Redonda, island A6 90
Redstone L5 95
Redvers A4 96
Redvers J11 104
Ree, lake B2 31
Reed, lake A2 96
Regensburg C4 40
Reggio di Calabria C3 38
Reggio nell'Emilia B1 38
Reghin C2 43
Regina F10 104
Régina B1 80
Registan, region A2 22
Rehoboth C3 70
Rehovot B2 26
Reigate Inset III 30
Reims D2 34
Reina Adelaida, archipelago B9 76
Reindeer, island C3 96
Reindeer, lake H3 104
Reindeer, river G4 104
Reinosa D1 37
Reliance G4 99
Remagen A3 40
Remich B2 33
Rémire B1 80
Remscheid A3 40
Rencontre East D5 98
Renfrew J2 102
Rennell, island B2 16
Rennes B2 34
Rennie D4 96
Reno, Nev. B2 126
Renous D2 97
Repentigny K5 103
Reserve H8 104
Resistencia D2 74
Reşiţa A3 43
Resolute J2 99
Resolution, island P4 99
Restigouche, river B1 97
Reston A4 96
Restoule F1 102
Réunion, island 55
Reus G2 37
Reuss, river C2 35
Reutlingen B4 40
Revelstoke N6 95
Reventazón, river C3 86
Revillagigedo, islands B4 84
Rexdale J5 102
Rexton E2 97
Rey, island C2 87
Reykjavik B3 96
Reykjavík, capital A2 52
Reynosa E2 84
Rezekne D2 46
Reznas, lake D2 46
Rhaetian Alps, mts. D2 35
Rharsa, salt marsh A2 57
Rhine, canal B1, B2 33
Rhine, river A3, A4 40
Rhineland-Palatinate A4 40
Rhode Island F1 126
Rhodes D3 51
Rhodes, island D3 51
Rhodope, mts. C4 50
Rhondda B3 30
Rhône, river D4 34
Rhône-Alpes D4 34
Rhum, island A1 30
Riaba A1 66
Ribe B3 32
Ribeira Brava B2 58
Ribeira Grande A1 58
Ribeirão Pires Inset II 81
Ribeirão Prêto D4 81
Riberalta A2 77
Rîbniţa B2 50
Rice, lake G3 102
Richard, lake C1 104
Richard-Toll B1 62
Richards Bay D2 71
Richards Landing A1 102
Richardson, mts. B1 105
Richardson, river E2 94
Richelieu, river C6 103
Richer C4 96
Richibucto E2 97
Richmond L6 95
Richmond D6 103
Richmond Hill F4, K5 102
Richmond Park D4 94
Richmond, capital, Va. F2 126
Ricobayo, reservoir D2 37
Rida A2 25
Rideau, lake J3 102
Rideau, river H6 102
Riesa C3 40
Rieti C2 38
Riga, capital C2 46
Riga, gulf B2, B3 46
Rigolet B2 98
Riiser-Larsen Ice Shelf, glacier B14 107
Riiser-Larsen, peninsula C16 107
Rijeka B2 48
Rila, mts. B3 50
Rimini C1 38
Rîmnicu Vîlcea C3 43
Rimouski H3 103
Rincón, bay C3 90
Rincón del Bonete, lake B2 75
Ringkøbing B2 32
Río Blanco B2 87
Rio Branco B2 81
Rio Claro A2 91
Río Cuarto C3 74
Rio de Janeiro D4, Inset I 81
Río Gallegos B7 74
Rio Grande C5 81
Rio Grande D2 90
Río Grande A2 87
Rio Grande (Río Bravo), river D2 84
Rio Grande do Norte E2 81
Rio Grande do Sul C4 81
Rio Verde C3 81
Riobamba B3 79
Ríohacha B2 78
Rioni, river B3 45
Riou, lake D1 104
Rîşcani A2 50
Rishiri, island Inset I 8
Rishra Inset II 20
Riske Creek L5 95
Ritchies, archipelago F6 20
Rivas B3 87
River Cess B3 63
River Hills C4 96
River John D2 100
Rivera C1 75
Rivercrest C4 96
Riverhurst D10 104
Rivers A4 96
Rivers Inlet J5 95
Riverside, Calif. B2 126
Riverside-Albert E3 97
Riverton C3 96
Riverview E2 97
Rivière Bleue G4 103
Rivière du Loup G4 101
Rivière du Rempart C2 69
Rivière Noire, mt. B3 69
Rivière-à-Pierre D4 103
Rivière-au-Renard M3 103
Rivière-aux-Rats D4 103
Rivière-du-Loup G4 103
Rivière-du-Portage E1 97
Rivière-Matawin D5 103
Rivière-Ste-Marguerite G3 103
Rivière-Verte A1 97
Riyadh, capital B1 24
Riyaq B2 26
Roanne D3 34
Roanoke, Va. F2 126
Roatán B1 86
Roatán, island B1 86
Robertsport A2 63
Roberval D3 103
Robinsonville C1 97
Roblin A3 96
Roboré C3 77
Robson, mt. N4 95
Roca, cape A3 36
Rocanville J10 104
Rocha C3 75
Rochdale C3 30
Rochefort B4 34
Rochester D4 94
Rochester, Minn. D1 126
Rochester, N.Y. F1 126
Rock Island D6 103
Rock, river D5 105
Rockcliffe Park H5 102
Rockford, Ill. E1 126
Rockglen E11 104
Rockhampton, Qld. E2 14
Rockland K2 102
Rocky Harbour C4 98
Rocky Island, lake B1 102
Rocky Mountain House C5 94
Rocky, mts. 82
Rockyford D5 94
Roddickton C4 98
Rodez C4 34
Rodney D5 102
Roermond D3 32
Roeselare B2 33
Rogersville D2 97
Roi, island B2 16
Roi Et C2 12
Rojo, cape A3 90
Rokel, river A1 63
Roland C4 96
Rolling Hills E6 94
Rollo, bay C2 100
Rolphton H1 102
Roma A2 71
Roma, Qld. D2 14
Roman D2 43
Romania 43
Rome, capital C2 38
Rømø, island B3 32
Roncador, cay Inset 78
Roncador, range C3 81
Ronde, island B1 91
Rondônia B3 81
Rongelap, island B1 16
Rongerik, island B1 16
Rønne E3 32
Ronne Ice Shelf, glacier B11 107
Roodeport C2 71
Roosevelt, island B6 107
Roosevelt Campobello Intl. Hist. Park C4 97
Roper, river C1 14
Roraima B1 81
Roraima, mt. A3 80
Rosa, mt. A1 38
Rosalie B3 90
Rosalind D5 94
Rosario C3 74
Roscommon B2 31
Roscrea C2 31
Rose Belle C3 69
Rose Blanche B5 98
Rose Hill B2 69
Rose Valley G8 104
Rose, island B1 18
Roseau, capital B3 90
Roseau, river B4 96
Rosebud D5 94
Rosemary D6 94
Rosenfeld C4 96
Rosenheim C5 40
Rosenort C4 96
Rosetown B9 104
Rosetta, river B1 56
Roskilde D3 32
Ross Ice Shelf, glacier A6 107
Ross River C4 105
Ross, island B5 107
Ross, river C4 105
Ross, sea B6 107
Rossburn A4 96
Rosseau, lake F2 102
Rossel, island B3 15
Rossendale B4 96
Rossignol, lake B3 100
Rossland O6 95
Rosslare C2 31
Rosso B3 58
Rosthern D8 104
Rostock C1 40
Rostov-na-Donu E3 44
Roswell, N. Mex. C2 126
Rotherham C3 30
Rothesay D3 97
Rotorua C2 15
Rotterdam B3 32
Roubaix C1 34
Rouen C2 34
Rouleau F10 104
Round Lake Centre H2 102
Round, island D1 69
Round, pond C5 98
Rounthwaite B4 96
Routhierville J3 103
Rouyn-Noranda A4 101
Rovaniemi C1 53
Rovigo B1 38
Rovno B1 47
Rovuma, river C1 68
Rowley D5 94
Roxas B4 12
Royal, canal C2 31
Ruacana, falls B1 70
Ruahine, range C2 15
Ruapehu, mt. C2 15
Rub al-Khali (Empty Quarter), desert C2 24
Rubtsovsk D6 44
Ruda Śląka D3 41
Rudnyy C1 23
Rufiji, river C2 68
Rufisque A2 62
Rügen, island C1 40
Ruggell B1 33
Ruhengeri B1 61
Ruhr, river B3 40
Ruhwa, river B2 61
Rukwa, lake B2 68
Rum, cay C3 89
Rumbek B3 59
Runaway Bay B2 88
Rundu C1 70
Rungue Inset 76
Rungwa, river B2 68
Rupel, river C1 33
Ruse D2 50
Russell A4 96
Russia 44
Rustavi C4 45
Rutana B2 61
Rutbah, ar- B2 24
Rutherglen F1 102
Rutland N6 95
Ruvubu, river C2 61
Ruvuma, river C3 68
Ruways, ar- B2, C1 25
Ruwenzori, range B3 61
Ruyigi C2 61
Ruzizi, river A1, A2 61
Ružomberok B2 42
Rwanda 61
Rweru, lake C2 61
Ryazan D3 44
Rybnik D3 41
Ryotsu C2 8
Rysy, mt. E4 41
Ryukyu, islands A4, Inset II 8
Rzeszów F3 41

S

's Hertogenbosch C3 32
Saale, river B3 40
Saar, river A4 40
Saarbrücken A4 40
Saaremaa, island B2 46
Saarland A4 40
Sab Abar A3 27
Šabac A2 49
Sabadell H2 37
Sabana de la Mar C1 89
Sabana Grande B2 90
Sabaneta A1 89
Sabha B2 56
Sable cape, Fla. E3 126
Sable River B4 100
Sabzevar D2 22
Sachigo, river B2 101
Sackville E3 97
Sacramento, capital, Calif. A2 126
Sadah A1 25
Sado, island C2 8
Sado, river A3 36
Safata, bay C3 18
Safed Koh, range D3 21
Safi B1 57
Safotu B1 18
Saga A3 8
Sagaing B2 12
Sagami, bay C3 8
Sagamihara C3 8
Saginaw, Mich. E1 126
Sagua la Grande C2 88
Saguenay, river F3 103
Sagunto F3 37
Sahara, desert 55
Saharanpur Panipat C3 20
Şahbuz A3 45
Sahel, region 55
Sahiwal D3 21
Sai Kung Inset 10
Saidpur B3 21
Saimaa, lake C2 53
St. Adolphe C4 96
St. Alban's D5 98
St. Albans C3, Inset III 30
St. Albert D4 94
St-Alexis-des-Monts C5 103
St-Ambroise E3 103
St. Ambroise B4 96
St-André B1 97
St-André G4 103
St. Andrews C2 30
St. Andrews B3 97
St-Angèle-de-Mérici J3 103
St. Ann's Bay B2 88
St. Anne, island Inset 70
St. Anthony D3 98
St-Antoine C6 103
St-Apollinaire E5 103
St-Augustin E3 101
St. Augustine A2 91
St. Augustine, Fla. E3 126
St. Austell B4 30
St. Barbe C3 98
St-Basile A1 97
St. Bernard's D5 98
St. Brendan's E5 98
St. Bride's D5 98
Saint-Brieuc B2 34
St. Brieux F8 104
St-Bruno E3 103
St-Camille-de-Lellis F5 103
St. Catharines F4 102
St. Catherine's E5 98
St. Catherine, mt. B2 91
St-Charles, lake K5 103
St. Clair, lake C5 102
St. Clair, river C5 102
St. Claude B4 96
Saint-Cloud Inset II 34
St. Cloud, Minn. D1 126
St-Côme C5 103
St-Constant J6 103
St. Croix B3 97
St-Cyprien H4 103
St-David-de-Falardeau E3 103
St. David's B2 91
St. David's B3 30
Saint-Denis Inset II 34
Saint-Dizier D2 34
St-Donat B5 103
St. Edward A2 100
St. Eleanors B2 100
St. Elias, mts. A5 105
Saint-Élie B1 80
St-Émile K5 103
Saint-Étienne D4 34
St. Eustache C4 96
St-Eustache H5 103
St-Fabien H3 103
St-Fabien-de-Panet F5 103
St-Félicien D3 103
St-Félix-d'Otis F3 103
St-François, lake E6 103
St-François, river D5 103
St-Gédéon F6 103
St. George C3 97
St. George's B5 98
St. George's, bay B5 98
St. George's, capital A2 91
St. George's, channel B2 15
Saint George's, channel C3 31
St. George, Utah B2 126
St. Georges, bay F2 100
St-Georges F5 103
Saint-Georges C2 80
St-Germain G4 103
Saint-Germain-en-Laye Inset II 34
St. Gotthard, pass C2 35
St. Gotthard, tunnel C2 35
St. Helens C3 30
St-Henri-de-Taillon E3 103
St-Hubert G4 103
St-Hyacinthe D6 103
St-Ignace-du-Lac C5 103
St-Isidore D1 97
St-Jacques A1 97
St-Jacques-de-Leeds E5 103
St-Jean, lake D3 103
St. Jean Baptiste C4 96
St-Jean-Chrysostome L6 103
St-Jean-de-Matha C5 103
St-Jean-Port-Joli F4 103
St-Jean-sur-Richelieu C6 103
St-Jérôme B6 103
Saint John C3 97
St. John, river B2 97
St. John's E5 98
St. John's, capital D5 90
Saint Joseph A3 90
St. Joseph E2 97
St. Joseph, island B1 102
St. Joseph, Mo. D2 126
St-Joseph-de-Beauce F5 103
St. Kitts (St. Christopher), island B2 90
St. Kitts and Nevis 90
St. Labre C4 96
St-Lambert J5 103
St. Laurent C4 96
St-Laurent J5 103
Saint-Laurent du Maroni A1 80
St. Lawrence D5 98
St. Lawrence, cape G1 100
St. Lawrence, gulf L4 92
St. Lawrence, river K4 92
St. Lawrence Islands N.P. J3 102
St-Lazare A4 96
St-Leonard J5 103
St-Léonard B1 97
St. Lewis D3 98
St. Lewis, river C3 98
Saint-Lô B2 34
Saint-Louis A1 62
St. Louis A2 100
St. Louis E8 104
St. Louis, Mo. D2 126
St-Louis, lake H6 103
St-Louis-de-Kent E2 97
St-Louis-de-Kent E2 97
St. Lucia 91
Saint Lucia, channel B1 91
St-Ludger F6 103
St. Ludger-de-Milot E3 103
St. Malo C4 96
St-Malo E6 103
Saint-Malo B2 34
Saint-Malo, gulf B2 34
Saint-Marc C1 89
St-Maredu-LacLong H4 103
St-Marcel F5 103
St-Marcellin H3 103
St. Margarets D2 97
St. Martin B3 96
St. Martin, lake B3 96
St. Martins D3 97
St. Mary's E5 98
St. Marys D4 102
St-Maurice, river C4 103
St-Michel F5 103
St-Michel-des-Saints C5 103
St-Milaire A1 97
St. Moritz D2 35
Saint-Nazaire B3 34
St-Nicolas E5 103
St-Pacôme G4 103
St-Pamphile G5 103
St-Pascal G4 103
St. Paul E4 94
St. Paul, capital, Minn. D1 126
St. Paul, river A2 63
St. Paul, river C3 98
St. Paul's A1 90
Saint Paul's, bay B2 36
St. Peters G2 100
St. Peters C2 100
St. Peters, bay C2 100
St. Peters, island B2 100
St. Petersburg D3 44
St. Petersburg, Fla. E3 126
St-Philémon F5 103
St. Pierre, island M4 92
St. Pierre-Jolys C4 96
St-Quentin B1 97
St-Raphaël F5 103
St-Rédempteur K6 103
St-Rémi-d'Amherst B5 103
St-Romuald L6 103
St. Shotts E5 98
St-Siméon G4 103
St. Stephen B3 97
St. Thomas D5 102
St-Tite-des-Caps F4 103
Saint-Tropez D5 34
St-Vallier F5 103
Saint Vincent, passage B4 91
St. Vincent, gulf Inset II 14
St. Vincent, island B2 91
St. Vincent and the Grenadines 91
St. Walburg A7 104
St-Zacharie F5 103
Ste-Agathe-des-Monts B5 103
Ste-Amélie B4 96
Ste-Anne-des-Monts K2 103
Ste-Anne-du-Lac A5 103
Ste-Apolline F5 103
Ste-Claire F5 103
Ste-Croix E5 103
Ste-Eulalie D5 103
Ste-Foy E5, K6 103
Ste-Luce H3 103
Ste-Marie E5 103
Ste-Monique E3 103
Ste-Rose-du-Nord F3 103
Ste-Thérèse H5 103
Ste-Véronique A5 103
Ste. Agathe C4 96
Ste. Anne C4 96
Ste. Rose du Lac B3 96
Ste-Anne-de-Madawaska A1 97
Saintes B4 34
Sajama, mt. A3 77
Sak, river B3 71
Sakai B3 8
Sakarya, river B2 27
Sakha (Yakutiya), republic C8 44
Sakhalin, island I4 44
Şaki B2 45
Sakishima, islands Inset II 8
Sakon Nakhon C2 12
Sal Rei D2 58
Sal, island D2 58
Sala'ilua A2 18
Salaberry-de-Valleyfield B6 103
Salacgriva C2 46
Salado, river B3, C2 74
Salaga B2 64
Salahiyah A2 27
Salalah B3 25
Salamá C4 85
Salamanca D2 37
Salamís, island Inset 51
Salar de Uyuni, salt flat A4 77
Salaverry B2 77
Salcedo B1 89
Saldanha A3 71
Saldus B2 46
Salé C1 57
Salekhard C5 44
Salelologa B2 18
Salem C6 20
Salem, capital, Oreg. A1 126
Salerno C2 38
Salerno, gulf C2 38
Salford C3 30
Salgótarján B1 43
Salibia B2 90
Salihorsk C3 47
Salima B2 68
Salina Cruz E4 84
Salina, Kans. D2 126
Salinas C3 90
Salines, point A2 91
Salisbury A2 90

	Key	Page
Salisbury	C3	30
Salisbury, island	N4	99
Salluit	A1	101
Sallum, as-	A1	56
Sally's Cove	C4	98
Salmon Arm	N6	95
Salmon River	A3	100
Salmon, Idaho	B1	126
Salmon, river	L4	95
Salo	B2	53
Salonta	A2	43
Saloum, river	B2	62
Salsette, island	Inset I	20
Salt Lake City, capital, Utah	B1	126
Salt Water, lake	Inset II	20
Salt, as-	A1	26
Salt, cay	D4	89
Salta	B1	74
Saltcoats	H9	104
Saltery Bay	K6	95
Saltillo, state capital	D2	84
Salto	B1	75
Salto del Guairá	E4	75
Salut, islands	B1	80
Salvador	E3	81
Salvage	E5	98
Salween, river	C2	10
Salyan	C3	45
Salzach, river	C3	39
Salzburg	C3	39
Salzburg Alps, range	C3	39
Salzgitter	B2	40
Samaná	C1	89
Samaná, bay	C1	89
Samaná, cape	C1	89
Samana, cay	C3	89
Samangan	B1	22
Samar, island	C4	12
Samar, sea	C3	12
Samara	D4	44
Samarian, hills	B1	26
Samarinda	C2	13
Samarqand	C3	23
Samarra	B2	24
Samawah, as-	C2	24
Sambalpur	D4	20
Sambre, river	C2	33
Samch'ŏk	C4	9
Samina, river	B2	33
Samoa		18
Samokov	B3	50
Sámos, island	C3	51
Samothráki, island	C1	51
Samsø, island	C3	32
Samsø, strait	C3	32
Samsonvale, lake	Inset III	14
Samsun	D2	27
Samtredia	B3	45
Samur, river	B2	45
San	C3	58
San Andrés, island	Inset	78
San Angelo, Tex.	C2	126
San Antonio	B4, Inset	76
San Antonio	A3	85
San Antonio	C2	90
San Antonio Oeste	B5	74
San Antonio, cape	D4	74
San Antonio, cape	A2	88
San Antonio, Tex.	D3	126
San Baudilio de Llobregat	G2	37
San Bernardino, Calif.	B2	126
San Bernardo	Inset	76
San Blas, mts.	C2	87
San Borja	A2	77
San Carlos	B4	12
San Carlos	C3	75
San Carlos	B3	87
San Carlos de Bariloche	A5	74
San Carlos, river	B2	86
San Clara	A3	96
San Cristóbal	B2	77
San Cristóbal	B2	79
San Cristóbal	B2	89
San Cristóbal de las Casas	F4	84
San Cristobal, island	B2	16
San Cristóbal, island	Inset	79
San Diego, Calif.	B2	126
San Felipe	D4	78
San Felipe	B1	84
San Félix	B3	76
San Fernando	B2	12
San Fernando	C4	37
San Fernando	B4	76
San Fernando	A2	91
San Fernando de Apure	C2	79
San Francique	A2	91
San Francisco	C3	74
San Francisco	B2	86
San Francisco de Macorís	B1	89
San Francisco, Calif.	A2	126
San Germán	A2	90
San Gimignano	B2	38
San Ignacio	B3	77
San Ignacio	A2	85
San Isidro	D2	90
San Jorge, gulf	B6	74
San José	B3	75
San José	C6	85
San José de Chiquitos	B3	77
San José de las Matas	A1	89
San José del Guaviare	B4	78
San Jose, Calif.	A2	126
San José, capital	B3	86
San José, river	B2	75
San Juan	B3	74
San Juan	B4	77
San Juan	A2	89
San Juan, capital	C2	90
San Juan, passage	D2	90
San Juan Bautista	D5	75
San Juan de Los Morros	C2	79
San Juan del Norte	C3	87
San Juan del Norte, bay	C3	87
San Juan del Sur	B3	87
San Juan, river	A3	78
San Juan, river	B3	87
San Lorenzo	D4	75
San Lorenzo	B2	79
San Lorenzo	B3	86
San Lorenzo	D2	90
San Lorenzo, cape	A3	79
San Lucas	C3	84
San Lucas, cape	B3	84
San Luis	B3	74
San Luis	D3	85
San Luis Potosí, state capital	D3	84
San Luis Río Colorado	B1	84
San Luis, lake	B2	77
San Marino		39
San Marino, capital	B1	39
San Marino, river	A1	39
San Martín, lake	A6	74
San Matías	C3	77
San Matías, gulf	C5	74
San Miguel	B2	86
San Miguel de Tucumán	B2	74
San Miguelito	C2	87
San Nicolás	C3	74
San Pablo	B3	12
San Pablo, river	B3	77
San Pawl il-Bahar	B2	36
San Pedro	D4	75
San Pédro	C4	63
San Pedro de Atacama	C2	76
San Pedro de las Colonias	D2	84
San Pedro de Macorís	C2	89
San Pedro Sula	A2	86
San Pedro, river	C2	85
San Pietro, island	B3	38
San Rafael	B3	74
San Remo	A2	38
San Salvador de Jujuy	B1	74
San Salvador, capital	A2	86
San Salvador, island	Inset	79
San Salvador, island	C3	89
San Salvador, river	A2	75
San Sebastián	F1	37
San Sebastián	B2	90
San Severo	C2	38
San Valentín, mt.	B8	76
San Vicente	B2	86
San Vito, cape	C3	38
San, river	E2	11
San, river	F3	41
Sanaa, capital	A1	25
Sanaga, river	B2	65
Sanandaj	B2	22
Sanaw	C1	25
Sancti Spíritus	C2	88
Sand, river	E3	94
Sandakan	D2	13
Sanday, island	Inset I	30
Sandilands	C4	96
Sandougou, river	B3	62
Sandoy, island	Inset	32
Sandspit	G4	95
Sandur	Inset	32
Sandwich, bay	C2	98
Sandy Bay	H5	104
Sandy Cove	A3	100
Sandy Lake	D3	94
Sandy Lake	A4	96
Sandy Lake	B2	101
Sandy Point	B2	89
Sandy Point Town	A1	90
Sandy, island	B2	18
Sandy, island	B2	91
Sandy, lake	C4	98
Sanford	C4	96
Sangha, river	D2	66
Sangmélima	B3	65
Sangre Grande	A2	91
Sangro, river	C2	38
Sangudo	C4	94
Sankosh, river	B2	19
Sankrail	Inset II	20
Sankt Gallen	D1	35
Sankt Pölten	D2	39
Sankuru, river	B2	67
Sannar	C2	59
Sanski Most	A1	48
Sant Julià de Lòria	A3	36
Sant'Antioco, island	B3	38
Santa Ana	A2	77
Santa Ana	A2	86
Santa Ana, range	C1	75
Santa Ana, volcano	A2	86
Santa Bárbara	A2	86
Santa Barbara, Calif.	B2	126
Santa Catarina	C4	81
Santa Clara	C2	88
Santa Coloma de Gramanet	H2	37
Santa Cruz	B3	77
Santa Cruz	A2	86
Santa Cruz de Tenerife	Inset I	37
Santa Cruz, island	Inset	79
Santa Cruz, islands	C2	16
Santa Cruz, river	A7	74
Santa Elena de Uairen	D3	79
Santa Elena, point	A4	79
Santa Fe	C3	74
Santa Fe, N. Mex.	C2	126
Santa Inés	Inset	76
Santa Inés, island	B9	76
Santa Isabel	C3	90
Santa Isabel, island	A1	16
Santa Isabel, peak	A1	66
Santa Lucía, river	B3	75
Santa Luzia, island	B2	58
Santa Maria	D2	58
Santa Maria	C4	81
Santa Maria di Leuca, cape	D3	38
Santa María, island	B2	18
Santa María, island	Inset	79
Santa Marta	B2	78
Santa Rita	B2	86
Santa Rosa	C4	74
Santa Rosa	B4	79
Santa Rosa de Copán	A2	86
Santa Rosa del Palmar	B3	77
Santa Rosalía	B2	84
Santana do Livramento	C5	81
Santander	E1	37
Santarém	A3	36
Santarém	C2	81
Santiago	B2	87
Santiago	B1	89
Santiago de Compostela	B1	37
Santiago de Cuba	E3	88
Santiago del Estero	C2	74
Santiago, capital	B4, Inset	76
Santiago, river	B1	77
Santo André	Inset II	81
Santo Antão, island	A1	58
Santo Domingo	B2	90
Santo Domingo de los Colorados	B3	79
Santo Domingo, capital	C2	89
Santo Tomás de Castilla	E4	85
Santos	D4, Inset II	81
Sanyati, river	B1	69
São Bernardo do Campo	Inset II	81
São Caetano do Sul	Inset II	81
São Domingos	A1	62
São Filipe	B4	58
São Francisco, river	D3	81
São Gonçalo	Inset I	81
São João de Meriti	Inset I	81
São José do Rio Prêto	D4	81
São Luís	D2	81
São Nicolau, island	B2	58
São Paulo	D4, Inset II	81
São Tiago, island	C3	58
São Tomé, capital	B4	63
São Tomé, island	B4	63
São Tomé, mt.	B4	63
São Tomé and Príncipe		63
São Vicente, cape	A4	36
São Vicente, island	A2	58
São Vincente	Inset II	81
Saona, island	D2	89
Saône, river	D3	34
Sapele	C5	65
Sapitwa, mt.	C3	68
Sapporo	Inset I	8
Sar, passage	B3	17
Sar-e Pol	B1	22
Sara Buri	B3	12
Sarajevo, capital	B2	48
Saramacca, river	B2	80
Sarandë	A4	49
Saransk	D4	44
Sarapiquí river	B2	86
Sarasota, Fla.	E3	126
Saratov	D4	44
Saravan	D4	11
Sarawak, state	C2	13
Saraya	D3	62
Sarbhang	B3	19
Sarcelles	Inset II	34
Sarda, river	A2	19
Sardinia, island	B2	38
Sargodha	D3	21
Sarh	B5	59
Sari	C2	22
Sariwŏn	A3	9
Sarjektjakko	C1	53
Sark, island	Inset II	30
Sarnia	C5	102
Saronic, gulf	Inset	51
Šar Planina, mts.	B3	49
Sarstoon, river	A4	85
Sarstún, river	D4	85
Sary Tash	C3	23
Sarygamysh Koli, lake	B2	22
Saryshaghan	D2	23
Sasamungga	A1	16
Sasaram	D4	20
Sasebo	A3	8
Saskatchewan, river	G3	92
Saskatoon	D8	104
Sassandra	C4	63
Sassandra, river	C2, C4	63
Sassari	B2	38
Sassnitz	C1	40
Sata, cape	A4	8
Satpura, range	C4	20
Satsuma, peninsula	A4	8
Sattahip	B3	12
Satu Mare	B2	43
Sauble Beach	D3	102
Saudhárkrókur	B2	52
Saudi Arabia		24
Saül	B2	80
Sault Ste. Marie	A1	102
Sault Ste. Marie, Mich.	E1	126
Sault-au-Mouton	G3	103
Saumur	B3	34
Saurimo	D3	70
Sauteurs	B2	91
Sava, river	B1, B2, C2	48
Savai'i, island	A2	18
Savalou	A3	64
Savan, island	B3	91
Savannah, Ga.	E2	126
Savannakhet	C3	11
Savé	B3	64
Savigny-sur-Orge	Inset II	34
Savinja, river	B2	48
Savona	B1	38
Savona	M6	95
Savonlinna	C2	53
Savu, sea	D2	13
Sawda, mt.	B2	24
Sawhaj	B2	56
Sawqirah	C2	25
Sawqirah, bay	C2	25
Saxony	C3	40
Saxony-Anhalt	B3	40
Sayabec	J3	103
Sayan, mts.	D6	44
Sayhut	C1	25
Sayward	K6	95
Saywun	B1	25
Sázava, river	B3	42
Scafell Pike, mt.	B2	30
Scarborough	C2	30
Scarborough	B1	91
Scarborough	F4, L5	102
Schaan	B2	33
Schaerbeek	C2	33
Schaffhausen	C1	35
Schefferville	D3	98
Schefferville	C3	101
Schelde, river	B2	33
Schellenberg	B1	33
Scheveningen	B2	32
Schiedam	B3	32
Schiermonnikoog, island	D1	32
Schleswig	B1	40
Schleswig-Holstein	B2	40
Schouwen, island	A3	32
Schreiber	C3	101
Schuler	E6	94
Schwäbisch Gmünd	B4	40
Schwedt	C2	40
Schweinfurt	B3	40
Schwerin	B2	40
Schweriner, lake	B2	40
Schwyz	C1	35
Scilly, islands	A4	30
Scone	B2	30
Sconser	A1	30
Scotstown	E6	103
Scotswood	A3	94
Scott, island	C5	107
Scottsbluff, Nebr.	C1	126
Scugog, lake	G3	102
Scunthorpe	C3	30
Scutari, lake	A1, A3	49
Sczcecinek	C2	41
Seaforth	D4	102
Seal Cove	C4	98
Seal, river	D1	96
Searchmont	A1	102
Seattle, Wash.	A1	126
Seawell	C4	91
Sebou, river	C1	57
Sebright	F3	102
Sechura, desert	A2	77
Seda, river	B3	36
Sedalia	E5	94
Sedan	D2	34
Sédhiou	B3	62
Sedley	F10	104
Seeley's Bay	J3	102
Sefadu	B1	63
Segbana	B2	64
Ségou	B3	58
Segovia	D2	37
Séguéla	C3	63
Segura, river	E3	37
Seinäjoki	B2	53
Seine, river	C2, Inset II	34
Sekake	B2	71
Sekondi-Takoradi	B4	64
Selebi-Phikwe	C2	69
Selenge Mörön, river	C2	11
Sélibaby	B4	58
Selínia	Inset	51
Selkirk	C4	96
Selvas, region	B2	81
Selwyn, mts.	C4	105
Seman, river	A3	49
Semara	B1	58
Semarang	C2	13
Sembawang	B1	13
Sembé	C3	66
Semeru, mt.	C2	13
Semey (Semipalatinsk)	E1	23
Semmering, pass	D3	39
Semois, river	D3	33
Sempach	C1	35
Sen, river	D2	11
Senaki	B3	45
Sendai	D2	8
Senegal		62
Senegal, river	B1, C2	62
Senkaku, islands	Inset II	8
Senmonorom	F3	11
Senne, river	C2	33
Senneterre	A4	101
Senta	B2	49
Seoul, capital	B4	9
Sepik, river	A2	15
Sept-Îles	C3	101
Septentrional, range	A1	89
Serangoon	B1	13
Serbia and Montenegro		49
Serbia, republic	B2	49
Seremban	A2	13
Serenje	C2	67
Sergipe	E3	81
Seria	A2	13
Serov	D5	44
Serowe	B2	69
Serpent, island	D1	69
Sérrai	B1	51
Serranilla, bank	Inset	78
Serravalle	B1	39
Serrekunda	C2	62
Serule	B2	69
Sese, islands	C4	61
Sesheke	A3	67
Seti, river	A2	19
Sétif	B1	57
Settat	C1	57
Setúbal	A3	36
Setúbal, bay	A3	36
Sevan, lake	C2	45
Sevastopol	C4	47
Seven Persons	E6	94
Seven Sisters Falls	C4	96
Severn, river	C3	30
Severn, river	B2	101
Severnaya Zemlya, islands	A6	44
Seville	D4	37
Sevran	Inset II	34
Sèvres	Inset II	34
Sewa, river	B2	63
Seward, Alaska	Inset I	126
Seychelles		70
Sfax	C2	57
Sfîntu Gheorghe	C3	43
Sha Tin	Inset	10
Shaanxi	D2	10
Shabwah	B1	25
Shache	A2	10
Shackleton Ice Shelf, glacier	C2	107
Shahr-e Kord	C3	22
Shaki	B3	65
Shalqar	B2	23
Sham, ash-	D1	25
Shamattawa	E2	96
Shamgong	B2	19
Shan, plateau	C2	12
Shanchung	B1	9
Shandong	E2	10
Shangani, river	A2	69
Shanghai	F2	10
Shannon	B2	31
Shannon, river	B2	31
Shantou	E3	10
Shanxi	E2	10
Shanxi	F3	10
Shaoguan	E3	10
Shaoxing	F3	10
Shaoyang	E3	10
Sharbot Lake	J3	102
Sharjah	C2	25
Shashe, river	C2	69
Shashi	E2	10
Shatt al-Arab, river	C2	24
Shaunavon	B11	104
Shawinigan	D5	103
Sheberghan	B1	22
Shediac	E2	97
Sheerness	E5	94
Sheet Harbour	E3	100
Sheffield	C3	30
Sheguiandah	D2	102
Sheho	G9	104
Shek Pik	Inset	10
Shelburne	B4	100
Shelburne	E3	102
Shelikhov, gulf	C9	44
Shell Lake	C7	104
Shellbrook	D7	104
Shelter Bay	N6	95
Shëngjin	A2	49
Shenyang	F1	10
Sherbro, island	A2	63
Sherbrooke	E2	100
Sherbrooke	E6	103
Sheridan, Wyo.	C1	126
Sherridon	A1	96
Sherwood Park	D4	94
Shetland, islands	Inset I	30
Sheva	Inset I	20
Shewa Gimira	B3	60
Shibar, pass	B2	22
Shibin al-Kawm	B1	56
Shijiazhuang	E2	10
Shikarpur	C4	21
Shikoku, island	B3	8
Shillong	F3	20
Shimizu	C3	8
Shimonoseki	A3	8
Shimonoseki, strait	A3	8
Shinano, river	C2	8
Shinas	C1	25
Shindand	A2	22
Shinyanga	B1	68
Shiono, cape	B3	8
Ship Cove	D3	98
Shippagan	E1	97
Shirane, mt.	C3	8
Shiraz	C4	22
Shire, river	B3	68
Shiretoko, cape	Inset I	8
Shizuoka	C3	8
Shkhara, mt.	B3	45
Shkodër	A1	49
Shkumbin, river	A2	49
Shoal Lake	A4	96
Sholapur	C5	20
Shostka	C1	47
Shreveport, La.	D2	126
Shrewsbury	C3	30
Shrirampur	Inset II	20
Shubenacadie	D2	100
Shubra al-Khaymah	B1	56
Shumen	E2	50
Shurugwi	B2	69
Shwebo	B2	12
Shymkent (Chimkent)	C2	23
Siahan, range	B4	21
Sialkot	E3	21
Siargao, island	C4	12
Šiauliai	B2	46
Sibbald	E5	94
Siberia, region	C7	44
Siberut, island	A2	13
Sibiti	B5	66
Sibiu	C3	43
Sibu	C2	13
Sibuyan, island	B3	12
Sibuyan, sea	B3	12
Sicamous	N6	95
Sichuan	D2	10
Sicily, island	C3	38
Sicily, strait	B3	38
Sico, river	C2	86
Sicuani	C3	77
Sidi bel Abbès	A1	57
Sidi Bou Zid	B3	57
Sidlaw, hills	B2	30
Sidney	L7	95
Sidney	B4	96
Sidon (Sayda)	A2	26
Sidra, gulf	C1	56
Sidvokodvo	B2	71
Siedlce	F2	41
Siegen	B3	40
Siempang	E1	11
Siemreab	B2	11
Siena	B2	38
Sieradz	D3	41
Sierra de Cayey, mts.	C2	90
Sierra de Loquillo, mts.	D2	90
Sierra Leone		63
Sierra Madre, mts.	B2	12
Sierra Madre, mts.	C5	85
Sierra Nevada de Santa Marta, mts.	B2	78
Sierra Nevada, mts., Calif.	A2	126
Sifton	A3	96
Siggiewi	B2	36
Sighetul Marmaţiei	B2	43
Sighişoara	C2	43
Siglufjördhur	B1	52
Siguatepeque	B2	86
Siguiri	D2	62
Siirt	E3	27
Sikanni Chief	L2	95
Sikasso	B3	58
Sikhote Alin, range	E8	44
Sikkim (state)	E3	20
Šilalė	B2	46
Silay	B4	12
Silesia, region	C3	41
Silet	B2	57
Silgarhi	B2	19
Silhouette, island	C1	70
Siliana	B1	57
Silifke	C3	27
Silisili, mt.	B2	18
Silistra	F1	50
Silkeborg	B2	32
Sillery	K6	103
Šilutė	A2	46
Silvassi	B4	20
Silver	C4	96
Silver City, N. Mex.	C2	126
Sima	B2	67
Simcoe, lake	E4	101
Simeulue, island	A1	13
Simferopol	C4	47
Simikot	B1	19
Simla	C2	20
Simon, lake	A6	103
Simonette, river	A4	94
Simonhouse	A2	96
Simpson, desert	C2	14
Sinai, peninsula	B2	56
Sinaloa	C3	84
Sincelejo	B2	78
Sinclair	A4	96
Sinclair Mills	M4	95
Sindhuli Garhi	C2	19
Siné, river	B2	62
Sines	A4	36
Singapore		13
Singapore, capital	B1	13
Singapore, island	B1	13
Singapore, strait	B2	13
Singen	B5	40
Singida	B1	68
Singur	Inset II	20
Sinope	C2	27
Sinpo	C2	9
Sint-Niklaas	C1	33
Sint-Truiden	D2	33
Sinŭiju	A2	9
Sió, river	B2	43
Siófok	B2	43
Sion	B2	35
Sioux City, Iowa	D1	126
Sioux Falls, S. Dak.	D1	126
Sioux Lookout	B2	101
Sipaliwini	A3	80
Siparia	A2	91
Siping	F1	10
Sipiwesk, lake	C1	96
Siple, island	B8	107
Siple, mt.	B8	107
Siquia, river	B2	87
Sirajganj	C4	21
Sirba, river	D2	64
Siret	D2	43
Siret, river	D2	43
Sirjan	D4	22
Sisaket	C3	12
Sisian	D3	45
Sisimiut (Holsteinsborg)	B2	106
Sisophon	B2	11
Siteki	B2	71
Sitka, Alaska	Inset I	126
Sittang, river	C2	12
Sittard	C4	32
Sittwe	B2	12
Siuna	B2	87
Sivas	D2	27
Siwah	A2	56
Sixaola, river	C3	86
Sjælland, island	C3	32
Skagen	C1	32
Skagerrak, strait	A3	53
Skaw, cape	C1	32
Skead	E1	102
Skeena, mts.	H3	95
Skeena, river	H4	95
Skeleton, coast	A1	70
Skellefteå	D2	53
Skellefteälven, river	C1	53
Skien	B4	52
Skierniewice	E3	41
Skikda	B1	57
Skíros, island	C2	51
Skive	B2	32
Skjern, river	B3	32
Skookumchuck	P6	95
Skopje, capital	B2	48
Skovorodino	D8	44
Skownan	B3	96
Skye, island	A1	30
Slagelse	C3	32
Slaná, river	C2	42
Slatina	C3	43
Slave Lake	C3	94
Slave, river	F2	92
Slavonia, region	C2	48
Slavonska Požega	C2	48
Slavonski Brod	D2	48
Sliema	C2	36
Slieve Donard, mt.	B2	30
Sligo	B1	31
Sliven	E3	50
Slobozia	D3	43
Slough	Inset III	30
Slovakia		42
Slovenia		48
Slovenskérudohorie, mts.	B2	42
Sluch', river	B1	47
Słupsk	C1	41
Småland, region	B3	53
Smallwood, reservoir	D3	98
Smeaton	F7	104
Smederevo	B2	49
Smilovichi	D3	47
Smiltene	C2	46
Smith River	J1	95
Smithers	J4	95

Key Page
Smithers Landing J3 95
Smiths Cove B3 100
Smiths Falls J3 102
Smithville F4 102
Smoky, river A3, A4 94
Smolensk D3 44
Smolevichi D2 47
Smolyan C4 50
Smoothstone, lake D6 104
Smoothstone, river D6 104
Snake, river C3 105
Snake, river B1 126
Snaring A4 94
Sneek C1 32
Sněžka, mt. B2 42
Śniardwy, lake E2 41
Snow Lake A2 96
Snowdon, mt. B3 30
Snowdrift F4 99
Snowflake B4 96
Snug Harbour D3 98
Snuol E3 11
Soan-kundo, islands B5 9
Sobaek, mts. B5 9
Sobat, river C3 59
Sobradinho, reservoir D3 81
Sobral D2 81
Soc Trang A5 11
Sochi E3 44
Socompa C2 76
Socorro, N. Mex. C2 126
Socotra, island C2 25
Söderhamn C2 53
Sofia, capital B3 50
Sofia, river B2 69
Sognafjord, fjord B3 52
Soissons C2 34
Sŏjosŏn, bay A3 9
Sokcho C3 9
Sokodé B2 64
Sokoto C1 65
Sokoto, plains C1 65
Sokoto, river C1 65
Sol, coast D4 37
Sola B1 18
Soldeu B2 36
Solihull C3 30
Solingen A3 40
Solomon Is. 16
Solomon, sea B2 15
Solosolo C2 18
Solway, estuary B2 30
Solwezi B2 67
Somalia 60
Sombe, beach E2 90
Sombor A2 49
Sombra C5 102
Somerset B4 96
Somerset, island K2 99
Someş, river B2 43
Somme, river C2 34
Somoto A2 87
Son La A2 11
Son, river D4 20
Sonarpur Inset II 20
Sønderborg B4 32
Sondrio B1 38
Songea C3 68
Songhua, river F1 10
Songkhla B5 12
Songköl D2 23
Sŏngnam B4 9
Songnim A3 9
Songwe, river B1 68
Sonora B1 84
Sonsonate A2 86
Sonsoral, island Inset 17
Sooke L7 95
Sopron A2 43
Sor, river B3 36
Sorel C5 103
Soria E2 37
Sorø C3 32
Soroca B1 50
Sorocaba D4 81
Sorong E2 13
Soroti C3 61
Sorraia, river A3 36
Sorrento C2 38
Sosnowiec D3 41
Soso, bay B3 17
Sota, river B2 64
Sotk C2 45
Sotouboua B2 64
Soubré C4 63
Soufrière B4 90
Soufrière A2 91
Soufrière, mt. B1 91
Soufrière, volcano A2 91
Souillac C4 69
Soungrougrou, river B3 62
Sources, mt. B1 71
Souris A4 96
Souris C2 100
Souris, river G11 104
Sous, plain B2 57
Sous, river B2 57
Sousúa B1 89
South Africa 71
S. Aulatsivik, island E3 98
South Australia C2 14
South Baymouth C2 102
South Bend, Ind. E1 126
South Branch B5 98
South Brook C4 98
South Carolina E2 126
South China, sea E4, Inset 10
South Comino, channel B2 36
South Dakota C1 126
South Downs, hills C3 30
South Dum-Dum Inset II 20
South Georgia, island 4
S. Gut St. Anns G1 100
South Henik, lake J4 99
S. Indian Lake D1 96
South Korea 9
South Magnetic Pole C3 107
South Male, atoll A3 19
South Malosmadulu, atoll A2 19
South Milford B3 100
S. Moose, lake B2 96
South Orkney, islands C12 107
South Ossetia, region B3 45
South Pole A17 107
South Rawdon D3 100
South River F2 102
South Ronaldsay, island Inset I 30
South Saskatchewan, river D8 104
South Shetland, islands C12 107
South Shields C2 30
South Taranaki, bight B2 15
South Uist, island A1 30
South West, cape A4 15
South, island A3 15
Southampton C4 30
Southampton D3 102
Southampton, island L4 99
Southend G4 104
Southend-on-Sea D3 30
Southern Alps, mts. A3 15
Southern Bug, river B2 47
Southern Uplands, mts. B2 30
Southland, plains A4 15
Southport C3 30
Southport B2 100
Sovetskaya Gavan E9 44
Soweto C2 71
Soya, point Inset I 8
Soyapango A2 86
Soyo B2 70
Sozh, river E3 47
Spa D2 33
Spain 37
Sousse C2 57
Spandau C2 40
Spanish C1 102
Spanish Town C3 88
Sparta B3 51
Spartansburg, S.C. E2 126
Spartivento, cape D3 38
Sparwood P6 95
Speightstown A2 91
Spence Bay K3 99
Spencer, gulf C3 14
Spences Bridge M6 95
Sperrin, mts. A2 30
Spessart, mts. B4 40
Spey, river B1 30
Speyer B4 40
Spiritwood C7 104
Spišská Nová Ves C2 42
Spithead, channel C4 30
Split C3 48
Split Lake D1 96
Splügen, pass D2 35
Spokane, Wash. B1 126
Spoleto C2 38
Spragge C1 102
Sprague D4 96
Spree, river C3 40
Spring Bay C2 102
Spring Coulee D6 94
Spring Hall A2 91
Springbok A2 71
Springdale C4 98
Springfield, capital, Ill. E2 126
Springfield, Mass. F1 126
Springfield, Mo. D2 126
Springhill C2 100
Springs C2 71
Springside H9 104
Springstein C4 96
Springwater B9 104
Spruce Grove D4 94
Spy Hill J10 104
Squamish L6 95
Square Islands D3 98
Sre Ambel B4 11
Srebrenica C1 48
Sredna Gora, mts. C3 50
Sremska Mitrovica A2 49
Sreng, river B2 11
Sri Jayawardenepura, capital A5 19
Sri Lanka 19
Srinagar B2 20
Stafford C3 30
Stand Off D6 94
Standard D5 94
Stanley C2 97
Stanmore E5 94
Stanovoy, range D8 44
Star City F8 104
Stara Zagora D3 50
Starbuck C4 96
Starbuck, island D2 17
Starnberg, lake B5 40
Start, point B4 30
Staubbach, falls B2 35
Stavanger B4 52
Stavropol E4 44
Stayner E3 102
Stead C4 96
Steen River B1 94
Stefanson, island G2 99
Steinbach C4 96
Steinkjer C3 52
Stellarton E2 100
Stellenbosch A3 71
Stendal B2 40
Stepanavan B2 45
Stephenville B5 98
Stettler D5 94
Stevenage Inset III 30
Stevenson, lake C2 96
Stewart H3 95
Stewart River B4 105
Stewart, island A4 15
Stewart, river B4, C3 105
Stewiacke D2 100
Steyr D2 39
Stikine G3 95
Stikine, river G2 95
Stirling B2 30
Stirling H3 102
Štip C2 48
Stockerau E2 39
Stockholm, capital C3 53
Stoeng Treng D2 11
Stoke-on-Trent C3 30
Stonecliffe H1 102
Stoneham E4 103
Stonewall C4 96
Stoney Point C5 102
Stony Mountain C4 96
Stony Plain D4 94
Stony Rapids E1 104
Storå, river B2 32
Storavan, lake C1 53
Store, strait C3 32
Storkerson, peninsula G2 99
Stornoway A1 30
Stornoway E6 103
Storsjön, lake B2 53
Storthoaks A4 96
Stoughton G11 104
Strakonice A3 42
Stralsund C1 40
Strangford B2 30
Stranraer B2 30
Strasbourg D2 34
Strasbourg F9 104
Stratford D4 102
Stratford E6 103
Stratford-upon-Avon C3 30
Strathclair A4 96
Strathlorne F1 100
Strathnaver L4 95
Strathroy D5 102
Straubing C4 40
Streymoy, island Inset 32
Stromboli, island C3 38
Stronsay, island Inset I 30
Struga A2 48
Struma, river A3 50
Strumica C2 48
Stryama, river C3 50
Stuart, lake K4 95
Stubbs B2 91
Stuie J5 95
Sturgeon C2 100
Sturgeon Falls D3 101
Sturgis H9 104
Stuttgart B4 40
Subotica A1 49
Suceava D2 43
Suchiate, river A5 85
Sucre, capital A3 77
Sudan 59
Sudbury E1 102
Sudd, region B3 59
Suddie B2 80
Sudeten, mts. B3 41
Sudirman, range E2 13
Suđuroy, island Inset 32
Sue, river B3 59
Suez B2 56
Suez, canal B1 56
Suez, gulf B2 56
Sugandha Inset II 20
Suhar C1 25
Sühbaatar C2 11
Suhl B3 40
Suir, river C2 31
Suita B3 8
Sukabumi B2 13
Sukang B3 13
Sukhnah, as- B2 27
Sukhothai B2 12
Sukhumi A3 45
Sukkur C4 21
Sula, islands D2 13
Sulaiman, range C4 21
Sulaybikhat, as- B2 24
Sulaymaniyah, as- C1 24
Sulayyil, as- B2 24
Sulima B2 63
Sullana A1 77
Sullivan, lake E5 94
Sulu, archipelago B5 12
Sulu, sea A4 12
Sülüktü A3 23
Sumatra, island B2 13
Šumava, mts. A3 42
Sumba, island D2 13
Sumbar, river B2 22
Sumbawa, island C2 13
Sumbawanga B2 68
Sumbe B3 70
Summerford D4 98
Summerland N6 95
Summerside B2 100
Summerville E5 98
Summit Lake K2 95
Summit Lake L4 95
Šumperk C3 42
Sumqayit C2 45
Sumy C1 47
Sun City C2 71
Sun Kosi, river C2 19
Sunch'ŏn B5 9
Sundarbans, region C7 21
Sunderland C2 30
Sunderland F3 102
Sundi C1 63
Sundown C4 96
Sundridge F2 102
Sundsvall C2 53
Sunnynook E5 94
Sunset House B3 94
Sunyani A3 64
Sup'ung, reservoir A2 9
Superior, lake J4 92
Superior, Wis. D1 126
Sur C1 25
Sur (Tyre) A2 26
Surab C4 21
Surabaya C2 13
Surakarta C2 13
Surat B4 20
Surat Thani B4 12
Sûre, river A2, B2 33
Surgut C5 44
Surigao C4 12
Surin C3 12
Suriname 80
Suriname, river B3 80
Surkhob, river B1 23
Surma, river E3 21
Surprise F1 95
Surt C1 56
Surtsey, island A3 52
Surud Ad, mt. B1 60
Sussex D3 97
Susuman C9 44
Sutlej, river D4 21
Sutton West F3 102
Suva, capital B3 17
Suvadiva, atoll A4 19
Suwałki F1 41
Suwanose, island A4 8
Suwar, as- B2 27
Suwayda, as- A3 27
Suwŏn B4 9
Suzano Inset II 81
Suzhou F2 10
Svalbard, islands 5
Svay Rieng D4 11
Svendborg C3 32
Šventoji, river C2 46
Svetozarevo B3 49
Svilengrad E4 50
Svishtov D2 50
Svitavy C3 42
Svobodnyy D8 44
Swabian Jura, mts. B4 40
Swains, island A1 18
Swakopmund B2 70
Swan Hills C4 94
Swan Lake B4 96
Swan River A3 96
Swan, lake A3 96
Swan, river A3 96
Swan, river Inset I 14
Swansea B3 30
Swaziland 71
Sweden 53
Swift Current D5 98
Swift Current C10 104
Swindon C3 30
Świnoujście B2 41
Switzerland 35
Swords C2 31
Sydney G1 100
Sydney, island B2 17
Sydney, N.S.W.,
capital E3, Inset IV 14
Syktyvkar C4 44
Sylhet E4 21
Syracuse (Siracusa) C3 38
Syracuse, N.Y. F1 126
Syrdarya, river A1, C2 23
Syria 27
Syrian, desert B1 26
Szczecin B2 41
Szeged C2 43
Székesfehérvár B2 43
Szekszárd B2 43
Szentes C2 43
Szolnok C2 43
Szombathely A2 43

T

Taabo, lake D3 63
Tabar, islands B2 15
Tabasará, mts. B2 87
Tabasco F4 84
Tabelbala A2 57
Taber D6 94
Tablas, island B3 12
Tabligbo B3 64
Taboão da Serra Inset II 81
Tábor B3 42
Tabora B2 68
Tabou C4 63
Tabriz B2 22
Tabuaeran, island D1 17
Tabuk A1 24
Tabusintac D1 97
Tabwemasana, mt. B2 18
Tacaná, volcano A4 85
Tacloban C4 12
Tacna C4 77
Tacoma, Wash. A1 126
Tacuarembó C1 75
Tacuarembó, river C1 75
Tacuarí, river D2 75
Tadjoura B2 60
Tadmur B2 27
Tadoussac G3 103
Taebaek-sanmaek, mts. C3 9
Taedong, river B3 9
Taegu C5 9
Taejŏn B4 9
Tafahi, island C1 17
Tafilah, at- A2 26
Taga A2 18
Taganrog, gulf D3 47
Tagish C5 105
Tagish, lake E1 95
Tagula, island B3 15
Tagus, river D3 37
Tahan, mt. B2 13
Tahat, mt. B2 57
Tahoua B3 59
Tai, lake F2 10
Tai'an E2 10
T'aichung B1 9
Taif, at- B2 24
T'ainan B2 9
Taipei, capital B1 9
Taitao, peninsula A8 76
T'aitung B2 9
Taiwan 9
Taiwan, strait E3 10
Taiyuan E2 10
Taizz A2 25
Tajikistan 23
Tajumulco, volcano B4 85
Tak B2 12
Taka, island B1 16
Takamaka Inset 70
Takamatsu B3 8
Takara, island A4 8
Takatsuki B3 8
Takev C5 11
Takipy A1 96
Takla Makan, desert B2 10
Takla, lake K3 95
Takua Pa B4 12
Takutu, river B4 80
Talagante Inset 76
Talak, region B2 59
Talamanca, range C3 86
Talara A1 77
Talas C1 23
Talaud, islands D1 13
Talavera de la Reina D3 37
Talca B5 76
Talcahuano B6 76
Taldyqorghan D2 23
Talish, mts. C3 45
Tall Afar B1 24
Tallahassee, capital, Fla. E2 126
Tallinn, capital C1 46
Taloqan B1 22
Talsi B2 46
Taltal B3 76
Taltson, river F4 99
Tamale B2 64
Tamanrasset B2 57
Tamarin B3 69
Tamaulipas E3 84
Tambacounda C3 62
Tambo, river C3, C4 77
Tâmega, river B2 36
Tampa, Fla. E3 126
Tampere B2 53
Tampico E3 84
Tampines B1 13
Tampok, river B2 80
Tamsagbulag D2 11
Tamu B1 12
Tamworth, N.S.W. E3 14
Tan-Tan B2 57
Tana, lake B1 60
Tana, river F1 61
Tana, river F1 52
Tanabe B3 8
Tanch'ŏn C2 9
Tandil D4 74
Tanega, island A4 8
Tanen, range B2 12
Tanezrouft, mts. A2 57
Tanga C2 68
Tanga, islands B2 15
Tangail C4 21
Tanganyika, lake A2 68
Tanggula, range C2 10
Tangier C1 57
Tangier E3 100
Tangshan E2 10
Tanimbar, islands E2 13
Tanjungpinang B1 13
Tanna, island C4 18
Tano, river A3 64
Tanshui B1 9
Tanta B1 56
Tanzania 68
Taongi, island B1 16
Taoudenni C1 58
T'aoyüan B1 9
Tapa C1 46
Tapachula F5 84
Tapajós, river C2 81
Tapanahoni, river B3 80
Tapeta B2 63
Taquari, river C3 81
Tara D5 44
Tara, river A3 49
Taraba, river F3 65
Tarakan C1 13
Taranto D2 38
Taranto, gulf D2 38
Tarapoto B2 77
Tararua, range C3 15
Tarat B2 57
Tarawa, capital A1 17
Tarbes C5 34
Taree, N.S.W. E3 14
Tarif B2 25
Tarija B4 77
Tarim, river B1 10
Tarin Kowt B2 22
Tarnobrzeg E3 41
Tarnów E3 41
Taroudant B2 57
Tarrafal C3 58
Tarragona G2 37
Tarrasa G2 37
Tarsus C3 27
Tartu D2 46
Tartus A2 27
Tarvo B3 77
Taseko, lake L5 95
Tash Kömür C2 23
Tashigang C2 19
Tashir B1 45
Tashkent, capital C2 23
Tasikmalaya B2 13
Tasman, bay B3 15
Tasman, sea E3 14
Tasmania D4 14
Tata C2 57
Tatabánya B2 43
Tatamagouche D2 100
Tataouine C3 57
Tatar, strait D9 44
Tatarstan, republic D4 44
Tathlina, lake E4 99
Tatla Lake K5 95
Tatlayoko Lake K5 95
Tatra, range B2 42
Tau, island A1 18
Taumaruni C2 15
Taunggyi C2 12
Taunton C3 30
Taunus, mts. B3 40
Taupo C2 15
Taupo, lake C2 15
Tauragė B2 46
Tauranga C2 15
Taureau, reservoir C5 103
Taurus, mts. B3 27
Tauu, islands B3 15
Tavan Bogd Uul, mt. A2 11
Taverny Inset II 34
Taveuni, island C2 17
Tavoy C3 12
Tavoy, point C3 12
Tawau D2 13
Tawi Tawi, island A5 12
Taxco E4 84
Tay Ninh B4 11
Tay, estuary C2 30
Tay, lake B2 30
Tay, river B2 30
Tay, river C4 105
Taymouth C2 97
Taymyr, peninsula B6 44
Taymyriya,
autonomous okrug B6 44
Taza C1 57
Tazin, lake A1 104
Tazin, river B1 104
Tbilisi, capital C4 45
Tchamba B2 64
Tchaourou B3 64
Tchentlo, lake K3 95
Tchibanga A2 66
Te Anau, lake A4 15
Tebicuary, river D5 75
Tecomán D4 84
Tecuci D3 43
Tedzhen C3 22
Tedzhen, river C3 22
Teepee Creek A3 94
Tees, river C2 30
Teeswater D3 102
Tefé B2 81
Tegal B2 13
Tegucigalpa, capital B2 86
Tehek, lake J4 99
Tehkummah D2 102
Tehran, capital C2 22
Tehuacán E4 84
Tehuantepec, gulf E4 84
Tehuantepec, isthmus F4 84
Teifi, river B3 30
Tekapo, lake B3 15
Tekeze, river B1 60
Tekirdağ A2 27
Tekong, island C1 13
Tel Aviv-Jaffa B1 26
Tela B2 86
Telavi C4 45
Telde Inset I 37
Telegraph Creek G2 95
Teles Pires, river C2 81
Telford C3 30
Telkwa J4 95
Telok Anson A2 13
Telšiai B2 46
Tema C4 64
Temagami, lake E1 102
Temburong, river C2 13
Temirtau D1 23
Tempisque, river A2 86
Temuco B6 76
Tena C3 79
Téna Kourou, mt. B3 64
Ténéré, desert C1 59
Tenerife, island Inset I 37
Tengiz, lake C1 23
Tenkodogo D3 64
Tennant Creek, N.T. C1 14
Tennessee E2 126
Tennessee, river E2 126
Tenojoki, river C1 53
Tenryu, river C3 8
Teotihuacán Inset 84
Tepexpan Inset 84
Tepic, state capital D3 84
Téra A3 59
Terai, region A2, C3 19
Teraina, island D1 17
Teramo C2 38
Teresina D2 81
Tereul F2 37
Termiz C3 23
Termoli C2 38
Ternate D1 13
Terni C2 38
Ternopil B2 47
Terrace H4 95
Terre Haute, Ind. E2 126
Terrebonne J5 103
Terreiro Velho C1 63
Terrenceville D5 98
Terschelling, island C1 32
Teseney A2 60
Teshio, river Inset I 8
Tesiyn, river B2 11
Teslić B1 48
Teslin C5 105
Teslin, lake C5 105
Teslin, river C5 105
Tessalit D1 58
Tessaoua B3 59
Testa del Gargano, point D2 38
Tete B3 68
Tête Jaune Cache N5 95
Tétouan C1 57
Tetovo A1 48
Teulada, cape B3 38
Teulon C4 96
Tewkesbury C3 30
Texarkana, Tex. D2 126
Texas D2 126
Texcoco Inset 84
Texel, island B1 32
Teyateyaneng A2 71
Tezoyuca Inset 84
Tezzeron, lake K4 95
Thaba-Tseka B2 71
Thabana Ntlenyana, mt. C2 71
Thai Nguyen A2 11
Thailand 12
Thailand, gulf B4, C4 12
Thames, river C3, Inset III 30
Thames, river D5 102
Thamesville D5 102
Thane Inset I 20

Key Page

Thanh Hoa A2 11
Thanjavur C6 20
Thar, desert C4 21
Thásos C1 51
Thásos, island C1 51
The Crane C4 91
The Hague B2 32
The Ovens C3 100
The Pas A2, C2 96
Thedford D4 102
Thekulthili, lake G4 99
Thelon, river H4, J4 99
Theodore H9 104
Thessalon B1 102
Thessaloníki B1 51
Thetford D3 30
Thetford Mines E5 103
Thicket C4 91
Thicket Portage C1 96
Thiès A2 62
Thika D4 61
Thimphu, capital A2 19
Thingvellir A2 52
Thio C2 18
Thíra, island C3 51
Thisted B2 32
Thlewiaza, river J4 99
Tholen, island B3 32
Thomaston Corner B3 97
Thompson C1, D2 96
Thompson, river M6 95
Thong Hoe A1 13
Thorhild D4 94
Thornhill K5 102
Thorold F4 102
Thrace, region D4 50
Thracian, plain C3 50
Three Kings, islands B1 15
Thule, air base B2 106
Thun B2 35
Thunder Bay C3 101
Thunersee, lake B2 35
Thuringia B3 40
Thuringian, forest B3 40
Thurso B1 30
Thurston, island B9 107
Ti'avea D2 18
Ti-n-Zaouâtene B2 57
Tiáhuac Inset 84
Tianjin E2 10
Tibati B2 65
Tiber, river C2 38
Tiberias B1 26
Tiberias (Galilee), lake A1, B1 26
Tibesti, massif B2 59
Tibet (Xizang) B2 10
Tibet, plateau B2 10
Tiburón, island B2 84
Tichit C3 58
Tichla A2 58
Ticino, river C2 35
Tide Head C1 97
Tidjikdja C3 58
Tien Shan, range A1 10
Tierra del Fuego, island C9 76
Tietê, river Inset II 81
Tignish A2 100
Tigre, river B1 77
Tigris, river B1 24
Tijuana A1 84
Tikal D2 85
Tikrit B2 24
Tiksi B8 44
Tiladummati, atoll A1 19
Tilburg C3 32
Tilbury C5 102
Tillabéry A3 59
Tilley E6 94
Tillsonburg E5 102
Tilomonte C2 76
Tilston A4 96
Timaru B3 15
Timbuktu C2 58
Timgad, ruins B1 57
Timişoara A3 43
Timmins D3 101
Timor, island D2 13
Timor, sea B1 14
Tindouf A2 57
Tingo María B2 77
Tinkissa, river C2 62
Tio C2 60
Tipitapa, river A2 87
Tipperary B2 31
Tirana, capital A2 49
Tiraspol B2 50
Tiree, island A2 30
Tîrgovişte C3 43
Tîrgu Jiu B3 43
Tîrgu-Mureş C2 43
Tîrgu Neamţ D2 43
Tîrgu Ocna D2 43
Tirich Mir, mt. D2 21
Tirso, river B2 38
Tiruchchirappalli C6 20
Tisa, river B2 49
Tisdale F8 104
Tista, river C2 21
Tisza, river C2 43
Titagarh Inset II 20
Titano, mt. B1 39
Titicaca, lake A3, D4 77
Titov Veles B2 48
Titova Mitrovica B3 49
Tivaouane A2 62
Tiverton B4 30
Tiverton D3 102
Tivoli B2 91
Tiznit B2 57
Tlaipan Inset 84
Tlalnepantla Inset 84
Tlaxcala, state capital E4 84
Tlemcen A1 57
Toa Payoh B1 13
Toad River K2 95
Toamasina B2 69
Toba Kakar, range C3 21
Tobago, cays A4 91
Tobago, island B1 91
Tobermory D2 102
Tobi, island Inset 17
Tobin, lake G7 104
Tobol, river C1 23
Tobolsk D5 44
Tobruk D1 56
Tocantins D3 81
Tocantins, river D2 81
Toco B2 91
Tocopilla B2 76
Tofino K6 95
Tofua, island B3 17
Togo 64
Tokachi, river Inset I 8
Tokaj C1 43
Tokara, islands A4 8
Tokat D2 27
Tŏkchŏk-kundo, islands A4 9
Tokmok D1 23
Tokorozawa C3 8
Toktogul C2 23
Toku, island C2 17
Tokuno, island Inset II 8
Tokushima B3 8
Tokuyama A3 8
Tokyo, capital C3 8
Tôlanaro B3 69
Toledo D3 37
Toledo, mts. D3 37
Toledo, Ohio E1 126
Toliara A3 69
Tolima, mt. B3 78
Tolland E4 94
Toltén, river B6 76
Toluca, state capital E4 84
Tolyatti D4 44
Tom Price, W.A. A2 14
Tomahawk C4 94
Tomakomai Inset I 8
Tomanivi, mt. B2 17
Tombua B5 70
Tomé B6 76
Tomelloso E3 37
Tomiko, lake F1 102
Tompkins B10 104
Tomsk D6 44
Tonalá F4 84
Tonbridge Inset III 30
Tone, river C2 8
Tonga 17
Tongariro, mt. C2 15
Tongatapu, island B4 17
Tonghua F1 10
Tongjosŏn, bay B3 9
Tongliao F1 10
Tongsa B2 19
Tongsa, river B2 19
Tonkin, gulf B2 11
Tonle Sap, lake B2,C3 11
Tonle Sap, river B2 11
Toowoomba, Qld. E2 14
Topeka, Kans. D2 126
Topley Landing J4 95
Torbay B4 30
Torbay E5 98
Torghay, plateau C1 23
Tormes, river D2 37
Torneälven, river D1 53
Torngat, mts. D3 98
Tornio B1 53
Torniojoki, river B1 53
Toronto, capital F4, K5 102
Tororo D3 61
Torquay G11 104
Torre del Greco C2 38
Torrejón de Ardoz Inset II 37
Torrelavega D1 37
Torrens, lake C2 14
Torrens, river Inset II 14
Torrente F3 37
Torreón D2 84
Torres, islands B1 18
Torres, strait D1 14
Torrington D5 94
Tórshavn Inset 32
Tortosa G2 37
Tortosa, cape G2 37
Tortuga, island C1 89
Toruń D2 41
Tõrva C2 46
Tory Hill G3 102
Tosa, bay B3 8
Totness A2 80
Tottori B3 8
Touggourt B1 57
Tougué C2 62
Toulaman, river B2 90
Touliu B2 9
Toulon D5 34
Toulouse C5 34
Toungoo C2 12
Toura, mts. C2 63
Tourcoing C1 34
Tournai B2 33
Tours C3 34
Toussoro, mt. B2 66
Toutes Aides B3 96
Tovuz A2 45
Towada, lake D1 8
Townsville, Qld. D1 14
Toxkan, river E2 23
Toyama C2 8
Toyama, bay C2 8
Toyohashi C3 8
Toyonaka B3 8
Toyota C3 8
Tozeur B3 57
Tqvarcheli A3 45
Trabzon D2 27
Tracadie-Sheila E1 97
Tracy C3 97
Tracy C5 103
Trafalgar E2 100
Trail O6 95
Tralee B2 31
Trang B5 12
Transantarctic, mts. B4 107
Transylvanian Alps, mts. C3 43
Trapani C3 38
Trasimeno, lake C2 38
Trat C3 12
Traun, river D2 39
Traverse City, Mich. E1 126
Trebinje B2 48
Treherne B4 96
Treinta y Tres C2 75
Trembleur, lake K4 95
Trenche, river C3 103
Trenčín B2 42
Trent, river C3 30
Trentino-Alto Adige B1 38
Trento B1 38
Trenton E2 100
Trenton H3 102
Trenton, capital, N.J. F1 126
Trepassey E5 98
Tres Puntas, cape B6 74
Treska, river B2 48
Treviso C1 38
Trier A4 40
Triesen B2 33
Triesenberg B2 33
Trieste C1 38
Trieste, gulf A3 48
Triglav, mt. A2 48
Trikala B2 51
Trim C2 31
Trincomalee C3 19
Trinidad B2 77
Trinidad B2 75
Trinidad C2 88
Trinidad, island A2 91
Trinidad, mts. C2 88
Trinidad and Tobago 91
Trinity East E5 98
Trinity, bay E5 98
Triolet C2 69
Tripoli (Tarabulus) A1 26
Tripoli, capital B1 56
Tripolitania, region B1 56
Triton D4 98
Trivandrum (Thiruvananthapuram) C7 20
Trnava A2 42
Trobriand, islands B2 15
Trois-Pistoles G3 103
Trois-Rivières D5 103
Troisvierges B1 33
Trollhättan B3 53
Trombay Inset I 20
Tromsø D2 52
Trondheim C3 52
Trondheimsfjord, fjord B3 52
Trongisvágur Inset 32
Troödos, mts. A2 27
Trossachs F11 104
Trout Creek F1 102
Trout Lake C3 94
Trout River B4 98
Trout, lake D4 99
Trout, lake B2 101
Trouville C2 34
Trowbridge C3 30
Troyes D2 34
Trujillo B2 77
Trujillo B2 79
Trujillo B2 86
Trujillo Alto C2 90
Truro B4 30
Truro D2 100
Trutch L2 95
Trutnov B2 42
Tsaratanana, mts. B1 69
Tsavo E5 61
Tsedike, river B3 71
Tsengwen, river B2 9
Tsetserleg C2 11
Tsévié B3 64
Tshabong A3 69
Tshane A3 69
Tshaneni B1 71
Tshikapa B2 67
Tshuapa, river B2 67
Tsiribihina, river B2 69
Tsiroanomandidy B2 69
Tsiteli-Tsqaro D4 45
Tskhinvali B3 45
Tsnori C4 45
Tsu, island A3 8
Tsuen Wan Inset 10
Tsugaru, strait D1, Inset I 8
Tsumeb C1 70
Tsumkwe D1 70
Tsuruga C3 8
Tsuruoka C2 8
Tuam B2 31
Tuas A1 13
Tuasivi B2 18
Tubarão D4 81
Tübingen B4 40
Tubmanburg A2 63
Tucson, Ariz. B2 126
Tucumcari, N. Mex. C2 126
Tucupita D2 79
Tucuruí, reservoir D2 81
Tuen Mun Inset 10
Tugela, river D2 71
Tuguegarao B2 12
Tuira, river D2 87
Tuktoyaktuk B3 99
Tuktut Nogait N.P. D3 99
Tukums B2 46
Tula D3 44
Tula, ruins D3 84
Tulcán C2 79
Tulcea E3 43
Tullamore C2 31
Tulsa, Okla. D2 126
Tulsequah F2 95
Tulsipur B2 19
Tultitlán Inset 84
Tulun D7 44
Tuma, river B2 87
Tumaco A4 78
Tumba, lake B2 67
Tumbes A1 77
Tumbler Ridge M3 95
Tumen, river C1 9
Tumuc-Humac, mts. A2, B3 80
Tumucumaque, range C1 81
Tunbridge Wells D3 30
Tundzha, river E3 50
Tungsten C4 99
Tunis, capital C1 57
Tunis, gulf C1 57
Tunisia 57
Tunja B3 78
Tupelo, Miss. E2 126
Tupiza A4 77
Tupungato, mt. B3 74
Tur, at- B2 56
Tura C7 44
Turan, lowland A2 23
Turayf A1 24
Turbo A2 78
Turda B2 43
Turfan, depression C1 10
Tŭrgovishte E2 50
Türi C2 46
Turin A1 38
Turin D6 94
Turkana (Rudolf), lake D2 61
Turkestan, mts. A1 23
Turkey 27
Turkmenbashi A2 22
Turkmenistan 22
Turks and Caicos Islands 89
Turks, islands D4 89
Turku B2 53
Turkwel, river C2 61
Turnberry A2 96
Turnbull B2 96
Turneffe, islands C2 85
Turnhout C1 33
Turnor Lake B4 104
Turnu Măgurele C4 43
Turquino, mt. E3 88
Tursunzoda A1 23
Turtle, lake B7 104
Turtleford B7 104
Tuscaloosa, Ala. E2 126
Tuscany B2 38
Tusket B4 100
Tuticorin C7 20
Tutong B2 13
Tutong, river B2 13
Tutuila, island A1, C2 18
Tuul, river C2 11
Tuvalu 16
Tuxtla Gutiérrez, state capital F4 84
Tuy Hoa B4 11
Tuya, lake G1 95
Tuz, lake C2 27
Tuzla B1 48
Tweed H3 102
Tweed, river C2 30
Twillingate D4 98
Twin Butte D6 94
Twin Falls, Idaho B1 126
Two Creeks A4 96
Tychy D3 41
Tynda D8 44
Tyndall C4 96
Tyne Valley B2 100
Tyne, river C2 30
Tyrrhenian, sea B2 38
Tyumen D5 44
Tyva, republic D6 44
Tywi, river B3 30

U

Uaboe B1 16
Ubangi, river B1 67
Ubayyid, al- C2 59
Ube A3 8
Úbeda E3 37
Úbeda E3 37
Uberaba D3 81
Uberlândia D3 81
Ubin, island B1 13
Ubon Ratchathani C3 12
Ucayali, river C2 77
Uccle C2 33
Uchiura, bay Inset I 8
Uchquduq B2 23
Ucluelet K7 95
Udaipur B4 20
Uddevalla B3 53
Uddjaur, lake C1 53
Udine C1 38
Udmurtiya, republic D4 44
Udon Thani C2 12
Udu, point C2 17
Uele, river C1 67
Uelzen B2 40
Ufa D4 44
Uga, river B2 70
Ugalla, river B2 68
Uganda 61
Uíge C2 70
Uitenhage C3 71
Ujae, island B2 16
Ujelang, island A2 16
Ujjain C4 20
Ujung Pandang C2 13
Ukhta C4 44
Ukmergė C2 46
Ukraine 47
Ulaan-Uul C2 11
Ulaanbaatar, capital C2 11
Ulaangom B2 11
Ulan-Ude D7 44
Ulansuhai, lake D1 10
Ulchin C4 9
Ulhas, river Inset I 20
Uliastay B2 11
Ulithi, atoll B2 15
Ullŭng-do, island D4 9
Ullapool B1 30
Ulm B4 40
Ulsan C5 9
Ulster, province C1 31
Ulu Dağ (Mt. Olympus), mt. B2 27
Ulúa, river B2 86
Ulubaria Inset II 20
Uluru (Ayers Rock) C2 14
Uman C2 47
Umbeluzi, river B2 71
Umboi, island A2 15
Umbria C2 38
Umeå D2 53
Umeälven, river C2 53
Umm al-Qaywayn C2 25
Umm Bab B3 25
Umm Qasr C2 24
Umm Said (Musayid) D4 25
Umniati, river B2 69
Umtata C3 71
Umuahia D5 65
Umzingwani, river B2 69
Una, river A1 48
Unayzah B1 24
Ungava, bay L3 92
Ungheni A2 50
Unión C2 76
Union, island A4 91
United Arab Emirates 25
United States 126
Unity A8 104
Unst, island Inset I 30
Upemba, lake C3 67
Upernavik B2 106
Upington B2 71
Upolu, island C2 18
Upper Arrow, lake O6 95
Upper Liard D5 105
Upper Lough Erne, lake A 30
Upper Musquodoboit E2 100
Upper Ohio B4 100
Uppsala C3 53
Ural, mts. D4 44
Ural, river B2 23
Uran Inset I 20
Uranium City B1 104
Urawa C3 8
Urganch B2 23
Urmia, lake B2 22
Uroševac B3 49
Uruapan D4 84
Urubamba, river C3 77
Uruguai, river C4 81
Uruguay 75
Uruguay, river D3 74
Urukthapel, island B3 17
Ürümqi B1 10
Usak B2 27
Ushuaia B7 74
Usk, river C3 30
Üsküdar B2 27
Usmas, lake B2 46
Ussuri, river E8 44
Ussuriysk E8 44
Ust-Ilimsk D7 44
Ust-Kamchatsk D10 44
Ust-Kut D7 44
Ust-Ordynskiy Buryat, autonomous okrug D7 44
Ust-Ordynskiy D7 44
Uster C1 35
Ústí nad Labem B2 42
Ustica, island C3 38
Ustka C1 41
Ustyurt, plateau A2, B2 23
Usulután B2 86
Usumacinta, river F4 84
Utah B2 126
Utah, beach B2 34
Utan Inset I 20
Utena C2 46
Utikuma, lake C3 94
Utila, island B1 86
Utrecht C2 32
Utsunomiya C2 8
Uttaradit B2 12
Utuado B2 90
Utupua, island C2 16
Uummannaq B2 106
Uvira C2 67
Uvs, lake B1 11
Uwajima B3 8
Uwaynat, al- B2 56
Uyo D5 65
Uyuni A4 77
Uzbekistan 23
Uzhhorod A2 47
Užice A3 49

V

Vaal, reservoir C2 71
Vaal, river B2 71
Vaalserberg, mt. D4 32
Vaasa B2 53
Vác B2 43
Vache, island B2 89
Vadodara B4 20
Vadsø F1 52
Vaduz, capital B2 33
Vágar, island Inset 32
Váh, river A2 42
Vahsh, river A1 23
Vaitupu, island C2 16
Vakhan, region C1 22
Val Comeau E1 97
Val Marie C11 104
Val-d'Or A4 101
Val-des-Bois A6 103
Valcourt D6 103
Valdecaño D2 37
Valdepeñas E3 37
Valdés, peninsula C5 74
Valdivia B6 76
Valemount N5 95
Valença A1 36
Valence D4 34
Valencia C1 79
Valencia F3 37
Valencia, gulf G3 37
Valenciennes C1 34
Valera B2 79
Valga D3 46
Valira d'Orient, river B2 36
Valira, river B2 36
Valjevo A2 49
Valka C2 46
Valladolid G3 84
Valladolid D2 37
Valle d'Aosta A1 38
Valledupar B2 78
Vallenar B3 76
Valletta, capital C2 36
Valley, river A3 96
Valmiera C2 46
Valparaíso B4, Inset 76
Van E2 27
Van, lake E2 27
Vancouver L6 95
Vancouver, island J6 95
Vanderhoof K4 95
Vänern, lake B3 53
Vanguard C11 104
Vanier H5 102
Vanier L5 103
Vanikolo, islands C2 16
Vanimo A2 15
Vannes B3 34
Vanrhynsdorp A3 71
Vanscoy D8 104
Vansittart, island M3 99
Vantaa B2 53
Vanua Balavu, island C2 17
Vanua Lava, island B1 18
Vanua Levu, island B2 17
Vanuatu 18
Varanasi D3 20
Varaždin C2 48
Vardar, river C2 48
Varde, river B3 32
Vardenis C2 45
Varkaus C2 53
Varna F2 50
Vasai Inset I 20
Vasai, creek Inset I 20
Vaslui D2 43
Vassar D4 96
Västerås C3 53
Vatican City 39
Vatnajökull, ice cap B2 52
Vättern, lake B3 53
Vatu Lele, island A3 17
Vaudreuil C6 103
Vaupés, river B4 78
Vava'u, island C2 17
Vavenby N5 95
Vavuniya B3 19
Vawkavysk B3 47
Växjö B3 53
Vayk C3 45
Vega C4 94
Vega Alta C2 90
Vega Baja C2 90
Vegreville D4 94
Veimandu, channel A3 19
Vejle B3 32
Velika Morava, river B2 49
Veliki, canal A2 49
Veliko Tŭrnovo D2 50
Vélingara B2 62
Vélingara B3 62
Vella Lavella, island A1 16
Vellore C6 20
Veneto B1 38
Venezuela 79
Venezuela, gulf B1 79
Venice C1 38
Venice, gulf C1 38
Venlo D3 32
Venta, river B1 46
Ventimiglia A2 38
Ventspils A2 46
Veracruz E4 84
Vercelli B1 38
Verde, river C3 75
Verdun D2 34
Verdun J6 103
Vereeniging C2 71
Verkhoyansk C8 44
Verkhoyansk, range C8 44
Vermillion, river C4 103
Vermont F1 126
Vernal, Utah C1 126
Verner E1 102
Vernon N6 95
Vernon Bridge C2 100
Vernon River C2 100
Véroia B1 51
Verona B1 38
Verona J3 102
Versailles C2, Inset II 34
Vert, cape A2 62
Verviers D2 33
Vesoul D3 34
Vesterålen, islands C2 52
Vestmanna Inset 32
Vestmannaeyjar A3 52
Vesuvius, volcano C2 38
Veszprém A2 43
Vetauua, island C1 17
Viana do Castelo A2 36
Vianden B2 33
Vibank G10 104
Viborg B2 32
Vicenza B1 38
Vich H2 37
Vichada, river C3 78
Vichy C3 34
Victoria D3 14
Victoria B6 76
Victoria A1 36
Victoria B2 100
Victoria Beach C4 96
Victoria Beach B3 100
Victoria Land, region B5 107
Victoria Nile, river C3 61
Victoria, capital Inset 70
Victoria, capital L7 95
Victoria, falls B3 67
Victoria, island F2 99
Victoria, lake B4, C4 61
Victoria, peak B3 85
Victoria, river C1 14
Victoria, Tex. D3 126
Victoriaville E5 103

	Key	Page
Vidin	A2	50
Viedma	C5	74
Viedma, lake	A6	74
Vieille Case	A1	90
Vienna, capital	E2	39
Vienne, river	C3	34
Vientiane, capital	B3	11
Vieques	D2	90
Vieques, island	E2	90
Vieques, passage	D2	90
Vieques, sound	E2	90
Vierzon	C3	34
Viet Tri	A2	11
Vietnam		11
Vieux Fort	B3	91
Vigan	B2	12
Vignemale, mt.	B5	34
Vigo	B1	37
Vijayawada	D5	20
Vijosë, river	A3	49
Vila do Conde	A2	36
Vila Nova de Gaia	A2	36
Vila Real	B2	36
Vila Real de Santo Antonio	B4	36
Vila, capital	C3	18
Vilaine, river	B3	34
Vilanculos	B4	68
Vilcabamba, mts.	C3	77
Viljandi	C2	46
Vilkaviškis	B2	46
Villa Ahumada	C1	84
Villa Hayes	D4	75
Villa María	C3	74
Villa Obregón	Inset	84
Villach	C4	39
Villahermosa, state capital	F4	84
Villalba	C2	90
Villarreal de los Infantes	F3	37
Villarrica	D4	75
Villavicencio	B3	78
Villazón	A4	77
Ville-Marie	A4	101
Villeneuve-Saint-Georges	Inset II	34
Villeroy	E5	103
Vilnius, capital	C2	46
Vilyuy, river	C7	44
Vilyuysk	C8	44
Viña del Mar	B4, Inset	76
Vincennes	Inset II	34
Vincente de Carvalho	Inset II	81
Vinces, river	B3	79
Vindelälven, river	C2	53
Vindhya, range	C4	20
Vinh	A2	11
Vinnitsa	B2	47
Vinson Massif, mt.	B10	107
Virden	A4	96
Virgin, river	C3	104
Virgin, islands		82
Virginia	F2	126
Virtsu	B2	46
Virunga, mts.	B1	61
Visakhapatnam	D5	20
Visayan, islands	B4	12
Visayan, sea	B4	12
Visby	C3	53
Viscount Melville, sound	F2	99
Viseu	B2	36
Vista	A4	96
Vista Hermosa	B4	78
Vistula, river	D2, E3	41
Vita	C4	96
Viterbo	C2	38
Viti Levu, island	A2	17
Vitoria	E1	37
Vitória	D4	81
Vitória da Conquista	D3	81
Vitsyebsk	E2	47
Vivian	C4	96
Vizcaíno, desert	B2	84
Vlaardingen	B3	32
Vladivostok	E8	44
Vlieland, island	B1	32
Vlissingen	A3	32
Vlorë	A3	49
Vltava, river	B3	42
Vöcklabruck	C2	39
Voinjama	B1	63
Vojvodina, province	A2	49
Volcano, islands	Inset III	8
Volga, river	E4	44
Volgograd	E4	44
Vologda	D3	44
Vólos	B2	51
Volta Redonda	D4	81
Volta, lake	C3	64
Volta, river	C3	64
Vonda	D8	104
Vorkuta	C5	44
Voronezh	D3	44
Vorotan, river	C3	45
Vorskla, river	C1	47
Vörts Järv, lake	D2	46
Võru	D3	46
Vosges, mts.	D2	34
Vostok, island	D3	17
Vranje	B3	49
Vratsa	B2	50
Vrbas	A2	49
Vrbas, river	B1	48
Vršac	B2	49
Vryburg	B2	71
Vukovar	D2	48
Vunaniu, bay	A3	17
Vung Tau-Con Dao	B4	11
Vunisea	B3	17

W

	Key	Page
Wa	A1	64
Waal, river	C3	32
Wabag	A2	15
Wabamun, lake	C4	94
Wabana	E5	98
Wabasca, river	C2	94
Wabe Gestro, river	C3	60
Wabe Shebele, river	D3	60
Wabowden	B2	96
Wabush	D4	98
Waco, Tex.	D2	126
Wad Madani	C2	59
Waddan	C2	56
Waddenzee, sound	C1	32
Waddington, mt.	K5	95
Wadena	G9	104
Wadi al-Malik, river	B2	59
Wadi as-Sirhan, depression	B2	26
Wadi Halfa	C1	59
Wafrah, al-	B3	24
Wagga Wagga, N.S.W.	D3	14
Waigeo, island	E2	13
Waikato, river	C2	15
Waimamaku	B2	15
Waingapu	D2	13
Wairau, river	B3	15
Waitaki, river	B3	15
Wajh, al-	A1	24
Wajir	F3	61
Wakasa, bay	B3	8
Wakaw	E8	104
Wakayama	B3	8
Wakefield	C3	30
Wakkanai	Inset I	8
Wakomata, lake	B1	102
Wakrah, al-	D3	25
Walachia, region	B3	43
Wałbrzych	C3	41
Walcheren, island	A3	32
Walden	D1	102
Waldersee	B4	96
Waldheim	D8	104
Walensee, lake	D1	35
Walkerton	D3	102
Wallace	D2	100
Wallaceburg	C5	102
Walsall	C3	30
Walton	C2	100
Walton	D4	102
Walvis Bay	B2	70
Wami, river	C2	68
Wanaka, lake	A3	15
Wanapitei, lake	E1	102
Wandering River	D3	94
Wando	B5	9
Wanganui	C2	15
Wanham	A3	94
Wapawekka, lake	F5	104
Wapawsik	B1	96
Wapiti, river	A4	94
Warangal	C5	20
Warbah, island	C1	24
Wardlow	E6	94
Ware	K2	95
Warman	D8	104
Warner	D6	94
Warren	C4	96
Warren	E1	102
Warren Landing	C2	96
Warri	C5	65
Warrington	C3	30
Warrnambool, Vic.	D3	14
Warsaw, capital	E2	41
Warta, river	B2, C2	41
Warwick	C3	30
Wasa	P6	95
Wasaga Beach	F3	102
Wasagaming	B4	96
Wash, bay	D3	30
Washago	F3	102
Washington	A1	126
Washington, cape	A3	17
Washington, capital, D.C.	F2	126
Waskada	A4	96
Waskaganish	A3	101
Waskesiu Lake	D7	104
Waspam	C1	87
Water Valley	C5	94
Water, cays	A3	89
Waterborough	C3	97
Waterbury, lake	F2	104
Waterford	C2	31
Waterhen, lake	B3	96
Waterloo	E4	102
Waterloo	D6	103
Watertown, N.Y.	F1	126
Watford	Inset III	30
Watford	D5	102
Wathaman, lake	G3	104
Watrous	E9	104
Watsa	C1	67
Watson	F8	104
Watson Lake	D5	105
Wau	A2	15
Wavre	C2	33
Waw	B3	59
Wawa	D3	101
Wawa, river	B1	87
Wawanesa	B4	96
Weagamow Lake	B2	101
Webbwood	D1	102
Webequie	C2	101
Webi Shabeelle, river	B3	60
Weddell, sea	B12	107
Wedgeport	A4	100
Weert	C3	32
Wei, river	D2	10
Weiden	C4	40
Weifang	E2	10
Weimar	B3	40
Weipa, Qld.	D1	14
Weitzel, lake	D3	104
Wekusko	B2	96
Wekusko, lake	B2	96
Weldiya	C2	60
Wellington	C2	71
Wellington	A2	100
Wellington, capital	B3	15
Wellington, island	A8	76
Wels	C2	39
Welsford	C3	97
Welshpool	B3	30
Welwyn	A4	96
Wembere, river	B1	68
Wenchi	A3	64
Weno	C2	15
Weno, island	C2	15
Wenshan	D3	10
Wentworth	D2	100
Wentzel, lake	C1	94
Wenzhou	F3	10
Werder	D3	60
Werra, river	B3	40
Weser, river	B2	40
Wesley	B2	90
Wesleyville	E4	98
West Antarctica	A8	107
West Devon	A2	100
West Frisian, islands	B1	32
West Ice Shelf, glacier	C1	107
West Palm Beach, Fla.	E3	126
West Point	A2	100
West Road, river	K4	95
West Siberian, plain	C5	44
West St. Modeste	C3	98
West Virginia	E2	126
Westbank	N6	95
Westbourne	B4	96
Western Australia	B2	14
Western Dvina, river	C2	46
Western Ghats, mts.	B5	20
Western Sahara		58
Western, channel	C5	9
Westerschelde, channel	A3	32
Westfield	C3	97
Westlock	D4	94
Westminster	Inset III	30
Weston	J5	102
Westport	B3	15
Westport	B2	31
Westport	J3	102
Westray	A2	96
Westray, island	Inset I	30
Wetar, island	D2	13
Wetaskiwin	D5	94
Wete	C1	68
Wetzlar	B3	40
Wewak	A1	15
Wexford	C2	31
Weyakwin	E6	104
Weyburn	G11	104
Weymouth	A3	100
Whakatane	C2	15
Whale Cove	K4	99
Whaletown	K6	95
Whangarei	B2	15
Wheatland	A4	96
Wheatley	C5	102
Wheeling, W. Va.	E1	126
Whistler	L6	95
Whitbourne	E5	98
Whitby	G4	102
White Fox	F7	104
White Lake	J2	102
White Nile, river	C3	59
White Rock	L6	95
White Sands	C3	100
White Volta, river	B1, D2	64
White, bay	C4	98
White, island	L3	99
White, river	A4	105
White, sea	C3	44
Whitecourt	C4	94
Whitefish Falls	D1	102
Whitefish, bay	A1	102
Whitehaven	B2	30
Whitehorse	C5	105
Whitelaw	A3	94
Whiteman, range	A2	15
Whitemouth	D4	96
Whitestone, river	B3	105
Whitewood	H10	104
Whitney	G2	102
Whitney mt., Calif.	B2	126
Wholdaia, lake	H4	99
Whyalla, S.A.	C3	14
Whycocomagh	F2	100
Wiarton	D3	102
Wichita Falls, Tex.	D2	126
Wichita, Kans.	D2	126
Wick	B1	30
Wicklow	C2	31
Wicklow Head, cape	D2	31
Wicklow, mts.	C2	31
Wiener Neustadt	E3	39
Wieprz, river	F3	41
Wiesbaden	B3	40
Wigan	C3	30
Wight, island	C4	30
Wilberforce	G2	102
Wilge, river	C2	71
Wilhelm, mt.	A2	15
Wilhelmina, canal	B3	32
Wilhelmina, mts.	A2	80
Wilhelmshaven	B2	40
Wilkes Land, region	C3	107
Wilkie	B8	104
William, river	B2	104
Williams Harbour	D3	98
Williams Lake	L5	95
Williamsport	C4	98
Williston, lake	K3	95
Willow Bunch	E11	104
Willow Creek	A11	104
Willowbunch, lake	E11	104
Wilmington, Del.	F2	126
Wilmington, N.C.	F2	126
Wilmot	B3	100
Wiltondale	C4	98
Wiltz	A2	33
Winchester	C3	30
Winchester	K2	102
Wind, river	B3	105
Windermere	O6	95
Windermere	F2	102
Windfall	B4	94
Windhoek, capital	C2	70
Windsor	Inset III	30
Windsor	C3	100
Windsor	C5	102
Windsor	D6	103
Windward Group	B2	58
Windward, islands	B4	91
Windward, passage	F3	88
Winefred, lake	E3	94
Winfield	N6	95
Wingham	D4	102
Winisk	C1	101
Winisk, lake	C2	101
Winisk, river	C2	101
Winkler	C4	96
Winneba	B4	64
Winnemucca, Nev.	B1	126
Winnipeg	C4, D2	96
Winnipeg Beach	C4	96
Winnipeg, lake	B3, C4, D2	96
Winnipeg, river	D4	96
Winnipegosis	B3	96
Winnipegosis, lake	A3	96
Winslow, Ariz.	B2	126
Winston-Salem, N.C.	E2	126
Winter Harbour	H6	95
Winterthur	C1	35
Wisconsin	D1	126
Wismar	B2	40
Witless Bay	E5	98
Witten	A3	40
Wittenberg	C3	40
Wittenberge	B2	40
Witu, island	A2	15
Wiwili	B2	87
Władysławowo	D1	41
Włocławek	D2	41
Woburn	F6	103
Wodzisław Śląski	D3	41
Woking	A3	94
Wolf, lake	C5	105
Wolfsberg	D4	39
Wolfsburg	B2	40
Wolfville	C2	100
Wollaston Lake	G2	104
Wollaston, lake	H2	104
Wollaston, peninsula	E3	99
Wollongong, N.S.W.	E3	14
Wolseley	G10	104
Wolverhampton	C3	30
Wong, river	A2	19
Wŏnju	B4	9
Wonowon	M3	95
Wŏnsan	B3	9
Wood Islands	C3	100
Woodbridge	J5	102
Woodlands	B1	13
Woodlands	C4	96
Woodlark (Muyua), island	B2	15
Woodnorth	A4	96
Woodridge	C4	96
Woods, lake	B3	101
Woodstock	B2	97
Woodstock	A2	100
Woodstock	E4	102
Woody Point	C4	98
Woomera, S.A.	C3	14
Worcester	C3	30
Worcester	A3	71
Worcester, Mass.	F1	126
Worms	B4	40
Wotho, island	B1	16
Wotje, island	B2	16
Wrangel, island	B10	44
Wrath, cape	B1	30
Wreck Cove	D5	98
Wrentham	D6	94
Wrigley	D4	99
Wrocław	C3	41
Wuhan	E2	10
Wuhu	E2	10
Wukari	E4	65
Wum	B2	65
Wuppertal	A3	40
Würzburg	B4	40
Wutivi, mt.	B1	63
Wuwei	D2	10
Wuxi	F2	10
Wuzhong	D2	10
Wuzhou	E3	10
Wye, river	C3	30
Wyndham, W.A.	B1	14
Wynyard	F9	104
Wyoming	C1	126

X

	Key	Page
Xaçmaz	C2	45
Xai-Xai	B5	68
Xam Nua	C1	11
Xangongo	C5	70
Xankändi	B3	45
Xánthi	C1	51
Xau, lake	B2	69
Xi'an	D2	10
Xi, river	E3	10
Xiamen	E3	10
Xiangfan	E2	10
Xiangkhoang	B2	11
Xiangtan	E3	10
Xigaze	B3	10
Xingu, river	C3	81
Xining	D2	10
Xinjiang Uygur	B1	10
Xinxiang	E2	10
Xinyang	E2	10
Xochimilco	Inset	84
Xuddur	A3	60
Xuzhou	E2	10

Y

	Key	Page
Ya'an	D2	10
Yablonovyy, range	D7	44
Yabucoa	D2	90
Yacuiba	B4	77
Yafran	B1	56
Yaguarí, river	C1	75
Yaguarón, river	D2	75
Yahk	O6	95
Yakima, Wash.	A1	126
Yaku, island	A4	8
Yakutsk	C8	44
Yala	B5	12
Yale	M6	95
Yalinga	B2	66
Yalta	C4	47
Yalu, river	B2	9
Yamagata	D2	8
Yamaguchi	A3	8
Yamal, peninsula	C5	44
Yamalo-Nenesiya, autonomous okrug	C5	44
Yambio	B4	59
Yambol	E3	50
Yamoussoukro, capital	D3	63
Yampi, sound	B1	14
Yamuna, river	C3	20
Yan, river	B3	19
Yanbu al-Bahr	A1	24
Yangambi	C1	67
Yangdŏk	B3	9
Yangon (Rangoon), capital	C3	12
Yangquan	E2	10
Yangtze, river	C2, D2	10
Yangzhou	E2	10
Yanji	F1	10
Yantai	F2	10
Yantra, river	D2	50
Yao	B3	8
Yaoundé, capital	B3	65
Yap, islands	A2	15
Yapen, island	E2	13
Yaque del Norte, river	A1	89
Yaque del Sur, river	A2	89
Yaqui, river	C2	84
Yare, river	D3	30
Yaren, capital	B3	16
Yariga, mt.	C2	8
Yarmouth	A4	100
Yaroslavl	D3	44
Yasawa, island group	A2	17
Yasuj	C3	22
Yata, river	A2	77
Yates	B4	94
Yatsushiro	A3	8
Yauco	B2	90
Yavarí, river	C1	77
Yaviza	D2	87
Yazd	C3	22
Yazd, region	C3	22
Ybbs, river	D2	39
Ye	C3	12
Yeboah	C3	30
Yecla	F3	37
Yeguas, point	D2	90
Yekaterinburg	D5	44
Yekepa	B2	63
Yell, island	Inset I	30
Yellow Grass	F11	104
Yellow, sea	F2	10
Yellowknife, capital	F4	99
Yemen		25
Yen Bai	A2	11
Yendi	B2	64
Yenisey, river	C6	44
Yeovil	C4	30
Yerevan, capital	B2	45
Yesilhrmak, river	D2	27
Yeu, island	B3	34
Yevlax	B2	45
Yevpatoriya	C3	47
Yevrey, autonomous oblast	E8	44
Yi, river	C2	75
Yialousa	C1	27
Yibin	D3	10
Yichang	E2	10
Yichun	F1	10
Yin Shan, mts.	E1	10
Yinchuan	D2	10
Yingkou	F1	10
Yining	B1	10
Ylikitka, lake	C1	53
Ylivieska	B2	53
Yoboki	B2	60
Yogyakarta	C2	13
Yojoa, lake	B2	86
Yokkaichi	C3	8
Yokohama	C3	8
Yokosuka	C3	8
Yola	G3	65
Yom, river	B2	12
Yomou	D4	62
Yonago	B3	8
Yonaguni, island	Inset II	8
Yŏngju	C4	9
Yonne, river	C2	34
Yopal	B3	78
York	C3	30
York	B2	100
York	K5	102
York Factory	E1	96
York, cape	D1	14
Yorkton	H9	104
Yoro	B2	86
Yoron, island	Inset II	8
Yoshino, river	B3	8
Yoshkar-Ola	D4	44
Yŏsu	B5	9
Yotvata	B3	26
Youghal	C3	31
Young	E9	104
Youngs Cove	D2	97
Ypané, river	D3	75
Ypoá, lake	D4	75
Ypres	A2	33
Ysyk-Köl, lake	E1	23
Yü Shan, mt.	B2	9
Yuan, river	D3	10
Yubari	Inset I	8
Yucatán, channel	A2	88
Yucatán, peninsula	G4	84
Yuen Long	Inset	10
Yueyang	E3	10
Yukon, river	D2	92
Yuma, Ariz.	B2	126
Yumen	C2	10
Yuna, river	B2	89
Yundum	B2	62
Yungas, region	A3	77
Yungho	B1	9
Yunnan	C3	10
Yurimaguas	B2	77
Yuscarán	B3	86
Yushu	C2	10
Yuzhno-Sakhalinsk	E9	44
Yverdon	A2	35

Z

	Key	Page
Zaanstad	B2	32
Zabbar	C2	36
Zabid	A2	25
Zabol	E3	22
Zabrze	D3	41
Zacapa	D5	85
Zacatecas, state capital	D3	84
Zacatecoluca	B2	86
Zadar	B3	48
Zafra	C3	37
Zagazig	B1	56
Zaghouan	C1	57
Zagreb, capital	B2	48
Zagros, mts.	B3	22
Zahedan	E4	22
Zahlah	A2	26
Zaječar	C3	49
Zákinthos, island	B3	51
Zakopane	D4	41
Zala, river	A2	43
Zalaegerszeg	A2	43
Zalău	B2	43
Zambales, mts.	B3	12
Zambezi	A2	67
Zambezi, river	A3, B3	67
Zambia		67
Zamboanga	B5	12
Zamboanga, peninsula	B5	12
Zamora	D2	37
Zamora	B5	79
Zamora, river	B4	79
Zamość	F3	41
Zanderij	B2	80
Zanjan	B2	22
Zanzibar	C2	68
Zao, mt.	D2	8
Zapadna Morava, river	B3	49
Zapatera, island	B3	87
Zaporizhzhia	D2	47
Zaqatala	B2	45
Zarafobod	A1	23
Zarafshon	B2	23
Zaragoza	F2	37
Zaranj	A2	22
Zareh Sharan	B2	22
Zaria	D2	65
Zarqa, az-	B1	26
Zarzis	C3	57
Zavidoviči	B1	48
Zaysan	E2	23
Zaysan, lake	E2	23
Zebbug	A1	36
Zeebrugge	B1	33
Zefat	B1	26
Zenica	B1	48
Zeravshan, mts.	A1	23
Zeravshan, river	A1, B2	23
Zermatt	B2	35
Zestaponi	B3	45
Zeta, river	A3	49
Zevulun, plain	B1	26
Zēzere, river	A3	36
Zhambyl (Dzhambul)	D2	23
Zhangjiakou	E1	10
Zhangye	D2	10
Zhanjiang	E3	10
Zhejiang	E3	10
Zhelaniya, cape	B5	44
Zhengzhou	E2	10
Zhenjiang	E2	10
Zhezqazgham	C2	23
Zhitomir	B1	47
Zhlobin	D3	47
Zhob, river	C3	21
Zhoda	C4	96
Zhu, river	E3	10
Zhuzhou	E3	10
Zibo	E2	10
Zielona Góra	B3	41
Zigong	D3	10
Ziguinchor	A3	62
Žilina	B2	42
Zillah	C2	56
Zillertal Alps, range	B3	39
Zima, lake	A2	94
Zimbabwe		69
Zinder	B3	59
Zion	C3	90
Zittau	C3	40
Ziway, lake	C3	60
Zlatibor, mts.	A3	49
Zlín	C3	42
Znojmo	C4	42
Zomba	C3	68
Zonguldak	B2	27
Zorzor	B2	63
Zouar	B2	59
Zouîrât	B2	58
Zrenjanin	B2	49
Zug	C1	35
Zugdidi	A3	45
Zugspitze, mt.	B5	40
Zuid-Willemsvaart, canal	C3	32
Zūjar, reservoir	D3	37
Zululand, region	D2	71
Zunyi	D3	10
Zürich	C1	35
Zürichsee, lake	C1	35
Zurrieq	B2	36
Zuwarah	B1	56
Zvishavane	B2	69
Zvolen	B2	42
Zvornik	C1	48
Zwedru	B2	63
Zwickau	C3	40
Zwolle	D2	32
Zyryanka	C9	44

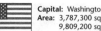

Capital: Washington, D.C. **Pop. (2002):** 288,368,698
Area: 3,787,300 sq. mi. **Largest City:** New York
9,809,200 sq. km. **Monetary Unit:** U.S. dollar

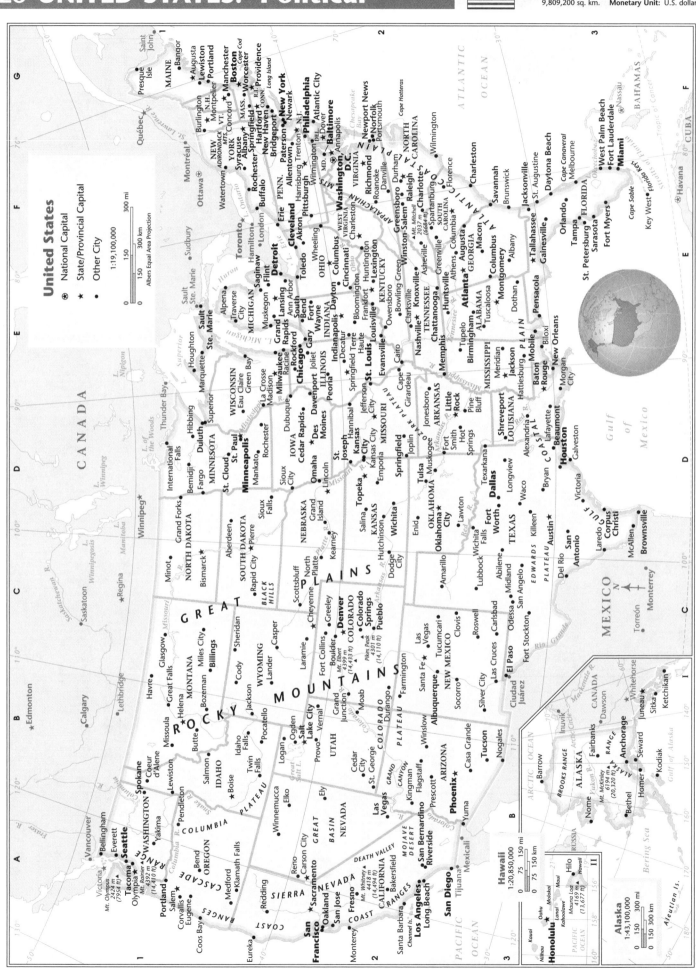

United States
⊛ National Capital
★ State/Provincial Capital
• Other City
1:19,100,000
Albers Equal Area Projection
0 150 300 km
0 150 300 mi

Hawaii
1:20,850,000
0 75 150 mi
0 75 150 km

Alaska
1:43,100,000
0 150 300 mi
0 150 300 km

© MapQuest.com, Inc.

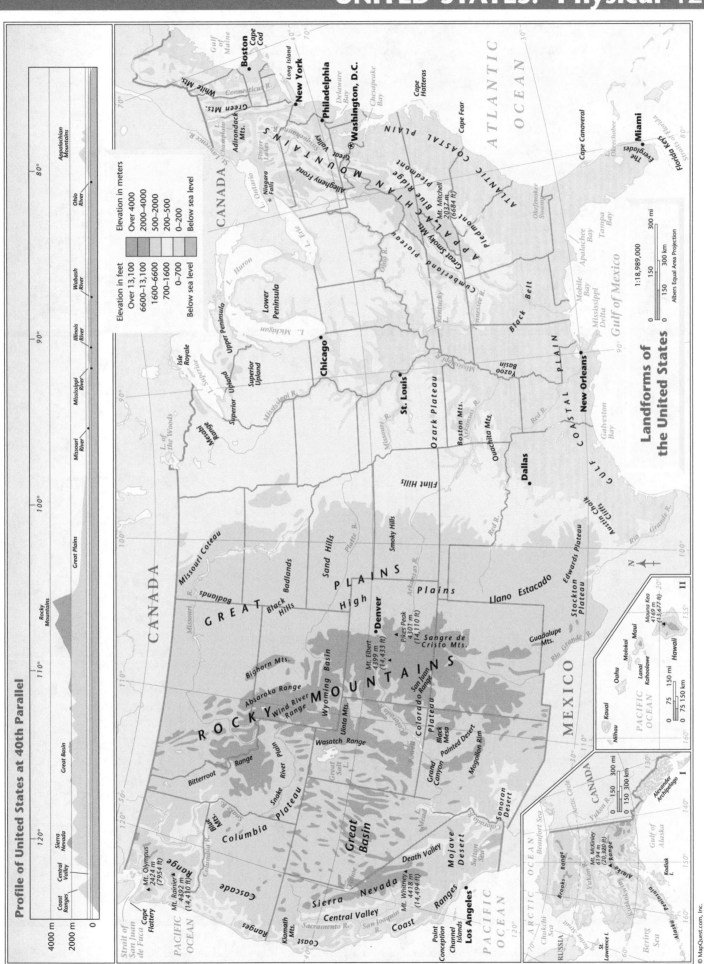

Profile of United States at 40th Parallel

4000 m

2000 m

0

Coast Ranges · Central Valley · Sierra Nevada · Great Basin · Rocky Mountains · Great Plains · Wabash River · Ohio River · Appalachian Mountains

Mississippi River · Illinois River · Missouri River

120° · 110° · 100° · 90° · 80°

Elevation in meters
- Over 4000
- 2000–4000
- 500–2000
- 200–500
- 0–200
- Below sea level

Elevation in feet
- Over 13,100
- 6600–13,100
- 1600–6600
- 700–1600
- 0–700
- Below sea level

Landforms of the United States

1:18,989,000

Albers Equal Area Projection

0   150   300 mi
0   150   300 km

© MapQuest.com, Inc.

Capital: Montgomery   Pop. (2002): 4,486,508
Area: 52,218 sq. mi.   Largest City: Birmingham
135,244 sq. km.   239,416

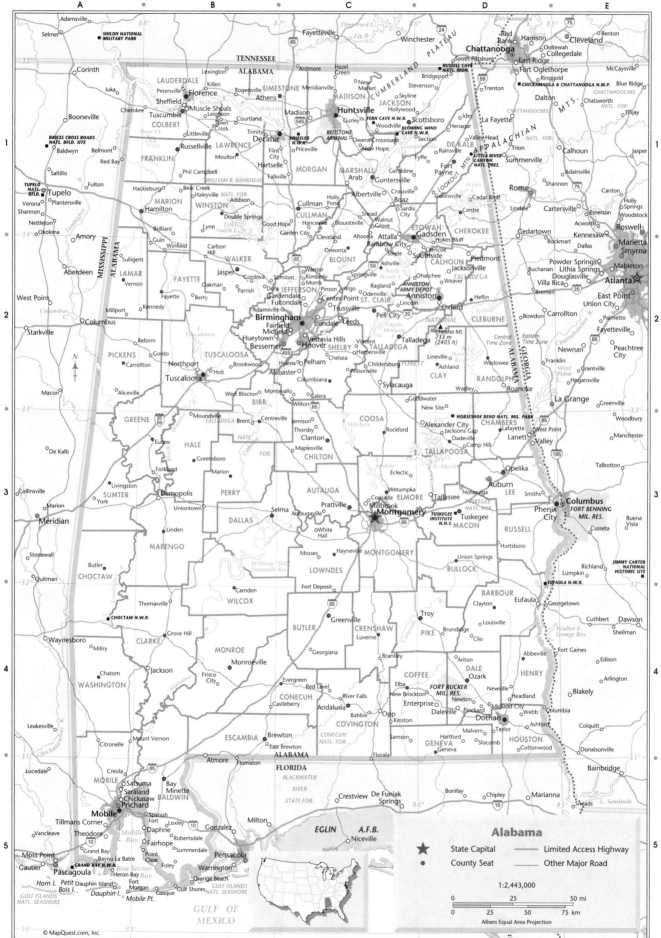

Alabama

★ State Capital   ── Limited Access Highway
• County Seat   ── Other Major Road

1:2,443,000

0   25   50 mi
0   25   50   75 km

Albers Equal Area Projection

© MapQuest.com, Inc.

Capital: Juneau
Area: 616,240 sq. mi.
1,596,049 sq. km.
Pop. (2002): 643,786
Largest City: Anchorage
268,983

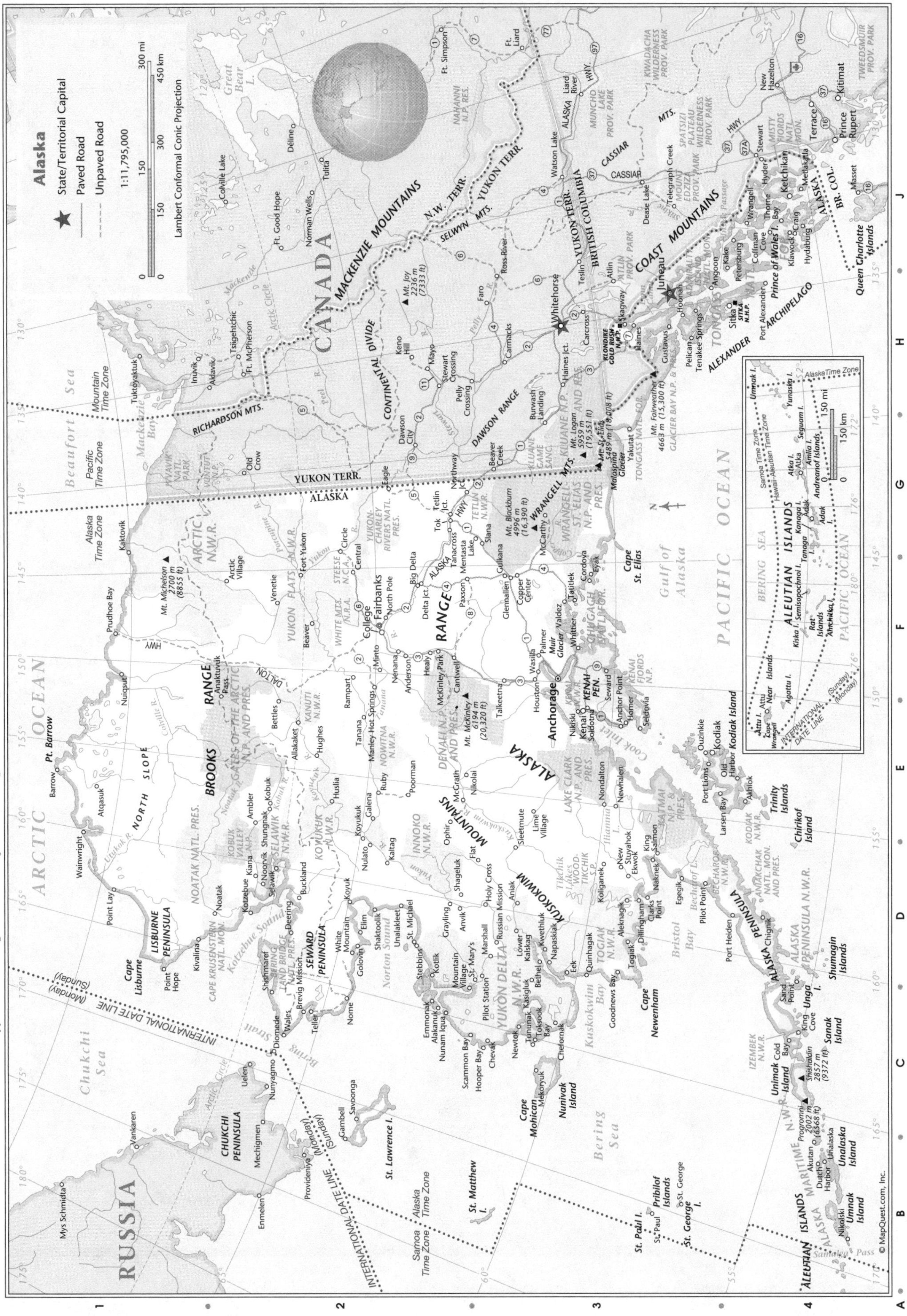

Alyaska
★ State/Territorial Capital
— Paved Road
--- Unpaved Road

300 mi
450 km

1:11,795,000
Lambert Conformal Conic Projection

CANADA

RUSSIA

ARCTIC OCEAN

PACIFIC OCEAN

Beaufort Sea

Chukchi Sea

Bering Sea

Gulf of Alaska

BROOKS RANGE

ALASKA RANGE

MACKENZIE MOUNTAINS

COAST MOUNTAINS

WRANGELL MTS.

N.W. TERR.

YUKON TERR.

BRITISH COLUMBIA

ALASKA

NORTH SLOPE

SEWARD PENINSULA

LISBURNE PENINSULA

KENAI PEN.

ALASKA PENINSULA

ALEUTIAN ISLANDS

KUSKOKWIM MOUNTAINS

INNOKO N.W.R.

YUKON DELTA N.W.R.

Pt. Barrow
Barrow
Prudhoe Bay
Kaktovik
Anchorage
Fairbanks
College
Juneau★
Whitehorse★
Nome
Kodiak
Kodiak Island

Mt. McKinley
6194 m
(20,320 ft)

Mt. St. Elias

Mt. Logan
5959 m
(19,551 ft)

DENALI N.P. AND PRES.

KLONDIKE GOLD RUSH N.H.P.

GLACIER BAY N.P. & PRES.

WRANGELL-ST. ELIAS N.P. AND PRES.

KATMAI N.P. & PRES.

LAKE CLARK N.P. AND PRES.

GATES OF THE ARCTIC N.P. AND PRES.

NOATAK NATL. PRES.

KOBUK VALLEY N.P.

SELAWIK N.W.R.

ARCTIC N.W.R.

YUKON FLATS N.W.R.

CONTINENTAL DIVIDE

INTERNATIONAL DATE LINE

Alaska Time Zone

Pacific Time Zone

Mountain Time Zone

Samoa Time Zone

Prince Rupert
Ketchikan
Sitka
Petersburg
Wrangell
Valdez
Cordova
Seward
Homer
Bethel
Dillingham
Unalaska
St. Paul I.
St. George I.
Pribilof Islands
Nunivak Island
St. Lawrence I.
St. Matthew I.
Cape Lisburne
Cape Newenham
Cape Mohican

Aleutian Islands inset:
BERING SEA
PACIFIC OCEAN
Alaska Time Zone
Hawaii-Aleutian Time Zone
Attu I.
Adak
Atka I.

© MapQuest.com, Inc.

Capital: Phoenix	Pop. (2002): 5,456,453
Area: 113,998 sq. mi.	Largest City: Phoenix
295,253 sq. km.	1,371,960

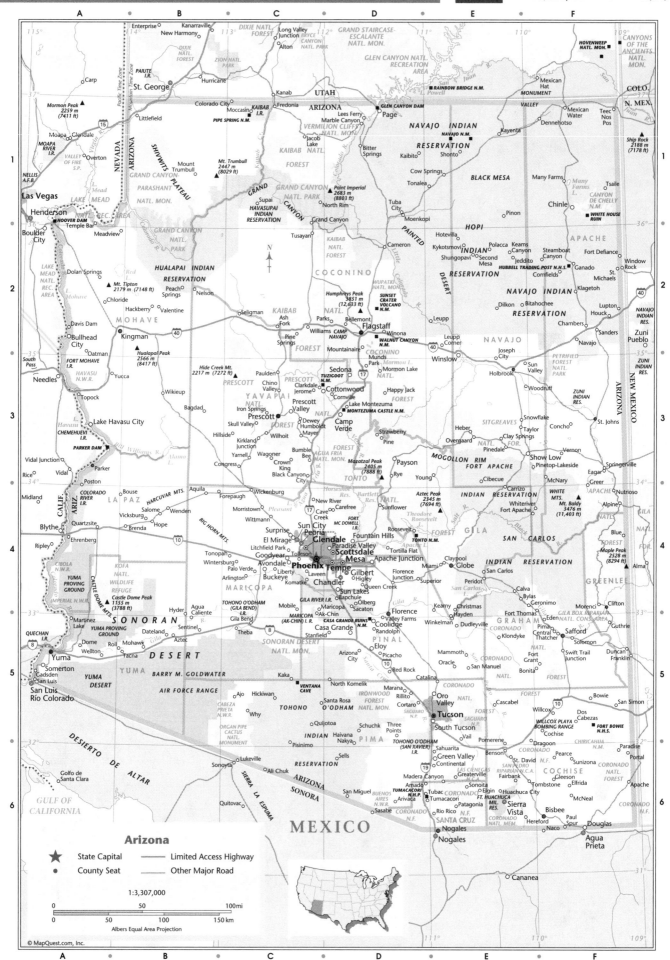

Arizona

★ State Capital   ══════ Limited Access Highway

• County Seat   ────── Other Major Road

1:3,307,000

0   50   100mi

0   50   100   150 km

Albers Equal Area Projection

© MapQuest.com, Inc.

Capital: Little Rock
Area: 53,178 sq. mi.
137,730 sq. km.
Pop. (2002): 2,710,079
Largest City: Little Rock
184,055

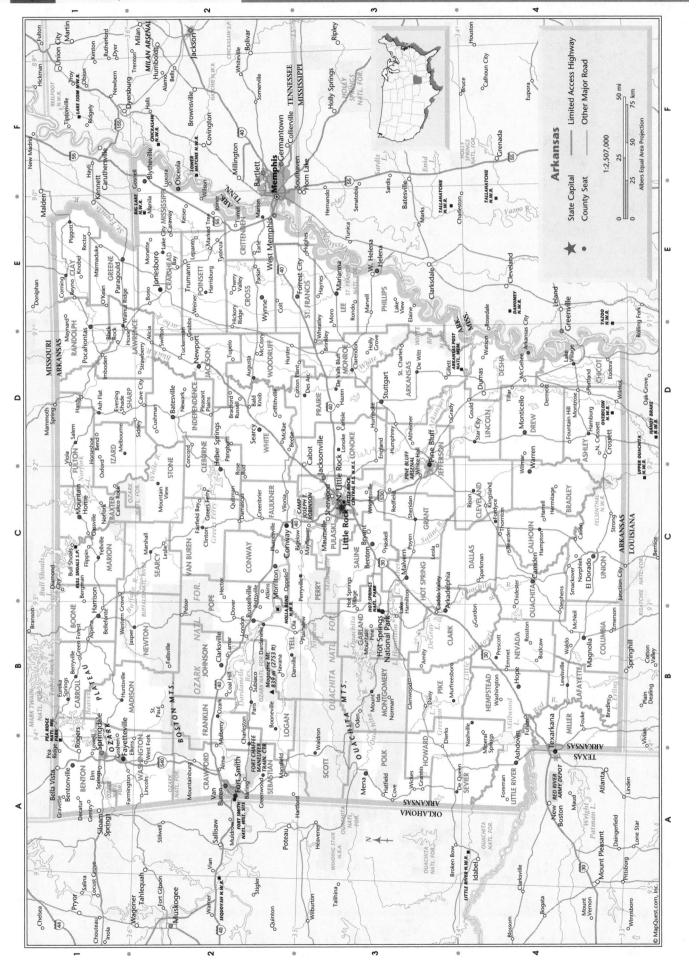

Arkansas

1:2,507,000

State Capital
County Seat

Limited Access Highway
Other Major Road

Albers Equal Area Projection

Capital: Sacramento
Area: 158,854 sq. mi.
411,429 sq. km.
Pop. (2002): 35,116,033
Largest City: Los Angeles
3,798,981

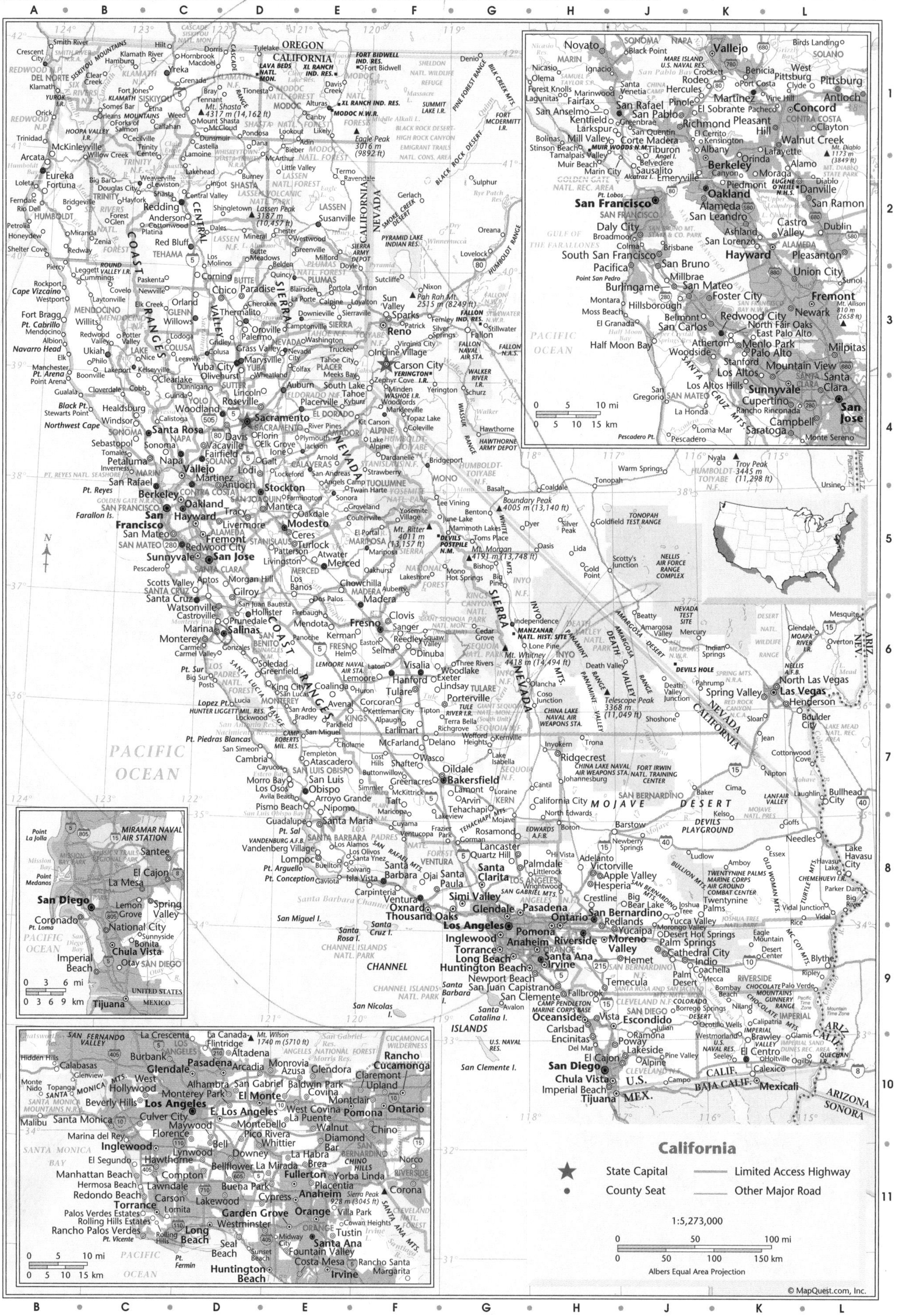

CALIFORNIA REPUBLIC

California

★ State Capital
• County Seat
—— Limited Access Highway
—— Other Major Road

1:5,273,000

0   50   100 mi
0   50   100   150 km

Albers Equal Area Projection

© MapQuest.com, Inc.

Capital: Denver
Area: 104,093 sq. mi.
269,599 sq. km.
Pop. (2002): 4,506,542
Largest City: Denver
560,415

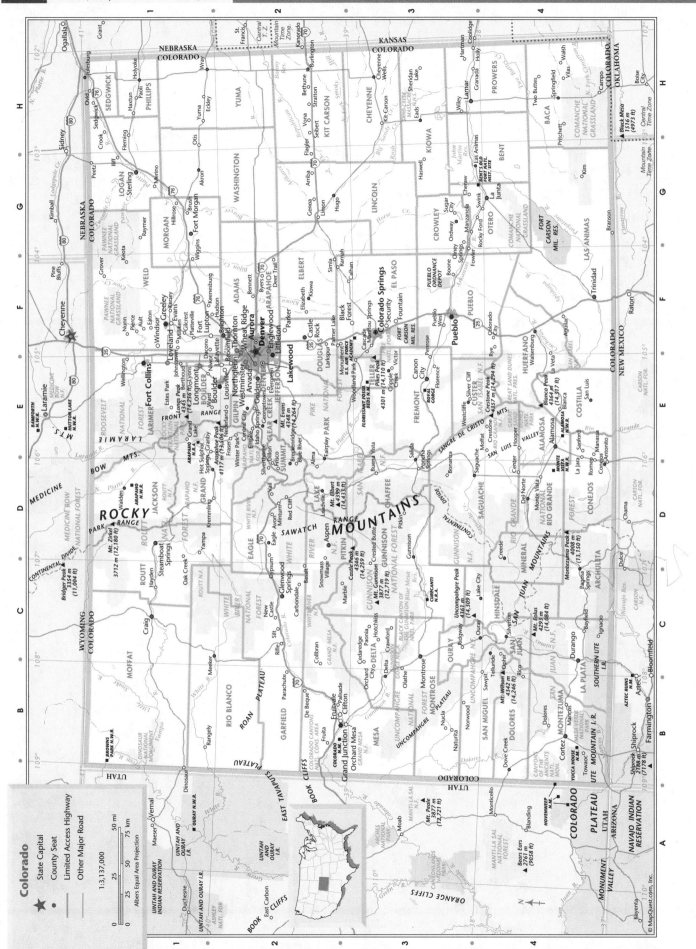

Colorado
★ State Capital
• County Seat
  Limited Access Highway
  Other Major Road

1:3,137,000
Albers Equal Area Projection

Capital: Hartford
Area: 5,543 sq. mi.
14,356 sq. km.

Pop. (2002): 3,460,503
Largest City: Bridgeport
140,104

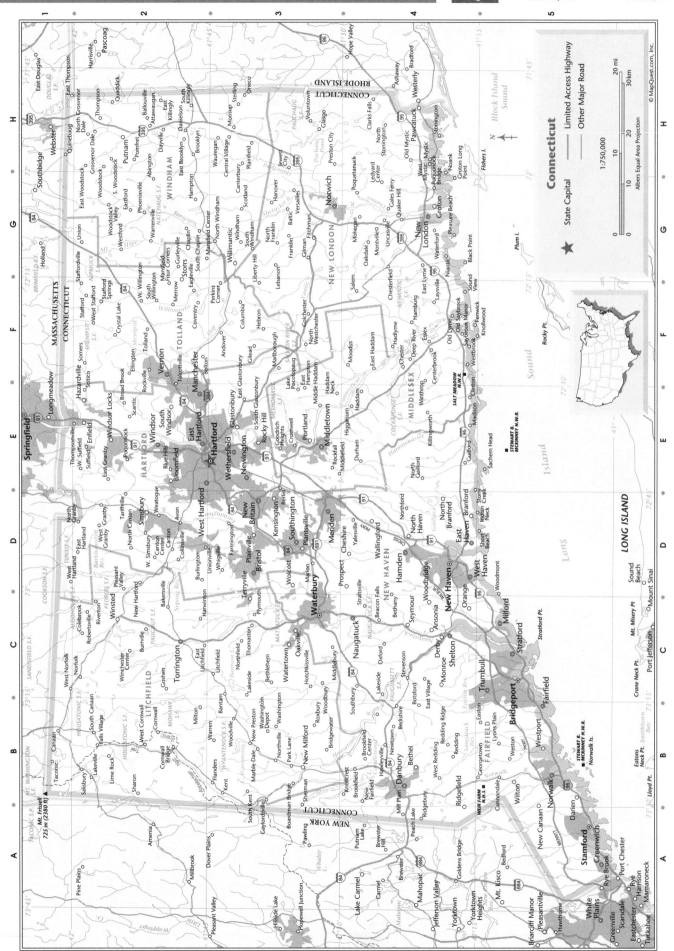

Connecticut

★ State Capital

— Limited Access Highway
— Other Major Road

1:750,000

Albers Equal Area Projection

© MapQuest.com, Inc.

Capital: Dover
Area: 2,396 sq. mi.
6,206 sq. km.

Pop. (2002): 807,385
Largest City: Wilmington
72,503

DELAWARE 135

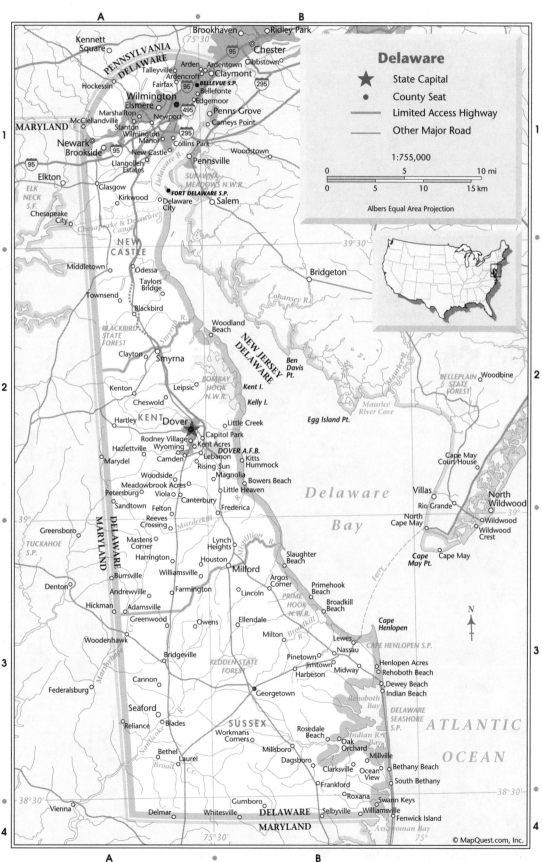

Delaware

★ State Capital
● County Seat
━━━ Limited Access Highway
─── Other Major Road

1:755,000

0   5   10 mi
0   5   10   15 km

Albers Equal Area Projection

© MapQuest.com, Inc.

Capital: Tallahassee
Area: 59,909 sq. mi.
155,163 sq. km.
Pop. (2002): 16,713,149
Largest City: Jacksonville
762,461

Florida

★ State Capital
● County Seat
— Limited Access Highway
— Other Major Road

1:3,135,000

0   25   50 mi
0   25   50   75 km
Albers Equal Area Projection

© MapQuest.com, Inc.

Capital: Atlanta
Area: 58,970 sq. mi.
152,731 sq. km.
Pop. (2002): 8,560,310
Largest City: Atlanta
424,868

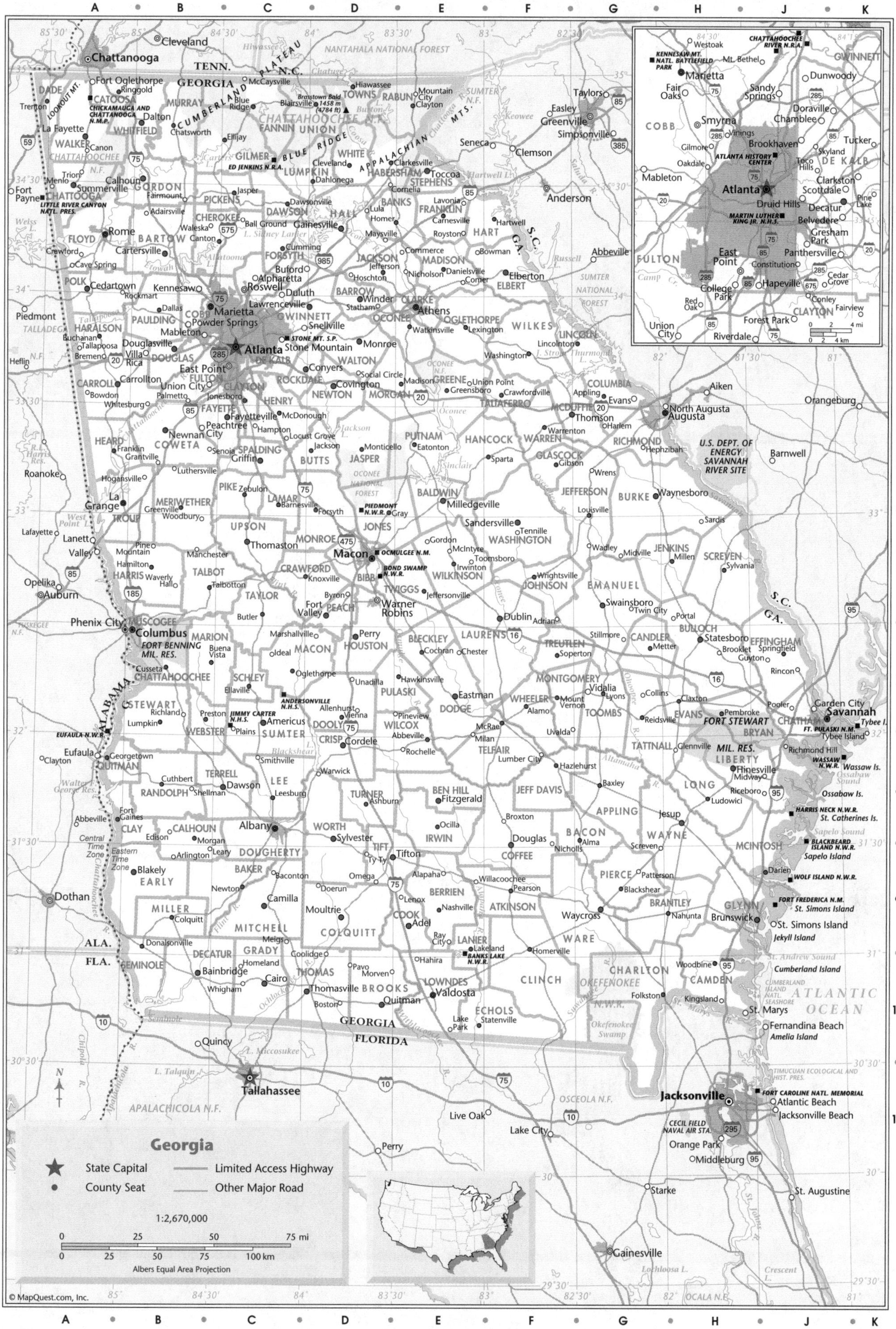

Capital: Honolulu
Area: 6,461 sq. mi.
16,734 sq. km.
Pop. (2002): 1,244,898
Largest City: Honolulu
378,155

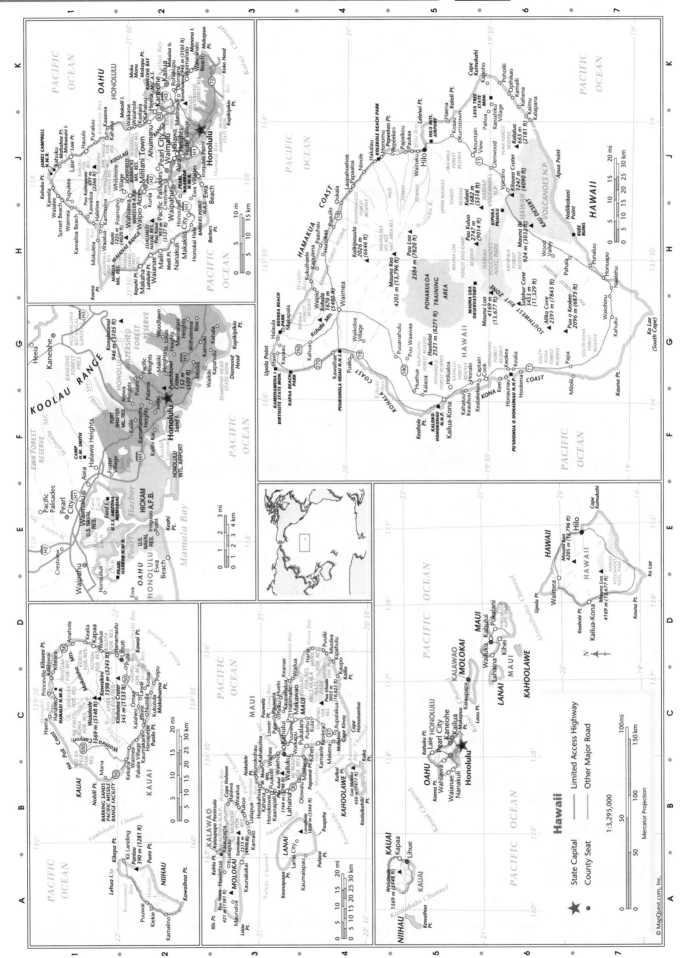

Hawaii

State Capital ★
County Seat ●

━━ Limited Access Highway
── Other Major Road

1:3,295,000
Mercator Projection

© MapQuest.com, Inc.

Capital: Boise **Pop. (2002):** 1,341,131
Area: 83,570 sq. mi. **Largest City:** Boise
216,445 sq. km. 189,847

Idaho

★ State Capital — Limited Access Highway
• County Seat — Other Major Road

1:3,295,000

0   50   100mi
0   50   100   150 km
Albers Equal Area Projection

©MapQuest.com, Inc.

CAN.
U.S.

MONTANA
WASHINGTON
OREGON
NEVADA
UTAH
WYOMING

Boise
Spokane
Lewiston
Clarkston
Coeur d'Alene
Sandpoint
Moscow
Pullman
Twin Falls
Idaho Falls
Pocatello
Chubbuck
Rexburg
Nampa
Caldwell
Ontario
Payette

Mt. Cleveland
3190 m
(10,466 ft)

Lolo Peak
2786 m
(9139 ft)

Warren Peak
3189 m
(10,464 ft)

Granite Peak
3228 m
(10,590 ft)

Sacajawea Peak
2998 m
(9839 ft)

Scott Peak
3473 m
(11,393 ft)

Borah Peak
3859 m
(12,662 ft)

Castle Peak
3601 m
(11,815 ft)

Ryan Peak
3595 m
(11,795 ft)

Hyndman Peak
3660 m
(12,009 ft)

Grand Teton
4280 m
(13,770 ft)

Cache Peak
3151 m
(10,339 ft)

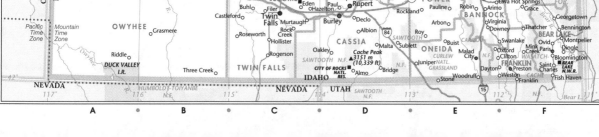

Capital: Springfield
Area: 57,914 sq. mi.
149,996 sq. km.
Pop. (2002): 12,600,620
Largest City: Chicago
2,886,251

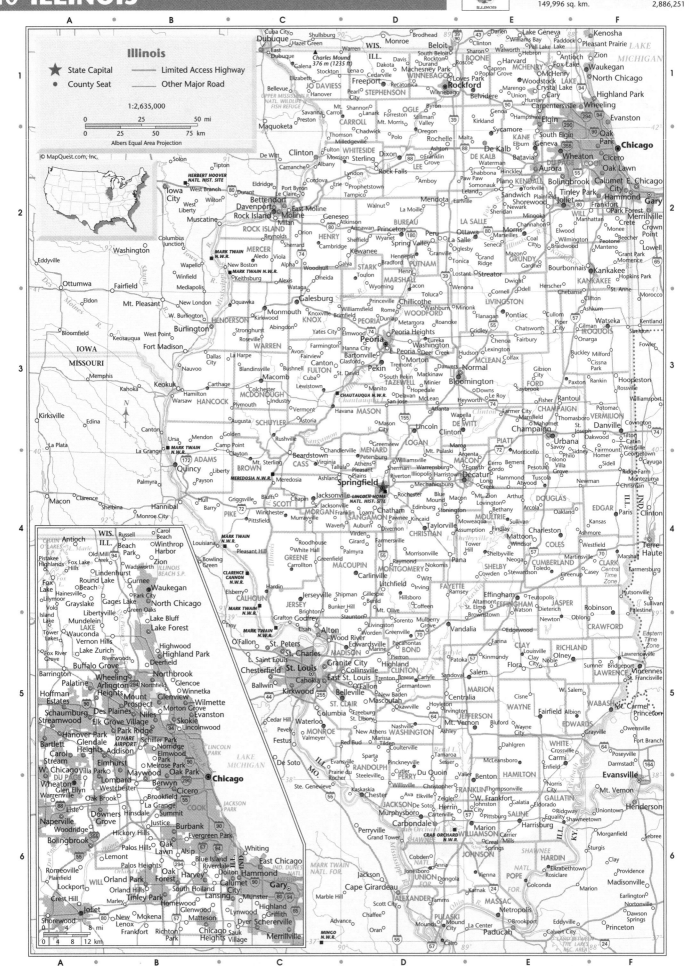

Illinois

★ State Capital   Limited Access Highway
● County Seat   Other Major Road

1:2,635,000

0   25   50 mi
0   25   50   75 km
Albers Equal Area Projection

© MapQuest.com, Inc.

Capital: Indianapolis
Area: 36,418 sq. mi.
94,322 sq. km.
Pop. (2002): 6,159,068
Largest City: Indianapolis
783,612

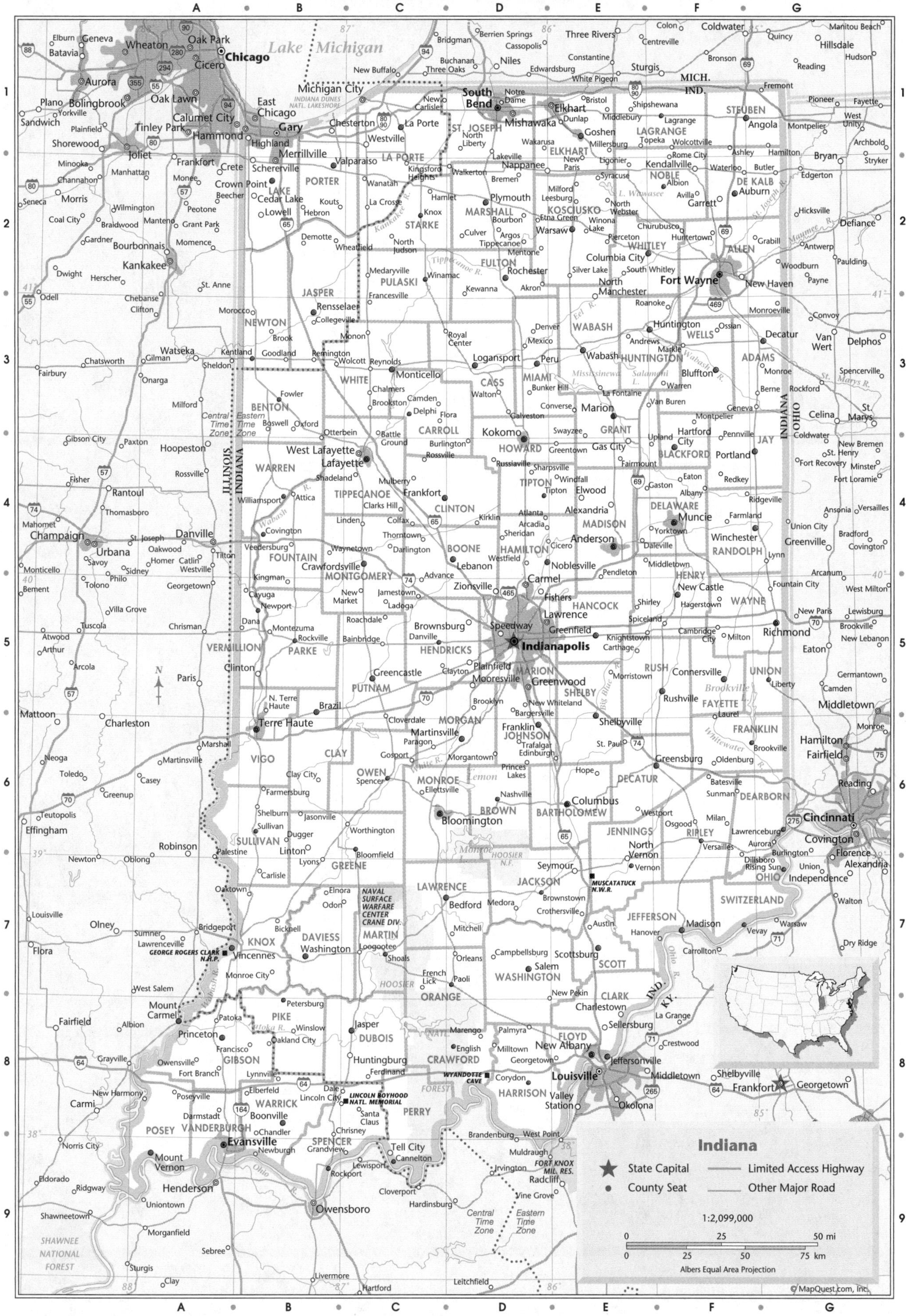

Indiana

★ State Capital   —— Limited Access Highway
● County Seat   —— Other Major Road

1:2,099,000

0   25   50 mi
0   25   50   75 km

Albers Equal Area Projection

© MapQuest.com, Inc.

Capital: Des Moines
Area: 56,271 sq. mi.
145,741 sq. km.
Pop. (2002): 2,936,760
Largest City: Des Moines
198,076

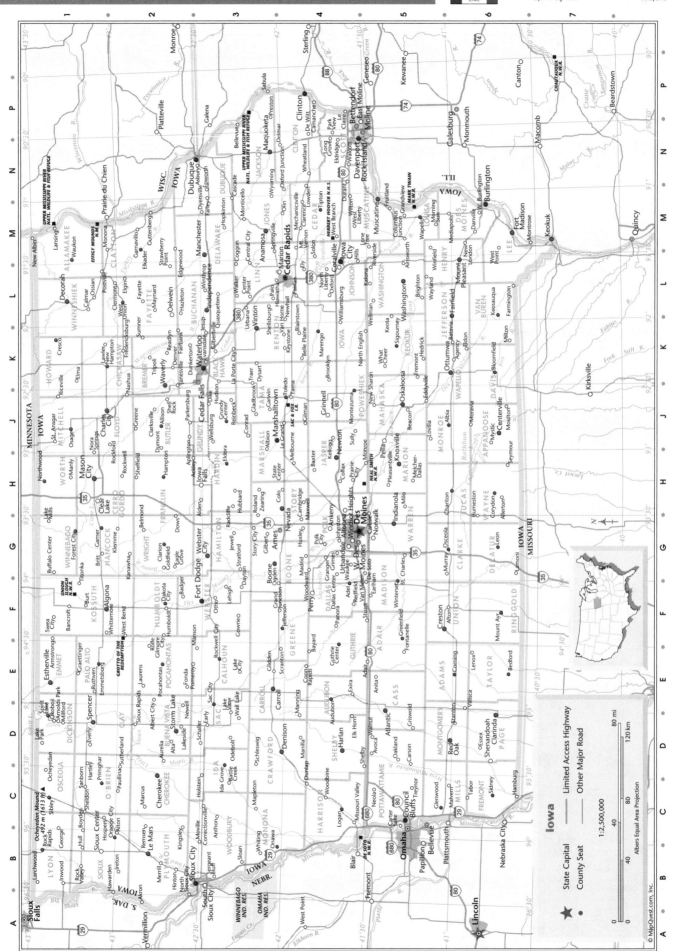

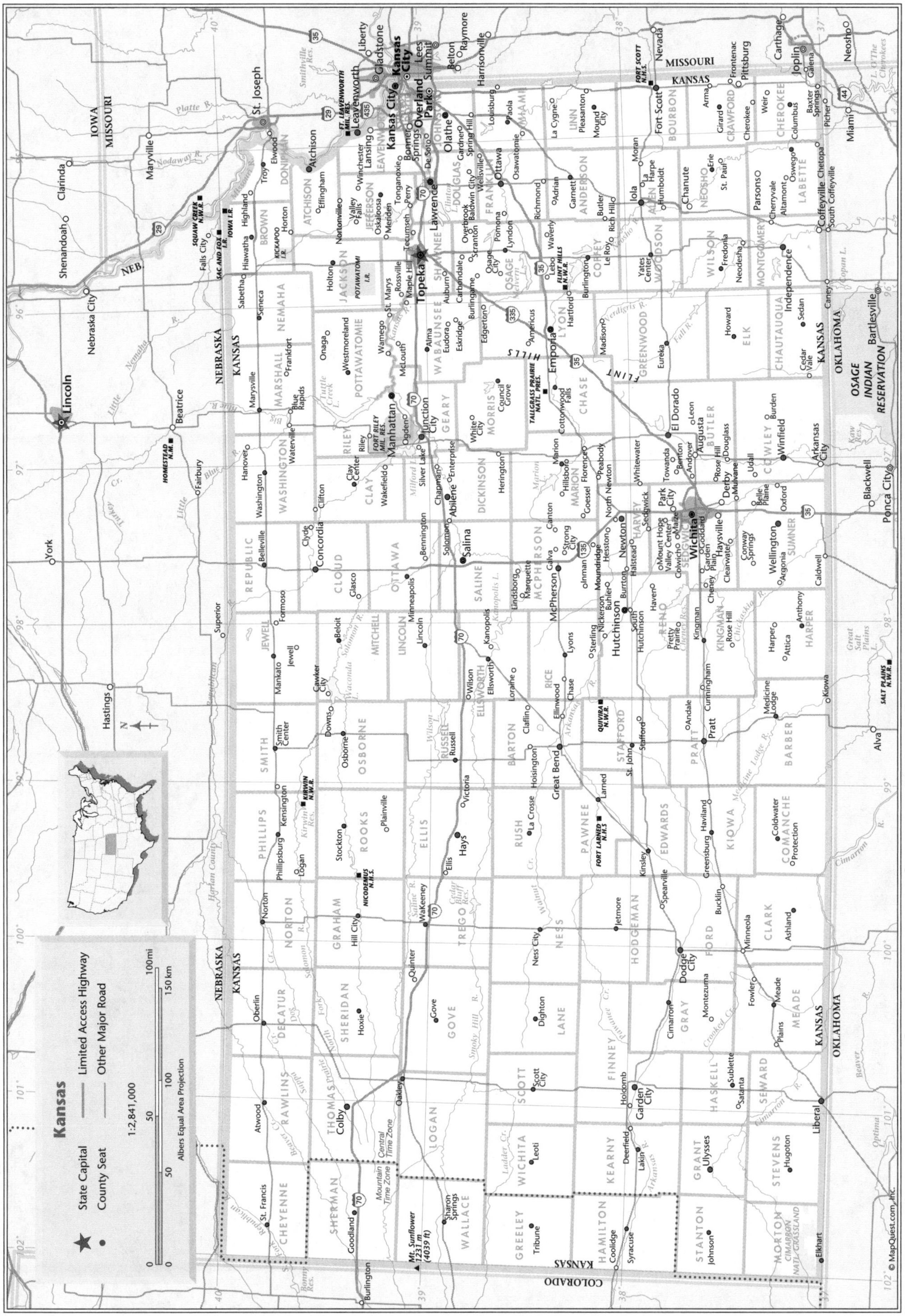

KANSAS

Capital: Topeka
Area: 82,276 sq. mi.
213,093 sq. km.
Pop. (2002): 2,715,884
Largest City: Wichita
355,126

Kansas

1:2,841,000
Albers Equal Area Projection

★ State Capital / Topeka
• County Seat

— Limited Access Highway
— Other Major Road

100 mi
150 km

© MapQuest.com, Inc.

Capital: Frankfort
Area: 40,409 sq. mi.
104,659 sq. km.
Pop. (2002): 4,092,891
Largest City: Louisville
529,548

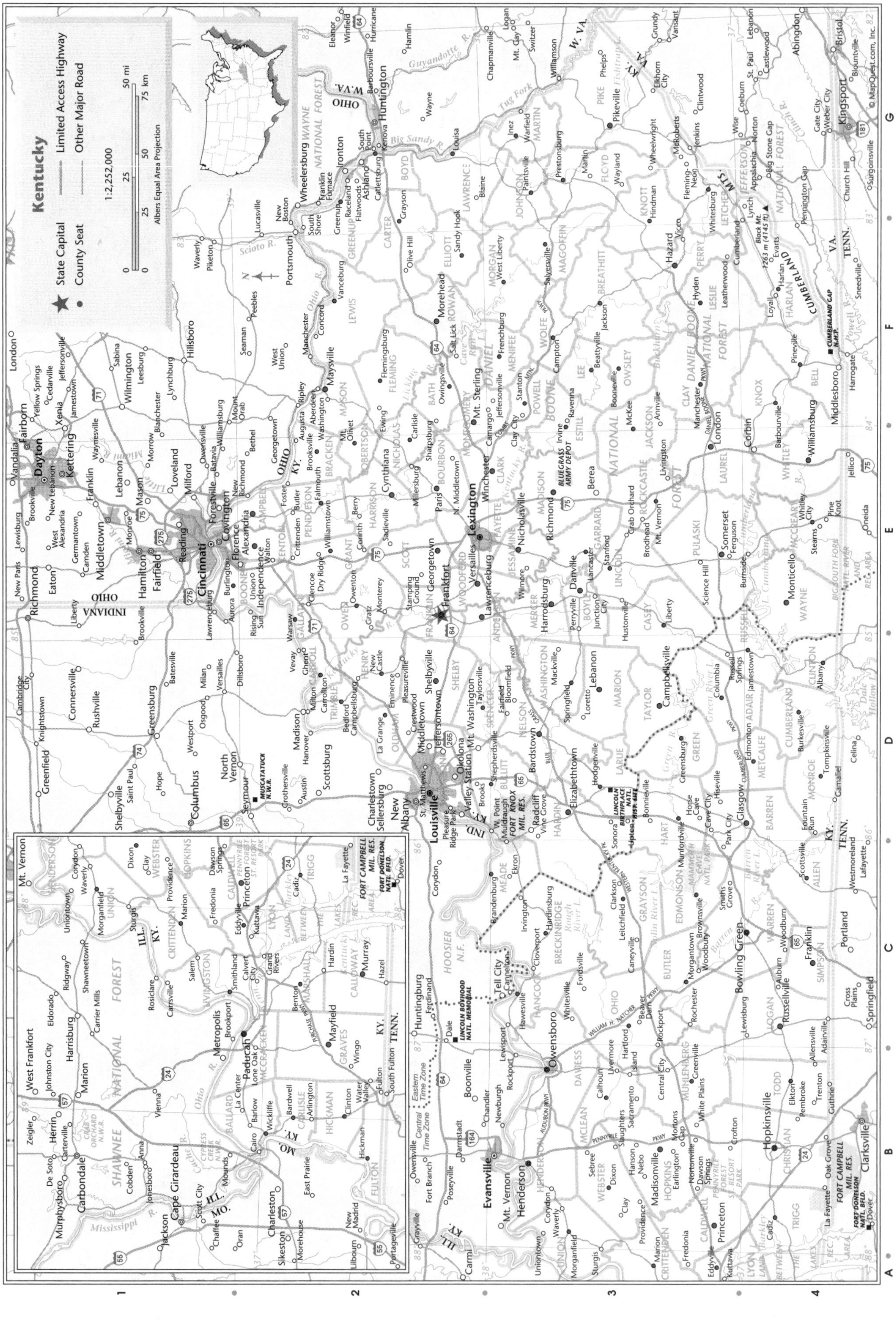

Kentucky

Limited Access Highway
Other Major Road

1:2,252,000

★ State Capital
• County Seat

Albers Equal Area Projection

0   25   50   75 km
0   25   50 mi

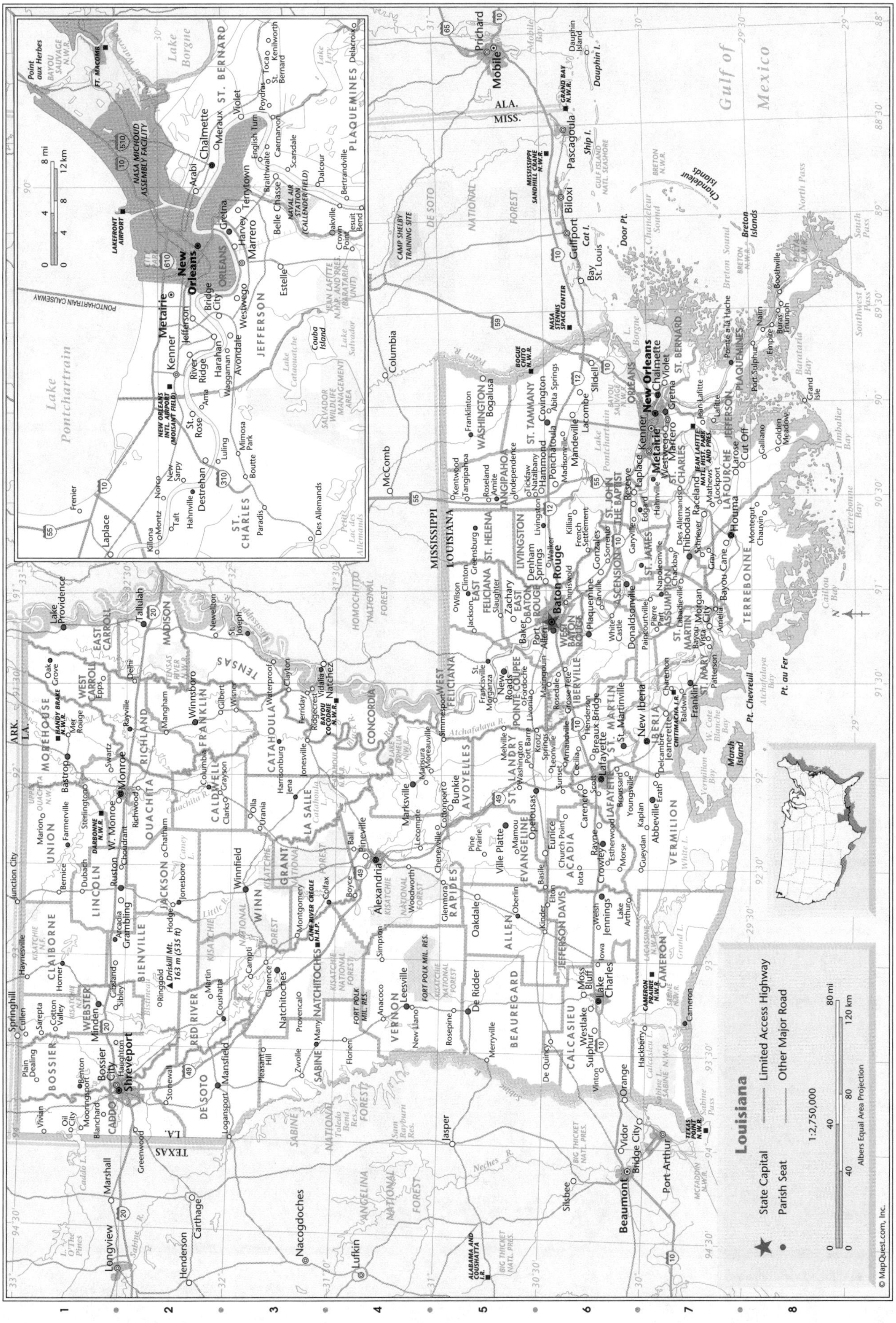

Capital: Baton Rouge
Area: 49,650 sq. mi.
128,593 sq. km.
Pop. (2002): 4,482,646
Largest City: New Orleans
473,681

Louisiana

1:2,750,000

★ State Capital
• Parish Seat

—— Limited Access Highway
—— Other Major Road

Albers Equal Area Projection

0   40   80 mi
0   40   80   120 km

© MapQuest.com, Inc.

(Map of Louisiana showing parishes, cities, rivers, and highways. Selected labels include:)

Inset — New Orleans area: Lake Pontchartrain, Pontchartrain Causeway, Metairie, Kenner, New Orleans, Gretna, Harvey, Marrero, Westwego, Jefferson, St. Charles, St. Bernard, Chalmette, Arabi, Meraux, Violet, Terrytown, Belle Chasse, NASA Michoud Assembly Facility, Lakefront Airport, New Orleans Intl. Airport (Moisant Field), Naval Air Station (Callender Field), Laplace, Des Allemands, Luling, Destrehan, Boutte

Cities and towns: Shreveport, Bossier City, Monroe, W. Monroe, Ruston, Grambling, Natchitoches, Alexandria, Pineville, Baton Rouge, Port Allen, Lafayette, New Iberia, Houma, Thibodaux, Morgan City, Franklin, Opelousas, Ville Platte, Eunice, Crowley, Jennings, Lake Charles, Sulphur, De Ridder, Leesville, Many, Minden, Springhill, Haynesville, Vivian, Oil City, Marshall, Longview, Henderson, Lufkin, Nacogdoches, Jasper, Beaumont, Port Arthur, Orange, Vidor, Bridge City

Parishes: CADDO, BOSSIER, WEBSTER, CLAIBORNE, UNION, MOREHOUSE, WEST CARROLL, EAST CARROLL, MADISON, LINCOLN, BIENVILLE, DESOTO, RED RIVER, NATCHITOCHES, SABINE, VERNON, BEAUREGARD, CALCASIEU, CAMERON, JEFFERSON DAVIS, ACADIA, ALLEN, EVANGELINE, ST. LANDRY, RAPIDES, GRANT, WINN, JACKSON, CALDWELL, OUACHITA, RICHLAND, FRANKLIN, CATAHOULA, LA SALLE, CONCORDIA, AVOYELLES, POINTE COUPEE, WEST FELICIANA, EAST FELICIANA, ST. HELENA, TANGIPAHOA, WASHINGTON, ST. TAMMANY, LIVINGSTON, ST. MARTIN, IBERIA, VERMILION, LAFAYETTE, ST. MARY, ASSUMPTION, TERREBONNE, LAFOURCHE, ST. CHARLES, ST. JAMES, ST. JOHN THE BAPTIST, ASCENSION, IBERVILLE, WEST BATON ROUGE, EAST BATON ROUGE, PLAQUEMINES, ST. BERNARD, ORLEANS, JEFFERSON

Forests / preserves: KISATCHIE NATIONAL FOREST, HOMOCHITTO NATIONAL FOREST, FORT POLK MIL. RES., SABINE NATIONAL FOREST, ANGELINA NATIONAL FOREST, BIG THICKET NATL. PRES.

Water features: Lake Pontchartrain, Lake Borgne, Lake Maurepas, Lake Salvador, Toledo Bend Res., Atchafalaya R., Mississippi R., Red R., Ouachita R., Terrebonne Bay, Timbalier Bay, Barataria Bay, Breton Sound, Chandeleur Sound, Gulf of Mexico

Neighboring states: ARK., TEXAS, MISSISSIPPI, ALA., MISS.

Driskill Mtn. (535 ft) 163 m

Capital: Augusta
Area: 33,738 sq. mi.
87,381 sq. km.
Pop. (2002): 1,294,464
Largest City: Portland
63,882

LAURENTIDES PROVINCIAL RESERVE

MT. CARLETON PROV. PARK

CANADA
U.S.

Baie-St-Paul
St-Pascal
Pohenegamook
Rivière-Bleue
Edmundston
St-Basile
Atlantic Time Zone
Eastern Time Zone

Mont-Carmel
La Pocatière
Madawaska
Grand Isle
St-Jacques

St-Ferréal-les-Neiges
St-Tite-des-Caps
St-Roch-des-Aulnaies
St-Jean-Port-Joli
St-Aubert
Frenchville
Lille
Ste-Anne-de-Madawaska

MT. STE-ANNE PROV. PARK
Ste-Anne-de-Beaupré
Beaupré
Fort Kent
Sinclair
Van Buren
St-Léonard

Château-Richer
Île d'Orléans
Cap-St-Ignace
Montmagny
St-Pamphile
Dickey
St. John
St. Francis
Soldier Pond
Stockholm
Hamlin
Grand Falls/Grand Sault

Charlesbourg
Québec
Ste-Perpétue
Eagle Lake
New Sweden

Lévis
St-Romuald
Winterville
Limestone
Plaster Rock

MOUNTAINS
ALLAGASH WILDERNESS WATERWAY
Perham
Caribou
Fort Fairfield
Perth-Andover

Ste-Claire
St-Paul-de-Montminy
Washburn
Portage
Presque Isle
Mapleton

St-Camille-de-Lellis
Clayton Lake
AROOSTOOK
Ashland
Westfield
Masardis
Mars Hill
Bridgewater

Lac-Etchemin
Ste-Justine
Munsungan L.
Squa Pan L.
Oxbow

St-Joseph-de-Beauce
Churchill L.
ALLAGASH WILDERNESS WATERWAY
Grand L.
Seboeis
Monticello

QUÉBEC
MAINE
Beauceville
St-Prosper
St-Zacharie
Chamberlain L.
Telos L.
Grand L. Matagamon
Littleton

Thetford Mines
Ste-Georges
St-Methode-de-Frontenac
Chesuncook L.
BAXTER STATE PARK
Smyrna Mills
Island Falls
Houlton
Hodgdon
Woodstock
Nackawic

La Guadeloupe
Lambton
St-Martin
Pittston Farm
North East Carry
Chesuncook Village
Patten
North Amity

FRONTENAC PROV. PARK
L. St-François
St-Gedeon
Seboomook
Mt. Katahdin 1606 m (5268 ft)
Sherman Station
Linneus
Orient

APPALACHIAN
Lac Mégantic
Moose River
Jackman
Rockwood
Moosehead
White Cap Mt. 1111 m (3644 ft)
Lily Bay
Millinocket
Sherman Mills
Haynesville

Coburn Gore
Long Pond
PISCATAQUIS
Kokadjo
Grindstone
North Amity
Danforth
McAdam

Snow Mt. 1204 m (3948 ft)
Moosehead
West Seboeis
Norcross
East Millinocket
Reed
Wytopitlock
Eaton
Vanceboro

SOMERSET
Lake Parlin
Shirley Mills
Greenville
Brownville Junction
PENOBSCOT
Kingman
Brookton

Eustis
The Forks
Monson
Sebec
Brownville
Seboeis
Lincoln
Lee
Springfield
Waite
PASSAMAQUODDY INDIAN TOWNSHIP I.R.

Stratton
Caratunk
Milo
Dover-Foxcroft
Lagrange
Howland
Burlington
Grand Lake Stream
Princeton
St. Stephen

Sugarloaf Mt. 1291 m (4237 ft)
Carrabassett
Bingham
Guilford
Charleston
South Lagrange
Passadumkeag
Olamon
Woodland
Calais
ST. CROIX ISLAND INTL. HIST. SITE

Saddleback Mt. 1255 m (4116 ft)
Kingfield
Solon
Wellington
Dexter
Hudson
Alexander
Perry
PASSAMAQUODDY PLEASANT POINT I.R.

Oquossoc
Rangeley
Salem
New Portland
Athens
Harmony
Corinna
Exeter Corners
East Corinth
PENOBSCOT I.R.
Milford
Old Town
Great Pond
Wesley
Eastport

Wilsons Mills
Phillips
Madison
New Vineyard
Hartland
Newport
Hermon
Kenduskeag
Orono
Amherst
WASHINGTON
Dennysville
Lubec

FRANKLIN
Byron
Weld
Mercer
Skowhegan
Norridgewock
Pittsfield
Carmel
Bangor
Brewer
East Holden
Green Lake
Waltham
Northfield
Whiting
West Quoddy Head

Upton
Andover
Farmington
Wilton
Hinckley
Burnham
Dixmont
Hampden
HANCOCK
Deblois
East Machias
Cutler

OXFORD
Rumford
Mexico
Dixfield
Chisholm
Oakland
Clinton
Fairfield
Unity
Brooks
Frankfort
Bucksport
Orland
Franklin
Harrington
Cherryfield
Columbia Falls
Machias
Cross I.

Berlin
Newry
Bryant Pond
Livermore Falls
Winslow
Waterville
China
Albion
Swanville
Stockton Springs
Ellsworth
Steuben
Milbridge
Jonesport

Gorham
Bethel
Gilead
Canton
Belgrade
KENNEBEC
South China
Searsmont
Belfast
Searsport
Trenton
Bar Harbor
Great Wass I.

WHITE MTN. NATL. FOR.
WHITE MTS.
N.H.
MAINE
North Waterford
Paris
Buckfield
Leeds
Winthrop
Augusta
Liberty
WALDO
Islesboro Island
Castine
Blue Hill
Somesville
Winter Harbor

Berlin
Norway
South Paris
Turner
Greene
Hallowell
Gardiner
Washington
Lincolnville
Camden
Sedgwick
ACADIA NATL. PARK
Mt. Desert I.
Southwest Harbor
Bass Harbor

Lovell
Oxford
Mechanic Falls
Lewiston
ANDROSCOGGIN
Whitefield
Jefferson
Union
North Haven
Deer Isle
Stonington
Swans I.
Atlantic
Frenchboro

North Conway
Fryeburg
Lisbon
Auburn
Richmond
Waldoboro
KNOX
Rockland
Thomaston
Camden
Isle au Haut
Long I.

Conway
Bridgton
Naples
Lisbon Falls
SAGADAHOC
Damariscotta
Wiscasset
LINCOLN
Owls Head
Vinalhaven I.
Vinalhaven
Isle au Haut
ACADIA NATL. PARK

Hiram
North Windham
Gray
Bath
Boothbay Harbor
Port Clyde
Matinicus I.

Kezar Falls
Cornish
Freeport
Brunswick
Yarmouth
Small Pt.
SEAL ISLAND N.W.R.

Limerick
CUMBERLAND
Falmouth
Casco Bay
Monhegan I.

Wolfeboro
Westbrook
Hollis Center
Portland
Casco Bay

Shapleigh
South Portland
Cape Elizabeth
Saco Bay

Springvale
Alfred
Saco
Biddeford
Old Orchard Beach

Farmington
Sanford
Kennebunk
Kennebunkport

Rochester
North Berwick
Berwick

Somersworth
Ogunquit

Dover
York
Durham
Newmarket
Kittery
Raymond
Epping
Portsmouth
Exeter

GULF
OF
MAINE

ATLANTIC
OCEAN

Maine

★ State/Provincial Capital
● County Seat
— Limited Access Highway
— Other Major Road

1:2,074,000

0   25   50 mi
0   25   50   75 km
Albers Equal Area Projection

© MapQuest.com, Inc.

Capital: Annapolis
Area: 12,297 sq. mi.
31,849 sq. km.
Pop. (2002): 5,458,137
Largest City: Baltimore
638,614

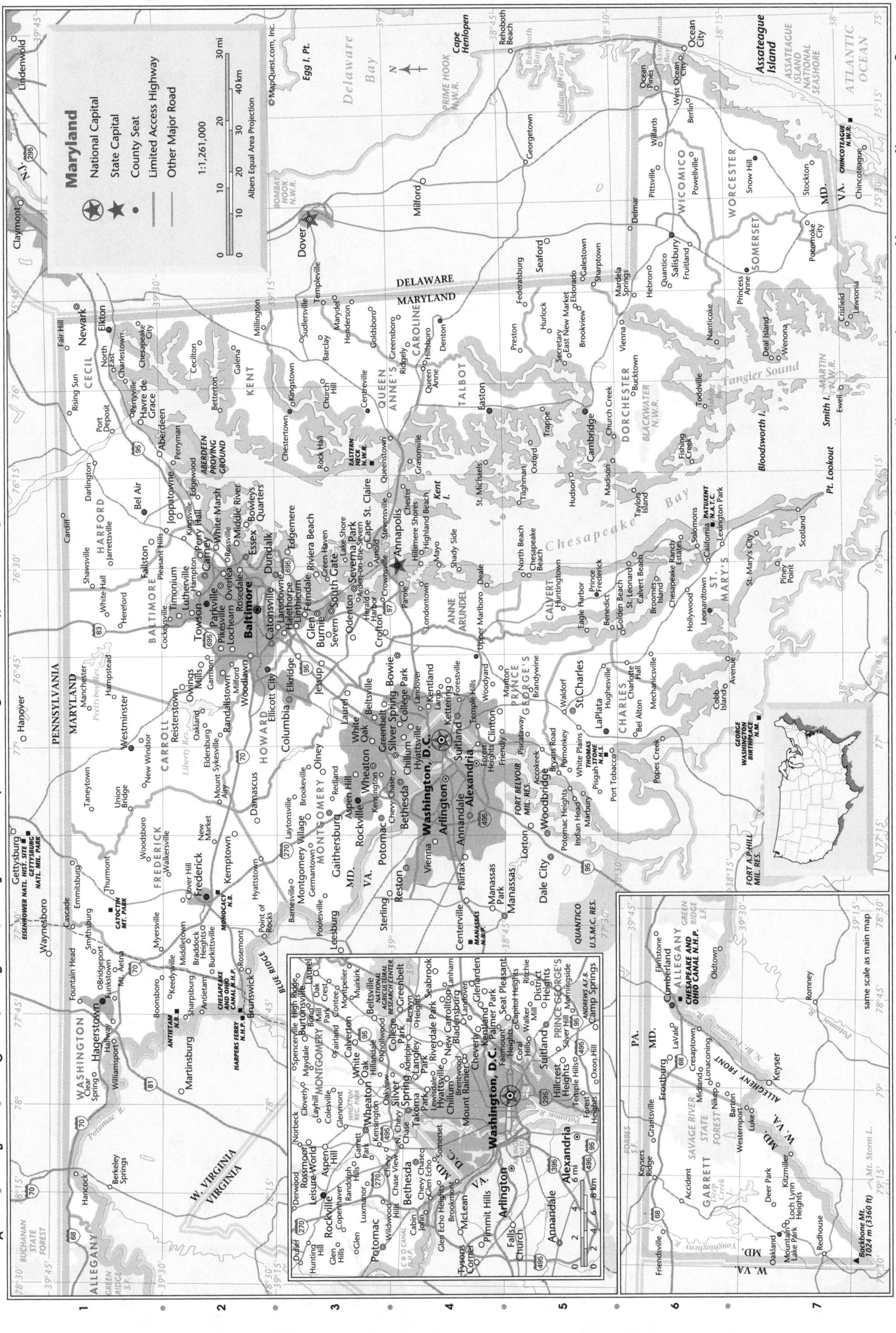

Maryland

- ★ National Capital
- ★ State Capital
- • County Seat
- Limited Access Highway
- Other Major Road

1:1,261,000

Albers Equal Area Projection

© MapQuest.com, Inc.

30 mi
40 km

ATLANTIC OCEAN

Chesapeake Bay

Delaware Bay

DELAWARE

MARYLAND

PENNSYLVANIA

W. VIRGINIA

VIRGINIA

Washington, D.C.

Baltimore

Annapolis

Hagerstown

Frederick

Cumberland

Ocean City

Assateague Island

ASSATEAGUE ISLAND NATIONAL SEASHORE

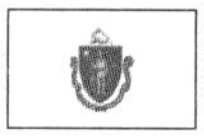

Capital: Boston
Area: 9,240 sq. mi.
23,931 sq. km.
Pop. (2002): 6,427,801
Largest City: Boston
589,281

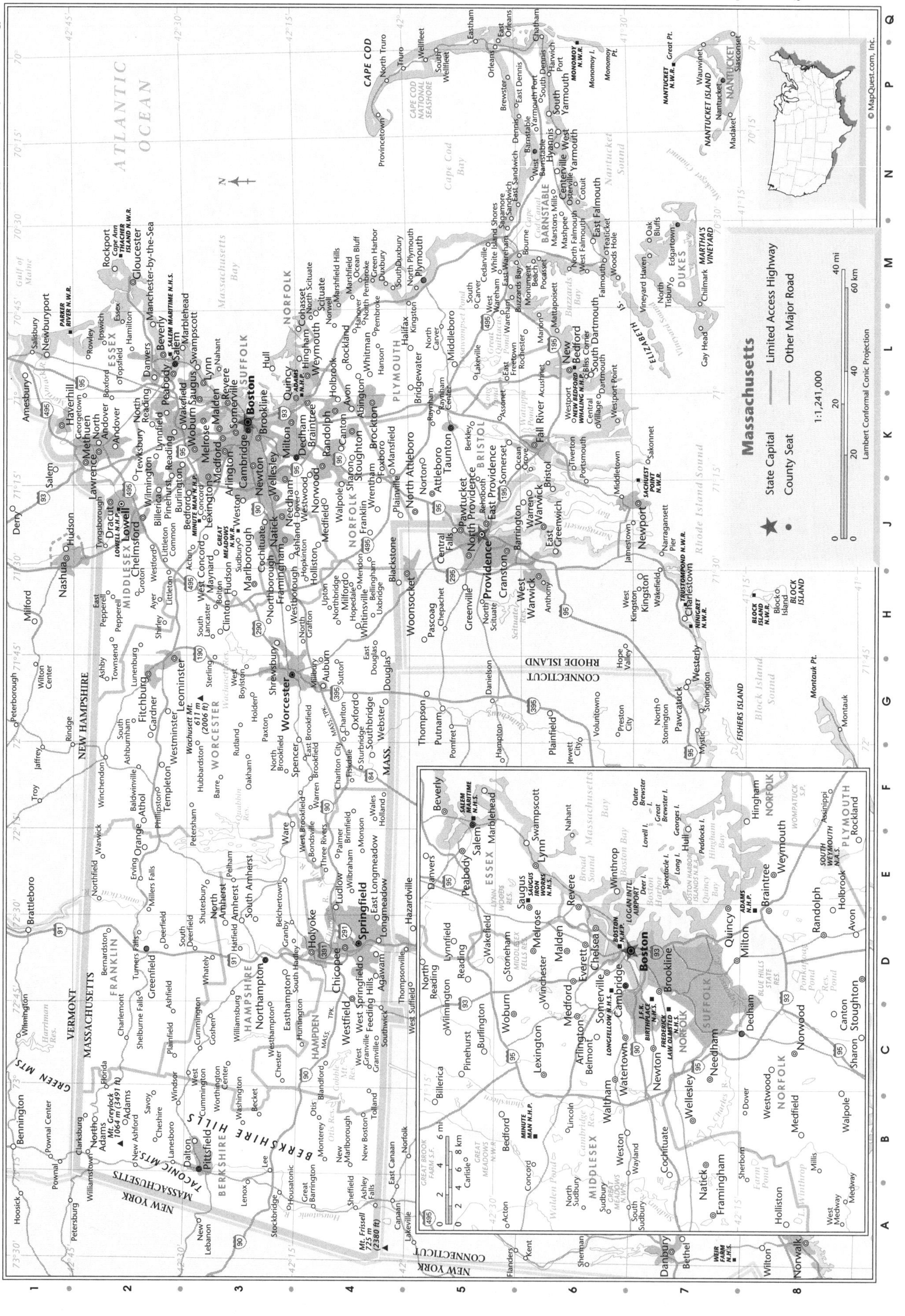

Massachusetts
State Capital
County Seat
Limited Access Highway
Other Major Road
1:1,241,000
Lambert Conformal Conic Projection
ATLANTIC OCEAN
CAPE COD
Boston
Worcester
Springfield
Providence
© MapQuest.com, Inc.

Capital: Lansing
Area: 96,716 sq. mi.
250,493 sq. km.
Pop. (2002): 10,050,446
Largest City: Detroit
925,051

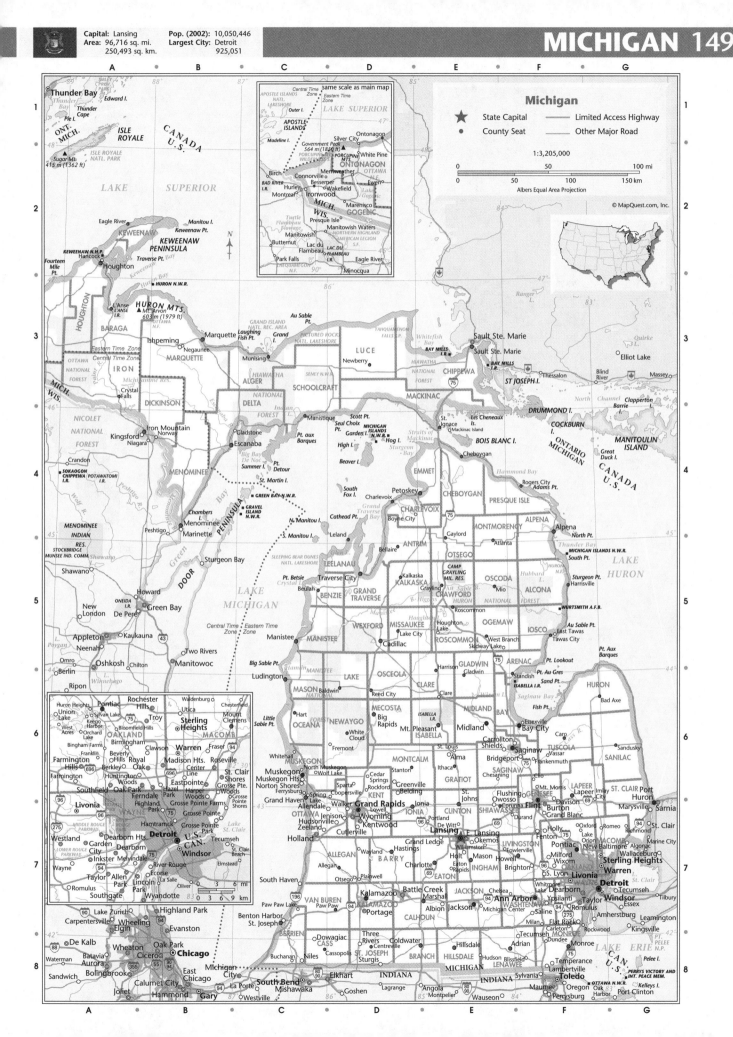

Michigan

★ State Capital
• County Seat
Limited Access Highway
Other Major Road

1:3,205,000

© MapQuest.com, Inc.

Albers Equal Area Projection

Capital: St. Paul
Area: 86,938 sq. mi.
225,168 sq. km.
Pop. (2002): 5,019,720
Largest City: Minneapolis
375,635

Minnesota

★ State Capital — Limited Access Highway
• County Seat — Other Major Road

1:2,773,000

| 0 | 40 | 80 mi |
| 0 | 40 | 80 | 120 km |

Albers Equal Area Projection

MANITOBA
MINNESOTA
LAKE OF THE WOODS
Lake of the Woods

KITTSON
ROSEAU
Warroad
Roseau
Baudette
Greenbush
Hallock
Karlstad
Stephen
Argyle
Warren

MARSHALL
RED LAKE INDIAN RES.
BELTRAMI
KOOCHICHING
Fort Frances
International Falls
Littlefork

PENNINGTON
Thief River Falls
RED LAKE INDIAN RES.
Upper Red L.
Lower Red L.
NETT LAKE IND. RES.

ST. LOUIS
SUPERIOR
QUETICO PROV. PARK
VOYAGEURS NATL. PARK
CAN.
U.S.
ONT.
MINN.

East Grand Forks
Grand Forks
Crookston
RED LAKE
Red Lake Falls
Red Lake
Redby
Ponemah
Blackduck

CHIPPEWA NATIONAL FOREST
ITASCA
DEER CREEK I.R.
Cook
VERMILION LAKE I.R.
Ely
Tower
Babbitt
COOK
LAKE
NATIONAL
SUPERIOR NATIONAL FOREST
RANGE

POLK
McIntosh
Fosston
CLEARWATER
Clearbrook
Bagley
Bemidji
LEECH LAKE IND. RES.
Cass Lake
Keewatin
Nashwauk
Marble
Bovey
Grand Rapids
MESABI RANGE
Mountain Iron
Chisholm
Eveleth
Virginia
Aurora
Hibbing
Buhl
Silver Bay

NORMAN
Ada
Twin Valley
Halstad
Ulen
Fertile
WHITE EARTH I.R.
MAHNOMEN
Mahnomen
HUBBARD
Walker
Deer River
Two Harbors
Lake Superior

CLAY
BECKER
Lake Park
Detroit Lakes
Frazee
Menahga
Park Rapids
Pine River
CASS
Emily
Cross Lake
Floodwood
Hermantown
Proctor
Cloquet
Duluth
Superior
FOND DU LAC I.R.
Carlton

Fargo
Moorhead
West Fargo
Glyndon
Dilworth
Hawley
Barnesville
Pelican Rapids
Perham
Sebeka
WADENA
Wadena
Verndale
New York Mills
Nisswa
Lake Shore
Pequot Lakes
Crosby
Aitkin
Deerwood
AITKIN
Moose Lake
RICE LAKE N.W.R.
CARLTON

WILKIN
Breckenridge
Wahpeton
Fergus Falls
OTTER TAIL
Battle Lake
Henning
Staples
East Gull Lake
Baxter
Brainerd
CROW WING
Mille Lacs
PINE
Sandstone
Hinckley

TAMARAC N.W.R.
Parkers Prairie
TODD
Bertha
Eagle Bend
Clarissa
Browerville
Randall
MORRISON
Pierz
MILLE LACS I.R.
Isle
Onamia
KANABEC
Mora
Ogilvie
Braham

GRANT
Elbow Lake
Evansville
Hoffman
Long Prairie
Little Falls
Royalton
Rice
ST. CROIX NATL. SCENIC RIVERWAY
Pine City
Rock Creek

DOUGLAS
Alexandria
Osakis
Holdingford
Melrose
Freeport
Sauk Centre
St. Stephen
Sartell
Foley
BENTON
Milaca
MILLE LACS
ISANTI
Cambridge
Harris
North Branch
CHISAGO
WISC. MINN.

TRAVERSE
LAKE TRAVERSE (SISSETON) INDIAN RES.
Browns Valley
Graceville
Wheaton
Clinton
BIG STONE
STEVENS
Chokio
Morris
Starbuck
Hancock
POPE
Glenwood
Benson
STEARNS
St. Cloud
St. Joseph
Waite Park
Sauk Rapids
Rockville
Cold Spring
Richmond
Paynesville
Watkins
Kimball
Annandale
Maple Lake
Clearwater
Becker
SHERBURNE N.W.R.
Elk River
St. Francis
Zimmerman
Stacy
Wyoming
Forest Lake
Center City
E. Bethel
ANOKA
Ramsey
Coon Rapids
Anoka

BIG STONE N.W.R.
Ortonville
Milbank
SWIFT
Appleton
Kerkhoven
Spicer
Atwater
Litchfield
MEEKER
WRIGHT
Buffalo
Monticello
Albertville
St. Michael
Corcoran

LAC QUI PARLE
Madison
Clara City
Montevideo
Dawson
CHIPPEWA
Willmar
KANDIYOHI
Kandiyohi
Raymond
Prinsburg
Cosmos
Hutchinson
Cokato
Howard Lake
Winsted
Lester Prairie
HENNEPIN
Plymouth
Minneapolis
Orono
Mound
St. Paul
WASHINGTON
Stillwater
Bayport

YELLOW MEDICINE
Granite Falls
Clarkfield
Canby
Sacred Heart
Renville
Danube
Olivia
Bird Island
Hector
RENVILLE
Brownton
Glencoe
MCLEOD
Buffalo Lake
Young America
Chanhassen
Shakopee
Prior Lake
Edina
Bloomington
Burnsville
Belle Plaine
Jordan
SCOTT
DAKOTA
Farmington
Lakeville
Hastings

LINCOLN
Hendricks
Ivanhoe
Tyler
Lake Benton
Balaton
PIPESTONE
Pipestone
FLANDREAU I.R.
LYON
Marshall
Minneota
Cottonwood
REDWOOD
Redwood Falls
Morgan
Wabasso
Lamberton
Walnut Grove
Tracy
MURRAY
Slayton
Westbrook
COTTONWOOD
Mountain Lake
Windom
Butterfield
WATONWAN
St. James
Madelia
BROWN
Sleepy Eye
Springfield
New Ulm
North Mankato
BLUE EARTH
Good Thunder
Lake Crystal
Amboy
Minnesota Lake
Winnebago
NICOLLET
St. Peter
Kasota
SIBLEY
Gaylord
Arlington
Winthrop
Gibbon
Henderson
Le Sueur
LE SUEUR
Montgomery
Cleveland
Le Center
Mankato
Janesville
WASECA
Waseca
Waterville
Elysian
Lake Elmo
St. Clair
Mapleton

ROCK
Luverne
Hills
NOBLES
Worthington
Adrian
Ellsworth
JACKSON
Lakefield
Heron Lake
Brewster
Jackson
Sherburn
Fairmont
MARTIN
Trimont
Truman
Welcome
Blue Earth
FARIBAULT
Wells
Easton
Winnebago
FREEBORN
Alden
Albert Lea
Glenville

Sioux Falls
Brookings
Sioux River

STEELE
Owatonna
Medford
Blooming Prairie
DODGE
Kasson
Dodge Center
Mantorville
West Concord
Claremont
MOWER
Austin
Brownsdale
Grand Meadow
Adams
Lyle

RICE
Faribault
Northfield
Dundas
Lonsdale
GOODHUE
Cannon Falls
Red Wing
Goodhue
Zumbrota
Pine Island
Kenyon
Morristown
Wanamingo
WABASHA
Wabasha
Plainview
Elgin
Oronoco
OLMSTED
Rochester
Eyota
Stewartville
Chatfield
DODGE

WINONA
Winona
Goodview
Stockton
St. Charles
Lewiston
La Crescent
FILLMORE
Preston
Spring Valley
Lanesboro
Harmony
Mabel
Spring Grove
Caledonia
HOUSTON
Houston
Hokah
Rushford

WISCONSIN
Osseo
Whitehall
Onalaska
La Crosse

NEW PRAGUE
Lonsdale
Le Sueur
Montgomery

Inset maps

ONTARIO
MINNESOTA
Central Time Zone
Eastern Time Zone
COOK
Eagle Mt. 701 m (2301 ft)
Brule L.
GRAND PORTAGE I.R.
GRAND PORTAGE N.M.
Pigeon River
Grand Portage
GRAND PORTAGE ST. FOR.
Hovland
Grand Marais
Lutsen
Lake Superior
same scale as main map

Fridley
North Oaks
White Bear Lake
Brooklyn Center
New Hope
Columbia Hts.
St. Anthony
Maplewood
Little Canada
Robbinsdale
HENNEPIN
Medicine Lake
Golden Valley
St. Louis Park
Hopkins
Edina
Minneapolis
RAMSEY
Falcon Heights
St. Paul
ST. PAUL DTN. AIRPORT
MINNEAPOLIS ST. PAUL INTL. AIRPORT
Richfield
Lilydale
Mendota
South St. Paul
Newport
DAKOTA
MALL OF AMERICA
Bloomington
FT. SNELLING
Eagan

IOWA
Estherville
Spirit Lake
Elmore
Kiester

N.DAK.
S.DAK.
MINN.
ONT.
MAN.

© MapQuest.com, Inc.

Capital: Jackson
Area: 48,282 sq. mi.
125,049 sq. km.
Pop. (2002): 2,871,782
Largest City: Jackson
180,881

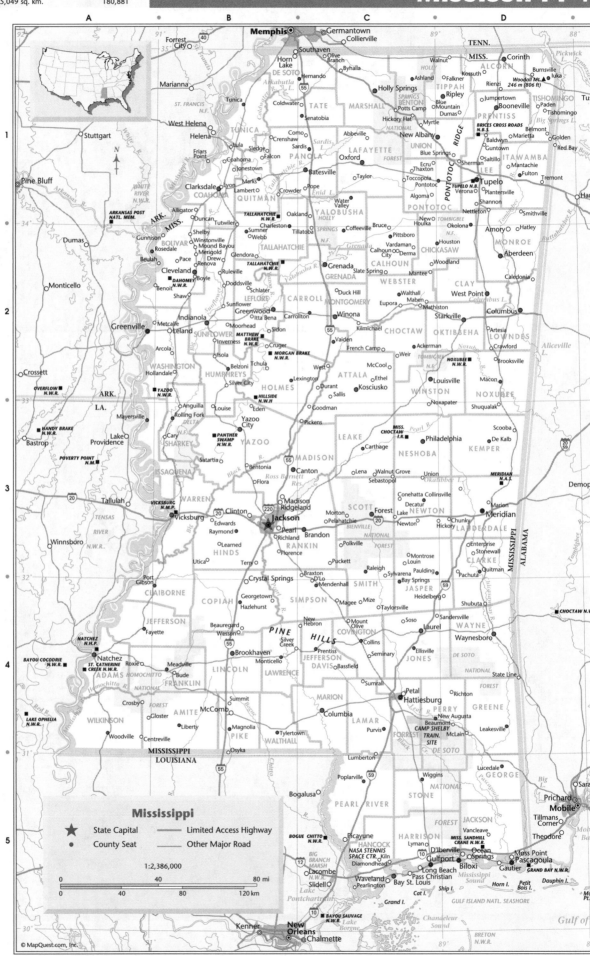

Mississippi

★ State Capital
• County Seat

━━━ Limited Access Highway
━━━ Other Major Road

1:2,386,000

0 — 40 — 80 mi
0 — 40 — 80 — 120 km

© MapQuest.com, Inc.

Capital: Jefferson City   **Pop. (2002):** 5,672,579
Area: 69,704 sq. mi.   **Largest City:** Kansas City
180,532 sq. km.   443,471

Missouri

Limited Access Highway
Other Major Road

★ State Capital
● County Seat

1:3,182,000

Albers Equal Area Projection

0   50   100 mi
0   50   100   150 km

©MapQuest.com, Inc.

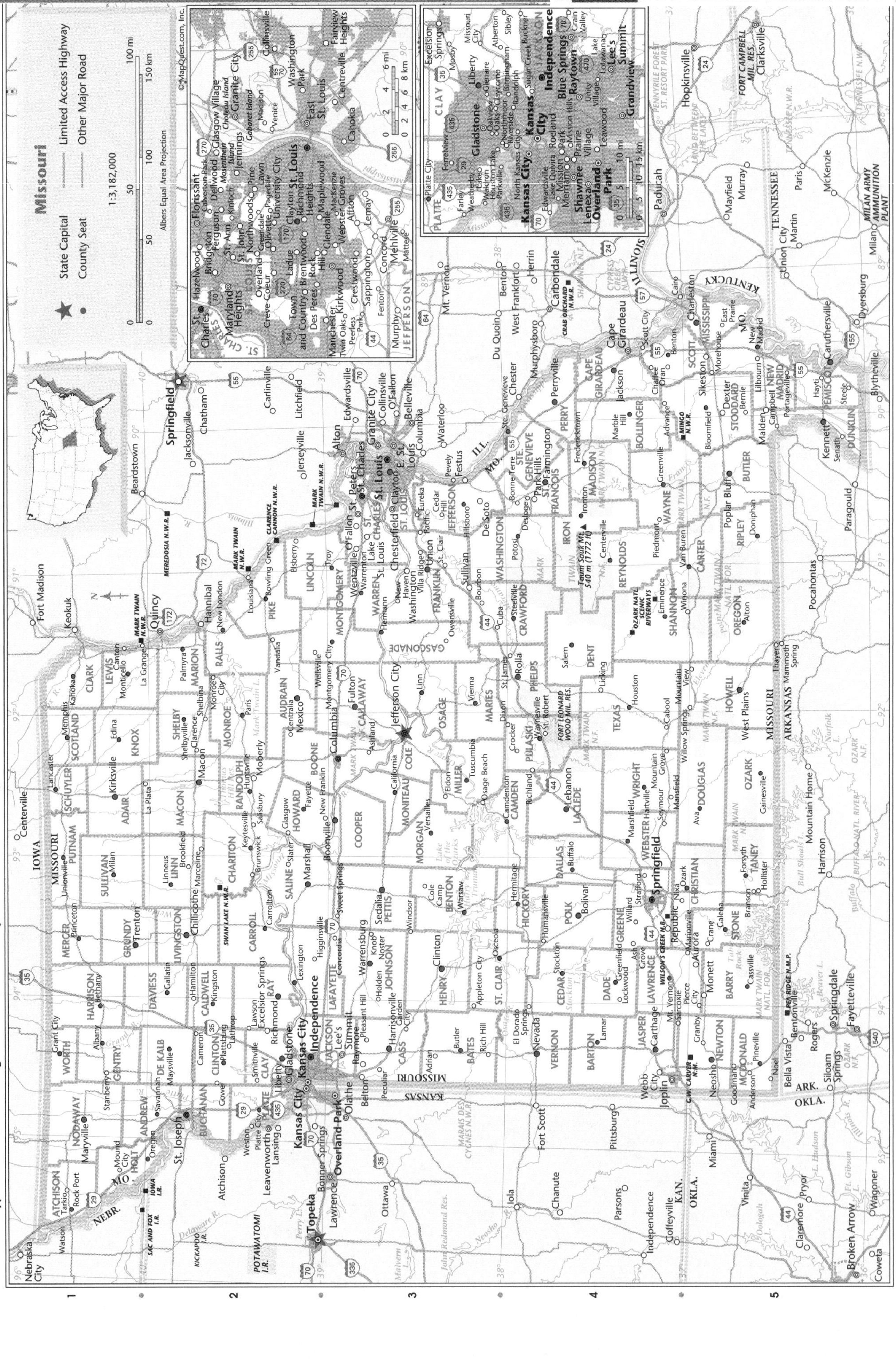

MONTANA

Capital: Helena
Area: 147,042 sq. mi.
380,836 sq. km.
Pop. (2002): 909,453
Largest City: Billings
92,008

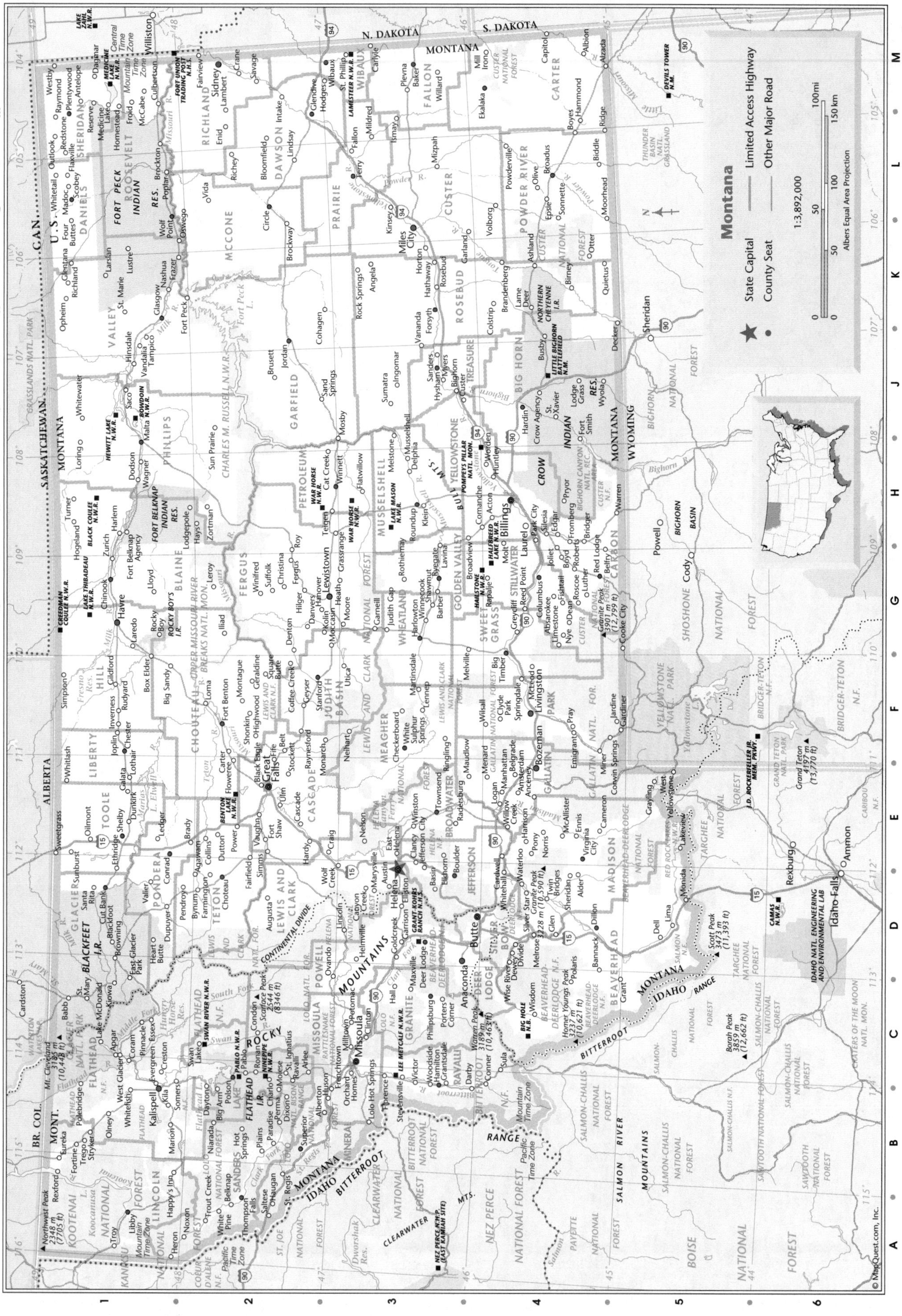

Montana

State Capital ★
County Seat ●

Limited Access Highway
Other Major Road

1:3,892,000
Albers Equal Area Projection

N. DAKOTA — Montana — S. DAKOTA

SASKATCHEWAN — CAN. / U.S.
ALBERTA
BR. COL. / MONT.
MONTANA / IDAHO
WYOMING

© MapQuest.com, Inc.

Capital: Lincoln   **Pop. (2002):** 1,729,180
Area: 77,353 sq. mi.   **Largest City:** Omaha
200,343 sq. km.   399,357

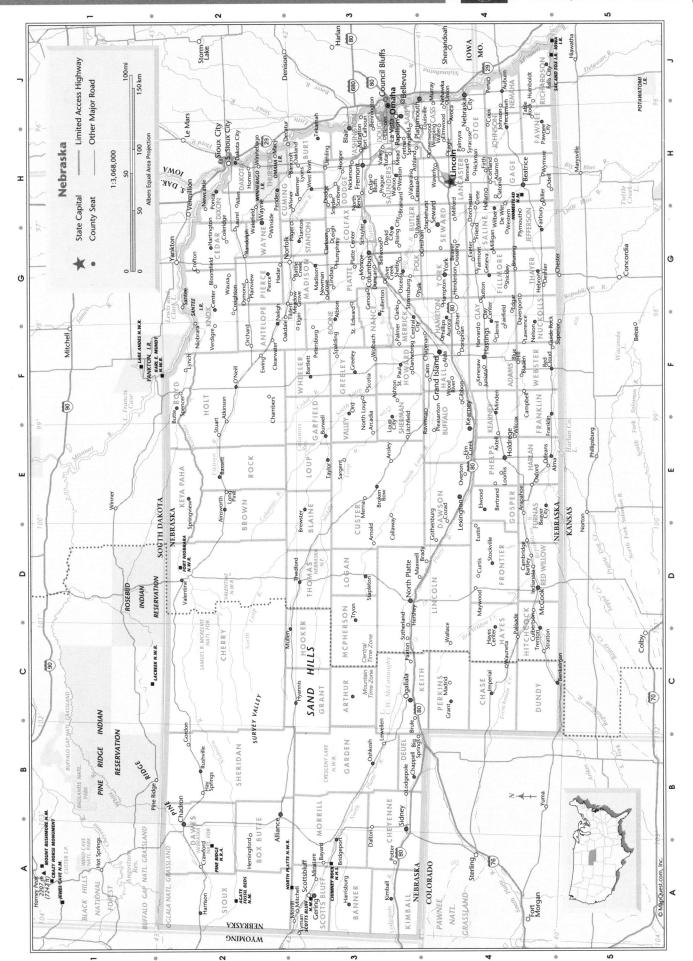

Nebraska

Limited Access Highway
Other Major Road

1:3,068,000
Albers Equal Area Projection

★ State Capital
● County Seat

Capital: Carson City
Area: 110,560 sq. mi.
286,348 sq. km.
Pop. (2002): 2,173,491
Largest City: Las Vegas
508,604

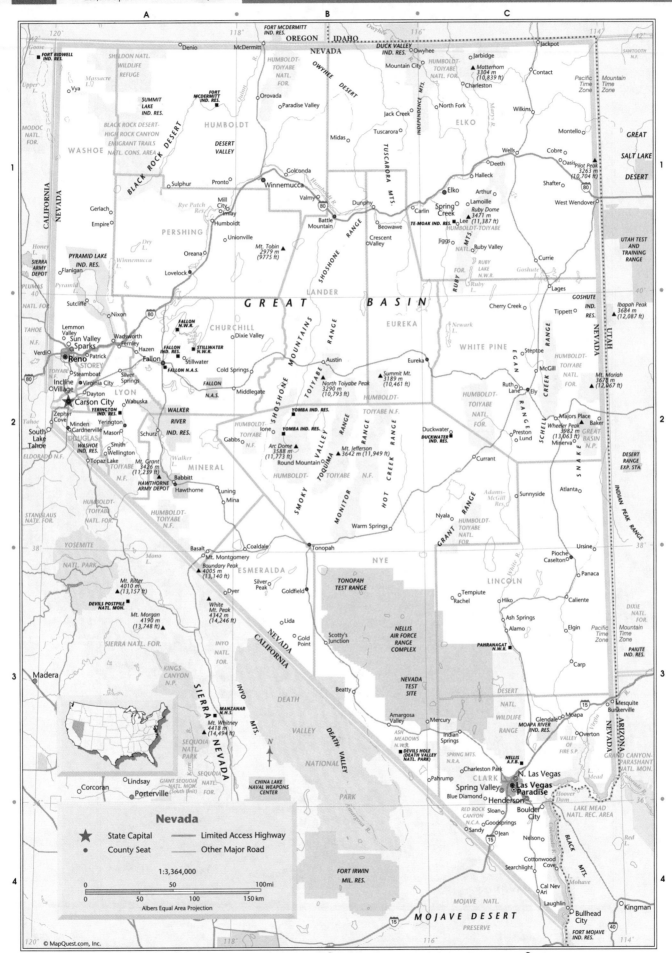

Nevada

★ State Capital
● County Seat
── Limited Access Highway
── Other Major Road

1:3,364,000

0   50   100mi
0 50 100 150 km

Albers Equal Area Projection

© MapQuest.com, Inc.

Capital: Concord
Area: 9,282 sq. mi.
24,040 sq. km.

Pop. (2002): 1,275,056
Largest City: Manchester
108,398

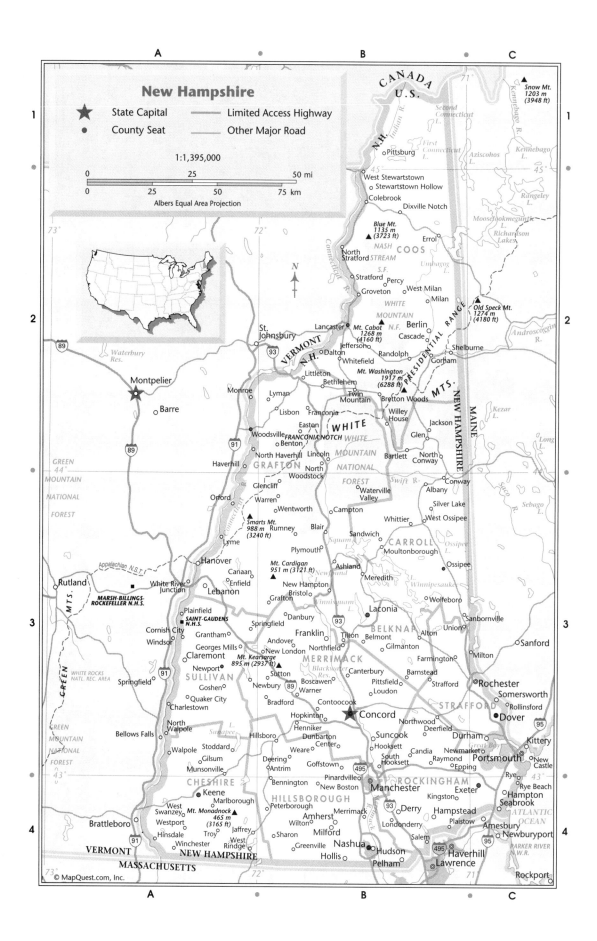

New Hampshire

★ State Capital
● County Seat

━━ Limited Access Highway
── Other Major Road

1:1,395,000

0   25   50 mi
0   25   50   75 km
Albers Equal Area Projection

Capital: Trenton
Area: 8,214 sq. mi.
21,274 sq. km.
Pop. (2002): 8,590,300
Largest City: Newark
277,000

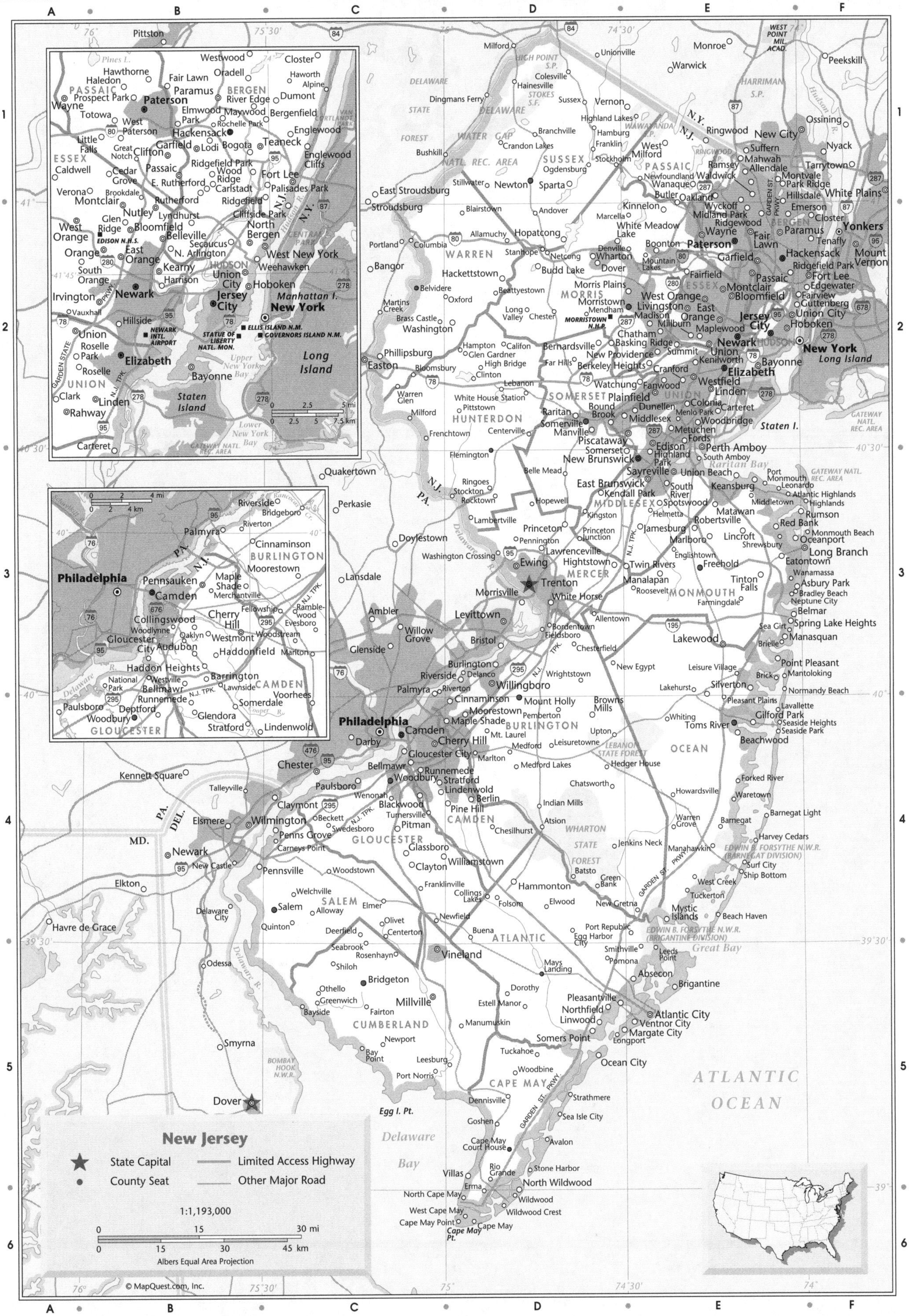

New Jersey

★ State Capital ― Limited Access Highway
● County Seat ― Other Major Road

1:1,193,000

0   15   30 mi
0 15 30 45 km

Albers Equal Area Projection

© MapQuest.com, Inc.

ATLANTIC OCEAN

Delaware Bay

Trenton

Newark

Jersey City

New York

Paterson

Camden

Philadelphia

Atlantic City

Cape May

Vineland

Toms River

Long Branch

Asbury Park

Elizabeth

New Brunswick

Princeton

Morristown

Dover

Millville

Bridgeton

Wildwood

Ocean City

Capital: Santa Fe   **Pop. (2002):** 1,855,059
Area: 121,589 sq. mi.   **Largest City:** Albuquerque
314,913 sq. km.   463,874

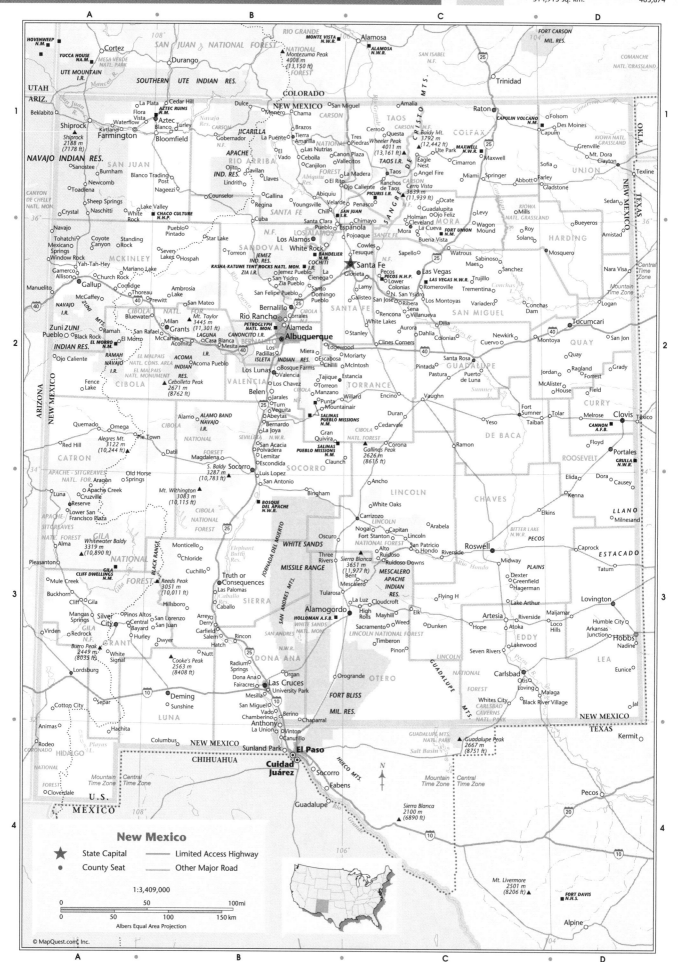

New Mexico

★ State Capital   ── Limited Access Highway
● County Seat   ── Other Major Road

1:3,409,000

0   50   100mi
0   50   100   150 km
Albers Equal Area Projection

© MapQuest.com, Inc.

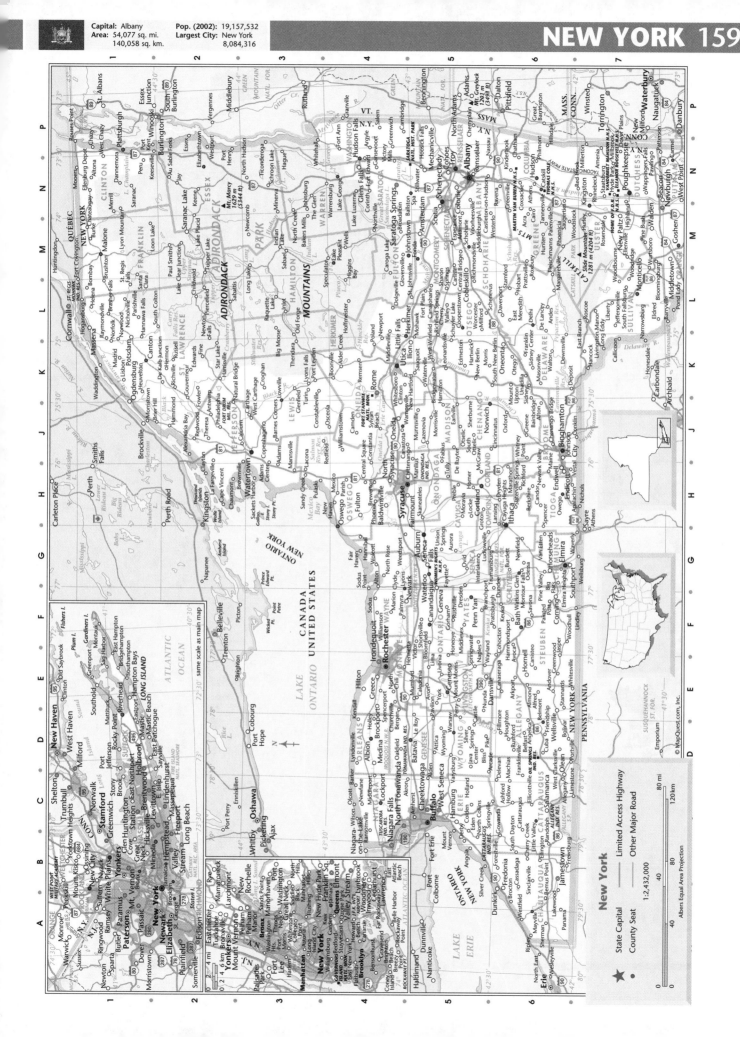

Capital: Albany
Area: 54,077 sq. mi.
140,058 sq. km.
Pop. (2002): 19,157,532
Largest City: New York
8,084,316

New York

State Capital
County Seat

Limited Access Highway
Other Major Road

1:2,432,000

Albers Equal Area Projection

© MapQuest.com, Inc.

Capital: Raleigh
Area: 52,670 sq. mi.
136,414 sq. km.
Pop. (2002): 8,320,146
Largest City: Charlotte
580,597

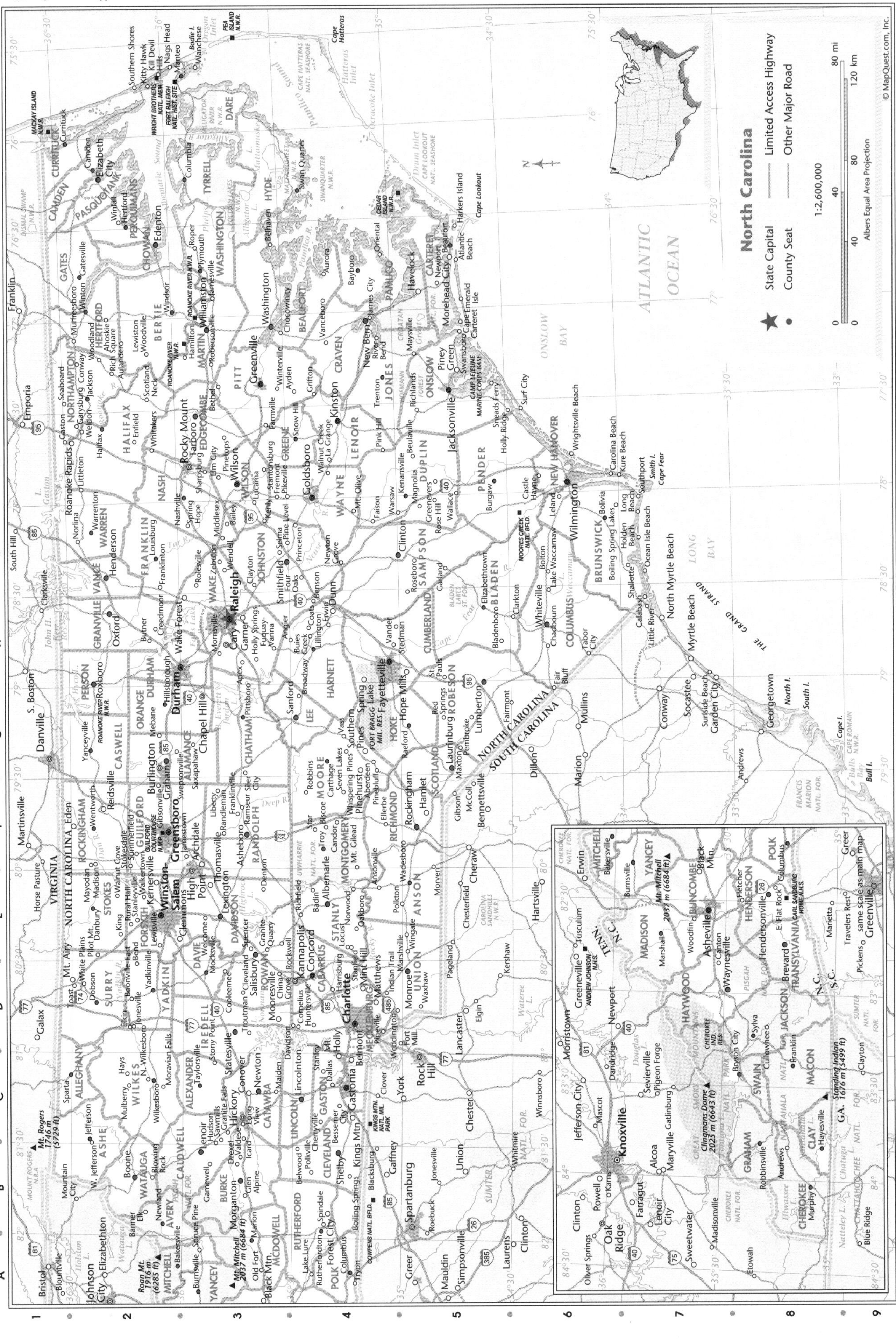

North Carolina

State Capital ★
County Seat ●
Limited Access Highway
Other Major Road

1:2,600,000
Albers Equal Area Projection

80 mi / 120 km

© MapQuest.com, Inc.

ATLANTIC OCEAN

VIRGINIA

NORTH CAROLINA

SOUTH CAROLINA

TENN.

GA.

Mt. Mitchell 2037 m (6684 ft)

Clingmans Dome 2025 m (6643 ft)

Capital: Bismarck	Pop. (2002): 634,110
Area: 70,699 sq. mi.	Largest City: Fargo
183,109 sq. km.	91,204

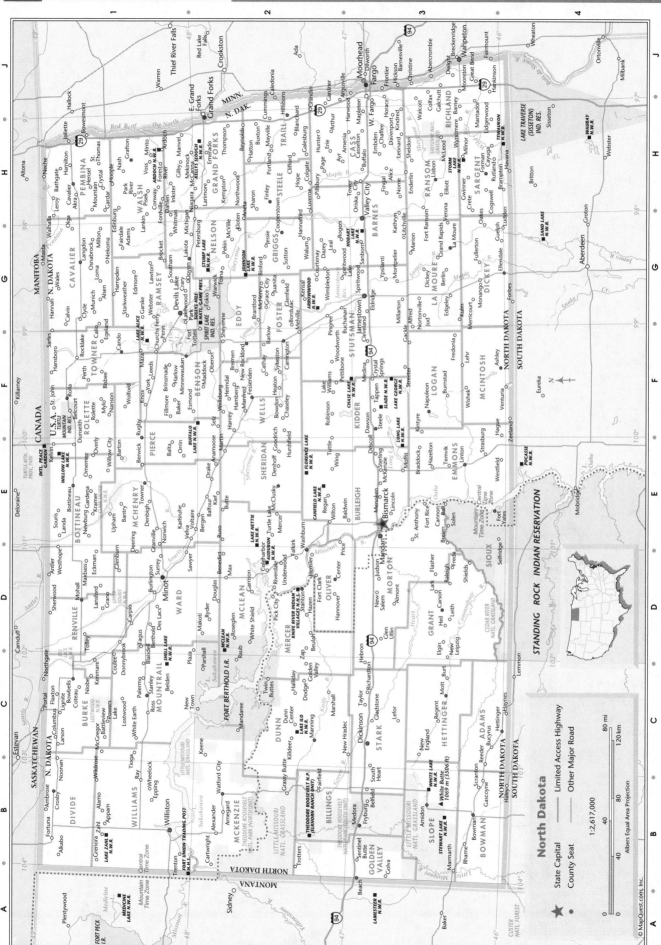

North Dakota

★ State Capital
● County Seat

Limited Access Highway
Other Major Road

1:2,617,000

Albers Equal Area Projection

STANDING ROCK INDIAN RESERVATION

© MapQuest.com, Inc.

Capital: Columbus
Area: 44,825 sq. mi.
116,096 sq. km.
Pop. (2002): 11,421,267
Largest City: Columbus
725,228

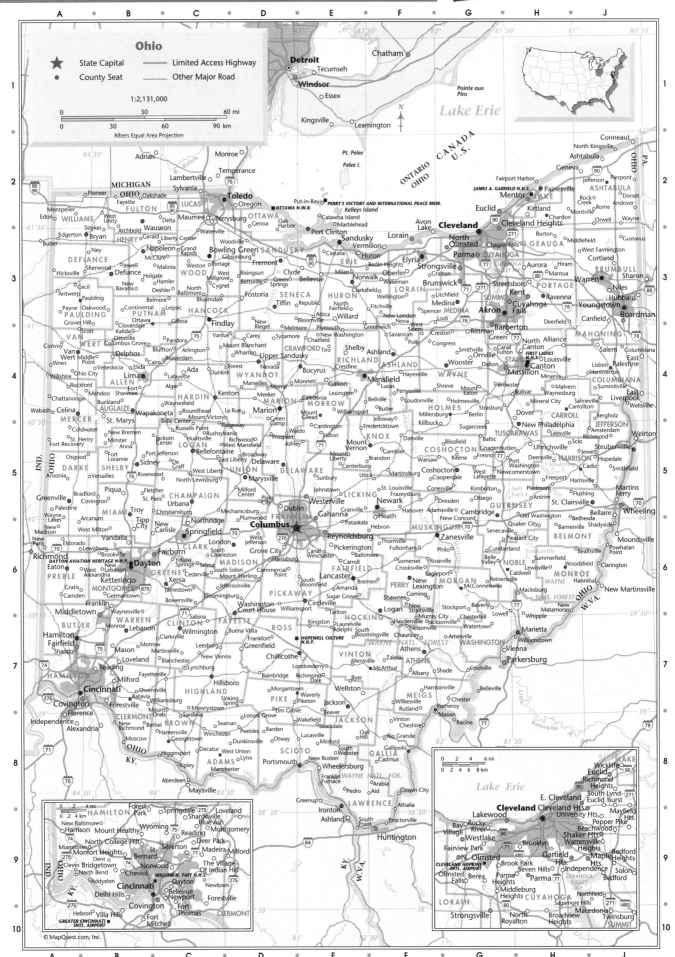

Ohio

★ State Capital
● County Seat
Limited Access Highway
Other Major Road

1:2,131,000

0   30   60 mi
0   30   60   90 km

Albers Equal Area Projection

© MapQuest.com, Inc.

Capital: Oklahoma City
Area: 69,898 sq. mi.
181,034 sq. km.
Pop. (2002): 3,493,714
Largest City: Oklahoma City
519,034

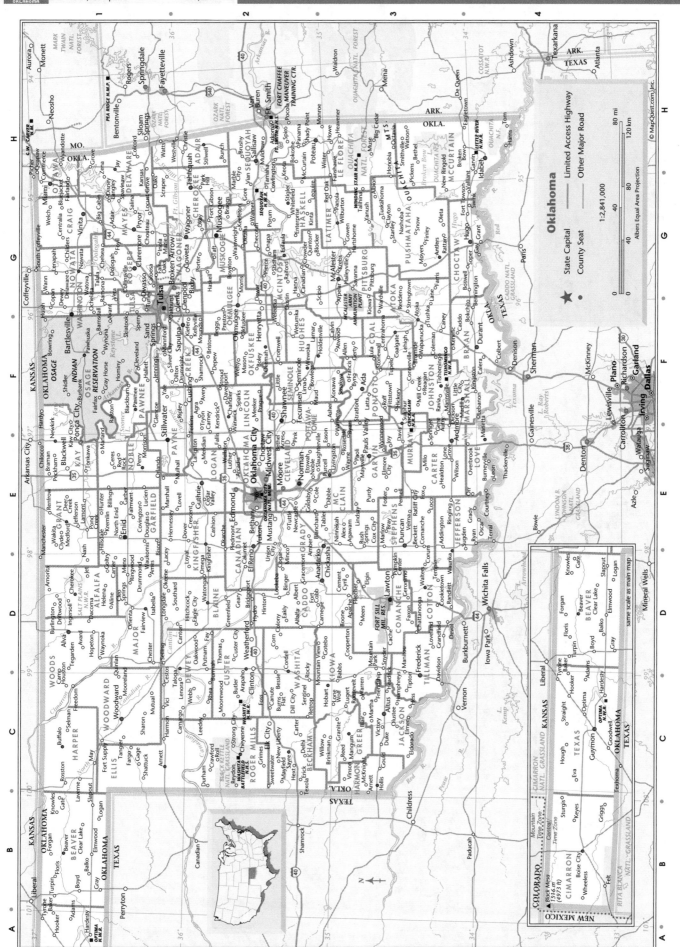

Oklahoma

1:2,841,000

★ State Capital
• County Seat

Limited Access Highway
Other Major Road

© MapQuest.com, Inc.

Albers Equal Area Projection

0   40   80 mi
0   40   80   120 km

Time Zone
Mountain / Central Time Zone

Capital: Salem
Area: 97,126 sq. mi.
251,554 sq. km.

Pop. (2002): 3,521,515
Largest City: Portland
539,438

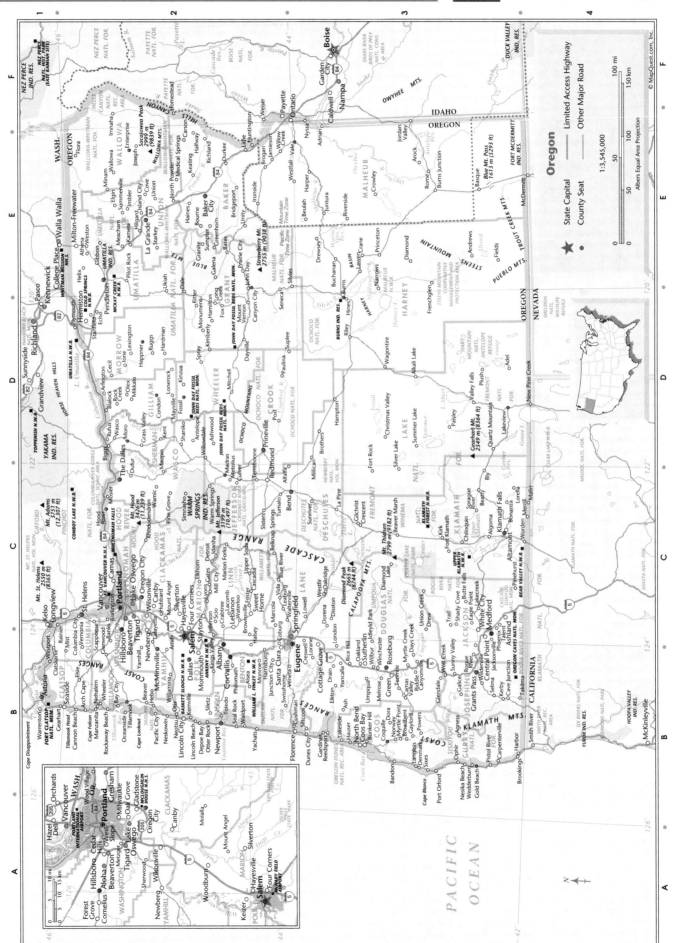

Capital: Harrisburg
Area: 46,055 sq. mi.
119,282 sq. km.
Pop. (2002): 12,335,091
Largest City: Philadelphia
1,492,231

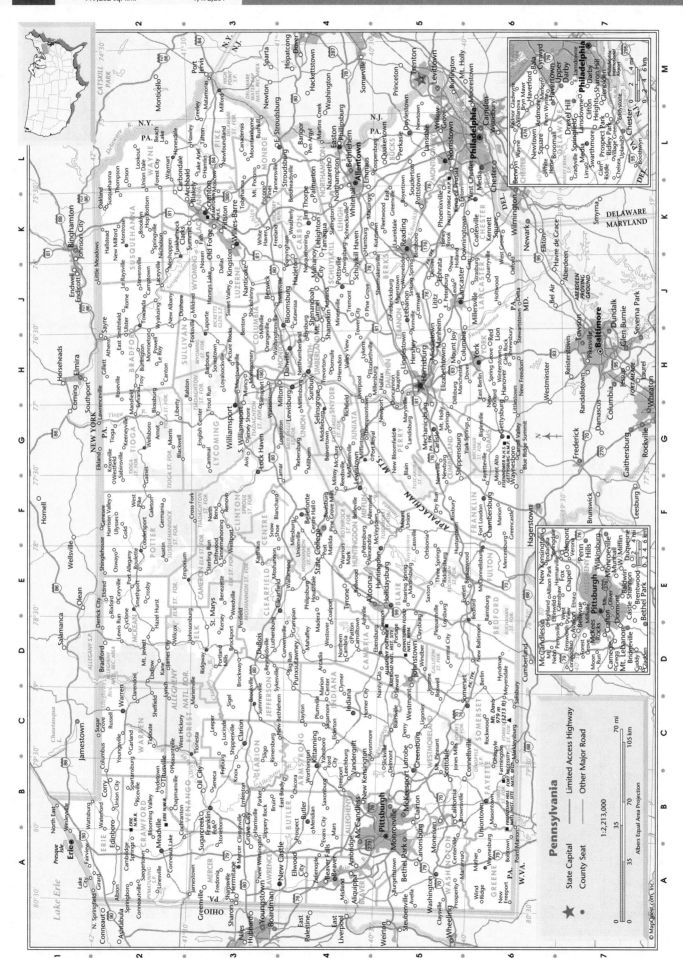

Pennsylvania

★ State Capital
• County Seat

Limited Access Highway
Other Major Road

1:2,213,000

Albers Equal Area Projection

© MapQuest.com, Inc.

Capital: Providence
Area: 1,231 sq. mi.
3,188 sq. km.
Pop. (2002): 1,069,725
Largest City: Providence
175,901

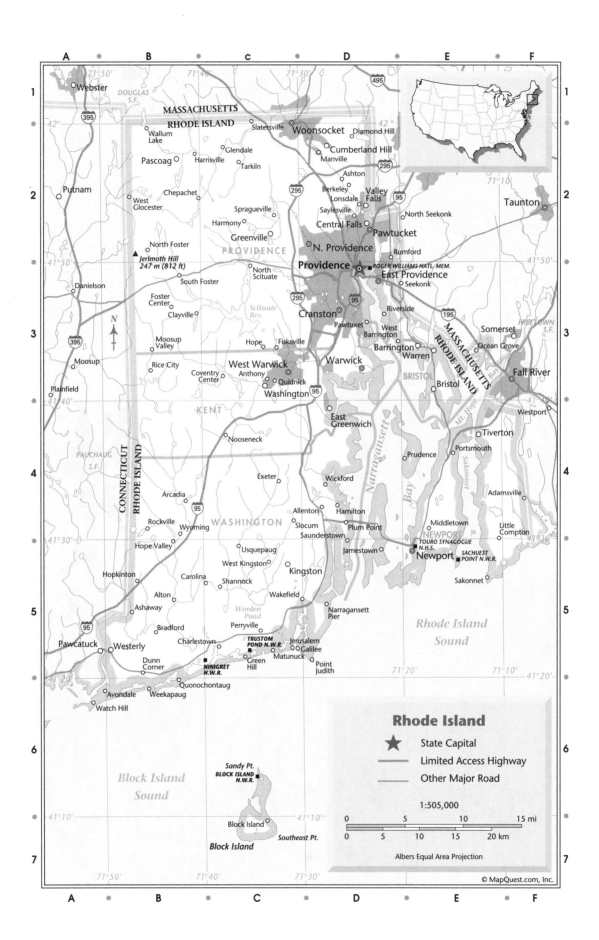

Rhode Island

★ State Capital
— Limited Access Highway
— Other Major Road

1:505,000

0   5   10   15 mi
0 5 10 15 20 km

Albers Equal Area Projection

© MapQuest.com, Inc.

Capital: Columbia
Area: 31,190 sq. mi.
80,781 sq. km.
Pop. (2002): 4,107,183
Largest City: Columbia
117,394

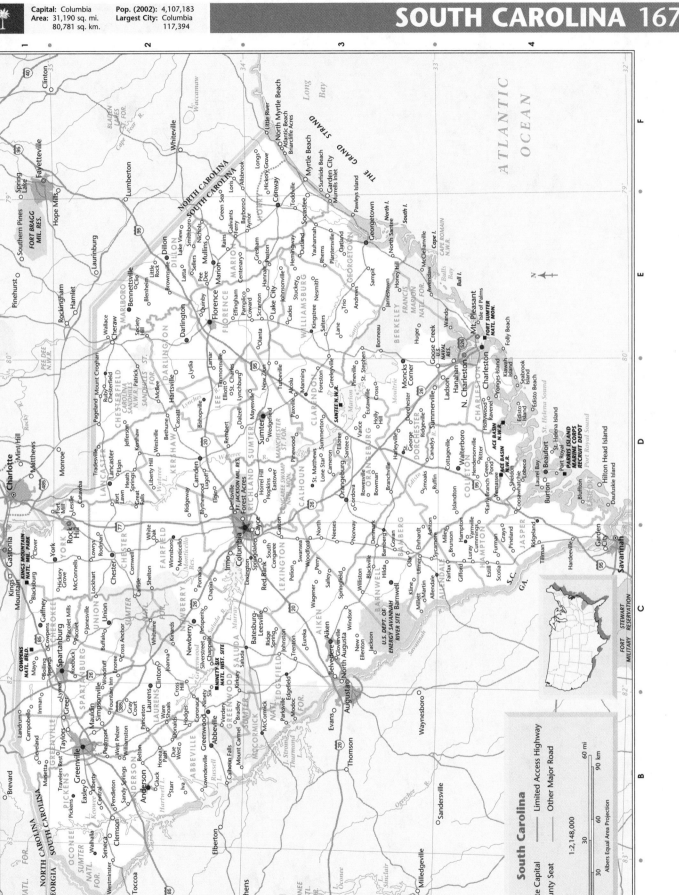

South Carolina

★ State Capital
● County Seat

— Limited Access Highway
— Other Major Road

1:2,148,000

Albers Equal Area Projection

MapQuest.com, Inc.

Capital: Pierre
Area: 77,116 sq. mi.
199,729 sq. km.

Pop. (2002): 761,063
Largest City: Sioux Falls
130,491

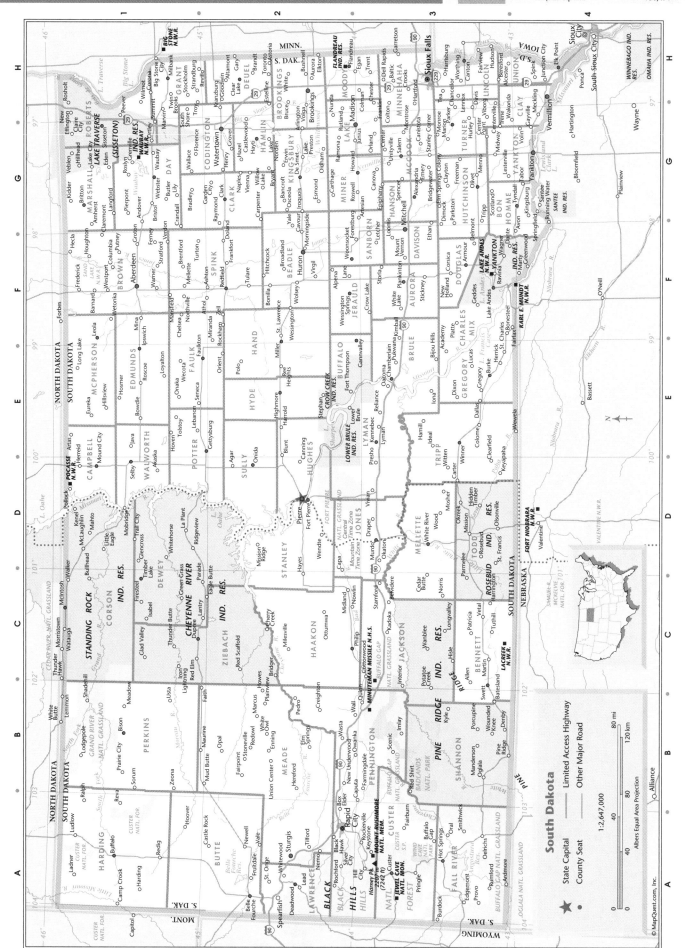

South Dakota

Scale 1:2,647,000

0   40   80 mi
0   40   80   120 km

Albers Equal Area Projection

★ State Capital
● County Seat

— Limited Access Highway
— Other Major Road

© MapQuest.com, Inc.

Capital: Nashville Pop. (2002): 5,797,289
Area: 42,143 sq. mi. Largest City: Memphis
109,150 sq. km. 648,882

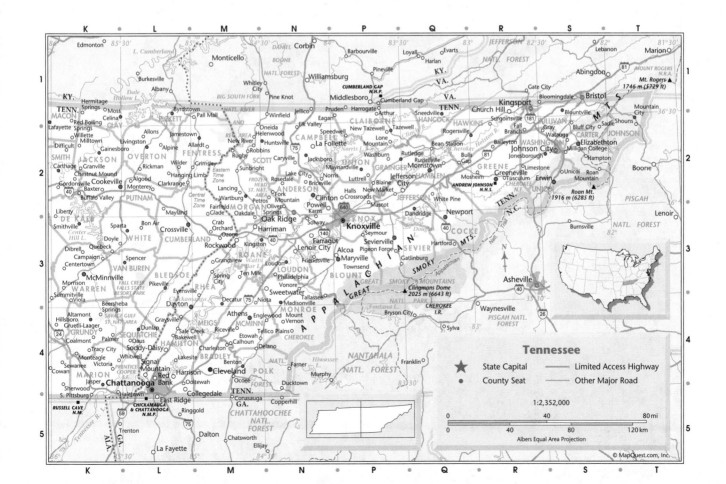

Tennessee

★ State Capital
• County Seat
Limited Access Highway
Other Major Road

1:2,352,000

0   40   80 mi
0   40   80   120 km
Albers Equal Area Projection

© MapQuest.com, Inc.

Capital: Austin
Area: 267,256 sq. mi.
692,188 sq. km.
Pop. (2002): 21,779,893
Largest City: Houston
2,009,834

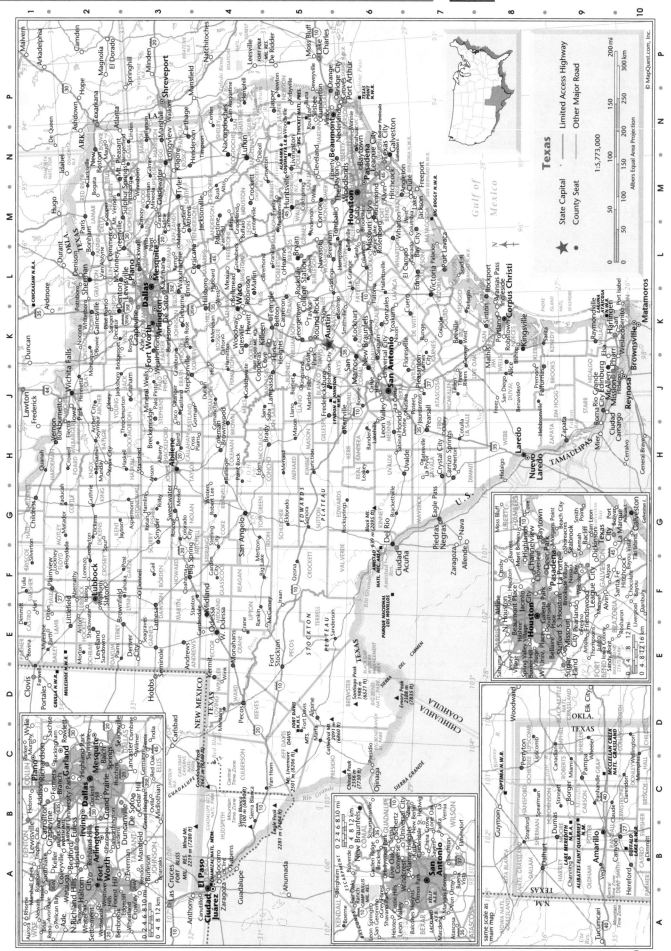

Texas

State Capital ★
County Seat ●

Limited Access Highway
Other Major Road

1:5,773,000
Albers Equal Area Projection

© MapQuest.com, Inc.

Gulf of Mexico

Capital: Salt Lake City
Area: 84,898 sq. mi.
219,884 sq. km.
Pop. (2002): 2,316,256
Largest City: Salt Lake City
181,266

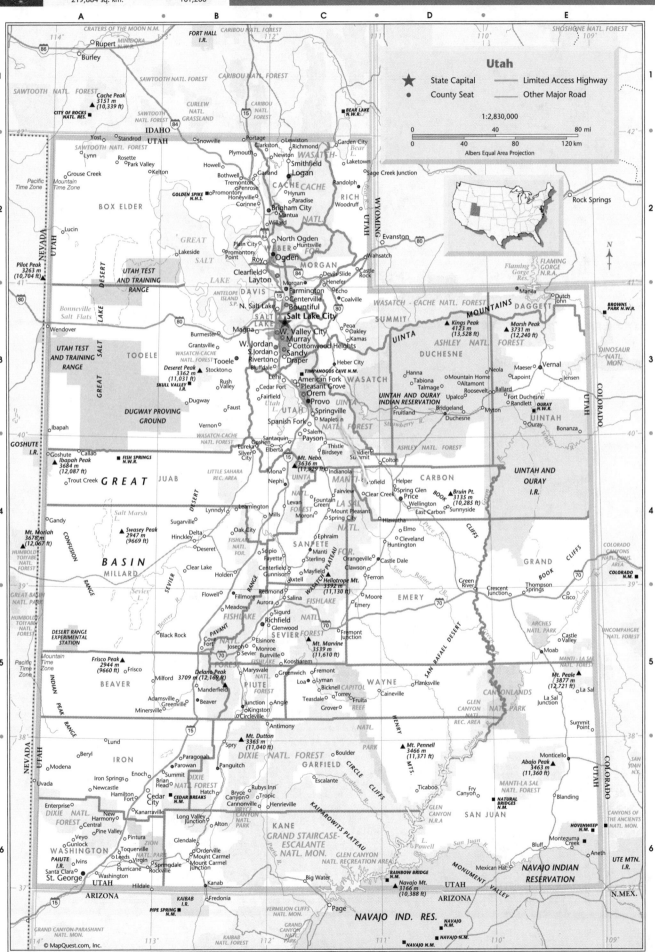

Utah

★ State Capital
● County Seat
━━ Limited Access Highway
━━ Other Major Road

1:2,830,000

0   40   80 mi
0   40   80   120 km
Albers Equal Area Projection

© MapQuest.com, Inc.

Capital: Montpelier
Area: 9,614 sq. mi.
24,900 sq. km.

Pop. (2002): 616,592
Largest City: Burlington
39,466

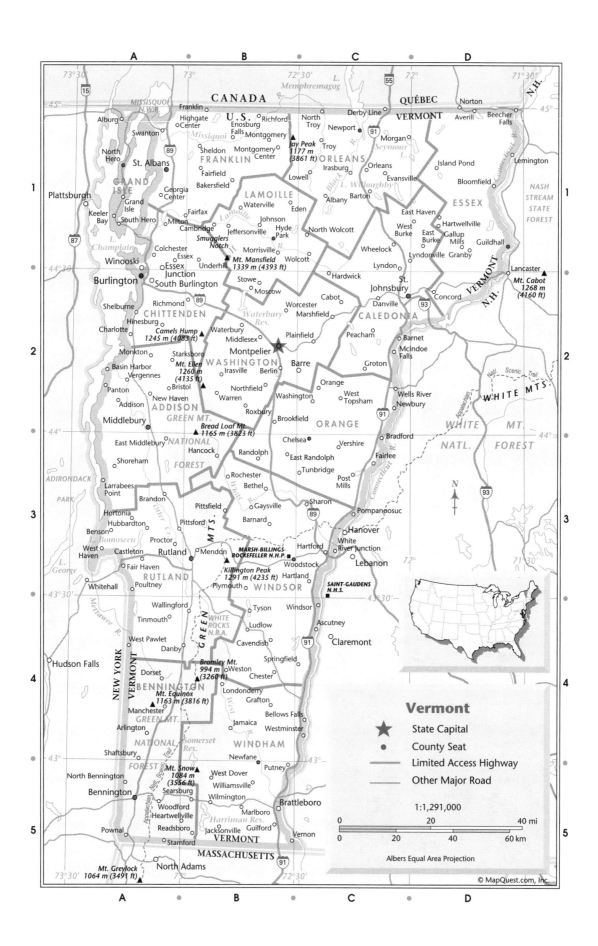

Vermont

★ State Capital
● County Seat
━━ Limited Access Highway
⋯⋯ Other Major Road

1:1,291,000

| 0 | 20 | | 40 mi |
| 0 | 20 | 40 | 60 km |

Albers Equal Area Projection

© MapQuest.com, Inc.

Capital: Richmond
Area: 42,328 sq. mi.
109,629 sq. km.
Pop. (2002): 7,293,542
Largest City: Virginia Beach
433,934

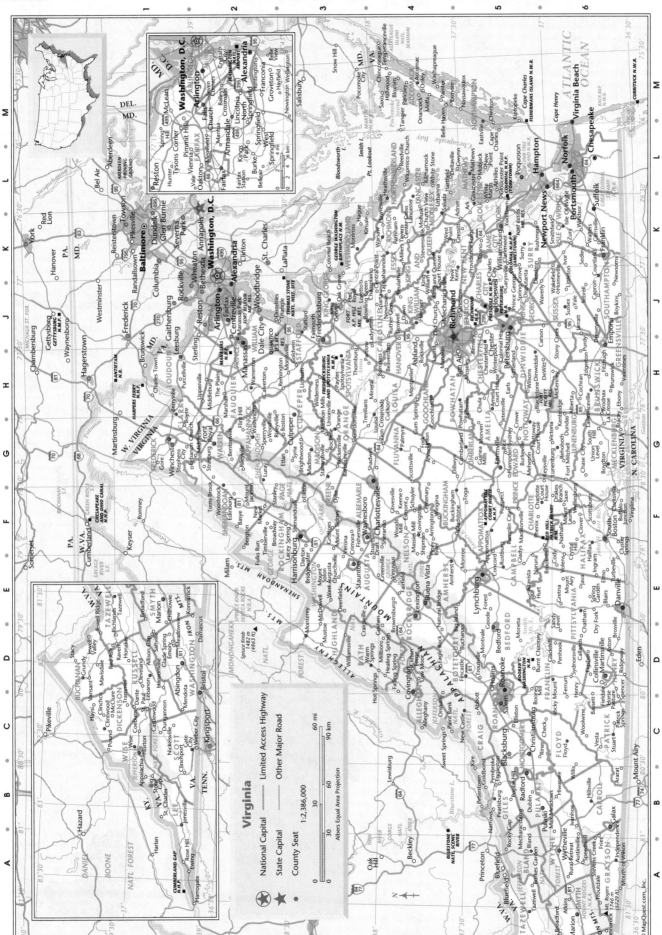

Virginia

National Capital ⭐

State Capital ★

County Seat ●

— Limited Access Highway

— Other Major Road

0   30   60 mi
0   30   60   90 km

Albers Equal Area Projection
1:2,386,000

© MapQuest.com, Inc.

Capital: Olympia
Area: 70,634 sq. mi.
182,941 sq. km.
Pop. (2002): 6,068,996
Largest City: Seattle
570,426

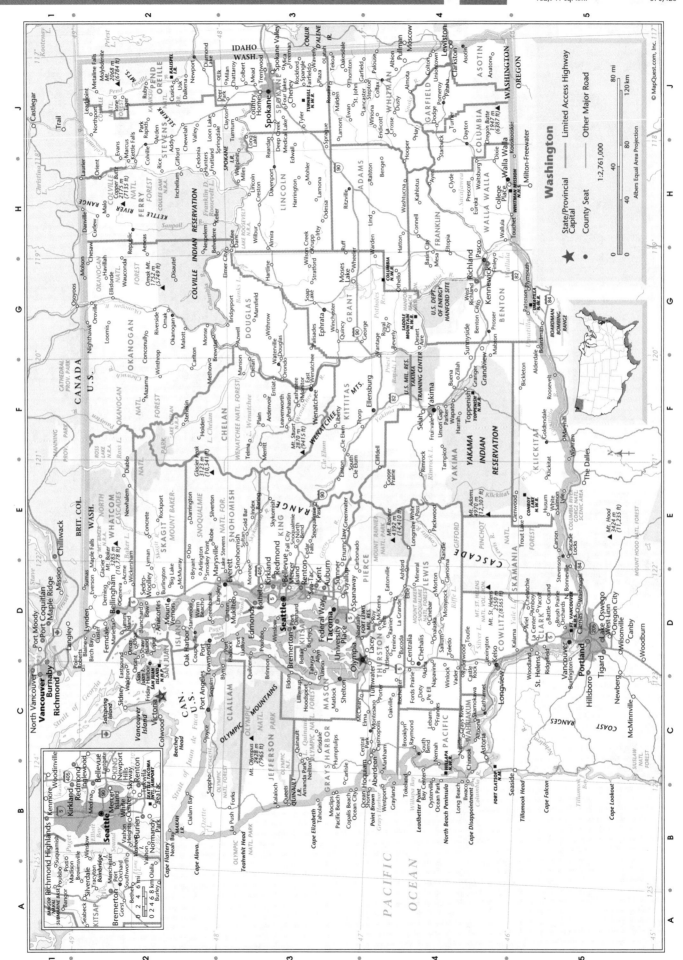

Capital: Charleston
Area: 24,230 sq. mi.
62,755 sq. km.
Pop. (2002): 1,801,873
Largest City: Charleston
51,702

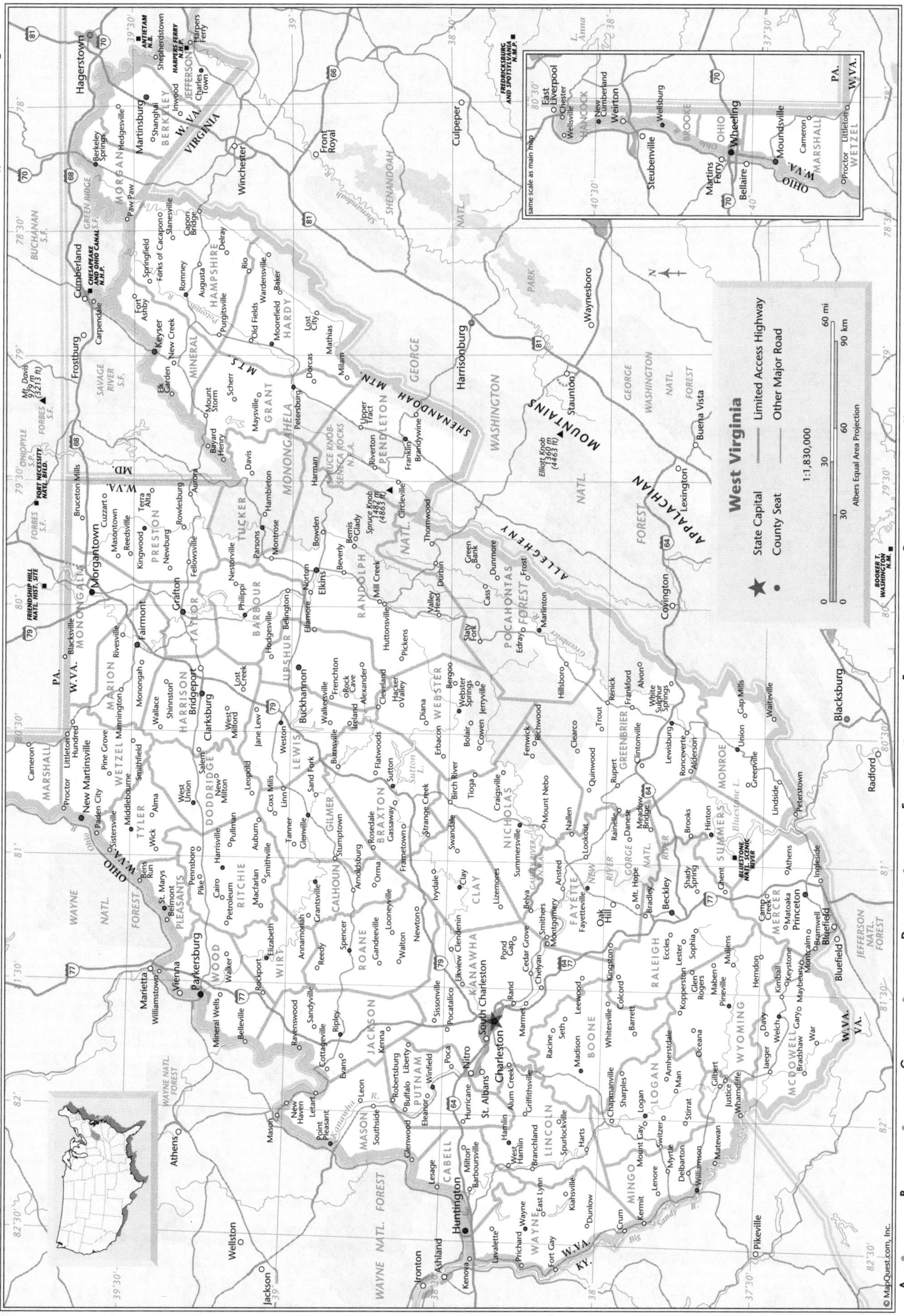

West Virginia

★ State Capital
• County Seat

Limited Access Highway
Other Major Road

1:1,830,000

Albers Equal Area Projection

0 30 60 90 km
0 30 60 mi

WISCONSIN 1848

Capital: Madison
Area: 65,498 sq. mi.
169,639 sq. km.
Pop. (2002): 5,441,196
Largest City: Milwaukee
590,895

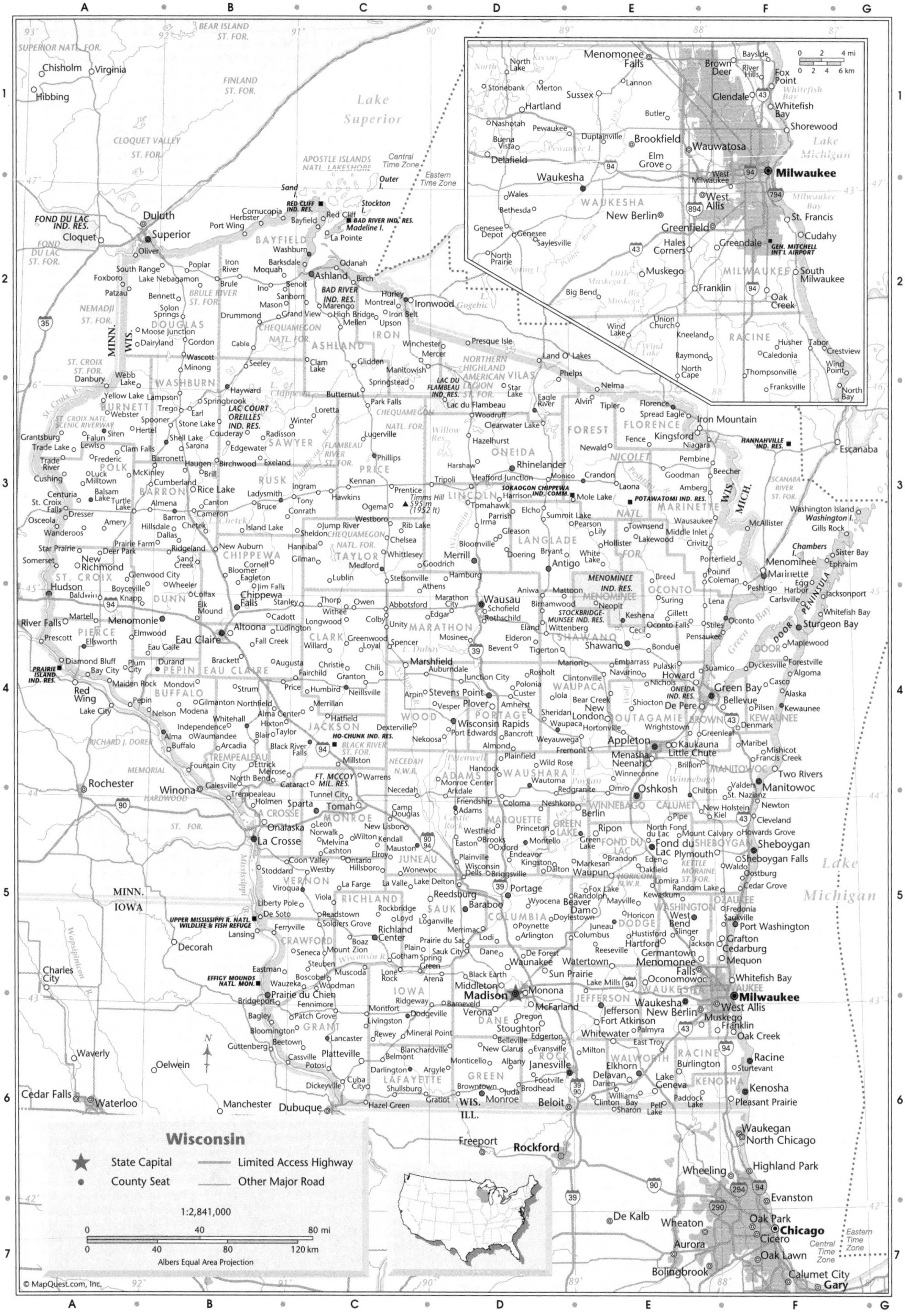

Wisconsin

★ State Capital
• County Seat
— Limited Access Highway
— Other Major Road

1:2,841,000

0   40   80 mi
0   40   80   120 km

Albers Equal Area Projection

© MapQuest.com, Inc.

Lake Superior

Lake Michigan

MINN.
WIS.
IOWA
ILL.
MICH.

Duluth, Superior, Ashland, Ironwood, Hurley, Bayfield, La Pointe, Washburn, Hayward, Rhinelander, Wausau, Eau Claire, Chippewa Falls, Menomonie, River Falls, Hudson, New Richmond, La Crosse, Onalaska, Tomah, Sparta, Winona, Rochester, Stevens Point, Wisconsin Rapids, Marshfield, Green Bay, De Pere, Appleton, Menasha, Neenah, Oshkosh, Fond du Lac, Sheboygan, Manitowoc, Two Rivers, Sturgeon Bay, Kewaunee, Beaver Dam, Portage, Baraboo, Reedsburg, Richland Center, Prairie du Chien, Platteville, Dodgeville, Madison, Monona, Middleton, Sun Prairie, Watertown, Waukesha, New Berlin, West Allis, Milwaukee, Franklin, Oak Creek, Racine, Kenosha, Beloit, Janesville, Monroe, Whitewater, Fort Atkinson, Jefferson, Stoughton

Milwaukee inset: Menomonee Falls, Brookfield, Wauwatosa, Waukesha, New Berlin, Greenfield, West Allis, Milwaukee, Whitefish Bay, Shorewood, Glendale, St. Francis, Cudahy, South Milwaukee, Oak Creek, Franklin, Muskego, Hales Corners, Greendale, Gen. Mitchell Int'l Airport

Chicago, Rockford, Freeport, De Kalb, Aurora, Evanston, Highland Park, Waukegan, North Chicago, Gary, Waterloo, Cedar Falls, Dubuque, Decorah

Capital: Cheyenne
Area: 97,813 sq. mi.
253,334 sq. km.
Pop. (2002): 498,703
Largest City: Cheyenne
53,658

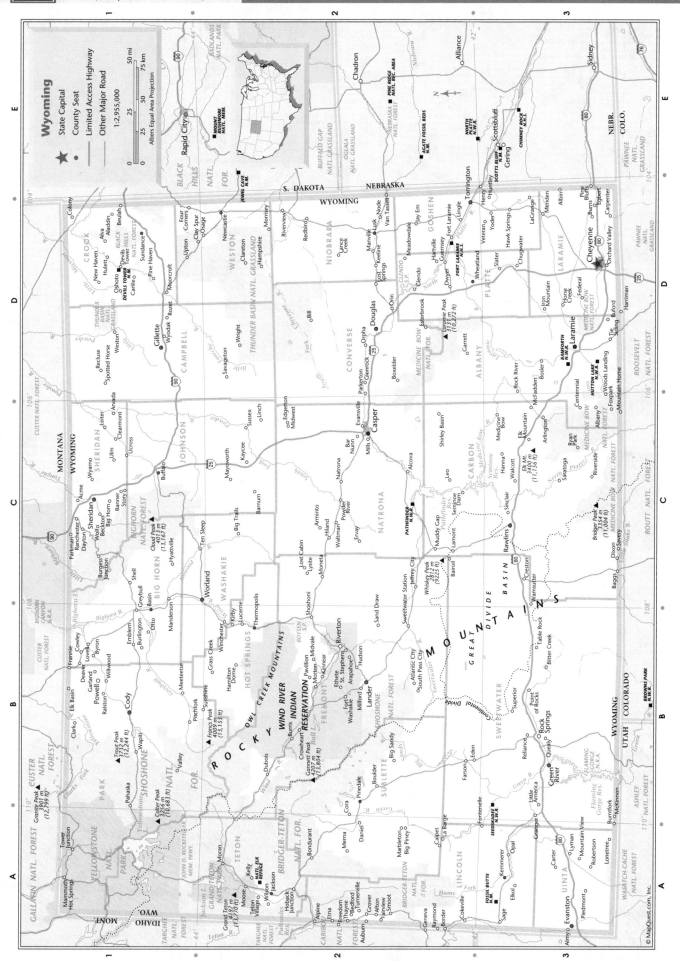

Wyoming

★ State Capital
● County Seat
— Limited Access Highway
— Other Major Road

1:2,955,000

Albers Equal Area Projection

© MapQuest.com, Inc.

Key

Abbreviations
N.H.P. National Historical Park
N.H.S. National Historic Site
N.M. National Monument
N.P. National Park
N.R.A. National Recreation Area

Alabama ... page 128

Cities and Towns
Abbeville D4
Adamsville C2
Alabaster C2
Albertville C1
Alexander City D3
Aliceville A2
Andalusia C4
Anniston D2
Arab C1
Ashford D4
Ashland D2
Ashville C2
Athens C1
Atmore B4
Attalla C1
Auburn D3
Bay Minette B5
Bayou La Batre A5
Bessemer C2
Birmingham C2
Blountsville C1
Boaz C1
Brent B3
Brewton B4
Bridgeport D1
Brundidge D4
Butler A3
Calera C2
Camden B4
Camp Hill D3
Carbon Hill B2
Carrollton A2
Center Point C2
Centre D1
Centreville B3
Chatom A4
Chelsea C2
Cherokee B1
Chickasaw A5
Childersburg C2
Citronelle A4
Clanton C3
Clayton D4
Clio D4
Collinsville D1
Columbiana C2
Cordova B2
Cottonwood D4
Creola A5
Crossville D1
Cullman C1
Dadeville D3
Daleville D4
Daphne B5
Decatur C1
Demopolis B3
Dora B2
Dothan D4
Double Springs B1
East Brewton B4
Elba C4
Enterprise D4
Eufaula D4
Eutaw B3
Evergreen C4
Fairfield C2
Fairhope B5
Falkville C1
Fayette B2
Flomaton B4
Florala C4
Florence B1
Foley B5
Fort Morgan A5
Fort Payne D1
Frisco City B4
Fultondale C2
Gadsden C1
Gardendale C2
Gasque B5
Geneva D4
Georgiana C4
Glencoe D2
Good Hope C1
Goodwater C2
Gordo B2
Grand Bay A5
Greensboro B3
Greenville C4
Grove Hill B4
Guin B2
Gulf Shores B5
Guntersville C1
Haleyville B1
Hamilton B1
Hanceville C1
Hartford D4
Hartselle C1
Hayneville C3
Hazel Green C1
Headland D4
Heflin D2
Helena C2
Henagar D1
Heron Bay A5
Hokes Bluff D2
Holt B2
Hoover C2
Hueytown B2
Huntsville C1
Irondale C2
Jackson B4
Jacksonville D2
Jasper B2
Jemison C3
Lafayette D3
Lanett D3
Leeds C2
Lincoln C2
Linden B3
Lineville D2
Livingston A3
Luverne C4
Madison C1
Marion B3
Meridianville C1
Midfield C2
Midland City D4
Millbrook C3
Mobile A5
Monroeville B4
Montevallo C2
Montgomery, *capital* C3
Moulton B1
Moundville B3
Muscle Shoals B1
New Hope C1
Newton D4
Northport B2
Oneonta C2
Opelika D3
Opp C4
Orange Beach B5
Oxford D2
Ozark D4
Parrish B2
Pelham C2
Pell City C2
Petersville B1
Phenix City D3
Phil Campbell B1
Piedmont D2
Pinson C2
Point Clear B5
Prattville C3
Priceville C1
Prichard A5
Ragland C2
Rainbow City C2
Rainsville D1
Reform A2
Roanoke D2
Robertsdale B5
Rockford C3
Russellville B1
Samson C4
Saraland A5
Sardis City C1
Satsuma A5
Scottsboro C1
Selma B3
Sheffield B1
Slocomb D4
Smiths D3
Southside C2
Spanish Fort B5
Springville C2
Stevenson D1
Sulligent A2
Sumiton B2
Sylacauga C2
Talladega C2
Tallassee D3
Taylor D4
Theodore A5
Thomasville B4
Thorsby C3
Tillmans Corner A5
Town Creek B1
Trinity B1
Troy D4
Trussville C2
Tuscaloosa B2
Tuscumbia B1
Tuskegee D3
Union Springs D3
Uniontown B3
Valley D3
Vernon A2
Vestavia Hills C2
Vincent C2
Warrior C2
Weaver D2
Wedowee D2
West Blocton B2
Wetumpka C3
Winfield B2
York A3

Other Features
Alabama, *river* B4
Appalachian, *mts.* D1
Bear Creek, *reservoir* B1
Black Warrior, *river* B3
Bon Secour, *bay* B5
Cahaba, *river* B3
Cheaha, *mt.* D2
Conecuh, *river* C4
Coosa, *river* D1
Dauphin, *island* A5
Guntersville, *lake* C1
Jordan, *lake* C3
Lewis Smith, *lake* B1
Logan Morgan, *lake* C2
Lookout, *mt.* D1
Martin, *lake* D3
Mitchell, *lake* C3
Mobile, *bay* A5
Neely Henry, *lake* C2
Pickwick, *lake* A1
R.L. Harris, *reservoir* D2
Russell Cave Natl. Monument D1
Tallapoosa, *river* D2
Tennessee, *river* A1
Tombigbee, *river* A4
Tuscaloosa, *lake* B2
Tuskegee Institute Natl. Hist. Site D3
Weiss, *lake* D1
Wheeler, *lake* B1
William "Bill" Dannelly, *reservoir* B3
Wilson, *lake* B1

Alaska ... page 129

Cities and Towns
Adak Inset
Anchorage F2
Barrow D1
Bethel C2
Big Delta F2
College F2
Cordova F2
Craig J3
Delta Jct. F2
Dillingham D3
Fairbanks F2
Haines H3
Homer E3
Juneau, *capital* J3
Kenai E2
Ketchikan J3
Kodiak E3
Kotzebue C1
McKinley Park F2
Metlakatla J3
Nikiski E2
Nome B2
North Pole F2
Palmer F2
Petersburg J3
Prudhoe Bay F1
Seward F2
Sitka H3
Skagway H3
Soldotna E2
Talkeetna E2
Tok G2
Unalaska B4
Valdez F2
Wasilla F2
Whittier F2
Wrangell J3

Other Features
Adak, *island* Inset
Admiralty Island Natl. Monument J3
Agattu, *island* Inset
Alaska, *gulf* F3
Alaska, *peninsula* C3
Alaska, *range* E2
Aleutian, *islands* A4, Inset
Alexander, *archipelago* H3
Amchitka, *island* Inset
Amlia, *island* Inset
Andreanof, *islands* Inset
Aniakchak N.M. and Preserve D3
Atka, *island* Inset
Attu, *island* Inset
Barrow, *point* D1
Beaufort, *sea* H1
Becharof, *lake* D3
Bering, *sea* B3
Bering, *strait* B2
Blackburn, *mt.* G2
Bristol, *bay* C3
Brooks, *range* D1
Cape Krusenstern N.M. C1
Chirikof, *island* D3
Chukchi, *sea* A1
Colville, *river* E1
Cook, *inlet* E3
Copper, *river* G2
Denali Natl. Park and Preserve E2
Fairweather, *mt.* H3
Gates of the Arctic N.P. and Preserve E1
Glacier Bay N.P. and Preserve H3
Iliamna, *lake* D3
Inside Passage, *waterway* J3
Kanaga, *island* Inset
Katmai Natl. Park and Preserve D3
Kenai, *peninsula* E2
Kenai Fjords Natl. Park F3
Kiska, *island* Inset
Klondike Gold Rush N.H.P H3
Kobuk, *river* D1
Kobuk Valley Natl. Park D1
Kodiak, *island* E3
Kotzebue, *sound* C1
Koyukuk, *river* D1
Kuskokwim, *bay* C3
Kuskokwim, *mts.* D2
Kuskokwim, *river* D2
Lake Clark Natl. Park and Preserve E2
Lisburne, *cape* B1
Lisburne, *peninsula* C1
Logan, *mt.* G2
Lynn, *canal* J3
McKinley, *mt.* E2
Malaspina, *glacier* G3
Michelson, *mt.* G1
Mohican, *cape* B2
Muir, *glacier* F2
Near, *islands* Inset
Noatak, *river* D1
Norton, *sound* C2
Nunivak, *island* B3
Porcupine, *river* G1
Pribilof, *islands* B3
Prince of Wales, *island* J3
Progromni, *volcano* C4
Rat, *islands* Inset
St. Elias, *mt.* G2
St. George, *island* B3
St. Lawrence, *island* A2
St. Matthew, *island* A2
St. Paul, *island* A3
Samalga, *pass* B4
Sanak, *island* C4
Seguam, *island* Inset
Semisopochnoi, *island* Inset
Seward, *peninsula* C1
Shishaldin, *volcano* C4
Shumagin, *islands* D4
Sitka N.H.P. H3
Stikine, *river* J3
Tanaga, *island* F3
Tanana, *river* E2
Tikchik, *lakes* D2
Trinity, *islands* E3
Umnak, *island* Inset
Unalaska, *island* B4
Unga, *island* C3
Unimak, *island* C4
Utukok, *river* C1
White Mts. Natl. Rec. Area F1
Wrangell, *mts.* G2
Wrangell-St. Elias N.P. and Preserve G2
Yukon, *river* D2
Yukon-Charley Rivers Natl. Preserve G2
Yunaska, *island* Inset

Arizona ... page 130

Cities and Towns
Ajo C5
Apache Junction D4
Avondale C4
Bagdad B3
Benson E6
Bisbee F6
Bitahochee E2
Buckeye C4
Bullhead City A2
Camp Verde D3
Carefree D4
Casa Grande D5
Catalina E5
Cave Creek D4
Chandler D4
Chinle F1
Chino Valley C3
Cibecue E3
Clarkdale C3
Claypool E4
Clifton F4
Colorado City C1
Coolidge D5
Cornville D3
Cow Springs E1
Crown King C3
Douglas F6
Dudleyville E5
Eagar F3
El Mirage C4
Eloy D5
Flagstaff D2
Florence D4
Fort Defiance F2
Fountain Hills D4
Ganado F2
Geronimo E4
Gila Bend C5
Gilbert D4
Globe E4
Goodyear C4
Grand Canyon C1
Greaterville E6
Green Valley E6
Guthrie F5
Happy Jack D3
Holbrook E3
Huachuca City E6
Kayenta E1
Kearny E4
Kingman A2
Kirkland Junction C3
Lake Havasu City A3
Lake Montezuma D3
Litchfield Park C4
Mammoth E5
Many Farms F1
Marana D5
Mesa D4
Miami E4
Nogales E6
Oracle E5
Oro Valley E5
Page D1
Paradise Valley D4
Parker A3
Payson D3
Peoria C4
Phoenix, *capital* C4
Pima F5
Pinetop-Lakeside F3
Prescott C3
Prescott Valley C3
Quartzsite A4
Queen Creek D4
Randolph D5
Sacaton D4
Safford F5
Sahuarita E6
St. David E6
St. Johns F3
San Carlos E4
Sanders F2
San Manuel E5
Scottsdale D4
Sedona D3
Sells D6
Show Low E3
Sierra Vista E6
Snowflake E3
Somerton A5
South Tucson E5
Springerville F3
Sun City C4
Sun Lakes D4
Superior D4
Surprise C4
Taylor E3
Tempe D4
Thatcher F5
Three Points D5
Tolleson C4
Tombstone E6
Tuba City D1
Tucson E5
Whiteriver F4
Wickenburg C4
Willcox F5
Williams C2
Window Rock F2
Winslow E3
Yuma A5

Other Features
Agua Fria, *river* C4
Alamo, *lake* B3
Apache, *lake* D4
Aztec Peak, *mt.* E4
Baldy, *mt.* F4
Bartlett, *reservoir* D4
Big Horn, *mts.* B4
Bill Williams, *river* A3
Black, *mesa* E1
Black, *river* E4
Canyon De Chelly N.M. F1
Casa Grande Ruins N.M. D5
Castle Dome, *mts.* A4
Castle Dome Peak, *mt.* A4
Chiricahua Natl. Monument F6
Colorado, *river* B2, D1
Coronado Natl. Mem. E6
Gila, *river* B5, D4, F4
Glen Canyon, *dam* D1
Glen Canyon Natl. Rec. Area D1
Grand, *canyon* C2
Grand Canyon Natl. Park B2, C1
Grand Canyon-Parashant N.M. B1
Harcuvar, *mts.* B4
Havasu, *lake* A3
Hide Creek, *mt.* C3
Hoover, *dam* A1
Hopi Indian Res. E2
Horseshoe, *reservoir* D4
Hualapai, *mt.* B2
Hubbell Trading Post N.H.S. F2
Humphreys Peak, *mt.* D2
Lake Mead Natl. Rec. Area B1
Little Colorado, *river* D2
Many Farms, *lake* F1
Maple Peak, *mt.* F4
Mazatzal Peak, *mt.* D3
Mohave, *lake* A2
Montezuma Castle N.M. D3
Monument, *valley* F1
Mormon, *lake* D3
Navajo Indian Res. E1, E2
Navajo Natl. Monument E1
Organ Pipe Cactus N.M. C5
Painted, *desert* D2
Parker, *dam* A3
Petrified Forest Natl. Park F3
Pipe Spring Natl. Monument C1
Pleasant, *lake* C4
Point Imperial, *mt.* D1
Powell, *lake* D1
Red, *lake* B1
Saguaro Natl. Monument E5
Salt, *river* E4
San Carlos, *lake* E4
San Pedro, *river* E5
Santa Cruz, *river* D5
Sonoran, *desert* B5
Sunset Crater Volcano N.M. D2
Theodore Roosevelt, *lake* D4
Tipton, *mt.* A2
Tonto Natl. Monument D4
Trumbull, *mt.* B1
Tumacacori Natl Hist. Park D6
Tuzigoot Natl. Monument C3
Ventana, *cave* C5
Verde, *river* D3
Virgin, *river* A1
Walnut Canyon Natl. Monument D2
White, *mts.* F4
White House, *ruin* F1
Wupatki Natl. Monument D2
Yuma, *desert* A5

Arkansas ... page 131

Cities and Towns
Alicia D2
Alma A2
Arkadelphia B3
Arkansas City D4
Ashdown A4
Ash Flat D1
Atkins C2
Augusta D2
Bald Knob D2
Barling A2
Batesville D2
Bay E2
Beebe D2
Bella Vista A1
Benton C3
Bentonville A1
Berryville B1
Blytheville F2
Bodcaw B4
Booneville B2
Brinkley D3
Bryant C3
Bull Shoals C1
Cabot D3
Camden C4
Caraway E2
Carlisle D3
Cave City D2
Charleston A2
Clarendon D3
Clarksville B2
Clinton C2
Conway C2
Corning E1
Crossett D4
Daisy B3
Damascus C2
Danville B2
Dardanelle B2
De Queen A3
Dermott D4
Des Arc D3
De Valls Bluff D3
De Witt D3
Dierks A3
Dumas D4
Earle E2
El Dorado C4
England D3
Eudora D4
Eureka Springs B1
Fairfield Bay C2
Fallsville B2
Farmington A1
Fayetteville A1
Fordyce C4
Foreman A4
Forrest City E2
Fort Smith A2
Fountain Hill D4
Gentry A1
Glenwood B3
Gosnell F2
Gould D4
Gravette A1
Greenbrier C2
Green Forest B1
Greenwood A2
Griffithville D2
Gurdon B4
Hamburg D4
Hampton C4
Harrisburg E2
Harrison B1
Haskell C3
Hatfield A3
Hazen D3
Heber Springs C2
Helena E3
Hope B4
Horseshoe Bend D1
Hot Springs National Park B3
Hot Springs Village B3
Hoxie E1
Hughes E3
Hunter D2
Huntsville B1
Jacksonville C3
Jasper B1
Jonesboro E2
Lake City E2
Lake Hamilton B3
Lake Village D4
Lepanto E2
Lewisville B4
Lincoln A1
Little Rock, *capital* C3
Lonoke D3
Luxora F2
McCrory D2
McGehee D4
McNeil B4
McRae D2
Magnolia B4
Malvern C3
Manila E2
Marianna E3
Marion E2
Marked Tree E2
Marshall C2
Marvell E3
Maumelle C3
Mayflower C3
Melbourne D1
Mena A3
Monticello D4
Morrilton C2
Mountain Home C1
Mountain View C2
Mount Ida B3
Mulberry A2
Murfreesboro B3
Nashville B4
Newport D2
North Crossett D4
North Little Rock C3
Oden B3
Osceola F2
Ozark B2
Paragould E1
Paris B2
Parkin E2
Pea Ridge A1
Pelsor B2
Perryville C2
Piggott E1
Pine Bluff D3
Pocahontas E1
Prescott B4
Rector E1
Rison C4
Rogers A1
Rose Bud C2
Russell D2
Russellville B2
St. Charles D3
St. Paul B2
Salem D1
Searcy D2
Sheridan C3
Sherwood C3
Siloam Springs A1
Smackover C4
Springdale A1
Springhill B4
Star City D4
Stuttgart D3
Texarkana A4
Tillar D4
Trumann E2
Tuckerman D2
Tupelo D2
Van Buren A2
Waldo B4
Waldron A3
Walnut Ridge E1
Warren C4
Washington B4
West Fork A2
West Helena E3
West Memphis E2
White Hall C3
Wynne E2
Yellville C1

Other Features
Arkansas, *river* D3
Arkansas Post Natl. Mem. D3
Beaver, *lake* B1
Black, *river* D2
Boston, *mts.* B2
Buffalo, *river* B1
Buffalo Natl. River C2
Bull Shoals, *lake* C1
Cache, *river* E2
Catherine, *lake* C3
Dardanelle, *reservoir* B2
DeGray, *lake* B3
Erling, *lake* B4
Fort Smith Natl. Hist Site A2
Greers Ferry, *lake* C2
Greeson, *lake* B3
Hamilton, *lake* B3
Hot Springs Natl. Park B3
Little Missouri, *river* B4
Little Rock Central H.S N.H.S. C3
Magazine, *mt.* B2
Maumelle, *lake* C3
Millwood, *lake* B4
Mississippi, *river* E3
Nimrod, *lake* B3
Norfork, *lake* C1
Ouachita, *lake* B3
Ouachita, *mts.* A3
Ouachita, *river* B3, C4
Ozark, *plateau* B1
Pea Ridge Natl. Mil. Park A1
Red, *river* B4
St. Francis, *river* E1
Saline, *river* C3
Table Rock, *lake* B1
White, *river* C2, D3

California ... page 132

Cities and Towns
Adelanto H8
Alameda K2
Alamo L2
Albany K1
Alhambra D10
Alpine J10
Altadena D10
Alturas E1
Anaheim E11, H9
Anderson C2
Antioch D4, L1
Apple Valley H8
Aptos D5
Arcadia D10
Arcata A2
Arnold E4
Arroyo Grande E7
Arvin G7
Ashland K2
Atascadero E7
Atherton K3
Atwater E5
Auberry F5
Auburn E4
Avalon G9
Avenal E6
Azusa E10
Bakersfield G7
Baldwin Park E10
Barstow H8
Bell D10
Bellflower D11
Belmont K3
Belvedere J1
Benicia K1
Berkeley C5, K2
Beverly Hills C10
Big Bear Lake J8
Bishop G5
Black Point J1
Blythe L9
Bonita C9
Boron H8

Key

Borrego Springs J9
Brawley K10
Brea E11
Bridgeport F4
Brisbane J2
Broadmoor J2
Buellton E8
Buena Park E11
Burbank C10
Burlingame J3
Burney D2
Buttonwillow F7
Calabasas B10
Calexico K10
California City H7
Calipatria K9
Calistoga C4
Cambria D7
Campbell L4
Canyon K2
Carlsbad H9
Carmel D6
Carmel Valley D6
Carpinteria F8
Carson D11
Castroville D6
Cathedral City J9
Cayucos E7
Central Valley C2
Ceres E5
Chester D2
Chico D3
Chino F10
Chowchilla E5
Chula Vista C9, H10
Claremont F10
Clayton L1
Clearlake C4
Cloverdale B4
Clovis F6
Clyde L1
Coachella J9
Coalinga E6
Cobb C4
Colfax E3
Colusa D3
Compton D11
Concord L1
Corcoran F6
Corning C3
Corona F11
Coronado B8
Corte Madera J1
Costa Mesa E11
Cottonwood C2
Covina E10
Cowan Heights E11
Crescent City A1
Crestline H8
Crockett K1
Culver City C10
Cupertino L4
Cypress D11
Daly City J2
Danville L2
Davis D4
Delano F7
Del Mar H10
Desert Hot Springs J9
Diablo L2
Diamond Bar E10
Dinuba F6
Dos Palos E6
Downey D11
Downieville E3
Dublin L2
Dunsmuir C1
Earlimart F7
East Los Angeles D10
Easton F6
East Palo Alto K3
El Cajon C8, J10
El Centro K10
El Cerrito K1
El Granada J3
Elk Grove D4
El Monte D10
El Segundo C11
El Sobrante K1
Emeryville K2
Encinitas H9
Escondido H9
Eureka A2
Exeter F6
Fairfax H1
Fairfield D4
Fallbrook H9
Ferndale A2
Firebaugh E6
Florence D11
Florin D4
Fort Bragg B3
Fortuna A2
Foster City K3
Fountain Valley E11
Frazier Park G8
Fremont D5, L3
Fresno F6
Fullerton E11
Galt D4
Garden Grove E11
Gilroy D5
Glendale D10, G8
Glendora E10
Glenview B10
Gonzales D6
Grass Valley D3
Greenacres F7
Greenbrae J1
Greenfield D6
Greenville E2
Gridley D3
Groveland E5
Guadalupe E8
Half Moon Bay J3
Hanford F6
Hawthorne C11
Hayfork B2
Hayward C5, L2
Healdsburg C4
Hemet J9
Hercules K1
Hermosa Beach C11
Hesperia H8
Hidden Hills B10
Hillsborough J3
Hollister D6
Holtville K10
Huntington Beach E11, G9
Huron E6
Ignacio J1
Imperial Beach B9, H10

Key

Independence G6
Indio J9
Inglewood C11, G9
Ingot C2
Inyokern H7
Ione E4
Irvine E11, H9
Isla Vista F8
Jackson E4
Joshua Tree J8
Julian J9
Kelseyville C4
Kensington K1
Kentfield J1
Kerman E6
Kernville G7
Kettleman City F6
King City D6
La Canada-Flintridge D10
La Crescenta D10
Lafayette K1
La Habra E11
La Honda K4
Lake Isabella G7
Lakeport C3
Lakeside J10
Lakewood D11
La Mesa C8
La Mirada D11
Lamont G7
Lancaster G8
La Puente E10
Larkspur J1
Laton F6
Lawndale C11
Lee Vining F5
Lemon Grove C8
Lemoore F6
Lincoln D4
Lindsay F6
Littlerock H8
Livermore D5
Livingston E5
Lockeford D4
Lodi D4
Loma Mar K4
Lomita C11
Lompoc E8
Lone Pine G6
Long Beach D11, G9
Los Altos K3
Los Altos Hills K4
Los Angeles D10, G8
Los Banos E5
Los Molinos C2
Los Osos E7
Lynwood D11
McCloud C1
McFarland F7
McKinleyville A2
Madera E6
Malibu B10
Mammoth Lakes G5
Manhattan Beach C11
Manteca D5
Marina D6
Marina del Rey C11
Marin City J1
Marinwood J1
Mariposa F5
Markleeville F4
Martinez C4, K1
Marysville D3
Maywood D10
Mecca J9
Mendota E6
Menlo Park K3
Merced E5
Midway City E11
Millbrae J3
Mill Valley J1
Milpitas L3
Miranda B2
Modesto E5
Mojave G7
Monrovia E10
Montara J3
Montclair F10
Montebello D10
Monte Nido B10
Monterey D6
Monterey Park D10
Monte Sereno L4
Moraga K2
Moreno Valley H9
Morgan Hill D5
Morongo Valley J8
Morro Bay E7
Moss Beach J3
Mountain View K3
Mount Shasta C1
Muir Beach H1
Napa C4
National City C9
Needles L8
Nevada City D3
Newark L3
Newberry Springs J8
Newport Beach H9
Nicasio H1
Nice C3
Nipomo E7
Nipton K7
Norco F11
North Edwards H7
North Fair Oaks K3
Novato H1
Oakdale E5
Oakhurst F5
Oakland K2, C5
Oceanside H9
Oildale F7
Ojai F8
Olema H1
Olivehurst D3
Ontario F10, H8
Orange E11
Orinda K1
Orland C3
Oroville D3
Otay C9
Oxnard F8
Pacheco L1
Pacifica J2
Palermo D3
Palmdale G8
Palm Desert J9
Palm Springs J9
Palo Alto K3
Palos Verdes Estates C11
Paradise D3
Pasadena D10, G8

Key

Patterson D5
Petaluma C4
Pico Rivera D10
Piedmont K2
Pine Valley J10
Pinole K1
Pismo Beach E7
Pittsburg L1
Placentia E11
Placerville E4
Pleasant Hill L1
Pleasanton L2
Pomona E10, H8
Port Costa K1
Porterville G6
Portola E3
Poway H10
Prunedale D6
Quartz Hill G8
Quincy E3
Ramona J9
Rancho Cucamonga F10
Rancho Palos Verdes C11
Rancho Rinconada L4
Rancho Santa Margarita F11
Red Bluff C2
Redding C2
Redlands H8
Redondo Beach C11
Redwood City C5, K3
Reedley F6
Richgrove F7
Richmond J1
Ridgecrest H7
Rio Dell A2
Riverside H9
Rodeo K1
Rolling Hills C11
Rolling Hills Estates C11
Rosamond G8
Roseville D4
Sacramento, *capital* D4
Salinas D6
San Andreas E4
San Anselmo H1
San Bernardino H8
San Bruno J2
San Carlos K3
San Clemente H9
San Diego B8, H10
San Francisco C5, J2
San Gabriel D10
Sanger F6
San Gregorio J4
San Jose D5, L4
San Juan Bautista D6
San Juan Capistrano H9
San Leandro K2
San Lorenzo K2
San Luis Obispo E7
San Mateo C5, K3
San Pablo J1
San Quentin J1
San Rafael C5, J1
San Ramon L2
Santa Ana E11, H9
Santa Barbara F8
Santa Clara L4
Santa Clarita G8
Santa Cruz C6
Santa Maria E8
Santa Monica C10
Santa Paula F8
Santa Rosa C4
Santa Venetia J1
Santa Ynez E8
Santee C8
Saratoga L4
Sausalito J2
Scotts Valley C5
Seal Beach D11
Sebastopol C4
Selma F6
Shafter F7
Shingletown D2
Shoshone J7
Simi Valley G8
Soledad D6
Solvang E8
Sonoma C4
Sonora E5
South Lake Tahoe F4
South San Francisco J2
Spring Valley C8
Squaw Valley F6
Stanford K3
Stinson Beach H1
Stockton D5
Sunnyvale C5, L4
Sunol L3
Sunset Beach D11
Susanville E2
Taft F7
Tamalpais Valley J1
Tehachapi G7
Temecula H9
Templeton E7
Terra Bella F7
Thermalito D3
Thousand Oaks G8
Tiburon J1
Tipton F6
Topanga B10
Torrance C11, G9
Tracy D5
Truckee E3
Tulare F6
Turlock E5
Tustin E11
Twain Harte E4
Twentynine Palms J8
Ukiah B3
Union City L3
Upland F10
Vacaville D4
Vallejo C4, K1
Vandenberg Village E8
Ventucopa F8
Ventura F8
Victorville H8
Villa Park E11
Vine Hill K1
Visalia F6
Vista H9
Walnut E10
Walnut Creek L1
Wasco F7
Watsonville D6
Weaverville C2
Weed C1
West Covina E10
West Hollywood C10

Key

Westminster E11
Westmorland K9
West Pittsburg L1
Westwood E2
Wheatland D3
Whittier D10
Willits B3
Willow Creek B2
Willows C3
Windsor C4
Wofford Heights G7
Woodlake F6
Woodland D4
Woodside K3
Wrightwood H8
Yorba Linda E11
Yosemite Village F5
Yreka C1
Yuba City D3
Yucaipa H8
Yucca Valley J8
Zenia B2

Other Features

Alameda, *river* L3
Alcatraz, *island* J2
Allison, *mt.* L3
Almanor, *lake* D2
Amargosa, *range* J6
Amargosa, *river* J7
Angel, *island* J1
Balboa, *park* B8
Berryessa, *lake* C4
Boundary, *peak* G5
Bullion, *mts.* J8
Cascade, *range* D1
Central, *valley* C2
Chabot, *lake* K2
Channel, *islands* F9
Channel Islands Natl. Park E9, F9
Chatsworth, *reservoir* B10
Chino, *river* F10
Chocolate, *mts.* K9
Clair Engle, *lake* C1
Clear, *lake* C3
Clear Lake, *reservoir* D1
Coast, *ranges* C2, D6
Colorado, *desert* J9
Colorado, *river* L9
Cucamonga, *river* F11
Death, *valley* H6
Death Valley Natl. Park H6
Devils Postpile Natl. Monument F5
Diablo, *mt.* L1
Eagle, *lake* E2
Eagle, *peak* E1
Eel, *river* B2
Estero, *bay* E7
Eugene O'Neill Natl. Hist. Site K2
Farallon, *islands* B5
Farallones, *gulf* H2
Giant Sequoia Natl. Mon. F6, G6
Golden Gate Natl. Rec. Area C5, J2
Goose, *lake* E1
Grizzly, *bay* L1
Half Moon, *bay* J3
Honey, *lake* E2
Humboldt, *bay* A2
Imperial, *valley* K9
Inyo, *mts.* H6
Irvine, *lake* F11
Joshua Tree Natl. Park K8
Kern, *river* G6
Kings, *river* F6
Kings Canyon Natl. Park G5
Klamath, *mts.* B1
Klamath, *river* B1
Lanfair, *valley* K7
Lassen, *peak* D2
Lassen Volcanic Natl. Park D2
Lava Beds Natl. Monument D1
McCoy, *mts.* L9
Mad, *river* B2
Manzanar Natl. Hist. Site G6
Merced, *river* E5
Middle Alkali, *lake* F1
Mission, *bay* B8
Mission Bay, *park* B8
Mojave, *desert* H7
Mojave, *river* J8
Mono, *lake* G4
Monterey, *bay* D6
Morgan, *mt.* G5
Morris, *reservoir* E10
Muir Woods Natl. Monument H1
Nacimiento, *reservoir* D7
Napa, *river* K1
Nicasio, *reservoir* H1
Old Woman, *mts.* K8
Oroville, *reservoir* D3
Otay, *river* C9
Panamint, *range* H6
Panamint, *valley* H6
Pescadero, *river* J4
Pinnacles Natl. Monument D6
Point Reyes Natl. Seashore B4
Redwood Natl. Park A1
Ritter, *mt.* F5
Sacramento, *river* C3
Salton, *sea* K9
San Antonio, *reservoir* D7
San Bernardino, *mts.* J8
San Clemente, *island* G10
San Diego, *bay* B9
San Diego, *river* B8
San Fernando, *valley* B10
San Francisco, *bay* J2
San Gabriel, *mts.* G8
San Gabriel, *reservoir* E10
San Joaquin, *river* E5
San Luis Obispo, *bay* E7
San Miguel, *island* E8
San Nicolas, *island* F9
San Pablo, *bay* J1
San Rafael, *mts.* F8
Santa Ana, *mts.* F11
Santa Barbara, *channel* E8
Santa Barbara, *island* F9
Santa Catalina, *island* G9
Santa Cruz, *island* F8
Santa Cruz, *mts.* J3
Santa Lucia, *range* D6
Santa Monica, *bay* B11
Santa Monica, *mts.* B10
Santa Monica Mts. N.R.A. B10
Santa Rosa, *island* E9
Santa Rosa and San Jacinto Mountains N.M. J9
Santiago, *river* F11
Sequoia Natl. Park G6
Shasta, *lake* C2
Shasta, *mt.* C1

Key

Sierra, *peak* F11
Sierra Nevada, *range* D3, G5
Siskiyou, *mts.* B1
Smith River N.R.A. B1
Tahoe, *lake* E3
Tehachapi, *mts.* G8
Telescope, *peak* H6
Trinity, *river* B2
Tule, *river* F6
Turtle, *mts.* L8
Upper, *lake* E1
Upper San Leandro, *reservoir* L2
Vizcaino, *cape* B3
Whiskeytown-Shasta-Trinity N.R.A. D1
White, *mts.* G5
Whitney, *mt.* G6
Wilson, *mt.* D10
Yosemite Natl. Park F5

Colorado ..... page 133

Cities and Towns

Akron G1
Alamosa E4
Arvada E2
Aspen D2
Aurora F2
Avon D2
Bennett F2
Berthoud E1
Black Forest F2
Boulder E1
Breckenridge D2
Brighton F2
Broomfield E2
Brush G1
Buena Vista D3
Burlington H2
Canon City E3
Carbondale C2
Castle Rock F2
Cedaredge C3
Center D4
Central City E2
Cheyenne Wells H3
Clifton B2
Colorado Springs F3
Conejos D4
Cortez B4
Craig C1
Crawford C3
Creede D4
Cripple Creek E3
Dacono F1
Del Norte D4
Delta B3
Denver, *capital* F2
Dinosaur A1
Dove Creek B4
Durango C4
Eads H3
Eagle D2
Eaton F1
Englewood F2
Estes Park E1
Evans F1
Evergreen E2
Fairplay E2
Florence E3
Fort Collins E1
Fort Lupton F1
Fort Morgan G1
Fountain F3
Frisco D2
Fruita B2
Fruitvale B2
Georgetown E2
Glenwood Springs C2
Golden E2
Grand Junction B2
Greeley F1
Gunnison D3
Gypsum D2
Haswell G3
Hayden C1
Holyoke H1
Hot Sulphur Springs D1
Hugo G2
Idaho Springs E2
Johnstown F1
Julesburg H1
Keota F1
Kiowa F2
Kit Carson H3
Lafayette E2
La Junta G4
Lake City C3
Lakewood E2
Lamar H3
Las Animas G3
Leadville D2
Limon G2
Littleton F2
Longmont E1
Louisville E2
Loveland E1
Manitou Springs F3
Meeker C1
Milliken F1
Monte Vista D4
Montrose C3
Niwot E1
Northglenn F2
Olathe C3
Orchard City C3
Orchard Mesa B2
Ordway G3
Ouray C3
Pagosa Springs C4
Palisade B2
Palmer Lake F2
Paonia C3
Parker F2
Platteville F1
Pritchett H4
Pueblo F3
Pueblo West F3
Rangely B1
Rifle C2
Rocky Ford G3
Saguache D3
Salida E3
San Luis E4
Security F3
Silverthorne D2
Silverton C4
Snowmass Village D2
Springfield H4
Steamboat Springs D1
Sterling G1
Telluride C4

Key

Thornton F2
Trinidad F4
Vail D2
Vilas H4
Walden D1
Walsenburg F4
Wellington E1
Westcliffe E3
Westminster E2
Wheat Ridge F2
Wiley H3
Windsor F1
Woodland Park E3
Wray H1
Yuma H1

Other Features

Animas, *river* C4
Apishapa, *river* F4
Arapahoe, *peak* E1
Arapaho Natl. Rec. Area E1
Arikaree, *river* G2
Arkansas, *river* F3
Bent's Old Fort Natl. Hist. Site G3
Black Canyon of the Gunnison Natl. Park C3
Blanca, *peak* E4
Blue Mesa, *reservoir* C3
Bonny, *reservoir* H2
Canyons of the Ancients N.M. B4
Castle, *peak* D2
Colorado, *plateau* A4
Colorado, *river* C2
Colorado Natl. Monument B2
Crestone, *peak* E4
Cucharas, *river* F4
Curecanti Natl. Rec. Area C3
Dinosaur Natl. Monument B1
Dolores, *river* B3
Elbert, *mt.* D2
Eolus, *mt.* C4
Evans, *mt.* E2
Florissant Fossil Beds N.M. E3
Front, *range* E1
Great Sand Dunes N.P. E4
Green, *river* B1
Gunnison, *mt.* C3
Gunnison, *river* B3
Hovenweep Natl. Monument B4
John Martin, *reservoir* G3
Laramie, *mts.* E1
Laramie, *river* E1
Little Snake, *river* B1
Longs, *peak* E1
Mancos, *river* B4
Medicine Bow, *mts.* D1
Mesa Verde Natl. Park B4
Montezuma, *peak* D4
North Fork Cimarron, *river* H4
North Fork Smoky Hill, *river* H2
North Platte, *river* D1
Park, *range* D1
Pikes, *peak* E3
Purgatoire, *river* G4
Rio Grande, *river* E4
Roan, *plateau* B2
Rocky, *mts.* D1
Rocky Mt. Natl. Park E1
Royal Gorge, *canyon* E3
Sand Creek Massacre N.H.S. H3
Sangre de Cristo, *mts.* E3
San Juan, *mts.* C4
San Luis, *valley* E4
Sawatch, *range* D2
South Fork Republican, *river* G2
South Platte, *river* E2, G1
Uncompahgre, *peak* C3
U.S. Air Force Academy F3
White, *river* B1
Wilson, *mt.* B4
Yampa, *river* B1
Yucca House Natl. Monument B4
Zirkel, *mt.* D1

Connecticut ..... page 134

Cities and Towns

Abington G2
Andover F3
Ansonia C4
Attawaugan H2
Avon D2
Bakersville C2
Ballouville H2
Baltic G3
Beacon Falls C4
Berkshire B4
Berlin E3
Bethany C4
Bethel B4
Bethlehem C3
Black Point G4
Bloomfield E2
Blue Hills E2
Boardman Bridge B3
Bolton F2
Botsford B4
Branford D4
Bridgeport C5
Bridgewater B3
Bristol D3
Broad Brook E2
Brookfield B4
Brookfield Center B4
Brooklyn H2
Burlington D2
Burrville C2
Cannondale B5
Canterbury H3
Canton D2
Canton Center D2
Centerbrook F4
Central Village H3
Chaplin G2
Cheshire D4
Chester F4
Chesterfield G4
Clarks Falls H4
Clinton E4
Colchester F3
Colebrook C2
Collinsville D2
Columbia F3
Cornwall B2
Cornwall Bridge B2
Coventry F2
Cromwell E3
Danbury B4
Danielson H2
Darien B5
Dayville H2

Key

Deep River F4
Derby C4
Durham E4
Eagleville F2
East Brooklyn H2
Eastford G2
East Glastonbury E3
East Granby E2
East Haddam F4
East Hampton E3
East Hartford E2
East Hartland D2
East Haven D4
East Killingly H2
East Litchfield C2
East Lyme G4
Easton B5
East Thompson H1
East Village C4
East Woodstock H2
Ellington F2
Enfield E2
Essex F4
Fairfield B5
Falls Village B2
Farmington D3
Fitchman G3
Flanders B3
Franklin G3
Gales Ferry G4
Gaylordsville B3
Georgetown B5
Gilead F3
Gilman G3
Glasgo H3
Glastonbury E3
Goodrich Heights E3
Goshen C2
Granby D2
Greenwich A5
Grosvenor Dale H2
Groton G4
Groton Long Point G4
Guilford E4
Gurleyville G2
Haddam E4
Haddam Neck E3
Hadlyme F4
Hamburg F4
Hamden D4
Hampton G2
Hanover G3
Hartford, *capital* E3
Harwinton C2
Hawleyville B4
Hazardville E2
Hebron F3
Higganum E4
Hotchkissville C3
Indian Neck D5
Jewett City H3
Kensington D3
Killingworth F4
Knollcrest B4
Knollwood F4
Lake Pocotopaug E3
Lakeside C3
Lakeside C4
Laysville F4
Lebanon G3
Ledyard Center G4
Liberty Hill F3
Lime Rock B2
Litchfield C3
Lyons Plain B5
Madison E4
Manchester E2
Mansfield Center G3
Mansfield Four Corners F2
Marble Dale B3
Marion D3
Meriden D3
Merrow F2
Middlebury C3
Middlefield E3
Middle Haddam E3
Middletown E3
Milford C5
Mill Plain A4
Milton B2
Mohegan G4
Monroe C4
Montville G4
Moosup H3
Mystic H4
Naugatuck C4
New Britain D3
New Canaan B5
New Fairfield B4
New Hartford D2
New Haven D4
Newington E3
New London G4
New Milford B3
Newtown B4
Niantic G4
Noank H4
Norfolk C2
North Branford D4
North Canton D2
Northfield C3
Northford D4
North Franklin G3
North Grosvenor Dale H2
North Guilford E4
North Haven D4
North Stonington H4
Northville B3
North Westchester F3
North Windham G3
Norwalk B5
Norwich G3
Oakdale G4
Oakville C3
Old Lyme F4
Old Mystic H4
Old Saybrook F4
Oneco H3
Orange C4
Oxford C4
Park Lane B3
Pawcatuck H4
Perkins Corner F3
Phoenixville G2
Plainfield H3
Plainville D3
Plantsville D3
Pleasant Valley D2
Pleasure Beach G4
Plymouth C3
Pomfret H2
Poquetanuck G4
Poquonock E2
Poquonock Bridge G4
Portland E3
Preston City H3
Prospect D4
Putnam H2
Quaddick H2
Quaker Hill G4
Redding B4
Redding Ridge B4
Ridgebury A4
Ridgefield B4
Riverton C2
Robertsville C2
Rockfall E3
Rockville F2
Rocky Hill E3
Roxbury B3
Sachem Head E4
Salem F4
Salisbury B2
Scantic E2
Scitico E2
Scotland G3
Seymour C4
Sharon B2
Shelton C4
Sherman B3
Short Beach D5
Simsbury D2
Somers F2
Sound View F4
Southbury C4
South Canaan B2
South Chaplin G2
South Glastonbury E3
Southington D3
South Kent B3
South Killingly H2
South Willington F2
South Windham G3
South Windsor E2
Stafford F2
Stafford Springs F2
Staffordville F2
Stamford A5
Sterling H3
Stevenson C4
Stony Creek E4
Storrs F2
Straitsville C4
Stratford C5
Suffield E2
Taconic B1
Talcottville F2
Tariffville D2
Terryville C3
Thompson H2
Thompsonville E2
Tolland F2
Torrington C2
Trumbull C5
Uncasville G4
Union G2
Unionville D2
Vernon F2
Versailles G3
Voluntown H3
Wallingford D4
Warren B3
Warrenville G2
Washington B3
Washington Depot B3
Waterbury C3
Waterford G4
Watertown C3
Weatogue D2
Westbrook F4
West Cornwall B2
Westford G2
West Granby D2
West Hartford E2
West Hartland D1
West Haven D4
West Mystic H4
West Norfolk C1
Weston B5
Westport B5
West Redding B4
West Simsbury D2
West Stafford F2
West Suffield E2
West Willington F2
Wethersfield E3
Whigville D3
Willimantic G3
Wilton B5
Winchester Center C2
Windham G3
Windsor E2
Windsor Locks E2
Winsted C2
Winthrop F4
Wolcott D3
Woodbridge C4
Woodmont D5
Woodstock H2
Woodstock Valley G2
Woodville B3
Yalesville D4

Other Features

Appalachian Natl. Scenic Trail B2
Bantam, *lake* C3
Barkhamsted, *reservoir* D2
Candlewood, *lake* B4
Connecticut, *river* E4
Easton, *reservoir* B4
Farmington, *river* D3
Frissell, *mt.* B1
Gaillard, *lake* D4
Hammonasset, *river* E4
Hop, *river* F3
Housatonic, *river* B4
Long Island, *sound* D5
Mt. Hope, *river* G2
Natchaug, *river* G2
Naugatuck, *river* C4
Nepaug, *reservoir* D2
Norwalk, *islands* B5
Norwalk, *river* B5
Quinebaug, *river* H3
Saugatuck, *reservoir* B4
Shenipsit, *lake* F2
Shetucket, *river* G3
Thames, *river* G4
Waramaug, *lake* B3
Weir Farm Natl. Hist. Site B5
Willimantic, *river* F2
Yantic, *river* F3

Delaware ....page 135

Cities and Towns

Adamsville A3
Andrewville A3
Argos Corner B3
Blackbird A2
Broadkill Beach B3
Brookside A1
Burrsville A3
Camden A2
Cannon A3
Canterbury A2
Capitol Park A2
Clarksville B3
Claymont B1
Collins Park A1
Delaware City A1
Dover, *capital* A2
Edgemoor A1
Elsmere A1
Fairfax A1
Georgetown B3
Glasgow A1
Gumboro B4
Harbeson B3
Harrington A3
Hartley A2
Hazlettville A2
Hickman A3
Hockessin A1
Indian Beach B3
Jimtown B3
Kirkwood A1
Kitts Hummock B2
Laurel A3
Lewes B3
Lincoln B3
Little Heaven B2
Llangollen Estates A1
Lynch Heights B3
McClellandville A1
Marshallton A1
Marydel A2
Mastens Corner A3
Middletown A2
Midway B3
Milford B3
Millsboro B3
Milton B3
Nassau B3
Newark A1
New Castle A1
Oak Orchard B3
Owens A3
Petersburg A2
Pinetown B3
Primehook Beach B3
Reeves Crossing A3
Rehoboth Beach B3
Reliance A3
Rosedale Beach B3
Roxana B3
Sandtown A2
Seaford A3
Selbyville B4
Smyrna A2
Stanton A1
Swann Keys B4
Talleyville A1
Taylors Bridge A2
Whitesville B4
Williamsville A3
Williamsville B4
Wilmington A1
Wilmington Manor A1
Woodenhawk A3
Woodland Beach B2
Workmans Corners B3

Other Features

Broadkill, *river* B3
Chesapeake & Delaware, *canal* A1
Delaware, *bay* B2
Delaware, *river* A1
Henlopen, *cape* B3
Indian River, *bay* B3
Mispillion, *river* B3
Murderkill, *river* A3
Nanticoke, *river* A3
Rehoboth, *bay* B3
Smyrna, *river* A2

Florida ....page 136

Cities and Towns

Alachua C2
Altamonte Springs D3
Anna Maria C4
Apalachicola A2
Apollo Beach C4
Apopka D3
Arcadia D4
Archer C2
Astor D2
Atlantic Beach D1
Auburndale D3
Aventura B3
Avon Park D4
Baldwin D1
Bal Harbour B3
Bartow D4
Bay Harbor Islands B3
Bayonet Point C3
Bee Ridge C4
Belle Glade E5
Belleview C2
Beverly Hills C3
Big Pine Key D7
Biscayne Park A3
Blountstown A1
Boca Raton E5
Bonifay C6
Bonita Springs D5
Boynton Beach E5
Bradenton C4
Brandon C4
Bristol A1
Bronson C2
Brooksville C3
Buckhead Ridge E4
Bunnell D2
Bushnell C3
Callaway C6
Cape Canaveral E3
Cape Coral D5
Carol City A3, E6
Chattahoochee A1
Chiefland C2
Chipley C6
Clearwater C4
Clermont D3
Clewiston E5
Cocoa E3
Cocoa Beach E3
Coconut Grove A3
Cooper City A2
Coral Gables A3, E6
Coral Springs E5
Crawfordville A1
Crescent City D2
Crestview B6
Cross City B2
Crystal River C3
Dade City C3
Dania B2
Davie A2, E5
Daytona Beach D2
De Bary D3
Deerfield Beach E5
De Funiak Springs B6
De Land D2
Delray Beach E5
Deltona D3
Destin B6
Dunedin C3
Dunnellon C2
East Naples D5
Eastpoint A2
Edgewater E3
El Portal A3
Elfers C3
Englewood C5
Eustis D3
Fellsmere E4
Fernandina Beach D1
Flagler Beach D2
Florida City E6
Fort Lauderdale B2, E5
Fort Meade D4
Fort Myers D5
Fort Myers Beach D5
Fort Myers Villas D5
Fort Pierce E4
Fort Walton Beach B6
Frostproof D4
Gainesville C2
Gifford E4
Golden Gate D5
Gonzalez A6
Goulds E6
Greenacres City E5
Green Cove Springs D2
Gretna A1
Gulf Breeze A6
Haines City D3
Hallandale B3, E6
Havana A1
Hawthorne C2
Hialeah A3, E6
Hialeah Gardens A3
High Springs C2
Hilliard D1
Holiday C3
Holly Hill D2
Hollywood A3, E5
Holmes Beach C4
Homestead E6
Homosassa Springs C3
Hudson C3
Immokalee D5
Indian Harbour Beach E3
Indian Rocks Beach C4
Indiantown E4
Inverness C3
Jacksonville D1
Jacksonville Beach D1
Jasper C1
Jensen Beach E4
Jupiter E5
Kendall A4, E6
Key Biscayne B4
Key Largo E6
Keystone Heights C2
Key West D7
Kissimmee D3
La Belle D5
La Crosse C2
Lady Lake D3
Lake Buena Vista D3
Lake Butler C1
Lake City C1
Lakeland D3
Lake Mary D3
Lake Panasoffkee C3
Lake Wales D4
Lake Worth E5
Land O' Lakes C3
Lantana E5
Largo C4
Lauderdale Lakes A2
Lauderdale-by-the-Sea B2
Lauderhill A2
Lawtey C1
Layton E7
Leesburg D3
Live Oak C1
Longboat Key C4
Lutz C3
Lynn Haven C6
Macclenny C1
Madison B1
Marathon D7
Marco D6
Margate E5
Marianna C6
Marineland D2
Mayo B1
Merritt Island E3
Miami A3, E6
Miami Beach B3, E6
Miami Lakes A3, A5
Miami Shores A3, A5
Miami Springs A3, A5
Middleburg D1
Milton A6
Mims E3
Miramar A3, E6
Monticello B1
Moore Haven D5
Mount Dora D3
Naples D5
Naples Manor D5
Naples Park D5
Naranja E6
New Port Richey C3
New Smyrna Beach E2
Niceville B6
Noma C5
North Bay Village A3
North Fort Myers D5
North Miami A3, E6
North Miami Beach A3
North Naples D5
North Port C4
Oakland Park B2, E5
Ocala C2
Ocoee D3
Okeechobee E4
Oldsmar C3
Olympia Hts. A3
Opa-Locka A3
Orange City D3
Orange Park D1
Orlando D3
Ormond Beach D2
Ormond-by-the-Sea D2
Otter Creek C2
Oviedo D3
Pace A6
Pahokee E5
Palatka D2
Palm Bay E3
Palm Beach E5
Palm Beach Gardens E5
Palm Coast D2
Palmetto C4
Palm Harbor C3
Panama City C6
Pembroke Park A3
Pembroke Pines A3
Pennsuco A3
Pensacola A6
Perrine E6
Perry B1
Pierson D2
Pine Castle D3
Plantation A2, E5
Plant City C3
Polk City D3
Pomona Park D2
Port Charlotte C5
Port Orange E2
Port St. Joe C7
Port St. Lucie E4
Port Salerno E4
Punta Gorda C5
Quincy A1
Raiford C1
Ridge Manor C3
Riverview C4
Riviera Beach E5
Rockledge E3
Royal Palm Beach E5
St. Augustine D2
St. Augustine Shores D2
St. Cloud D3
St. Pete Beach C4
St. Petersburg C4
San Carlos Park D5
Sanford D3
Sanibel C5
Sarasota C4
Satellite Beach E3
Sebastian E4
Sebring D4
Silver Springs C2
Sneads A1
South Miami A3
South Venice C4
Springfield C6
Spring Hill C3
Starke C2
Stuart E4
Sunrise A2
Surfside B3
Sweetwater A3, E6
Tallahassee, *capital* A1
Tamarac A2, E5
Tampa C3
Tarpon Springs C3
Tavares D3
Tavernier E7
Temple Terrace C3
Titusville E3
Treasure Island C4
Trenton C2
Umatilla D3
Venice C4
Vero Beach E4
Vilano Beach D2
Virginia Gardens A3
Warrington A6
Wauchula D4
Webster C3
Weeki Wachee C3
Welaka D2
West Melbourne E3
West Miami A3
Weston A2
West Palm Beach E5
West Pensacola A6
Westwood Lakes A3
Wildwood C3
Williston C2
Wilton Manors B2
Winter Garden D3
Winter Haven D3
Winter Park D3
Woodville A1
Yulee D1
Zephyrhills C3

Other Features

Amelia, *island* D1
Apalachee, *bay* A2
Apalachicola, *bay* A2
Apalachicola, *river* A1
Aucilla, *river* B1
Big Cypress, *swamp* D5
Biscayne, *bay* B3, E6
Biscayne Natl. Park E6
Boca Chica Key, *island* D7
Caloosahatchee, *river* D5
Canaveral, *cape* E3
Canaveral Natl. Seashore E3
Castillo de San Marcos N.M. D2
Cedar Keys, *islands* B2
Charlotte, *harbor* C5
Chattahoochee, river A1
Choctawhatchee, *bay* B6
Crooked, *island* C6
De Soto Natl. Memorial C4
Deadman, *bay* B2
Dog, *island* A2
Dry Tortugas Natl. Park C7
Elliott Key, *island* E6
Escambia, *river* A5
Everglades, *swamp* A5, E6
Everglades Natl. Park E6
Fisher, *island* B3
Florida, *bay* E6
Florida, *straits* E7
Florida Keys, *islands* D7
Fort Caroline Natl. Memorial D1
Fort Matanzas Natl. Monument D2
Gasparilla, *island* C5
George, *lake* D2
Gulf Islands Natl. Seashore A6
Homosassa, *bay* C3
Indian, *river* B6
Iron, *mt.* D4
Istokpoga, *lake* D4
John F. Kennedy Space Center E3
Key Biscayne, *island* B3
Key Largo, *island* E6
Kissimmee, *lake* D4
Lochloosa, *lake* D2
Marquesas Keys, *islands* C7
Mexico, *gulf* B5, B6
Ochlockonee, *river* A1
Okeechobee, *lake* E5
Okefenokee, *swamp* C1
Peace, *river* D4
Pensacola, *bay* A6
Ponce de Leon, *bay* D6
Romano, *cape* D6
Sable, *cape* D6
St. Andrews, *bay* B6
St. George, *island* A2
St. Johns, *river* D2
St. Joseph, *bay* C7
St. Marys, *river* D1
St. Vincent, *island* A2
San Blas, *cape* C7
Sands Key, *island* E6
Sanibel, *island* C5
Santa Rosa, *island* A6
Seminole, *lake* A1
Sugarloaf Key, *island* D7
Suwannee, *river* C1, C2
Talquin, *lake* A1
Tamiami, *canal* A3
Tampa, *bay* C4
Virginia Key, *island* B3
Waccasassa, *bay* C2
Withlacoochee, *river* B1
Yellow, *river* A6

Georgia ....page 137

Cities and Towns

Abbeville E8
Adairsville B3
Adel E9
Alamo F7
Albany C8
Alma G8
Alpharetta C3
Americus C7
Appling G4
Arlington B9
Ashburn D8
Athens E4
Atlanta, *capital* C4, J3
Augusta H5
Bainbridge B10
Barnesville C5
Baxley G8
Belvedere K3
Blackshear G9
Blairsville D2
Blakely B9
Blue Ridge C2
Boston D10
Bremen A4
Brookhaven J2
Brunswick H9
Buchanan A4
Buena Vista B7
Buford C3
Butler C6
Byron D6
Cairo C10
Calhoun B2
Camilla C9
Canton B3
Carnesville E3
Carrollton A4
Cartersville B3
Cedar Grove J3
Cedartown A3
Chamblee J2
Chatsworth B2
Clarkesville D2
Clarkston K2
Claxton H7
Clayton E2
Cleveland D2
Cochran E7
College Park H3
Colquitt B9
Columbus B7
Commerce E3
Conley J4
Constitution J3
Conyers D4
Cordele D8
Cornelia D2
Covington D4
Crawfordville F4
Cumming C3
Cusseta B7
Cuthbert B8
Dahlonega D2
Dallas B4
Dalton B2
Danielsville E3
Darien J9
Dawson C8
Dawsonville C3
Decatur K3
Donalsonville B9
Doraville K2
Douglas F8
Douglasville B4
Druid Hills J3
Dublin F6
Dunwoody J2
Eastman E7
East Point C4, H3
Eatonton E5
Elberton F3
Ellaville C7
Ellijay C2
Evans G4
Fair Oaks H2
Fairview K4
Fayetteville C5
Fitzgerald E8
Folkston G10
Forest Park J4
Forsyth D5
Fort Gaines A8
Fort Oglethorpe A2
Fort Valley D6

Key
Franklin ... A5
Gainesville ... D3
Garden City ... J7
Georgetown ... A8
Gibson ... F5
Gilmore ... H2
Glennville ... H8
Gordon ... E6
Gray ... D5
Greensboro ... E4
Greenville ... B5
Gresham Park ... J3
Griffin ... C5
Hahira ... E10
Hamilton ... B6
Hampton ... C5
Hapeville ... J3
Hartwell ... F3
Hawkinsville ... E7
Hazlehurst ... F8
Hephzibah ... G5
Hiawassee ... D2
Hinesville ... H8
Hogansville ... B5
Homer ... D3
Homerville ... F9
Irwinton ... E6
Jackson ... D5
Jasper ... C3
Jefferson ... E3
Jeffersonville ... E6
Jesup ... H8
Jonesboro ... C4
Kennesaw ... B3
Kingsland ... H10
Knoxville ... D6
La Fayette ... A2
La Grange ... A5
Lakeland ... E9
Lavonia ... E3
Lawrenceville ... D4
Leesburg ... C8
Lexington ... E4
Lincolnton ... G4
Locust Grove ... C5
Louisville ... G5
Ludowici ... H8
Lumber City ... F8
Lumpkin ... B7
Lyons ... G7
Mableton ... B4, G2
McDonough ... C5
McIntyre ... E6
Macon ... D6
McRae ... F7
Madison ... E4
Manchester ... B6
Marietta ... B4, H1
Marshallville ... D7
Metter ... G7
Milledgeville ... E5
Millen ... H6
Monroe ... D4
Monticello ... D5
Morgan ... B8
Moultrie ... D9
Mount Vernon ... F7
Mt. Bethel ... J1
Nashville ... E9
Newnan ... B5
Newton ... C9
Oakdale ... H2
Ocilla ... E8
Oglethorpe ... C7
Panthersville ... K3
Peachtree City ... B5
Pearson ... F9
Pembroke ... H7
Perry ... D7
Pooler ... J7
Powder Springs ... B4
Preston ... B7
Quitman ... E10
Red Oak ... H4
Reidsville ... G7
Richland ... B7
Richmond Hill ... J8
Rincon ... J7
Ringgold ... A2
Riverdale ... J4
Rochelle ... E8
Rockmart ... A3
Rome ... A3
Roswell ... C3
Royston ... E3
Sandersville ... F6
Sandy Springs ... J2
Savannah ... J7
Scottdale ... K3
Skyland ... J2
Smyrna ... H2
Snellville ... D4
Social Circle ... D4
Soperton ... F7
Sparta ... F5
Springfield ... J7
St. Marys ... H10
St. Simons Island ... J9
Statenville ... E10
Statesboro ... H7
Statham ... D4
Stone Mountain ... C4
Summerville ... A3
Swainsboro ... G6
Sylvania ... H6
Sylvester ... D8
Talbotton ... B6
Tennille ... F6
Thomaston ... C6
Thomasville ... D10
Thomson ... G5
Tifton ... E9
Toccoa ... E2
Toco Hills ... J2
Trenton ... A2
Trion ... A2
Tucker ... K2
Tybee Island ... K8
Unadilla ... D7
Union City ... B4, H4
Union Point ... E4
Valdosta ... E10
Vidalia ... G7
Vienna ... D7
Villa Rica ... B4
Wadley ... G6
Warner Robins ... D6
Warrenton ... F5
Washington ... F4
Watkinsville ... E4
Waycross ... G9
Waynesboro ... G5

Key
Westoak ... H1.
Winder ... D4
Woodbine ... H10
Wrens ... G5
Wrightsville ... F6
Zebulon ... C5

Other Features
Alapaha, *river* ... E9
Allatoona, *lake* ... B3
Altamaha, *river* ... G8
Andersonville Natl. Hist. Site ... C7
Appalachian, *mts.* ... D2
Blackshear, *lake* ... D8
Blue, *ridge* ... C2
Brasstown Bald, *mt.* ... D2
Burton, *lake* ... D2
Carters, *lake* ... B2
Chattahoochee, *river* ... A5, A9, G3
Chattahoochee River N.R.A. ... J1
Chattooga, *river* ... E2
Chatuge, *lake* ... D1
Chickamauga and Chattanooga Natl. Military Park ... A2
Coosa, *river* ... D2
Cumberland, *island* ... J10
Cumberland Island Natl. Seashore ... J10
Ed Jenkins Natl. Rec. Area ... C2
Etowah, *river* ... B3
Flint, *river* ... C9
Fort Frederica Natl. Monument ... J9
Fort Pulaski Natl. Monument ... K7
Hartwell, *lake* ... F2
Jackson, *lake* ... D5
Jekyll, *island* ... J9
Jimmy Carter Natl. Hist. Site ... C7
J. Strom Thurmond, *lake* ... G4
Lookout Mt., *ridge* ... A2
Martin Luther King Jr. N.H.S. ... J3
Ocmulgee Natl. Monument ... D6
Ochlockonee, *river* ... C10
Ocmulge, *river* ... E7
Oconee, *lake* ... E5
Oconee, *river* ... F6
Ogeechee, *river* ... F5
Ohoopee, *river* ... G7
Okefenokee, *swamp* ... G10
Ossabaw, *island* ... J8
Russell, *lake* ... F3
St. Catherines, *island* ... J8
St. Marys, *river* ... H10
St. Simons, *island* ... J9
Sapelo, *island* ... J9
Savannah, *river* ... H5
Seminole, *lake* ... B10
Sidney Lanier, *lake* ... C3
Sinclair, *lake* ... E5
Stone Mt. State Park ... C4
Suwannee, *river* ... F10
Tallapoosa, *river* ... A4
Tybee, *island* ... K7
Walter F. George, *reservoir* ... A8
Wassaw, *island* ... J8
Weiss, *lake* ... A3
West Point, *lake* ... A6
Withlacoochee, *river* ... E10

Hawaii ... page 138

Cities and Towns
Ahuimanu ... J2
Aiea ... F1, J2
Captain Cook ... G6
Crestview ... E1, J2
Eleele ... C2
Ewa ... D2, J2
Ewa Beach ... E2, J3
Foster Village ... F1, J2
Haena ... C1, J5
Halawa ... B3
Halawa Heights ... F1, J2
Haleiwa ... H1
Hana ... D4
Hanamaulu ... D1
Hanapepe ... C2
Hauula ... J1
Heeia ... G1, K2
Hilo ... E7, J5
Holualoa ... G5
Honalo ... G5
Honokaa ... H4
Honolulu, *capital* ... C5, F2, J2
Iroquois Point ... E2, J2
Kaanapali ... B3
Kahana ... B3, J1
Kahului ... C3, D6
Kailua ... C5, K2
Kailua-Kona ... D7, F5
Kalaheo ... C2
Kalaoa ... F5
Kalaupapa ... B3
Kaneohe ... C5, G1, K2
Kapaa ... A5, D1
Kaunakakai ... A3
Keaau ... J5
Kealakekua ... G5
Kealia ... D1, G6
Kekaha ... B2
Kihei ... C4, D6
Kilauea ... C1
Koloa ... C2
Kualapuu ... A3
Kula ... C4
Lahaina ... B3, D6
Laie ... C5, J1
Lanai City ... B3
Lawai ... C2
Lihue ... A5, D2
Maili ... H2
Makaha ... H2
Makakilo City ... H2
Makawao ... C3
Maunawili ... K2
Mililani Town ... J2
Mokuleia ... H1
Mountain View ... J5
Nanakuli ... B5, H2
Pacific Palisades ... E1, J2
Pahala ... H6
Papaikou ... J5
Pearl City ... C5, E1, J2
Pepeekeo ... J5
Pohakupu ... K2
Pukalani ... C3, D6
Pupukea ... J1
Volcano ... J6
Waialua ... B3, H1
Waianae ... B5, H2
Waihee ... C3
Waikiki ... G3
Waikoloa Village ... G4

Key
Wailua ... C3, D1
Wailuku ... C3, D6
Waimalu ... E1, J2
Waimanalo ... K2
Waimanalo Beach ... K2
Waimea ... C2, D6, H1
Waipahu ... E1, J2
Waipio ... H4
Waipio Acres ... J2
Whitmore Village ... J2

Other Features
Alenuihaha, *channel* ... D6
Alika Cone, *mt.* ... G6
Diamond Head, *point* ... G3
Ford, *island* ... E1
Haleakala Natl. Park ... C4, D6
Hamakua, *coast* ... H4
Hawaii, *island* ... E6, G5
Hawaii Volcanoes Natl. Park ... E7, H6
Hilo, *bay* ... J5
Hualalai, *mt.* ... G5
Kaala, *mt.* ... H1
Kaena, *point* ... B5, H1
Kahoolawe, *island* ... B4, D6
Kahului, *bay* ... C3
Kaikipauula, *mt.* ... H4
Kailua, *bay* ... K2
Kaiwi, *channel* ... C5, K3
Ka Lae (South Cape), *cape* ... D7, G7
Kalalua, *mt.* ... J6
Kalaupapa, *peninsula* ... B3
Kalaupapa Natl. Hist. Park ... B3
Kaloko-Honokohau Natl. Hist. Park ... F5
Kamakou, *mt.* ... B3
Kau, *desert* ... H6
Kauai, *channel* ... B5, D2
Kauai, *island* ... A5, B1
Kaulakahi, *channel* ... A5, B1
Kawaikini, *mt.* ... C1
Kiholo, *bay* ... G4
Kilauea, *crater* ... J6
Kilohana, *crater* ... C2
Kinau, *cape* ... C4
Kipuka Puaulu, *mt.* ... H6
Kohala, *coast* ... F5
Kohala, *mt.* ... G4
Kohala, *mts.* ... G4
Kona, *coast* ... F6
Konahuanui, *mt.* ... G2, K2
Koolau Range, *mts.* ... F1, J1
Kulani, *mt.* ... H5
Kumukahi, *cape* ... E7, K5
Lanai, *island* ... B3, C6
Lehua, *island* ... A1
Lua Makika, *mt.* ... B4
Maalaea, *bay* ... C4
Makaleha, *mts.* ... C1
Makapuu, *point* ... C5, K2
Mamala, *bay* ... E2, J3
Maui, *island* ... C3, D6
Mauna Iki, *mt.* ... H6
Mauna Kea, *mt.* ... E6, H5
Mauna Loa, *mt.* ... D7, H6
Maunalua, *bay* ... K3
Mokolii, *island* ... J2
Mokuauia, *island* ... J1
Mokulua, *island* ... K2
Moku Manu, *island* ... K2
Molokai, *island* ... A3, C5
Molokini, *island* ... C4
Na Pali, *coast* ... B1
Niihau, *island* ... A2, A5
Oahu, *island* ... B5, D2, K1
Pearl, *harbor* ... E2
Punchbowl, *crater* ... G2
Pu'uhonua O Honaunau N.H.P. ... G6
Puu Kainapuaa, *mt.* ... J1
Puu Kaua, *mt.* ... H2
Puukohola Heiau Natl. Hist. Site ... G4
Puu Kukui, *mt.* ... B3
Puu Kulua, *mt.* ... H5
Puu Loa, *mt.* ... H5
Puu O Keokeo, *mt.* ... G6
Puu Ulaula, *mt.* ... C4
Sand, *island* ... F2
Sulphur Cone, *mt.* ... G6
U.S.S. Arizona Memorial ... E1
Upolu, *point* ... D6, G3
Waialeale, *mt.* ... A5, C1
Waianae Range, *mts.* ... H1
Wailuku, *river* ... H5
Waimea, *canyon* ... C2
West Maui, *mts.* ... B3

Idaho ... page 139

Cities and Towns
Aberdeen ... E7
American Falls ... E7
Ammon ... F6
Arco ... D6
Banks ... A5
Bellevue ... C6
Bennington ... F7
Blackfoot ... E6
Boise, *capital* ... A6
Bonners Ferry ... A1
Buhl ... C7
Burley ... D7
Caldwell ... A6
Cascade ... A5
Challis ... C5
Chubbuck ... E7
Coeur d'Alene ... A2
Council ... A5
Driggs ... F6
Dubois ... E5
Eagle ... A6
Emmett ... A6
Fairfield ... C6
Filer ... C7
Fish Haven ... F7
Fruitland ... A6
Fruitvale ... A5
Garden City ... A6
Garden Valley ... B5
Glenns Ferry ... B7
Gooding ... C7
Grangeville ... A4
Hailey ... C6
Hayden ... A2
Idaho City ... B6
Idaho Falls ... E6
Jerome ... C7
Kamiah ... A3
Kellogg ... A2
Ketchum ... C6
Kuna ... A6
Laclede ... A1
Lewiston ... A3

Key
McCall ... A5
Malad City ... E7
May ... D5
Middleton ... A6
Montpelier ... F7
Moscow ... A3
Mountain Home ... B6
Murphy ... A6
Nampa ... A6
New Plymouth ... A6
Nezperce ... A3
Orofino ... A3
Osburn ... A2
Paris ... F7
Parma ... A6
Patterson ... D5
Pauline ... E7
Payette ... A5
Pinehurst ... A2
Pocatello ... E7
Post Falls ... A2
Preston ... F7
Priest River ... A1
Rathdrum ... A2
Rexburg ... F6
Rigby ... F6
Rupert ... D7
St. Anthony ... F6
St. Maries ... A2
Salmon ... D4
Sandpoint ... A1
Shelley ... E6
Shoshone ... C7
Soda Springs ... F7
Sugar City ... F6
Sun Valley ... C6
Thatcher ... F7
Twin Falls ... C7
Wallace ... B2
Weiser ... A5
Wendell ... C7

Other Features
American Falls, *reservoir* ... E7
Bear, *lake* ... F7
Bear, *river* ... F7
Big Lost, *river* ... D6
Bitterroot, *range* ... B3, D4
Blackfoot, *reservoir* ... F7
Blackfoot, *river* ... F6
Bruneau, *river* ... B7
Cache, *mt.* ... D7
Caribou, *range* ... F6
Cascade, *reservoir* ... A5
Castle, *mt.* ... C5
Clearwater, *mts.* ... B3
Clearwater, *river* ... B4
Craters of the Moon N.M. ... D6
Dworshak, *reservoir* ... A3
Grays, *lake* ... F6
Hagerman Fossil Beds N.M. ... C7
Hells, *canyon* ... A5
Hells Canyon Natl. Recreation Area ... A4
Kootenai, *river* ... A1
Lemhi, *river* ... D5
Lochsa, *river* ... B3
Middle Fork Salmon, *river* ... B5
Minidoka Internment Natl. Mon. ... C7
Nez Perce N.H.P. ... A3, B3
North Fork Clearwater, *river* ... B3
Owyhee, *mts.* ... A6
Owyhee, *river* ... A6
Palisades, *reservoir* ... F6
Payette, *lake* ... A5
Payette, *river* ... A5
Pend Oreille, *lake* ... A1
Pend Oreille, *river* ... A1
Priest, *lake* ... A1
Ryan, *mt.* ... C6
St. Joe, *river* ... A2
Salmon, *river* ... B4
Salmon River, *mts.* ... C5
Sawtooth, *range* ... B5
Sawtooth Natl. Recreation Area ... C5
Scott, *mt.* ... E5
Snake, *river* ... A4
South Fork Selway, *river* ... B3
Teton, *river* ... F6
Weiser, *river* ... A5
Yellowstone Natl. Park ... F5

Illinois ... page 140

Cities and Towns
Abingdon ... C3
Addison ... B5
Albion ... E5
Aledo ... C2
Alsip ... B6
Altamont ... E4
Alton ... C5
Amboy ... D2
Anna ... D6
Antioch ... A4, E1
Arcola ... E4
Arlington Heights ... A5
Arthur ... E4
Ashland ... C4
Athens ... D4
Atlanta ... D3
Atwood ... E4
Auburn ... D4
Aurora ... E2
Barrington ... A5
Barry ... B4
Bartlett ... A5
Bartonville ... D3
Batavia ... E2
Beach Park ... B4
Beardstown ... C3
Beecher ... F2
Belleville ... D5
Belvidere ... E1
Bement ... E4
Benld ... D4
Benton ... E6
Berwyn ... B6
Bethany ... E4
Bloomington ... D3
Blue Island ... B6
Bolingbrook ... A6, E2
Bourbonnais ... F2
Braidwood ... E2
Breese ... D5
Bridgeport ... F5
Brighton ... C4
Brookfield ... B6
Buffalo Grove ... B5
Bunker Hill ... D4
Burbank ... B6
Bushnell ... C3

Key
Byron ... D1
Cahokia ... C5
Cairo ... D6
Calumet City ... C6, F2
Cambridge ... C2
Canton ... C3
Capron ... E1
Carbondale ... D6
Carlinville ... D4
Carlyle ... D5
Carmi ... E5
Carol Stream ... A5
Carpentersville ... E1
Carrier Mills ... E6
Carrollton ... C4
Carterville ... D6
Carthage ... B3
Cary ... E1
Casey ... F4
Catlin ... F3
Centralia ... D5
Cerro Gordo ... E4
Champaign ... E3
Channahon ... E2
Charleston ... E4
Chatham ... D4
Chenoa ... E3
Chester ... D6
Chicago ... B5, F2
Chicago Heights ... B6
Chillicothe ... D3
Christopher ... D6
Cicero ... B6, F2
Clifton ... F3
Clinton ... E3
Coal City ... E2
Colchester ... C3
Collinsville ... D5
Columbia ... C5
Crest Hill ... A6
Crete ... F2
Crystal Lake ... E1
Cuba ... C3
Danville ... F3
Decatur ... E4
Deerfield ... B5
De Kalb ... E2
Delavan ... D3
De Soto ... D6
Des Plaines ... B5
Dixon ... D2
Dolton ... B6
Downers Grove ... B6
Du Quoin ... D5
Dwight ... E2
Earlville ... E2
East Dubuque ... C1
East Moline ... C2
East Peoria ... D3
East St. Louis ... C5
Edwardsville ... D5
Effingham ... E4
Elburn ... E2
Eldorado ... E6
Elgin ... E1
Elizabethtown ... E6
Elk Grove Village ... B5
Elmhurst ... B5
Elmwood ... D3
Elmwood Park ... B5
Erie ... C2
Eureka ... D3
Evanston ... B5, F1
Evergreen Park ... B6
Fairbury ... E3
Fairfield ... E5
Farmer City ... E3
Farmington ... C3
Fisher ... E3
Flora ... E5
Forreston ... D1
Forsyth ... E4
Fox Lake ... A4, E1
Fox Lake Hills ... A4
Fox River Grove ... A5
Frankfort ... B6, F2
Freeburg ... D5
Freeport ... D1
Fulton ... C2
Gages Lake ... B4
Galena ... C1
Galesburg ... C3
Galva ... C2
Geneseo ... C2
Geneva ... E2
Genoa ... E1
Georgetown ... F4
Gibson City ... E3
Gillespie ... D4
Gilman ... F3
Girard ... D4
Glen Ellyn ... A5
Glencoe ... B5
Glendale Heights ... A5
Glenview ... B5
Glenwood ... B6
Godfrey. ... C5
Golconda ... E6
Granite City ... C5
Granville ... D2
Grayslake ... A4
Grayville ... E5
Green Oaks ... B4
Greenup ... E4
Greenville ... D5
Gridley ... E3
Gurnee ... B4
Hainesville ... A4
Hamilton ... B3
Hampshire ... E1
Hanover Park ... A5
Hardin ... C4
Harrisburg ... E6
Harristown ... D4
Harvard ... E1
Harvey ... B6
Havana ... C3
Hennepin ... D2
Henry ... D2
Herrin ... D6
Herscher ... E2
Heyworth ... E3
Hickory Hills ... B6
Highland ... D5
Highland Park ... B5, F1
Highwood ... B5
Hillsboro ... D4
Hinckley ... E2
Hinsdale ... B6
Hoffman Estates ... A5
Homer ... F3
Homewood ... B6

Key
Hoopeston ... F3
Huntley ... E1
Island Lake ... A5
Jacksonville ... C4
Jerseyville ... C4
Johnston City ... E6
Joliet ... A6, E2
Jonesboro ... D6
Justice ... B6
Kankakee ... F2
Kaskaskia ... D6
Kewanee ... D2
Kincaid ... D4
Knoxville ... C3
Lacon ... D2
La Grange ... B6
La Harpe ... C3
Lake Bluff ... B5
Lake Forest ... B5
Lake Zurich ... A5
Lanark ... D1
La Salle ... D2
Lansing ... B6
Lawrenceville ... F5
Lemont ... B6
Lena ... D1
Le Roy ... E3
Lewistown ... C3
Lexington ... E3
Libertyville ... B5
Lilymoor ... A4
Lincoln ... D3
Lincolnwood ... B5
Lindenhurst ... A4
Lisle ... A6
Litchfield ... D4
Lockport ... A6
Lombard ... B6
Louisville ... E5
Loves Park ... D1
Lynwood ... C6
McHenry ... E1
Machesney Park ... D1
Mackinaw ... D3
McLeansboro ... E5
Macomb ... C3
Macon ... E4
Mahomet ... E3
Manhattan ... F2
Manito ... D3
Manteno ... F2
Marengo ... E1
Marion ... E6
Marissa ... D5
Marley ... B6
Maroa ... E3
Marseilles ... E2
Marshall ... F4
Mascoutah ... D5
Mason City ... D3
Matteson ... B6
Mattoon ... E4
Maywood ... B5
Melrose Park ... B5
Mendota ... D2
Metamora ... D3
Metropolis ... E6
Milan ... C2
Milford ... F3
Minonk ... D3
Minooka ... E2
Mokena ... B6
Moline ... C2
Momence ... F2
Monmouth ... C3
Monticello ... E3
Morris ... E2
Morrison ... D2
Morton ... D3
Morton Grove ... B5
Mound City ... D6
Mounds ... D6
Mount Carmel ... F5
Mount Carroll ... D1
Mount Morris ... D1
Mount Olive ... D4
Mount Prospect ... B5
Mount Pulaski ... D3
Mount Sterling ... C4
Mount Vernon ... E5
Mount Zion ... E4
Moweaqua ... D4
Mundelein ... A5
Murphysboro ... D6
Naperville ... A6
Nashville ... D5
Neoga ... E4
New Athens ... D5
New Baden ... D5
New Lenox ... B6
Newton ... E5
Niles ... B5
Nokomis ... D4
Normal ... E3
Norridge ... B5
Northbrook ... B5
North Chicago ... B4, F1
Northfield ... B5
Oak Brook ... B6
Oak Forest ... B6
Oak Lawn ... B6, F2
Oak Park ... B5, F2
Oakwood ... F3
Oblong ... F4
O'Fallon ... D5
Oglesby ... D2
Okawville ... D5
Old Mill Creek ... B4
Olney ... E5
Onarga ... F3
Oquawka ... C3
Oregon ... D1
Orion ... C2
Orland Hills ... B6
Orland Park ... B6
Ottawa ... E2
Palatine ... A5
Palestine ... F4
Palos Heights ... B6
Palos Hills ... B6
Pana ... D4
Paris ... F4
Park City ... B4
Park Forest ... F2
Park Ridge ... B5
Pawnee ... D4
Paxton ... E3
Pecatonica ... D1
Pekin ... D3
Peoria ... D3
Peoria Heights ... D3
Peotone ... F2

Key
Peru D2
Petersburg D4
Pinckneyville D5
Pittsfield C4
Plainfield A6, E2
Plano E2
Polo D2
Pontiac E3
Princeton D2
Princeville D3
Prophetstown D2
Quincy B4
Rantoul E3
Red Bud D5
Richton Park B6
Riverdale B6
Riverton D4
Riverwoods B5
Roanoke D3
Robinson F4
Rochelle D2
Rochester D4
Rock Falls D2
Rock Island C2
Rockford D1
Rockton D1
Rome D3
Romeoville A6
Roodhouse C4
Roscoe D1
Rosiclare E6
Rossville F3
Round Lake Beach A4
Rushville C3
Russell B4
St. David C3
St. Elmo E4
St. Joseph E3
St. Libory D5
Salem E5
Sandoval D5
Sandwich E2
Sauk Village C6
Savanna C1
Savoy E3
Schaumburg A5
Schiller Park B5
Seneca E2
Sesser D5
Shawneetown E6
Shelbyville E4
Sheridan E2
Sherman D4
Shorewood A6, E2
Skokie B5
Somonauk E2
South Beloit D1
South Elgin E2
South Holland B6
South Jacksonville C4
Sparta D5
Spring Valley D2
Springfield, *capital* D4
Staunton D4
Steeleville D5
Sterling D2
Stockland F3
Stockton C1
Streamwood A5
Streator E2
Sullivan E4
Summit B6
Sycamore E2
Taylorville D4
Teutopolis E4
Tilton F3
Tinley Park B6, F2
Toledo E4
Tolono E4
Toluca D3
Toulon D2
Tower Lakes A5
Tremont D3
Trenton D5
Tuscola E4
Urbana E3
Vandalia D5
Vernon Hills B5
Vienna E6
Villa Grove E4
Villa Park B5
Virden D4
Virginia C4
Volo A4
Wadsworth B4
Walnut D2
Wapella E3
Warren D1
Warrensburg D4
Warrenville A6
Warsaw B3
Washington D3
Waterloo C5
Watseka F3
Wauconda A5
Waukegan B4, F1
Waverly D4
Westchester B6
West Chicago A5
West Frankfort E6
Westville F3
Wheaton A6, E2
Wheeling B5, F1
White Hall C4
Wilmette B5
Wilmington E2
Winchester C4
Winnebago D1
Winnetka B5
Winthrop Harbor B4
Woodridge A6
Wood River C5
Woodstock E1
Wyoming D2
Yorkville E2
Zeigler D6
Zion B4, F1

Other Features
Carlyle, *lake* D5
Chautauqua, *lake* C3
Chicago, *river* B5
Clinton, *lake* E3
Crab Orchard, *lake* D6
Des Plaines, *river* A6, B4
Du Page, *river* A6
Fox, *lake* A4
Fox, *river* E2
Illinois, *river* D3
Ind. Dunes Natl. Lakeshore C6
Kankakee, *river* E2
Kaskaskia, *river* E4
Lincoln Home Natl. Hist. Site D4
Marie, *lake* A4
Michigan, *lake* F1
O'Hare, *airport* B5
Ohio, *river* D6
Orland, *lake* B6
Rend, *lake* D5
Rock, *river* D2
Sangamon, *river* C3
Shelbyville, *lake* E4
Spoon, *river* C3
Wabash, *river* E6

Indiana .... page 141

Cities and Towns
Albany F4
Albion F2
Alexandria E4
Anderson E4
Angola G1
Arcadia D4
Argos D2
Atlanta D4
Attica B4
Auburn F2
Aurora G6
Austin E7
Avilla F2
Bargersville D5
Batesville F6
Bedford D7
Berne G3
Bicknell B7
Bloomfield C6
Bloomington C6
Bluffton F3
Boonville B8
Bourbon D2
Brazil B5
Bremen D2
Brookston C3
Brookville F6
Brownsburg D5
Brownstown D7
Butler G2
Cambridge City F5
Cannelton C9
Carmel D5
Chandler B8
Charlestown E8
Chesterton B1
Churubusco F2
Cicero D4
Clayton C5
Clinton B5
Cloverdale C5
Columbia City E2
Columbus E6
Connersville F5
Corydon D8
Covington B4
Crawfordsville C4
Crothersville E7
Crown Point B2
Culver D2
Dale C8
Daleville E4
Danville C5
Darmstadt A8
Decatur G3
Delphi C3
Demotte B2
Dunlap E1
East Chicago B1
Eaton E4
Edinburgh E6
Elkhart E1
Ellettsville C6
Elwood E4
English D8
Evansville A9
Fairmount E4
Farmland F4
Ferdinand C8
Fishers D5
Flora C3
Fort Branch A8
Fort Wayne F2
Fowler B3
Frankfort C4
Franklin D6
Fremont G1
French Lick C7
Galveston D3
Garrett F2
Gary B1
Gas City E4
Geneva G3
Georgetown E8
Goshen E1
Greencastle C5
Greenfield E5
Greensburg F6
Greentown E4
Greenwood D5
Hagerstown F5
Hammond A1
Hanover F7
Hartford City F4
Hebron B2
Highland B1
Hope E6
Huntertown F2
Huntingburg C8
Huntington F3
Indianapolis, *capital* D5
Jasonville B6
Jasper C8
Jeffersonville E8
Kendallville F2
Kentland B3
Kingsford Heights C2
Knox C2
Kokomo D3
Kouts B2
Lafayette C4
Lagrange F1
Lakeville D1
La Porte C1
Lawrence D5
Lawrenceburg G6
Lebanon D4
Liberty G5
Ligonier E2
Lincoln City B8
Linton B6
Logansport D3
Loogootee C7
Lowell B2
Madison F7
Marion E3
Martinsville D6
Merrillville B2
Michigan City C1
Middlebury E1
Milan F6
Milford E2
Mishawaka D1
Mitchell D7
Monon C3
Monticello C3
Montpelier F3
Mooresville D5
Mount Vernon A9
Mulberry C4
Muncie F4
Nappanee D2
Nashville D6
New Albany E8
Newburgh B9
New Carlisle C1
New Castle F5
New Haven F2
Newport B5
New Whiteland D5
Noblesville D4
North Judson C2
North Liberty D1
North Manchester E2
North Terre Haute B5
North Vernon E6
Notre Dame D1
Oakland City B8
Odon C7
Orleans D7
Osgood F6
Ossian F3
Otterbein B3
Oxford B3
Paoli D7
Pendleton E4
Peru D3
Petersburg B8
Plainfield D5
Plymouth D2
Portland G4
Princeton A8
Redkey F4
Rensselaer B3
Richmond G5
Rising Sun G7
Rochester D2
Rockport B9
Rockville B5
Rushville F5
Salem D7
Schererville B2
Scottsburg E7
Sellersburg E8
Seymour E7
Shadeland C4
Shelbyville E5
Sheridan D4
Shoals C7
South Bend D1
South Whitley E2
Speedway D5
Spencer C6
Sullivan B6
Syracuse E2
Tell City C9
Terre Haute B6
Thorntown C4
Tippecanoe D2
Tipton D4
Union City G4
Upland F4
Valparaiso B2
Veedersburg B4
Vernon E7
Versailles F6
Vevay F7
Vincennes A7
Wabash E3
Wakarusa E1
Walkerton D2
Warsaw E2
Washington B7
Waterloo F2
Westfield D4
West Lafayette C4
Westport E6
Westville C1
Williamsport B4
Winamac C2
Winchester G4
Winona Lake E2
Woodburn G2
Worthington C6
Yorktown F4
Zionsville D5

Other Features
Big Blue, *river* E5
Brookville, *lake* F5
Eel, *river* E3
George Rogers Clark N.H.P. A7
Indiana Dunes Natl. Lakeshore B1
Kankakee, *river* C2
Lemon, *lake* D6
Lincoln Boyhood Natl. Memorial C8
Maumee, *river* G2
Michigan, *lake* B1
Mississinewa, *lake* E3
Monroe, *lake* D6
Ohio, *river* A9
Patoka, *river* B8
St. Joseph, *river* G2
Salamonie, *lake* E3
Tippecanoe, *river* C2
Wabash, *river* A8
Wawasee, *lake* E2
White, *river* C6
Whitewater, *river* F6

Iowa .... page 142

Cities and Towns
Ackley H2
Adel F4
Akron A2
Albia J5
Algona F1
Allison J2
Alta D2
Altoona H4
Ames G3
Anamosa M3
Ankeny G4
Asbury N3
Atlantic D5
Audubon E4
Avoca D5
Batavia K5
Bayard E4
Bedford E6
Belle Plaine K4
Bellevue P3
Belmond G2
Bettendorf P4
Bloomfield K6
Boone G3
Brighton L5
Britt G1
Brooklyn K4
Burlington M6
Camanche P4
Carlisle G5
Carroll E3
Carter Lake C5
Cascade N3
Cedar Falls K3
Cedar Rapids L4
Center Point L3
Centerville J6
Chariton H5
Charles City J1
Cherokee C2
Clarinda D6
Clarion G2
Clarksville J2
Clear Lake H1
Clinton P4
Colfax H4
Columbus Junction M5
Coon Rapids E4
Coralville L4
Corning E6
Corydon H6
Council Bluffs C5
Cresco K1
Creston F5
Dakota City F2
Dallas Center G4
Davenport N4
Decorah L1
Denison D4
Denver K2
Des Moines, *captial* G4
De Witt N4
Dubuque N2
Dunlap C4
Durant N4
Dyersville M3
Eagle Grove G2
Eldora H3
Eldridge N4
Elgin L2
Elkader M2
Emmetsburg E1
Epworth N3
Estherville E1
Evansdale K3
Fairfield L6
Farley M3
Fayette L2
Forest City G1
Fort Dodge F2
Fort Madison M6
Garner G1
Gilmore City F2
Glenwood C5
Greenfield F5
Grimes G4
Grinnell J4
Grundy Center J3
Guthrie Center E4
Guttenberg M2
Hampton H2
Harlan D4
Hartley D1
Hawarden B1
Hiawatha L3
Holstein C3
Hudson K3
Hull B1
Humboldt F2
Huxley G4
Ida Grove D3
Independence L3
Indianola G5
Iowa City L4
Iowa Falls H2
Jefferson F4
Jesup K3
Johnston G4
Kalona L5
Keokuk M7
Keosauqua L6
Knoxville H5
Lake City E3
Lake Mills G1
Lake View D3
Lamoni G6
La Porte City K3
Laurens E2
Le Claire P4
Le Mars B2
Lenox E6
Leon G6
Logan C4
Lovilia J5
Madrid G4
Manchester M3
Manly H1
Manning D4
Manson E2
Mapleton C3
Maquoketa N3
Marengo K4
Marion L4
Marshalltown J3
Mason City H1
Mediapolis M5
Melcher-Dallas H5
Milford D1
Missouri Valley C4
Monona M1
Monroe H4
Montezuma J4
Monticello M3
Mount Ayr F6
Mount Pleasant L6
Mount Vernon M4
Moville B3
Muscatine M5
Nashua J2
Nevada H3
New Hampton K1
New London M6
Newton H4
Nora Springs J1
North Liberty L4
Northwood H1
Norwalk G5
Oakland D5
Oelwein L2
Ogden F3
Onawa B3
Orange City B1
Osage J1
Osceola G5
Oskaloosa J5
Ottumwa K5
Park View N4
Parkersburg J2
Pella J5
Perry F4
Pleasantville H5
Pocahontas E2
Polk City G4
Postville L1
Prairie City H4
Primghar C1
Red Oak D5
Reinbeck J3
Remsen C2
Rock Rapids B1
Rock Valley B1
Rockwell City E3
Sac City E3
Sanborn C1
Sergeant Bluff B3
Sheldon C1
Shell Rock J2
Shenandoah D6
Sibley C1
Sidney C6
Sigourney K5
Sioux Center B1
Sioux City B2
Spencer D1
Spirit Lake D1
Storm Lake D2
Story City G3
Strawberry Point L2
Stuart F4
Sumner K2
Tama J4
Tipton M4
Toledo J4
Traer K3
Urbandale E4
Villisca E6
Vinton K3
Walcott N4
Wapello M5
Washington L5
Waterloo K3
Waukee G4
Waukon M1
Waverly K2
Webster City G2
West Branch M4
West Burlington M6
West Des Moines G4
West Liberty M4
West Union L2
Williamsburg L4
Wilton M4
Windsor Heights G4
Winterset F5
Woodbine C4

Other Features
Big Sioux, *river* A1
Boone, *river* G2
Cedar, *river* K3
Chariton, *river* H6
Clear, *lake* H1
Coralville, *lake* L4
Des Moines, *river* F3
Effigy Mounds Natl. Monument M1
Floyd, *river* B2
Fox, *river* K6
Herbert Hoover Natl. Hist. Site M4
Iowa, *river* K4
Little Sioux, *river* D2
Maple, *river* D2
Mississippi, *river* M2
Missouri, *river* B4
Rathbun, *lake* J6
Red Rock, *lake* J5
Saylorville, *reservoir* G4
Skunk, *river* L5
Spirit, *lake* D1
Storm, *lake* D2
Turkey, *river* L2
Wapsipinicon, *river* K2
West Nishnabota, *river* K2

Kansas .... page 143

Cities and Towns
Abilene E3
Adrian G3
Alma F3
Andover E4
Anthony D4
Arkansas City E4
Arma H4
Ashland C4
Atchison G2
Atwood A2
Augusta F4
Baldwin City G3
Baxter Springs H4
Belle Plaine E4
Belleville E2
Beloit D2
Bonner Springs H2
Buhler E3
Burlington G3
Butler G3
Caldwell E4
Caney G4
Carbondale G3
Chanute G4
Chapman E3
Cheney E4
Cherryvale G4
Chetopa G4
Cimarron B4
Clay Center E2
Clearwater E4
Clifton E2
Coffeyville G4
Colby A2
Coldwater C4
Columbus H4
Concordia E2
Conway Springs E4
Coolidge A3
Cottonwood Falls F3
Council Grove F3
Derby E4
De Soto H3
Dighton B3
Dodge City B4
Douglass F4
El Dorado F4
Elkhart A4
Ellinwood D3
Ellis C3
Ellsworth D3
Emporia F3
Erie G4
Eudora F3
Eureka F4
Florence F3
Fort Scott H4
Fredonia G4
Frontenac H4
Galena H4
Garden City B4
Gardner H3
Garnett G3
Girard H4
Goddard E4
Goodland A2
Gove B3
Great Bend D3
Greensburg C4
Halstead E4
Harper D4
Hays C3
Haysville E4
Herington F3
Hesston E3
Hiawatha G2
Hill City C2
Hillsboro E3
Hoisington D3
Holcomb B4
Holton G2
Horton G2
Howard F4
Hoxie B2
Hugoton A4
Humboldt G4
Hutchinson E3
Independence G4
Iola G4
Iuka D4
Jetmore C3
Johnson A4
Junction City F2
Kansas City H2
Kansas City H2
Kingman D4
Kinsley C4
La Crosse C3
Lakin A4
Lansing H2
Larned C3
Lawrence G3
Leavenworth H2
Leoti A3
Liberal B4
Lincoln D2
Lindsborg E3
Lorraine D3
Louisburg H3
Lyndon G3
Lyons D3
McPherson E3
Maize E4
Manhattan F2
Mankato D2
Marion E3
Marysville F2
Meade B4
Medicine Lodge D4
Minneapolis E2
Mound City H3
Moundridge E3
Mulvane E4
Neodesha G4
Ness City C3
Newton E3
North Newton E3
Norton C2
Oakley B2
Oberlin B2
Ogden F2
Olathe H3
Osage City G3
Osawatomie H3
Osborne D2
Oskaloosa G2
Oswego G4
Ottawa G3
Overland Park H3
Paola H3
Park B2
Park City E4
Parsons G4
Peabody E3
Phillipsburg C2
Pittsburg H4
Plainville C2
Pratt D4
Rich Hill G3
Rose Hill D4
Rose Hill E4
Russell D3
Sabetha G2
St. Francis A2
St. John D3
St. Marys F2
Salina E3
Scott City B3
Sedan F4
Sedgwick E4
Seneca F2
Sharon Springs A3
Silver Lake F2
Smith Center D2
South Hutchinson E4
Spring Hill H3
Stafford D4
Sterling D3
Stockton C2
Sublette B4
Syracuse A4
Tecumseh G2
Tonganoxie G2
Topeka, *capital* G2
Towanda F4
Tribune A3
Troy G2
Ulysses A4
Valley Center E4
Valley Falls G2
Wakeeney C2
Wamego F2

Key
Washington E2
Waterville F2
Wellington E4
Wellsville G3
Westmoreland F2
Wichita E4
Winfield F4
Yates Center G4

Other Features
Arkansas, *river* A4, D3
Big Blue, *river* F2
Cedar Bluff, *reservoir* C3
Cheney, *reservoir* E4
Chikaskia, *river* D4
Cimarron, *river* A4
Clinton, *lake* G3
Fall, *river* F4
Flint Hills F4
Fort Larned Natl. Hist. Site C3
Fort Scott Natl. Hist. Site H4
Kanapolis, *lake* E3
Kansas, *river* F2
Kirwin, *reservoir* C2
Little Blue, *river* E1
Marion, *lake* E3
Medicine Lodge, *river* C4
Melvern, *lake* G3
Milford, *lake* F2
Missouri, *river* G2
Neosho, *river* G3
Nicodemus Natl. Hist. Site C2
North Fork Solomon, *river* B2
Republican, *river* D1
Saline, *river* C2
Smoky Hill, *river* B3
Solomon, *river* D2
South Fork Republican, *river* A2
Sunflower, *mt.* A2
Tuttle Creek, *lake* F2
Verdigris, *river* F3
Waconda, *lake* D2
Wilson, *lake* D3

Kentucky ... page 144

Cities and Towns
Aberdeen F2
Albany D4
Alexandria E2
Allensville B4
Ashland G2
Auburn C4
Augusta E2
Barbourville F4
Bardstown D3
Bardwell E3
Beattyville F3
Beaver Dam C3
Bedford D2
Benton C2
Berea E3
Berry E2
Booneville F3
Bowling Green C4
Brandenburg C3
Brooks D2
Brooksville E2
Brownsville C3
Burkesville D4
Burlington E1
Butler E2
Cadiz B4, C2
Calhoun B3
Calvert City C2
Campbellsville D3
Campton F3
Carlisle E2
Carrollton D2
Carrsville C1
Catlettsburg G2
Cave City D3
Central City B3
Clay City F3
Clinton B2
Columbia D3
Concord F2
Corbin E4
Corinth E2
Covington E1
Crestwood D2
Cumberland G4
Cynthiana E2
Danville E3
Dawson Springs B3, C1
Dixon B3, C1
Dry Ridge E2
Earlington B3
Eddyville A3, C2
Edmonton D4
Ekron C3
Elizabethtown D3
Elkton B4
Eminence D2
Fairfield D3
Falmouth E2
Flatwoods G2
Flemingsburg F2
Florence E2
Foster E2
Frankfort, *capital* E2
Franklin C4
Frenchburg F3
Fulton B2
Georgetown E2
Glasgow D3
Gratz E2
Grayson G2
Greensburg D3
Greenup G2
Greenville B3
Guthrie B4
Hardinsburg C3
Harlan F4
Harrodsburg E3
Hartford C3
Hawesville C3
Hazard F3
Henderson B3
Hickman B2
Hindman G3
Hiseville D3
Hobson D3
Hodgenville D3
Hopkinsville B4
Horse Cave D3
Hyden F3
Independence E2
Inez G3
Irvine F3
Jackson F3
Jamestown D4
Jeffersontown D2
Jeffersonville F3
Jenkins G3
Junction City E3
La Fayette B4, C2
La Grange D2
Lancaster E3
Lawrenceburg E2
Leatherwood F3
Lebanon D3
Leitchfield C3
Lewisport C3
Lexington E2
Liberty E3
Livermore B3
Livingston E3
London E3
Louisa G2
Louisville D2
McKee F3
Mackville D3
Madisonville B3
Manchester F3
Marion A3, C1
Mayfield B2
Maysville F2
Middlesboro F4
Middletown D2
Monterey E2
Monticello E4
Morehead F2
Morganfield B3, C1
Morgantown C3
Mt. Olivet E2
Mt. Sterling F2
Mt. Vernon E3
Mt. Washington D2
Muldraugh C3
Munfordville D3
Murray C2
Nebo B3
New Castle D2
Nicholasville E3
Oak Grove B4
Okolona D2
Olive Hill F2
Owensboro B3
Owenton E2
Owingsville F2
Paducah C2
Paris E2
Patesville C3
Phelps G3
Pikeville G3
Pine Knot E4
Pineville F4
Pleasure Ridge Park D2
Prestonsburg G3
Princeton B3, C2
Providence B3, C1
Raceland G2
Radcliff D3
Richmond E3
Rochester C3
Russell Springs D3
Russellville C4
St. Matthews D2
Salyersville F3
Sandy Hook F2
Scottsville C4
Sebree B3
Shelbyville D2
Shepherdsville D3
Slaughters B3
Smithland C1
Somerset E3
South Shore G2
Springfield D3
Stanford E3
Stanton F3
Sturgis A3, C1
Taylorsville D2
Tompkinsville D4
Valley Station D2
Vanceburg F2
Versailles E2
Vicco F3
Vine Grove D3
Walton E2
Warsaw E2
West Liberty F3
Wheelwright G3
Whitesburg G3
Whitley City E4
Wickliffe B2
Williamsburg E4
Williamstown E2
Wilmore E3
Winchester E3
Woodbury C3
Zion B3

Other Features
Barkley, *lake* B4, C2
Barren, *river* C3
Barren River, *lake* C4
Big Sandy, *river* G2
Big South Fork Natl. River and Rec. Area E4
Buckhorn, *lake* F3
Cave Run, *lake* F2
Cumberland, *lake* E4
Cumberland, *river* E4
Cumberland Gap Natl. Hist. Park F4
Dale Hollow, *lake* D4
Fish Trap, *river* G3
Green, *river* B3, D3
Green River, *lake* D3
Kentucky, *lake* C2
Kentucky, *river* D2, E3
Licking, *river* F2
Lincoln Birthplace Natl. Hist. Site D3
Mammoth Cave Natl. Park C3
Nolin River, *lake* C3
Ohio, *river* F2
Rough, *river* C3
Rough River, *lake* C3
Tennessee, *river* C2
Tug Fork, *river* G3

Louisiana ... page 145

Cities and Towns
Abbeville E7
Abita Springs J6
Alexandria F3
Ama Inset
Amelia G7
Amite J5
Arabi Inset
Arcadia D1
Arnaudville F6
Avondale Inset
Baker G5
Baldwin F7
Ball E4
Basile D6
Bastrop F1
Baton Rouge, *captial* G6
Bayou Cane H7
Bayou Vista G7
Belle Chasse Inset
Bentley E3
Bernice D1
Bertrandville Inset
Bogalusa K5
Bossier City B1
Boyce D4
Braithwaite Inset
Breaux Bridge F6
Bridge City Inset
Broussard F6
Bunkie E5
Buras K8
Caernarvon Inset
Cameron C7
Carencro E6
Carville G6
Cecilia F6
Chalmette Inset, K7
Charenton F7
Chauvin H8
Church Point E6
Clinton G5
Colfax D3
Columbia E2
Cottonport E5
Coushatta C2
Covington J6
Crowley E6
Crown Point Inset
Cullen C1
Cut Off J7
Dalcour Inset
Delcambre F7
Delhi G2
Denham Springs H5
De Quincy C6
De Ridder C5
Des Allemands J7
Destrehan Inset
Donaldsonville H6
Edgard H6
Elton D6
English Turn Inset
Erath E7
Estelle Inset
Eunice E6
Farmerville E1
Ferriday F3
Franklin F7
Franklinton J5
Frenier Inset
Galliano J8
Garyville H6
Glenmora D5
Golden Meadow J8
Gonzales H6
Grambling D1
Grand Isle K8
Gray H7
Greensburg H5
Greenwood B2
Gretna Inset, J7
Gueydan E6
Hackberry C6
Hahnville Inset, J7
Hammond J5
Harahan Inset
Harrisonburg E2
Harvey Inset
Haughton C1
Haynesville C1
Henderson F6
Homer C1
Houma H7
Independence J5
Inniswold G6
Iota D6
Iowa C6
Jackson G5
Jeanerette F7
Jean Lafitte J7
Jefferson Inset
Jena E3
Jennings D6
Jesuit Bend Inset
Jonesboro D2
Jonesville F3
Kaplan E6
Kenilworth Inset
Kenner Inset, J7
Kentwood J5
Killona Inset
Kinder D6
Krotz Springs F5
Labadieville H7
Lacombe K6
Lafayette E6
Lafitte J7
Lake Arthur D6
Lake Charles C6
Lake Providence G1
Laplace Inset, J6
Larose J7
Lecompte E4
Leesville C4
Livingston H5
Lockport H7
Logansport B3
Luling Inset
Mamou E5
Mandeville J6
Mansfield B3
Mansura E4
Many C3
Marion E1
Marksville E4
Marrero Inset, J7
Melder D4
Melville F5
Meraux Inset
Metairie Inset, J7
Mimosa Park Inset
Minden C1
Monroe E1
Montegut H8
Montz Inset
Morgan City G7
Moss Bluff C6
Napoleonville G7
Natalbany J5
Natchitoches C3
Newellton G2
New Iberia F6
New Llano C4
New Orleans Inset, J7
New Roads G5
New Sarpy Inset
Norco Inset
Oakdale D5
Oak Grove G1
Oakville Inset
Oberlin D5
Oil City B1
Olla E3
Opelousas E5
Paincourtville G6
Paradis Inset
Patterson G7
Plaquemine G6
Point a la Hache K7
Ponchatoula J6
Port Allen G5
Port Barre F5
Port Sulphur K8
Poydras Inset
Raceland H7
Rayne E6
Rayville F2
Reserve H6
Richwood E2
Ringgold C2
River Ridge Inset
Ruston D1
St. Bernard Inset
St. Francisville G5
St. Joseph G3
St. Martinville F6
St. Rose Inset
Scarsdale Inset
Schriever H7
Scott E6
Shreveport B2
Simmesport F5
Slidell K6
Springhill C1
Stonewall B2
Sulphur C6
Sunset E6
Swartz F1
Taft Inset
Tallulah G2
Terrytown Inset
Thibodaux H7
Toca Inset
Vidalia G3
Ville Platte E5
Vinton B6
Violet Inset, K7
Vivian B1
Waggaman Inset
Walker H6
Washington E5
Welsh D6
Westlake C6
West Monroe E1
Westwego Inset, J7
White Castle G6
Winnfield D3
Winnsboro F2
Zachary G5
Zwolle B3

Other Features
Atchafalaya, *bay* G8
Atchafalaya, *river* F5
Barataria, *bay* K8
Bistineau, *lake* C2
Black, *river* F4
Borgne, *lake* Inset, K6
Breton, *islands* L8
Caddo, *lake* A1
Caillou, *bay* G8
Calcasieu, *lake* C7
Caney, *lake* E2
Cane River Creole Natl. Hist. Park D3
Catahoula, *lake* E3
Chandeleur, *islands* M7
Driskill, *mt.* C2
Grand, *lake* D7
Jean Lafitte N.H.P. and Preserve J7
Little, *river* D2
Marsh, *island* F7
Mississippi, *river* G3
Ouachita, *river* E2
Pearl, *river* K5
Pontchartrain, *lake* Inset, J6
Red, *river* C3
Sabine, *lake* B7
Sabine, *river* B5
Terrebonne, *bay* H8
Timbalier, *bay* J8
Toledo Bend, *reservoir* B4
Vermilion, *bay* F7
West Cote Blanche, *bay* F7
White, *lake* E7

Maine ... page 146

Cities and Towns
Alfred B5
Amherst D4
Athens C4
Auburn B4
Augusta, *capital* C4
Bangor D4
Bar Harbor D4
Bass Harbor D4
Bath C5
Belfast C4
Berwick B5
Biddeford B5
Boothbay Harbor C4
Brewer D4
Bridgton B4
Brunswick C4
Bucksport D4
Calais E3
Camden C4
Cape Elizabeth B5
Caribou D2
Chisholm B4
Clinton C4
Conway A4
Damariscotta C4
Dexter C3
Dixfield B4
Dover-Foxcroft C3
East Millinocket D3
Eastport F4
Ellsworth D4
Fairfield C4
Falmouth B5
Farmington B4
Fort Fairfield E2
Fort Kent D1
Frankfort D4
Franklin D4
Freeport B5
Frenchboro D4
Frenchville D1
Fryeburg B4
Gardiner C4
Greene B4
Hallowell C4
Hampden D4
Houlton E2
Howland D3
Kennebunk B5
Kittery B5
Lewiston B4
Lincoln D3
Lisbon Falls B4
Livermore Falls B4
Machias E4
Madawaska D1
Madison C4
Mars Hill E2
Mechanic Falls B4
Mexico B4
Milbridge E4
Milford D4
Millinocket D3
Milo D3
Norridgewock C4
North Amity E3
North Berwick B5
North Conway A4
North East Carry C3
North Windham B5
Norway B4
Oakland C4
Old Orchard Beach B5
Old Town D4
Orono D4
Oxford B4
Patten D3
Portland B5
Presque Isle D2
Richmond C4
Rockland C4
Rumford B4
Saco B5
Sanford B5
Skowhegan C4
South Paris B4
South Portland B5
Springvale B5
Thomaston C4
Van Buren E1
Waldoboro C4
Waterville C4
Westbrook B5
Westfield E2
Wilsons Mills A4
Wilton B4
Winslow C4
Winthrop C4
Wiscasset C4
Woodland E3
Yarmouth B5
York B5

Other Features
Acadia Natl. Park D4
Androscoggin, *river* B4
Appalachian, *mts.* A3
Aroostook, *river* D2
au Haut, *island* D4
Aziscohos, *lake* A3
Baskahegan, *lake* E3
Baxter State Park D2
Big, *lake* E3
Casco, *bay* B5
Chamberlain, *lake* C2
Chesuncook, *lake* C2
Churchill, *lake* C2
Cross, *island* E4
Deer, *island* D4
Elizabeth, *cape* B4
Flagstaff, *lake* B3
Grand, *lake* E3
Grand Matagamon, *lake* D2
Grand Seboeis, *lake* D2
Great Wass, *island* E4
Islesboro, *island* D4
Katahdin, *mt.* D3
Kennebec, *river* C3
Long, *island* D4
Maine, *gulf* C4
Matinicus, *island* D4
Mattawamkeag, *river* D2
Millinocket, *lake* D3
Monhegan, *island* C4
Moosehead, *lake* C3
Mooselookmeguntic, *lake* B4
Mt. Desert, *island* D4
Munsungan, *lake* D2
Nicatous, *lake* D3
Pemadumcook, *lake* C3
Penobscot, *bay* D4
Penobscot, *river* D3
Piscataquis, *river* C3
Richardson, *lakes* B4
Saco, *bay* B5
Saco, *river* B5
Saddleback, *mt.* B4
St. Croix, *river* E3
St. John, *river* C2
Sebago, *lake* B5
Sebec, *lake* C3
Seboeis, *lake* D3
Seboomook, *lake* C3
Snow, *mt.* B3
Sugarloaf, *mt.* B3
Swans, *island* D4
Telos, *lake* C2
Umbagog, *lake* A4
Vinalhaven, *island* D4
West Grand, *lake* E3
West Quoddy Head, *peninsula* F4
White Cap, *mt.* C3

Maryland ... page 147

Cities and Towns
Aberdeen K2
Accident A6
Accokeek F5
Adelphi C4
Annapolis, *capital* J4
Arden-on-the-Severn H3
Arnold J3
Aspen Hill B3, F3
Avenue G7
Baltimore H2
Bel Air J1
Beltsville C3, G3
Berlin P6
Berwyn Heights C4
Bethesda B4, F4
Bladensburg C4
Boonsboro D1
Bowie G4
Bowleys Quarters J2
Braddock Heights D2
Brandywine G5
Brentwood C4
Brunswick D2
Bucktown K6
Burtonsville C3
Cabin John A4
California J6
Calverton C3
Cambridge K5
Cape St. Claire J3
Camp Springs C5
Carney H2
Cascade D1
Catonsville H2
Centreville K3
Chesapeake Beach H5
Chesapeake Ranch Estates J6
Chestertown K3
Cheverly C4
Chillum C4, G4
Clinton G4
Clover Hill E2
Cloverly C3
Cockeysville H2
Colesville C3
College Park C4, G4
Columbia G3
Contee D3
Copenhaver A3
Coral Hills C5
Cresaptown C6
Crisfield L7
Crofton H3
Crownsville H3
Cumberland D6
Damascus F2
Deale H4
Delmar M6
Denton L4
Derwood A3
District Heights D5
Dufief A3
Dundalk H2
Easton K4
Edgemere J3
Edgewood J2
Eldersburg G2
Elkridge G3
Elkton L1
Ellicott City G2
Emmitsburg E1
Essex J2
Fair Hill L1
Fallston J1
Federalsburg L5
Ferndale H3
Forest Heights B5, G4
Forestville G4
Fountain Head D1
Frederick E2
Friendsville A6
Frostburg C6
Fruitland M6
Gaithersburg F3
Garrison G2
Germantown E3
Glen A3
Glenarden D4
Glen Burnie H3
Glen Echo Heights B4
Glen Hills A3
Glenmont B3
Golden Beach H6
Grantsville B6
Grasonville K4
Green Haven H3
Greenbelt D4, G3
Greensboro L4
Hagerstown D1
Halfway C1
Hampstead G1
Hampton H2
Hancock B1
Havre de Grace K1
Herald Harbor H3
High Ridge D3
Hillandale C3
Hillcrest Heights C5
Hillsmere Shores J4
Hughesville G5
Hunting Hill A3
Hurlock L5
Hyattstown E2
Hyattsville C4, G4
Indian Head F5
Jarrettsville J1
Jessup G3
Joppatowne J2
Kemptown E2
Kensington B3, F3
Kentland D4, G4
Kettering G4
Keysers Ridge B6
Kingstown K3
Kingsville J2
Knollwood C3
Lake Shore J3
Landover C4, G4
Langley Park C4
Lanham D4
Lansdowne H3
LaPlata G5
Largo G4
Laurel D3, G3
LaVale C6
Lawsonia L7
Layhill B3
Leonardtown H6
Lewisdale C4
Lexington Park J6
Linthicum H3
Lochearn H2
Londontown H4
Lutherville H2
Luxmanor B3
Manchester G1
Marlton G4
Maydale C3
Middle River J2

Key
Middletown D2
Milford G2
Montgomery Village F3
Montpelier D3
Mount Aetna D1
Mountain Lake Park A7
Mount Airy F2
Mount Rainier C4
Muirkirk D3
New Carrollton D4
Norbeck B3
North Chevy Chase B4
North East L1
Oak Crest D3
Oakland A7
Oakland G2
Oakview C3
Ocean City P6
Ocean Pines P6
Odenton H3
Olney F3
Overlea H2
Owings Mills G2
Oxon Hill C5
Palmer Park D4
Parkville H2
Parole H4
Perry Hall J2
Perryman K2
Perryville K1
Pikesville H2
Pleasant Hills J2
Pocomoke City M7
Poolesville E3
Potomac A3, F3
Potomac Heights F5
Preston L5
Prince Frederick H5
Princess Anne M7
Randallstown G2
Randolph Hills B3
Redhouse A7
Reisterstown G2
Rising Sun K1
Ritchie D5
Riverdale C4
Riviera Beach H3
Rock Hall K3
Rockville A3, F3
Rosedale H2
Rossmoor Leisure World B3
Rossville J2
St. Charles G5
St. Michaels K4
Salisbury M6
Seabrook D4
Seat Pleasant D5
Severn H3
Severna Park H3
Shady Side H4
Shawsville H1
Silver Hill C5
Silver Spring B4, F4
Snow Hill N7
South Gate H3
Spencerville C3
Stevensville J3
Suitland C5, G4
Sykesville G2
Takoma Park C4
Taneytown F1
Temple Hills C5, G4
Thurmont E1
Timonium H2
Towson H2
Upper Marlboro H4
Waldorf G5
Walker Mill D5
Walkersville E2
Westernport B7
Westminster F1
West Ocean City P6
Wheaton B3, F3
White Marsh J2
White Oak C3, G3
White Plains G5
Wildwood Hills A3
Williamsport C1
Woodlawn G2
Woodyard G4

Other Features
Allegheny Front, *mt. ridge* C7
Antietam Natl. Battlefield D2
Appalachian Natl. Scenic Trail D2
Assateague Island Natl. Seashore P7
Assawoman, *bay* P6
Backbone, *mt.* A7
Chesapeake, *bay* J5
Chesapeake and Ohio Canal N.H.P. A4, D2
Chester, *river* K3
Chincoteague, *bay* N7
Choptank, *river* K4
Deep Creek, *lake* A6
Liberty, *reservoir* G2
North Branch Potomac, *river* C7
Nanticoke, *river* L6
Patapsco, *river* H3
Patuxent, *river* H4
Potomac, *river* G6
Susquehanna, *river* J1
Thomas Stone Natl. Hist. Site F5
Wicomico, *river* G6
Youghiogheny, *river* A6

Massachusetts page 148

Cities and Towns
Abington L4
Acton A5, J3
Acushnet L6
Adams B2
Amesbury L1
Amherst D3
Andover K2
Arlington C6, K3
Ashby G2
Ashfield C2
Ashland J3
Assinippi F8
Assonet K5
Athol F2
Attleboro J5
Auburn G4
Avon D8, K4
Ayer H2
Baldwinville F2
Barnstable N6
Becket B3
Bedford B5, J3

Key
Belchertown E3
Bellingham J4
Belmont C6
Berkley K5
Bernardston D2
Beverly F5, L2
Billerica B5, J2
Blackstone H4
Blandford C4
Bliss Corner L6
Bolton H3
Bondsville E4
Boston, *capital* D6, K3
Boxford L2
Braintree E8, K4
Brewster P5
Bridgewater L5
Brimfield F4
Brockton K4
Brookfield F4
Brookline C7, K3
Burlington C5, K2
Buzzards Bay M5
Cambridge D6, K3
Canton C8, K4
Carlisle B5
Cedarville M5
Centerville N6
Central Village K6
Charlton G4
Charlton City G4
Chatham Q6
Chelmsford J2
Chelsea D6
Cheshire B2
Chester C3
Chicopee D4
Chilmark M7
Clarksburg B2
Clinton H3
Cochituate B7, J3
Cohasset L4
Concord B6, J3
Cotuit N6
Dalton B3
Danvers E5, L2
Dartmouth K6
Dedham C7, K4
Dennis P6
Douglas H4
Dover B8, J4
Dracut J2
Duxbury M4
East Brookfield F4
East Dennis P6
East Douglas H4
East Falmouth M6
East Freetown L5
Eastham Q5
Easthampton D3
East Longmeadow D4
East Orleans Q5
East Pepperell H2
East Wareham M5
Edgartown M7
Erving E2
Essex L2
Everett D6
Fall River K6
Falmouth M6
Feeding Hills D4
Fiskdale F4
Fitchburg G2
Florida B2
Foxboro K4
Framingham A7, J3
Franklin J4
Gardner G2
Gay Head L7
Georgetown L2
Gloucester M2
Granby D3
Granville C4
Great Barrington A4
Greenfield D2
Green Harbor M4
Halifax L5
Hamilton L2
Hanover L4
Hanson L4
Haverhill K1
Hingham F8, L4
Holbrook E8, K4
Holland F4
Holliston A8, J4
Holyoke D4
Hopedale H4
Hopkinton H4
Hubbardston G3
Hudson H3
Hull F7, L3
Huntington C4
Hyannis N6
Ipswich L2
Kingston M5
Lakeville L5
Lawrence K2
Lee B3
Lenox A3
Leominster G2
Lexington C6, K3
Lincoln B6
Littleton H2
Littleton Common J2
Longmeadow D4
Lowell J2
Ludlow E4
Lunenburg H2
Lynn E6, L3
Lynnfield D5, K2
Madaket P7
Malden D6, K3
Manchester-by-the-Sea L2
Mansfield K4
Marblehead F5, L3
Marion L6
Marlborough H3
Marshfield M4
Marshfield Hills M4
Mashpee N6
Mattapoisett L6
Maynard J3
Medfield B8, J4
Medford D6, K3
Medway A8
Melrose D6, K3
Mendon H4
Methuen K2
Middleboro L5
Milford H4
Millis B8
Milton D7, K3

Key
Monson E4
Monterey B4
Monument Beach M6
Nahant E6, L3
Nantucket P7
Natick B7, J3
Needham C7, K3
New Ashford B2
New Bedford L6
New Boston B4
Newburyport L1
New Marlborough B4
Newton C7, K3
North Adams B2
North Amherst D3
Northampton D3
North Andover K2
North Attleboro J5
Northborough H3
Northbridge H4
North Brookfield F3
North Carver L5
North Falmouth M6
Northfield E2
North Grafton H4
North Pembroke L4
North Plymouth M5
North Reading D5, K2
North Scituate L4
North Sudbury A6
North Tisbury M7
Norton K5
Norwell L4
Norwood C8, K4
Oakham F3
Ocean Bluff M4
Ocean Grove K6
Orange E2
Orleans Q5
Osterville N6
Otis B4
Oxford G4
Palmer E4
Paxton G3
Peabody E5, L2
Pelham E3
Pembroke L4
Pepperell H2
Petersham F3
Pinehurst C5, K2
Pittsfield B3
Plainfield C2
Plainville J4
Plymouth M5
Pocasset M6
Provincetown P4
Quincy E7, K3
Randolph D8, K4
Raynham K5
Raynham Center K5
Reading D5, K2
Rehoboth K5
Revere E6, K3
Rochester L6
Rockland E8, L4
Rockport M2
Rutland G3
Sagamore M5
Salem F5, L2
Salisbury L1
Sandwich N5
Saugus E6, K3
Savoy B2
Scituate L4
Sharon C8, K4
Sheffield A4
Shelburne Falls D2
Sherborn B8
Shirley H2
Shrewsbury H3
Shutesbury E3
Somerset K5
Somerville D6, K3
South Amherst D3
Southbridge F4
South Carver M5
South Deerfield D3
South Dennis P6
South Duxbury M4
South Lancaster H3
South Sudbury A7
South Wellfleet P5
South Yarmouth P6
Spencer G4
Springfield D4
Sterling G3
Stoneham D5
Stoughton D8, K4
Sturbridge F4
Sudbury A6, J3
Sutton G4
Swampscott E6, L3
Taunton K5
Teaticket M6
Templeton F2
Tewksbury K2
Three Rivers E4
Tolland B4
Topsfield L2
Truro P5
Turners Falls D2
Tyngsborough J2
Upton H4
Uxbridge H4
Vineyard Haven M7
Wakefield D5, K2
Wales F4
Walpole C8, J4
Waltham C6, B6
Ware F3
Wareham M5
Warren F4
Warwick E2
Washington B3
Watertown C6
Wauwinet P7
Wayland B7
Webster G4
Wellesley B7, J3
West Barnstable N6
Westborough H3
West Boylston G3
West Brookfield F4
West Concord J3
West Cummington C3
West Falmouth M6
Westfield D4
Westford J2
West Granville C4
Westhampton C3
West Medway A8

Key
Westminster G2
Weston B6, J3
Westport K6
Westport Point K6
West Springfield D4
West Wareham L5
Westwood C8, K4
West Yarmouth P6
Weymouth E8, L4
Whately D3
White Island Shores M5
Whitinsville H4
Whitman L4
Wilbraham E4
Williamstown B2
Wilmington C5, K2
Winchendon F2
Winchester C6
Windsor B2
Winthrop E6
Woburn C5, K3
Worcester G3
Worthington Center C3
Wrentham J4
Yarmouth Port P6

Other Features
Adams Natl. Hist. Park E8, L4
Ann, *cape* M2
Berkshire, *hills* B4
Boston, *bay* E6
Boston, *harbor* E7
Boston Harbor Islands N.R.A. E7
Boston Natl. Hist. Park D6
Buzzards, *bay* M6
Cape Cod, *bay* N5
Cape Cod, *canal* M5
Cape Cod Natl. Seashore P5
Charles, *river* B7
Chicopee, *river* D4
Cobble Mt., *reservoir* C4
Cod, *cape* P4
Connecticut, *river* E2
Deer, *island* E7
Elizabeth, *islands* L7
Frederick Law Olmsted N.H.S. C7
Georges, *island* E7
Greylock, *mt.* B2
Hingham, *bay* E7
Housatonic, *river* A4
J.F.K. Birthplace Natl. Hist. Site D7
Long, *island* E7
Longfellow Natl. Hist. Site D6
Lowell Natl. Hist. Park J2
Maine, *gulf* M1
Martha's Vineyard, *island* M7
Massachusetts, *bay* F6, M3
Merrimack, *river* K1
Minute Man Natl. Hist. Park B6, J3
Monomoy, *island* P6
Muskeget, *channel* N7
Nantucket, *island* P7
New Bedford Whaling N.H.P. L6
Neponset, *river* C7
Otis, *reservoir* B4
Peddocks, *island* E7
Quabbin, *reservoir* F3
Quincy, *bay* E7
Salem Maritime N.H.S. F5, L2
Saugus Iron Works N.H.S. E6
Shawsheen, *river* B6
Spectacle, *island* E7
Swift, *river* E4
Taconic, *mts.* A2
Wachusett, *reservoir* G3
Wachusett, *river* G3
Walden, *pond* B6

Michigan page 149

Cities and Towns
Adrian E8
Albion E7
Algonac G7
Allegan D7
Allendale C7
Allen Park A7
Alma E6
Alpena F4
Ann Arbor F7
Atlanta E5
Bad Axe G6
Baldwin D6
Battle Creek D7
Bay City F6
Belding D6
Bellaire D5
Belleville F7
Benton Harbor C7
Berkley A6
Bessemer C2
Beulah C5
Beverly Hills A6
Big Rapids D6
Birmingham A6
Blissfield F8
Bloomfield Hills A6
Boyne City D4
Bridgeport F6
Brighton F7
Buchanan C8
Burton F6
Cadillac D5
Carleton F7
Caro F6
Carrollton F6
Cassopolis C8
Cedar Springs D6
Center Line B6
Centreville D8
Charlevoix D4
Charlotte E7
Cheboygan E4
Chelsea E7
Chesaning E6
Chesterfield C6
Christmas C3
Clare E6
Clawson B6
Clio F6
Coldwater D8
Connorville C2
Coopersville D6
Crystal Falls A3
Cutlerville D7
Davison F6
Dearborn A7, F7
Dearborn Hts. A7
Detroit B7, F7
De Witt E7
Dowagiac C8

Key
Dundee F8
Durand F7
Eagle River A2
East Lansing E7
Eastpointe B6
East Tawas F5
Eaton Rapids E7
Ecorse B7
Escanaba B4
Essexville F6
Farmington A6
Farmington Hills A6
Fenton F7
Ferndale B6
Ferrysburg C6
Flat Rock F7
Flint F6
Flushing F6
Fowlerville E7
Frankenmuth F6
Franklin A6
Fraser B6
Fremont D6
Garden City A7
Gaylord E4
Gladstone B4
Gladwin E6
Grand Blanc F7
Grand Haven C6
Grand Ledge E7
Grand Rapids D7
Grayling E5
Greenville D6
Grosse Pointe B7
Grosse Pointe Farms B6
Grosse Pointe Park B7
Grosse Pointe Shores B6
Grosse Pointe Woods B6
Hamtramck B7
Hancock A2
Harper Woods B6
Harrison E5
Harrisville F5
Hart C6
Hastings D7
Hazel Park B6
Highland Park B7
Hillsdale E8
Holland C7
Holly F7
Holt E7
Houghton A2
Houghton Lake E5
Howell F7
Hudson E8
Hudsonville D7
Huntington Woods A6
Huron Heights A6
Imlay City F6
Inkster A7
Ionia D6
Iron Mountain A4
Ironwood C2
Ishpeming B3
Ithaca E6
Jackson E7
Jenison D7
Kalamazoo D7
Kalkaska D5
Keego Harbor A6
Kentwood D7
Kingsford A4
Lake City D5
Lake Orion F7
Lambertville F8
L'Anse A3
Lansing, *capital* E7
Lapeer F6
Lincoln Park A7
Livonia A7, F7
Lowell D7
Ludington C6
Madison Hts. B6
Manistee C5
Manistique D2
Marenisco C2
Marine City G7
Marquette B3
Marshall E7
Marysville G7
Mason E7
Melvindale A7
Menominee B4
Merriweather D2
Michigan Center E7
Midland E6
Milan F7
Milford F7
Mio E5
Monroe F8
Mount Clemens B6
Mount Morris F6
Mount Pleasant E6
Munising C3
Muskegon C6
Muskegon Hts. C6
Negaunee B3
New Baltimore G7
Newberry D3
Niles C8
North Muskegon C6
Norton Shores C6
Norway B4
Oak Park A6
Okemos E7
Ontonagon D1
Orchard Lake A6
Otsego D7
Owosso E6
Oxford F7
Paw Paw D7
Paw Paw Lake C7
Petoskey E4
Plainwell D7
Pontiac A6, F7
Portage D7
Port Huron G7
Portland E7
Rapid River C4
Reed City D6
Richmond G7
River Rouge B7
Rochester Hills A6
Rockford D6
Rockwood F7
Rogers City F4
Romeo F7
Romulus F7
Roscommon E5
Roseville B6
Royal Oak B6
Saginaw F6

Key
St. Clair G7
St. Clair Shores B6
St. Ignace E4
St. Johns E6
St. Joseph C7
St. Louis E6
Saline F7
Sandusky G6
Sault Ste. Marie E3
Shields E6
Silver City D1
Skidway Lake E5
Southfield A6
Southgate A7
South Haven C7
South Lyon F7
Sparta D6
Spring Lake C6
Standish F6
Stanton D6
Sterling Heights F7
Sturgis D8
Sylvan Lake A6
Tawas City F5
Taylor A7, F7
Tecumseh F7
Temperance F8
Three Rivers D7
Traverse City D5
Troy B6
Union Lake A6
Utica B6
Vassar F6
Wakefield C2
Waldenburg B6
Walker D7
Warren B6, F7
Wayland D7
Wayne A7
West Acres A6
West Branch E5
Westland A7
White Cloud D6
Whitehall C6
White Pine D2
Whitmore Lake F7
Williamston E7
Wixom F7
Wolf Lake C6
Wyandotte B7
Wyoming D7
Ypsilanti F7
Zeeland C7

Other Features
Arvon, *mt.* A3
Au Sable, *river* E5
Beaver, *island* D4
Big Bay De Noc, *bay* C4
Big Sable, *point* C5
Bois Blanc, *island* E4
Cass, *river* F6
Chambers, *island* B4
Detroit, *river* B7
Drummond, *island* F4
Erie, *lake* G8
Escanaba, *river* B3
Glen, *lake* D5
Gogebic, *lake* D2
Government Peak, *mt.* D1
Grand, *island* C3
Grand Island Natl. Rec. Area C3
Grand Traverse, *bay* D4
Green, *bay* B5
Hamlin, *lake* C5
Hammond, *bay* E4
Higgins, *lake* E5
High, *island* D4
Hog, *island* D4
Houghton, *lake* E5
Hubbard, *lake* F5
Huron, *bay* A3
Huron, *lake* G5
Huron, *mts.* A3
Indian, *lake* C3
Isle Royale, *island* A1
Isle Royale Natl. Park A2
Keweenaw, *bay* A3
Keweenaw, *peninsula* A2
Keweenaw, *point* B2
Keweenaw Natl. Hist. Park A2
Lookout, *point* F5
Manistee, *river* D5
Manitou, *island* B2
Menominee, *river* B4
Michigamme, *reservoir* A3
Michigan, *lake* C5
North Manitou, *island* C4
Paint, *river* A3
Pictured Rocks Natl. Lakeshore C3
Porcupine, *mts.* D2
Saginaw, *bay* F6
St. Clair, *lake* G7
St. Martin, *island* C4
Sleeping Bear Dunes Natl. Lakeshore C5
South Fox, *island* D4
South Manitou, *island* C4
Straits of Mackinac E4
Sturgeon, *bay* D4
Superior, *lake* A2
Thunder, *bay* F5
Whitefish, *bay* E3
Wixom, *lake* E6

Minnesota page 150

Cities and Towns
Ada A3
Aitkin D4
Albany C5
Albert Lea D7
Albertville D5
Alexandria B5
Annandale C5
Anoka D5
Appleton A5
Arlington C6
Aurora E3
Austin E7
Babbitt F3
Bagley B3
Barnesville A4
Baudette C2
Baxter C4
Bayport E6
Belle Plaine D6
Bemidji C3
Benson B5
Big Lake D5
Bird Island C6

Key
Blooming Prairie D7
Bloomington D6
Blue Earth C7
Brainerd C4
Breckenridge A4
Brooklyn Center E5
Buffalo D5
Burnsville D6
Caledonia F7
Cambridge D5
Canby A6
Cannon Falls E6
Carlton E4
Center City E5
Chanhassen D6
Chaska D6
Chatfield E7
Chisholm E3
Clara City B6
Clarks Grove D7
Clearwater C5
Cloquet E4
Cokato C5
Cold Spring C5
Columbia Hts F5
Coon Rapids D5
Corcoran D5
Crookston A3
Crosby D4
Dawson A6
Detroit Lakes B4
Dilworth A4
Dodge Center E6
Duluth E4
Eagan F6
Eagle Lake D6
East Bethel D5
East Grand Forks A3
Edina D6
Elbow Lake B5
Elk River D5
Ely F3
Evansville B4
Eveleth E3
Eyota E7
Fairmont C7
Falcon Heights F5
Faribault D6
Farmington D6
Fergus Falls A4
Foley D5
Forest Lake E5
Fosston B3
Fridley F5
Gaylord C6
Glencoe C6
Glenwood B5
Golden Valley E5
Goodview F6
Grand Forks A3
Grand Marais F3
Grand Portage F4
Grand Rapids D3
Granite Falls B6
Hallock A2
Hastings E6
Hawley A4
Hayfield E7
Hermantown E4
Hibbing E3
Hokah F7
Hopkins E5
Hovland F4
Howard Lake C5
Hutchinson C6
International Falls D2
Ivanhoe A6
Jackson B7
Janesville D6
Jordan D6
Kasson E6
Kenyon E6
La Crescent F7
Lake Crystal C6
Lakefield B7
Lakeville D6
Le Center D6
Le Sueur D6
Lewiston F7
Litchfield C5
Little Canada F5
Little Falls C5
Long Prairie C5
Lonsdale D6
Lutsen E3
Luverne A7
McIntosh B3
Madelia C6
Madison A5
Mahnomen B3
Mankato D6
Mantorville E6
Maple Grove E5
Maple Lake C5
Mapleton D7
Maplewood F5
Marshall B6
Melrose C5
Mendota F6
Milaca D5
Minneapolis D6
Minneota B6
Montevideo B6
Montgomery D6
Monticello D5
Moorhead A4
Mora D5
Morris B5
Mound D6
Mountain Iron E3
Mountain Lake C7
New Hope E5
Newport F6
New Prague D6
New Ulm C6
Nisswa C4
North Branch E5
Northfield D6
North Mankato C6
North Oaks F5
Olivia C6
Orono D6
Oronoco E6
Ortonville A5
Osakis B5
Owatonna D6
Park Rapids B4
Paynesville C5
Pelican Rapids A4
Perham B4
Pigeon River F4
Pine City E5
Pine Island E6
Pipestone A7
Plainview E6
Plymouth D5
Preston E7
Princeton D5
Prinsburg B6
Prior Lake D6
Proctor E4
Ramsey D5
Red Lake Falls A3
Red Wing E6
Redwood Falls B6
Renville B6
Richfield F6
Robbinsdale E5
Rochester E6
Roseau B2
Rushford F7
St. Anthony F5
St. Charles E7
St. Cloud C5
St. Francis D5
St. James C7
St. Joseph C5
St. Louis Park E5
St. Michael D5
St. Paul, *capital* D6
St. Peter D6
Sandstone E4
Sartell C5
Sauk Centre C5
Sauk Rapids C5
Shakopee D6
Silver Bay F3
Slayton B7
Sleepy Eye C6
South St. Paul F5
Spring Valley E7
Springfield C6
Staples C4
Stewartville E7
Stillwater E5
Thief River Falls A2
Tracy B6
Truman C7
Two Harbors F3
Tyler A6
Virginia E3
Wabasha E6
Wadena B4
Waite Park C5
Walker C3
Warren A2
Warroad B2
Waseca D6
Waterville D6
Wells D7
Wheaton A5
White Bear Lake F5
Willmar B5
Windom B7
Winnebago C7
Winona F6
Winsted C6
Winthrop C6
Worthington B7
Wyoming E5
Young America D6
Zimmerman D5
Zumbrota E6

Other Features
Big Fork, *river* D2
Brule, *lake* E4
Buffalo, *river* A4
Chippewa, *river* B5
Clearwater, *river* B3
Cloquet, *river* F3
Des Moines, *river* B6
Eagle, *mt.* E4
Grand Portage Natl. Monument F4
Gull, *lake* C4
Lake of the Woods, *lake* C1
Leech, *lake* C3
Little Fork, *river* D2
Lower Red, *lake* B3
Lower Whitefish, *lake* C4
Mall of America F6
Mesabi, *range* D3
Mille Lacs, *lake* D4
Minnesota, *river* B6
Mississippi, *river* C3
Mud, *lake* B2
Namakan, *lake* E2
Pipestone Natl. Monument A6
Pokegama, *lake* D3
Rainy, *river* C2
Red River of the North, *river* A3
Root, *river* E7
Rum, *river* D5
St. Croix, *river* E5
St. Louis, *river* E3
Superior, *lake* F3
Upper Red, *lake* C2
Vermilion, *range* F3
Voyageurs Natl. Park E2
Winnibigoshish, *lake* D3

Mississippi ....page 151

Cities and Towns
Aberdeen D2
Ackerman C2
Alligator B1
Amory D2
Ashland C1
Baldwyn D1
Bassfield C4
Batesville C1
Bay St. Louis C5
Bay Springs C4
Beauregard B4
Belmont D1
Belzoni B2
Biloxi D5
Blue Springs D1
Booneville D1
Brandon C3
Braxton C3
Brookhaven B4
Bruce C2
Calhoun City C2
Canton B3
Carrollton C2
Carthage C3
Centreville A4
Charleston B1
Clarksdale B1
Cleveland B2
Clinton B3
Coahoma B1
Coffeeville C2
Coldwater C1
Collins C4
Collinsville D3
Columbia C4
Columbus D2
Como C1
Corinth D1
Crystal Springs B4
Decatur C3
De Kalb D3
Diamondhead C5
D'Iberville D5
Doddsville B2
Drew B2
Durant C2
Eden B3
Edwards B3
Ellisville C4
Eupora C2
Falcon B1
Falkner D1
Fayette A4
Flora B3
Florence B3
Forest C3
Friars Point B1
Fulton D1
Gautier D5
Glendora B2
Gloster A4
Golden D1
Goodman C3
Greenville A2
Greenwood B2
Grenada C2
Gulfport C5
Hattiesburg C4
Hazlehurst B4
Hernando C1
Hollandale B2
Holly Springs C1
Horn Lake B1
Houston D2
Indianola B2
Itta Bena B2
Iuka D1
Jackson, *capital* B3
Jonestown B1
Kiln C5
Kosciusko C2
Kossuth D1
Laurel C4
Leakesville D4
Learned B3
Leland B2
Lena C3
Lexington B2
Liberty B4
Long Beach C5
Louisville C2
Lucedale D5
Lula B1
Lumberton C4
Lyman C5
McComb B4
McCool C2
Macon D2
Madison B3
Magee C4
Magnolia B4
Mantee C2
Marion D3
Marks B1
Mayersville A3
Meadville B4
Mendenhall C4
Meridian D3
Monticello B4
Montrose C3
Moorhead B2
Morton C3
Moss Point D5
Mound Bayou B2
Natchez A4
Nettleton D1
New Albany D1
New Augusta C4
Newton C3
Ocean Springs D5
Okolona D1
Olive Branch C1
Oxford C1
Paden D1
Pascagoula D5
Pass Christian C5
Paulding C3
Pearl B3
Pearlington C5
Pelahatchie C3
Petal C4
Philadelphia C3
Picayune C5
Pickens C3
Pittsboro C2
Polkville C3
Pontotoc D1
Pope C1
Poplarville C5
Port Gibson B4
Prentiss C4
Purvis C4
Quitman D3
Raleigh C3
Raymond B3
Richland B3
Ridgeland B3
Ripley D1
Rolling Fork B3
Rosedale A2
Ruleville B2
Sallis C3
Saltillo D1
Sardis C1
Satartia B3
Seminary C4
Senatobia C1
Shannon D1
Shaw B2
Shelby B2
Shubuta D4
Silver Creek B4
Slate Spring C2
Southaven B1
Starkville D2
Summit B4
Sumner B2
Sylvarena C3
Taylorsville C4
Tchula B2
Tillatoba C2
Toccopola C1
Tunica B1
Tupelo D1
Tutwiler B1
Tylertown B4
Union C3
Vaiden C2
Vancleave D5
Verona D1
Vicksburg B3
Walthall C2
Water Valley C1
Waveland C5
Waynesboro D4
Wesson B4
West C2
West Point D2
Wiggins C3
Winona C2
Woodland C2
Woodville A4
Yazoo City B3

Other Features
Arkabatula, *lake* B1
Big Black, *river* B3
Big Springs, *lake* D1
Big Sunflower, *river* B2
Bogue Chitto, *river* B4
Buttahatchee, *river* D2
Cat, *island* C5
Chickasawhay, *river* D4
Coldwater, *river* B1
Columbus, *lake* D2
Enid, *lake* C1
Grenada, *lake* C2
Gulf Island Natl. Seashore D5
Homochitto, *river* A4
Horn, *island* D5
Leaf, *river* C4
Mississippi, *river* B1
Mississppi, *sound* D5
Natchez Natl. Hist. Park A4
Noxubee, *river* D2
Okatibbee, *lake* D3
Pascagoula, *river* D5
Pearl, *river* C3
Petit Bois, *island* D5
Pickwick, *lake* D1
Pontotoc, *mt. ridge* D1
Ross Barnett, *reservoir* C3
Sardis, *lake* C1
Ship, *island* D5
Tallahatchie, *river* B1
Tombigbee, *river* D1
Tupelo Natl. Battlefield D1
Vicksburg Natl. Mil. Park B3
Woodall, *mt* D1
Yazoo, *river* B2

Missouri ....page 152

Cities and Towns
Adrian B3
Affton H3
Albany B1
Alton E5
Anderson B5
Appleton City B3
Ashland D3
Atherton J4
Aurora C5
Ava D5
Barnett D3
Belton B3
Benton G4
Bernie G5
Bethany B1
Birmingham J4
Bloomfield G5
Blue Springs J4
Bolivar C4
Bonne Terre F4
Boonville D3
Bowling Green E2
Branson C5
Brentwood H2
Bridgeton H2
Brookfield C2
Buckner J4
Buffalo C4
Butler B3
Cabool D4
California D3
Calverton Park H2
Camdenton D4
Cameron B2
Campbell F5
Canton E1
Cape Girardeau G4
Carrollton C2
Carthage B4
Caruthersville G5
Cassville C5
Cedar Hill F3
Centerville F4
Centralia D2
Chaffee G4
Charleston G5
Chesterfield F3
Chillicothe C2
Claycomo J4
Clayton F3, H2
Clinton C3
Columbia D3
Concord H3
Concordia C3
Crestwood H3
Creve Coeur H2
Cuba E3
Dellwood H2
Desloge F4
De Soto F3
Des Peres G2
Dexter G5
Dixon D3
Doniphan F5
East Prairie G5
Edina D1
Eldon D3
El Dorado Springs B4
Elsberry F2
Eminence E4
Eureka F3
Excelsior Springs B2, J3
Farley H3
Farmington F4
Fayette D2
Fenton G3
Ferguson H2
Festus F3
Florissant H2
Forsyth C5
Fredericktown F4
Fulton E3
Gainesville D5
Galena C5
Gallatin C2
Gladstone B2, J3
Glasgow D2
Glasgow Village H2
Glendale H3
Grain Valley J4
Granby B5
Grandview J4
Grant City B1
Greenfield C4
Greenville F4
Hamilton C2
Hannibal E2
Harrisonville B3
Hartville D4
Hayti G5
Hazelwood H2
Hermann E3
Hermitage C4
Higginsville C2
Hillsboro F3
Holden C3
Hollister C5
Houston E4
Huntsville D2
Independence B2, J4
Ironton F4
Jackson G4
Jefferson City, *capital* D3
Jennings H2
Joplin B4
Kahoka E1
Kansas City B2, H4
Kennett F5
Keytesville D2
Kingston B2
Kinloch H2
Kirksville D1
Kirkwood H3
Knob Noster C3
Ladue H2
Lake Lotawana J4
Lake St. Louis F3
Lamar B4
Lancaster D1
La Plata D1
Lathrop B2
Lawson B2
Lebanon D4
Lee's Summit B3, J4
Lemay H3
Lexington C2
Liberty B2, J3
Licking E4
Lilbourn G5
Linn Creek D3
Linneus C2
Louisiana E2
Mackenzie H3
Macon D2
Malden G5
Manchester G3
Mansfield D4
Maplewood H3
Marble Hill G4
Marceline D2
Marionville C5
Marshall C2
Marshfield D4
Maryland Heights H2
Maryville B1
Mattese H3
Maysville B2
Mehlville H3
Memphis D1
Mexico E2
Milan C1
Millard D1
Moberly D2
Monett C5
Monroe City E2
Montgomery City E3
Monticello E1
Mosby J3
Mound City A1
Mountain Grove D4
Mountain View E4
Mt. Vernon C4
Murphy G3
Neosho B5
Nevada B4
New Haven E3
New London E2
New Madrid G5
Nixa C4
North Kansas City H4
Northwoods H2
Oaks J4
O'Fallon F3
Olivette H2
Oregon A2
Osage Beach D3
Osceola C3
Overland H2
Owensville E3
Ozark C4
Pacific F3
Pagedale H2
Palmyra E2
Paris D2
Park Hills F4
Parkville H4
Peculiar B3
Peerless Park G3
Perryville G4
Pevely F3
Piedmont F4
Pierce City C5
Pine Lawn H2
Pineville B5
Platte City B2, H3
Plattsburg B2
Pleasant Hill B3
Poplar Bluff F5
Portageville G5
Potosi F4
Princeton C1
Randolph J4
Raymore B3
Raytown J4
Republic C4
Rich Hill B3
Richland D4
Richmond C2
Richmond Heights H2
Riverside H4
Rock Hill H2
Rock Port A1
Rolla E4
St. Ann H2
St. Charles F3, G2
St. Clair F3
Ste. Genevieve F4
St. James E3
St. John H2
St. Joseph B2
St. Louis F3, H2
St. Peters F3
St. Robert D4
Salem E4
Salisbury D2
Sappington H3
Sarcoxie B4
Savannah B2
Scott City G4
Sedalia C3
Senath F5
Seymour D4
Shelbina D2
Shelbyville D2
Shirley F4
Sikeston G5
Slater C2
Smithville B2
Springfield C4
Stanberry B1
Steele G5
Steelville E4
Stockton C4
Stoutsville E2
Sugar Creek J4
Sullivan E3
Sweet Springs C3
Tarkio A1
Thayer E5
Town and Country G2
Trenton C1
Troy F3
Tuscumbia D3
Union F3
Unionville C1
Unity Village J4
University City H2
Van Buren E5
Vandalia E2
Versailles D3
Vienna E3
Villa Ridge F3
Waldron H3
Warrensburg C3
Warrenton E3
Warsaw C3
Washington E3
Watson A1
Waynesville D4
Weatherby Lake H3
Webb City B4
Webster Groves H3
Wellsville E2
Wentzville F3
West Plains E5
Weston B2
Willard C4
Willow Springs E4
Windsor C3

Other Features
Bull Shoals, *lake* D5
Eleven Point, *river* E5
Fox, *river* E1
G.W. Carver Natl. Monument B5
Grand, *river* B1
Harry S. Truman, *reservoir* C3
Lake of the Ozarks, *lake* D3
Mark Twain, *lake* E2
Meramec, *river* E4
Mississippi, *river* G4
Missouri, *river* C2
Osage, *river* B4, D3
Ozark Natl. Scenic Riverways E4
Platte, *river* B2
St. Francis, *river* F4
Stockton, *lake* C4
Table Rock, *lake* C5
Taum Sauk, *mt.* F4
Thomas Hill, *reservoir* D2
Weldon, *river* C2

Montana...................page 153

Cities and Towns
Anaconda D3
Baker M3
Belgrade E4
Big Timber F4
Billings H4
Boulder D3
Bozeman E4
Bridger H4
Broadus L4
Butte D3
Chester F1
Chinook G1
Choteau D2
Circle L2
Columbus G4
Conrad E1
Crow Agency J4
Cut Bank D1
Deer Lodge D3
Dell D5
Dillon D4
East Helena E3
Ekalaka M4
Evergreen B1
Forsyth K3
Fort Benton F2
Gardiner F4
Glasgow K1
Glendive M2
Great Falls E2
Hamilton B3
Hardin J4
Harlowton G3
Hathaway K3
Havre G1
Helena, *capital* D3
Kalispell B1
Lame Deer K4
Laurel H4
Lewistown G2
Libby A1
Lincoln D3
Livingston F4
Lolo Hot Springs B3
Malta J1
Miles City L3

Key
Missoula C3
Orchard Homes B3
Philipsburg C3
Plentywood M1
Polson B2
Pony E4
Red Lodge G4
Ronan B2
Roundup H3
Rudyard F1
St. Regis A2
Scobey L1
Shelby E1
Sidney M2
Somers B1
Stanford F2
Superior B2
Terry L3
Thompson Falls A2
Townsend E3
West Yellowstone E5
Whitefish B1
Wibaux M3
Wolf Point L1

Other Features
Bighorn, *river* J4
Bighorn Canyon Natl. Rec. Area H4
Bitterroot, *river* B3
Bull, *mts.* H3
Canyon Ferry *lake* E3
Clark Fork, *river* D3
Cleveland, *mt.* C1
Custer Battlefield Natl. Monument J4
Elwell, *lake* E1
Flathead, *lake* B2
Flathead *river* B1
Fort Peck, *lake* K2
Fresno, *reservoir* F1
Glacier Natl. Park C1
Granite Peak, *mt.* D4
Granite Peak, *mt.* G4
Grant-Kohrs Ranch N.H.S. D3
Homer Youngs Peak, *mt.* C4
Hungry Horse, *reservoir* C1
Koocanusa, *lake* A1
Kootenai, *river* A1
Little Missouri, *river* M5
Madison, *river* E4
Marias, *river* E1
Middle Fork, *river* C1
Milk, *river* D1
Missouri, *river* G2
Musselshell, *river* H3
Northwest Peak, *mt.* A1
Pompeys Pillar Natl. Mon. H3
Powder, *river* L3
Rocky, *mts.* C2
St. Mary, *river* C1
St. Regis, *river* B2
Scarface Peak, *mt.* C2
South Fork, *river* C2
Swan, *river* C2
Teton, *river* E2
Tongue, *river* K4
Upper Missouri River Breaks N.M. G2
Warren Peak, *mt.* C4
Yellowstone, *river* L3
Yellowstone Natl. Park F5

Nebraska ....page 154

Cities and Towns
Ainsworth E2
Albion G3
Alliance B2
Alma E4
Ashland H3
Atkinson F2
Auburn J4
Aurora F4
Bartlett F3
Bassett E2
Beatrice H4
Beaver City E4
Bellevue J3
Benkelman C4
Blair H3
Brewster E3
Bridgeport A3
Broken Bow E3
Burwell E3
Butte F2
Center G2
Central City F3
Chadron B2
Chapman F3
Chappell B3
Clay Center F4
Columbus G3
Cozad E4
Crete H4
Dakota City H2
David City G3
Elkhorn H3
Elwood E4
Exeter G4
Fairbury G4
Falls City J4
Franklin F4
Fremont H3
Fullerton G3
Geneva G4
Gering A3
Gibbon F4
Gordon B2
Gothenburg D4
Grand Island F4
Grant C4
Greeley F3
Gretna H3
Guide Rock F4
Harrisburg A3
Harrison A2
Hartington G2
Hastings F4
Hayes Center C4
Hebron G4
Holdrege E4
Hyannis C3
Imperial C4
Kearney F4
Kimball A3
La Vista A3
Leigh G3
Lexington E4
Lincoln, *capital* H4
Loomis E4
Loup City F3
McCook D4
Madison G3
Milford G4
Minden F4
Mitchell A3
Mullen C2
Nebraska City J4
Neligh F2
Nelson F4
Norfolk G2
North Platte D3
Oakland H3
Ogallala C3
Omaha J3
O'Neill F2
Ord F3
Osceola G3
Oshkosh B3
Papillion H3
Pawnee City H4
Paxton C3
Pender H2
Pierce G2
Plainview G2
Plattsmouth J3
Plymouth H4
Ponca H2
Prague H3
Ravenna F3
Red Cloud F4
Rushville B2
St. Paul F3
Schuyler G3
Scottsbluff A3
Seward G4
Sidney B3
South Sioux City H2
Springfield H3
Springview E2
Stanton G3
Stapleton D3
Stockville D4
Superior F4
Sutton G4
Syracuse H4
Taylor E3
Tecumseh H4
Tekamah H3
Thedford D3
Trenton C4
Tryon D3
Valentine D2
Valley H3
Wahoo H3
Waverly H4
Wayne G2
West Point H3
Wilber H4
Wisner H3
Wymore H4
York G4

Other Features
Agate Fossil Beds N.M. A2
Arikee, *river* B5
Big Blue, *river* G5
C.W. McConaughy, *lake* C3
Calamus, *reservoir* E3
Calamus, *river* E2
Cedar, *river* F3
Chimney Rock Natl. Hist. Site A3
Elkhorn, *river* E2, G3
Harlan Co., *lake* E4
Homestead Natl. Monument H4
Lewis and Clark, *lake* G2
Little Blue, *river* G4
Loup, *river* F3
Middle Loup, *river* D3
Missouri, *river* J4
Niobrara, *river* B2, E2
North Loup, *river* C2, E3
North Platte, *river* B3
Pine, *mt. ridge* B2
Pine Ridge Natl. Rec. Area A2
Platte, *river* D4, G3
Republican, *river* D4
Sand, *hills* C3
Scotts Bluff Natl. Monument A3
South Fork Republican, *river* B5
South Loup, *river* E3

Nevada ....page 155

Cities and Towns
Alamo C3
Battle Mountain B1
Beatty B3
Boulder City C4
Carlin B1
Carson City, *capital* A2
Elko C1
Ely C2
Eureka C2
Fallon A2
Fernley A2
Gardnerville A2
Goldfield B3
Hawthorne A2
Henderson C3
Incline Village A2
Las Vegas C3
Laughlin C4
Lovelock A1
McGill C2
Mesquite C3
Minden A2
North Fork C1
North Las Vegas C3
Pahrump C3
Paradise C3
Pioche C3
Reno A2
Silver Peak B3
Sparks A2
Spring Creek C1
Spring Valley C3
Sun Valley A2
Tonopah B2
Virginia City A2
Wells C1
West Wendover C1
Winnemucca B1
Yerington A2
Zephyr Cove A2

Other Features
Arc Dome, *mt.* B2
Black Rock, *desert* A1
Boundary Peak, *mt.* A3
Colorado, *river* C4
Desert, *valley* C1
Egan, *range* C2
Goshute, *lake* C1
Grant, *mts.* C2
Grant, *mt.* A2
Great Basin B2
Great Basin Natl. Park C2
Hoover Dam C3
Hot Creek, *range* B2
Humboldt, *river* B1
Independence, *mts.* C1
Jefferson, *mt.* B2
Lake Mead Natl. Rec. Area C3
Marys, *river* C1
Matterhorn, *mt.* C1
Mead, *lake* C3
Mohave, *lake* C4
Monitor, *range* B2
Moriah, *mt.* C2
North Toiyabe Peak, *mt.* B2
Owyhee, *desert* B1
Owyhee, *river* B1
Pilot Peak, *mt.* C1
Pyramid, *lake* A1
Quinn, *river* B1
Ruby, *mts.* C1
Ruby Dome, *mt.* C1
Rye Patch, *reservoir* A1
Schell Creek, *range* C2
Shoshone, *mts.* B2
Shoshone, *range* B1
Smoky, *valley* B2
Snake, *range* C2
Summit, *mt.* B2
Tahoe, *lake* A2
Tobin, *mt.* B1
Toiyabe, *range* B2
Toquima, *range* B2
Tuscarora, *mts.* B1
Virgin, *river* C3
Walker, *lake* A2
Wheeler Peak, *mt.* C2
White, *river* C3

New Hampshire ....page 156

Cities and Towns
Albany B3
Amherst B4
Antrim B3
Barnstead B3
Bartlett B2
Benton B2
Berlin B2
Blair B3
Bradford B3
Bretton Woods B2
Bristol B3
Candia B3
Cascade B2
Claremont A3
Concord, *capital* B3
Contoocook B3
Conway B3
Cornish City A3
Dalton B2
Deerfield B3
Deering B3
Derry B4
Dixville Notch B2
Dover C3
Dunbarton Center B3
Durham C3
Easton B2
Enfield A3
Epping B3
Exeter C4
Farmington B3
Franklin B3
Gilmanton B3
Glencliff B2
Gorham B2
Groveton B2
Hampstead B4
Hampton C4
Hanover A3
Haverhill A2
Henniker B3
Hillsboro B3
Hinsdale A4
Hollis B4
Hooksett B3
Hudson B4
Jackson B2
Jaffrey A4
Jefferson B2
Keene A4
Laconia B3
Lancaster B2
Lebanon A3
Littleton B2
Loudon B3
Lyman B2
Manchester B4
Meredith B3
Merrimack B4
Milan B2
Milford B4
Monroe A2
Munsonville A3
Nashua B4
Newbury A3
New Castle C3
New London B3
Newmarket C3
Newport A3
North Conway B2
Northfield B3
North Haverhill A2
North Walpole A3
North Woodstock B2
Orford A3
Ossipee B3
Pelham B4
Percy B2
Peterborough B4
Pinardville B4
Pittsfield B3
Plymouth B3
Portsmouth C3
Quaker City A3
Randolph B2
Raymond B3
Rochester C3
Rumney B3
Rye C4
Sandwich B3
Sharon B4
Shelburne B2
Silver Lake B3
Somersworth C3
South Hooksett B3
Springfield A3
Stewartstown Hollow B2
Strafford B3
Stratford B2
Suncook B3
Sutton B3
Tilton B3
Warner B3
Waterville Valley B3
Westport A4
West Rindge A4
West Stewardstown B2
Whittier B3
Willey House B2
Winchester A4
Wolfeboro B3
Woodsville A2

Other Features
Appalachian Natl. Scenic Trail A3
Blackwater, *reservoir* B3
Blue, *mt.* B2
Cabot, *mt.* B2
Cardigan, *mt.* B3
Connecticut, *river* A3
First Connecticut, *lake* B1
Franconia, *notch* B2
Great, *bay* C3
Indian, *river* B1
Kearsarge, *mt.* B3
Merrimack, *river* B4
Monadnock, *mt.* A4
Newfound, *lake* B3
Ossipee, *lake* B3
Presidential, *mt. range* B2
Saint-Gaudens Natl. Hist. Site A3
Second Connecticut, *lake* B1
Smarts, *mt.* A3
Squam, *lake* B3
Sunapee, *lake* A3
Swift, *river* B3
Umbagog, *lake* B2
Washington, *mt.* B2
White, *mts.* B2
Winnipesaukee, *lake* B3
Winnisquam, *lake* B3

New Jersey ....page 157

Cities and Towns
Absecon E5
Allendale E1
Allentown D3
Alloway C4
Alpine C1
Asbury Park E3
Atlantic City E5
Atlantic Highlands E3
Atsion D4
Avalon D5
Barrington B3
Basking Ridge D2
Batsto D4
Bay Point C5
Bayonne E2
Bayside C5
Beachwood E4
Beattyestown D2
Beckett C4
Belle Mead D3
Belleville B2
Bellmawr B3, C4
Belmar E3
Belvidere C2
Bergenfield B1
Berkeley Heights E2
Berlin D4
Bernardsville D2
Blackwood C4
Blairstown D2
Bloomfield E2
Bogota B1
Boonton E2
Bordentown D3
Bound Brook D2
Bradley Beach E2
Brass Castle C2
Brick E3
Bridgeboro C3
Bridgeton C5
Brielle E3
Brigantine E5
Brookdale B1
Browns Mills D4
Budd Lake D2
Buena D4
Burlington D3
Butler E1
Caldwell A1
Camden B3, C4
Cape May D6
Cape May Court House D5
Carlstadt B1
Carneys Point C4
Carteret B2
Carteret E2
Cedar Grove B1
Centerton C4
Centerville D2
Chatham E2
Cherry Hill B3, C4
Chesilhurst D4
Chesterfield D3
Cinnaminson B3, D4
Clark A2
Clayton C4
Cliffside Park C2
Clifton B1
Clinton D2
Closter F2
Colesville D1
Collings Lakes D4
Collingswood B3
Colonia E2
Cranford E2
Deerfield C4
Delanco D3
Denville E2
Deptford B4
Dover D2
Dumont C1
Dunellen E2
East Brunswick E3
East Orange E2
East Rutherford B1
Eatontown E3
Edgewater F2
Edison E2
Egg Harbor City D4
Elizabeth E2
Elmer C4
Elmwood Park B1
Elwood D4
Emerson E2
Englewood C1
Englewood Cliffs C1
Englishtown E3
Erma D6
Estell Manor D5
Evesboro C3
Ewing D3
Fair Lawn B1, E2
Fairfield E2
Fairton C5
Fairview F2
Fanwood E2
Farmingdale E3
Fellowship C3
Fieldsboro D3
Flemington D3
Folsom D4
Fords E2
Forked River E4
Fort Lee F2
Franklin D1
Franklinville C4
Freehold E3
Frenchtown C2
Garfield E2
Gilford Park E4
Glassboro C4
Glen Gardner D2
Glen Ridge B2
Glendora C4
Gloucester City B3, C4
Goshen D5
Great Notch B1
Green Bank D4
Greenwich C5
Guttenberg F2
Hackensack E2
Hackettstown D2
Haddon Heights B3
Haddonfield B3
Hainesville D1
Haledon B1
Hamburg D1
Hammonton D4
Hampton D2
Harrison B2
Haworth C1
Hawthorne B1
Hedger House D4
High Bridge D2
Highland Lakes E1
Highland Park E3
Highlands F3
Hightstown D3
Hillsdale E1
Hillside B2
Hoboken E2
Hopatcong D2
Hopewell D3
Howardsville E4
Indian Mills D4
Irvington B2
Jamesburg E3
Jenkins Neck D4
Jersey City E2
Keansburg E3
Kearny B2
Kendall Park D3
Kenilworth E2
Kinnelon E2
Lakehurst E3
Lakewood E3
Lambertville D3
Lavallette E4
Lawnside B3
Lawrenceville D3
Leeds Point E5
Leisure Village E3
Leisuretowne D4
Leonardo E3
Lincroft E3
Linden E2
Lindenwold B4, C4
Linwood D5
Little Falls B1
Livingston E2
Lodi B1
Long Branch F3
Long Valley D2
Lyndhurst B2
Madison E2
Mahwah E1
Manahawkin E4
Manalapan E3
Manasquan E3
Manumuskin D5
Manville D2
Maple Shade B3, D4
Maplewood E2
Marcella E2
Margate City E5
Marlboro E3
Marlton C3, D4
Matawan E3
Mays Landing D5
Maywood B1
Medford Lakes D4
Mendham D2
Menlo Park E2
Merchantville B3
Metuchen E2
Middlesex E2
Middletown E3
Midland Park E2
Milford C2
Millburn E2
Millville C5
Monmouth Beach F3
Montclair E2
Montvale E1
Moorestown C3, D4
Morris Plains E2
Morristown E2
Mountain Lakes E2
Mount Holly D4
Mount Laurel D4
Mystic Islands E4
National Park B3
Neptune City E3
Netcong D2
Newark E2
New Brunswick E3
New Egypt D3
Newfield C4
New Gretna E4
Newfoundland E1
New Providence E2
Newton D1
Normandy Beach E3
North Arlington B2
North Bergen B2
North Cape May D6
Northfield D5
North Wildwood D5
Nutley B2
Oakland E2
Oaklyn B3
Ocean City D5
Oceanport E3
Ogdensburg D1
Olivet C4
Oradell B1
Orange B2
Othello C5
Oxford D2
Palisades Park B1
Palmyra B3, C3
Paramus B1, E2
Park Ridge E1
Passaic E2
Paterson E2
Paulsboro A4, C4
Pemberton D4
Pennington D3
Penns Grove C4
Pennsauken B3
Pennsville B4
Perth Amboy E2
Phillipsburg C2
Piscataway E2
Pine Hill D4
Pitman C4
Pittstown D2
Plainfield E2
Pleasant Plains E4
Pleasantville D5
Point Pleasant E3
Pomona D5
Port Monmouth E3
Port Norris C5
Princeton D3
Princeton Junction D3
Prospect Park B1
Quinton C4
Rahway A2
Ramblewood C3
Ramsey E1
Raritan D2
Red Bank E3
Ridgefield B2
Ridgefield Park B1, E2
Ridgewood E2
Ringoes D3
Ringwood E1
Rio Grande D5
River Edge B1
Riverside C3, D3
Riverton B3, C3
Robertsville E3
Rochelle Park B1
Rocktown D3
Roselle A2
Roselle Park A2
Rumson F3
Runnemede B4, C4
Rutherford B1
Salem C4
Sayreville E3
Seabrook C5
Sea Girt E3
Sea Isle City D5
Seaside Heights E4
Seaside Park E4
Secaucus B2
Ship Bottom E4
Shrewsbury E3
Silverton E3
Smithville E5
Somerdale B4
Somers Point D5
Somerset E3
Somerville D2
South Amboy E3
South Orange A2
South River E3
Sparta D1
Spotswood E3
Spring Lake Heights E3
Stanhope D2
Stillwater D1
Stockholm D1
Stratford B4, C4
Strathmere D5
Summit E2
Surf City E4
Sussex D1
Swedesboro C4
Teaneck B1
Tenafly F2
Tinton Falls E3
Toms River E4
Totowa B1
Trenton, *capital* D3
Tuckahoe D5
Tuckerton E4
Turnersville C4
Twin Rivers E3
Union E2
Union Beach E3
Union City E2
Upton D4
Vauxhall A2
Ventnor City E5
Vernon E1
Verona A1
Villas D5
Vineland C5
Voorhees C4
Waldwick E1
Wanamassa E3
Wanaque E1
Waretown E4
Warren Glen C2
Warren Grove E4
Washington D2
Washington Crossing D3
Watchung E2
Wayne A1, E2
Weehawken B2
Welchville C4
Wenonah C4
Westfield E2
West Milford E1
Westmont B3
West New York C2
West Orange E2
West Paterson B1
Westville B3
Westwood B1
Wharton D2
White Horse D3
White House Station D2
White Meadow Lake D2

Key
Whiting E4
Wildwood D6
Wildwood Crest D6
Williamstown D4
Willingboro D3
Woodbine D5
Woodbridge E2
Woodbury B4, C4
Woodlynne B3
Wood Ridge B1
Woodstown C4
Woodstream C3
Wrightstown D3
Wyckoff E1

Other Features
Cape May, *point* D6
Cooper, *river* B4
Delaware, *bay* C5
Delaware, *river* D3
Delaware Water Gap N.R.A. D1
Edison Natl. Hist. Site B2
Gateway Natl. Rec. Area F3
Great, *bay* E5
Hudson, *river* C2
Morristown Nat. Hist. Park D2
Pines, *lake* B1
Raritan, *bay* E3
Statue of Liberty N.M. B2

New Mexico ....page 158

Cities and Towns
Acoma Pueblo B2
Acomita B2
Alameda B2
Alamogordo C3
Albuquerque B2
Anthony B4
Artesia C3
Aztec B1
Bayard A3
Belen B2
Bernalillo B2
Bloomfield B1
Bosque Farms B2
Carlsbad C3
Carrizozo C3
Central A3
Chaparral B3
Chimayo C1
Clayton D1
Clovis D2
Corrales B2
Deming B3
Dulce B1
Elida D3
Elk C3
Elkins C3
Espanola B2
Estancia B2
Eunice D3
Fairacres B3
Farmington A1
Floyd D2
Fort Sumner C2
Gallup A2
Grants B2
Greenfield C3
Hobbs D3
Hurley A3
Jal D3
Jemez Pueblo B2
Kirtland A1
La Luz C3
Las Cruces B3
Las Vegas C2
Lordsburg A3
Los Alamos B2
Los Chavez B2
Los Lunas B2
Los Padillas B2
Lovington D3
Lower Colonias C2
Lower San Francisco Plaza A3
Maxwell C1
Mayhill C3
Mesilla B3
Milan B2
Mora C2
Moriarty B2
Mosquero D2
Navajo A2
Polvadera B2
Portales D2
Questa C1
Ranchos De Taos C1
Raton C1
Reserve A3
Rio Rancho B2
Roswell C3
Ruidoso C3
Sabinoso C2
San Felipe Pueblo B2
San Miguel B1
San Miguel B3
Santa Fe, *capital* C2
Santa Rosa C2
Santo Domingo Pueblo B2
Shiprock A1
Silver City A3
Socorro B2
Springer C1
Sunland Park B4
Taos C1
Tesuque C2
Tierra Amarilla B1
Truth or Consequences B3
Tucumcari D2
Tularosa B3
University Park B3
Ute Park C1
Valencia B2
Waterflow A1
Zuni Pueblo A2

Other Features
Abiquiu, *reservoir* B1
Alegres, *mt.* A2
Aztec Ruins Natl. Monument B1
Baldy, *mt.* C1
Bandelier Natl. Monument B2
Black, *mt. range* B3
Burro, *mt.* A3
Caballo, *reservoir* B3
Canadian, *river* C1
Capulin Volcano N.M. D1
Carlsbad Caverns Natl. Park C3
Cebolleta, *mt.* B2
Cerro Vista, *mt.* C1
Chaco Culture Natl. Hist. Park B1
Cimarron, *river* D1
Conchas, *lake* C2
Contintal Divide, *mt. ridge* B2
Cooke's, *mt.* B3
Elephant Butte, *res.* B3
El Malpais Natl. Monument B2
El Morro Natl. Monument A2
Fort Union Natl. Monument C2
Gallinas, *mt.* C2
Gila, *river* A3
Gila Cliff Dwellings N.M. A3
Guadalupe, *mts.* C3
Jornada Del Muerto B3
Kasha-Katuwe Tent Rocks N.M. B2
Llano Estacado, *plateau* D3
Navajo, *reservoir* B1
Navajo Indian Res. A1
Pecos, *river* C2, C3
Pecos, *plains* C3
Pecos N.H.P. C2
Petroglyph Natl. Monument B2
Playas, *lake* A4
Reeds, *mt.* B3
Rio Grande, *river* C1
Rio Hondo, *river* C3
Rio Puerco, *river* B2
Salinas Pueblo Missions N.M. B2
San Andres, *mts.* B3
San Juan, *river* A1
Sangre De Cristo, *mts.* C1
Shiprock, *mt.* A1
Sierra Blanca, *mt.* C3
South Baldy, *mt.* B3
Sumner, *lake* C2
Taylor, *mt.* B2
Wheeler, *mt.* C1
White Sands Natl. Monument B3
Whitewater Baldy, *mt.* A3
Withington, *mt.* B3
Zuni, *mts.* A2

New York ....page 159

Cities and Towns
Adams H3
Adams Center H3
Akron C4
Albany, *capital* N5
Albion D4
Alden D5
Alfred E6
Allegany D6
Altamont M5
Amsterdam M5
Angola B5
Arcade D5
Astoria A3
Athens N6
Attica D5
Auburn G5
Avon E5
Bainbridge J6
Baldwinsville H4
Ballston Spa N4
Batavia D4
Bath F6
Beacon N7
Bedford-Stuyvesant A4
Belle Harbor A4
Belmont D6
Bensonhurst A4
Big Flats G6
Binghamton J6
Bloomfield F5
Bolivar D6
Boonville K4
Breezy Point A4
Brentwood C1
Brewerton H4
Bridgehampton E1
Brighton Beach A4
Broadalbin M4
Brockport E4
Brocton B6
Bronx A3, B1
Bronxville A2
Brooklyn A4, B2
Buffalo C5
Cairo M6
Calcium J2
Caledonia E5
Cambridge P4
Camden J4
Canajoharie L5
Canandaigua F5
Canarsie A4
Canastota J4
Canisteo E6
Canton K1
Carmel N7
Carthage J3
Castleton-on-Hudson N5
Catskill N6
Cayuga Heights H6
Cazenovia J5
Cedarhurst B4
Central Square H4
Chatham N6
Cheektowaga C5
Chittenango J4
Churchville E4
Clayton H2
Clinton K4
Clyde G4
Cobleskill L5
Cohoes N5
College Point A3
Colonie N5
Coney Island A4
Cooperstown L5
Corinth N4
Corning F6
Cortland H5
Coxsackie N6
Cuba D6
Dannemora N1
Dansville E5
Delhi L6
De Ruyter J5
Deposit K6
Dolgeville L4
Dover Plains N7
Dryden H6
Dundee G6
Dunkirk B6
East Atlantic Beach B4
Eastchester A2
East Hampton E1
East Islip C2
East New York A4
East Northport C1
East Patchogue D1
Eden C5
Elizabethtown N2
Ellenville M7
Elmira G6
Elmira Heights G6
Elmont B4
Endicott H6
Endwell H6
Fairmount H4
Far Rockaway B4
Fayette G5
Fine K2
Flatbush A4
Flushing A3
Fonda M5
Fort Edward N4
Fort Plain L5
Franklin Sq. B4
Franklinville D6
Fredonia B6
Freeport C2
Frewsburg C6
Friendship D6
Fulton H4
Geneseo E5
Geneva G5
Glen Cove B1
Glens Falls N4
Gloversville M4
Goshen M7
Gouverneur K2
Gowanda C6
Granville P4
Gravesend A4
Great Neck B1
Greece E4
Greene J6
Greenport E1
Greenwich P4
Groton H5
Hamburg C5
Hamilton J5
Hampton Bays E1
Hancock K7
Harlem A3
Hempstead B2
Herkimer L4
Hicksville C1
Highland N7
Hilton E4
Holbrook C1
Holland C5
Holley D4
Homer H5
Hoosick Falls P5
Hornell E6
Horseheads G6
Houghton D6
Howard Beach A4
Hudson N6
Hudson Falls N4
Huntington Station C1
Hurley M7
Ilion K4
Inwood B4
Irondequoit E4
Ithaca H6
Jamaica B2
Jamestown B6
Johnson City J6
Johnstown M4
Keeseville P1
Kew Gardens A4
Kinderhook N6
Kingston N7
Lake George N4
Lake Placid M2
Lake Pleasant M4
Lakewood B6
Lansing H5
Larchmont B2
Lawrence B4
Le Roy D5
Levittown C1
Liberty L7
Lima E5
Lindenhurst C2
Little Falls L4
Little Valley C6
Livingston Manor L7
Livonia E5
Lockport C4
Long Beach B2
Long Eddy K7
Long Island City A3
Long Lake M3
Loon Lake M1
Lowville K3
Lynbrook B4
Lyons G4
Malone M1
Mamaroneck B2
Manhasset Hills B3
Manhattan A3
Manlius J4
Manorhaven B3
Massapequa C2
Massena L1
Mastic D1
Mastic Beach D1
Mattituck E1
Mayville A6
Mechanicville N5
Medina D4
Mexico H4
Middleburgh M5
Middleport D4
Middletown M7
Millbrook N7
Mineola B1
Mohawk K5
Monroe A1
Montauk F1
Monticello L7
Montour Falls G6
Moravia H5
Mount Kisco B1
Mount Morris E5
Mount Vernon B1, C5
Munnsville J5
Nassau N5
Newark F4
Newburgh M7
New City C1
Newfane C4
New Hartford K4
New Hyde Park B3
New Paltz M7
New Rochelle B3
New York B3
Niagara Falls B4
Norfolk L1
North Collins C5
North Hills B3
North Syracuse H4
North Tonawanda C4
Norwich J5
Norwood L1
Nunda E5
Nyack B1
Oakfield D4
Ogdensburg K1
Olcott C4
Olean D6
Oneida J4
Oneonta K6
Ossining B1
Oswego H4
Owego H6
Oxford J6
Ozone Park A4
Painted Post F6
Palmyra F4
Pawling N7
Peekskill B1
Pelham A3
Pelham Manor A3
Penn Yan F5
Perry D5
Peru N1
Philadelphia J2
Philmont N6
Phoenix H4
Pine Bush M7
Plattsburgh P1
Port Henry P2
Port Jefferson D1
Port Morris A3
Port Washington B3
Potsdam L1
Poughkeepsie N7
Pulaski H3
Queens B4
Randolph C6
Ransomville C4
Ravena N6
Red Hook N6
Rensselaer N5
Rhinebeck N7
Richfield Springs L5
Riverhead D1
Rochester E4
Rockaway Point A4
Rocky Point D1
Rome K4
Rosendale M7
Rouses Point P1
Rye B2
Sackets Harbor H3
Sag Harbor E1
St. George A2
St. Johnsville L4
Salamanca C6
Sands Point B3
Saranac Lake M2
Saratoga Springs N4
Saugerties N6
Sayville D2
Schenectady N5
Schoharie M5
Scotia N5
Seneca Falls G5
Sherburne K5
Shortsville F5
Sidney K6
Silver Creek B5
Skaneateles H5
Sodus F4
Southampton E1
South Fallsburg L7
Southold E1
Southport G6
Spencerport E4
Springville C5
Stillwater N5
Stony Brook C1
Suffern A1
Syracuse H4
Throgs Neck A3
Ticonderoga P3
Troy N5
Trumansburg G5
Tupper Lake M2
Unadilla K6
Utica K4
Valley Stream B2
Victory Mills N4
Voorheesville N5
Walden M7
Walton K6
Wampsville J4
Wappingers Falls N7
Warrensburg N4
Warsaw D5
Warwick A1
Waterloo G5
Watertown J3
Waterville K5
Watkins Glen G6
Waverly G6
Wayland E5
Weedsport G4
Wellsville E6
West Carthage J3
Westfield A6
West Point N7
West Seneca C5
Whitehall P3
White Plains B1
Whitesboro K4
Whitestone A3
Williamsburg A4
Wilson C4
Wolcott G4
Woodmere B4
Woodstock M6
Yonkers B1
Yorktown Heights B1

Other Features
Adirondack, *mts.* L2
Adirondack Park M2
Appalachian Natl. Scenic Trail A1
Black, *lake* J2
Black, *river* K3
Cannonsville, *reservoir* K6
Catskill, *mts.* L7
Catskill Park L6
Cayuga, *lake* G5
Champlain, *lake* P1
Chenango, *river* J6
Cranberry, *lake* L2
Delaware, *river* K7
Eleanor Roosevelt N.H.S. N7
Erie, *canal* J4
Erie, *lake* A5
Fire Island Natl. Seashore D2
Fishers, *island* F1
Fort Stanwix Natl. Monument K4
Galloo, *island* H3
Gardiners, *island* F1
Gateway Natl. Rec. Area B2
Genesee, *river* D6
George, *lake* N3
Governors Island Natl. Mon. A4
Great Sacandaga, *lake* M4
Hinckley, *reservoir* K4
Home of F.D.R. Natl. Hist Site N7
Hudson, *river* M3
Indian, *lake* M3
J.F.K. Int'l Airport A4
Keuka, *lake* F5
Long, *island* E1
Long, *lake* M3
Long Island, *sound* C1
Marcy, *mt.* N2
Martin Van Buren Natl. Hist. Site N6
Mettawee, *river* P3
Mohawk, *river* L5
Oneida, *lake* J4
Ontario, *lake* E3
Pepacton, *reservoir* L6
Piseco, *lake* L4
St. Lawrence, *river* K1
Salmon River, *reservoir* J3
Saratoga, *lake* N4
Saratoga Natl. Hist. Park N4
Schoharie, *reservoir* M6
Schroon, *lake* N3
Slide, *mt.* M7
Staten, *island* A2
Stony, *island* H3
Susquehanna, *river* J6
Thomas Cole Natl. Hist. Site N6
Thousand, *islands* H2
Tupper, *lake* L2
Unadilla, *river* K5
Upper Saranac, *lake* M2
Vanderbilt Mansion N.H.S. N7
West Point Military Academy A1
Women's Rights N.H.P. G5

North Carolina ....page 160

Cities and Towns
Aberdeen G4
Ahoskie L2
Albemarle E4
Andrews C8
Angier H3
Apex H3
Archdale F3
Asheboro F3
Asheville E7
Atlantic Beach M5
Ayden L4
Badin E4
Bakersville A2
Bayboro M4
Beaufort M5
Belhaven M3
Belmont C4
Benson H4
Bessemer City C4
Bethel L3
Biscoe F4
Black Mt. A3
Bladenboro H5
Blowing Rock B2
Boiling Spring Lakes J6
Boiling Springs B4
Bolivia J6
Boone B2
Brevard E8
Bryson City C8
Buies Creek H4
Burgaw K5
Burlington G2
Burnsville A3
Butner H2
Camden N2
Canton E7
Carolina Beach K6
Carthage G4
Cary H3
Chadbourn H6
Chapel Hill G3
Charlotte D4
Cherryville C4
China Grove D3
Clayton J3
Clemmons E3
Clinton J5
Coats H4
Columbia N3
Columbus A4
Concord D4
Conover C3
Cornelius D4
Creedmoor H2
Cullowhee D8
Currituck N2
Dallas C4
Danbury E2
Davidson D3
Denton E3
Dobson D2
Drexel B3
Dunn H4
Durham H2
E. Flat Rock E8
Eden F2
Edenton M2
Elizabeth City N2
Elizabethtown H5
Elkin D2
Elm City K3
Emerald Isle M5
Enfield K2
Erwin H4
Fairmont G5
Farmville K3
Fayetteville H4
Fletcher E8
Forest City B4
Four Oaks J4
Franklin C8
Franklinton J2
Fremont K3
Fuquay-Varina H3
Gamewell B3
Garner H3
Gastonia C4
Gatesville M2
Gibsonville F2
Goldsboro K4
Graham G2
Granite Falls C3
Granite Quarry E3
Greensboro F2
Greenville L3
Grifton L4
Halifax K2
Hamlet F5
Harkers Island M5
Harrisburg D4
Havelock M5
Hayesville C8
Hays C2
Henderson J2
Hendersonville E8
Hertford N2
Hickory C3
High Point E3
Hillsborough G2
Hope Mills H5
Hudson C3
Huntersville D4
Icard C3
Indian Trail D4
Jackson L2
Jacksonville L5
Jamestown F3
Jefferson C2
Jonesville D2
Kannapolis D4
Kenansville K5
Kenly J3
Kernersville E2
Kill Devil Hills P2
King E2
Kings Mt. C4
Kinston K4
Kitty Hawk P2
La Grange K4
Laurinburg G5
Leland J6
Lenoir B3
Lewisville E2
Lexington E3
Liberty F3
Lillington H4
Lincolnton C4
Locust E4
Long Beach J7
Long View C3
Louisburg J2
Lumberton G5
Madison F2
Maiden C3
Manteo P3
Marion A3
Marshall E7
Marshville E5
Matthews D4
Maxton G5
Mayodan F2
Mebane G2
Mint Hill D4
Mocksville D3
Monroe D5
Mooresville D3
Moravian Falls C2
Morehead City M5
Morganton B3
Mt. Airy D2
Mt. Gilead F4
Mt. Holly D4
Mt. Olive J4
Mulberry C2
Murfreesboro L2
Murphy B8
Nags Head P3
Nashville K3
New Bern L4
Newland B2
Newport M5
Newton C3
Norwood E4
North Wilkesboro C2
Oxford H2
Pembroke G5
Pinehurst G4
Pinetops K3
Pineville D4
Piney Green L5
Pittsboro G3
Plymouth M3
Polkville B4
Raeford G5
Raleigh, *capital* H3
Randleman F3
Red Springs G5
Reidsville F2
River Bend L4
Roanoke Rapids K2
Robbinsville C8
Robersonville L3
Rockingham F5
Rockwell E3
Rocky Mount K3
Rolesville J3
Rose Hill J5
Roseboro H5
Roxboro H2
Rural Hall E2
Rutherfordton B4
Salisbury E3
Sanford G4
Sawmills C3
Scotland Neck L2
Selma J3
Seven Lakes F4
Sharpsburg K3
Shelby B4
Siler City G3
Smithfield J3
Sneads Ferry L5
Snow Hill K4
Southern Pines G4
Southern Shores P2
Southport J7
Sparta C1
Spencer E3
Spindale B4
Spring Lake H4
Spruce Pine A3
St. Pauls H5
Stanley C4
Stanleyville E2
Statesville D3
Stokesdale F2
Stony Point C3
Summerfield F2
Swan Quarter N4
Sylva D8

Key
Tabor City ... H6
Tarboro ... K3
Taylorsville ... C3
Thomasville ... E3
Toast ... D2
Trenton ... L4
Troutman ... D3
Troy ... F4
Valdese ... B3
Wadesboro ... E5
Wake Forest ... H3
Wallace ... K5
Wanchese ... P3
Warrenton ... J2
Warsaw ... J5
Washington ... L3
Waxhaw ... D5
Waynesville ... D7
Weddington ... D4
Welcome ... E3
Weldon ... K2
Wendell ... J3
Wentworth ... F2
W. Jefferson ... C2
Whiteville ... H6
Wilkesboro ... C2
Williamston ... L3
Wilmington ... K6
Wilson ... K3
Windsor ... M2
Winfall ... N2
Wingate ... E5
Winston-Salem ... E2
Winterville ... L3
Winton ... M2
Woodfin ... E7
Wrightsville Beach ... K6
Yadkinville ... D2
Yanceyville ... G2
Zebulon ... J3

Other Features
Albemarle, *sound* ... N3
Alligator, *lake* ... N3
Alligator, *river* ... N3
B. Everett Jordan, *lake* ... G3
Bodie, *island* ... P3
Cape Fear, *river* ... H5
Cape Hatteras Natl. Seashore ... P4
Cape Lookout Natl. Seashore ... N5
Chatuga, *lake* ... C8
Clingmans Dome, *mt.* ... C7
Dan, *river* ... F2
Deep, *river* ... F3
Falls Lake, *reservoir* ... H3
Fear, *cape* ... K7
Fontana, *lake* ... C7
Fort Raleigh Natl. Hist. Site ... P3
Gaston, *lake* ... K1
Great, *lake* ... L5
Great Smoky Mts. Natl. Park ... C7
Hatteras, *cape* ... P4
Hatteras, *inlet* ... P4
Highrock, *lake* ... E3
Hiwassee, *lake* ... B8
Hyco, *lake* ... G2
John H. Kerr, *reservoir* ... H1
Lookout, *cape* ... M5
Mattamuskeat, *lake* ... N3
Mitchell, *mt.* ... A3
Nantahala, *lake* ... C8
Neuse, *river* ... J4
Norman, *lake* ... D3
Ocracoke, *inlet* ... N4
Oregon, *inlet* ... P3
Pamlico, *river* ... M4
Pamlico, *sound* ... P4
Phelps, *lake* ... N3
Roan, *mt.* ... A2
Roanoke, *river* ... K2
Rocky, *river* ... E4
Smith, *island* ... K7
Standing Indian, *mt.* ... C8
Tar, *river* ... J2
Waccamaw, *lake* ... J6
Wright Brothers Natl. Memorial ... P2
Yadkin, *river* ... D2

North Dakota ... page 161

Cities and Towns
Ashley ... F3
Beach ... A3
Belcourt ... F1
Beulah ... D2
Bismarck, *capital* ... E3
Bowman ... B3
Cando ... F1
Carrington ... F2
Casselton ... H3
Cavalier ... H1
Center ... D2
Cooperstown ... G2
Crosby ... B1
Devils Lake ... G1
Dickinson ... C3
Ellendale ... G3
Fargo ... J3
Fessenden ... F2
Finley ... H2
Forman ... H3
Fort Yates ... E3
Garrison ... D2
Grafton ... H1
Grand Forks ... H2
Harvey ... F2
Hazen ... D2
Hettinger ... C3
Hillsboro ... H2
Jamestown ... G3
Lakota ... G1
La Moure ... G3
Langdon ... G1
Larimore ... H2
Linton ... E3
Lisbon ... H3
McClusky ... E2
Mandan ... E3
Mayville ... H2
Mohall ... D1
Mott ... C3
Napoleon ... F3
New Rockford ... F2
New Town ... C1
Oakes ... G3
Park River ... H1
Rolla ... F1
Rugby ... F1
Stanley ... C1
Stanton ... D2
Steele ... F3

Key
Tioga ... C1
Towner ... E1
Valley City ... H3
Wahpeton ... J3
Washburn ... D2
Watford City ... B2
West Fargo ... J3
Williston ... B1

Other Features
Cannonball, *river* ... D3
Devils, *lake* ... G1
Fort Union Trading Post N.H.S. ... A1
Green, *river* ... B2
Heart, *river* ... D3
Intl. Peace Garden ... E1
James, *river* ... F2
Jamestown, *reservoir* ... G2
Knife, *river* ... C2
Knife River Indian Villages N.H.S. ... D2
Little Missouri, *river* ... B3
Long, *lake* ... E3
Maple, *river* ... G3, H2
Missouri, *river* ... D2
Oahe, *lake* ... E3
Pembina, *river* ... G1
Sakakawea, *lake* ... C2
Sheyenne, *river* ... E2, G2, H3
Souris, *river* ... D1
Theodore Roosevelt N.P. ... B2, B3
White Butte, *mt.* ... B3
Wild Rice, *river* ... H3

Ohio ... page 162

Cities and Towns
Aberdeen ... C8
Ada ... C4
Akron ... G3
Alliance ... H4
Ansonia ... A5
Antrim ... H5
Antwerp ... A3
Arabia ... F8
Arcanum ... A6
Archbold ... B2
Arlington ... C4
Ashland ... F4
Ashtabula ... J2
Athens ... F7
Aurora ... H3
Avon Lake ... F2
Baltimore ... E6
Barberton ... G3
Barnesville ... H6
Batavia ... B7
Bay Village ... G9
Beachwood ... J9
Bedford ... J9
Bedford Heights ... J9
Bellaire ... J5
Bellefontaine ... C5
Bellevue ... E3
Bellville ... E4
Berea ... G9
Berlin Heights ... F3
Bethel ... B8
Beverly ... G6
Blanchester ... C7
Blissfield ... G5
Blue Ash ... C9
Bluffton ... C4
Boardman ... J3
Bowling Green ... C3
Bradford ... B5
Bremen ... F6
Brewster ... G4
Bridgetown ... B9
Broadview Heights ... H10
Brook Park ... G9
Brooklyn ... H9
Brookville ... B6
Brunswick ... G3
Bryan ... A3
Bucyrus ... E4
Burton ... H3
Cadiz ... J5
Caldwell ... G6
Cambridge ... G5
Camden ... A6
Canal Fulton ... G4
Canal Winchester ... E6
Canfield ... J3
Canton ... H4
Cardington ... E5
Carey ... D4
Carrollton ... H4
Cedarville ... C6
Celina ... A4
Centerburg ... E5
Chagrin Falls ... H3
Chardon ... H2
Chesterhill ... G7
Cheviot ... B9
Chillicothe ... E7
Cincinnati ... A7
Circleville ... E6
Cleveland ... G2
Cleveland Heights ... G2
Cleves ... A9
Clyde ... E3
Coldwater ... A5
Columbiana ... J4
Columbus, *capital* ... D6
Columbus Grove ... B4
Congress ... F4
Conneaut ... J2
Cortland ... J3
Coshocton ... G5
Covington ... B5
Crestline ... E4
Creston ... G4
Crooksville ... F6
Cuyahoga Falls ... H3
Dalton ... G4
Dayton ... B6
De Graff ... C5
Deer Park ... C9
Defiance ... B3
Delaware ... D5
Delhi Hills ... B9
Delphos ... B4
Delta ... C2
Deshler ... C3
Dover ... H4
Dresden ... F5
Dublin ... D5
Dunkinsville ... D8
E. Cleveland ... H8
East Liverpool ... J4
East Palestine ... J4

Key
Eaton ... A6
Edgerton ... A3
Elida ... B4
Elyria ... F3
Euclid ... G2
Fairborn ... C6
Fairfield ... A7
Fairport Harbor ... H2
Fairview Park ... G9
Findlay ... C3
Fitchville ... F3
Forest ... C4
Forest Park ... B8
Forestville ... B7
Fort Recovery ... A5
Fort Shawnee ... B4
Fostoria ... D3
Franklin ... B6
Fredericktown ... E5
Fremont ... D3
Fresno ... G5
Gahanna ... E5
Galion ... E4
Gallipolis ... F8
Gambier ... F5
Garfield Hts. ... H9
Geneva ... J2
Genoa ... D2
Georgetown ... C8
Germantown ... B6
Gibsonburg ... D3
Grafton ... F3
Granville ... E5
Green ... G4
Green Springs ... D3
Greenfield ... D7
Greenville ... A5
Greenwich ... E3
Grove City ... D6
Hamilton ... A7
Hannibal ... J6
Harrisburg ... D6
Harrison ... A9
Heath ... F5
Hebron ... F6
Hicksville ... A3
Hillsboro ... C7
Hiram ... H3
Holgate ... B3
Hubbard ... J3
Huron ... E3
Independence ... H9
Jackson ... E7
Jackson Center ... B5
Jefferson ... J2
Jeffersonville ... C6
Johnstown ... E5
Keene ... G5
Kent ... H3
Kenton ... C4
Kettering ... B6
Kimbolton ... G5
Kirtland ... H2
Lakewood ... G9
Lancaster ... E6
Lebanon ... B7
Leipsic ... C3
Lewisburg ... A6
Lexington ... E4
Lima ... B4
Lisbon ... J4
Lodi ... G3
Logan ... F6
London ... D6
Lorain ... F3
Loudonville ... F4
Louisville ... H4
Loveland ... B7
Lucasville ... E8
Lyndhurst ... J8
McArthur ... F7
McConnelsville ... G6
Macedonia ... J10
Macksburg ... H6
Madeira ... C9
Manchester ... C8
Mansfield ... E4
Maple Hts. ... J9
Marietta ... H7
Marion ... D4
Martins Ferry ... J5
Marysville ... D5
Mason ... B7
Massillon ... G4
Maumee ... C2
Mayfield Hts. ... J9
Mechanicsburg ... C5
Medina ... G3
Mentor ... H2
Miamitown ... B9
Middleburg Heights ... G9
Middlefield ... H3
Middletown ... B6
Milan ... E3
Milford ... B7
Millersburg ... G4
Minerva ... H4
Minster ... B5
Monfort Heights ... B9
Monroe ... B7
Montgomery ... C9
Montpelier ... A2
Mount Gilead ... E4
Mount Healthy ... B9
Mount Orab ... C7
Mount Sterling ... D6
Mount Vernon ... E5
Napoleon ... B3
Nelsonville ... F7
Newark ... F5
New Baltimore ... B9
New Boston ... E8
New Bremen ... B5
New Carlisle ... B6
Newcomerstown ... G5
New Concord ... G6
New Lebanon ... B6
New Lexington ... F6
New London ... F3
New Paris ... A6
New Philadelphia ... H5
New Richmond ... B8
Newtown ... C9
Niles ... J3
North Baltimore ... C3
North Canton ... H4
North College Hill ... B9
North Kingsville ... J2
North Olmsted ... G3
North Royalton ... H10
Northfield ... J9
Northridge ... C6

Key
Norwalk ... E3
Norwood ... C9
Oak Harbor ... D2
Oak Hill ... E8
Oberlin ... F3
Olmsted Falls ... G9
Oregon ... D2
Orrville ... G4
Orwell ... J2
Otsego ... G5
Ottawa ... B3
Painesville ... H2
Parma ... G3
Parma Heights ... H9
Pataskala ... E6
Paulding ... A3
Peebles ... D8
Pepper Pike ... J9
Perrysburg ... C2
Pickerington ... E6
Piketon ... E7
Pioneer ... A2
Piqua ... B5
Plain City ... D5
Plymouth ... E4
Pomeroy ... F7
Port Clinton ... E2
Portsmouth ... E8
Powhatan Point ... J6
Ravenna ... H3
Reading ... B7
Reynoldsburg ... E6
Richmond Heights ... J8
Richwood ... D5
Ripley ... C8
Rittman ... G4
Roseville ... F6
Russells Point ... C5
Sabina ... C7
Sagamore Hills ... J9
St. Bernard ... C9
St. Clairsville ... J5
St. Henry ... A5
St. Louisville ... F5
St. Marys ... B4
St. Paris ... C5
Salem ... J4
Salineville ... J4
Sandusky ... E3
Selma ... C6
Seven Hills ... H9
Shadyside ... J6
Shaker Hts. ... J9
Sharonville ... C9
Shelby ... E4
Shreve ... F4
Sidney ... B5
Silverton ... C9
Smithville ... G4
Solon ... J9
Somerset ... F6
South Charleston ... C6
South Euclid ... J8
South Point ... E9
Springdale ... C9
Springfield ... C6
Steubenville ... J5
Strasburg ... G4
Streetsboro ... H3
Strongsville ... G3
Stryker ... B3
Sugarcreek ... G5
Sunbury ... E5
Sylvania ... C2
The Village of Indian Hill ... C9
Tiffin ... D3
Tipp City ... B6
Toledo ... C2
Troy ... B5
Twinsburg ... J10
Uhrichsville ... H5
University Hts. ... J9
Upper Sandusky ... D4
Urbana ... C5
Utica ... F5
Van Wert ... A4
Vandalia ... B6
Venedocia ... B4
Vermilion ... F3
Versailles ... B5
Wapakoneta ... B4
Warren ... J3
Warrensville Heights ... J9
Warsaw ... G5
Washington Court House ... D6
Waterville ... C2
Wauseon ... B2
Waverly ... E7
Waynesville ... B6
Wellington ... F3
Wellston ... E7
Wellsville ... J4
West Alexandria ... A6
West Jefferson ... D6
West Lafayette ... G5
West Liberty ... C5
West Milton ... B6
West Salem ... F4
West Union ... C8
West Unity ... B2
Westerville ... E5
Westlake ... G9
Weston ... C3
Wheelersburg ... E8
Wickliffe ... J8
Wilkesville ... F7
Willard ... E3
Williamsburg ... B7
Williamsport ... D6
Williamsport ... E4
Wilmington ... C7
Woodsfield ... H6
Woodville ... D3
Wooster ... G4
Wyoming ... C9
Xenia ... C6
Yellow Springs ... C6
Youngstown ... J3

Other Features
Clendening, *lake* ... H5
Cuyahoga Valley N.P. ... G3, H9
Dayton Aviation N.H.P. ... B6
Erie, *lake* ... G1
First Ladies Natl. Hist. Site ... H4
Hocking, *river* ... F7
Hopewell Culture N.H.P. ... E7
James A. Garfield N.H.P. ... H2
Kelleys, *island* ... E2
Mohican, *river* ... F4
Muskingum, *river* ... G6
Ohio, *river* ... J6

Key
Salt Fork, *lake* ... H5
Sandusky, *river* ... D3
Scioto, *river* ... D4
Senecaville, *lake* ... H6
William H. Taft Natl. Hist. Site ... C9

Oklahoma ... page 163

Cities and Towns
Ada ... F3
Agawam ... E3
Altus ... C3
Alva ... D1
Anadarko ... D2
Antlers ... G3
Apache ... D3
Arapaho ... D2
Ardmore ... E3
Arkoma ... H2
Atoka ... F3
Barnsdall ... F1
Bartlesville ... F1
Beaver ... B1
Bethel Acres ... E2
Bixby ... G2
Blackwell ... E1
Blanchard ... E2
Boise City ... B4
Bristow ... F2
Broken Arrow ... G1
Broken Bow ... H3
Buffalo ... C1
Cache ... D3
Calera ... F4
Carnegie ... D2
Catoosa ... G1
Chandler ... F2
Checotah ... G2
Chelsea ... G1
Cherokee ... D1
Cheyenne ... C2
Chickasha ... E2
Choctaw ... E2
Chouteau ... G1
Claremore ... G1
Cleveland ... F1
Clinton ... D2
Coalgate ... F3
Collinsville ... G1
Comanche ... E3
Commerce ... H1
Cordell ... D2
Corum ... D3
Coweta ... G2
Cushing ... F2
Davis ... E3
Dewey ... G1
Drumright ... F2
Durant ... F4
Eagletown ... H3
Edmond ... E2
Elk City ... C2
Enid ... E1
Eufaula ... G2
Fairfax ... F1
Fairview ... D1
Farris ... G3
Fittstown ... F3
Floris ... B1
Forgan ... B1
Fort Gibson ... G2
Frederick ... D3
Geary ... D2
Glenpool ... G2
Granite ... C3
Grove ... H1
Guthrie ... E2
Guymon ... C4
Harmon ... C1
Hartshorne ... G3
Haskell ... G2
Healdton ... E3
Heavener ... H3
Hennessey ... E1
Henryetta ... F2
Hobart ... C2
Holdenville ... F2
Hollis ... C3
Hominy ... F1
Hooker ... A1
Hugo ... G3
Idabel ... H4
Inola ... G1
Jay ... H1
Jenks ... G1
Joy ... E3
Kingfisher ... E2
Konawa ... E3
Krebs ... G3
Laverne ... C1
Lawton ... D3
Lenora ... C1
Lindsay ... E3
Locust Grove ... G1
Lone Grove ... E3
Loveland ... D3
Lovell ... E1
McAlester ... G3
McCurtain ... H2
McKnight ... C3
Madill ... F3
Mangum ... C3
Mannford ... F1
Marietta ... E4
Marlow ... E3
Medford ... E1
Midwest City ... E2
Minco ... E2
Moore ... E2
Muldrow ... H2
Muskogee ... G2
Mustang ... E2
Newcastle ... E2
Newkirk ... E1
Norman ... E2
Nowata ... G1
Oakhurst ... F1
Okeene ... D1
Okemah ... F2
Oklahoma City, *capital* ... E2
Okmulgee ... G2
Owasso ... G1
Panama ... H2
Pawhuska ... F1
Pawnee ... F1
Perkins ... E2
Perry ... E1
Picher ... H1
Piedmont ... E2
Ponca City ... E1
Poteau ... H2
Prague ... F2

Key
Pryor Creek ... G1
Purcell ... E2
Roll ... C2
Sallisaw ... H2
Sand Springs ... F1
Sapulpa ... F1
Sayre ... C2
Seminole ... F2
Shattuck ... C1
Shawnee ... F2
Skiatook ... F1
Slaughterville ... E2
Snyder ... D3
Sparks ... F2
Spiro ... H2
Stanley ... G3
Stigler ... G2
Stillwater ... E1
Stilwell ... H2
Stratford ... F3
Stroud ... F2
Sulphur ... F3
Tahlequah ... H2
Talihina ... G3
Tecumseh ... F2
Tishomingo ... F3
Tonkawa ... E1
Tulsa ... G1
Turley ... G1
Tuttle ... E2
Vian ... H2
Vinita ... G1
Wagoner ... G2
Walters ... D3
Wanette ... E3
Warner ... G2
Warren ... C3
Watonga ... D2
Watova ... G1
Waukomis ... E1
Waurika ... D3
Weatherford ... D2
Westville ... H1
Wetumka ... F2
Wewoka ... F2
Wilburton ... G3
Wilson ... E3
Woodward ... C1
Wynnewood ... E3
Yale ... F1
Yukon ... E2

Other Features
Arkansas, *river* ... F1
Black Mesa, *mt.* ... B4
Broken Bow, *lake* ... H3
Canadian, *river* ... C2
Canton, *lake* ... D1
Chickasaw Natl. Rec. Area ... E3
Cimarron, *river* ... C1
Fort Gibson, *lake* ... G1
Hugo, *lake* ... G3
Illinois, *river* ... H2
Kaw, *lake* ... F1
Keystone, *lake* ... F1
North Canadian, *river* ... C1
Oklahoma City Natl. Memorial ... E2
Oologah, *lake* ... G1
Ouachita, *mts.* ... G3
Red, *river* ... C3
Sooner, *lake* ... F1
Texoma, *lake* ... F4
Washita Battlefield N.H.S. ... C2
Winding Stair Natl. Rec. Area ... H3

Oregon ... page 164

Cities and Towns
Albany ... B2
Aloha ... A2
Altamont ... C3
Ashland ... C3
Astoria ... B1
Baker City ... E2
Bandon ... B3
Beaverton ... A2, C2
Bend ... C2
Brookings ... B3
Brownsville ... C2
Burns ... D3
Canby ... A2, C2
Canyon City ... E2
Cedar Hills ... A2
Central Point ... C3
Clatskanie ... B1
Condon ... D2
Coos Bay ... B3
Coquille ... B3
Cornelius ... A2
Corvallis ... B2
Cottage Grove ... B3
Creswell ... B3
Crowley ... E3
Dallas ... B2
Eagle Point ... C3
Elgin ... E2
Enterprise ... E2
Eugene ... B2
Florence ... B3
Forest Grove ... A2
Fossil ... D2
Four Corners ... A2, C2
Glendale ... B3
Gold Beach ... B3
Grants Pass ... B3
Green ... B3
Gresham ... B2
Harbor ... B3
Harrisburg ... B2
Hayesville ... A2, C2
Heppner ... D2
Hermiston ... D2
Hillsboro ... A2, C2
Hines ... D3
Homestead ... F2
Hood River ... C2
Hubbard ... C2
Jacksonville ... C3
Jefferson ... C2
John Day ... E2
Junction City ... B2
Juntura ... E3
Keizer ... A2
Klamath Falls ... C3
Lafayette ... B2
La Grande ... E2
Lakecreek ... C3
Lake Oswego ... A2, C2
Lakeside ... B3
Lakeview ... D3
Lebanon ... C2

Key
Lexington D2
Lincoln Beach B2
Lincoln City B2
McMinnville B2
Madras C2
Meacham E2
Medford C3
Metzger A2
Mill City C2
Milton-Freewater E2
Milwaukie A2
Molalla A2
Monument D2
Moro D2
Mount Angel A2, C2
Mount Vernon D2
Myrtle Creek B3
Myrtle Point B3
Newberg A2, C2
Newport B2
North Bend B3
Nyssa E3
Oak Grove A2
Oakridge C3
Ontario F2
Oregon City A2, C2
Pendleton E2
Philomath B2
Phoenix C3
Pilot Rock E2
Portland A2, C2
Post D2
Prineville D2
Rainier C1
Redmond C2
Reedsport B3
Riley D3
Rogue River B3
Roseburg B3
Rufus D2
St. Helens C2
Stanfield D2
Salem, *capital* A2, B2
Santa Clara B2
Scappoose C2
Seaside B2
Seneca E2
Shady Cove C3
Sherwood A2
Silverton A2, C2
Springfield C2
Stayton C2
Sunriver C3
Sutherlin B3
Sweet Home C2
Talent C3
The Dalles C2
Tigard A2, C2
Tillamook B2
Toledo B2
Umpqua B3
Union E2
Vale E3
Veneta B2
Vernonia B2
Waldport B2
Warm Springs C2
Warrenton B1
Waterloo C2
West Slope A2
White City C3
Willamina B2
Wilsonville A2, C2
Woodburn A2
Wood Village B2

Other Features
Abert, *lake* D3
Blue, *mts.* E2
Calapooya, *mts.* C3
Cascade, *range* C3
Cascade-Siskiyou Natl. Mon. C3
Clackamas, *river* C2
Coast, *mt. ranges* B2
Columbia, *river* D2
Coos, *bay* B3
Crater, *lake* C3
Crater Lake Natl. Park C3
Crescent, *lake* C3
Crooked, *river* D2
Davis, *lake* C3
Deschutes, *river* C2
Diamond Peak, *mt.* C3
Gearhart Mtn., *mt.* D3
Green Peter, *lake* C2
Harney, *basin* D3
Harney, *lake* D3
Hells, *canyon* F2
Hells Canyon Natl. Rec. Area F2
Hood, *mt.* C2
Jefferson, *mt.* C2
John Day, *river* C2
John Day Fossil Beds N.M. D2
Klamath, *mts.* B3
Lookout, *cape* B2
McLoughlin house N.H.S. A2
Malheur, *lake* E3
Malheur, *river* E3
Molalla, *river* B2
Multnomah, *waterfalls* C2
Ochoco, *mts.* D2
Oregon Caves Natl. Monument B3
Oregon Dunes Natl. Rec. Area B3
Owyhee, *lake* E3
Owyhee, *river* E3
Powder, *river* E2
Pudding, *river* A2
Pueblo, *mts.* E3
Rogue, *river* B3
Sacajawea Peak, *mt.* E2
Silvies, *river* D3
Siuslaw, *river* B3
Snake, *river* F2
South Umpqua, *river* B3
Steens, *mts.* E3
Strawberry Mt., *mt.* D2
Summer, *lake* D3
Thielsen, *mt.* C3
Tillamook, *bay* B2
Trout Creek, *mts.* E3
Umatilla, *lake* D2
Upper Klamath, *lake* C3
Waldo, *lake* C3
Wallowa, *mts.* E2
Willamette, *river* A2

Pennsylvania ....page 165

Cities and Towns
Albion A2
Aliquippa A4
Allensville F4
Allentown L4
Allison Park E6
Altoona E4
Ambridge A4
Annville H5
Archbald K2
Ardmore M6
Arnot G2
Ashland J4
Athens H2
Austin E2
Avalon D7
Avis G3
Bala Cynwyd M6
Baldwin E7
Bangor L4
Barnesboro D4
Beaver A4
Beaver Falls A4
Beavertown G4
Bedford E5
Bellefonte F4
Belleville F4
Bellevue D7
Bellwood E4
Berlin D6
Berwick J3
Berwyn L6
Bethel Park A5, D7
Bethlehem L4
Birdsboro K5
Blairsville C5
Blakely K3
Bloomsburg J4
Blossburg G2
Boalsburg F4
Boothwyn L7
Boswell C5
Boyertown K5
Bradford D2
Brentwood E7
Bridgeville D7
Brockport D3
Brockway D3
Brodheadsville L4
Brooklyn K2
Brookville C3
Broomall L6
Brownsville B5
Bryn Mawr L6
Burgettstown A5
Butler B4
California B5
Cambridge Springs A2
Canonsburg A5
Canton H2
Carbondale K2
Carlisle G5
Carnegie D7
Carroll Valley G6
Carrolltown D4
Castle Shannon E7
Catawissa J4
Chambersburg F6
Chelsea L7
Chester L6, L7
Clairton B5
Clarion C3
Clarks Summit K2
Claysburg E5
Clearfield E3
Clifton Heights L7
Clymer C4
Coatesville K6
Columbia H5
Connellsville B6
Conyngham J4
Coopersburg L5
Coraopolis D7
Cornwall J5
Corry B2
Coudersport E2
Crafton D7
Cresson D5
Crosby E2
Cuddy D7
Curwensville D4
Dallas K3
Danville H4
Darby M7
Delmont B5
Denver J5
Derry C5
Dillsburg G5
Dormont D7
Dover H5
Downingtown K5
Doylestown L5
Drexel Hill M7
DuBois D3
Duncannon G5
Duquesne E7
Dushore J2
East Greenville K5
East Lansdowne M7
Easton L4
East Petersburg J5
East Stroudsburg L3
Ebensburg D4
Eddystone L7
Edinboro A2
Effinwild E6
Elizabethtown H5
Elizabethville H4
Elkland G2
Ellwood City A4
Elysburg H4
Emlenton B3
Emmaus L4
Emporium E2
Emsworth D7
Ephrata J5
Erie A1
Etna E7
Evans City A4
Everett E5
Exton K5
Fayetteville F6
Fleetwood K5
Ford City B4
Forest City L2
Forest Grove D7
Forksville H2
Fox Chapel E7
Franklin K3
Freeport B4
Galeton F2
Gettysburg G6
Girard A2
Gladden D7
Gladwyne M6
Glenolden M7
Glen Riddle L7
Glen Rock H6
Gradyville L7
Greencastle F6
Greensburg B5
Greenville A3
Gregg D7
Grove City A3
Hallstead K2
Hamburg K4
Hanover H6
Harmarville E6
Harrisburg, *capital* H5
Harrisville A3
Harveys Lake J3
Haverford M6
Havertown M6
Hazel Hurst D2
Hazleton K4
Hermitage A3
Herndon H4
Hershey H5
Highland D6
Hollidaysburg E5
Homer City C4
Honesdale L2
Huntingdon E5
Hyndman D6
Indiana C4
Indianola E6
Jersey Shore G3
Jim Thorpe K4
Johnsonburg D3
Johnstown D5
Kane D2
Kennett Square K6
King of Prussia L5
Kingston K3
Kittanning B4
Kutztown K5
Lake City A1
Lancaster J5
Lansdale L5
Lansdowne M7
Laporte J3
Latrobe C5
Lebanon J5
Leechburg B4
Lehighton K4
Levittown M5
Lewisburg H4
Lewistown F4
Ligonier C5
Lima L7
Linglestown H5
Lititz J5
Littlestown G6
Lock Haven G3
Lykens H4
McCandless A4, D6
McConnellsburg E6
McKees Rocks D7
McKeesport B5
Macungie K4
Mahanoy City J4
Manchester H5
Manheim J5
Mansfield G2
Mars A4
Martinsburg E5
Marysville H5
Masontown B6
Matamoras M3
Meadville A2
Mechanicsburg G5
Media L6, L7
Mercer A3
Mercersburg F6
Meridian B4
Merion M6
Meyersdale C6
Middleburg G4
Middletown H5
Midland A4
Mifflinburg G4
Mifflintown G4
Mifflinville J3
Milford M3
Millersburg H4
Millersville J6
Millheim G4
Millvale E7
Milroy F4
Milton H3
Minersville J4
Monessen B5
Monroeville B5, F7
Mont Alto F6
Montgomery H3
Montoursville H3
Montrose K2
Moon Run D7
Moscow K3
Mt. Carmel J4
Mt. Holly Springs G5
Mount Joy H5
Mt. Lebanon D7
Mt. Nebo D6
Mt. Oliver E7
Mt. Pleasant B5
Mt. Pocono L3
Mount Union F5
Muncy H3
Munhall E7
Myerstown J5
Nanticoke J3
Nanty Glo D5
Nazareth L4
Nesquehoning K4
New Bloomfield G5
New Castle A4
New Freedom H6
New Holland J5
New Kensington B4, F6
New Oxford G6
Newport G5
Newtown M5
Newtown Square L6
Newville G5
New Wilmington A3
Norristown L5
North East B1
Northampton L4
North Springfield A1
Northumberland H4
Oakmont E7
Oil City B3
Old Forge K3
Orwigsburg J4
Oxford J6
Palmerton K4
Patton D4
Pen Argyl L4
Penn Hills F7
Penn Wynne M6
Perkasie L5
Philadelphia L6, M7
Philipsburg E4
Phoenixville K5
Picture Rocks H3
Pine Grove J4
Pittsburgh B5, E7
Pittston K3
Pleasantville B3
Pleasantville D5
Point Marion B6
Polk B3
Port Allegany E2
Port Matilda E4
Portage D5
Portland Mills D3
Pottstown K5
Pottsville J4
Powell H2
Prospect Park L7
Punxsutawney D4
Quakertown L5
Quarryville J6
Radnor L6
Rainsburg D6
Reading K5
Red Lion H6
Renovo F3
Reynoldsville D3
Ridgway D3
Ridley Park L7
Roaring Spring E5
St. Marys D3
Saxonburg B4
Sayre H2
Schnecksville K4
Schuylkill Haven J4
Scottdale B5
Scranton K3
Selinsgrove H4
Shamokin H4
Sharon A3
Sharon Hill M7
Sharpsville A3
Sheffield C2
Shenandoah J4
Shippensburg F5
Shoemakersville K5
Shrewsbury H6
Sinking Spring J5
Slatington K4
Slippery Rock A3
Smethport E2
Somerset C5
Souderton L5
South Williamsport G3
Spring Grove H6
Springdale F6
Springfield L7
State College F4
Stewartstown H6
Strasburg J6
Stroudsburg L4
Sugarcreek B3
Sunbury H4
Susquehanna K2
Swarthmore L7
Sykesville D3
Tamaqua K4
Tionesta C3
Titusville B2
Tobyhanna L3
Towanda J2
Tower City H4
Tremont J4
Trevorton H4
Troy H2
Tunkhannock K2
Tyrone E4
Union City B2
Uniontown B6
Upland L7
Valley View H4
Vandergrift B4
Verona E7
Village Green L7
Villanova L6
Warren C2
Washington A5
Waterford B2
Watsontown H3
Waymart L2
Wayne L6
Waynesboro F6
Waynesburg A6
Weatherly K4
Wellsboro G2
Wesleyville A1
West Chester K6
West Grove K6
West Mifflin E7
Westmont D5
West Pike E2
West View E7
Whitehall K4
White Horse J6
Wilcox D2
Wilkes-Barre K3
Wilkinsburg F7
Williamsport G3
Willow Grove L5
Windber D5
Womelsdorf J5
York H6
York Springs G5
Youngsville C2
Zelienople A4

Other Features
Allegheny, *reservoir* D2
Allegheny, *river* B3
Allegheny Natl. Rec. Area C2
Allegheny Portage Railroad N.H.S. D5
Appalachian, *mts.* F5
Clarion, *river* C3
Conemaugh, *river* C4
Davis, *mt.* C6
Delaware, *river* L2
Delaware Water Gap N.R.A. M3
Eisenhower Natl. Hist. Site G6
Erie, *lake* A1
Friendship Hill Natl. Hist. Site B6
Gettysburg Natl. Mil. Park G6
Johnstown Flood Natl. Memorial D5
Juniata, *river* F5
Lehigh, *river* K3
Ohio, *river* A4
Presque Isle, *island* A1
Raystown, *lake* E5
Schuylkill, *river* K5
Steamtown Natl. Hist. Site K3
Susquehanna, *river* J2
Tioga, *river* G2
Valley Forge Natl. Hist. Park L5

Rhode Island ....page 166

Cities and Towns
Adamsville F4
Allenton D4
Alton B5
Anthony C3
Arcadia B4
Ashaway B5
Ashton D2
Avondale A6
Barrington E3
Berkeley D2
Bradford B5
Bristol E3
Carolina C5
Central Falls D2
Charlestown C5
Chepachet B2
Clayville B3
Coventry Center C3
Cranston D3
Cumberland Hill D2
Diamond Hill D2
Dunn Corner B5
East Greenwich D4
East Providence D3
Exeter C4
Fiskeville C3
Foster Center B3
Galilee C5
Glendale C2
Green Hill C5
Greenville C2
Hamilton D4
Harmony C2
Harrisville B2
Hope C3
Hope Valley B5
Hopkinton B5
Jamestown D5
Jerusalem C5
Kingston C5
Little Compton E4
Lonsdale D2
Matunuck C5
Middletown E4
Moosup Valley B3
Narragansett Pier D5
Newport E5
Nooseneck C4
North Foster B2
North Providence D2
North Scituate C3
Pascoag B2
Pawtucket D2
Pawtuxet D3
Perryville C5
Plum Point D4
Point Judith D5
Portsmouth E4
Providence, *capital* D3
Prudence E4
Quidnick C3
Quonochontaug B6
Rice City B3
Riverside D3
Rockville B4
Rumford D2
Sakonnet E5
Saunderstown D5
Saylesville D2
Shannock C5
Slatersville C1
Slocum C4
South Foster B3
Spragueville C2
Tarkiln C2
Tiverton E4
Usquepaug C5
Valley Falls D2
Wakefield C5
Wallum Lake B2
Warren E3
Warwick D3
Washington C3
Watch Hill A6
Weekapaug B6
West Barrington D3
Westerly B5
West Glocester B2
West Kingston C5
West Warwick C3
Woonsocket C1
Wyoming B4

Other Features
Block, *island* C7
Block Island, *sound* B6
Mt. Hope, *bay* E4
Narragansett, *bay* D4
Rhode Island, *sound* E5
Roger Williams Natl. Mem. D3
Sakonnet, *river* E4
Scituate, *reservoir* C3
Touro Synagogue N.H.S. E5

South Carolina ....page 167

Cities and Towns
Abbeville B2
Aiken C3
Allendale C3
Anderson B2
Andrews E3
Bamberg C3
Barnwell C3
Batesburg-Leesville C3
Beaufort D4
Belton B2
Belvedere C3
Bennettsville E2
Bishopville D2
Blacksburg C1
Blackville C3
Boiling Springs C1
Brownsville E2
Buffalo C2
Burton D4
Calhoun Falls B2
Camden D2
Cayce C3
Central B2
Charleston E4
Cheraw E2
Chester C2
Chesterfield D2
Clemson B2
Clinton C2
Clover C1
Columbia, *capital* C2
Conway E3
Cowpens C1
Darlington E2
Denmark C3
Dentsville D2
Dillon E2
Easley B2
Edgefield C3
Elgin D2
Enoree C2
Estill C4
Fairfax C4
Florence E2
Folly Beach E4
Forest Acres D2
Forestown D3
Fort Mill D1
Fountain Inn B2
Furman C4
Gaffney C1
Garden City F3
Georgetown E3
Gifford C4
Gloverville C3
Goose Creek D3
Great Falls D2
Greeleyville E3
Greenville B2
Greenwood B2
Greer B2
Hampton C4
Hanahan D4
Hardeeville C4
Harleyville D3
Hartsville D2
Hickory Grove C2
Hickory Grove F3
Hilda C3
Hilton Head Island D4
Holly Hill D3
Hollywood D4
Honea Path B2
Horrel Hill D3
Inman B1
Irmo C2
Isle of Palms E4
Jackson C3
Jefferson D2
Joanna C2
Johnsonville E3
Johnston C3
Kershaw D2
Kiawah Island D4
Kingstree E3
Kline C3
Ladson D4
Lake City E3
Lancaster D2
Landrum B1
Lane E3
Latta E2
Laurel Bay D4
Laurens B2
Lexington C3
Liberty B2
Little River F3
Little Rock E2
Loris F2
Lugoff D2
Lyman B2
Lynchburg D2
McBee D2
McClellanville E3
McCormick B3
Manning D3
Marion E2
Mauldin B2
Mayesville D3
Mayo C1
Moncks Corner D3
Mt. Pleasant E4
Mullins E2
Murrells Inlet E3
Myrtle Beach F3
Neeses C3
New Ellenton C3
Newberry C2
Nichols E2
Ninety Six B2
North Augusta C3
North Charleston E4
North Myrtle Beach F3
Norway C3
Olanta E3
Olar C3
Orangeburg D3
Pacolet C2
Pacolet Mills C2
Pageland D2
Pamplico E3
Patrick D2
Pelion C3
Pendleton B2
Pickens B2
Piedmont B2
Pinewood D3
Pomaria C2
Port Royal D4
Ravenel D4
Red Bank C3
Ridgeland D4
Ridgeville D3
Ridgeway D2
Rock Hill C2
Roebuck C2
Rowesville D3
Ruby D2
St. George D3
St. Matthews D3
St. Stephen E3
Salley C3
Salters E3
Saluda C3
Santee D3
Sellers E2
Seneca B2
Simpsonville B2
Socastee E3
Society Hill E2
South Congaree C3
Spartanburg C2
Springfield C3
Starr B2
Stuckey E3

Key
Summerville D3
Sumter D3
Surfside Beach F3
Swansea C3
Sycamore C3
Taylors B2
Timmonsville E2
Travelers Rest B2
Trenton C3
Turbeville D3
Union C2
Varnville C4
Wagener C3
Walhalla A2
Walterboro D4
Ware Shoals B2
Westminster A2
Whitmire C2
Williamston B2
Williston C3
Winnsboro C2
Woodruff B2
Yemassee D4
York C2

Other Features
Bull, *island* E4
Bulls, *bay* E4
Cape, *island* E3
Congaree Swamp N.M. D3
Cowpens Natl. Bfld. C1
Edisto, *river* D3
Fort Sumter Natl. Monument E4
Greenwood, *lake* C2
Hartwell, *lake* B2
J. Strom Thurmond, *lake* B3
Keowee, *lake* B2
Kings Mt. Natl. Mil. Park C1
Long, *bay* F3
Lynches, *river* D2
Marion, *lake* D3
Monticello, *reservoir* C2
Moultrie, *lake* D3
Murray, *lake* C2
Ninety Six Natl. Hist. Site B2
North, *island* E3
Port Royal, *sound* D4
Russell, *lake* B2
St. Helena, *sound* D4
Saluda, *river* C2
Santee, *river* E3
Savannah, *river* C3
South, *island* E3
The Grand Strand F3
Wateree, *lake* D2
Wateree, *river* D2

South Dakota ....page 168

Cities and Towns
Aberdeen F1
Alexandria G3
Armour F3
Belle Fourche A2
Beresford H3
Black Hawk A2
Box Elder A2
Britton G1
Brookings H2
Burke E3
Canton H3
Chamberlain E3
Cherry Creek C2
Clark G2
Clear Lake H2
Custer A3
Deadwood A2
Dell Rapids H3
De Smet G2
Dupree C1
Elk Point H4
Faulkton E1
Flandreau H2
Fort Pierre D2
Freeman G3
Gettysburg E1
Hartford H3
Highmore E2
Hot Springs A3
Howard G2
Huron F2
Ipswich E1
Kadoka C3
Lake Andes F3
Lead A2
Lemmon B1
Lennox G3
Leola F1
Madison G2
Martin C3
Milbank H1
Miller E2
Mitchell G3
Mobridge D1
Murdo D3
Onida D2
Parker G3
Parkston G3
Philip C2
Pierre, *capital* D2
Pine Ridge B3
Plankinton F3
Platte F3
Rapid City A2
Redfield F2
Rosebud D3
Salem G3
Selby D1
Sioux Falls H3
Sisseton G1
Spearfish A2
Sturgis A2
Timber Lake C1
Tyndall G4
Vermillion H4
Volga H2
Wagner F3
Watertown G2
Webster G1
Wessington Springs F2
White River D3
Winner E3
Woonsocket F2
Wounded Knee B3
Yankton G4

Other Features
Andes, *lake* F3
Angostura, *reservoir* A3
Bad, *river* C2
Badlands Natl. Park B3
Belle Fourche, *reservoir* A2
Belle Fourche, *river* A2
Big Sioux, *river* G2
Big Stone, *lake* H1
Black, *hills* A2
Bois de Sioux, *river* H1
Cheyenne, *river* C2
Francis Case, *lake* F3
Grand, *river* C1
Harney Peak, *mt.* A3
James, *river* F1
Jewel Cave Natl. Monument A3
Keya Paha, *river* D3
Lewis and Clark, *lake* G4
Little Missouri, *river* A1
Little White, *river* D3
Minuteman Missile N.H.S. B3, C3
Missouri, *river* E3
Moreau, *river* B1
Mount Rushmore Natl. Memorial A3
North Fork Grand, *river* B1
Oahe, *lake* D2
Pine, *ridge* B3
Sharpe, *lake* E2
South Fork Grand, *river* A1
Traverse, *lake* H1
Vermillion, *river* G3
Waubay, *lake* G1
White, *river* D3
Whitewood, *river* G2
Wind Cave Natl. Park A3

Tennessee ....page 169

Cities and Towns
Adamsville E4
Alamo C3
Alcoa P3
Algood L2
Altamont K4
Arlington B4
Ashland City G2
Athens M4
Bartlett B4
Baxter K2
Bells C3
Benton M4
Bethel Springs D4
Bethpage J2
Blaine P2
Blountville S1
Bluff City S2
Bolivar D4
Brentwood H2
Bristol S1
Brownsville C3
Bruceton E2
Buffalo Valley K2
Byrdstown L1
Camden E2
Campaign K3
Carthage K2
Caryville N2
Celina K1
Centerville G3
Charlotte G2
Chattanooga L4
Church Hill R1
Clarksville G1
Cleveland M4
Clinton N2
Collegedale L4
Collierville B4
Columbia G3
Conasauga M4
Cookeville L2
Covington B3
Cowan J4
Crossville L3
Dandridge Q2
Dayton L3
Decatur M3
Decaturville E3
Decherd J4
Dickson G2
Dover F2
Dresden D2
Dunlap L4
Dyer C2
Dyersburg C2
East Ridge L4
Elizabethton S2
Englewood N4
Erin F2
Erwin S2
Estill Springs J4
Etowah M4
Fairfield Glade M2
Farragut N3
Fayetteville H4
Forest Hills H2
Frankewing H4
Franklin H3
Gainesboro K2
Gallatin J2
Gatlinburg P3
Germantown B4
Gleason D2
Goodlettsville H2
Granville K2
Graysville L4
Greeneville R2
Greenfield D2
Grimsley M2
Gruetli-Laager K4
Halls C3
Halls Crossroads P2
Hampshire G3
Harriman M3
Hartsville J2
Henderson D4
Hendersonville H2
Humboldt D3
Huntingdon E3
Huntsville N2
Jacksboro N2
Jackson D3
Jamestown M2
Jasper K4
Jefferson City Q2
Jellico N1
Johnson City S2
Jonesborough S2
Karns N3
Kenton C2
Kingsport R1
Kingston M3
Kingston Springs G2
Knoxville P3
Lafayette J1
La Follette N2
Lake City N2
Lakewood H2
La Vergne H2
Lawrenceburg G4
Lebanon J2
Lenoir City N3
Lewisburg H4
Lexington E3
Linden F3
Livingston L2
Loretto G4
Loudon N3
Lynchburg J4
McEwen F2
McKenzie D2
McKinnon F2
McMinnville K3
Madisonville N3
Manchester J4
Martin D2
Maryville P3
Mascot P2
Maynardville P2
Medon D4
Memphis A4
Middleton D4
Milan D3
Millersville H2
Milligan College S2
Millington B4
Monterey L2
Morristown Q2
Mosheim R2
Mountain City T1
Mount Juliet H2
Mount Pleasant G3
Munford B4
Murfreesboro J3
Nashville, *capital* H2
Newbern C2
New Johnsonville F2
New Tazewell P2
Nolensville H3
Norris N2
Oak Hill H2
Oak Ridge N2
Oliver Springs N2
Oneida M2
Overall J3
Paris E2
Parsons E3
Pegram G2
Pigeon Forge P3
Pikeville L3
Portland H1
Powell N2
Pulaski G4
Reagan E3
Red Bank L4
Ridgely C2
Ripley B3
Rockwood M3
Rogersville R2
Rutherford D2
Rutledge Q2
Savannah E4
Selmer D4
Sevierville P3
Sewanee K4
Shelbyville H4
Signal Mountain K4
Smithville K3
Smyrna H3
Sneedville Q1
Soddy-Daisy L4
Somerville C4
South Fulton D2
South Pittsburg K4
Sparta L3
Spencer L3
Spring City M3
Spring Hill H3
Springfield H1
Stanton C4
Surgoinsville R2
Sweetwater N3
Taft H4
Tazewell P2
Tellico Plains N4
Tennessee Ridge F2
Tiptonville C2
Tracy City K4
Trenton D3
Trimble C2
Tullahoma J4
Tusculum R2
Union City C2
Wartburg M2
Waverly F2
Waynesboro F4
Westmoreland J1
White House H2
White Pine Q2
Whitwell K4
Winchester J4
Woodbury J3

Other Features
Andrew Johnson Natl. Hist. Site R2
Appalachian, *mts.* N4
Appalachian Natl. Scenic Trail Q3
Barkley, *lake* F1
Big South Fork Natl. River and Rec. Area M1
Center Hill, *lake* K3
Cherokee, *lake* Q2
Chickamauga & Chattanooga Natl. Mil. Park L5
Chickamauga, *lake* M3
Clinch, *river* Q2
Clingmans Dome, *mt.* Q3
Cumberland, *river* G2
Dale Hollow, *lake* L1
Douglas, *lake* Q3
Duck, *river* H3
Great Smoky, *mts.* P3
Great Smoky Mts. Natl. Park Q3
Holston, *river* R2
Kentucky, *lake* F2
Mississippi, *river* B3
Norris, *lake* P2
Roan, *mt.* S2
Shiloh Natl. Mil. Park E4
Tennessee, *river* E5, K5
Watts Bar, *lake* M3
Woods, *reservoir* J4

Texas ....page 170

Cities and Towns
Abernathy F2
Abilene H3
Addison C1
Alamo Heights B7
Albany H3
Algoa F9
Alice J8
Alpine D5
Alvin M6
Amarillo B9
Anahuac N6
Anderson M5
Andrews E3
Angleton M6
Anson H3
Anthony A3
Aransas Pass K8
Archer City J2
Arlington L3
Asherton H7
Aspermont G2
Atascosa A7
Athens M3
Atlanta N2
Austin, *capital* K5
Avondale A1
Azle K3
Bacliff G9
Baird H3
Balch Springs C2
Balcones Heights A7
Ballinger H4
Bandera H6
Barrett F8
Bastrop K5
Batesville H7
Bay City M7
Bayou Vista G10
Baytown N6
Beaumont N5
Beaumont Place F8
Beaver C8
Bedford B2
Beeville K7
Bellaire E8
Bellmead K4
Belton K4
Benavides J8
Benbrook A2
Benjamin H2
Bergheim A6
Big Lake F4
Big Spring F3
Bishop K8
Boerne J6
Bogata M2
Bonham L2
Borger C9
Bovina E1
Bowie K2
Bracken B6
Brackettville G6
Brady H4
Breckenridge J3
Brenham L5
Briar A1
Bridge City P5
Bridgeport K2
Brookshire M6
Brookside Village F9
Brownfield E2
Brownsville K10
Brownwood J4
Bryan L5
Buckingham C1
Buena Vista B7
Buffalo L4
Bulverde A6
Buna P5
Bunker Hill Village E8
Burkburnett J1
Burleson A3
Burleson K3
Burnet J5
Caldwell L5
Cameron L5
Canadian D9
Canton M3
Canutillo A4
Canyon B9
Carrizo Springs H7
Carrollton B1
Carthage N3
Castle Hills A6
Castle Hills J6
Cedar Hill B3
Cedar Park K5
Center N4
Centerville M4
Chandler M3
Channelview F8
Channing B9
Childress G1
Chocolate Bayou F10
Cisco J3
Clarendon C10
Clarksville M2
Claude C9
Cleburne K3
Cleveland M5
Clifton K4
Cloverleaf F8
Clute M6
Cockrell Hill B2
Coldspring M5
Coleman H4
College Station L5
Colleyville A2
Colorado City G3
Columbus L6
Comanche J4
Combine D2
Commerce L2
Conroe M5
Converse B6
Cooper M2
Copperas Cove K4
Corpus Christi K8
Corsicana L3
Cotulla H7
Crane E4
Crockett M4
Crosby F8
Crosbyton F2
Crowell H2
Crowley A3
Crystal City H7
Cuero K6
Daingerfield N2
Dalhart B8
Dallas L3
Dalworthington Gardens B2
Danbury F10
Dayton N5
Decatur K2
Deer Park F8
Del Rio G6
Denison L2
Denton K2
Denver City E3
De Soto L3
Devine J6
Diboll N4
Dickens G2
Dickinson F9
Dilley H7
Dimmitt E1
Dublin J3
Dumas B9
Duncanville B2
Eagle Lake L6
Eagle Pass G7
Eastland J3
Eden H4
Edgecliff A3
Edinburg J9
Edna L7
El Campo L6
Eldorado G5
El Paso A4
Electra J1
Elgin K5
Elsa J9
Emory M3
Ennis L3
Euless B2
Everman A3
Fabens A4
Fair Oaks Ranch A6
Fairfield L4
Falfurrias J8
Farmers Branch B1
Farwell D1
Ferris C3
Flatonia K6
Floresville J6
Floydada F2
Forest Hill A2
Fort Davis D5
Fort Stockton E5
Fort Worth K3
Franklin L4
Fredericksburg J5
Freeport M7
Freer J8
Friendswood F9
Gail F3
Gainesville K2
Galena Park F8
Galveston N6
Ganado L6
Garden City F4
Garden Ridge B6
Gardendale B7
Garland C2
Gatesville K4
George West J7
Georgetown K5
Germann C3
Giddings L5
Gilmer N3
Gladewater N3
Glen Rose K3
Glenn Heights B3
Goldthwaite J4
Goliad K7
Gonzales K6
Gorman J3
Graham J2
Granbury K3
Grand Prairie B2
Grand Saline M3
Grapeland M4
Grapevine B1
Grapevine K3
Greenville L2
Groesbeck L4
Groves P6
Groveton M4
Guthrie G2
Hallettsville L6
Haltom City A2
Hamilton J4
Hamlin G3
Harker Heights K4
Harlingen K9
Haskell H2
Hearne L5
Hebbronville J8
Helotes A6
Hemphill P4
Hempstead L5
Henderson N3
Henrietta J2
Hereford B10
Hewitt K4
Hico J4
Hidalgo J9
Highland Park C2
Highlands F8
Hillsboro K3
Hitchcock F9
Hitchcock M6
Hollywood Park A6
Hondo H6
Houston M6
Hubbard L4
Huntsville M5
Hurst A2
Hutchins C2
Idalou F2
India C3
Ingleside K8
Iowa Park J2
Irving B2
Jacinto City F8
Jacksboro J2
Jacksonville M4
Jasper P5
Jayton G2
Jefferson N3
Jersey Village E8
Johnson City J5
Jourdanton J7
Juliff E9
Junction H5
Karnes City K7
Katy M6
Kaufman L3
Keller A2
Kermit D4
Kerrick B8
Kerrville H5
Kilgore N3
Killeen K4
Kingsland J5
Kingsville K8
Kirby B7
Kirbyville P5
Knox City H2
Kountze N5
La Grange L6
Lake Jackson M7
Lakehills J6
La Marque G9
Lamesa F3
Lampasas J4
Lancaster C3
La Porte F9
La Pryor H7
Laredo H8
League City M6
Leakey H6
Leon Springs A6
Leon Valley J6
Levelland E2
Lewisville L2
Liberty N5
Linden N3
Lipscomb D8
Littlefield E2
Live Oak B6
Livingston N5
Llano J5
Lockhart K6
Lockney F1
Longview N3
Lubbock F2
Lufkin N4
Luling K6
Lumberton N5
Mabank L3
McAllen J9
McCamey E4
Macdona A7
McKinney L2
Madisonville M5
Mangus Corner A7
Mansfield B3
Manvel F9
Marble Falls J5
Marfa C5
Marlin L4
Marshall N3
Mason H5
Matador G1
Mathis K8
Memphis C10
Menard H5
Mentone D4
Meridian K4
Merkel G3
Mertzon G4
Mesquite F3
Mesquite L3
Mexia L4
Miami C9
Midland E4
Midlothian B3
Mineola M3
Mineral Wells J3
Mission J9
Missouri City M6
Monahans E4
Mont Belvieu G8
Montague K2
Morgans Point G8
Morton E2
Moss Bluff G8
Mt. Houston F8
Mt. Pleasant N2
Mt. Vernon M2
Muleshoe E1
Munday H2
Murphy C1
Nacogdoches N4
Nassau Bay F9
Navasota L5
Nederland N6
New Berlin C7
New Boston N2
New Braunfels J6
Newton P5
Nixon K6
Nocona K2
North Houston E8
North Richland Hills A2
Odessa E4
Olmos Park A7
Olney J2
Olton E1
Orange P5
Ovilla B3
Ozona F5
Paducah G1
Paint Rock H4
Palacios L7
Palestine M4
Palo Pinto J3
Pampa C9
Panhandle C9
Pantego B2
Paris M2
Parita B7
Parker C1
Pasadena M6
Pearland F9
Pearsall H7
Pecos D4
Pelican Bay A2
Perryton C8
Pharr J9
Pilot Point L2
Pittsburg N2
Plains E2
Plainview F1
Plano L2
Pleasanton J7
Port Arthur P6
Port Bolivar G9
Port Isabel K9
Portland K8
Port Lavaca L7
Post F2
Poteet J6
Premont J8
Presidio C6
Quanah H1
Quitman M3
Ranger J3
Rankin F4
Raymondville K9
Red Oak C3
Refugio K7
Reno A2
Richardson C1
Richland Hills A2

Key
Richmond M6
Rio Grande City J9
Roanoke A1
Robert Lee G4
Robinson K4
Robstown K8
Roby G3
Rockdale L5
Rockport K7
Rocksprings G5
Rockwall L3
Roma H9
Roscoe G3
Rosenberg M6
Rosharon E9
Rotan G3
Round Rock K5
Rowlett C2
Rusk M4
Sabinal H6
Sachse C1
St. Hedwig B7
San Angelo G4
San Antonio J6
San Augustine N4
San Benito K9
Sanderson E5
San Diego J8
Sandy Point E9
Sanger K2
San Geronimo A6
San Leon G9
San Marcos K6
San Saba J4
Sansom Park A2
Sarita K8
Satsuma E8
Sayers B7
Schertz B6
Schumansville C6
Seabrook F9
Seadrift L7
Seagoville C2
Seagraves E3
Sealy L6
Seguin K6
Selma B6
Seminole E3
Seymour H2
Shallowater E2
Shavano Park A6
Sherman L2
Shoreacres G9
Sierra Blanca B4
Silsbee N5
Silverton F1
Sinton K7
Slaton F2
Smith Point G9
Smithville K5
Snyder G3
Socorro A4
Sonora G5
South Houston F9
Southlake A1
Southside Place E8
Southton B7
Spearman C8
Spring Valley E8
Spur G2
Stafford E9
Stamford H3
Stanton F3
Stephenville J3
Sterling City G4
Stratford B8
Sugar Land E9
Sulphur Springs M2
Sundown E2
Sunnyvale C2
Sweetwater G3
Tahoka F2
Taylor K5
Temple K4
Texarkana N2
Texas City N6
The Woodlands M5
Thompsons E9
Three Rivers J7
Throckmorton H2
Tilden J7
Tomball M5
Trinity M5
Trophy Club A1
Tulia F1
Tyler M3
Universal City J6
University Park C2
Uvalde H6
Van Alstyne L2
Van Horn C4
Vega B9
Vernon H1
Victoria L7
Vidor N5
Von Ormy A7
Waco K4
Waskom N3
Watauga A2
Waxahachie L3
Weatherford K3
Webster F9
Wellington D10
Weslaco K9
West K4
West Columbia M6
West Odessa E4
Westover Hills A2
West University Place E8
Westworth A2
Wharton L6
Wheatland A3
Wheeler D9
White Settlement A2
Whitesboro L2
Wichita Falls J2
Willis M5
Wills Point L3
Wilmer C3
Windcrest B6
Winnie N6
Winnsboro M3
Winters H4
Wolfforth F2
Woodville N5
Woodway K4
Wylie D1
Yoakum K6
Zapata H9
Zuehl B7

Other Features
Alibates Flint Quarries N.M. B9
Amistad, *reservoir* F6
Amistad Natl. Rec. Area G6
Balcones, *escarpment* A6
Big Bend Natl. Park D6
Big Thicket Natl. Preserve N5
Black, *mt.* G6
Canadian, *river* C9
Cathedral, *mt.* D5
Chamizal Natl. Mem. A4
Chinati Peak, *mt.* C6
Dallas-Fort Worth Intl. Airport B2
Davis, *mts.* C5
Eagle Peak, *mt.* B5
Edwards, *plateau* G5
Emory Peak, *mt.* D6
Falcon, *reservoir* H9
Fort Davis Natl. Hist. Site D5
Galveston, *bay* G9
Galveston, *island* N6
Guadalupe, *mts.* C3
Guadalupe Mts. Natl. Park C4
Guadalupe Peak, *mt.* C4
Kemp, *lake* H2
Lake Meredith Natl. Rec. Area C9
Livermore, *mt.* C5
Livingston, *lake* M5
Lyndon B. Johnson N.H.P. J5
Meredith, *lake* C9
Nueces, *river* J7
O.H. Ivie, *lake* H4
Padre Island Natl. Seashore K8
Pecos, *river* E4
Pelican, *island* G9
Red, *river* H1
Red Bluff, *lake* D4
Rio Grande, *river* F6
Sabine, *pass* P6
Sabine, *river* P5
Sam Rayburn, *reservoir* N4
Santiago Peak, *mt.* D6
Sierra Del Carmen, *mt.* D6
Stockton, *plateau* E5
Toledo Bend, *reservoir* P4

Utah ....page 171

Cities and Towns
American Fork C3
Beaver B5
Bicknell C5
Blanding E6
Bluffdale C3
Bountiful C3
Brigham City C2
Castle Dale C4
Cedar City A6
Centerville C3
Clearfield B2
Coalville C3
Cottonwood Heights C3
Delta B4
Draper C3
Duchesne D3
East Carbon D4
Enoch A6
Ephraim C4
Farmington C3
Ferron C4
Fillmore B5
Garland B2
Grantsville B3
Gunnison C4
Heber City C3
Helper D4
Hildale A6
Huntington D4
Hurricane A6
Hyrum C2
Ivins A6
Junction B5
Kanab B6
Lapoint E3
Layton C2
Lehi C3
Lewiston C2
Loa C5
Logan C2
Long Valley Junction B6
Maeser E3
Magna B3
Manila E3
Manti C4
Mapleton C3
Moab E5
Monroe B5
Monticello E6
Morgan C2
Mount Pleasant C4
Murray C3
Myton D3
N. Salt Lake C3
Nephi C4
North Ogden C2
Ogden C2
Orangeville C4
Orem C3
Panguitch B6
Parowan B6
Payson C3
Plain City B2
Pleasant Grove C3
Price D4
Provo C3
Randolph C2
Richfield B5
Richmond C2
Riverton C3
Roosevelt D3
Roy B2
St. George A6
Salem C3
Salina C5
Salt Lake City, *capital* C3
Sandy C3
Santa Clara A6
Santaquin C4
Smithfield C2
South Jordan C3
Spanish Fork C3
Springville C3
Sugarville B4
Tooele B3
Tremonton B2
Vernal E3
Washington A6
Wellington D4
West Jordan C3
West Valley City C3
Willard B2

Other Features
Abajo Peak, *mt.* E6
Arches Natl. Park E5
Bear, *lake* C2
Bear, *river* C2
Beaver, *river* B5
Bonneville Salt Flats A3
Bruin Point, *mt.* D4
Bryce Canyon Natl. Park B6
Canyonlands Natl. Park E5
Capitol Reef Natl. Park C5
Cedar Breaks Natl. Monument B6
Colorado, *river* E5
Delano Peak, *mt.* B5
Deseret Peak, *mt.* B3
Dinosaur Natl. Monument E3
Dutton, *mt.* B5
Escalante, *river* C6
Flaming Gorge, *reservoir* E2
Flaming Gorge Natl. Rec. Area E2
Frisco Peak, *mt.* A5
Glen Canyon Natl. Rec. Area D6
Golden Spike Natl. Hist. Site B2
Grand Staircase-Escalante N.M. C6
Great, *basin* A4
Great Salt, *lake* B2
Great Salt Lake, *desert* A3
Green, *river* D4
Heliotrope, *mt.* C4
Henry, *mts.* D6
Ibapah Peak, *mt.* A4
Kings Peak, *mt.* D3
Marsh Peak, *mt.* E3
Marvine, *mt.* C5
Monument, *valley* D6
Natural Bridges Natl. Monument E6
Navajo, *mt.* D6
Navajo Indian Res. E6
Nebo, *mt.* C4
Paria, *river* C6
Pavant, *range* B5
Peale, *mt.* E5
Pennell, *mt.* D6
Powell, *lake* D6
Price, *river* D4
Rainbow Bridge Natl. Monument D6
Salt Marsh, *lake* A4
San Juan, *river* D6
San Rafael, *river* D4
Sevier, *desert* B4
Sevier, *lake* A5
Strawberry, *river* D3
Swasey Peak, *mt.* A4
Timpanogos Cave N.M. C3
Uinta, *mts.* D3
Utah, *lake* C3
Wasatch, *plateau* C5
White, *river* E3
Zion Natl. Park A6

Vermont ....page 172

Cities and Towns
Addison A2
Albany C1
Ascutney C4
Averill D1
Bakersfield B1
Barnard B3
Barnet C2
Barre C2
Basin Harbor A2
Beecher Falls D1
Bellows Falls C4
Bennington A5
Benson A3
Berlin B2
Bethel B3
Bloomfield D1
Bradford C3
Brandon A3
Brattleboro B5
Bristol A2
Brookfield B2
Burlington A2
Cabot C2
Cambridge B1
Castleton A3
Cavendish B4
Charlotte A2
Chelsea C3
Colchester A1
Concord D2
Danby B4
Danville C2
Dorset A4
East Burke D1
East Haven D1
East Middlebury A3
East Randolph B3
Eden B1
Enosburg Falls B1
Essex A1
Essex Junction A1
Evansville C1
Fair Haven A3
Fairfax B1
Fairfield B1
Fairlee C3
Franklin B1
Gallup Mills D1
Gaysville B3
Georgia Center A1
Grafton B4
Granby D1
Grand Isle A1
Groton C2
Guildhall D1
Guilford B5
Hancock B3
Hanover C3
Hardwick C2
Hartford C3
Hartland C3
Hartwellville D1
Heartwellville A5
Highgate Center A1
Hinesburg A2
Hortonia A3
Hubbardton A3
Hyde Park B1
Irasburg C1
Irasville B2
Jacksonville B5
Jamaica B4
Jeffersonville B1
Johnson B1
Keeler Bay A1
Larrabees Point A3
Lemington D1
Londonderry B4
Lowell C1
Lyndon C1
Lyndonville C1
McIndoe Falls C2
Marlboro B5
Mendon B3
Middlebury A2
Middlesex B2
Milton A1
Monkton A2
Montgomery B1
Montgomery Center B1
Montpelier, *capital* B2
Morgan C1
Morrisville B1
Moscow B2
Newbury C2
Newfane B4
New Haven A2
Newport C1
North Bennington A5
Northfield B2
North Hero A1
North Wolcott C1
Norton D1
Orange C2
Panton A2
Peacham C2
Pittsfield B3
Pittsford A3
Plainfield C2
Plymouth B3
Pompanoosuc C3
Post Mills C3
Poultney A3
Pownal A5
Proctor A3
Putney B5
Randolph B3
Readsboro B5
Richford B1
Richmond A2
Rochester B3
Roxbury B2
Rutland B3
St. Albans A1
St. Johnsbury C2
Searsburg B5
Shaftsbury A4
Sharon C3
Shelburne A2
Sheldon B1
Shoreham A3
South Burlington A2
South Hero A1
Springfield C4
Stamford A5
Starksboro A2
Swanton A1
Tinmouth A4
Troy C1
Tunbridge C3
Tyson B4
Underhill B1
Vergennes A2
Vernon B5
Vershire C3
Warren B2
Washington C2
Waterbury B2
Waterville B1
Wells River C2
West Burke D1
West Dover B5
West Haven A3
Westminster C4
Weston B4
West Pawlet A4
West Topsham C2
Wheelock C1
White River Junction C3
Williamsville B5
Wilmington B5
Windsor C4
Winooski A1
Wolcott C1
Woodford A5
Woodstock B3
Worcester B2

Other Features
Appalachian Natl. Scenic Trail A5
Black, *river* C1
Bomoseen, *lake* A3
Bread Loaf, *mt.* B2
Bromley, *mt.* B4
Camels Hump, *mt.* B2
Champlain, *lake* A1
Connecticut, *river* C3
Ellen, *mt.* B2
Equinox, *mt.* A4
Green, *mts.* B4
Harriman, *reservoir* B5
Jay Peak, *mt.* B1
Killington Peak, *mt.* B3
Lamoille, *river* B1
Mansfield, *mt.* B1
Marsh-Billings-Rockefeller N.H.P. B3
Mettawee, *river* A3
Missisquoi, *river* B1
Seymour, *lake* C1
Smugglers Notch, *pass* B1
Snow, *mt.* B5
Somerset, *reservoir* B4
Waterbury, *reservoir* B2
West, *river* B4
White, *river* B3
White Rocks N.R.A. B4
Willoughby, *lake* C1

Virginia ....page 173

Cities and Towns
Abingdon D1
Accomac M4
Achilles L5
Alberta H6
Alexandria J2
Allison Gap D1
Altavista E5
Amelia Court House H5
Amherst E4
Annandale M2
Appalachia B1
Appomattox F5
Arlington J2
Ashland H4
Baileys Crossroads M2
Bassett C6
Basye F2
Bedford D5
Belleair L2
Belle Haven M4
Belle View M2
Bensley J5
Berryville H1
Big Stone Gap B1
Blacksburg B5
Blackstone H5
Bland A5
Bloxom M4
Bluefield A5
Bon Air H4
Bowling Green J3
Boyce G1
Boydton G6
Boykins J6
Bridgewater F3
Bristol D2
Brodnax G6
Brookneal F5
Brunswick H6
Buckingham F4
Buena Vista E4
Burke L2
Burkeville G5
Callands D6
Cape Charles L5
Castlewood C1
Centreville J2
Charles City J5
Charlotte Court House F5
Charlottesville F4
Chase City G6
Chatham E6
Cheriton M5
Chesapeake L6
Chester J5
Chesterfield H5
Chilhowie E1
Chincoteague M4
Christiansburg C5
Chula H5
Claremont K5
Clifton Forge D4
Clinchco C1
Clintwood C1
Coeburn C1
Collinsville D6
Colonial Beach K3
Colonial Hts. J5
Concord E5
Courtland J6
Covington C4
Crewe G5
Crimora F3
Crystal City M2
Crystal Hill F6
Culpeper G3
Cumberland G4
Dale City J2
Danville E6
Dendron K5
Dillwyn G4
Dinwiddie H5
Drakes Branch F6
Dublin B5
Dumfries J2
Dungannon C1
Eastville M5
Elkton F3
Emory D1
Emporia H6
Ewing A1
Fairfax J2
Fairfax Station L2
Falls Church M2
Falmouth J3
Farmville G5
Ferrum D6
Figsboro D6
Fincastle D4
Fishersville F3
Flint Hill G2
Floyd C6
Forest E5
Fort Mitchell G6
Franconia M2
Franklin K6
Fredericksburg J3
Fries B6
Front Royal G2
Galax B6
Gate City C1
Glade Spring D1
Gloucester K5
Gloucester Point L5
Goochland H4
Gordonsville G3
Goshen D4
Gretna E6
Grottoes F3
Groveton M2
Grundy D1
Halifax F6
Hampton L5
Hanover J4
Harrisonburg F3
Harrogate A1
Heathsville L4
Hollins D5
Hopewell J5
Horse Pasture D6
Huntington M2
Hurt E5
Independence A6
Isle of Wight K6
Jetersville G5
Jonesville B1
Kenbridge G6
King and Queen Courthouse K4
King George J3
Kings Park L2
King William J4
Lancaster L4
Lawrenceville H6
Lebanon D1
Leesburg H1
Lexington E4
Lincolnia M2
Louisa G4
Lovingston F4
Lunenburg G6
Luray G2
Lynchburg E5
McLean M1
Madison G3
Manakin H4
Manassas J2
Manassas Park J2
Mantua L2
Marion A6
Martinsville D6
Mathews L5
Mechanicsburg A5
Mechanicsville J4
Meherrin G5
Millboro D4
Monterey D3
Montross K3
Mount Jackson F2
Narrows B5
New Castle C4
New Kent K4
New Market F2
Newport News L6
Newsoms J6
Norfolk L6
North Springfield M2
Norton C1
Nottoway Court House G5
Oakton L2
Onancock M4
Orange G3
Palmyra G4
Pearisburg B5
Petersburg J5
Peterstown B5
Pimmit Hills M1
Poquoson L5
Portsmouth L6
Powhatan H4
Prince George J5
Pulaski B5
Purcellville H1
Radford B5
Raven D1
Reston J2
Richlands D1
Richmond, *capital* J4
Ridgeway D6
Roanoke D5
Rocky Mount D6
Rustburg E5
Ruther Glen J4
Salem C5
Saltville D1
Saluda K4
Shenandoah F3
Smithfield K6
South Boston F6
South Hill G6
Spotsylvania H3
Springfield M2
Spring Hill M1
Stafford J3
Stanardsville G3
Staunton E3
Sterling J1
Stony Creek J6
Strasburg G2
Stuart C6
Stuarts Draft E3
Suffolk K6
Surry K5
Sussex J6
Tappahannock K4
Tazewell A5
Timberville F2
Triangle J2
Tysons Corner M1
Vale L1
Verona E3
Victoria G6
Vienna L1
Virginia Beach M6
Warm Springs D3
Warrenton H2
Warsaw K4
Washington G2
Waverly J5
Waynesboro F3
Weber City C1
Wellington M3
West Point K4
West Springfield M2
Williamsburg K5
Winchester G1
Wise C1
Woodbridge J2
Woodstock F2
Wytheville A6
Yorktown K5

Other Features
Allegheny, *mts.* D3
Anna, *lake* H3
Appalachian, *mts.* C5
Appomattox Court House N.H.P. F5
Arlington Natl. Cem. M2
Assateague Island Natl. Seashore M4
Booker T. Washington N.M. D5
Charles, *cape* M5
Chesapeake, *bay* L5
Colonial Natl. Hist. Park K5
Fredericksburg & Spotsylvania Natl. Mil. Park H3
Gaston, *lake* G6
George Washington Birthplace N.M. K3
Henry, *cape* M6
Iron, *mts.* A6
James, *river* K5
John H. Kerr, *reservoir* F6
Manassas Natl. Battlefield Park H2
Mount Rogers Natl. Rec. Area A6
Petersburg Natl. Battlefield J5
Potomac, *river* K3
Rappahannock, *river* J3
Rogers, *mt.* A6
Shenandoah, *mts.* E3
Shenandoah, *river* F3
Shenandoah Natl. Park G2
Smith Mtn., *lake* D5
York, *river* K5

Washington ....page 174

Cities and Towns
Aberdeen C4
Amboy D5
Anacortes D2
Arlington D2
Asotin J4
Auburn D3
Bangor A1
Battle Ground D5
Bellingham D2
Belvedere H2
Benton City G4
Bethel A2
Birch Bay D2
Blaine D2
Boardman G5

Key

Bothel D3
Bremerton D3
Brewster G2
Bridgeport G3
Bucoda D4
Burien B2
Burlington D2
Camas D5
Cashmere F3
Castle Rock D4
Cathlamet C4
Central Park C3
Centralia D4
Chehalis D4
Chelan F3
Cheney J3
Chewelah J2
Clarkston J4
Cle Elum F3
Clinton D3
Colfax J4
College Place H4
Colville J2
Connell H4
Cosmopolis C4
Country Homes J3
Coupeville D2
Davenport H3
Dayton J4
Deer Park J3
Dusty J4
Eastgate B2
Easton E3
Eastsound D2
East Wenatchee F3
Eatonville D4
Edmonds D3
Ellensburg F3
Elma C3
Elmer City H3
Enumclaw E3
Ephrata G3
Everett D2
Everson D2
Fall City E3
Federal Way D3
Ferndale D2
Fords Prairie C4
Forks B3
Four Lakes J3
Friday Harbor C2
Fruitvale F4
Goldendale F5
Gorst A2
Grandview G4
Granger F4
Hoquiam C3
Inglewood C2
Kelso D4
Kenmore B1
Kennewick G4
Kent D3
Kettle Falls H2
Kirkland D3
Lacey D3
La Grande D4
Lake Stevens D2
Leavenworth F3
Lexington D4
Longmire E4
Longview D4
Lynden D2
Mabton G4
McKenna D4
McMurray D2
Markham C4
Marysville D2
Medical Lake J3
Medina B2
Mercer Island D3
Merritt F3
Monroe D3
Montesano C4
Moses Lake G3
Mount Vernon D2
Mukilteo D3
Newhalem E2
Newport J2
Newport Hills B2
Normandy Park B2
North Bend E3
Oak Harbor D2
Ocean Park B4
Ocean Shores B3
Okanogan G2
Olalla B2
Olympia, *capital* D3
Omak G2
Opportunity J3
Orchards D5
Oroville G2
Othello G4
Oysterville B4
Pasco G4
Plymouth G5
Pomeroy J4
Port Angeles C2
Porter C4
Port Hadlock D2
Port Ludlow D3
Port Orchard D3
Port Townsend D2
Poulsbo D3
Prosser G4
Pullman J4
Puyallup D3
Quincy G3
Raymond C4
Redmond D3
Renton D3
Republic H2
Richland G4
Richmond Highlands B1
Ridgefield D5
Ritzville H3
St. John J3
Seabeck A2
Sea-Tac D3
Seattle D3
Sedro-Woolley D2
Selah F4
Sequim C2
Shelton C3
Silverton E2
Skyway B2
Smokey Point D2
Snohomish D3
Snoqualmie E3
South Bend C4
Southworth B2
Spanaway D3
Spokane J3
Stanwood D2
Stevenson E5
Sultan E3
Sumas D2
Sumner D3
Sunnyside F4
Suquamish A1
Tacoma D3
Tekoa J3
Tenino D4
Tiger J2
Toppenish F4
Tracyton A2
Trentwood J3
Tukwila B2
Tumwater D4
Union Gap F4
University Place D3
Vancouver D5
Vashon B2
Walla Walla H4
Wapato F4
Warden G4
Washougal D5
Waterville F3
Wenatchee F3
Westport B4
West Richland G4
White Center B2
White Salmon E5
Winslow D3
Woodinville B1
Woodland D5
Yakima F4
Yelm D4
Zillah F4

Other Features

Adams, *mt.* E4
Bainbridge, *island* B2
Baker, *mt.* E2
Banks, *lake* G3
Cascade, *range* E4
Chelan, *lake* F2
Chewuch, *river* F2
Columbia, *river* G2
Copper Butte, *mt.* H2
Cowlitz, *river* E4
Disappointment, *cape* B4
Elliott, *bay* B2
Flattery, *cape* B2
Franklin D. Roosevelt, *lake* H2
Glacier Peak, *mt.* E2
Grays, *harbor* B4
Green, *river* E3
Hanford Reach Natl. Mon. G4
Hood, *canal* C3
Kettle River, *range* H2
Klickitat, *river* E4
Lake Chelan Natl. Rec. Area F2
Lake Roosevelt Natl. Rec. Area H2
Lewis, *river* E4
Mt. Baker Natl. Rec. Area E2
Mount Rainier Natl. Park E4
Mt. St. Helens Natl. Vol. Mon. D4
North Cascades Natl. Park E2
Okanogan, *river* G2
Olympic, *mts.* C3
Olympic Natl. Park C3
Olympus, *mt.* C3
Omak, *mt.* G2
Orcas, *island* D2
Oregon Butte, *mt.* J4
Ozette, *lake* B2
Pasayten, *river* F2
Pend Oreille, *river* J2
Potholes, *reservoir* G3
Priest Rapids, *lake* G4
Puget, *sound* B1, D2
Rainier, *mt.* E4
Riffe, *lake* D4
Rimrock, *lake* E4
Ross, *lake* F2
Ross Lake Natl. Rec. Area F2
Sacajawea, *lake* H4
St. Helens, *mt.* D4
San Juan, *island* C2
Sanpoil, *river* H2
Selkirk, *mts.* J2
Skagit, *river* E2
Skykomish, *river* E3
Snake, *river* J4
Spokane, *river* H3
Strait of Juan de Fuca B2
Stuart, *mt.* F3
Umatilla, *lake* G5
Vashon, *island* B2
Wallula, *lake* H4
Washington, *lake* B1
Wenatchee, *lake* F3
Wenatchee, *mts.* F3
Wenatchee, *river* F3
White, *pass* E4
Whitman Mission Natl. Hist. Site H4
Willapa, *bay* B4
Yakima, *river* F4
Yale, *lake* D4

West Virginia .... page 175

Cities and Towns

Ansted D4
Barboursville B4
Beckley D5
Belington G2
Berkeley Springs K1
Bluefield D6
Bradley D5
Bridgeport F2
Buckhannon F3
Charles Town L2
Charleston, *capital* C4
Chester K4
Circleville G3
Clarksburg F2
Clay D4
Clendenin D4
Craigsville E4
Davis H2
East Liverpool K4
Edray F4
Eleanor C3
Elizabeth D2
Elkins G3
Fairmont F2
Fayetteville D4
Fort Ashby J2
Franklin H3
Gary C6
Glenville E3
Grafton F2
Grantsville D3
Hamlin B4
Harpers Ferry L2
Harrisville D2
Hinton E5
Huntington B4
Hurricane B4
Inwood K2
Kenova A4
Keyser J2
Kingwood G2
Lewisburg F5
Logan C5
Madison C4
Mannington F1
Marlinton F4
Marmet C4
Martinsburg L2
Matewan B5
Middlebourne E2
Milton B4
Montgomery D4
Moorefield J2
Morgantown G1
Moundsville K6
Mt. Hope D5
Mullens D5
Newburg G2
New Cumberland K4
New Haven C3
New Martinsville E1
New Milton E2
Nitro C4
Oak Hill D5
Oceana C5
Orma D3
Paden City E1
Parkersburg C2
Parsons G2
Pennsboro E2
Petersburg H3
Peterstown E6
Philippi F2
Pineville C5
Point Pleasant B3
Princeton D6
Rainelle E5
Ravenswood C3
Reedy D3
Richwood E4
Ripley C3
Romney J2
Ronceverte F5
Rupert E5
St. Albans C4
St. Marys D2
Salem E2
Shady Spring D5
Shepherdstown L2
Shinnston F2
Sistersville E1
Slanesville J2
South Charleston C4
Spencer D3
Summersville E4
Sutton E3
Terra Alta G2
Union E5
Vienna C2
Wayne B4
Webster Springs F4
Weirton K5
Welch C6
Wellsburg K4
Wellsville K4
West Milford F2
Weston F2
West Union E2
Wheeling K5
White Sulphur Springs F5
Whitesville C5
Williamson B5
Williamstown D2
Winfield C4

Other Features

Allegheny, *mts.* G4
Big Sandy, *river* B5
Bluestone, *lake* E5
Bluestone Natl. Scenic River E5
Gauley River Natl. Rec. Area D4
Greenbrier, *river* E4
Harpers Ferry Natl. Hist. Park L2
Kanawha, *river* B3
New River Gorge Natl. River D5
Ohio, *river* E1
Potomac, *river* J2
Shenandoah, *mts.* H4
Spruce Knob, *mt.* G3
Spruce Knob-Seneca Rocks N.R.A. H3
Sutton, *lake* E3

Wisconsin .... page 176

Cities and Towns

Abbotsford C4
Adams D5
Algoma F4
Alma B4
Altoona B4
Amery A3
Antigo D3
Appleton E4
Arcadia B4
Ashland C2
Augusta B4
Baldwin A4
Balsam Lake A3
Baraboo D5
Barronett A3
Bayside F1
Beaver Dam E5
Belleville D6
Bellevue F4
Beloit D6
Bennett B2
Berlin E5
Bethesda D2
Big Bend E2
Black River Falls C4
Bloomer B3
Bloomville D3
Boscobel C5
Breed E3
Brillion E4
Brodhead D6
Brookfield E1
Brown Deer F1
Bryant D3
Buena Vista D1
Burlington E6
Butler E1
Cadott B4
Cameron B3
Canton B3
Carlsville F4
Cedarburg F5
Cedar Grove F5
Chelsea C3
Chetek B3
Chili C4
Chilton E4
Chippewa Falls B4
Cleveland F5
Clinton E6
Clintonville E4
Colby C4
Coloma D5
Columbus D5
Conrath B3
Cornell B3
Cornucopia B2
Crandon E3
Crestview F2
Cuba City C6
Cudahy F2
Cumberland A3
Darlington C6
De Forest D5
De Pere E4
Delafield D1
Delavan E6
Denmark F4
Dodgeville C6
Duplainville E1
Durand B4
Eagle River D3
Easton D5
East Troy E6
Eau Claire B4
Edgar C4
Edgerton D6
Elkhorn E6
Ellsworth A4
Elm Grove E1
Elroy C5
Evansville D6
Fennimore C6
Florence E3
Fond du Lac E5
Forestville F4
Fort Atkinson E6
Fox Lake E5
Fox Point F1
Fredonia F5
Friendship D5
Galesville B4
Genesee D2
Genesee Depot D2
Germantown E5
Gillett E4
Glendale F1
Grafton F5
Green Bay F4
Greendale F2
Greenfield F2
Green Lake E5
Greenleaf E4
Hales Corners E2
Hamburg D3
Harrison D3
Hartford E5
Hartland D1
Hayward B2
Hillsboro C5
Hollister E3
Holmen B5
Horicon E5
Hortonville E4
Howard E4
Howards Grove F5
Hudson A4
Hurley C2
Husher F2
Jackson E5
Janesville D6
Jefferson E6
Juda D6
Jump River C3
Juneau E5
Kaukauna E4
Kenosha F6
Keshena E4
Kewaskum E5
Kewaunee F4
Kiel E5
Kneeland F2
Lac du Flambeau D3
La Crosse B5
Ladysmith B3
Lake Delton D5
Lake Geneva E6
Lake Mills E5
Lampson B3
Lancaster C6
La Pointe C2
Little Chute E4
Lodi D5
Lomira E5
McFarland D6
Madison, *capital* D5
Maiden Rock A4
Manitowish C2
Manitowoc F4
Marathon City D4
Marinette F3
Markesan E5
Marshfield C4
Mason B2
Mattoon D3
Mauston C5
Mayville E5
Medford C3
Menasha E4
Menomonee Falls E5
Menomonie B4
Mequon F5
Merrill D3
Middleton D5
Milton E6
Milwaukee F5
Mineral Point C6
Mishicot F4
Modena B4
Mole Lake E3
Mondovi B4
Monona D5
Monroe D6
Montello D5
Montfort C6
Mosinee D4
Muscoda C5
Muskego E6
Neenah E4
Neillsville C4
Nekoosa D4
New Berlin E6
New Glarus D6
New Holstein E5
New Lisbon C5
New London E4
New Richmond A3
Newton F5
Niagara F3
North Fond du Lac E5
North Lake D1
North Prairie D2
Oak Creek F6
Oconto F4
Oconto Falls E4
Odanah C2
Omro E4
Onalaska B5
Oostburg F5
Oregon D6
Osceola A3
Oshkosh E4
Paddock Lake E6
Palmyra E6
Park Falls C3
Pell Lake E6
Peshtigo F3
Pewaukee E1
Phillips C3
Platteville C6
Pleasant Prairie F6
Plover D4
Plymouth F5
Polonia D4
Portage D5
Port Edwards D4
Porterfield F3
Port Washington F5
Port Wing B2
Poynette D5
Prairie du Chien B5
Prairie du Sac D5
Prescott A4
Princeton D5
Pulaski E4
Racine F6
Randolph E5
Random Lake F5
Raymond F2
Reedsburg D5
Rhinelander D3
Rice Lake B3
Richland Center C5
Ridgeway D5
Ripon E5
River Falls A4
River Hills F1
Rothschild D4
St. Croix Falls A3
St. Francis F2
Sauk City D5
Saukville F5
Saylesville D2
Schofield D4
Shawano E4
Sheboygan F5
Sheboygan Falls F5
Shell Lake B3
Shorewood F1
Slinger E5
South Milwaukee F2
Sparta C5
Spencer C4
Spooner B3
Spread Eagle E3
Spring Green C5
Stanley C4
Stevens Point D4
Stonebank D1
Stoughton D6
Sturgeon Bay F4
Sturtevant F6
Summit Lake D3
Sun Prairie D5
Superior A2
Sussex E1
Tabor F2
Thompsonville F2
Thorp C4
Tomah C5
Tomahawk D3
Tony C3
Two Rivers F4
Verona D6
Viroqua C5
Wales D2
Wanderoos A3
Washburn C2
Watertown E5
Waukesha E6
Waunakee D5
Waupaca D4
Waupun E5
Wausau D4
Wautoma D4
Wauwatosa E1
Wauzeka C5
West Allis F6
West Bend E5
Westby C5
West Milwaukee F1
Weyauwega E4
Whitehall B4
Whitewater E6
Williams Bay E6
Wind Lake E2
Wind Point G2
Winneconne E4
Wisconsin Dells D5
Wisconsin Rapids D4
Wrightstown E4

Other Features

Apostle Islands Natl. Lakeshore C1
Big Muskego, *lake* E2
Castle Rock, *lake* D5
Chetek, *lake* B3
Chippewa, *lake* B3
Door, *peninsula* F4
Dubay, *lake* D4
Flambeau, *river* C3
Green, *bay* F4
Madeline, *island* C2
Michigan, *lake* G5
Mississippi, *river* B5
Outer, *island* C1
Peshtigo, *river* E3
Petenwell, *lake* D4
Pewaukee, *lake* D1
Poygan, *lake* E4
St. Croix Natl. Scenic Riverway A3
Sand, *island* C2
Spring, *lake* D2
Stockton, *island* C2
Superior, *lake* C1
Timms Hill, *mt.* C3
Winnebago, *lake* E4
Wisconsin, *river* D3
Wolf, *river* E4
Yellow, *river* C4

Wyoming .... page 177

Cities and Towns

Afton A2
Basin B1
Boxelder D2
Buffalo C1
Byron B1
Casper C2
Cheyenne, *capital* D3
Cody B1
Cokeville A2
Deaver B1
Douglas D2
Evanston A3
Evansville C2
Gillette D1
Glenrock D2
Green River B3
Greybull B1
Jackson A2
Kemmerer A3
Lander B2
Laramie D3
Lovell B1
Lusk D2
Lyman A3
Medicine Bow C3
Mills C2
Newcastle D2
Pinedale B2
Powell B1
Rawlins C3
Reliance B3
Riverton B2
Rock Springs B3
Saratoga C3
Sheridan C1
Sundance D1
Thermopolis B2
Torrington D2
Wamsutter C3
Wheatland D2
Worland C1

Other Features

Absaroka, *range* A1
Belle Fourche, *river* D2
Big Sandy, *river* B2
Bighorn, *lake* B1
Bighorn, *mts.* C1
Bighorn, *river* B1
Bighorn Canyon Natl. Rec. Area B1
Bridger Peak, *mt.* C3
Clarks Fork Yellowstone, *river* B1
Cloud Peak, *mt.* C1
Colter Peak, *mt.* A1
Continental Divide, *mt. ridge* B3
Devils Tower Natl. Monument D1
Elk, *mt.* C3
Flaming Gorge, *reservoir* B3
Flaming Gorge Natl. Rec. Area B3
Fort Laramie Natl. Hist. Site D2
Fossil Butte Natl. Monument A3
Francs Peak, *mt.* B2
Gannett Peak, *mt.* B2
Grand Teton, *mt.* A2
Grand Teton Natl. Park A2
Great Divide, *basin* B3
Green, *river* B3
Greybull, *river* B1
Jackson, *lake* A2
Laramie, *mts.* C2
Laramie, *river* D3
Laramie Peak, *mt.* D2
Little Bighorn, *river* C1
Little Missouri, *river* D1
Little Powder, *river* D1
Little Snake, *river* C3
Medicine Bow, *river* C2
North Platte, *river* D2
Nowood, *river* C1
Owl Creek, *mts.* B2
Pathfinder, *reservoir* C2
Powder, *river* D1
Rocky, *mts.* B2
Seminoe, *reservoir* C3
South Fork Cheyenne, *river* D2
South Fork Powder, *river* C2
Sweetwater, *river* B2
Teton, *river* A2
Tongue, *river* C1
Trout Peak, *mt.* B1
Whiskey Peak, *mt.* C2
Wind, *river* B2
Wind River, *range* B2
Yellowstone, *lake* A1
Yellowstone Natl. Park A1